High Clouds Soaring, Storms Driving Low

The Letters of Ruth Moore

Edited and with an Introduction by

Sanford Phippen

BLACKBERRY PRESS

Nobleboro, Maine *1993*

ACKNOWLEDGMENTS

Hal Borland for the right to quote from his book, *Hill Country Harvest,* J. B. Lippincott Pub. Co., Philadelphia, 1967.

Gordon Bok for re-print rights to his song "Turning Toward the Morning." Words and music © 1975 Gordon Bok

Faber & Faber, Ltd. (London, England), original publishers of *Adamastor* by Roy Campbell, 1931; reprinted by Greenwood Press, Westport, Conn., 1971.

Mark Melnicove, for re-print rights to "Tongue of Granite, Tongue of Salt," originally published in *Killick Stones: A Collection of Maine Island Writing,* Island Institute, Rockland, Maine, 1987.

Joel White, for permission to re-print E. B. White's letter to Dorothy Lobrano Guth, originally published in *The Letters of E. B. White* edited by Dorothy Lobrano Guth, Harper & Row, New York, 1976. Also, for permission to quote from E. B. White in the Introduction and for permission to re-print E. B. White's letter to Ruth Moore.

ISBN: 0-942396-66-9

Blackberry Books RR 1, Box 228 Nobleboro, Maine 04555

Book design by Judith Cooper, Mind's Eye Design

Printed in the United States of America
Thomson-Shore, Ann Arbor, Michigan

To

Esther Moore Trask

and

Edward M. "Ted" Holmes

THE WORKS OF RUTH MOORE

Novels

The Weir, 1943
Spoonhandle, 1946
The Fire Balloon, 1948
Candlemas Bay, 1950
Jeb Ellis of Candlemas Bay, 1952
A Fair Wind Home, 1953
Speak to the Winds, 1956
The Walk Down Main Street, 1960
Second Growth, 1962
The Sea Flower, 1965
The Gold and Silver Hooks, 1969
"Lizzie" and Caroline, 1972
The Dinosaur Bite, 1976
Sarah Walked Over the Mountain, 1979

Poetry

Cold as a Dog and the Wind Northeast, 1958
Time's Web, 1972
The Tired Apple Tree, 1990

Anthologies in which Ruth Moore's work appears

White Pine and Blue Water, 1950
The Best Maine Stories, 1986
Maine Speaks, 1989

Contents

Introduction

The title of this book is Ruth's from the following passage in her novel *Spoonhandle:*

> Winter in a northern seacoast land is interlude. Day after day in the changing weather, high clouds soaring, storms driving low, the land huddles into itself. Salt water curdles into slush against the shore, then, slowly, into grainy pale-green ice, fissured by tides and flung in crumpled blocks up and down the beaches. The spruces crack and snap on a windless evening and let go their loads of snow, so that a wood lot in the cold seems to be talking to itself in a language of small stirrings, whispers and sighs. There is nothing people can do with land like that, bitten four feet deep with frost, secret and uncommunicative under snow.
>
> Winter is a time of gear-overhauling in the fishhouses, snug with fires built in oil drum stoves, of building traps and painting buoys, of mending the dragnet that the shark tore through. The shark himself is keen in the memory and the gaping hole he made is here and now. But the warm weather, the summertime, lost in the blizzard that drives the small drift under the windowsill, is as unreal as a ghost until it comes again. The talk above the tapping hammers is gusty and loud, but to a man going home to supper, walking through the snowy twilight is like

> walking through a dream, and the house looming in blown whiteness is a house of sleep.
>
> Winter is the time of wood-cutting, the hollow thung of the axes like bells among the tree boles; the clean track of the woodsled and the brown dung of the horses in the snow; the frosty maple-butt flying apart on the chopping-block at a touch of the ax.
>
> In the early mornings, blue with snow and coming light, the deer comes to the orchard, digging with her cold hoofs for the frozen buried apples; and in the time after the gear is overhauled and the wood is cut and the boat is painted, content comes out or loneliness bites deep, depending on whether people are content or lonely.
>
> —*Spoonhandle,* pp. 257-258

In several of her letters collected here, Ruth Moore describes herself as "the-eyes-that-watch-from-the-underbrush;" and it's that special vantage point that makes passages such as the above so lovely and vivid. In a 46-year career as a popular writer, Ruth granted very few interviews for publication, only two for broadcast, and gave no public readings or talks. She didn't even show up for her two honorary doctorates from the University of Maine and Unity College.

About the prospects of her first radio interview with Mary Margaret McBride, one of the pioneers of "Talk Radio," in New York on NBC in 1943, she wrote to her mother, "I guess you can listen if you want to, but I won't recommend it, because the Lord knows what they'll get me to say, and it probably won't sound the least like me. It isn't a talk—it's an interview. They ask questions about whether I thought up the book while I was standing on my head in a haystack, or did it just come to me, and I say, no, a little bird let drop on my hat one day and it just knocked the idea out of me, and all that. You get the idea. Maybe it'll fall through, the broadcasting, I mean, and I hope so, for I'd rather take a good licking. Makes me feel like a cussed fool. And probably I'll sound like one. Or I'll have the jitters so hard I'll sound like a machine gun."

Ruth's attitude toward the media didn't change until late in her career, when her Maine publisher, Gary Lawless, began to re-publish her novels in paperback; then, to help out Lawless, she consented to several major interviews with the likes of *Down East* magazine, the *Maine Times,* and the *Puckerbrush Review.* For *Puckerbrush,* when interviewer Betsy Graves asked Ruth what she should call her—"Miss Moore," or whatever—Ruth replied, "Just call me Ruth. Everybody does."

Ruth's rule for life seemed to be: "Keep it simple. I always try to, much the best way." Plain and simple on the surface, but complex, contradictory, contrary, and multi-faceted underneath. As with any fine artist, it's just as important to note what Ruth left out as it is to see what she kept in.

Born on July 21, 1903, on Gott's Island into a family that had lived and worked on the island for five generations, Ruth was the eldest daughter of weir fisherman Philip "Fripper" Moore and his wife, Lovina "Viney" Joyce Moore. With her older brother Harvey, or "Harve," and her two younger sisters, Esther ("Tug") and Louise ("Wee"), she attended grammar school on the island; for her high schooling, 1917–1921, she left the island to board with relatives in Ellsworth, where she attended Ellsworth High School. In a family where everyone had a nickname, Ruth's was "Uppy," because when her first-born nephew, Harvey Dow, nicknamed "Tink," would stand in front of her, he'd say, "Up, up, up."

Ruth hated Ellsworth High School; as a contemporary schoolmate of hers, Sylvia McDonald Young, remembers, "The snooty Ellsworth kids made fun of her, because she was an 'island girl,' because of the way she talked, her homemade and unfashionable bright-colored clothes, and also because she was very smart and outspoken."

On vacations and during summers, Ruth would be back on Gott's Island where she helped her parents and siblings with the work not only of a fishing and farming family, but with feeding the summer people as well. The Moores took in boarders, had a small restaurant and store in their house, and maintained the island post office.

Because she was several years older than her two sisters, she would often watch them and do the housework while Lovina Moore worked. Ruth's sister Louise Dow recalls, "She was the best sister in the world. She would always be there if you needed help; but we used to give her a hard time when she was keeping house."

One family of summer folk from New Jersey with whom Ruth became very close was the Holmes clan, which included Betty Holmes and her younger half-brother Edward, or "Ted." Ruth shared many adventures with the Holmes kids. Betty later persuaded Ruth to go to live near her in New York and Ted grew up to become a Maine author, too.

Another Gott's Island summer family, the Davidsons, were instrumental in encouraging Ruth to go to college. Mr. Davidson was the head of St. Stephens Academy, now Bard College, in New York State. Ruth never went to Bard (though her niece Emily Trask did); she chose to attend the New York State College for Teachers at Albany, now the State University of New York at Albany, graduating in 1925.

Mary Kamenoff was Ruth's sorority sister and roommate in college who became the first of several important "Marys" in Ruth's life. Others included Mary Dillon, who hired Ruth at The Reader's Digest and became a good friend; Mary White Ovington of the NAACP; Mary Grahn of the Yale School of Drama; and Mary Clarke, another good friend.

Graduating in 1925 as an English major with an Economics minor, Ruth taught high school English and Latin at Central Islip on Long Island for one year after college. She found out that neither teaching nor Long Island were for her and moved in 1926 to a small apartment on Minetta Lane in Greenwich Village. She worked mainly as a secretary; and her most interesting and important job at this time in 1927 was as a live-in secretary to Mary White Ovington, one of the founders of the National Association for the Advancement of Colored People (NAACP). The Ovington family had summered for years on Gott's Island. At one point, Ruth went to Atlanta to catalogue the number of lynchings that were taking place there, a rather dangerous undertaking.

From 1929 to 1930, Ruth worked as Assistant Campaign Manager for the NAACP, reporting directly to James Weldon Johnson, noted poet, author of *God's Trombones,* and then head of the Association. Ruth helped to plan and carry through a campaign for the raising of $100,000 and she also designed pamphlets and brochures and wrote copy for them. During the summer months of 1930, Ruth worked as a special investigator in two criminal cases involving murder. One investigation necessitated extensive travel through the southern states, specifically Arkansas and Tennessee where she was able to unearth information which set in motion the freeing of two young "colored boys" wrongly accused of murder.

In 1931, Ruth returned to Maine; and for the school year 1931–32, she enrolled as a candidate for the M.A. degree in English at the University of Maine in Orono. She dropped out after completing only the fall semester. While at Orono, she worked as a secretary in the English department.

None of her letters written to her family from college and when she first lived in New York have been found. Ruth's sister Esther remembers that their mother kept Ruth's letters in a trunk that was lost when they moved from Gott's Island to the mainland in 1927.

The Ruth Moore letters collected here begin in 1930, when she had returned to Gott's Island for a summer. Though her family had left their year-round home there (along with most of the other native families) for work and life on Mount Desert Island and the mainland, the Moores still owned property and houses on Gott's. In McKinley (now Bass Harbor), the Moore family at first rented various places. In the summer, Ruth would live on the island. She worked at different jobs on Gott's and in McKinley to add to the family income.

In 1932, Ruth returned to New York City, where she had another apartment in Greenwich Village, this time at 123 Waverly Place, which she shared with Julia Faye, another young writer-in-the-making. Ruth's first success as a writer had come in 1929 in New York when she had a long poem entitled "Voyage" published in the *Saturday Review of Literature*. During the Depression years of the early 1930s, Ruth worked again as a secretary and at other odd jobs, but when she could, she wrote poems and short stories.

From 1932–1935, Ruth worked as a private secretary to Dr. John Haynes Holmes, a liberal minister, playwright and lecturer, who lived in Brooklyn, New York. For Dr. Holmes, Ruth handled an exceptional volume of daily correspondence, edited his manuscripts, and acted as manager for his nationwide lecture tours, handling bookings and so on.

In 1936, Ruth was hired by Alice Tisdale Hobart, a popular novelist of the time who had achieved a significant success with her best-selling *Oil for the Lamps of China,* published in 1934 and made into an equally successful film in 1935. With Mr. and Mrs. Hobart (he had retired from the Standard Oil Company), Ruth moved to Washington, D.C., where she worked for a short time until moving again with the Hobarts to California. The Hobarts bought a ranch in Martinez, California, where they raised walnuts, grapes, and other fruit. Ruth was not only private secretary to Mrs. Hobart; she also helped run the Hobarts' ranch for them.

Ruth's cousin, Carl Moore, who had also grown up on Gott's Island, was then part of the crew that was building the Golden Gate Bridge in nearby San Francisco, and Ruth saw him frequently.

Soon after she moved to California, Ruth received word that her father had died. Philip Moore had been suffering for a long time from angina and heart trouble. Much as she wanted to, Ruth did not return home right away. In fact, during this time, she returned home infrequently. Transportation between East and West coasts was time-consuming, difficult, and very expensive in those days.

In 1940, when she was home for a visit, Ruth met Eleanor Mayo, fourteen years Ruth's junior, who had been one of sister Esther's students at Pemetic High School in Southwest Harbor. Esther introduced them. Eleanor was a budding young writer herself, and they quickly became friends. They went back to California together and Ruth continued working for the Hobarts until the next year when she and Eleanor moved back east to New York City. They both found work and stayed there until 1942. That year, Ruth was hired by *The Reader's Digest,* at first answering letters from readers and later helping to condense other writers' books. Ruth and Eleanor moved out of the city to Westchester County, first to Pleasantville, where the *Digest* is located, and later to White Plains.

In 1943, *The Weir,* Ruth's first novel, was published by William Morrow and Company, and in 1945, Eleanor's first novel, *Turn Home,* was published, also by Morrow. Ruth continued to work for the Digest until 1946. She once said that what she learned from condensing other people's books was how "to cut out the fluff and get on with the story." In 1946, her second novel, *Spoonhandle,* became a best-seller and was purchased by 20th Century-Fox studios, to be filmed the following year in Vinalhaven as *Deep Waters.* With the $50,000 she was paid for the film rights, Ruth could leave her job at the *Digest* and spend her time working on her own stories.

20th Century-Fox hired Ruth to come to Hollywood to write the screenplay for *Deep Waters* and other screenplays as well, but she didn't succeed. She hated the work and hated the movie studio system, and she told them so. When *Deep Waters* was released, Ruth was very upset over the stupid mistakes and inaccuracies in the film. "They butchered my book," she claimed, and was very embarrassed by the movie. Possibly because of her outspoken criticism of the movie to Darryl Zanuck, then studio head, and to others in the movie business, she didn't have much luck, afterward, in selling her novels to Hollywood. Ruth could be the worst enemy of her own career in this way. "She wouldn't compromise her standards just to sell a book," says her niece, Muriel Davisson.

In 1947, Ruth and Eleanor returned to Maine, where they bought 23 acres of shorefront in Tremont (now Bass Harbor) on the road to Bass Harbor Head Light. With a great deal of help from Eleanor's father, Fred Mayo, they proceeded to build their own house.

Throughout the 1950s, 1960s, and 1970s, Ruth and Eleanor had a happy life there. They enjoyed continued success with their writing; cultivated a number of close friendships, literary and otherwise; did some traveling abroad and a lot of gardening at home; collected rocks and Native American artifacts; and kept busy with the comings and goings of relatives and friends.

According to her niece Emily Trask-Eaton, Ruth always took a great interest in the younger generation. "She was a teacher," says Emily. She encouraged Emily with her music and Emily's brother Brian with geology. Ruth was lovable, always telling stories to her nieces and nephews and later to their children. Emily says, "She made each of us feel special ... what 'Uppy' taught me was that there was a bigger world—and you can be part of it—and still live here in Maine." She understood and encouraged it. "She never inhibited me and that is why I treasured her so much." Emily says, "I can tell you with conviction that she was psychic and knew many things that she never told but just watched them unfold. I don't know for how long she acknowledged her abilities, but I do know she was grappling with it at the end of her life. I suspect it had something to do with the way she calmly accepted the end of her life."

Ruth's first reviewers heralded her as a writer "... who is blessed with a good ear and immune to the temptation to romance or fake" and "... an author who may not be a Dreiser, but who is, in her way, as forthright and fearless as he." Her work on The Weir was described as "... not as soft and as noble as others, but it's as honest as the work of Grant Wood, and as uncompromising."

Ruth lived to see herself compared favorably to William Faulkner, John Steinbeck, Erskine Caldwell, and Flannery O'Connor. At one point, the New York Times declared, "It is doubtful if any American writer has ever done a better job of communicating a people, their talk, their thoughts, their geography, and their way of life."

About her writing, Ruth herself said, "The only thing I really try to do is not to tell a lie about a place. If I'm describing something, I know what I'm describing. I just tell the truth about what there is . . ."

Most of the early letters, 1930s–'40s, are to Ruth's mother, Lovina, whom she addressed as "Marm," "Mom," "Mum," "Momma," "Mummer," and "Ma"; and most of the later letters are to John C. Willey, her editor and friend for forty-some years. Ruth was a very private person who didn't keep most of her personal letters and who didn't disclose her most private feelings.

When she's away from Maine, she writes about how homesick she is for it; and when she's back in Maine, she complains about the "millions of tourists" driving by her door, stealing out of her garden, and interrupting her privacy.

Ruth relished a good, wild storm. Whether it was an earthquake in California or a blizzard Downeast, she was fascinated, per usual, with the powers of Nature.

The language of her letters is as salty and colorful as in her novels and poetry. The voice, the humor, and the concerns are the same as well. Ruth's novels are full of details, and so are her letters: details of the weather, the surrounding flora and fauna, the people and places of her life, her daily existence. She mentions her cats in many of her letters.

Ruth makes up words like "frivoling" and "grimpsy"; and she uses expressions like "sucks to them," "hen-minded," and "busted a gusset." She's forever "swotting away," "whizzling around," and "yattering on."

She opened and closed most of her letters in the same way ("Thank you for your pleasant letter . . ."), and when she had a good joke or a good line, she was bound to repeat it any number of times. I've edited out some of these repetitious lines and passages. Also, with her sharp tongue, Ruth could offend and hurt. Some of her unflattering and mean remarks have been cut, too.

However, most of her colorful cuss words and some condescending references, especially to Blacks, Jews, Asians, and Italians, have been left intact. Ruth herself might have objected to publishing these objectionable references, or at least she might have been rather embarrassed by them, but I think she would probably have objected more to anyone's "prettifying" her language.

In her introduction to *The Letters of E.B. White*, the editor and Ruth's good friend Dorothy Lobrano Guth quotes from Mr. White: "I was born in a

WASP's nest and learned to speak by listening to my elders. When I was a child, my bigotry—if you want to call it that—was benign, built-in, and standard. And although I began, early on, to question the social structure, it is quite apparent from these letters that I did nothing about revising the vocabulary of implied condescension. Not until mid-century, when I was a lad of fifty, did America finally get around to questioning its complacent attitudes and objectionable speech."

I'm sure Ruth, who also questioned the social structure most of her life, concurred with Mr. White.

Editing Ruth Moore's letters has been a great honor and a labor of love that has taken me all over the place ever since Gary Lawless first approached me, after Ruth's memorial service at Bass Harbor in May 1990, about attempting the job. As my contribution to the service, I had read one of Ruth's letters to me.

Besides Gary, there are many other people to thank for their assistance during this project.

First of all, Ruth's family: her sister Esther Moore Trask, her niece and literary executor Emily Trask-Eaton, her grandnephew Sven Davisson, her niece Muriel Davisson, her sister Louise Moore Dow, and her nephew Brian Trask. For information regarding Ruth's years at *The Reader's Digest,* Mary Dillon; and for the years with William Morrow and Company, Dorothy Lobrano Guth.

For information regarding John C. Willey: Lawrence Hughes, Dorothy Lobrano Guth, Cookie Goulart of Cherryfield Public Library, Elizabeth Janeway, Ann Monsarrat, Morris West, Jon Cleary, Herb and Merrie Ann Ledbetter, Jim Frick and the University of Maine Alumni Association, Joe Foster, and Gardner and Virginia Grant.

For general and bibliographical information: Muriel Sanford and her staff of the Special Collections Department of Fogler Library at the University of Maine; The Harry Ransom Humanities Research Center at the University of Texas at Austin (where Ruth's papers are stored); Vicky Erker and the Reference Department of the Bangor Public Library; Jean Blake and the staff of the Orono Public Library; the Hancock Point Library; and Travis Taylor for helping me with the research.

Because there were so few personal letters to include in this collection, I asked a number of friends, relatives, and colleagues from Ruth's life and career to share their reminiscences, most of which are included in Appendix A. In alphabetical order these are: Betty Holmes Baldwin, Gordon Bok, Miriam Colwell, Dennis Damon, Sven Davisson, Margaret Dickson, Jackson Gillman, John Gould, Betsy Graves, Edward "Ted" Holmes, Marilis Hornidge, Constance Hunting, Gary Lawless, Harris McLean, Newman "Slim" Moore, Kendall Morse, Donald Mortland, Elisabeth Ogilvie, Eunice Phillips, Dorothy Simpson, and LaRue Spiker.

For information about the early years on Gott's Island and after in New York City: Betty Holmes Baldwin, Ted Holmes, and Constance and Daniel McCarthy.

Thanks to Joel White for giving me permission to include E.B. White's letter about Ruth; to Mary Kamenoff for information about Ruth's college years in Albany; and to Roger Angell for information regarding Ruth's association with *The New Yorker*.

Finally, I would like to thank my mother, Elizabeth Phippen, my sister Susan Springer, and my friends Steve and Myrna Coffin, Farnham "Mike" Blair, Betsy Graves, Constance Hunting, Condon Rodgers, Mark Rose, and Alice Janick for being, as always, so understanding, thoughtful, supportive, and helpful over the past two years.

Sanford Phippen
Hancock and Orono, Maine
November 1992

1930s

Ruth Moore's letters begin with a neatly hand-written one to Edward "Ted" Holmes. The letter is un-dated, but Ted thinks it must be the fall of 1930 when he was a student at Dartmouth and Ruth was home on Gott's Island and in Bass Harbor (McKinley then), after having lived and worked in New York since 1925, when she graduated from Albany.

Haskell "Hick" Smith, also known as "Hack," was a Native American who came to Gott's Island and stayed with local character and handyman, Mont Gott. *The Last Mile* was a play about capital punishment written by J. Wexley. *Ghosts* is the play by Henrik Ibsen, and George Pierce Baker was the professor at Harvard who ran the famous workshop for young playwrights.

Pearl Dow married Louise Moore, Ruth's youngest sister; and Captain Eldredge was a local man for whom Pearl worked. *Et dona ferentes* is Latin for "even when bearing gifts."

TO EDWARD M. HOLMES

The Island
Sunday Fall 1930? (no date)

Dear Ted,

Hick came this morning *et dona ferentes*—ten lobsters, *not* the long green kind, in a paper bag. He was washed, I think because your father made out a cheque to him to the order of "Hick" Smith. His name is Haskell, he would have the world know.

I saw *The Last Mile*, so don't lose sleep. I think the play is tragedy, though it does rather give one to wish that the classic gent who concocted that definition had given us a bit more scope—something to pull and haul on, as the sailors say.

Not to quarrel with him—but aren't there some situations, certainly tragic, that don't come under his heading? Take *Oswald* in *Ghosts*. He was destroyed by a chain of circumstances which he failed to control, but his failure was due not so much to a defect in his character as to an unpleasant physical legacy from an indiscreet papa. In other words, the circumstances were such that he couldn't possibly have controlled them, had he no defects at all. Or take the case of the man whose partner ruined him in business and ran away with his wife. Instead of whining, he found another job, worked at it until his health broke, and died friendless and still without a murmur in the paupers' infirmary. Treated with more dignity and seriousness, such a theme would be tragedy? And the tragedy would be in the strength, not the weakness, of your protagonist's character.

Shades—oh, deep, dark, shades—of George Pierce Baker! I'm all mixed up.

Pearl said that Captain Eldredge had had your letter and had asked him about you. I gather he gave you a star recommendation—for so slight an acquaintance. As usual, I have stewed up another idea. If we can wangle it, it ought to insure everything—*assure,* I should say. Pearl asked me if I'd write your father and see if he'd take him on as a boatman for next summer. He wants a job near home, so that he can be with Louise. But, of course, your father doesn't know when he's going to put his boat into commission, or whether it will be before August, I suppose; I think I heard your mother say that you all might be here longer, next season. Suppose Pearl took his old job on the yacht next April, worked it until your father wanted him—supposing he does want him and then let you step into his shoes. You see, Pearl couldn't manage, being a family man, unless he has an all summer's job. He couldn't, honestly, take his old yacht job, knowing he would leave it at the busiest time, without someone to take his place. And as you can't begin until June anyway, that would insure an opening for you when you wanted it. It would have to be arranged with the captain, of course. I'll talk to Pearl and let you know. Not to appear conceited, I think it's a slam of an idea.

The island is nice now. Colors are changing, and sea-birds are beginning to fly over, very low. They say it means a hard winter when birds do that. I hope it means at least twenty feet of snow, and soon, so that one can't get out to go to New York. I'm writing—like a fool—for the first time in months. How goes college?

Sincerely, *Ruth*

Prohibition was the law of the land in 1930, and a number of local Maine folk were earning extra money as rum-runners. Ted Holmes' summer job for 1931 was to play the drums on a boat going to Europe. The "World" was *The New York World,* for whom Franklin Pierce Adams wrote a humor column. Monty and Hacky were Mont Gott and Haskell Smith.

TO EDWARD M. HOLMES

McKinley, Maine
October 1930? (no date)

Dear Ted,

This unprecedented promptness is begot by a desire to encourage your Maine week-end. Do you have Washington's Birthday? Any time will do, but W.B. seems to be a holiday, and by judicious cutting you might squeeze out an extra day then. Esther writes that she will be here for three days. If you want to make it earlier or later you can—I'm not exactly sandwiching my week-end parties. Bring a feller if you want to. Or a girl, or anything. And, if not too impossible, bring skis. At present, the Lord seems to be supplying the snow. Two days of it, and still blizzing.

Let's see ... what didn't I write to your mother? Horrid little habit she has of passing my letters around *in familia,* so to speak. Completely destroys my leisurely method of writing the same letter to everybody. WELL, certainly not this:

Our leading citizens observe the New Year through a rosy mist ... a booze-boat went ashore in a squall at Winter Harbor ... All one had to do was to back a truck down to almost any beach along the coast and load up with first class rye. The cases were strewn in heaps. Captain and crew took a sneak on the first train out, and it was some time before the Federal people got wind of the disaster, so that there were no hindrances. McKinley has reeled—and reeked—for days. One old Bacchus sat in a snowbank in front of the schoolhouse, groggily offering drinks to all passers-by at five cents the glass—he had a six-gallon jug. There was one tale—which I do not vouch for—of a Manset farmer who concealed seven cases in his spring ... A snow-and-rock slide came, unbeknownst ... He watered his cows. Later, five of the poor things were seen lying flat on their backs by the bars, their legs waving feebly in the air. Believe it or not; I choose to not. It smacks of the Maine creative spirit. Then there was the wild pursuit of two of our fellow townsmen by the Federal agents, through Somesville and along the Ellsworth road, in two Fords. The pursued had ten six-gallon cans in their rumble seat. The Federals were gaining. At sixty miles an hour, or whatever it was, one of the pursued climbed out on the running-board, extracted one of the cans, and dropped it in the road. The Federals hit it, got a shower bath of whiskey, wabbled, and came on. The second can went under their front wheel and burst a tire. So that was that. They got clean away, and came home three days later seeing purple skinks. Comic opera simply isn't in it with a Maine town in winter.

So Eldredge, the old flounder, didn't answer your letter. Just as well. You seem to be nicely fixed for the summer. You men-folk do have all the nice times ... I'm positively ill-humored with jealousy. Doing the Atlantic with a drum sounds so jolly ... comparable only to doing parts of it with a cabin-cruiser. Some day I'm going to shuck off this weak femininity and do Cape Horn in a knockabout or something. Last year in New York I knew a tremendously nice man who wanted me to sail to Nova Scotia in a sloop. It was a darb of a boat ... we had a couple of short trips on the Hudson, and I lost my heart to it. But neither of us was enthusiastic about holy wedlock (some of the best of sailors do *not* make husbands), and naturally, Mrs. Grundy's bristles stood up at the idea. Unreasonable, when one has such terrific attacks of things like small-boatitis, to be so ingebecitated. One of these days "impelled by a terrific attack of passion," I *shall* "throw the kitchen clock into the sea."

Well, go along with your drum, do. From June to October, *I'm* going to look after an elderly lady with diabetic inclinations.

Dear me, I really don't mean to sound plaintive. After all, elderly diabetic ladies have infinite possibilities, and (Big Secret) I'm going to California in October, if nothing upsets the applecart. My system reels at the thought of more New York, and there are no jobs in Maine. Plans are more than indefinite, as yet; but those are my inclinations.

Skiing alone is excellent recreation, as I very well know. The country around here is limited—woody, unless one wanders far afield—but there are several hills, not terribly thrilling descents, but fair. How do you suppose the Perpendicular Trail would be? You know, I have a secret urge to do some winter climbing. If you *should* happen to come up ... do you suppose we'd break our cussed necks on that trail?

I think a house-party at the island's a rosy idea, and I don't believe the island will object to the mob. A mere week ought to give it the jitters. Between you and me, I think a little dose of young blood will do it good.

Have you happened to see A.J. Williers' *By the Way of Cape Horn*? I haven't had the book, but pictures and a bit of the text were printed in the (God wot) February number of the Nat'l Geog. Mag. Sounded good. And there's a new poetry book out, *Adamastor*, by Roy Campbell. It's quite robust and very noisy:

"Then to the largest of that bony tribe,
'O merry bird,' one shouted, 'work your will!
I offer my clean body as a bribe
That when upon its flesh you've gorged your fill

"'You'll take my heart and bear it in your beak
To where my sweetheart combs her yellow hair
Beside the Vaal; and if she bids you speak,
Tell her you come to represent me there.

"'Tell her I fought as blindly as the rest,
That none of them had wronged me whom I killed,
And she must seek within some other breast
The promise that I leave her unfulfilled.

"'I should have been too tired for love or mirth,
Stung as I am, and sickened by the truth—
Old men have hunted beauty from the earth,
Over the broken bodies of our youth!'"

Not exactly first rate, I suppose, but quite effective as a war poem. It's a good bit longer—these are the last stanzas. Called "Hialmar," which means simply nothing, I believe.

I enclose a bit which came out in the *World* last summer. It's attributed to me, but "Elspeth" is really Dorothy Parker. I've had infinite congratulations on having crashed F.P.A.'s column. Wouldn't you think people would know? In the first place, I haven't done any free verse, and in the second place, I swear I could do better by the island ... Haw.

My typewriter has the gallops, particularly with "a's." I trust you to bridge the gaps. *Grand Hotel*, I've heard, is interesting. I was stricken because the Theatre Guild put on *Roar China*, and I not there to see it.

If you come up, I demand to be taught vingt-et-un—or do you play it on a wheel?

Wit' roses, *Ruth*

The Monty and the Hacky had a quarrel ... but the Monty didn't call the Hacky "little prig." Hacky called him a "damn sneakin' codfish" ... and he called

Hacky ... well, Monty always was original.
I read as how Dartmouth won the winter meet.

Ruth called her father, Philip Moore, by a family nickname, "Fripper." Philip had been inside for four years because he had angina and couldn't do physical labor. "The Colonel" was Ruth's employer in New York City at the time, for whom she worked as a secretary. Julia Faye, a friend and fellow writer, shared an apartment with Ruth in New York. "Winnie" Clark was the Superintendent of Schools in Southwest Harbor. The next letters were written from 123 Waverly Place, New York City, New York.

TO PHILIP MOORE

March 2, 1936

Dear Fripper,

Well, it certainly was a surprise to me to get a letter from you—I don't believe you've written since I have, have you? It sure was nice to hear you and Mom over the telephone the other night. You both sounded pretty darned good to me. I sure do have foul luck about striking Tuggy at home though, don't I? The others told me that I'd have a better chance of finding her home if I waited until later, but once I got the idea I couldn't wait, and besides, you and mom would have been to bed. So one way and another, we made out pretty well.

I was so sorry to hear that you've been kind of under the weather lately. I guess you ought to have taken it a little bit easier when you first started in doing out-doors again. Of course a man can't expect to start right in and chop down a million trees and wrastle 'em into cordwood, the first few weeks he works out-doors after four years inside. You take it easier, old dear, until you get fixed up. If mom runs out of wood, I'll come home and chew down some alders. Let me know how you feel and what the doctor says—though I expect you'll be feeling all O.K. again by the time you get this. If you don't, you let me know, and I'll come home and cut the damn wood myself, job or no job.

I've had a cussed time with the old Colonel. He's got about as much sense as a backhouse-hole cover, if you know what I mean, and he never knows until tomorrow what he's going to do today. About three weeks after I got back from home, he went away on a lecture trip, and on the night before he left he told me that I was laid off without pay until he got back—ten days, he was planning to be gone. It was a dirty trick, because he did it without a moment's notice, and my rent was due and I was pretty broke. So I 'lowed to myself that, come what would, I'd find another job before he got back. And then I went and got a tough cold and was laid up for ten days, and was just beginning to crawl around again when he called up for me to come back to work.

Well, then his divorced wife went to court and the judge awarded her the custody of his two children, who had been living with him up to this time; so she came and took the kids to Philadelphia. He just couldn't bear it, poor old soul, so he went on a bat which lasted for about two weeks, and by the end of that time I couldn't stand the business any longer, so I quit for good—or so I thought. It was getting pretty bad—he was drunk all the time and he didn't always remember his manners. So around the middle of February, I was out of a job. I hunted the town over, and found one or two pretty good prospects which didn't pan out and then, last Monday, the Colonel's grown-up daughter [...] called me up and wanted to know if I'd come and have a talk with her, so I did. It seemed they'd put the poor old Colonel to bed and straightened him out, and they'd tried about five secretaries for him and none of 'em would stay; so she and this Mrs. K[.] who is a friend of his, came to me and said, "Look here, you've handled the Colonel better than anybody ever has, and wouldn't you consider coming back and doing the work, because he's not well and he really can't have just an ordinary woman around him." Well, that made me pretty smart, so I said I would come back for awhile, and that's where I am now. I don't know how long I'll be there, for the old Colonel is really pretty sick, and I think the family will probably take him south, or abroad or something, when he gets better. But this Mrs. K[.] who talked to me about coming back to him, said, among other things, that if I would go back and work for him as long as he needed me, she'd guarantee me a good job when his job petered out. So I'm getting along all right now, though I was pretty blue and broke all through February, which was one reason why I didn't feel much like writing any letters. You know how it is. I feel swell now, and on top of the world.

I'm sending along a little mazooka to pay you the five I owe you with a little interest—or did I borrow ten from you? Anyway, here's ten, and I hope it will help some. I would have sent it before if the damned job hadn't acted up so. I think I can send some more before too long, if things keep on going well. If they don't, I'll come home myself, which probably would be pleasanter if not so practical. Don't you and mom worry too much about expenses, because if things pan out for me, and I think they will, I'll have a nice job here [...]. Don't worry too much, anyway. You and mom have had your share of work, and it's about time the both of you had some good time. We aren't always going to be so broke, old dear, so don't be counting on it. I've had some breaks this month—sold a couple of poems to Julia's magazine, and I think her editor wants some more as soon as she sees these, and she pays me ten dollars apiece for them. It's a good magazine to sell to, because they pay well, and they have a circulation of 100,000, so it gives work a good chance to be seen. The American Association of the Blind sent me a letter last week or so, asking if they could have permission to reprint one of my poems in braille, which means that it will go into books and magazines for the blind all over the country. I don't know whether it's a compliment or not to feel that the blind are the only ones who read your stuff—what do you think?

Well, I mustn't tell you all the whole news-bag, or I won't have anything left to write to mom. Be a nice egg and write to me again—you might get another letter out of me, you never can tell. I hope you get all over your pip, or whatever, and feel like a bird by the time you get this.

Lots of love, dear, *Uppy*

Helen is Helen Moore, Ruth's cousin. "Sweeney" was a teacher in Southwest Harbor. "Junior" was Lester Radcliffe, Harvey "Harve" Moore's stepson; Ann was Harve's daughter. "Tinky" (Harvey Jr.) and Carlton David are Louise Moore Dow's sons, Ruth's nephews.

TO MRS. LOVINA MOORE

March 2, 1936

Dear Missus Moore,

I've gone and written a letter to Phil, and covered about two month's news in it, but I guess there's still a little bit left for you and me to chew over. We always do manage to find something, don't we?

I've been a base-born slut about writing letters since I got back, but I really do mean to write them, and I did get you called up a couple of times, so you weren't completely deserted. But of course, you do write to me every week, and somebody ought to kick me in the tail. Julia does every once in a while, but it doesn't seem to do much good. Well, anyway ... I done it and I'll probably do it again, though I certainly don't mean to. It isn't the writing that's such a job, it's the finding the time and the getting started. I expect Tuggy won't ever speak to me again—or will she?

I've told Philip all about the job, so you can read his letter for that. What's the news about Sweeney? If she does leave, would Tug go and see Clark for me about getting her job, or had I better write him? It kind of catches me with my pants down, because if this Mrs. K[.] lives up to her promises, she will get me a really good job—she is the head of an organization called the Fashion Group, which has headquarters all over Radio City, and she knows magazine editors well enough to call them by their first names. However, if Sweeney does leave her job, and Clark would let me have it, of course I would take it. Because I haven't any intention of spending my life in New York City. And because, too, it would have to be a pretty good job that I'd get down here to get as much ahead of the game as I would if I was up there. So if Sweeney [...] leaves, you get Tug to see Clark quick and wire me, if he says yes.

The pillow covers are swell. The patterns are lovely. Where did you get them, or did you and Tug conjure them up? I haven't had time to sew them onto pillows yet, but I plan to this weekend, when I have a moment. Since I went back to work for the Colonel, I've been starting at twelve o'clock noon, and working right through till eleven or twelve at night, most evenings. So I haven't had much time at home, and is Julia sore! She thinks the Colonel ought to be strung up by the neck, and I guess maybe he had. However, the poor old soul is sick, and sick in his mind, too, I guess.

We've got an elevator strike down here which covers almost the whole city. Practically every elevator operator in town has walked out on his job, and you should hear some of the Park Avenue boys and girls who live on the thirty-second floor yelp. In our building here at Waverly Place the elevators are running, but the front door is locked and we all have to come in through the back way, and the elevator starts from the second floor, so that any of the local union people who may be spotting the building from the outside, see all the people who live in the house come in and start walking up the stairs, so they don't throw bricks through the windows. It's all very exciting. I hope they don't stop the elevators up at 405 Park, where I work, because the Colonel's apartment is on the ninth floor, and I don't want to horse these aching old bones up nine flights of stairs. However, the elevator man up there told me tonight that they were just waiting for word from the union to walk out. So, I expect next time you hear from me I'll be writing from the stairs, halfway up.

Helen is here for a few days. She was staying at a hotel, but Julia invited her to stay here, so she will be here until Wednesday, I think. She's well, and having a nice time. I would have invited her myself, but I didn't think of it.

Love to Tug, and Louise and the babies and all the rest. I will write again soon, really I mean it, and next time it will be a nicer letter because I won't have told Phil all the news first.

Love, *Uppy*

Julia wants to add a line, so

Julia: Here I am—and hello, everybody! Did you think we were quite cuckoo the other night, the lot of us calling gayly to Maine? But we were having such a good time that we simply had to call you. We had the radio going full blast and were dancing around like mad when somebody said, "Let's call Maine"; whereupon the Moore family plus myself trailed downstairs to the phone en masse, leaving Helen's two gentlemen up here to cool their heels until our return. It's such a thrill to hear the operators all along the line answering, and then finally your voice over all those miles and miles. When I think of all the sea I churned along through last summer before I arrived at Bar Harbor, I get a special kick out of it. Hope you're all fine and dandy, and give my special love to Junior and Ann for those darling Valentine greetings they sent to me. I took them to the office to show the word from Ann's Quacky, the Duck, and everybody wanted to hear more about Ann—which they did. Lots of love to Tinky, and Louise and all. I am going to write Louise one of these days, for I must have some special news of young David. Say cheerio to Tuggy for me and my best to Mr. Moore. Must sign off, as I have already written too much, and Ruth is stamping her foot over there, I think.

Merritt Hayden and Jack Hapworth were Esther's boyfriends. The Prices were summer people. Lucy Rhoads bought Enoch Moore's house. Goddard was Ruth's boyfriend from Brookline, Massachusetts, whom she met in New York City. Bill Thurston was Philip Moore's employer. Tena was the wife of Bert Moore, Philip's brother, and Preston was Preston Ford, Tena's second husband. Ted Holmes married Jane Colyer in 1936.

TO ESTHER MOORE

April 28, 1936

Dear Tug,

Well, as usual, we haven't done so good—me especially. But you know how 'tis about this writing letters—same old mullarkey, I suppose, isn't it? So I shan't waste time saying what a lazy hound I am, as you already know it. I've been feeling lousy for the last two weeks—had a cold on the chest, which I don't seem to get rid of, though it's better now than it was. I expect I need some cod liver oil, or something. Julia says castor oil, the rat, and she'd have it down me, too, if I didn't sleep with my mouth shut. But I will be all right as soon as we have some warm weather—so far, we've had it chilly and rainy with only a few good days here and there.

You sound as if things were picking up a little bit. I'm so glad to hear about the boy-friend, because it must make things seem much less dull. He sounds like the real McCoy, and apparently everybody thinks so, too. I can't tell you how glad I am that Merritt is of the past now. In a way, I do feel sorry for him; but I'm afraid I have to believe that he had it coming to him. Jack sounds like somebody you can depend on—any guy who can put out a burning automobile with only an army shirt gets my vote every time. My, my, that's somep'n though ... go out to park, and have the car start to burn! Tch, tch! What a gal!

Well, let's see what the news is with me. The Colonel came back from England on the 8th of April, and I had work until the 20th, when he was off again on a lecture trip to the Middle West. He was worse than hell this time, nerves all gone to pot and kept likkered up all the time; so when he told me that I was to be laid off again without pay while he was gone this time, I said O.K., you better get somebody else when you get back. So he offered to put me on half-pay if I'd stay, so, like a fool, I did. He is coming back on the first of May, and after that I don't know what his plans are. I know I am sick of all his works and ways. I have had one or two leads for other jobs, but there hasn't been anything definite as yet. Of course, it's only a matter of time, as you can always find a job if you look for it and can hang on financially until you do. Of course, that's the reason why I have hung onto the Colonel.

Frankly, I haven't made up my mind what I ought to do this summer. What I want to do is to come home the last of May and stay until September. I cashed in that poor old neglected life insurance and got a nice fat pot—$164.22—most of which I plunked into the bank as an anchor to windard, just in case.

So I'd have enough to carry me over the summer all right. But the plain fact is, I don't want to risk being stranded next fall without a job and with no dough, for that would mean staying at home and living off the family, and I don't see how I can do that with them so broke. In the first place, it wouldn't be right, and in the second place, I'd most likely go nuts without any job. I don't really think Clark will give me a job; he has some kind of a nigger in the woodpile, god knows what it is. I've written him about it, all nicely, and I could come home in June and plan to stay. But he's so darned evasive about it—I wish he had the guts to come out and say no, in so many words, and tell me why. I'd think a lot better of him if he'd be direct for once. I told him so in my letter, so when he gets around to answer it, if he does this year, maybe we'll know the wherefores of the situation.

Meanwhile, I've got a couple of irons or so in the fire besides, so far as writing is concerned, and something may come of it, though of course you can't depend on it. I've got a story with *Scribner's Magazine*, and a kid's story with *St. Nicholas,* and Reynal and Hitchcock has my manuscript of poems. They may take 'em and they may all come bouncing back in my lap. If I do sell some, and get a little encouragement, I am going to plan to come home anyway, the last of May or the first of June, and spend the summer writing like a fool.

So you see. Things just ain't decided. About that civil service notice—I don't know how c.s. jobs are run in Maine, but I took a state exam last fall for an employment job and passed it quite high on the list. So I inquired around, and found out that they check up on how you vote and in this state if you didn't vote Democrat, straight, you don't even get considered. Hell, I didn't have a chance—I didn't even vote Republican. Like every other kind of job, I guess, it's a matter of pull. Of course, if you could get somebody with a lot of political pull to go around and see the representative from our district, and say, "Look here, here's a girl who ought to have a job," why then it might make a difference. Otherwise, you might as well piss up the stovepipe as take a civil service exam. Which expresses how I feel about it, having taken one and passed it. Of course, though, politics in New York State are stinko. Maybe they aren't so bad in Maine. I hope not.

Tell mom I wrote to the Prices down in Moylan Park, Pa., about the old place, and have been waiting for an answer. But I haven't heard from them, and I guess it's probably because they haven't any dough. They didn't sound so rich, last summer, you remember. But, you know, if the heirs are thinking of selling the place for just $1000—which is a steal—especially if they let all that land go for that—I would bet you my red undershirt that they could get at least $2000 for it from Miss Lucy Rhoads. I wish Pa would write her and ask her about it. She mentioned the old place last summer and how she would like to have it. Her address, the last I knew, was 103 Putnam Street, Quincy, Mass. I think it would be better for Pa to write her, because she thinks so much of him. I think Tena has got a gall, because as I see it, she's taking advantage of her relatives when they haven't any of them got much dough, and $250 looks like a lot. And the fact remains that Tena is older than Preston, and when she dies the place will be out of the family for good and all, and god knows what he'd do with it. However, it isn't any of my business, I suppose, except I do think the heirs are awful fools to think of selling for a thousand dollars. The point is, $250 is going to last each one of them such a little time, and when it's gone, they won't have anything.

I think I have lost Goddard for good and all this time. He came back to me, unannounced, the middle of March, and seemed to be very upset, so I let him hang around. Last week he asked me to go dancing with him, but didn't make any very definite arrangements, and, of course, a week ago Saturday I came down with this cold and didn't dare get snaked out in low evening clothes. So I wrote him a note and said the date was off, and he came down the next Monday as sore as a pimple, and said that he had a table reserved at the French Casino and an order in at the florist's, which he had had to cancel. Well, I didn't believe it for a minute—not the way that one glues on to his dimes. So I said so. Says I, "If you had a table at the French Casino and had had an order in at the florist's, it would be the first time, my good man, that I would have made the acquaintance of either one through any effort of yours; and I'm damned if I believe a word of it." So he went off, very mad, and I haven't seen him since, and I thought Julia was going to die laughing.

I sound like a very mean skunk in this letter, but I guess it's only my snotty nose. I will be my sweet self again, as soon as the snuffles go. Share this letter with the folks, especially with mom, because it really ought to be hers; I will write her as soon as my news bag fills up again. I do so hope things break so I can come home this summer, and I think they will, though I'm trying not to count too much on things, in case they don't.

By the way, Ted Holmes is getting married on the 27th of June and he and Jane are going to spend their honeymoon at the island. Ain't that somep'n?

Love to all the kids, etc. *Uppy*

Why don't Fripper have a talk with Bill and ask him to put in a dime for me with Winnie Clark and the school board?

Carl Moore was Ruth's cousin and Helen's brother. Philip had deeded his part of Enoch Moore's house to Esther and Ruth. Bert and Tena wanted to buy the house and the land—between 50 and 60 acres—for $1000, but Ruth refused to sign the deed. Joe was Julia's brother. Aunt Ede was Edith Kelley, Philip Moore's sister.

TO LOVINA MOORE

May 1936

Dear Ma,

Well, you'll be surprised to hear from me again so soon, and I guess it is kind of unusual. Maybe the heat's gone to my head. I can't imagine you folks having it so cold—I enclose a clipping which shows what *we* got down here. Dawgone, it does seem as though the Lord was pouring it on, when here it is only the end of May. We'll all be little lumps of grease, if this keeps up. Julia and I and Joe went over to play tennis yesterday at one of the city courts. It wasn't so bad out there as there was a little breeze, but every once in a while a gust would come and it would pick up this little fine dust off the courts and just about choke us to death. When we got home we looked like niggers.

By the way, I sent you that box of bulbs and seeds, so for goodness sakes, plant 'em before it's too late. I never thought you and Tug would think it belonged to somebody else, but it's just like me for not letting you know. I wish when you plant 'em you'd mark the dahliahs with their names, so we can tell which is which—be sort of fun to see what they do. Lord, I wish I could pop in and help you. Wouldn't it be a rosy time! The chances look kind of slim now, though I hate to admit it. I've had a couple of bites at jobs, and one of them has finally come through. It's a good one, and if I didn't want to come home so much, I'd be tickled to death. As it is, I just feel like sticking out my tongue at any kind of work.

This job that has come through is with quite a well-known novelist, Mrs. Alice Tisdale Hobart. She's written two best-sellers, River Supreme and Oil for the Lamps of China, which was in the movies. You may have seen it. It was quite a popular movie. She lives down in Washington, D.C., and if I take the job, it will mean living at her country place outside of Washington, for the summer. She wants a secretary and someone who can edit the manuscript of her next novel. Of course, that's right down my alley. I've done one batch of manuscript for her, and she liked it a lot. She will pay me a hundred dollars a month and all living expenses, which, of course, is too darned good to pass up. However, it is only a summer job, which will last until October. After that, I would plan to take a vacation and come home for a month, and then come back here and find a job for the winter. The way things are, with all of us so broke and one thing and another, I feel that that's about the only thing I can do. I wish that damned old Colonel I worked for all last winter would get the piles, or something, so bad he couldn't sit down—at least, until he pays me the back salary he owes me. He kept putting me off on my last two salary checks, and when I left I couldn't collect a cent from him. I suppose there's a place in hell for rich old crooks like him to fry in, but it seems a long time to have to wait for justice, and kind of indefinite, too.

Well, that's the set-up right now. I know you'll be disappointed, because I've had a sneaking feeling all along that something would break so I could have at least part of the summer at home. Now we'll have to wait until the last of September or October first. I suppose that's better than nothing. If I go to Washington, she wants me on June 1.

I'll let you know, if I go, and what my address will be. Julia is sore as a boil at the idea, and thinks I ought to stay here in New York and wait until a job comes through here. She doesn't say much about it, but I can tell how she feels. I suppose a job would come if you waited long enough for it, but living is so expensive here, and money just melts away, and I don't feel that I can wait much longer. If nothing else breaks before the first of June, I expect I'll go to Washington. Of course, if will be kind of interesting to live down there for a while. I've never been there—only passed through a couple of times, and I expect what with the campaign for the presidential election going on, things will be kind of exciting. Though they say that Washington is blistering hot in summer, I don't believe it could be much worse than little ole New York. From what the weather forecasters say about the heat this summer here, the devil's decided to save expenses this summer, by shutting down hell and moving in until October.

Helen and Carl both write me that they have decided not to sign the deed to sell the old place, so that lets me off of the responsibility. Carl said that after he read the deed he changed his mind about it, because he hadn't realized before that there was so much land involved. I expect Uncle Bert and Aunt Tena will be as sore as a boil, and I'm awfully sorry if they are. But that quit-claim deed that was fixed up for Tug and me to sign, reads that we give up all claim of any kind whatever to the property "forever," and I don't want to sign any deed that shuts me out for that long. I haven't heard a word from Aunt Ede, but I had a long letter from Bert. He was kind of huffy. He didn't say anything in the second letter that wasn't in the first one he wrote me. The only thing he said about the three suggestions I made for putting some strings on the property was "Your suggestions are all right, but I think they should have been brought up before so much trouble was gone to." I don't see why it isn't possible to get together on at least one of them, without going to too much additional trouble; all he'd have to do is have a new deed drawn up which would include whichever suggestion the heirs decide on. Of course, his idea is to get rid of the whole property, clip and clean, and get his cut and call it a day. In a way, I don't blame him; but I don't feel that I want to give up my interest "forever." So that's that. Maybe it's a good idea if I don't show my puss around there this summer.

It is an awful shame about gramp's face being so bad. I do wish something might be done about it. It seems terrible for gram to be looking after him alone, but I suppose she'd rather do it as long as she can. [...] I'd take him right to Boston now, while he still has the strength to go and not wait any longer. Or could he manage to go now?

Goddard has crawled up out of the cracks in the floor again. I don't know why. I'm getting so I can't stand the sight of him. He has got a lovely idea into his head that if I'd just sleep with him once it would solve all the problems and we could plan to get married at the end of this summer. My answer to that is NUTS! So I told him to pick up his dolls and dishes and go play somewhere else, though I don't know how long it will last this time. He bought a new sailboat that he paid five hundred dollars for, and then he came creeping around to take me out to dinner and asked me if I'd pay for my own dinner-check, as he was saving his money. So I told him No, I'd decided not to eat for the next month or so, as I was saving mine, too. Honestly, I could puke.

Well, I guess that's all that's in my news-bag. I'm getting so I sound like an old grouch, but I guess I'll get over it. Tell Tug I got her letter and will answer it soon. When does her school close? Tell Fripper if he'd rather I'd sign the deed I will, though I gather from your letters that he feels about the same as the rest of us do. Lots of love to all the kids and the rest. Wee said she was going to send me a snapshot of little David as soon as she got a good one. I hope she does as I'm crazy to see how he looks now. Tell Tinky when you see him that he owes me a letter.

Love, *Uppy*

Newman is Ruth's cousin, and Helen and Carl's brother; Alice was their mother. Liz was Uncle Bert Moore's wife.

TO PHILIP MOORE

May 1936

Fripper, dear,

I was so glad to get your letter, because I have been wanting to get a word from you. I feel bad about this business of the old place, and as sorry as the devil that Uncle Bert is so tore out. Of course he has paid the lion's share of the taxes for a long time, and he ought to have the most say. I don't blame him for being sore.

The main reason why I held back was because mother wrote me that when Uncle Bert brought up the deed for you to sign, you didn't want to sign, and that you and he had quite a little chew over it. She said that she didn't want to sign herself, that Newman had signed but was sorry he had and that he was going to write Helen and Carl and ask them not to, and that Tug wasn't in favor of it either. I thought if that was the way everybody felt, what was the use? Besides, since other people weren't in favor of it, I don't see how Uncle Bert can blame the whole thing on me. Alice has just written to Helen that she is very glad Helen refused, and that if she had thought it over, she wouldn't have signed it herself. So there you are. I wonder why you have changed your mind about it. Is it because of the taxes, or do you feel that there will be hard feelings if Tena doesn't get the place?

About the taxes. Helen and Carl were both here a week or so ago, and I told them as strong as I could make it that if we were going to be the ones who wouldn't sign, then we would have to take the responsibility of the taxes. They agreed to divide up the sum of the back taxes between the five of us—

Helen, Carl, Newman, Tug, and I—if Newman and Tug would agree to do it, too, and I think they will. Helen was going to write Newman about it, and she also wrote Oscar Tolman to get the exact sum of taxes that is due. Uncle Bert says sometimes $175 is due, and then he says $200 is due, and the lord knows just what the right sum is. Helen has sent me a copy of Oscar Tolman's letter and according to him it's as follows:

Due on	1934 taxes	$34.36
	1935	$73.60
		$107.96

Then Tolman goes on to say, "On the 1936 tax of $23.04, $12.16 is heirs of Holsey N. Moore; $10.88 is heirs of Laura Moore. This property has been taxed to the five heirs."

What does he mean by that? Are the taxes for 1936 lower? That doesn't seem right. That would mean that the tax for 1936 is $52.72. Will you find out from him just exactly what the tax total due is, and let me know?

I told Helen and Carl that it was a thing to be thought over pretty seriously, and that they had no right to stand out if they didn't plan to take responsibility. They both say that they will pay without fail.

Carl has a good job and so has Helen and there is no reason why they shouldn't chip in and I think they will. They both told me that they had been given to believe that their father's share of the taxes had been taken out of the money that grammie Moore left, each year. As to that, I don't know; but it does seem kind of odd to me that all that money was put into repairs last year, and the taxes left unpaid. I don't see what Bert was thinking of, really I don't. But after all, he has seen to it that the taxes were paid for a long time, and I don't suppose that he ought to be criticized. I am fixing up a written agreement for the five of us to sign, guaranteeing the backtaxes, to be paid this year. I'll write Uncle Bert that that's what we're doing, and see that at least part payment is made before the end of the summer. Do you think that that will be all right? After all, there is nothing that can be done now to make him less sore, and I'm awful sorry about it. I shouldn't have taken the stand I did at all, if I hadn't felt that everyone felt more or less the way I did.

I haven't been able to do more this spring than just pay my expenses, as my job fell through back in March. I have been working off and on since then, but nothing to brag about. Now, however, I have got a bang-up job down in

Washington, which I have just written mother about, and won't repeat, so things will be better, and I will be able to take some responsibility, not only for the old place, but for the mortgage and taxes on our place. I won't get home until October this year, or possibly the last of September, and that's just about killing me, because I get homesick when I don't get home in the summer. But we've got to have the dough, and I don't see any other way out of it. I am going to Washington next Monday, June 1—just had a letter this morning clinching the thing up for good. Be sure you keep my address and give it to mother—

Care of Mrs. E.T. Hobart
Tilden Gardens
3031 Sedgewick Street
Washington, D.C.

I suppose you saw the letter from Mr. Price about renting one of the houses on the island. What do you think about it? He didn't get my letter I wrote him before about buying the old place, as I sent it to the wrong address and it was returned to me. So I was glad to hear from him. I wrote him yesterday telling him the old place was for sale for $2500, as mother mentioned in her letter. Is that all right? He is not a rich man, but they were all so enthusiastic about the place last year, and asked over and over what the selling price was, and all I could tell them then was $5000, which was what I understood the heirs wanted. He said last year if I remember, that $2500 would be a good price. I have to wait to hear from him, before I can know any more definitely, of course. I also told him that I hoped he would be able to rent the old place this summer. Mother said in her letter that the stove there had gone to pieces and bedding was needed, and of course the well would have to be cleaned out. I told Mr. Price that I thought the heirs wanted to rent very much, but did not know whether they were able to stand the expense of making the place rentable for the summer. Will you find out from Uncle Bert what he wants to do? I think the Prices and the Stephenses might pay $60 for the month they want to use it. I believe that is all we could ask, in fairness, for what they would be getting. I said that in case the heirs didn't want to go to the expense of getting the old place in shape, Mr. Price could have our house for a month for $50. Is that all right with you? I hardly knew what to tell him, as it is so hard to make arrangements two ways by letter. Will you talk it over with Uncle Bert and let me know definitely as soon as you can? So far as the bedding goes, I expect, if they wanted to rent the old place, we could help out with bedding from our house; it would be an easy matter for Newman or somebody, or for you and Uncle Bert yourselves to go down there and clean out the well; and as for a stove, why not borrow the stove that is now rusting away in Alice's house, if she is willing? It would do it good to be cleaned up and used. Tug and Helen could go down before July 15 and give the house a good cleaning. In that way it could be got into shape again, and if the Prices and the Stephenses came one summer and had a good time and felt they liked it, they might, if not buy the place, at least, rent it for some summers to come.

I will write to Uncle Bert and ask him if he will talk the matter over with you. I hope I can write him so that he will be a little less mad, but I doubt if I can, what with Liz prodding him all the time.

Will you break out your old fountain pen again and answer this letter as soon as you can get the facts?

I'm sorry as unpremeditated hell if I have kicked up a family row. As I said before, I shouldn't have done it if I hadn't thought it was the right thing to do. Three years ago when the bottom was out of real estate all over the country, an offer of $1000 for the place would have been O.K. But now things are picking up. I have talked with two real estate companies here in town, and they say that anyone would be a fool to let such an old house and so much land go for a song; they say that if we advertise, there is no doubt but we could sell it for a better price. Well, we can't advertise now, because none of us have the dough, but later, maybe we can, if Mr. Price doesn't bite on. I have got Mrs. Murray interested in it too, to the extent that she told me that if we got up against it and couldn't pay the taxes, she would lend me the money to do it. But I don't want to borrow unless I have to.

Of course, $250 would come in handy right now. But, old dear, that $250 would last a few months and then it would be gone, and then nobody would have anything. Land costs taxes, of course, but it's something that is always there to go back to, in case anyone has to. As for sentiment, that has a place, too, but nobody would be any quicker than I to sell the old place, out of the family or not, if we were offered a fair price for it. My feeling is that Tena could perfectly well afford to pay a fair price for it; but the less said about that the better.

This is a long letter; but there was a lot to say. You sound kind of down, and I don't blame you, but don't get any more worried than you can help. I have a feeling that things are beginning to break for us. I am all set for the summer and probably longer, and I will be able to help out if things go too wrong. Perhaps you will be able to find something to do, but don't think of taking anything that will be too awful hard outdoor work. After the rinktum you had this spring, you want to be careful.

Lots of love, and keep your snoot wiped, old dear,
Uppy

Admiral Byrd and his family summered in the Bass Harbor area, and Esther did typing for him. "Little Johnnie" is Harvey's son. The following letters were written from Tilden Gardens, 3031 Sedgewick Street, Washington, D.C.

TO ESTHER MOORE

June 9, 1936

Dear Tuggy,

Somebody owes somebody a letter, and I've forgotten who 'tis, so I guess it's probably me. The heat of Washington is enough to drove memory out of anybody's head, so you mustn't be surprised. It is a very pretty city, but the climate of it sits on your chest. All the nice fat figger I got last winter from drinking beer with the Fayes is running off the end of my spine, and I expect I'll look like Ginger Rogers at the end of the summer.

Is your school done? I expect it closed Friday, didn't it? What are your summer plans, if any? Have any of the old crowd of professors and Byrds turned up to have any stenography done? When the first of June came around, I was pretty homesick, but I couldn't have passed this job up. It was too darned swell. Did you read *Oil for the Lamps of China*, or see the movie? It was a best seller, I guess, and if I know anything about it, this one Mrs. Hobart's working on now is going to be, too. She is such a nice person, and it is such a relief to work for somebody who's human, after old Teeterballs [...]. We are working now on the final corrected copy of the manuscript, getting it ready for the printer. That will be done in August, and then I'm going to help with the proof, and after that, I'll be done, and will be home for a month, if I can wrangle it, and I think I can. As I told mother in my last letter, I expect to be there most of September. Well, I haven't had any opinion from you yet as regards the old place rinktum. What did you think about it? I got an ugly-mad letter from Aunt Tena which I meant to send home in ma's letter, but forgot to put in. Apparently she thinks I'm to blame for the whole thing, and I suppose I am, but somehow I don't give a cuss. I had a letter from Lucy Rhoads yesterday, saying her father was mildly interested, but what was likely to happen was that she could devil him into buying the place for her. She is in Wilmington, now, and I asked her to come over here and visit me for a weekend, and we could talk about it. She seemed to think the thing was in the bag. Wouldn't that be swell? I'd like to see her have the place, since it can't stay as it is, I suppose, with everybody in the family, except you and I and the cousins boiling mad about it and flinging insults. If Lucy comes over here, and I can get to talk to her, I feel sure I can get results. Maybe the letter I wrote her will get 'em anyway.

I'm waiting to hear from Pa about renting the old place to the Prices. Bert wrote me the hell with it, or words to that effect. He's washed his hands of it all in the last three letters I've had from him. I don't blame him for being mad, really, and I have a lot of sympathy for him. I never could get mad at him, really, he's such a loveable soul, and I've always been keen about him. But I wish I could get some definite answer out of somebody, so I could write Mr. Price. Will you and ma put your heads together and see if it's possible at all to fix it up to rent? If it is out of the question entirely, I'll write Price that he can have our house. I set a price of $50 rent on it when I wrote him—that is, in case he couldn't get the old place. I expect I better write him that he can't have the old place anyway, as that would simplify matters all around. But I'll wait until I hear from you before writing him. Of course, way off here, I can't do much of anything, and if we rented either of the houses, you'd have to do the honors about getting whichever one of them it is fixed up. When I hear definitely from the Prices, I'll tell them to write to you for all further information and arrangements, shall I? If nothing comes from all these customers we seem to have raked up, and nobody buys the house, do you think we who have stood out against Tena's buying it could club together on the taxes? Helen and Carl have agreed to put in a fifth each on the amount due, and I will, and I thought you and Newman, if able, would like to do it too. I can't find out what the actual sum is, but if it's $175, that would be $35 apiece. I thought we might arrange it in the fall, say October, when all of us will be working again—if all of us are. I think I can manage to save enough out of this summer's job to carry my part, and also make some kind of a payment on our own house. Will you dig around and find out what the actual, total sum of taxes on the old place is due? I asked Pa for it, but you know how long it takes him to make up his mind to write.

Well, all this is old potatoes, and I'm getting kind of sick of it, as I expect everybody else is. Write me where you stand, and what your opinion is. Aunt Tena will probably arrive sometime this summer, trailing clouds of gloom and injury, and you will probably hear a bellyful. However, I still believe I done right, begosh.

It is awful hot here today. I got thinking about the island while I was having my lunch, and almost cried into the soup. Boy, would it be nice and cool there, today! I'd go down and crawl into the upper pool with just my nose out, and wouldn't come out for a week. Heigh ho. September's comin', kid, September's comin'.

How are all the kids? Tell Tinky and Wee and Pearl they all owe me a letter. I'd love to get some mail, I'm lonesome as a tick on an elephant's back, and I don't know anybody in Washington. Tell Wee she ought to write me and tell me about David. Nobody's mentioned him, how much he weighs, or how he's growing or anything, in the last two months. I expect he and little Johnnie and Ann are so big they can't get into a clothes-basket, now. Wee was going to send me a picture of the baby, when she got one. Tell her I'm still open-minded about it.

Goddard wrote he had stood it as long as he could and was coming down this weekend, so whether he will turn up or not, I don't know. I expect I'd even be glad to see him, the way I don't know any lewd companions down here. However, I'm meeting people all the time, and I suppose shan't feel lonesome after a while. Just the same, kid, it would be nice to lay my eyes on, say, you, for instance.

How's Jack? Give him my regards. Is Newky back yet? Have you been down to the island? Now I must get back to my copying and do a little work.

Love, old bison, and write
soon.*Uppy*

Atlantic is a village on Swan's Island. "Tene" is a nickname for Tena.

TO LOVINA MOORE

Washington, D.C.
June 1936? (no date)

Dear Mom,

I got your letter written in Atlantic and meant to write before, but the new job is keeping me awfully busy and Washington is so hot. I do wish you didn't have to go through all that, it must be awful, and hard on your lameness, too. Poor old Gramp. I didn't realize before that things had got so bad. It seems so terrible that nothing can be done. I wish I could be home to help out, for it is too much for you. [. . .] Write me how things go and give my love to Gram. I feel so sorry for her.

I had a nasty letter from Aunt Tena which I enclose. You better burn it up. I'm sorry she's up a tree, but I still don't regret stopping the sale. Bert wrote me, too, again, saying he doesn't care what we do with the old place this summer. I wrote him and Tena about the Prices wanting to rent. What do you think? Shall we let them have our house, or would it be worth while to fix up the old place? I don't suppose Pa will get around to answering the questions in my letter till along in the fall sometime. The old bird. Poke him up about it, will you? At this distance, I can't do much, and I'd like to have things settled so I could write Mr. Price. Isn't it swell that Mr. Rhoads is interested? Lord, I wish he'd buy it. Couldn't we haw haw up our sleeves then? Boy!

What I can't understand is that if Tene was buying it just to be bighearted, why is she so mad? I wouldn't have thought so myself, if she hadn't gone up a tree about it. I'm getting a little sick, myself, of having knock-notes from my uncles, my cousins and my aunts, and the next one that comes is going to get a good rousing answer. Pooh to it! I can get mad myself—and what's more I've got a college education—same thing that ruined me, as Tene once said. However, I haven't answered her letter, and don't believe I shall.

The new job is swell. I've been awfully busy so far. It is mostly working on the manuscript of her new book, getting it ready for the printers. She isn't very well—has a bad back and does her writing lying down with a pad and pencil on her stomach. So her stuff comes to me in awful shape, and I take it and type it, and take out mistakes, etc. Quite a lot the same as I did for Miss Ovington last summer, only this is more fun to work on because Mrs. Hobart is a much brighter woman than Miss Ovington. Mrs. H. and her husband have a lovely apartment, all furnished with Chinese stuff she brought from China. They lived in China for sixteen years—Mr. Hobart was head of the Standard Oil Company there. He is quite a boy. When they were in China, they were living in Nanking at the time the Chinese got stirred up by the Reds and started to kill all the white people in the town. Mrs. Hobart and Mr. Hobart and John Davis, the American Consul, along with about twenty others, were trapped in Mr. H.'s house, and they laid on the floor for two days while the Chinese shot bullets through the walls. When, finally they (the Chinese) got into the house, they took Mr. Hobart and the Consul and stood them up against a wall, and were aiming their rifles to fire, when Mr. Hobart made a funny crack at them and made them laugh. So then they got to talking with him, and he kidded them along until the British gunboats, which were coming, arrived and let off a couple of shells over the city. The Chinks started to run, and while they were scared off for a while, the whole crowd sneaked out of the house, let themselves down by sheets tied together over the city wall, and got away to the gunboat. The idea was that if Mr. Hobart hadn't made that funny crack, the whole crowd would have been shot. Lord, it's enough to curdle your blood. Mrs. H. wrote the story of it in a book called *Within the Walls of Nanking*. It makes swell reading. I will try to get a copy of it to send to you.

For the first week I was here I lived at their apartment, but I now have a room around the corner, as they are getting ready to move to their country place and the place is being packed up. Mr. H. is going to California the middle of July—he has a new job there, in Berkeley, and Mrs. H. is going in September. After he goes, possibly before, I will be moved out to the country place for the rest of the summer, where we will shut ourselves off and work on the final copy of the book. It's a lovely place, 18 miles from Washington on the Potomac River. When the book is done, my job will be, and then I expect I will get home for most of the month of September.

Well, it's bedtime and I must saw off. I hope by the time you get this things will be better for Gramp. Anyone can't wish anything else, I suppose, seeing he is so bad off. Write me how it is, and be careful of yourself, dear.

Love, *Uppy*

TO LOVINA MOORE

June 1936? (no date)
Wednesday

Dear Mom,

I've been so rushed, though I did mean to write you right after Gramp died. I'm glad it's over, though I do think it was awful for him to have to suffer so, poor old soul. How is Gram? I am going to write her, though I expect a few letters aren't going to make her any the less lonesome. I wish I could have been home. Seems awful to be way off here like this, sometimes. But shucks, I suppose I'm lucky to have the job. It's a grand job and lots of fun to do, but

I sure do miss being around this summer. They don't often come like last summer, do they?

I'm sending along a letter I had from the county attorney in Ellsworth. It looks as if Lucy were going to buy the place, but I'm not hatching out any eggs until I see the deed signed and know that you folks have the purchase price sewed up in your stockings. I was over to Wilmington last Sunday—a week ago—and I had a lovely time. They certainly are nice people. Mr. Rhoads was just as nice to me as he could be. He certainly thinks an awful lot of Fripper. He said something about giving him a job to work on his place this summer, by the way—but of course it doesn't do to count on things until they come through. I do hope he does. Lucy was rooting for it hammer and tongs, and it wouldn't surprise me if it happened.

Mr. Rhoads himself wasn't keen on buying the old place. He said he had so much real estate now he didn't know what to do with it. But Lucy wants it like the devil for herself, and I think she will buy it—$2,000—for she has some money of her own. However, let's not get our mouths watering, because you never can tell what will go wrong. Some of the heirs may be so mad at me that they won't sign, and that would be too bad. Cutting off their noses to spite their faces, I expect it would be. But I don't believe they'll do that, do you?

Of course, what I would like to do is write to Uncle Bert and put the whole matter up to him. But from what I hear, he doesn't want any of my works or ways. I'm sorry, awful sorry, he feels so. Perhaps you and Fripper can show him the letter from Percy Clarke and my answer to it, and see what he says. So far as Aunt Tena is concerned, what I would say if Lucy does buy the place for $2000 is "Haw, haw, haw!" That letter of hers sure did make me mad. After all, what I did was for the good of all concerned, though I won't go so far as she did and say that I "had no selfish motive" at all. Damn it, we want to get as much as we can out of the place, seeing we have to sell it. So far as I'm concerned, myself, I don't want to sell it at all. Lord sakes, don't it mean anything to anybody concerned that that land has been in the family since the seventeen-hundreds, or something? I suppose that's what's known as "sentimental tomrot," but land is land. It stays where it's put. The money you get for it doesn't. And when the money's gone, then what? You haven't a roof over your head. However, nobody else seems to feel like that but me, and you, so I guess we might as well haul in our horns. $2,000 isn't much but it's better than $1,000, if I do say so as shouldn't. But one thing I'm going to say right now is this—in ten years we're going to be awfully sorry we sold that place for $2,000. We need the dough right now, but I'll bet the whole two thousand that we could double it in a few years from now. Real estate is going up by leaps and bounds, especially in country places. [...]

The job goes on nicely, though we're awful busy and it's awful hot. It goes up to 91 or two and sometimes 98, and stays that way. Doesn't even cool off at night. I have been going out to Mrs. Hobart's country place some, but until Mr. Hobart goes to California on the 15th, there isn't room for me to spend nights, as it's a small house. What with the heat, I've lost five pounds, but I could afford it. I feel all right, but kind of tired.

I plan to go up to New York this week-end and pick up some things and see Julia and Joe and have a nice time. I've stuck fairly close to work, and it's time I had some fun.

I must write to Wee. She sent me a lovely snapshot of the baby, and I was so glad to get it. He is a love, and how his Uppy would like to see him! Tinky was going to write to me—tell him, if you see him, I'm still looking for a letter. That Tug is as bad as Fripper. They both better be put in a bag and shook and see which one comes out first—is that letter they started to me still lying around? But I expect they're both busy, as I am sometimes.

I'm glad the garden is coming so nice. I'll bet it looks pretty from the sitting-room window. I expect the lilacs and the horse chestnut and the apple blossoms are all gone now. I thought of how pretty they looked all in blossom together, last June. Has the cow come in yet? It sure will be nice to have her fresh, won't it? What are you going to do with the bossy?

Well, give my love to Harve and his nips and to Wee and hers, and all the rest. I'll write again pretty soon.

Lucy and her father are coming up soon after the 4th. By the way, I had a letter from Mr. Price—he wasn't so sure of coming, but would let us know. Of course, after they got us all hot and bothered, the rats. However, I'll let you know as soon as I hear for sure.

Love, *Ruth*

Mr. Percy T. Clarke, Hancock County Attorney, wrote to both Ruth and her father on behalf of Miss Lucy R. Rhoads of Wilmington, Delaware about the possible purchase of their property on Gott's Island.

TO PERCY T. CLARKE

July 1, 1936

Mr. Percy T. Clarke
Attorney At Law
Ellsworth, Maine

Dear Mr. Clarke:

I have your letter of June 29 with regard to Miss Rhoads' request for information about heirship and title to the old Moore estate on Gott's Island. The heirship situation is somewhat complicated, as there are quite a number of heirs, but I believe there will be no trouble in obtaining a release deed at any time. The title to the property is clear, so far as I know. We have always believed so, and we have the necessary deed. There are some back taxes due for 1935 and 1936, to the amount of some $175. These, however, the heirs have agreed to pay this year ... I mentioned this matter of the back taxes to Miss Rhoads when I saw her last week.

It seems best that I give you a complete list of heirs and their addresses. I have been in touch with them, and will, of course, cooperate with you in any way possible. There are not minors among the heirs at present, although two of the original heirs—Enoch N. Moore and Laura A. Moore—have since died. I enclose this list herewith.

If there is anything more I can do in the way of information, please let me know. My father, Philip Moore, lives in McKinley, and you may address him there if you wish to get in touch with him. I know he would be glad to drive over and talk with you any time.

Very sincerely yours,
Ruth Moore

HEIRS (AS OF 1936) **to the Moore Estate on Gott's Island, Me.**

Albert D. Moore—McKinley, Maine.

Mrs. Howard N. Kelley, Worcester, Mass. (I find I have mislaid her address, but will secure it and send it as soon as I can. My father in McKinley has it, however.)

Heirs of Holsey N. Moore (deceased, 1921)

Mrs. Alice P. Moore Kings' Daughters Home, Bangor, Maine
Miss Helen Moore, McKinley, Maine
Mr. Newman Moore, McKinley, Maine

Mr. Carl Moore c/o Murray, 157 William Street, Catskill, N.Y.
Esther Moore, McKinley, Maine
Ruth Moore Tilden Gardens, 3031 Sedgwick Street, Washington, D.C.
(My sister Esther and myself now have legal title to the share of Philip Moore, our father, which was deeded to us in 1932.)
My aunt, **Mrs. Preston Ford,** of West Palm Beach, Florida, a few weeks ago deeded her share to Mrs. Howard Kelley, of Worcester.
Edwin M. Moore, the eldest son, died a number of years ago. His share was bought in, I believe, by the other heirs.

Gertie is an aunt of Ruth Moore's on her mother's side of the family. "Loosh" is Miss Lucia Leffingwell, a summer resident of Gott's Island.

TO LOVINA MOORE

Friday, July 9, 1936

Dear Mom,

It's so hot that I'm beginning to siss, and I don't believe I've got a brain in my head, but I want to get your letter answered before I fry completely. Lord knows what the temperature is today—thermometers are busted, I guess—but it feels hotter than it did yesterday and yesterday was 104. What a lousy climate! It's no wonder to me that the government's gone to pot. Located down here, it's a miracle that things aren't worse than they are.

I got yours and Pa's letters, and they were so nice. I had to laugh over Pa mourning because he had to burn up the letter he started. Why, the old rip, I ought to have had that one and a couple more in between, before he got around to write the one I got. He's worse than I am—and as for that Tug, when I get my flippers on her, I'm going to make her so she won't squeak, even if you push on the right button. You tell her so, huh? Tell her she's a double-jointed puke, and one of these days she's going to meet up with Miss Uppy about it. So there.

I had a letter from Lucy just before she left for Maine. I suppose you've seen her by now, and know the best—or the worst. She wrote me that she had left some money in the bank where she could draw it out at three weeks' notice. Doesn't seem as though she'd go to all that trouble, or say quite so much about it, if she weren't pretty well decided about buying; but as I said before, I don't want to count any chickens before they hatch out ducks. I would laugh like hell if she did buy, on account of Aunt Tene's flying off the handle and giving her share to Aunt Ede. I would bet a brass button that she will be so mad she would like to knock the beejeezus out of me. But after that letter she wrote me, I can't seem to feel too horrible bad about it.

Well, well. So you got a bossy. Name's "Depression" I hear. Well, that's nice and appropriate. It must be good to be having milk again. I'm glad to hear that the new bulbs I sent home are doing well. I don't know what color the glads will be—I hope, assorted, as I asked for that. They ought to do real well out there by the rhubarb. I hope they do better than the cabbage patch we had last summer, out there.

It's like late August down here. Everything looks dry and yellow, the way it does in late summer. Blackberries are way past ripe, and all the fruit is ripe. Corn is in season, too. Seems funny to see all those things getting ripe so early in the year. It's nothing unusual, down here, though—though maybe things are a little ahead of time on account of the heat. I never saw or felt anything like the heat of the past two days. Even New York at its balmiest can't hold a candle to this. I read in the paper that they had it 102.3 yesterday there, which was only two degrees behind us. Boy, I'll bet Julia's stewing. She hates hot weather almost as much as I do. I was up there last week-end. Mrs. Hobart gave me an extra day off over the Fourth, so I had from Friday night until Tuesday morning. We had a nice time. Didn't do very much, as we were both kind of tired, but sat around and gassed and had a nice time. Sunday, Julia and I and Joe went out to a beach on Staten Island and sat around on the sand. (Well the radio just announced that at noon today, the temperature was 100 here. Yesterday, at noon, it was only 97, so I'll bet by now it's at least a hundred and six. Well, September's on the way, boys, but I bet I get home half-stewed.)

The Hobarts have gone to the country, and Mrs. H. said it was too hot to work, so she didn't leave me much manuscript to do. So I'm living the life of Riley. Here I sit with the electric fan going and as naked as a carrot. I expect if anybody should peek in, they'd see sights, but I also expect if anybody peeked in anywhere today, they'd see sights. The only people I know of who've got any clothes on are the people working in the government, and they say Franklin likes them to wear their pants, as he shocks easy.

Mr. Price wrote me that they were undecided, as yet about coming, so there's no news there.

How is gram getting along? What do you hear from her? I expect she's pretty lonesome, poor old dear. Is Gertie still with her, and do you know what she plans to do? I haven't heard from her, and plan to write again as soon as I can get to it.

I wish I could have been there on the 4th to see Tinky and his fireworks. We had such a nice time and he was so cute last year. I was thinking this morning, gee, I'll bet it's nice and cool down on the island. Boy, wouldn't it be nice, with just your head sticking out of the upper pool! I expect Ted and his wife are down there—have you seen them? Jane is nice, I think. Though it must be kind of unpopulated down there—I expect they don't mind that. Who's there, this summer? Has Loosh come yet?

Well, I'll quit, I guess and see if I can get into the bathtub. Maybe that'll cool things off some. Tell Fripper I'll answer his letter in a day or so. It was nice to hear from him. If Lucy makes up her mind, do let me know pronto, won't you?

Love to all the kids, *Uppy*

TO LOVINA MOORE

Saturday, July 10, 1936

Dear Mom,

Something I forgot to mention in my letter yesterday … When I saw Julia in New York, she was still undecided about her vacation, which starts on the 6th of August, and I suggested that she spend part of it up with you folks. I think she would like to, as she thinks the world of you, but she said she was afraid you wouldn't want her if I wasn't there. I told her not to be foolish, of course you did—that's so, isn't it?

If she came for, say, a couple of weeks, she would expect to pay board and her expenses—said she wouldn't think of coming without doing so; so I told her that would be all right, if she wanted to, and, of course, if she comes, you mustn't refuse to let her, because she would plan on paying it wherever she goes.

If you feel that you'd like to have her for a boarder for a couple of weeks in August, I thought maybe you'd like to drop her a line and tell her to come on up. She is kind of bashful and shy about some things, and I think she'd love to come, only she's kind of holding back about what she calls "running in on you," even though she would expect to pay board.

I haven't said an awful lot about it—thought I'd see what you thought, first. I expect you've got quite a family, now, and if it seems like too much, why, don't think of it, but it would be better than boarding that road man, anyhow. She wouldn't be much trouble, because what she wants to do, mostly, is to rest.

It's still awful hot here—105 yesterday and 102 today. Boy, I never saw anything like it. It's so hot the concrete roads are exploding—they say it's as much as your life's worth to walk around down town—you're likely to get a faceful of concrete most any time. Well, I don't expect to wander around much. The only thing you can do is just sit still. I hope it doesn't last much longer.

Will write again soon, Love, *Uppy*

Latty Cove is in West Tremont.

TO LOVINA MOORE

c/o Harry Tavenner
R.F.D. Route #2
Herndon, Virginia
August 11, 1936

Dear Mum,

At last I've got a few minutes—we've been working almost day and night to get the book ready for the publisher, but today we're taking some time off. I'm ashamed to think of how long it's been since I've written. I've been here at Mrs. Hobart's country place since the middle of July. It's an awfully pretty place, on the Potomac River, 18 miles from Washington, out in Virginia, and I have a nice little cottage all to myself. Mrs. Hobart and the maid are in the big house—we're all by ourselves now, as Mr. Hobart has gone to California. He has a new job out there, and Mrs. H. is going out to be with him after the book goes to the publisher in September.

I like it here a lot better than in Washington. It's not so hot, and you can wear old clothes. Of course there are a lot of bugs—they have more bugs in the South than any place I ever saw, and, of course, mere screens won't keep them out. Yesterday I looked up from my work—I was typing on the front porch—and there was a lizard running up the inside of the screen. Ugh-uh! But, of course, there isn't anything poison around—they just make you creep and crawl up and down the back. Yesterday, Edna, the maid, who is colored and black as your hat, found a snake in her room. I thought I'd die laughing.

It wasn't anything but a garter snake, like we have out by the rhubarb, but it like to scared her to death. She was sitting in her rocking-chair and it "crep' 'long the rug," she says, "so I to'inter him with de heel o' my shoe. I kilt 'im, aw right, but he like to scairt me white." She WAS almost white when she came out lugging the snake on a stick. Mrs. Hobart and I were working on the terrace, and out comes Edna with this snake. We didn't dare to laugh until she got out of sight, but when she did, we both like to died. All you could see was the whites of Edna's eyes.

Well, let's see. Lots of news in your letter. Has Tuggie got the new job sewed up? I expect if she gets it, you folks will be kind of lonesome next winter. But I suppose she ought to go, if it comes through. She's too smart a kid to stay put too long in Southwest. Tell her I'll answer her letter the next breathing spell I get. The deal on the old place has apparently gone through. I had a letter from Lucy, saying she was sending home for her money to be sent to Percy Clark, and having him send it to me. I wish she wouldn't have it sent to me, as all I could do out here is endorse it over to Pa or Uncle Bert and send it right back. So I'm writing her to have Clark send the check to Pa. I kind of wish her lawyer would see to dividing it up according to the rightful amount each heir should have. I can't help feeling that it would save a lot of chewing that way, but I don't suppose it makes an awful lot of difference. The agreement was, of course, that the taxes would come off of the sale price—that is, that we would pay them in the amount now due. I didn't discuss the furniture in the house, with Lucy, Pa and Uncle Bert will have to decide about that. Personally, I feel that most of the furniture should go with the house—except for what has a sentimental value to any of the heirs. There will be some things there, of course, that really shouldn't be sold to anyone. Boy, oh, boy, I hate to think of the chaw that will go on when the heirs try to divide that furniture up. However, I shan't say anything about it, as I've spoke my piece.

Isn't it nice that Admiral Byrd has bought the Latty Cove place? It's kind of a feather in Tremont's cap, isn't it? I hope he means what he says about being a citizen of Tremont, and I hope the town fathers won't sock him with taxes. I guess they won't.

I don't know just when I will be home, as we can't say just when the job will be over. Mrs. Hobart said the other day that we might not be through the page-proof until Sept. 15, but I don't think it will be quite that long. I think it will probably be right after Labor Day, but am not sure. I'll let you know, of course. I can hardly wait, it does seem so long, although the summer has gone fast, and the job has been nice. I've enjoyed working for Mrs. Hobart, she is a very nice lady, and I wish she were going to be in New York this winter, so that the job will go on. But it isn't much of a substitute for last summer, is it? I want to stay at home a month, if I can. There is a job in a publishing house, which may break in October, and if it does, I'll be sitting in a butter-tub.

Too bad Lucy's father makes such a fuss about her, isn't it? She is a grand girl, and he hasn't any reason to. It must make it awfully difficult for her. The letter I had from her didn't sound any too happy. I am going to write her as soon as I can get a moment.

The letter from Gram was kind of nice. I read most of it. She sounded kind of blue, as well she might, but in general, it was a swell letter, and I want to answer it.

The kids sound grand. I can hardly wait to see them. How's Ann and Johnnie? I expect great big now. Julia wrote me she had got a chance to go to Bermuda with a friend, so she had decided to do that instead of going to Maine. She sailed on Saturday of last week, and I expect is having a slick time. Though she wrote me that for a while it was a toss-up which she'd do. She was tickled pink with the letter you folks wrote.

Well, you have quite a family, haven't you, at the house now? How are things going? Is it still dry up there? We have had a lot of rain. There's the prettiest field not far from here—alfalfa, about three miles of it, growing over three little hills—the greenest field I ever saw. How is the corn doing? I'll get some of it this year, won't I? Always before I've had to leave just as it was coming on. Now I must close, as it's dinner time.

Lots of love, and *see you soon, Uppy*

Ruth had arthritis in her back and spent a lot of time in a brace. She went to Bermuda with Lucy Rhoads.

TO LOVINA AND PHILIP MOORE

c/o Herman Walker
Windermere, Bermuda, 1936 (no date)

Dear Momma and Poppa,

We got here yesterday after a swell trip down. It's the prettiest place I ever saw and the water is the color of the handsomest green ink that ever came out of a bottle. It's so hot that you have to be careful you don't fry but you don't notice it very much. The island is only fifteen miles long and people travel around on bicycles and in buggies. We're going up to the north end of it today and go in swimming.

I stopped with Betty in Boston and saw the doctor and he said my back was a lot better and to stop and see him on my way back the last of the month. He said that he thought by then I could leave the brace off. He changed all my exercises and now I have to take them twice a day. Thursday I went into New York and spent Friday night with Julia. We left Saturday at three o'clock and it was swell. The boat was the "Monarch of Bermuda," a whackin' big one. It was raining and mizzling when we left the harbor, and I went to bed early as I kind of felt the motion of the boat. We woke up Sunday morning to the best kind of a day—got into the Gulf Stream at about 11 o'clock a.m., and it began to be warm.

Love to everybody. I'll write again before the next boat goes back. I'm fine and having a grand time.

Love *Uppy*

"Steve" was Audrey, Harvey Moore's wife. Junior was Lester Radcliffe, Harvey's stepson.

TO LOVINA MOORE

123 Waverly Place NYC
Nov. 27, 1936

Dear Mom,

I feel pretty low about this change of plan, and I guess from Tug's note, you folks do too. I wish it hadn't turned out this way. Of course I'm keen to go to California—who wouldn't be?—but I kind of hate to have things so jumbled up and hustled around. However, I'm enclosing Mrs. Hobart's letter and telegram so you can see just how things came about. I got back from Bermuda on Friday, the 20th, a week earlier than I'd planned, as Lucy changed her mind about staying three weeks. When I got back here, I wired Mrs. Hobart I was back, as she had said in an earlier letter that she would have a letter waiting for me when I got back from Bermuda, with some instructions about doing some things for her in New York. She sent me the enclosed telegram, and two days later I got the enclosed letter, with a sheet of instructions laying out some publicity plans for me to attend to here. I'd planned to make at least a flying trip home and be there over Thanksgiving and at least a couple of days, but with the work I had to do I couldn't manage it. It makes kind of a mess, because I've got things of Tug's I ought to return, I want to get the radio back to back to Pearl and Louise, my typewriter's up there and a few other things I want, and all in all, it means sailing off under a kind of jack-ass rig. But I don't see how I could do any different, as you'll see from reading Mrs. H.'s letter. She wired me Monday to come ahead, arriving on Saturday the 5th. So I've got a reservation on the 11:55 train Tuesday night. That gets into Chicago at around four the next day, and the train for the west leaves Chicago at 9:45 that night. I get into Berkeley at 7:33 Saturday morning. I wish you'd have a letter there waiting for me—c/o Hobart, 834 Euclid Avenue,—for it's a darned long trip, and right now I feel as lonesome as an old goat. It wouldn't be so bad if I could see you all like we planned, but from this point it seems like a long ways away. I bet you had a swell Thanksgiving dinner—did Newky wallop the heads off of the old roosters? Julia and I had ours in Shrafft's restaurant, and it was a glum affair, because she wanted to go home, too.

There are fifty thousand things to say, and I guess I better begin at the beginning and get them all down one by one, before I start telling about Bermuda. I'm packing a box of clothes to send home, and will stick in all of Tug's clothes I borrowed. I don't know whether Steve can use that old winter coat or not. It's in pretty lousy shape and she'll have to have it cleaned and aired. The rest of the junk you and Tug better look over and see if you can use. Maybe she can wear some of it, but most of it is about ready to go into your rugs. Will you have a look around and see if I left any duds besides that pair of pajamas? Sometime soon you might stick them and that envelope full of poems in my room and my leather coat into a bundle and mail them out. There's no hurry about it, as I won't be settled there for a week or so. I will have to leave the typewriter until I come home next May. It would get busted in the mail, I'm afraid. Besides, Mrs. H. has a portable that I can borrow. I'm going to write Louise and Pearl—I think I can have the radio boxed and sent. If it's carefully packed, I think it will arrive all right. I'm sticking a couple of pieces of coral I brought from Bermuda into the box of clothes. It's kind of pretty and I want you to see it.

How about the deed? I hope to the Lord everything has gone through and that you folks have got your money. I wrote to Carl when I was in Bermuda, telling him to send Uncle Bert a power of attorney to sign the deed for him. Lord knows if he has done it, as it seems to take at least a month for anything to percolate through anybody's head. I'm writing Uncle Bert, telling him to get the thing through as quick as he can, if he wants it to go through at all. Lucy is getting kind of mad because she doesn't get any action. It's a long story. She is the salt of the earth, but she is hen-minded, there's no question about it, and you can't depend on her from one day to the next. I think she is in a kind of state of mind where she is suspicious of everybody. It's too bad, for she is a swell girl, and I think she must be pretty unhappy. I promised her as soon as I had any news to write her, but I think it would be nice if Pa wrote her, as she feels kind of sore because she hasn't heard from him. She seems to think he doesn't want her to have the place, although I have talked my head off persuading her that he does. If he would write her, it might smooth things out in that direction. I didn't dare mention a job for Pearl down there, the way she seems to feel about last summer. She says she couldn't get any satisfaction out of anybody—Fripper wouldn't do anything, and Newman wanted six dollars a day, and she asked Pearl to see about having the cistern fixed and she hasn't even heard from him as to whether it's been done. I talked her out of a lot of her resentment, but it seemed best to let the matter rest until the deed was signed and the money paid. She doesn't intend to do anything until next summer down there, anyway; and personally, I wouldn't want to be responsible for Pearl leaving a steady job to work for her, because he wouldn't ever know how long his job would last from one day to the next. As I say, she can't be depended on to know her mind. At the same time, Lucy's a kind-hearted old thing, and means well. You can't help liking her. But darned if she doesn't give a good bucket of milk and then kick it over,—can't seem to help it.

I had a swell time in Bermuda—Lucy arranged everything, bought the tickets, reserved and paid for the stateroom on the boat, and fixed everything up for us to travel in style. I thought it was pretty darned swell of her, as it was, to give anyone a trip like that. So I told her so—said I certainly did appreciate it, because I never could have afforded it myself. And darned if the girl didn't begin to gripe about how much money it cost her, and how broke she was, and how she never should have come, and how she wondered if we'd ever have enough money to pay our expenses back again; and she not only griped once about it, she kept it up, until I was so sick of hearing about money that I nearly puked. Why, I don't believe that she was two jumps ahead of the poorhouse. Well, I had a little money with me, as you know, so I finally told her that if things were so bad with her, I'd contribute a share of the expenses. No, she wouldn't hear of it, of course not, it was her trip, what did I think, and so on and so on. But she did take a little here and there—would I tip the steward, and would I pay for the lunches, and well, she'd left her pocketbook in her bag, and did I mind paying just this once, until it looked as if I was paying not only my own expenses, but part of hers. Gosh, it was comical. Finally, I got to the place where I didn't dare to spend any more, as I was planning to come up to Maine after we got back and had to keep something for the fare, so I told her so. She went right off the handle. Well, she didn't know how we were going to get home—She was broke. We'd have to take the next boat back, or we wouldn't get there at all. Well, I happened to know that she had the return ticket and stateroom all bought and salted away, and besides, I was onto her by this time, so I didn't bother my head much. I said, well, in that case, we'd better go earlier than we planned, and let's take the Monarch back, arriving Friday the 20th. So she decided to do that. And then that afternoon, what does sister Lucy do but go out and buy an English bicycle, costing the Lord knows how much money, they're awfully expensive, and you pay duty on them to get them into this country—must've cost all together around a hundred dollars—and come toting it home as pleased as a baby with a new sucker. When I saw it, I laid right down on the floor and laughed until I was hoarse, because I thought it was one of the funniest things that ever happened. Of course, it wasn't any of my business what she bought, and I didn't give a cuss, but after this big poverty build-up, it did seem kind of out of place, and the idea of Lucy and a bicycle was kind of quaint anyway. I rolled on the floor and yowled—honest to God, I thought I'd die. It sure does take all kinds to make a world, doesn't it? Of course, Lucy's not broke—she's lousy with money, not that it's any of my business, so to speak. I don't know why she acted the way she did, but I'm pretty sure it was a state of mind, and that she honestly didn't do it to be mean. Maybe for the time being, she did feel kind of poor, having spent a little more than she should've out of her monthly income. You can't expect people who have money to feel about it the way ordinary people do, anyhow. To me, it was so damn funny that I get tears in the eyes every time I think of it—especially so, since I happen to know that she fell off the bicycle into a match-me-if-you-can bush (that's a kind of bush they have in Bermuda), and got a black and blue spot on one cheek of her tail and had to sit sideways the rest of the trip. It was a swell black and blue spot—looked like a great big black hand, poor old soul.

Well, all in all, Lucy was kind of tough to handle, but I had a rosy time—just about the best time I ever had in my life. We left New York on Saturday noon, Nov. 7, in a cold rain and drizzle. Julia saw us off and treated us to a cocktail in the Hotel Pennyslvania before we left. (Lucy said she liked Julia a lot, but she was afraid she drank. I said what made her think so, and Lucy said she didn't know, but Julia had kind of a look in her eye that made her look as if she drank a great deal too much. Of course, when we got back from Bermuda, Lucy took Julia aside and told her that I had been drunk from the time we got on the boat on the trip down until we got off it on the arrival back, and Julia was so mad she almost hit her, so I had to explain to Julia that that was the way Lucy was. You can imagine Julia—her eyes snapped and crackled, and she was so mad she quivered.) Well, to get back to the trip ... We went to bed Saturday night and it was so cold it would skin you and pouring rain. Sunday morning we woke up to a lovely sunny summer day, warm wind blowing, blue sky, and the ocean on all sides of us, a deep, calm blue. We got into the Gulf Stream about twelve o'clock. I wish you could have seen it. It's about the bluest thing I ever saw—instead of being green when you look down into it, the way our ocean water is, it's a kind of light navy blue. Swell. No prettier than the water off the island, though—just a different color. We arrived off Saint Georges, Bermuda, at eight the next morning, and I looked out of the porthole just in time to see the tender haul up alongside. She was about ten feet away from the porthole when I looked, a boat about the size of the Westport, and you wouldn't believe it, but honestly, the water was so clear and clean under her, that you could see all of her keel and her propellers just as if you were looking through glass. There were old coral reefs all around, and some of them were twenty feet below the surface, but you could see them all clear. The water was the darndest color—a kind of clear, pale green, shading up to clear, dark blue. I never saw anything like it in my life.

We had breakfast and went out on deck, and there was Bermuda off the starboard bow. It's a long, high island—or, at least it looks like one island, but really it's a lot of little ones all pushed together. The whole thing is about fifteen miles long. The channel into Hamilton Harbor is less than an eighth of a mile wide in some places—the old liner just about scrapes the edges when she goes coasting up it. *The Monarch* is a whackin' big boat, too, 29,000 tons. All kinds of boats came out of Hamilton to meet her—little sailboats, motorboats, speedboats. We left the sailboats and motorboats behind, but the speed boats coasted alongside us all the way in—we stood on the sun-deck, about fifty feet above the water, and it was like looking down on them from the top of a mountain. Everybody was yelling and excited, and waving things. The shore was lovely to look at—it's all green with palm trees and dark cedars, and the houses all look as if they were made out of white frosting. It was so pretty to look at that I almost cried. And of course, the water—you can see bottom in five miles of it.

The boat docks at Hamilton, right up against the main street of the town. It's a town a little bigger than Southwest, and it smells like bananas and oranges. And oh, boy, was it *hot!* Clear, and blue sky, and hot! We had to have our baggage inspected by the customs, so that they'd know we weren't smuggling in any diamonds, and then we got into a little motor boat that was there to meet us from the house where we were going to board. It was a flat, open-sided boat, with the front glassed in, not a bit like our boats, and the bottom had glass set into it, so you could look down and see the fish and coral, as you went along. The boatman was a Portuguese as black as a nigger—his name was Faustine. He took us over to Windermere, which is a little creek and a beach about a mile and a half from Hamilton. Gosh, it was pretty. Great big hedges full of flowers, ten feet high, poinsettias growing all along the shore, hibiscus and oleanders, orange trees with oranges on them ... boy! The house where we stayed was run by an Englishwoman named Mrs. Walker. She was a nice woman, I thought, though Lucy said she suspected her of being immoral and running around with men. So far as I could see, she was pretty nice, and had a good time showing her boarders how to get around and see the sights of Bermuda. Believe me, they are something to see. There aren't any automobiles, of course, except a few owned by the government. If you want to go anywhere, you either hire a bicycle, or you telephone for a carriage. I went around by bicycle, as the carriages are pretty expensive. I expect I looked as funny as anybody, riding a bicycle, but then, everybody else did too, including Lucy. We had some swell trips—we rode one day up to St. George's and back, and another day around the south shore. All the roads are made of white limestone, as white as snow, almost, and most of them run along the tops of cliffs around the shore. The sun is so bright and hot that you have to wear dark glasses all the time, or the light on those white roads would blister your eyeballs. I never saw rocks like the ones along those cliffs—they're all porous and eaten away—look like sponges. Sometimes you'll see a place where the water has eaten in around a cliff, leaving it all hollowed out like a big archway. We went down on the rocks one day at low tide—you have to walk pretty carefully, or the sharp edges will cut the soles of your shoes to pieces, and if you fall down, it's just too bad, because you get skivered. I'll bet if Lucy fell down once she fell down fifty times in Bermuda—she looked as if she had been to war, poor old soul, though she was a good sport about it. Well, at low tide, you see all kinds of rock pools full of fish—some of the pools are ten feet deep, all full of colored fish—damndest thing I ever saw, pink, blue, yellow fish and crabs. One crab I saw was a kind of cerise with yellow spots—he looked like something after you'd had a turrible hangover.

Of course we went in swimming every day. The last four days we had bad weather, which was a shame. It rained and got a little chilly—the Bermudians like to froze, but it seemed to me just about like our weather at home in June. I got a nice tan, which is now fast fading away, and felt swell. My back hasn't bothered me a bit, except it's been a little stiff since I got back, on account of the cold weather.

All in all, it was simply swell. I met some nice folks, and saw a grand place, and however Lucy acted up, she didn't spoil it, and say what you will, it was swell of her to give me the chance to go. I'm sorry she's so tough a proposition, but I don't believe she can help it. She talks awful about her father, so maybe I'm getting off easy if all she tells Julia is that I'm an old drunk. She doesn't believe it, of course. She just seems to have a kind of need to gossip about people.

I must saw off now and do some packing. I expect I won't have time to write again before I leave, but I certainly will have plenty of time on the train. Did you get the letter I wrote you from Bermuda? I wish I could see you all—you don't know how much. It's kind of tough, after I'd planned to come home for a month longer. Write me how things are—834 Euclid Avenue, Berkeley, Calif., and all my love,

Uppy

The next letters were written from 834 Euclid Avenue, Berkeley, California.

TO LOVINA MOORE

Jan. 2, 1937

Mom, dear,

Well, I guess this is about the worst I ever did, isn't it? Of course I've been busy, but the most of it is, I was just rotten homesick after I got here, and somehow or other I didn't feel like putting pen to paper. But I guess you would rather have had a glum letter than no letter at all. Mrs. Hobart has been sick, and I have had my hands full, too. She has a maid, but it takes time to run that establishment, and when I first got here, the first three weeks, Mr. Hobart was away in Utah, so she was alone. I don't think I ever had anyone so glad to see me in my life—except you, of course. She felt rotten and lonesome, and hung on to me like a lifeline. I was with her at first from the time we got up in the morning until she finally got to sleep at night, and it kind of wore me out, so to speak. But she is better now and feels quite herself again. It was a kind of breakdown, after putting in such a summer of tough work on the book, I think. Things are going smoothly again, and now I have time on my hands. It is a swell country out here, but kind of hard to get used to. I haven't ever seen anything like it, and at first, didn't feel at home here a bit.

Our house is up on top of a—well, back home, we'd call it a mountain, but back here it's a hill. The road goes up to it in a steep spiral, and the street car meets itself going down, and I don't see how they ever had the nerve to build that car on straight lines, for how it ever makes those turns, I can't see. There isn't a road in the whole city that goes more than a block without turning off in an S turn or a right angle. I wish my good Tuggie could see me driving a car out here … my ghost of gimlets, if anybody had told me!!! It's a 1936 Buick, and it's as big as a boxcar, and honest to God, it's a wonder my hair isn't white. The first time I went out in it—having done just the amount of driving that I did on Tug's car at home—I went with a friend of Mr. Hobart's, who has driven a car out here all his life. Gosh, if you ever put that man on a clear, straight road, with no hills, he'd break his neck. Well, he took me out at night, and headed us up a road called Skyline Boulevard. Well, we got about three quarters of the way up this mountain and it was going steeper all the time and talk about curves! Boy, not even banked and five or six hundred feet to drop. So I said I wasn't a very good driver, and hadn't we better try something easier. "Easier!" says he. "Why, this is the easiest thing I know of." So I ground my teeth and shut my eyes, and slammed the old thing into second and let 'er trickle, and when I came to, we were on top of the mountain about to start down on the other side. So I says, "If this is Heaven we've got to, I'm gonna stay here." It turned out to be the top of Grizzly Peak. Gawd! And it turned out, the man was right. It is the easiest thing they've got. We turned around to go down, and there was a road sign, and if you think it said "Bad Hill" or "Dangerous," you got another guess. It said, believe it or not, "Grade." Grade! my sainted godmother. It said "Grade!"

Well, nobody needs to worry about me now, for I've been driving every day and I'm just getting over being nervous and can handle the car quite nicely. And gosh, is it a beautiful car. You feel as if you had all the power in the world under your foot, and the engine hardly makes a sound. Mr. Hobart got it last year and broke it in beautifully, and lord, you could take off and fly in it. I do just wish, Tug, you could see the garage I have to go into. The house is built into a side-hill, and the garage is down the hill. There's a little narrow driveway past the side of the house—you have to hit it just exactly or you scrape. It drops about thirty feet in a distance of about forty feet, glory, is that thing steep! And when you get down, you have to back and fill and turn that great arc of a Buick around in a little dime of a back yard to fit it inside the garage alongside of Mr. Hobart's big coupe. When those two cars are in there, there isn't four inches of space between them. As I said, my hair isn't white, but it will turn so on the day when I take a couple of miles of paint off of either one of those two Buicks. Well, I guess that's enough about that, but it certainly does me good to get it out of my system. Talk about being nervous for the first ten days or so! If a goose had said boo to me I would have jumped into the next county.

Pa certainly has been having a rotten time. Looks as though if it wasn't one thing it was another. Is he feeling better now? I expect part of it is the cold weather, and he'll pick up his dominoes when it comes spring. At least, he won't have to worry so much about a few bucks to get through the winter on, now that the Lucy deal has gone through. I got the check from Bert and am sending it along endorsed. Why on earth didn't Bert give it right to you? I suppose he thought he had to have everything according to law, but it was kind of stretching a point to mail the dough all the way out here and back. How does everybody feel, now that the dust is cleared away and they've all got their two cents? Have you heard anything from Lucy? That sheep deal is the pay-off, isn't it. How they doin'? And what will happen if Newky gets a call to work and has to leave? Well, no use to borrow trouble, I spose.

I didn't have time to do a gosh darn bit of shopping for Christmas, because I had to do all the boss's shopping and do up about five million bundles for her, and by the time it was over I was so sick of it that I thought, well, everybody will hate me, but I can't do up another thing. Besides, by the time I got any time, there wouldn't have been time for the packages to get there anyway. I got all the nice things from home, and feel like a schlemiel; but I've decided now to wait until I can get over to San Francisco, and then do something about it. By the time it got to be Christmas Eve I was so cussed homesick that I didn't feel like doing a thing; I expect I would have felt better about it if I could've got some shopping done. Did Tinky get skates? I want him to have some, if he didn't, but I can't get them here because nobody ever saw any ice, and the kids go roller-skating instead. When I get paid on the 15th of this month, I think I'll send the money to Tug and let her get a few things for the kids. It's lousy not to do anything. The picture of the house was swell, and you couldn't have sent anything I'd have liked better.

This is a funny country, and I don't know whether I'll ever get used to it or not. It isn't very warm now. It's what they call the rainy season and it rains a lot and is cold. Temperature is about 45, but you feel it, boy, do you feel it. Mornings when I got to take the streetcar to work, I shiver and shake. Of course, it isn't anything like what you're having. There's a lot of frost, but it never seems to hurt any of the things. Some flowers are in blossom, and there are palm trees and a lot of green hedges and things. It doesn't seem quite real to me—but I guess I will get used to it. When I think it over, I believe I'd rather have snow; though I suppose you have enough to make up for it.

I have got a little apartment of my own now, 2511 Hearst Avenue, but I'm having my mail all go to the Hobarts', because I don't know how long I'll be here. It's not a very satisfactory place, but there aren't very many places to live here, as most people own their own houses, and the only apartments are full of students, on account of the University of California being in Berkeley. When the school term is over, you can get almost any place you want, very cheap. So I may hold in here and wait until the semester ends and then make a change.

I had Christmas Dinner at the Hobarts', and it was a nice party, and I got invited to a cocktail party with some friends of theirs on Christmas night. It's kind of a hard place to get acquainted in, but then, I guess any place is when you first come to it. And I'm so busy that I really don't have much time to play.

Mrs. Hobart is going to come East in March to go to the hospital again for awhile, and if I get the breaks I may get to come with her. Don't count on it too much, for if things are too rushing, if the book is sold to the movies, for instance, I will have to stay here and take care of things. On the other hand, she may need to have me make the trip with her, depending on how she feels. Wouldn't it be swell if I could manage to come then? Oh, boy. But as I say, don't plan on it too much. Probably I shouldn't mention it, but I can't help counting on it a little myself. California is nice, but it's a long ways away to be.

Love to the kids and keep your rhubarb up, Fripper, and I'll try not to be so long before I write again.

Uppy

Tapley was Dr. Thomas Tapley of Tremont who delivered many babies on Gott's Island. He began his career as a veterinarian.

TO ESTHER MOORE

January 1937? (no date)

Tug, dear,

I just got your letter this morning. Lord, I hadn't any idea things were so bad with Fripper. I expect I've felt the way we all have for so long, that it was mostly his mind, and I don't, somehow, believe that we can be blamed for thinking so. And of course, Tapley, the old idiot, confirmed it. Why the hell he couldn't have told us in the first place, if he knew, I can't see. Perhaps this angina is something that's developed out of the minor heart ailment that Tapley told me Pa had, and Tapley isn't to blame. But if he had told us that it was serious, it would have changed our whole point of view about it, we would have treated Pa like a sick man instead of having so much doubt about him. And that would have made him happier, to say nothing of us, now. Perhaps Tapley had some scruples about alarming us, but it would seem to have been carried a little too far. If I had known, for instance, I would have split my schedule wide open and come home after I got back from Bermuda, and I might have arranged with Mrs. Hobart to wait until January or longer before getting away off here to hellangon, where it's almost impossible for me to get back in a hurry. Well, no use to blame the doctor, but I have a feeling that I would like to kick the old bastard's teeth out.

I have a feeling that since Pa feels as he does about having another doctor, and would probably be scared out of his shirttails if we did have one, that probably we'd better let things ride. Angina is unmistakable, I'm told, and probably even Tapley can diagnose it. I would say that the best thing to do is to take as good care of him as we can and keep his courage up all we can, and not alarm him with new treatments and doctors. If we let him think we think he's bad off, it's going to make him a lot more unhappy, and while I can guess just how low in his mind he is, having seen it, if we can only build up what little courage he has left, he might pull through it. Angina doesn't need to be fatal for a long time, and I know a couple of men who have had it for years. If he goes to a hospital, I think it would probably be the end of him, he'd be so miserable. Doesn't that seem sensible to you? Of course, if the rest of you think he ought to go to one, I'll chip in and help with some money. By the way, in my letter yesterday, I forgot to enclose the money Bert sent. Here it is. I've endorsed it to you so that you can get it cashed for Pa. Seems simpler that way, because you'll probably have to get it cashed anyhow.

Of course, old dear, if things get too tough, I can come home. I would love to. But of course, it's expensive, and the best I could do would be about a hundred dollars. Two hundred, if I planned to come back, and I would have to, because this is the only job I got. I won't do it unless things turn out so that it's absolutely necessary. You let me know how that part of it stands, won't you? If taking care of Pa seems to be doing mother in too much, or if you think I'm pretty much needed, you let me know, and I'll wangle it if it takes the last peso, job or no job. Anyway, keep me posted as often as you can, won't you? Mrs. Hobart is planning to come east in March, and I think I will wangle to come with her.

It is a lovely day here, warm and sunny—too lovely to feel so down in the mouth. I wish I could have every one of you here, sitting in the sun with me. Mrs. Hobart is away gone to Salt Lake City on a business trip with her husband, and Bessie, the maid, and I are keeping house. Bessie is a stout colored dame, of the ilk that has to be watched or she walks off with the house. Someday I'm going to paste her one, but I think I'll wait until the boss gets back, so she can get someone in to pick up the pieces.

Now I must saw off and do some work. Write as often as you can, for it's kind of anxious out here so far away. Of course, I would pull a stunt like not writing for a month after I got here, right now. I feel kind of lazy about that, but there's nothing to be done about it, I guess. Someone ought to kick me. Perhaps someone will someday.

Love to all the kids and mom. Is Newky still around? I hope so. I expect he'll stick, as long as he's so much needed as he is now. I had dinner with Carl last night. He is doing well, but I think we're both finding it pretty lonesome. His mother wrote and wants to use her money she got on the old place to pay her fare out here with and come to live with him, and Carl was fit to tie. He's petrified for fear she'll appear to him some day. The Lord help him if she does, for he couldn't begin to support her, and there isn't any work for her out here.

Well, cheerio, old sock, and keep your tonnage down.

Up

Yang and Yin was the novel by Alice Tisdale Hobart that Ruth worked on in Washington. Warner Oland played Charlie Chan in the movies and the *Fu Manchu* series was a popular movie series. *Eyeless in Gaza* is a novel by Aldous Huxley. The Golden Gate Bridge was opened in 1937.

TO ESTHER MOORE

January 1937? (no date)

POISONAL

Tuggie, my Lamb,

I wrote Mom a letter that could be showed around, but this one you better read to Mom, and then drop it in the stove. There are a lot of things I want to glab about, and it's just as well if the menfolks see the other letter, huh?

From your letter and Mom's I gather that Pa's trouble is kind of serious. Is there anything that ought to be done, a hospital, or what? Or had we better just let things ride? I could help stump up some cash, later on, if it's needed. That seems to be about the only thing I can do, from this far away. What does Jack think about it—does he figure that Tapley is all right and is doing everything that could be done, or ought we to have somebody else? Maybe I'm taking the glum side, but I do feel pretty glum and worried about it. Maybe you better keep me posted, when you get time, huh?

I've been rotten, as usual, about writing, but I've felt all haired up ever since I came. Homesick wasn't the name for it the first two weeks. Everything was so darned different, and if I hadn't been as busy as a cat with pups I'd have turned around and taken the next train back. I'm getting more used to things now, and the homesickness is wearing off, but lord, I thought I'd croak for awhile. I was so glad to get your letter—you wouldn't know it, would you, from the way I answered it by return mail. But I guess you know the state of mind where you're constitutionally unable to touch pen to paper. Anyway, I sent post cards on the way out.

I gathered from your letter that it was kind of hellish. I can imagine just how it must be. In a good many ways, I kind of wish this job wasn't at the ends of the earth away from home. But, of course, I would have been seven kinds of a fool if I had passed it up. It is swell, and the boss is grand. They don't come any nicer than she is, and after the lousy breaks of the past few years, it seemed as if I just about had to string along with her. The job is darned interesting. *Yang and Yin* is now rated as second national best seller, outstripped only by *Gone With The Wind*. When *GWTW* loses it impetus, the publishers' weekly prophesies that the boss's book will be first. How did you like it when you got it finished?

As soon as the boss gets over this spell of sickness she's had, she's going to start on another book, and that will be something for me in the way of research, for she is going to do something about the Chinese in America, and I will have some work to do over in San Francisco's Chinatown, which is a swell place—like a foreign country. And the Chinese, whatever Warner Oland and Fu Manchu may have done to their reputation, are a hell of a nice people.

Thanks for *Eyeless in Gaza*. Did you read it? Somehow it seems kind of perverted to me. That fox-terrier incident was about as sickening a thing as I've run across. Ugh-uh! What do you want for Christmas? As I explained in the other letter, things ganged up for me just before the great holiday, and I didn't get a chance to shop. Hell, as a matter of fact, I was damned low. You know the way you get. But would you rather have a little dough than something that would have to be done up and sent? Honest, I did up so many packages just before Christmas, that the idea of some more of them kind of gags me. So I expect I'll crash through with some cash, after next payday. Maybe everybody concerned would rather have it anyway.

How's Jack? Give my love to the old coot. This is the country of a coupla young people, my lambs, in case you'd like to know. Carl's working on the

Golden Gate Bridge, and getting six dollars a day for unskilled labor. And living's kind of cheap. Of course, he had to wangle his way into the labor union and has to pay union dues, but that's duck soup if you know your way around. However, I suppose I'm kind of talking kind of impossible, I guess. I never planned that you should have to take so many of them, old dear, and I hope you'll kind of keep in the back of your noodle that you and I are kind of taking them together. I'm off at the ends of the earth, but I can help out with cash, when needed, now, praise be. Let me know how things stand, off'n on, huh? It is so cussed hard to get these things across in a letter; and when I was home I was kind of low, what with my back and all. The back is better, by the way. Looks like I could take off the brace in a couple months or so. But look, Tug. Don't feel stuck, huh? If you need to, write me. I sound like calamity, don't I? I don't mean to, because there isn't calamity, and perhaps it sounds so because I've been low in my mind and am just beginning to work out of it and feel human again. The mind is a bog of mud sometimes, my good wumman, and you've been on mine for a piece of time now. O.K.?

I've just about scared myself to death a couple of times driving the boss's car, but that's coming along all right now. When you drive out to see me your next vacation, me lass, you're going to see *somep'n* in the way of precipices. Lord! There isn't a piece of ground within a hundred miles of here that isn't straight up and down a hill—hill, they call it. Jee-sus! You can imagine what I did, in the beginning, with a Buick about thirty feet long. For about two weeks I had a permanent cold chill, though now I'm beginning to slam the old thing around a little better. Driving over to San Francisco is the next thing, and I don't look forward to that; because in San Francisco you not only have precipices, but you have traffic. Alas, little did I think when I used to shiver over turning the car around in our driveway at home that I'd come to this.

Give my love to the kids, when you see them, and write when you can, for I'm as lonesome as an old goat.

Love, *Ruth The old procrastinator*

TO LOVINA MOORE

Dear Mom,

I got Tug's telegram this morning, and it does sound so awful bad, and I guess it is. I feel as if I should come home, but don't know quite what to do—

whether I should hustle along as fast as possible, or wait until I hear from you again. I'm alone here—Mrs. Hobart's away for ten days, somewhere in Utah. She will be in Salt Lake City, I don't know just when, and I've left word for her to get in touch with me as soon as she arrives. I haven't enough money for the railroad fare. If I only hadn't mailed that check home, but I mailed it yesterday in the after noon before I called up at night. And then, of course, maybe I ought to be glad I mailed it, for we need it to use, I know. It's an awful tough spot, mom. I've hauled all the strings I know, but my hands are tied until I can get in touch with Mrs. Hobart. Of course you folks couldn't tell me over the phone, as it's so close by, and I couldn't tell from Tug's telegram how long it would be, or whether the doctor could tell. The only thing I can do is just sit here until I hear from somebody. You and Tug keep me posted as often as you can, won't you? Gosh, it was good to hear all of you, even at three thousand miles off. For awhile, I thought Louise was you, your voices are so much alike.

I wish to heaven if Tapley had known what was wrong he could have told me when I had that talk with him, and when I see him I'm going to tell him so. Mrs. Hobart would have rearranged her schedule, I know, and then I would be right there now, as I planned to be, instead of coming out here in December instead of January. I wouldn't think so much about it, if Tapley hadn't played the same trick on the Holmeses. What ails him, anyway? Well, perhaps he didn't know, but if he didn't he ought to go out of business.

Mom, I wonder if I ought to spend the money to come. I will have to borrow it from Mrs. Hobart—two hundred dollars, pretty near, and I will be paying it back to her at just the time when we will be needing money badly. Of course, I won't let that stop me. Lord knows, I'd be glad to do it, and probably shall do it. But I have to stop and think of how handy that two hundred would come in later, when we will all be needing it. What do you think—what do you want me to do? If things are just too much, and you want me, I expect you'd better say you do, and I'll come. But it is such an undertaking that I'm hesitating a little, where if it were only nearer I'd come a-flying and be there by now. I've about decided to wait until I hear from you again, though it kind of takes it out of me, just to sit around and wait, especially when it's so far away and takes so long to get word. Tug's telegram said it was only a matter of time, she thought. Does that mean days or weeks or doesn't the doctor know?

I'll write again, just as soon as I hear from Mrs. Hobart and find out what I can do. Write me, honey, and lots of love. If I'd only realized things were so bad, I could have made better plans, but of course nobody did, did they?

Uppy

Philip Moore died in January, 1937.

TO LOVINA MOORE

Feb. 1937 (no date)

Mom, dear,

I would have written last night, only I wanted to be sure first whether I was coming home or not. I've decided not to, but I want to hear from you before I give up the idea altogether. I had a letter from Wee, today, and I was awful glad to get it. She said you were fine, but kind of tired. I expect you are, for from what Wee said, you didn't take much rest. Are you all right, dear? Seems as if I couldn't wait to hear from you. Just as soon as you get rested a little, you write me, won't you? I thought first I would try to come home, but it does look like too much money; and if everything pans out as I want it to, and I think it will, I will be home for about three weeks in March, as Mrs. Hobart is coming east, and I think she will bring me with her. Money's an awful thing, isn't it? But I do believe that's the wisest thing to do, if you think so, too. Mrs. Hobart telephoned me to be sure to go now if it was necessary; she would be glad to lend me the money. She's swell, and has been awfully nice. She almost cried over the phone. But she needs me here pretty badly now, would have to get somebody else in, but that wouldn't cut any ice with her, or me either, if you'd rather I came east now. You let me know, won't you?

I'm all right myself, kind of heavy-hearted, as you all are. It just happened I was here alone, for a week, until the boss gets back from her trip, and that wasn't so good. But Carl came over to spend the weekend, and really, he was a godsend. I never knew Carl could be so nice. He felt awful bad, too. We took the car and went for a long drive into the mountains, and I don't think we spoke more than twice all the way. But it was good to have somebody around.

Wee wrote me all about it, an awful nice letter, and of course I was crazy to know anything there was to know, as there isn't much room in telegrams, and I knew you and Tug must both have an awful lot to do, but would write when you could. Up until the night I called up, I didn't realize that Pa was so bad, as I guess none of you did in time to write me. I knew from Tug's night letter that he was awfully sick, but I didn't have any idea it would be so soon. But I'm glad it was and that he didn't have to suffer like that any longer. I expect I will have a letter from you pretty soon, won't I, dear? It was so good to hear your voice over the telephone the other night, and worth the price. It didn't cost an awful lot, by the way. I could have got out of it for $5 if I had talked only three minutes, but the time seemed too short. And it was, it only cost $9.70, and I'm glad I did it, because it was the next thing to being right there with you. I knew, of course, you wouldn't be able to tell me much over the phone, but I talked with you all, and did it seem good!

I'm working good and hard, with Mrs. Hobart away, but it has been good to have something to do that took up my mind. Work is a pretty good thing, and I have lots of it, with the book getting to be so successful.

Did you get the check all right? I put it in Tug's letter. I can't decide whether it's a good thing I sent it off the day before I heard, because if I hadn't I would have used it to come home with. I expect we'll need it, and probably it's a good thing I had sent it, but if I hadn't, I would've been on the way home as sure as god.

I felt pretty bad not to have been there, for it has been too tough on you, and while it's hard for me to be alone out here, it's easier than it's been for you. Wee wrote that all the relatives had been around, as of course they should have been—Alice and Ede and Howard, etc. But it must have been tough. Carl said he bet you'd rather see the devil coming than his mother, and I can just imagine how it was. I did so wish you didn't have to have them around at such a time. Must have been hell. Thank the lord that part of it is over.

It is so hard to say what your heart and head are full of, in a letter, honey, and I don't guess I'll try. If I was there we could talk all we wanted to, couldn't we, but talking is so different from a letter. Poor old dear, it's so hard to realize he's gone, but I guess we just have to take it.

I know you want to know about me, and I'm fine. The work's going well and I do like it so much. If only it wasn't so far away, this job would be perfect. They can talk all they want to about "sunny" California, but it has rained here for three days, and been the coldest weather they have any record of. This morning I looked out of the window and it was snowing like hell, and you know, the snow looked kind of good. It didn't snow long—turned to rain—but while it snowed, it sure did snow. Looked like one of our old-fashioned blizzards for about fifteen minutes. Of course, this is the season when it rains anyway, around the San Francisco region. The thermometer went down to 24 above day before yesterday, and you would have thought it was 24 below, the way people yelled about it. Of course, none of the houses are built for cold weather, and it was kind of hard to keep warm. I didn't dare to take the car out on these hills after it got so cold, as the ice on these curves isn't so good. But the cold weather won't last long, and it will be sunny again in a few days probably. I wish I could send you some of it, for I expect it is awful cold in Maine.

Mrs. Hobart will be back Wednesday night, and I will be glad to see her, for it's been pretty lonesome. But it isn't so bad for me as it must be for you, dear. I wish I could be there.

Lots of love to Tug and Harve, and Wee, and write when you can, mom dear.

Uppy

TO LOVINA MOORE

January 1937? (no date)

Mom, dear,

I didn't get your letter off so soon as I meant to, as it has been an awful busy week. Mr. and Mrs. Hobart got back from Salt Lake City and they both came down with the grippe at once. I've been putting in quite a lot of time taking care of them, as, of course, there was nobody else, and they were both quite sick, running temperatures, and having to stay in bed. My goodness, sometimes I feel as if I had come out here to run a hospital, but, of course, I don't mind doing it, as they are both so awfully nice to me and do so much. So far, I haven't had a sign of a cold and don't believe I am going to catch it. Maybe that rouser of a cold I had in October was the cold to end all colds. Gosh, I hope so. So far, I feel fine. Have lost a little weight, but not very much, and will probably get it back again after a time. I'm working quite hard, and having to do a lot of running around, although mostly I can do it in the car, so it isn't so bad. I'm getting to be quite a good driver, but I can't say I'm perfect, specially on these hills.

I was awful glad to get your letter. Anything from home these days is pretty darn welcome. Of course, it always was, but specially so now, since I can't be there. Writing letters is such a kind of inadequate business. You can't think how to say what you want to say; but they're a darn sight better than nothing.

I know how you feel when you say you can't make it seem real. I can't either. But it's an awful lot harder for you, it must be, because you have been right there through it, and I haven't. Sometimes it seems as if I'd bust if I didn't come home; but there, I mustn't talk about it. I was talking yesterday with Mrs. Hobart about coming east with her in March, and she said she would take me if she possibly could. It seems to depend on whether the book sells to the movies or not. Of course, a lot depends on her own health—if she isn't well enough to come alone, she will have to take me with her. I know she will if she can possibly manage. I feel as if I really out to come then, let alone being half crazy to. But I suppose I will have to wait for a little while to find out for sure. I never do seem to know what I'm going to do, do I? Well, it's that way most always, when you have to consider somebody else's plans. I will let you know the minute I know for sure.

I'm glad you and Tuggie are bunking in together. That's a nice little room, and she and I had such a nice time when we slept up there together. I think about you so much and wonder if you are surely all right, and anything that you do to make it seem like company seems too important, somehow. It is always harder when everything is over, and you have more time to think, and right now is the hardest time we will have. We'll all feel better after awhile, when the shock has had some time to wear off a little. We don't any of us know how to accept a thing like this, because we've never had it before. But I will stop talking about it—I don't suppose it makes any of us feel any better, except that we get it off our chests. I've been just about busted to talk to somebody. Mrs. Hobart has been swell, but of course she isn't like one of your own.

Well, I have finally found a place to live and I moved in yesterday and today. It is the top floor of a small, two-story house, about two blocks below where the boss lives. I have two rooms, a large living-room and a bedroom, a bathroom and a kitchen and a fairly large hall. It's quite nice. It has a little coal stove which I'm using now, but which I won't have to use much as soon as the cold snap is over. They call it a cold snap out here—the coldest it's been is 24 above, but that is cold enough to ruin most of the orange and lemon crops. Too bad, because most of the people below here live off of their fruit ranches, and I guess they will have a tough time.

This place was unfurnished, but the landlord lent me a bed, and a table and a couple of chairs, and Mrs. Hobart gave me a lot of curtains and some things, and I'm pretty well fixed up without having to buy much. The rent is $25 a month, which is the best I could do; but most things are a lot less than they were in New York. It is the nicest place I've ever had, as a rented place—has a little upstairs sun-porch, and a lovely view. It's high up on the hill back of the city of Berkeley, and at night you can see all the lights of Oakland and Berkeley, and the big double line of light on the bridge going across the bay to San Francisco. In the daytime you can see all of San Francisco Bay and the Golden Gate and the big new bridge across the Golden Gate. I like it an awful lot, and of course it's nice and close to work.

* * *

I've had nice letters from a lot of people. The Holmeses, and Vera and Jennie both wrote me, and I had a printed condolence card from Nannie Dow. Even Winnie crashed through and wrote. Everybody is being awfully nice. Julia wired me. Poor Julia, she has been lonesome as an old crow since I came west, and her letters sound awful kind of unhappy. She will snap out of it, I think. I think she and Joe have had some kind of a dust-up, as she wrote me she had the apartment up for sublet, and was thinking of going on her own. Gosh, I feel as if I had walked off the other end of the earth, just at the time when everybody needed me most.

You would laugh if you could hear the people who live out here growling and complaining about the cold weather. After all, nobody's going to freeze to death with the temperature just a degree or so below freezing. But the entire population is huddled over an electric heater, and you would think to hear them that icicles were coming out of their ears. I have to laugh. I wonder what kind of weather you are having. It must be kind of a mild winter, from what I hear.

Well, Marm dear, I guess I will saw off and turn in. Look, let me know how heavy the expenses were, will you? Tell Tuggie I will write her pretty soon, when I have some more news in the bag. How is the old gal?

All my love, dear, *Uppy*

P.S.: Gosh, how I wish I could run in and see you all tonight. Would we be glad to see each other, or would we!

Louise Robbins was a young girl, killed getting off the schoolbus, and Frank Colson was the bus driver.

TO ESTHER MOORE

March 9, 1937

Tuggy, my old hair-restorer,

How you do? Darn, I haven't written you for so long, I feel as if I ought to make sure I've got your address right. As usual, I've told marm all the news, but I guess I can make out. The earthquake was the big news this week, and it sure does make a good story to tell. Don't let marm worry, as there isn't a chance that there'll be another.

Well, it sure has been a winter around here. Seems as if it never rains but it pours, all right, this year. I was so sorry to hear about Louise Robbins, and it did seem so unnecessary, but those things always do, of course. I bet some of those skates who go tearing around there in cars stopped to do a little thinking, but on second thought, probably those were just the ones who didn't. Was Frank Colson a rough driver, or was it just one of those things? I have got so I dare to drive the Buick thirty miles an hour on the straightaway, but of course that isn't often, as there isn't any straightaway around here, unless you go over the mountains to the valley on the other side. Poor old Mr. Clark! Well, I don't suppose his being dead excuses any of the passes he made when he was alive, but I sure am sorry for the old codger. Is the new supt. a right guy, or have you seen him yet? It must seem awfully queer not to have Mr. Clark around.

Marm writes me about the job at Dartmouth. Any news about it yet, and have you made up your mind? It sure is an awful hard thing to decide, isn't it? I swear, I don't know what to advise you. If it pays any money, it sounds as if it might be an awfully nice job, and would get you out of teaching and into something you would an awful lot rather do. What does Jack think about it, and what would the situation be there—would you two have to be separated, or could something be arranged? Marm writes that he is leaving the CCC the last of March and going to work with his brother, or something. Would that be away somewhere? Rockland, I expect, wouldn't it? If that's the case, I expect you'll find it pretty lonesome around McKinley without him, though you could probably manage to see each other week-ends. Darn, I do wish I could have managed to get home this March, for there are so many things to talk over, and it is so hard to talk them over in a letter. Of course, you have to decide things yourself, but maybe I could help in the clarification of things. And of course it is pretty difficult for you to know what's the right thing to do. I would be way off here at the ends of the earth.

There are so many things involved, it's kind of hard to know where to begin, isn't it? It's a situation that you and I and Marm must talk over and think about together, and see what's the best thing to do for all of us. You and I'd be sunk if Marm got to feeling that all the pins were being knocked out from under her at once, and these last months have been pretty tough ones for all concerned. If Marm were like a lot of people, she'd be making a fuss about it, but being Marm, she'd rather fry than let on she's lonesome, or needs anybody around. I could wish, in a way, that the question of your going away hadn't come up for a few months or so, but there it is, and a job won't wait, and we have to look the situation in the eye. If the job pays enough to make it worth your while, and all things considered including Jack, you want to take it and get out of teaching, which you do not like and probably ought not to do, I think probably you ought to take it. If it isn't anything extra so far as money goes, probably you ought to wait awhile. I would ask for $30 or $35 a week, if I were you, because there are so many considerations involved, that it would be worth that to you, if you take it. Before I closed the deal, I'd write to Admiral Byrd and tell him what is in the wind. I would say frankly that I'd rather work for him, and if there were a chance of his being able to offer you a permanent job, as well as just a summer job, you would wait for it. You might possibly run into something pretty nice that way; and that would mean that your work at least in summer, would be near home. Then you could be at home this summer, and while I'm there for my vacation, we could talk the matter all over and the three of us decide what to do. It's too bad the job's breaking so soon, isn't it, in a way? Would you think it a good idea to write President Hopkins, telling him just what the situation is, and asking him if there would be any chance of the job's being open the first of September? You will probably work for Admiral Byrd this summer, if you're around, won't you? And that would give us a little more time to get squared around.

I would love it if Marm could come out and visit me next winter, and if she wants to, and thinks she wouldn't be too lonesome daytimes when I'm away, I wish we could plan for it. It looks as if I would be here with Alice, or wherever she is, and her plan is to live here, for quite some time; for I love the job and it is the very thing for me to do. The rest of you would probably cuss me if I got Marm to come so far away for even a few months; but it would be a lovely trip for her and a change, and it ought to be just grand to have her with me. We can talk it over when I come home. By that time, I will be fixed up in my apartment, and we would have a rosy old time together. I think I could fix things so she wouldn't be homesick.

In the meantime, if the job does break and you feel you want to take it or that it's too good a chance to lose, the three of us will have to get together on some arrangement so she won't be there alone, for coming right now, I don't believe she ought to, for it would be too darned lonesome for her. Also, you and I could chip in together on some expense money, couldn't we, so that she'd feel comfortable about that. So far, I've been settling up some back bills and haven't been very helpful, have I. But I can and will be, whenever needed.

You write me what you decide to do, and I'll lay my plans accordin'. You and Marm can talk it over. Don't let it get to be too much of a conflict, lambie pie, or try to decide on all the variations of the problem at once. Let me know, huh?

Love and write soon, *Uppy*

TO LOVINA MOORE

March 9, 1937

Dear Marm,

I haven't been very good about writing the last few weeks, have I? I expect you have looked and looked for a letter; but I had been kind of holding off until everything was decided about the Eastern trip. For quite a while, Mrs. Hobart couldn't tell whether she could take me with her or not, and I was so crazy to go that I didn't dare to breathe. Then she had a bad spell of lameness and had to go earlier than she planned to; and that meant that I had to take over all her business and all the things that were on the fire which she couldn't settle up before she left. For awhile I was pretty heartsick, for somehow I couldn't bear to disappoint you again, especially right now, for if ever two people needed to see each other, you and I do. But the trip has been put off for me for awhile; Alice says she will give me my vacation—a month with pay—as soon as she possibly can arrange it, so we will have to wait. It's a bad business, for I know how lonesome your are, and have had a little taste of it myself. Alice will be back on the 25th of March, and in the meantime I am so busy I don't know which way to pee. Among other things, I have got to handle a big afternoon tea for a member of the British nobility, on March 17, a Lady Hosie who is stopping here on her way home from China. Alice planned to give the tea for her and had made all the arrangements, and then, of course, had to go east to the hospital. So that leaves little Uppy with half the high society of Berkeley and San Francisco on her hands. Oh, I will do it and keep my nose as high as anybody's, but I'd rather be home with you to plant the beans this spring. Alice doesn't do that sort of thing very much, but this lady is an old friend of hers and she has got to entertain her while she's here, or I have. I don't think my vacation will be very far off, but I am not going to make any plans or say for sure when it will be until I know, this time. It's awful to have to disappoint people so much, but I know Alice will arrange the vacation as soon as she can. She is a dear, and is awfully nice to me, and it isn't her fault that the trip fell through.

Well, we had an earthquake, out here. I hope the newspapers back east didn't spread it all over the front page and scare you to death. I thought of sending you a telegram to say that I was all right, just in case they did put out scare-heads about it. But then I thought probably they wouldn't, as it didn't do much damage here, and that's what makes them spill over on the ink. It happened about half past two in the morning. I was sleeping down in my apartment that night—sometimes when Mr. and Mrs. Hobart are both away, I stay at 834, but Sunday night I was at home. I woke up with a funny feeling of things moving, and stuck my head out of the blankets just in time to see the stove do a nose dive into the middle of the floor, and all the stovepipe come down on top of it. At the same time, a heavy full-length looking glass that the landlord lent me, fell into the bathtub. It made an awful noise. I thought to myself, "Well, I certainly am having a lordly nightmare, and it must be that canned salmon I had for supper, and I hope to God I *am* asleep." But then the little table beside my bed apparently walked under its own power out into the middle of the room and fell over, and I was awake enough by then to realize that the room was going up and down like a boat, and that something very, very peculiar was going on. So I bounced out of bed, and found I had to go to the toilet very bad, and just made it, but, marm, don't ever sit on the John during an earthquake, for it is a very, very horrible sensation. While I was sitting there, with the thing going up and down under me, it struck me funny, for I thought how I must look, and when I got through laughing, everything was as quiet as it must have been before I woke up. I went out on the sun porch, and it was as pretty a night as you ever saw, great big stars and a little bit of a moon just coming up in the east. I thought to myself, "I guess I was asleep after all," but, no, there was the stove turned bottom up, and all the furniture ske-wiff. And then all along the hill back of the house lights began to come on in the houses, and people began to talk in very high voices. And the funniest thing of all, all up and down the hill, back of my house and in front of it, you could hear one toilet flushing after another, where people had to go and go quick. It was about the stillest night I ever saw and noises carried. I heard a man say in a kind of astonished voice, "My God, Annie, I've pissed all over the mattress." I know who he was, as his house is just across the street from mine, and I've seen him going out and in—he's a professor of philosophy down at the University of California. Boy, would I love to ask him one of these days if he's got his mattress dried out yet.

Well, I sat there on the sun porch for about fifteen minutes, and nothing happened and it was kind of cold, so I thought I might as well go back to bed, and just as I got up to go in, the thing began again, only sort of easy and swaying this time. I hung onto the door frame waiting for it to get worse, but it didn't—just swayed the house a little and rattled the windows, and then stopped. So then I knew there wasn't anything more to worry about, because if the second shock is lighter than the first one, it means it's only a settling shock, and the worst is over. So by and by I did go back to bed, and went to sleep and slept until morning. And by gosh, I must have been some scared, because I don't remember getting dressed at all, but when I woke up in the morning, I had on all my clothes, even to my coat and hat. Gosh, I laughed for half an hour, because I must have looked darned funny, asleep there with my hat on.

As it turned out, we got the worst of it where I lived, because the center of the tremor was on Keith Avenue, which is one block from my house. Some chimneys fell down and plate glass windows broke, and of course, a lot of plaster was damaged, but nobody was hurt, except the people who peed themselves, and now it all seems as if it never could have happened. The Hobarts' house wasn't damaged, except for some bad cracks in the plaster.

Well, the geologists say that we won't have another one for years, and that's all right with me. So don't let it worry you. It's all over, and now that it is, I wouldn't have missed it for anything, for it certainly was something to see. There's a big cherry tree that goes up along side of my sun porch, which is all covered with blossoms now, and when that second shock came, it sent a whole thick shower of petals flying down all over the porch. However, one of the things is enough for awhile, and I can get along for a few years without another.

Well, I guess that's pretty near all the news. I was over in San Francisco to the movies last Saturday and saw *The Good Earth*. It's a grand picture, about China. Afterwards, we went to Chinatown to dinner and ate in a Chinese restaurant, with chopsticks. My gosh, imagine trying to eat soup with a couple of pencils. Chinatown is a swell place, and I liked it a lot. There were a couple of Chinese students from the University of California with us, and they showed us all the things that people who don't know their way around don't usually get to see. We went to a Chinese fire sale, where a lot of Chinese were rummaging around these great big tables all covered with silk pants and coats and carved boxes and ivory back-scratchers, and all jabbering at once, and, boy, it was fun to see them.

My goodness, the Moores do seem to all be rounding up new jobs, don't they? I hope Harve will like his, as it sounds like an awful good one. Of course, he does hate summer people, but maybe if he strikes a nice summer man, it won't be quite so bad. Some of them are all right, though sometimes they do come like old aunt Greer, or whatever her name is, over at Manset. I do wish Pearl could find something to do like that. I don't believe he and Lucy would ever get along; and the reason I didn't do more about it when I saw Lucy last fall, was because I don't think you can depend on her for a minute. She is an awful nice girl, but she is addle-headed. I will write her about the sheep, and see if I can get her to say what she wants done with them. Of course it is silly and unbusiness-like for her to neglect to tell you, and not to send you any money for their board. But that is what she is like. On thinking it over, though, maybe this would be a better plan. She has been kind of on the outs with me ever since the Bermuda trip, when I kicked over the traces a little about paying for her cocktails all the time—I wrote you about it. I'll tell you what to do. You write her and say that you haven't heard from her about the sheep, and that they ought to be let run the first of April, and that you have got to have some instructions about what to do. Say that if you don't hear from her, you will have to conclude that she hasn't received your letter, and that you think perhaps the best thing for you to do will be to write her father and see if he will send her the message from you. Don't say it in a threatening way, as of course you won't, as Lucy has to be handled. Something like this: "I keep wondering if you have received my letters, and feel a little worried about it, as of course you ought to have this information at once. Perhaps you are away somewhere, and I wonder if I ought not to try to reach you through your father and ask him to pass the information on to you, as I am very anxious for you to have it. But I will wait a week or so, hoping to hear from you."

That will fetch her if anything will, because last fall she was terrified for hear her father would find out about her having bought the place. As a matter of fact, when I found out that she was, I tried to persuade her not to do it, as I felt kind of funny about it, but there was no stopping her. However, it's done now, and I guess the old man will have to scratch his mad place.

I'm so glad to hear that all the sick ones are better. I'm writing Tuggie, as I owe her a letter. Tell that Wee she owes me one, the old alligator.

Lots of love dear, and I will come home as soon as I possibly can manage it. Gosh, may it be soon, for I'm achin' to see you.

Uppy

P.S. I wrote to Tuggie some ideas about the Dartmouth job, so you two better share letters.

TO LOVINA MOORE

March 1937? (no date)

Well, mom, dear, I sure am late getting this off, but I had a humdinger of a cold and it developed into the grippe so I had to stay in bed for ten days and it kind of put me back in me doin's. You know, it's the first real cold I've had since I've been in California—one of the real old whoopin' kind. I guess, though, it was really kind of a flu bug, for Earle went on a trip to Texas and came home with it and he was in bed for a long time. I'm all right now, feeling fine, and no cough now, but, boy I had a honey for a while. Didn't do me any harm and I had ten days vacation in bed, but I had an awful snotty nose.

How you gitt'n 'long, hon? Just think, we're most up over March hill. And what do you know—I got my reservation on the *Challenger* the other day to come east, leaving here on the 5th of July. Ain't that sompin? Just about three months left, and I'll come trickling in like the old bad penny. Seems a long time to wait, but not so long as it was, and I'll have two months home, this year. I got my reservation early, because a lot of people are travelling this year, on account of the fair.

I have got the loveliest tree in blossom you ever saw and I do wish you could see it. It's an acacia, and the leaves are a kind of grey green and the blossoms lie along them just like yellow snow. You know that soft kind of snow, when it's beginning to melt a little and look all woolly? Well, if you can think of that kind of pale yellow, that's what my tree looks like I expect you haven't even begun to think of garden, yet, but it won't be long now, will it? Are you going to have your vegetable garden this year? But there, it's foolish to ask, of course you are, and wouldn't I love to help plant it. I have got marigolds in blossom, and say, marm, you ought to get you some "Lemon Queen" marigold seeds—calendulas, really, I guess. They are the handsomest things—yellow blossoms about four inches across, and the plants grow great big. Burpee's have them—that's where we got ours.

How's Tug? Darn, I mean to write her every week, and I guess she thinks I'm an old foo'. Lord love the scamp, though, I will get a letter off one of these days. I owe her one, and I owe Wee one, too. That Tinky is the only one who owes me a letter. When I get home I'm going to have one of his ears off if he doesn't write me pretty soon. …

Everything is lovely and green here now, and all the farmers around the valley are beginning to plow. You can't hear yourself think for the clicketty-clacketty of tractors. The darn things make an awful racket. John is plowing our vineyard today. I kind of hate to see the grass plowed under, for it means living in a plowed field for the rest of the year. This is the prettiest time we have out here, before the dry summer turns everything brown and hot. Well, I'll be away through the worst of the heat and dryness, so I don't have any kick coming, do I? Won't we have the swell time, though?

Are you still by your lonesome, or did you manage to wangle Gram back for another visit? I wonder a lot how you are getting along, and if you get too lonesome there all by yourself. This living alone isn't what it's cracked up to be, but I expect there's a lot of things worse. It does seem too bad that you and I can't be together, hon, doesn't it? I wish we could, and perhaps we can, someday. Anyway, the way it is now, we get a little bit of each year together, and that's better than a poke in the tail, isn't it? I expect the folks get around to see you pretty often, and Tinky wrote me that he is keeping you company quite often week-ends. The little scamps, how I'd like to see them all.

I haven't been to the San Francisco Fair yet. The boss went with her brother—he's out here visiting her now from Washington—and I guess she thought it was pretty nice. He's awfully nice, by the way, not a bit like her sister, more like Alice herself. I expect I'll have to pick up and go one of these days, but I'm always so busy, and it's hard to find time. Saturdays and Sundays, when I'm least busy, the darn place is so crowded that you have to step on the tops of people's heads to get around, I hear, and I never was awfully keen on traipsing around in big crowds. Well, maybe I'll get to it someday.

Well, I must saw off, hon, and git a-goin'. I sneaked away this morning to write to you, because I'm going over to town this morning and can get the letter off on the air mail. Give my love to all the worms, and lots to you.

Uppy

TO LOVINA MOORE

April 1937? (no date)

Marm, dear,

It was so good to get your nice letter and to have all the news. Tuggie's probably back by now, isn't she? I'm keen to hear how the basketball team came out. She sure has done awfully well with them this year, hasn't she? I hope they beat everybody and come home with medals pinned all over them. What news of the job at Dartmouth, and has she made up her mind what to do yet? I wonder what you think of my idea about having you visit me next winter. Of course, it's just an idea, so far, and I don't know how you'll feel about it. Me, I'd love it, and we can talk it over when I come home. Probably it seems kind of far away to you, and you may not want to do it at all, but, gee, it sure would be nice for us to have some time together again, wouldn't it? Well, we can see how the land lies when I get there. I don't know yet just when it will be, as usual. Alice gets back from the east coast on Thursday. I sure will be glad to see her. It seems as if she has been gone a year, though it's only since the 25th of February. I've been busy's a bee, though, so the time's gone quite fast, and Mr. Hobart's been home most of the time. He's an awful nice man. He gets home from his office usually just before I leave at night, and he always invites me to have a cocktail with him. He's lonesome as a goat without Alice, and I don't blame him, for it doesn't seem like the same place with her away.

Well, Lady Hosie arrived last Friday, and she sure is a nice old coot. She had to leave Saturday morning, but she is coming back next week to see Alice, so I put off giving the tea until then. I sure was glad to do it, too. The old gal seemed to like me a lot—said I was the nicest American she's seen in this country. Might have been a back-handed compliment, as I don't think she likes Americans very well—doesn't understand them, I guess. However, she kissed me goodbye, which surprised me considerably. I warn't never kissed goodbye by the British nobility before. However, I kissed back, not to be outdone. We have been having awful rains here and the countryside is just about melting away. Every once in a while a hill will let go and come blop down into the highways and such a mess! They say it's the last of the rainy season, and after this we won't have any rain at all until November. Never saw such a country. I had the jitters for awhile after the earthquake, but things seem to stay pretty steady, and they say now that there won't be another one for thirty years. Well, that's all right with me, too.

I have got my place all fixed up again, and it does look nice. Alice sent me a lovely set of dishes from Altman's in New York. She sure does spoil me, but, darn, I like it. It's a service for six, plates, cups and saucers, oatmeals, bread-and-butter plates and platters and vegetable dishes, in a lovely bright pattern, and it sure does dress up my kitchen shelf. It was awfully nice of her, wasn't it? She's all the time doing things like that—likes to, says it makes her feel good.

When she was in the hospital in Boston, she wrote me that Helen was there—said she had been down to see her. I guess the poor kid is having a rotten time with her back, has about the same thing I had, only it seems to be worse. Alice wrote that the doctor had given her a steel back-brace that had more bars to it than hers (Alice's), which probably means a kind of a tough thing to wear. Well, I thought I was bad off with that back-pad. I'm still wearing it, by the way, but it looks as if I'll be able to take it off in a month or so. Alice also wrote that Betty Holmes had been in to call on her, and while she was in New York, she called up Julia and took her out to lunch, so I expect she will have all kinds of messages for me when she gets back on Thursday. I set out to write to Tug and tell her that if she could manage it she might drive down to Boston a week-end and see Alice while she was there, seeing I hadn't been able to come; but I thought better of it, as it would have cost dough and the going is so bad up there this time of year. It would have been next best to seeing Tug myself, though, as Alice could have brought me word. However, I'll be back myself before too long. It all depends upon Alice's affairs, and how much business turns up before the summer. Sometime after she gets back, she wrote me, she may have to go down to Hollywood and that means

I will drive down the coast in the Buick and be with her while she's there. That'll be a lot of fun, won't it? I don't know whether *Yang and Yin* has sold to the movies—she won't know until she gets back, but I think it probably will. The darn thing has sold thousands all over the country, and the movies always buy the best-sellers. If it does, it will mean that I will get a raise in salary. Whoopee!

Little David sure has been having a tough winter, hasn't he? He doesn't seem to be over one thing before something else turns up. Too darn bad, and I expect Louise has been having a busy time. How's Tinky getting along? Nothing much ever the matter with that one, I guess—he's always been blooming ever since I took him off of Eagle Grand, the scamp. If you see him, you better tell him he owes me a letter. Did the kids get the valentines I sent? Too bad Steve is having such a time getting over her grippe. I expect she is better by now. I do hope so. Maybe the mild winter you've been having has got something to do with it. Have you got the wood out yet? Alice wrote that there had been some snow around Boston and New York, and I thought maybe that meant you had been having some, too. Tell Newky I sure would hate to think of him backing out of that swamp junk by junk.

How are you getting on with the papering and house-cleaning? What rooms are you going to do besides your bedroom? I hope you'll be careful, hon, and not do too much, and you will let the kids help you with the papering, won't you? Don't duff into it too hard and get your side out of kilter will you? Papering's awful hard work, with all the reaching. But it will be nice to have it done, won't it, and I do wish I could be there to help. I wouldn't have been much good at it last fall, but now my back's an awful lot better, and I expect it'll be back to normal after a while. Once in a while I get a twinge, but it's nothing to what it was last year. I wonder what causes a thing like that—it would almost seem it was something in the family, what with Helen having it too.

Carl's still around—he comes over from San Francisco Sundays and we take in a movie. He's getting along pretty well—doesn't stay long on one job, but always manages to find another. He's working for an advertising company now, piling boxes, or something. I wish he could stay put for awhile. It seems funny he doesn't, but between you and me, I don't think he likes to work hard enough, quite, to do the kind of work he's doing out here, and, of course, when his company lays off men, Carl's always one of the first to get the bounce. Well, I wish he'd get over it, and buckle down. If the supply of jobs ever runs out, he'll be up a tough row of stumps. After all, it's three thousand miles back to where people know him.

Julia wrote me that her editor had used up all the poems of mine they had and wanted some more, so I have got to get down to business and write some jingles. I have been so busy since I came here that I haven't thought very much about writing, though every once in a while Alice cracks down and bawls me out for not trying harder. When she gets back, she is going to have me come in the morning at eleven o'clock, only she says I have got to promise to spend the two hours between nine and eleven in writing. Seems to think I ought to. Well, I expect I had. If I'm ever going to do anything with it, I ought to begin pretty soon, and I showed some stories to Alice and she said there was no reason in the world why they wouldn't sell, if I got down to business and went to town on it. Well, maybe she's right and maybe she isn't.

I've been spending a lot of time this month going around the country-sides—when it hasn't been raining—looking for some land for the Hobarts to build a house on. Believe you me, it's a tough job. The real estate game in this country is something to scare you—of course it's one of the big brooks to catch suckers in, just the same as in Florida. I hunted for about a month, and found just what Alice wanted—six acres of wild land outside of Berkeley, on what is known as Grizzly Peak. It was a swell place. The price for the six acres was $6500, according to the real estate company. Mr. Hobart made them an offer on it, and they jumped it to $8000. So he told me to tell them what they could do with it, and I did—not in so many words, but they got told. That's the way they do—you make an offer, and the price jumps a couple of thousand dollars. So now they have decided not to build for a while, but to take an apartment in San Francisco next fall, and in the meantime, keep an eye open for some land out in the mountains, where they can have a country place to go during the hot weather. It makes you sick to see the way the real estate people are handling the land—they'll take sixty-five acres of lovely wild mountainside, and cut it up into fifty foot lots—they expect to get right around $2000 a lot, and I guess they can, all right, the way people seem to be going crazy about real estate out here. Of course you can't blame anyone for doing business, but it does seem too bad. Of course what will happen is what happened in Florida—the bottom will drop out of real estate one of these days, and then you can buy lots at a nickel a throw. But just now it's kind of tough on people who want to build a house and don't want to be taken for a buggy ride by the real estate sharks.

Well, I must saw off for awhile, and go do some work. Tell Tuggy I'm keen to hear from her about the job. I'm keen to hear from most anybody these days, as I haven't got over the disappointment of not being able to come east with Alice. It sure did do me in for awhile, but of course, nothing to do about it. A job's a job, and somebody had to stay here. I know she would have taken me if she could—she felt awful bad because she couldn't. Bye, honey, and don't work too hard on the papering.

Love, *Uppy*

TO LOVINA MOORE

May 12, 1937

Marm, dear,

Yes, I'm still here and up to my old tricks again. Somebody ought to get behind me with a picked stick, though I don't know as it would do much good. The last month has been just one hustle and bustle, and I've been so busy I've hardly taken time out to take a bath and eat. The first thing that happened, the maid got to raising Cain and Alice had to let her go, and we had a rosy old time finding another one, so for a couple weeks I did her work as well as mine. Alice helped as much as she could, but it tires her so that she isn't much account, and I tell you, I sure did rastle my old bones around keeping up. The second week, Mr. Hobart was away, so there were just the two of us at home, so it wasn't so hard. Then, just as we found another maid—found a dandy, too, a middle-aged woman who works like a trooper and is awfully nice to have around—Alice got another sick spell, and this one was quite a bad one. She had to have a lot of looking after, and is just beginning to get better. Lord knows, I don't mind the extra work, but it sure is too bad she has such a tough time. She has bad pain, all up and down her back, and I know it just about kills her, but she doesn't peep about it. The only way I can tell is sometimes she gets a funny look around the eyes. She said the other day that she made up her mind ten years ago that it was bad enough for one person to have to have pain, so she decided she wouldn't ever drag other people in on it, too. The climate here isn't very good for that kind of thing. She and Earle are going away in the morning on one of his business trips to be gone a couple of weeks, and she thinks the dry valley where they are going will put her on her feet again.

Well, it looks as if I were going to be a farmer again. The Hobarts have bought a ranch in a valley about twenty miles back in the hills from Berkeley. Boy, is it a swell place. It has eighteen acres of fruit trees—pears, almonds, grapes, and walnuts. They want me to run it for them. Of course, I'm crazy to, but darn, I don't know anything about fruit. I can raise a pretty good mess of beans and potatoes, but fruit is something else again. The pears are an awful headache—you have to spray them six times a year, and then when they get good and ripe you have to pick them practically in ten minutes and ship them off or they rot on you; and maybe just as you get ready to pick them, a good breeze comes up and plop they go onto the ground which spoils them. The grapes aren't much of a money-making crop either. Everybody raises grapes, and the best price you can hope for is $35 a ton. Yes, I said a *ton*. Doggone, can you imagine how many grapes there must be in a ton? However, this place averages a ton of grapes to the acre, and there are eight acres. The nut crops are money-makers, though. The almond trees are just loaded down, and last year the price of almonds was twenty-five cents a pound. We can count on at least three tons of almonds this year, which ought to keep us in shoes. Earle has made me a very good proposition—he'll give me half of what the place makes, and I figure, in a good year, with no crop failures, it ought to be close to a thousand dollars. That's in addition to what I'm making now. So while it looks like a thundering lot of work, especially since I'm so green at it, I guess I'll take it on and see how I do. I could use some extra money, all right. Besides, it will be fun—you know how I go for farming.

There is a nice ranch house on the place, quite small—four rooms—which is going to be my house. Alice and Earle are going to build another house about fifty feet behind it for themselves. They figure they'll need more room than that, and there wouldn't be room enough for all of us in the little house anyway, especially when Alice's family comes to visit. They are having the inside of the little house torn out and remodeled for me—gee, it's going to be slick—a great big living room with a fireplace and big windows looking off toward the mountains, a bedroom, a kind of little combination study and place to work, a kitchen and a bathroom. It sure is nice of them to go to all that trouble and expense. The house would have done all right as it was, and I tried to get them to leave it, it was plenty good enough for me. But Alice said, no, I was taking over a big job for them, and she was going to see that I had the most comfortable place she could give me to work in. Boy, swell people, what? I guess they like me. They seem to.

It will take four months to get the house ready to live in—that is to get the big house built. The little house ought to be ready by the first of July. I expect we'll be going over there some before then. We want to get Alice over there as much as possible, as it's the hot, dry climate she needs. It's awful good for my old bones, too. My old back feels twice as limber over there as it does here in Berkeley.

I talked over plans for my vacation with Alice a week or so ago. This ranch business has thrown all our plans off for a while and so has Alice's sick spell. The hefty part of the fruit harvest comes in late August and all of September, so I'll have to be here then. The pears—blast 'em—come in July. I suggested June to Alice and at first she said O.K. that would be a good time, and of course I'm crazy to come then, because it's so soon and June's such a lovely month. But she looked kind of funny and I asked her if it was positively all right for me to go east then, and she finally cried a little, and said she knew she was being a pig, but she didn't see how she could get along without me for a month so soon, and I had to own up that I didn't either. Of course, she's been sick, and carrying on alone looks like a big job. So then she said if I could possibly hold out until the last of September, she would lay her plans to come east with me and go to the hospital—she has to go every six months, you know—and she would plan things so that I would have a full month at home. And, also, she would pay my way there and back, which is something to be considered. Between you and me, she probably would anyway. The way things are now, if I just had the month, I'd be five days coming and five days going, which would cut down the time at home to just about three weeks. Well, I don't know. Waiting four more months will seem a long time for you and me both. I wish I knew what was the right thing to do. It's one of these situations where you just plain don't. I know she'll let me come in June if I say I want to, but on the other hand, I know the work, and I know just how hard it will be for her, coming just after she's been sick. And she is doing for me just about three times more than you'd ever expect of a boss. How do you feel about it? I think I'll let things ride for awhile, and see how she feels when she gets back from this trip. I had my mouth all set to see the lilacs down on the island for one thing, to say nothing of some folks around I'm just about splitting my buttons off to see. Guess you know who they are. S'pose we'll bust before September, marm, dear?

I had two letters from Tena, of all people. She and Uncle Piss are in Los Angeles, and are going to be up around here the last of this month. I guess the hatchet must be buried, butter wouldn't melt in her mouth. Well, it's all right with me. She was the one who was mad. I suppose they'll turn up someday soon. Seems kind of mean not to be gladder about it, but my name's been took in vain too many times for me to feel very hoop-te-do over the occasion. I suppose I better write her.

I got Tug's nice letter—which she owed me, darn her tripe, give the devil his due—and will write her next time, when I haven't emptied the news bag to you. You and she seem to be getting along pretty well. … I suppose you'll put in a few seeds here and there, won't you? Gosh, you never know until you buy vegetables all the time out of a store what an item they can run up to. Well, Newk did a good chore getting the wood cut for you. …

The kitchen paper is slick. I'll bet it looks nice on, and I would give my liver to see it. Your knees must be an awful lot better, marm. They're either better, or you're going through torture doing all that papering. Still, when I was home last year, I don't believe you could have done any papering, no matter how you drove yourself, could you? Look, honey, don't you go and do too much of that hard stuff, now. You take it a little easier. There must be some youngster around who'll come in and do the barn work. Lugging water for the cow is too hard for either you or Tug to do.

The new radio sounds as if you might be having a good time with it. I'm awful glad you got one. I've got a little one that Alice gave me and I have a lot of fun with it. Hope mine is still doing its stuff for Wee—and Pearl. I'm so glad I had the sense to leave it for them, for I know they take a lot of pleasure with it, and I couldn't have carted it way out here. By the way, my furniture that I left in New York would have cost more than it was worth to send home. I wish you could have had it. I think Julia is using it. If Tug ever happens to drive down to New York, she could fill up the rear end of her car with odds and ends that you might like to have. There's a set of dishes and she might be able to get in the chair. But it really needs a truck, and that would cost more than the junk would be worth. I told Julia to use what she wanted of it and get rid of the rest to the second hand man, but I don't think she has sold any of it, as, being Julia, she couldn't wait to get to the post office to send me the money. She's moved, by the way. She and Joe have separate places now, and she lives at 224 Sullivan Street, same apartment house I used to live in.

Well, I thought by this time, I'd be getting a little ahead, but lo and behold, I have had to have my eyes examined and new glasses, and my teeth fixed, and it is the same old story. I was going to put off the dentist, but Alice got after me and said it didn't pay. Besides, if I am ever going to have that bridgework put in, I have to have it done soon, as your gums shrink after so long and then it can't be done. So I've dropped down the ladder again a little, though not so much as I have been, in my time. One thing after another, isn't it? Managing the farm though, and the extra it will bring in, will give me some margin, after this fall, and gosh, that will be nice. I got the letter from the Union Trust and am going to send them a payment out of this month's paycheck. How does that mortgage stand, now, anyhow? Never mind, I'll ask the bank to send me a statement. I'm not sure just how much it is. It was nice of you and Tug to take care of the interest. I thought I'd send them fifteen dollars this time, and maybe a little more later on.

Well, it's getting late and I'm about at the bottom of the news bag and tomorrow I've got seventeen things to do. It's a typical day. In the morning I've got to go down to Oakland and see Earle's lawyer for him—take down some stuff to be signed and put on record. Then I've got to come flying back, haul the mail out of the box and answer it. After lunch, I'll drive forty miles out in the country to hunt up an Italian man named Philomena, who's going to cultivate the farm for us this time, and battle with him over the dough he wants for to do it. The big chiseler wants $2.50 an hour for himself and his tractor. Hell, I'd plough it up with my nose for that. I'll probably tell him so, which will tickle him, and he'll come down to $2. So I'll give him a check for twenty hours work, and kid him along, and come on home. Philomena's a swell guy—great big fat man, with his pants down under his belly—like Rube Lancaster. Earle says his chest has slipped. Philomena has 200 acres of grapes under cultivation and about fifteen all the same age. His wife gave me a drink of white wine when I was out there last time, and it like to blew the top of my head off. I asked her if she hadn't made a mistake and got the ammonia bottle instead, and Philomena laughed his head off and says, "Swell a da grape!" She feeds him on lye and cucumber juice. Well, that's sure what his wine tasted like. He got to kidding his wife and she bawled him out in Italian and then she flipped around to me and says, "Philomena, he no good. All belly." And

Philomena says, "Big belly, she swell. Gotta da big fig-leaf tattooed on it." And he fetched himself a whack. "Right on a da belly. Getta him in the navy." So I thought it was about time I came home. He'd have been showing it to me next.

Somehow or other, I spose I've got to find out how you raise fruit. Earle thinks it might be a good idea if I took a course down at the University of California School of Agriculture, but I shouldn't be surprised if I could find out a lot from the farmers who live around. Darned if I see how I'll ever get enough time to take courses. Well, anyhow, it looks as if it would be a lot of fun. When you see Pearl, you might tell him the Old Maid's raising her own nuts, now, and pfft.

Give my love to all the kids and so on. Tell Tinky I remember I owe him a letter. His was grand. He sure has learned how to write, hasn't he?

Lots of love *Uppy*

Kathleen Norris was a very popular "woman's writer," who wrote such novels as *Belle-Mere, Hands Full of Living, The Foolish Virgin, The Fun of Being a Mother,* etc., in the 1930s–40s.

TO EDWARD M. HOLMES

Spring 1937? (no date)

Dear Popa,

I got to wondering what might the news be with you and Jane, also if I owed you a letter, which I do. I have been what you might call laboring in the vineyard and the day has not yet been made which has hours enough to get my labor into. In addition to what I was doing when I wrote you last, I am now manager of a fruit ranch back in the hills, to which we will move as soon as our house is built. It is, in many ways, a curious situation, for while I have raised many's the good mess of beans and potatoes, I do not know anything about the horrifying angles of farming in a god-forsaken land where it rains for six months and turns into desert the other six. Nevertheless, there sits the harvest, at least it's beginning to turn into harvest so fast that the most I can do is to sit with my breath in short pants. Five acres of pears. (Pears are a headache. There is an insect called "Thrips" which crawls up out of the ground and lays eggs. You put arsenic on him six times a season.) Eight acres of grapes, interspersed with walnuts. You go around with a flit gun and put sulphur on the grapes. You get up at 3 A.M. to do this, as at other times of day there is wind. Three acres of almonds. And there, my popa, is a crop. We can count (if they don't rot, or an earthquake doesn't shake them off the trees, or if thrips doesn't get immune to arsenic this season, on 350 boxes of pears. 50 cents a box. Hell, and all that work! Grapes will grow a ton to the acre. You get $35 a ton for them. Yes, I said a ton. Did you ever think how many grapes there were in a ton? The walnut trees aren't bearing well this year. So pfft to them. But the almond trees are already needing to be propped up, and according to estimates, we can figure at least three tons of nuts, and almonds, my popa, my very dear, good popa, bring twenty-five round copper cents a pound. And, nothing can happen to them, because the only thing that can happen to almonds is frost to the blossoms in the early spring. So, when we get the proceeds from this year's nuts, we are going to hire a caterpillar tractor and haul out all them goddam pear trees and put in almonds. And that is the reason you have not heard from me in all these years, because I have been learning about thrips and where the hell you can get a man to come in with a flit gun.

It is swell country out there. Valley, with mountains. Hotter than the red leathered plush seats of hell in the daytime. Cool at night. Clear air in your lungs. Hills all now covered with yeller poppies. Floor of the valley all cultivated orchards. Olives. Apricots. Grapes. Nuts! And how I have worked on the damn place. I'm running it fifty-fifty profits (if any) for the boss. It is a very swell arrangement, as it means getting out of this town for good, living for nine months a year on the ranch and three in San Francisco. Berkeley is a lousy place all full of women who look like Kathleen Norris. Literary teas. International House. Real estate men burbling about the "view." Fifty-foot lots. The Mobilized Women of Berkeley. Can't buy water-cress. Can't buy chicory. Oranges are ten cents a dozen, but what oranges! Julia Altrocchi, who wrote a poem called "Snow-Covered Wagons." Blerck!

Over in the valley, the neighbors are Italiano. Meestair Callero makes white wine. His wife bakes long narrow loaves of bread, crusty outside, brown inside, white in the middle. Meester Filomeo has 200 acres of grapes under cultivation. Meestair Filomeo has a bunch of grapes tattooed on his stomach, his navel being the lead-grape. His wife told me, "Filomeo," says she, "he iss no good. He is all belly." "Ten a da bambino," roars Filomeo, fetching her a swat on the rump. "Soch good pipple as you," says he to me, "da grape, da nut, she iss not for you. You raisa da bambino—ha! I find you beeg Italiano!" "Swell!" says I.

I don't know when I'll get east—probably September. What does on with you and how is Jane and how does the writing go? Carl is back on the bridge, or was, three weeks ago, when I last saw him. There is not much more news with me. I have been through an earthquake—minor, but god preserve us from a major one—and my ears are full of Mt. Diablo 'dobe. It is full summer here, but I miss trees and woods and the spring coming slowly. I would like to hear the water running, and see a northwest day and the lilacs at the island. The Pacific is a grey sea, no subtlety. Oh, big, yes. California is all right to spend week-ends, but I wouldn't want to live there. Nevertheless, I am living there, and very well, too, and happily, I might say. But I protest against the panegyrics that rise romantically over this really, (except for Yosemite) very ordinary state, as compared with some I could mention.

Yrs. *Moma*

"Ma" Kenway was a neighbor of the Moores on Gott's Island.

TO LOVINA MOORE

June 4, 1937

Marm, dear,

I've been out at the ranch all day, running around in pants and having a swell time. Earle and I tore down an old woodshed, and I cleaned out a henhouse and got covered with lice, so I crawl all over. Today was the first day that the people who owned the place before weren't there, so we had it all to ourselves. Gosh, it's a nice place. I picked half a bushel of great big red cherries, and I do wish I could drop in on you tonight with a peck of them. There are two cherry trees, and they are the handsomest cherries you ever saw. The ranch is going to be a swell lot of fun. There is all kinds of fruit on it, besides the four big crops of walnuts, grapes, pears, and almonds. We have two apricot trees, five different kinds of plums, some olives, figs, apples and prunes, all loaded down. I do wish you could see it. It's lovely, with all that fruit. Nothing but the cherries ripe yet, though.

My little house is going to be swell. Alice and Earle are going to live in it this summer—until they get their house built. Their house is going to be up on the hill, about a hundred yards back of mine. It's going to be a swell house—California style, built around a patio, with outdoor fireplaces and things, but I like mine better, because it looks like a Maine house. It has five rooms and a bath, all on one floor. A great big living room with a fireplace, two bedrooms, a storeroom, kitchen and bathroom. Running water, and bathtub and so forth. I have a wood range for heating and an electric stove to cook on. Alice is furnishing it for me, and the things are so nice, you just can't believe that anyone would go to all that trouble. Well, she and Earle are swell people, and I guess they must like me. Of course, I work for it, but most bosses don't appreciate things to quite that extent. I put in a pretty long day, but of course I love the work. The ranch is quite something to manage, and of course, I do all of Alice's secretarial work as well. Today, I had the spraying men in to spray the pears. I wish you could have seen the outfit. Three men and a sprayer and two mules, and they went through that pear orchard like a dose of salts. There are two bug hoses and a gas pump and a tank of arsenic. You have to watch them all the time to see they do it right—they're Italians, and they're likely to skimp a little if you don't watch them. But, lord, are they fun! Old Philomena, the boss Italian, hauled out his jug of wine and gave me a swig, and they all laughed a lot and told stories, and in the end, they did a swell job of spraying. Next week I have the same gang in to disc-harrow the whole eighteen acres. That job grizzles me, for I have to pay $2.50 an hour for the job, and it will take about 30 hours. After that, a gang has to go through the vineyard and spray sulpher on the grapevines to kill powdery mildew, which is a disease all California grapes have if you don't sulpher them; after that's done, somebody has to go through the walnut trees and prop them up so that the weight of the crop won't break down the trees. Then there won't be much more to do—say those jobs don't last more than a month—until the pears are ripe in July. The pears have to be picked by a crew of men who know how, just at the right time, or phooey! they rot. As soon as the pears are picked, the almonds will come along—almonds aren't so ticklish to handle, but the process is pretty complicated. First, your crew of pickers knocks them off the trees on to a big sheet of canvas. They put a sheet of canvas around each tree on the ground, and when the nuts are knocked off that tree they pour them onto big trays to dry. Then you have trucks come and haul them to the huller over in Concord. If you let them dry and least bit too long, you lose about half their weight, and your profit's gone. We've got a swell crop of almonds. We ought to get about four tons of nuts, and they sell for 25 cents a pound—maybe thirty cents, this year. After the walnuts, the grapes. The grapes are a thundering big job, and cost a lot to pick. We figure on about ten tons of grapes. The last grapes go in about the third week in September, after which, I will pick up my goody-two-shoes, and head for home, to see you all and will I have earned a vacation!

We had a nice picnic and a nice ride and came on home. Preston is an awful fast driver, and you know me; but I enjoyed the picnic. Tene feels awful bad about Pa—she talked an awful lot, whenever she could get me alone, about how if only he had let her know about the Davis house, she would have bought the mortgage. Well, as to that, I don't know. But I figure she really thinks, now, she would have, so why say anything mean? So I told her that it would have been swell if she could have, but that I didn't think Pa would have accepted it, though he might have. Between you and me, I don't think she remembers telling me in the summer of 1930 that she wished she could help out, but she just didn't have the money. However, people are funny, and I think she really does feel awful bad.

I can't help thinking of you folks these busy days, and wishing I could get home. This is the nicest time of year in Maine, isn't it? If I ever stopped long enough, I'd be as homesick as a peep. Every once in a while I think about the kids, and have to give a gullup. But I'm sunk—I can't possibly leave now, with all this fruit on my hands, and of course it's a swell job and swell fun, for I really do love raising fruit, even if the pears do rot if you take time off to get a night's sleep. Well, as soon as the boss's house is up, and I move into my own house with the extra bedrooms, I wouldn't be surprised if I had some company. If you feel that coming out here this winter would be too far away from the babies and too lonesome, I am going to wangle it so you and Tug can drive out for a swell trip next year, when Tug has her summer vacation. As a matter of fact, Alice suggested that the other day. I would love to have both of you come, and maybe by that time Jack will have a vacation, and could come along too. Boy, wouldn't that be swell! If I were in my house this summer, and we could manage it, it would be nice this year, but we will all be living in my house until October.

The kids sound swell. David and Johnnie must be quite boys now, and Ann probably grows like a weed. As for my boy Tink, I probably won't know him when I get home. I hope you will get your garden in pretty soon. It seems a shame not to, and you take such comfort with it, besides, it helps out so much. I would like to see the house, now that you have got it all cleaned and papered,

I'll bet it looks swell. We are going to paint and paper the ranch house, but I'll bet we won't have such a good time as you and I did the last time we papered. Oh, well, the only trouble with this job is that it is so far away from home; but I guess we can't have everything.

Did you get down to the island with your flowers? Somehow, I almost hope you didn't, though that sounds kind of foolish, for it couldn't have helped making you feel pretty bad. Still, it would be nice to know that the lot looks nice, when anybody can't do very much else. Somehow, I haven't ever been able to convince myself about the whole thing, and I expect I shan't be able to until I get home. But I mustn't make you feel bad.

Wasn't it too bad about Mr. Rhoads? I suppose Lucy will be rarin' to go down at the island now that she has some dough to chew on. What ever happened to the sheep? It's the cross of my life that I won't be at the island this summer, to hear the fireworks the day those sheep gnaw up "Ma" Kenway's garden.

Well, honeybunch, I must wash off these damn hen-lice and go to bed. I'm tired's an old goat. All my love, and write when you can.

Uppy

TO LOVINA MOORE

Martinez, Calif.
Sunday, June 5, 1937

Marm, dear,

Got your nice letter yesterday, and it was lovely to have it. I haven't got a word to say about anybody's not writing, but the weeks do slip by so fast, don't they? We are settled at the ranch at last, and the past few weeks have been simply a madhouse, what with the old ranch house to fix up and all the fruit to take care of. We had to move over from Berkeley sort of all in a heap, as Alice got sick from the damp climate, and had to come before the house was ready. Two old Italian people had lived in it before and it was *filthy*, honey. We got a couple of scrubbers in and after they'd washed it from top to bottom with lye, I undertook to paper it, and papered four rooms, with Fitz, a colored man, to help me. It was a lot of fun, but hard work, though it sure does look nice now. Alice was going to hire professional paperhangers, but they charge 8.00 a day, and I knew I could do it—I ought to be able to, after the paper you and I have put on together, oughtn't I? The living room came out lovely—we put on a light yellow paper with a big gray peony on it and painted the woodwork pale gray, and it is one of the best looking rooms I ever saw. It is going to be my house after the new house is built, and Alice and Earle move up there. It has a lovely fireplace. The kitchen has a wood stove, an electric cook stove and hot and cold water. Next summer, I am going to plan, if I possibly can, to have you and Tug drive out here for Tug's vacation, (that is, if I don't wangle to get you out here before that). If I should plan, for instance, next summer, not to come home for my vacation, but to use the money to have you and Tug come out here, we could have a slick time—go up and see Yosemite, and the Grand Canyon, and see each other too, which I'd rather, wouldn't you? But of course that's a long time off, and so far, I can't look forward to much of anything else but coming home in September. When the last almond goes rattling down the chute, little Uppy ain't going to be there to hear more than the first click or so. I can't tell just exactly the date, as nobody knows just what week in September the almonds and grapes will be ripe. But I expect to start east somewhere between the 15th and the 25th. And does that sound good!

Ranch life is swell. There's an awful lot of work to do, and I've got to hire a man next week to help harvest the pears. Marm, I wish you could see the fruit on this place. Yesterday I picked seven bushels of dead ripe apricots off of three trees, and they were the loveliest things—great big golden globes, and talk about sweet and juicy! From where I'm sitting writing, I can see a little plum tree about six feet tall, that is so loaded with plums you can't see the leaves hardly. We've had to prop it up. The plums are almost ripe—they're going to be dark reddish-purple, but now they're a kind of rich red. We've picked two lots of plums already, and Alice's housekeeper put up 72 quarts of plum jam and jelly. Part of the apricots we put up, and the rest we gave away to some friends of Earle's at the bank. It's no use to try to sell apricots in this country. Every ranch has hundreds of bushels of them. Next week the pears will be ready to pick. It will be quite a job. You pick them green. We expect to harvest about seven tons, and ship them east on consignment through the California Fruit Exchange. That way we'll get about $1.35 for them—if the market in New York and Chicago is any good. If it isn't we may end up owing the railroad money for freight. By $1.35, I mean by the box. Well, I do wish I could hand you over two or three bushels of stuff to put up. Golly, you look around at these ranches and you see hundreds of bushels of fruit just going to waste—a lot of stuff the ranchers get so little for that it doesn't pay them to pick.

I'm having my hands full just now, running the ranch and doing Alice's work, too. Alice's sister is here, just back from Japan with a lot of pictures and material she's going to work into a new history of Japan, and I'm doing the typing. If you could follow me around for a day, you wouldn't wonder that you never got a letter. But I put my foot down today. She's an old hellion—Alice's sister is, I mean. Typical old maid, not a bit like Alice.

The news from home sounds as though everybody was doing all right. You sound kind of down in the mouth, honey. Wish I could be there for awhile. I expect you get lonesome. I get kind of homesick sometimes, but try to think about September. We'll have a rosy time, you and I and Tug. How is the old gal? I guess I owe her a letter. I can't wait to see you all. The kids must be swell now. Wouldn't it be so, that the only job I ever had that was absolutely swell and just the thing for me, would be so far away from home? I guess you can't have everything, and I'm awfully lucky to have got this work, but sometimes I feel as if it were off at the end of the earth.

The green has all gone out of California now, and we've got brown hills, brown roads and brown ploughed ground. In the spring after the rains, the whole countryside turns a lovely bright green, but of course the rains stop in April, and everything dries up. The only green on our ranch now is the green leaves on the trees. Everything else is tan or brown. We cultivate the whole 18 acres, so that under the trees and around the house is all brown 'dobe. Tomorrow I've got a man coming with a tractor and a weed-cutter to go over the place again—we've got a weed coming up all over the place, which they tell me is the worst pest you can have. Its roots go down thirty feet, and it kills your trees by taking all the moisture out of the ground. Of course, in a country where it doesn't rain from April to December, you've got to keep all the moisture you can for your trees. So far, we've paid out $240 for cultivation alone, and this weed-cutting will cost about $60 more. I hope to God the price of nuts goes up and stays.

It seems funny not to have any rain, ever, and sometimes I get sick of sun, sun, sun, every day. This morning when I woke up it was overcast and it sure did seem good. But the sun came out again about ten o'clock. By golly, I'd like to be right in the middle of a good old Maine fog for about three days. Of course, we can get all the fog we want by going over to San Francisco, as that has fog about all the time this time of year. But Pacific Ocean fog stinks like an old backhouse. I don't know why, but it does.

* * *

Ted wrote me that he and Jane were planning to be at the island through Sept. and that some of the rest of the family might be there earlier. I haven't heard from Betty since January, so don't know what she may be doing, or what her plans are. Julia went to Guatemala in Central America for her vacation. I expect she came back all fizzing over about it. I bet she saw some tarantulas, and I sure would like to see Julia within a yard or two of a tarantula. I'll bet she'd go off like a gun.

Well, tell Tuggie and the kids to drop me a line, and by the way, notice that I have a new address now. Lots of love, honey, and keep your shirt on. We'll all be together in September.

Uppy

TO LOVINA MOORE

Walnut Creek, Calif.
Jan. 15, 1938

Dear Marm,

Well, time certainly does fly so, you can't keep up with it. I expect you feel as if I had flew into the middle of next week, and darn it, I almost feel as if I had, too. I meant to write for Christmas, at the time, and I almost didn't remember either Christmas or New Year's. Kind of funny, when we always made so much of it, isn't it? Poor Alice has been awfully sick, and we have been worried and busy. The doctors decided that I was as good as a trained nurse—I can't imagine why, as I don't know very much along those lines—but anyhow, they did, and I have been taking care of her. For the last week she has been better, but I have been just about tired out. About a month ago she began to be sick with a fever and pain in her stomach, and I guess at first they were afraid of typhoid fever. But it wasn't that, and the doctor got to fuddy-duddying around with samples, etc., and he found the eggs of this Oriental parasite in her movements. Seems she must have picked up the critter sometime when she was living in China. It was a kind of tapeworm, only a little tiny bit of a thing. She had to take a very hefty dose to kill it off—it grows by its mouth to the inside of the intestines—and the dose pretty near polished her off, as well as little Henry and Frederick. But anyway, we got 'em, and honestly, I never saw such a mess of critters in my life. There must have been thousands of them—all wiggling together. Of course, me, I had to look—couldn't let anything as interesting as that get by. Made you go all crinkle-crinkle. Well, she is getting better, now, and I do hope she won't get anything else. She has had a miserable winter. I'm fine and healthy, but tired, though I've got rested some this past week. I would have written before, hon, but I just couldn't seem to think. We did get a little fun out of it, in one way, though. John, the hired man, had to take a fruit jar full of s—t over to the doctor each morning. It was all wrapped up, so of course he didn't know what he was taking, and I was quite p'lite (for me) and didn't kid him about it. Well, it seems that over in China the farmers fertilize their lettuce and other vegetables with human dung, and in some cities where the houses are built along canals, these farmers go along in a boat from house to house, and the housewives bring down their slopjars and dump 'em right into the boat. When the boat is full, the farmer rows it home and puts it on his garden. So if you happen to be in that part of China, and meet one of these boats rowing along, it makes a real pretty sweet posy-smell, and somebody or other made up the name "honey-boat" for them. Nice custom.

Well, anyway, on John's day off, I had to run the sample over to the doctor's office. Earle brought it down when he left for his office in town, early in the morning and left it, all neatly wrapped up (in a fruit jar), and left it on my doorstep. There was a folded paper under it, that had something typed on it, so I read it and it went like this:

MASTERS LICENSE

This is to certify that RUTH (SUPE) MOORE having satisfactorily passed the necessary tests is hereby granted a MASTERS LICENSE to operate "HONEY BOATS" under steam, gas or sail on any ocean, tidal river or inland waters.

Given under my hand and seal this 25th day of December, 1937

GEORGE WASHINGTON

I took it up to show Alice and sick as she was, she almost rolled out of bed laughing.

Well, it did seem for a while as if for once I might be able to get something done for Christmas, but I didn't even get letters written. There wasn't any chance of getting away to get to town, and I don't know's I'd have had the energy to wrap anything up, just at that time. It seems awful, somehow, and I'm awfully glad you folks didn't, because it makes me feel better. I have got a big box of assorted nuts done up that we raised here, and the next time I can get to the express office at Martinez, I will send them along. They're not much of a Christmas present, at this late date; as a matter of fact, I was going to send them, Christmas or not, as soon as I could get to town. I've been pretty tied down. Alice didn't want anybody but me to take care of her, especially when she had a fever, so I haven't been getting out much. But it will be different from now on, now that she is getting better.

How I did wish I could have got home for Christmas this year. I know it must have seemed pretty lonesome to you. Seems almost as if I hadn't been there at all this year, I was home such a finickin' short time. But we had a good time, what time I did make it for, didn't we? Alice talks some of coming this year in June, but I just don't dare to make any plans ahead. So much of her planning depends on her health now. We'll have to see what the gods and the summer bring forth.

You sound nice and cheerful, dear, and I take it you and Tuggie are makin' it all right. Is Gram still with you? Give her my love. Nice Tug hasn't had any more colds. How's her thyroid trouble—is it bothering her much these days? I have been as healthy as a horse. I had a little cold last week but it wasn't bad, and I guess it was just that I was tired. I'm nice and comfortable here in the ranch house. It has been cold, but my sweet peas came up. They haven't grown any—seem to stay about two inches high and the leaves don't unfold, but they will, as soon as we get a little sun. We have had an awful lot of fog here in the valley this winter, more than usual, they tell me. But of course Californians always say that, when you get a little rain or fog. Last year it snowed about an inch in this valley, and you would have thought it had snowed duck-tird, the way everybody carried on. Mrs. Mack, the housekeeper, is living in the other side of the ranch house. I'm glad of it, as it makes company for me, and I think Alice arranged it because she was afraid I'd get lonesome down here. Of course, their house is only a hundred feet or so away from this one, but it does make it nice to have somebody in the same house with you. I have a fire in the fireplace tonight and it does seem cozy; but I wish you and Tug could be here to share it with me. Well, maybe next year, if the goose hangs high, huh?

I have thought of you a lot, and wondered how you were making out with all that barn work, and if the weather has been cold, and if Tuggie has had to paddle through the snow very much this winter. I guess you haven't had much snow, from what you say, though by this time you may have had blizzards. You sound from one or two of your letters as if you weren't letting any grass grow under your feet. You mustn't go on working jags like that, marm. I don't suppose work ever hurt anybody, in moderate amounts, but you sounded as if you'd done enough in that one day for a couple of miners and a coal-heaver. Work's an awful good thing—I'd be awful lonesome out here, if it wasn't for mine. Alice is beginning to write her new novel, now that she feels better and that means more work for me. Well, I like it all. I'd rather be busy than a loafer, any day, wouldn't you?

The babies must all be swell and growing fast. I do wish I could see them. The twins must be grand about now. Do they still look as much alike, or has Louise got bracelets on them now, so you can tell them apart? Give them all a big smacker for Uppy when you see them.

Since the rains started the hills have all come up to green grass and they are lovely—green as a sarpint's back—when you can see them for fog. Today was nice, though—blue sky, and warm. We have got our vineyard all pruned and the pears and almond trees pruned. The orchards look nice. From the buds, it looks as if we would have pretty good crops this year. I am going to try to get a flower garden started—as a matter of fact, I have been trying to get the time to read up on plants that will grow with very little water. Later on, John and I are going to build a picket fence around my house—the way it is now, if I started a garden, the first time the Spik milkman came he would drive his truck over it—I don't think he will drive over a picket fence, but I wouldn't put it past him.

The box came all right, just as nice as it was the day I packed it. I will send you the ten dollars for the rest of the price of the rugs, just as soon as Alice gets to feeling a little stronger. She thought they were swell, and they are lovely on the floors. I hope you will get around to doing some more this winter, as we could use three more and never bat an eye. Braided ones are all right, if the hooked ones are too hard on your knees. People out here are crazy about them, and I know I can sell all you want to make. I expect fifteen dollars would be top price for a hooked one, maybe more for a big hooked one. It's a cheap country, in every way, I find. Between you and me, it can't hold a candle to back east, either the people or the country. I hope this letter doesn't get lost in the mail and read by a Californian, or I will be stretched by the neck. But, about the rugs, if you want to send them along, when you finish them, I will take care of the freight and see that you get paid for them. By the way—will you let me know again what the freight was on that box? I want to send it to you, but I can't find your letter.

Well, my old news-bag's a-flapping empty, and I'm tired enough to cry, so I guess I'll quit and go to bed. Seems like you're all an awful ways away, dear, and I do wish I could be with you more, these days. If you get feeling blue, or up against it, or anything, you write right to me, won't you? I know I'm an old hog for not writing oftener. I will try to, now that things have straightened out a little. But sometimes, these past weeks, it has seemed as though sometimes I would kerflummux and pass out. I'm not used to taking care of a sick person, especially anyone who is very sick; but there, I ought to have more guts. Alice is a darling and she and Earle have done an awful lot to make me happy. If it wasn't so far away from home, this job would really be swell. They gave me a grand phonograph for Christmas—an RCA Victor electric one—and it is sure a fine machine. I wish I had some of my records here; but darn it, I don't want to get too much junk out here. Between you and me, I'd never settle down in California for good. If I get everything out here, there'll be too much to move back when I come. As I damnwell am, sometime!

By the way, I have a norful unpleasant feeling that I may not have sent Louise the money for my Signet stockings. I thought I did, at least I remember getting a money order, but I can't remember mailing the letter, and if she didn't get it , I'll be sure I didn't. I went to town just before Alice was taken sick, and my mind's been so full ever since, that I just plain can't remember. If she hasn't got it, do let me know, and I'll sure make it right, quick. I must be getting old, I'm so forgetful.

Well, love to everybody, and much to you. I wish you and I could have an old git-together, tonight, dear, don't you?

Uppy

TO LOVINA MOORE

Martinez, Calif.
Sunday April 1938? (no date)

Dear Marm,

Well, I guess I better put another letter in the mailbox for you and Tinky to find. I've thought so often of you and him piking down in the dark with the flashlight.

It's so nice he can spend some nights and week-ends together with you, and I'll bet the two of you have a swell time. Didn't he write a nice letter, though. I was so tickled with it I sat right down and answered it right off, and I expect he has got it by this time.

We have been having hard rain and quite a lot of fog. So far, it has been dry winter, and most of the fruit farmers were pretty worried for fear there wouldn't be enough rainfall to see us through the summer. But it's making up for it now, all right. The fields are all bright green and the wild mustard is beginning to blossom. Some different from last year, though. At this time last year the grass and mustard in the orchard was up to your waist, and now it is only about three inches high. But I guess it will be wet enough to see us through.

Alice and I are baching it this month, as Earle has gone to Texas on business. He will be back around the 23rd. It seems funny for just the two of us to be by ourselves so long, and he is such a nice soul to have around that we miss him.

I expect the World's Fair, that opens next week, will be something to see. I never was very much on anything like that, but I guess I will have to go to see this, as if railroad fares were going to be down this year, and that I am thankful for. Last year I paid $168 something for my ticket, but this year it looks as if $135 would cover it. No great loss without some small gain, I guess. . . .

How are things going with you? I thought maybe you could use a little extra dough this winter, but for the Lord's sake, marm, twenty dollars a month coming in extra is little enough for anybody to get along on. I wish I could send more. I can spare it all right, this year, and I would rather you had it than park it away somewhere. Are you and Tug going to be O.K. about the taxes? Let me know if you can't make it, or if you need more. I have got a dentist bill this month, or I would take care of them, but if it seems like too much, I will do it next month.

The papers have been full of all the blizzards they have been having in the "East," which out here means around Chicago. Seems funny, doesn't it, when Chicago seems out west to us? Have you been having much snow and ice, and has Tug been able to get home any? She will be having her Easter vacation, pretty soon, won't she? Honest, I ought to write to that kid, I ought to be shot, the way I let letters go. But never mind, we love each other just the same, and we both know it, but I expect she would love to have a letter. I did get one written to Wee, and she answered it, and I'm not a bit better off, except it was lovely to have her letter.

Have you been able to get Gram to come back to stay with you? Poor soul, I don't blame her for getting homesick, I do myself. But it is too bad when she could have such a nice comfortable home for herself with you and be company, that she can't feel contented. But darn, I expect she feels the same about living in McKinley as we would to pull up stakes and go live somewhere else. You know, marm, I think you never should even consider giving up the house until you want to, as long as we can keep it. You've always had a place of your own, and I don't believe it would be happy for you to go live anywhere else. I think when you get to be an old, old lady with long green whiskers, you might begin to think about it; but as long as you want the house and are not too lonesome there when you have to be alone, I think you ought to keep it. But only as long as you want to, understand. Sometimes I wonder if you don't get too lonesome there, specially nights.

Things are fine with me. I'm working like a tick in a mattress, and hardly have time to think. There's an awful lot of work to be done in the garden, and things are beginning to grow like fools, including weeds. I went over to San Francisco the other day and had a hair-do and blew myself to a movie, and we had a party the other afternoon and had some people out from Berkeley. But mostly we just work along. I will be glad when vacation comes, and it won't be so awful long now, will it? I'm planning to leave here around the first to the fourth of July and I will be home until the first of September. Won't that be kippy, boy!

Lots of love, and here is a little more dough. I wish the twenty had about five ciphers after it, boy, wouldn't we go to town!

Love, *Uppy*

TO LOVINA AND ESTHER MOORE

New York Central Train En Route
Chicago, Illinois
September 2, 1938

Dear Mum and Tug,

Here I am at the halfway point—at least it seems halfway, though it's really only a third—2000 miles to go. I wanted to stay in Boston with Alice as long as I could, so I took the last train out of Boston for Chicago and it was a slow old thing that wandered all over Southern Canada. We did get going once—about thirty miles an hour, but I think that must have been because a cow mooed and scared the engineer. Anyway, it didn't last long. We got here at ten minutes past six, Chicago time, but my clock said 8:10. You set your clock back an hour, and I was on daylight saving. So that let the New York Central out. Damn 'em, they charged me a dollar for breakfast, so I ate a dollar's worth and made it last all day. The waiter's eyes like to popped out of his head. I guess he thought I was one of the starving Armenians.

I stayed in Boston from Monday morning to Wednesday night. Alice is much better, but she's got to stay in the hospital until the fifteenth. Poor lamb, she's as lonesome as an old goat, and if you'd like to write to her, marm, she'd be awfully glad to hear from you. Her address is Mrs. E.T. Hobart, Robert Brigham Hospital, 125 Parker Hill Avenue, Boston. If it weren't for my darn nuts, I'd have stayed with her, but I've got to get back and see to 'em. Earle wrote that we had worms in the pears again—100 boxes went through all right, but the rest all got thrown out. Blast it, California's a darn buggy hole, anyway. I haven't heard just what the extent of the damage was, but it was probably plenty. And we sprayed the damn things five times, too, till they were so white they looked as if it had snowed arsenic!

Well, I got three hours more to wait before my train leaves. I was going to take in a movie, but I'm tired and it's a long ways uptown. All the stations in Chicago seem to be down by the "Winnego Works," and the street outside looks like bum heaven. I stuck my head out to take in a little walk and the first thing I saw was a big fat man standing on the sidewalk peeing in the gutter. Didn't even have the manners to use a lamppost. So I came away from there.

Everything looks awfully pretty and green all across the country. There's been so much rain. All the brooks and rivers are high and the corn in Indiana and Michigan is something to see. Wish you were along, both of you, we would all be having so much better a time, wouldn't we?

Write to me when you can, and I'll try to keep the insides of the old pen from drying out. It was swell to be home for just that little time, even, though from here it doesn't seem like any time at all.

Lots of love, *Uppy*

In the letter that follows, Ruth refers to the disastrous Hurricane of 1938 that devastated New England. The following letters were written from Martinez, California

TO LOVINA MOORE

Sunday night Oct. 4, 1938

Dear Mum,

Well, this morning we got our first rain of the season—began at five o'clock and rained until about eight, a steady pour. It seemed awfully good to hear it and to smell things getting wet, though we're a little worried about the grapes—we still have about ten tons in the field to pick, and if it rains very much it will rot them. Gosh, farming is a toss-up, isn't it? I guess we will get them in all right. The rains are coming early this year—last year it didn't rain until the first of November. We haven't picked any walnuts yet, but rain won't hurt them, unless it sets in a rains for two or three days, which it won't, this time of year.

It was so nice to get your lovely long letter, and to have Tuggy's, too. Tuggy writes a swell letter, doesn't she? Sounds as if she were enjoying her job, and isn't that good? Well, it's about time she had one she can enjoy. I had a nice letter from her that I haven't answered yet. I must get busy and do it, for it's mean to let letters go so long unanswered. I don't mean to, really, as you know.

I expect you are alone again, with Aunt G. gone back to the island. I hope it isn't too lonesome for you. I expect it does get so, sometimes, and I wish we knew somebody who could come and stay—somebody who'd be good company and not too much bother. Of course, Tug will be coming home weekends this fall, and that will help a lot, won't it? Wish I could. But I expect you keep busy day times and go to bed early nights. I am as busy as a bee. Sometimes I wonder how I'm going to get everything done. We are putting in gardens this fall, and it does seem funny to get all the little plants started, when it seems as if any day now it ought to begin to be cold. I have got a lovely bed of little marigold plants just beginning to come up, and they will just hum along with this rain.

I sent the Union Trust fifty dollars yesterday on the mortgage, and I hope that will hold them for awhile. If the interest does come due this month, I think I will either wait until next month or maybe see if Tug can handle it. Do you think she could? I hate to ask her, for I know she's probably still sailing close to the wind. If it isn't convenient, they will just have to wait until the first of November. I guess that is perhaps what we had better do, for I just remembered that Tug is still making car payments. So don't say anything about it to her, and I will send it in at the end of Oct. It must be hard for her to keep paying out that eighteen dollars every month, and she'll be glad when it's done, I guess.

Nice that your vegetable garden is turning out so good. Too bad the potatoes didn't. I expect to hear most any time that you have had a frost, and I hate to think of it, for the flowers must be lovely now. They were swell when I was home, but from what you say in your letter they must have done quite a lot more blossoming. Too bad the season isn't longer. We ought to be able to whack up—say I swap you three months of warm weather and you send me some snow. I hate to think how long it is since I have really seen snow. We had some last winter on the top of Mt. Diablo, but it was twenty miles away and on the top of a mountain.

I have been feeling swell since I got back. They gave me some new exercises when I saw the doctor in Boston, and they seem to be helping my back more than any I have ever had. It really begins to feel strong again, and it isn't stiff in the mornings any more. They think I should wear the brace a while longer—they always do—but it is ever so much better—the back, I mean. And of course I'm so used to the brace that I don't much care any more whether I have it on or not. ...

Well, honey, I do wish I could drop in tonight for a good old glab with you. I was kind of homesick—always am when I first get back. Earle and I and Mrs. Mack kept house for three weeks until Alice got home, and it was kind of lonesome, though Mrs. Mack is awfully nice and good company. Alice got back the 27th. She is very much better and it does seem good to have her feeling good and out of pain. She has gained ten pounds and looks nice and rosy. She was tickled to death to have that letter from you—she let me read it, and it was a lovely letter, dear. She is going to answer it, just as soon as she gets settled. It missed her at the hospital and they forwarded it here, so she got it when she got home.

Some kind of a darn bug has bit me right on the titty, and golly, does it itch! Doggone them, I wish they'd stay off of some places. Bad enough to get bites in places that show, but when they get that cagy, fun's fun.

Well, I think of you lots, old dear, and wonder how you're getting along. How does the mailbox work? I want to drop a letter into it pretty often, and will try to. After the crops are in, I won't be so darn rushed. I got the knocking poles all right, and we have got the almonds picked and shipped. Tomorrow John is going to knock walnuts and then get after the grapes. I have got to drove over to Concord—about ten miles from here—to get a lot of bags for the nuts. It is still and cloudy again tonight, and I shouldn't wonder if we got more rain. Too bad if we do, but after the way the pears acted, I'm not going to do any more worrying. Some year I hope we can break even of this ranch. You know, I wish you could have seen those pears—the ones we had to lose. Great big things, deep yellow, and looked perfect. There weren't so very many of them that had worms, either, only of course the ones that did made the whole lot not fit to ship. We figured that the ranch raised ten tons of pears. Think of it! I almost howl when I do.

Say, that was some hurricane they had down the coast, wasn't it? Just think of having a storm like that in New England. A good many of those places that had so many houses wiped all over the map were places I knew quite well, like West Hampton, L.I., and Westerly and Providence, R.I. It must have been a horrible thing, and I will admit, I looked pretty sharp in the papers to see if it reached as far north as Maine, until I got your letter. Maine's a pretty good old place, isn't it, and damn it, I wish I was in it.

Well, dear, I must close now and do my accounts and go to bed. Be a good girl and don't sleep with the boys and don't get lonesome, and write when you can. Lots of love,

Uppy

Aunt Clisty was an elderly woman in Bass Harbor.

TO LOVINA MOORE

Nov. 1938

Mommer, dear,

As usual, my good intentions ain't done me a mite of good. I meant to write and send you this check a week ago. Earle went to Salt Lake City, and when he goes away, it always means that I have more to do—my evenings aren't my own, and I just never get things done. But you know I love you just the same, and mean to write, even if you don't hear from me till the cows come home. It's been so nice to get your lovely long letters. I'm so excited about all the things that are going on, and I can always count on getting all the news, for you seem to be able to get everything in, and you always know just what I like to hear about. It's so nice that you've had such a nice fall. I expect by now you got all your garden stuff under cover. It seems so funny now to be thinking of you folks getting ready for winter. I have just got through cultivating the chrysanthemums, and I wish you could see them. Alice bought a hundred plants from the greenhouse and we put them out on the hillside by the house. They are all in blossom now, and they are a sight. Great big bronze-y and yellow blossoms, some of them half as big as your head. For the last two weeks, John has been carting away the old adobe dirt around the house and walks and filling it in with nice sandy loam from the other side of the ranch, and we're just now starting to plant it with the things that will bloom in winter out here—winter stock, calendulas, sweet peas, verbenas, sweet alyssum, and lots of different kinds of shrubs. It will look lovely when we get it done. Of course, though, it does seem kind of unnatural, and maybe you won't believe me, but I had a darn sight rather have a good cold snowy winter, even if you do have to wrap up and tie mittens over your nose. I haven't seen any snow now for going on three years, except a little patch of it that appeared on the mountain, twenty miles away from here, last winter. Well, you can't have everything. I haven't had any colds, either. And perhaps it is nice to be able to go out and dig in the garden on the 8th of November, in a summer shirt and a thin pair of slacks.

Isn't Aunt Tene doing herself proud, though? You know you could have knocked me over with a feather. But every once in a while, she does something like that—like putting Helen through college—which is pretty darn fine. I think she feels quite a lot for her family, don't you? After all, she's been away from home, and far away, too, for a pretty long time, and I know just how she feels. Sometimes you get mad at her—I know I was, when she wrote me that nasty letter about the old place, but maybe she had something on her side. Well, it sure will be swell for Louise and Pearl and the youngsters. To have a bigger house and some land to play around in, and I guess that John Gott place is quite a good house, isn't it? Has it got electricity? Well, if it hasn't, perhaps someday they will be able to have it put in. I'm crazy to hear from Louise. I guess I better write her. I expect they feel pretty happy, don't they?

In some ways, I hate to have you take Aunt Clisty, but maybe it would be a good thing, although what bothers me is for you to have such a mess to take care of. You just aren't easy in your mind unless you have somebody to look after, are you, dear? Well, I can see that, too. After a woman's brought up a family, and done a smashing good job of it, too—because we're pretty nice, all of us, aren't we?—it's pretty much of a jolt to wake up some morning and find that family's all grown up and on its own. Of course, that's the natural and normal thing to have happen, and when you come to think of it, it couldn't happen any other way. But that doesn't make it any the less lonesome. If you were an old lady with one tooth and all ready to come unshackled, I'd say give up the place and come to live with one of us. We talked that over last summer. But as I told Louise, you're full of beans, and keeping the house and cow and garden is just what you ought to do. You and I both feel the same way about work. We both love to work, and we wouldn't be easy in our minds or happy without it. I hope I always have to and you feel the same way. I guess it's all decided now that I'm coming home for two months next summer, and we'll have that to look forward to. Having Aunt Clisty there won't make a bit of difference, if you want her. We'll all turn to, Tuggie and I and you, and help look out for her. The poor old soul will feel as if she's gone to heaven, with some decent care at last.

Well, honeybun, I'm feeling fine and busy as a bee. The crops are all in—we didn't do very well with the grapes, as we couldn't sell them, that is all of them. We've got about four tons spoiling on the vines. There was some kind of a legal mix-up that just about ruined the sale of all the wine grapes in California. But we got about $200 for the walnuts, and I guess the almonds will bring a good price—we haven't heard from them yet, except for an advance payment of $35. I will send you some more dough the first of December, and let me know if you run short before then.

Lots of love, dear, and tell everybody to write.

Uppy

TO LOVINA MOORE

Dec. 17, 1938

Momma, dear,

Well, the old goose is a-gitt'n fat, isn't he? Snuck up behind me, too, the dope. He always does. As usual, I'm way behind hand with my letter. I did enjoy your lovely long one so much, and it was awful nice to hear from Gram. Wish we could swap weather for awhile. I was out working in the garden this afternoon, putting manure around the iris bed. The little irises have come up and they will be in blossom by February, and since the rains started everything has begun to be green, just like spring. Maybe you won't believe it, but I'd a darn sight rather have seen that good old blizzard you wrote about. It'll be three years this winter since I saw snow last, for I came out here in December, 1936, and I hadn't seen any since the winter of '35. Well, I guess most everyone wants something different from what they've got, when it comes to weather, don't they? I expect Tuggie will be coming home pretty soon for her Christmas vacation. Does she have a nice long one? Wouldn't it be fun if we could all have it together! Perhaps someday we can, because I wouldn't be surprised if I got a winter vacation, instead of a summer one, someday. Gosh, you old honeybunch, how I would like to see you! I thought over getting some things to send home for Christmas, but it still doesn't look as if I am going to get to San Francisco before then, and I know all the various families will understand if I send you money instead. You do just what you want with it—if you need it for anything you use it, or if you want to spend it for Christmas, you spend it. Anyway, I want you and Gram to have a nice Christmas. I will send you another twenty bucks the first or thereabouts of January, depends on when I get paid. I wanted to get the kids some cowboy hats, but darn it, the stores out here want two or three dollars apiece for them. Maybe I will get out in the country back of here one of these days. I guess the kids will all think they don't have much luck with my presents.

The Hobarts are going to give me a trip to Yosemite National Park for Christmas. Isn't that swell? I'm going up with a crowd that's going skiing, and I expect I will do some skiing too, if I don't fall on my foolish neck. I guess, after all, I'll see some snow this winter. They say Yosemite is something to see almost any time of year, and I've always wanted to see it. I can use a little vacation, too, for since I came back the boss and I have both been working like fools. She has got her next book about half done, and it has to be done by June, so there isn't any time to play around in the sand pile. One thing, she is feeling an awful lot better than she did last year, but she still isn't very strong, though she seems to be getting better all the time. I do hope she will get entirely well, for it is a devilish shame for anybody so nice to have to go through so much. I think she still has quite a lot of pain in her back, but she doesn't say much about it. Some people would growl and complain all over the place, but she doesn't say much about it. Some people would growl and complain all over the place, but she never says a word. She is able now to do quite a lot of work in the garden, and that's good for her. I do wish you could see our garden, mom. The frost took all the chrysanthemums, but we've got petunias and calendulas and forgetmenots and verbenas in blossom, and lots of new little plants coming up. It doesn't seem possible, this time of year, does it? After the rain began, I sowed the front yard to lawn grass and it's all coming up now, just a little thin sheet of green over the brown ground.

We have fallen heir to a new family of cats—a lean old skinny-tailed mother cat and three generations of her kittens. Apparently she only has one kitten at a time and keeps them all with her, for one is about her size, one half grown, and one ittle-bitty. They must be all hers, for she nurses them all at once, and I wish you could see the poor old soul, stretched out with all shapes and sizes of kittens sucking on her at once. The littlest one is just about the shape of Tom Bumbo—remember him? Looks like him, too, only he's black with a white vest. The mother cat takes them out in the fields to hunt mice, and they parade off in a line, first mama, then big brother, and so on, down to the baby. Alice saw them marching off across the terrace the other day and she about rolled on the floor laughing. How's Maggie, by the way? She presented any new families lately?

I'm getting along nicely, feel fine, and my back's just about well. I still do exercises and stick my big toe into my ear ten times on one side and ten times on the other, night and morning, but that's only just to keep limber. I think my back's strong now as it ever was, and it is a relief not to have it bothering all the time.

John is beginning to prune the fruit trees and the grapes. His wife has been sick, and he's been awfully worried about her, but I guess she's going to get better. He had to send her to the hospital, and that just about scared him to death. She's got something wrong with her heart, and for a while he thought he was going to lose her. He thinks an awful lot of her. For about a week he couldn't do his work or think about anything, but he's kind of coming back now. You'd have died to hear him bawl out the greenhouse man for bringing Alice some second-hand plants. Alice ordered three snowberry bushes, and when the man brought them they turned out to be so old the stalks were all rotten. John says to the man, "By Gawd, if them ain't some plants. Why, them plants is older'n what I be."

The man thought he could calm him down, so he says, "Well, that hadn't ought to be anything against them."

"Hell," says John, "Maybe it ain't, but I don't 'low I'll grow no more."

You tell all the folks, will you, marm, that I'm wishing I wasn't such a long ways from home this Christmas. It was lovely to have all the news about the various youngsters—how they're doing and all. Have Louise and Pearl moved yet, or are they going to wait until spring? I expect they can't wait to get into their new house. And isn't it nice that Harve has been doing so well lobstering. I'd like to see the old bub. Golly, I'll never forget as long as I live the way he sat on Hollis Reed. That was one lovely job. Sometimes I think of it now and laugh.

Well, it doesn't do a bit of good to run on and on, saying how much you'd like to see folks at Christmastime, does it? I must close now and go peep-py. My fire's burned down, and the room's cooling off anyway. Boy, the nights here are coolish-like, even if we have got flowers in the garden!

Lots of love, honey. Give my love to the whole push, will you, and lots to Gram.

Uppy

TO EDWARD M. AND JANE HOLMES

Christmas Eve 1938? (no date)

Dear Ted and Jane,

It follows no tradition that all the letters I should write you should be drunken letters, as last year the only epistle sent you should be full of cheer; but only that from this barbarian country where on December 25 the grass is green and birds sing in the fields, I should be homesick for sleet and snow on Christmas Eve, and the elements howling around a New England chimney, and thus when bidden to a party, consisting of the Man In a New and Unsullied Country and Very Happy That He Is No Part of A Decadent East, Where Seeds of Decay Have Blossomed Into A Pusillanimous Whisker Growth On the Face of the Earth, I should in my dismay drink ten old fashioneds and come home to unfold my typewriter and my shaken soul to my nearest and dearest, however far apart. It is that in a country where on Christmas Eve the radio should play *Silent Night* and *O Little Town of Bethlehem,* there comes on a program called the *Drip Hour*, advertising Barbasol. It is that they do not sing the Christmas carols in this country, but they give away 100-piece sets of china and Oldsmobiles. It is that it is not my kind of a country, and I am wondering what it must be like in New York and Maine tonight, however cold and bitter the wind around the cornices and the spruce trees. It is that there may be a war with Japan, and I do not, instinctively, like the idea of a Japanese, however wizened, with a bayonet. And it is that I am wondering how goes the struggle, of which I am no longer a part, having gone over to a protected existence, where jobs do not matter. It is that I am not sorry I have done so, as security is a good thing and full of peace and orchards full of fruit, (or will be), and an opportunity for the spirit to obey its impulses and be the more rested for the respite. It is strange for me, even when drunk on ten old-fashioneds. My house is now a spacious one, quiet, in fields; the sitting-room looks no end like a New England parlor—not so prim, but lived in and comfortable; the place where I work and live and write, a little; and study music; and wonder how it was with me on other Christmas Eves, when I was just as drunk, but curiously resentful. I am not resentful now, only a little drunk and sentimentally homesick; thinking it still a strange barbaric country and the people unsophisticated; it is like the Pathetique Symphony played upon an accordion.

Ted, I wonder how the writing goes. I read "Death in Maine" with deep interest; and saw in it what was meant, I think. For me, it does not need rewriting, because it is a personal thing about things I know. But I know why you are re-working it, so that it will have a more universal appeal. Where you deal with the things of Maine, your writing is superb; you have caught the peculiar mood of the place, which you and I know well; that could not be bettered, except as an artist thinks he can better his work by continual work upon it. To sell, of course, the story needs reorganization; as it gets across those things of Maine only to people like you and me, who know them. I would like to see it when you have finished it. If you can send a copy, so much the better, or I will wait a year, until I come east again. I believe you are on the right track; and I say so not as one who would encourage you with phrases. I would not be that cruel. So far, you have done well. The stories of yours I have seen have had more artistry in them than most of the things people have sold for money, through pull. I know you will not be satisfied until you sell stories and get the recognition from established sources that a writer needs for his further creative energy; that is a good way to feel, and I know you will not give up until you get your satisfaction, either in one way or another. I do not know how you will reconcile the success the world demands of a person with your own peculiar idealism; perhaps you will not. I hope you will. I wish you did not have to feel that financial success must depend upon the success of your work in the light of other people's judgment. I do not think that the judgment of the publishing world is worth very much; they are not the kind of people who should have that judgment in their hands. I may say this because I have not succeeded with them myself; I do not think so entirely. I read the book reviews, and I do not know any group of people who are so effete and do-less as the book reviewers. What success is in the writing world, I do not know; financial success it may be; but I suspect there is more than that. You will know when you have it. In the meantime, I yell you on. This is no doubt sentimental; I have meant to say, however, for a long time, that your courage, and Jane's, in living your way of life, has been a marvel to me in this day of hostages to fortune.

Jane, Christmas Eve is an odd time to be drunk, when one should be thinking of hanging up one's stocking and of the time when you got spanked by your grandmother for insisting you saw Santa Claus come down the chimney. My grandmother, God rest her, was a White Ribboner, and never knew that particular solace which comes from ten old-fashioneds in a strange and barbaric country. I not only had the ten old-fashioneds, but I drove the boss home over a mountain afterward; it must be the climate. In New York ten o.f.s would have had me under the table, taps up. My child, you were always amused at me, because in the inception of our acquaintance, so to speak, I had always had a beer. I expect I will never be sophisticated about drinking, and will always behave as if I were a hen who laid an ostrich egg, and so proud, God help her. However, I always felt best when I had had beer, and it was only that my grandmother had been a White Ribboner that I bragged when I was drunk, and still do. I wanted to say, a moment ago, that I believe there are not very many women in this age of female selfishness—you know, as a general rule, I don't like the way women act to men—who would do what you are doing, not that you do not take it for granted and should. It is perhaps brash of me to mention it, although I don't apologize, only to reiterate that it does this haggard old spirit swell, my child. How goes the Christmas tree idea for Maine, and shall you both go there for good in the spring, as you talked of? I hope so. It is not the usual thing, but why should one stick to what has always been done by one's people? Me, I can't be a part of the island for a long time, as once I planned. It is better to do those things by twos. Not that I have given up the idea. I am saving my dough.

Well, my children, it is the witching hour of the night. The whole state of Calif. has been to bed so long that they all are beginning to twitch for morning. Morning coming over Mt. Diablo would not surprise me, either, though I am not twitching. My fire is not a spruce log, it is a live-oak. I am a sentimental old New Englander, hide-bound. I would like a Christmas Eve with snow and sleet like the enclosed; though it is very nice and unusual to see green grass and our cover-crop of blue vetch standing up on its little stems; well, God bless us all and a Merry Christmas. Let me know how all goes with you, and much love,

Moma

1940s

The letters resume after Ruth had moved East, and was sharing an apartment with Eleanor Mayo. At the time Ruth wrote this letter, she was working on her first novel *The Weir*. Junior was Junior Sprague, who, with his brother Sonny, were state wards who boarded with Lovina Moore for several years. Junior joined the Navy. Orville Trask was Esther Moore's husband. Mrs. Stoddard was the editor of *American Girl* magazine. The following letters were written from 120 East 10th Street, New York City.

TO LOVINA MOORE

Feb. 6, 1942

Dear mumma,

Your nice long letter came the other morning and I sure was glad to see it. You always tell me every smidgin of news, and it's the next best thing to a trip home. As usual, I'm way behind you, but I do try to make up for it in length. Don't know whether I can outdo you this time though or not. Your letter was a pretty long one. Gol dag it, I sure do wish I could be there with you this winter. You keep telling about the snow, and it fairly makes my tongue hang out—I expect you don't feel the same way. We have had just two farting little snow storms, that covered the streets with about an inch of slush, and that's all. Makes me mad, the first winter I spend in the east after all those make-believe winters out west, and it has to be a mild one. That is, it's mild down here. Lots of gray weather, and not much sun, and a couple of days now and then when it's cold. It was four above the other morning, but that's the most it's been. I kind of shivered and shook in my shoes, but so far I haven't minded the cold half so much as I thought I would. I have had a cold this week, though, and the snottiest nose in New York County and I don't know but State. However, it's better now, and I only missed one day of work.

The job crawls along about as usual. It's kind of tiresome, and not half so much fun as chopping alders—maybe Sonny won't agree with me there—but it pays my share of the rent and keeps me in beer, and doughnuts. I finally got paid for that short story that Mrs. Stoddard finally made up her mind to buy—you remember "Pennies in the Water." You were hoping so I'd sell it and so was I, and by God, I did. Got fifty bucks for it, believe it or not. Well, if I could have known that before I left home last fall, maybe I could have made up my mind to stay there this winter, and I don't know but I wish I had. Eleanor and I are both making pretty good money, but the rent is so high, and you wouldn't believe what they charge you now down here for just plain food.

So if I had just a plain cheap job up there in Maine I'd probably come out just as well as I am here, and could be at home with more time to write. I have been writing evenings, for the last three months, and have got my novel almost done. I don't know whether it will sell or not, but for the love of God, marm, *pray*. It ought to sell, and if it does, by God, we'll all be rich. Believe you me, if I could get ahead a little, I'd make some of the debts fly in our family. Well, no use to count chickens. I do wish I could send you a little dough, but I guess you're doing pretty well, you old devil. Where on earth did you squeeze out enough dough to pay those back taxes? Is my face *red!* Well, dear, I'll try to pay you back in a little while. I don't mean to be squawking poverty, it sounds horrid, but before I got paid for the short story, it was kind of hard sledding for a while—nothing too bad, you know, but just kind of scrape-y.

Eleanor has got quite a nice job with a printing shop, the Craftype Company. She has got an awful nice boss. When she first went to work there, she worked two days until Friday, which was her first payday, and they paid her for almost a whole week. Golly, I wonder why nothing like that ever happens to me! I have had, by and large, the scrummiest collection of bosses that God ever put gall into. Well, it's probably part my fault, I guess. I always expect too much, and then when people turn out to have a smushy place, I feel too bad. These people I work for now are nice and hard-boiled, and we don't call each other darling, and I leave on the tick of five o'clock, and is that swell. I like them a lot.

There's an old lady lives across the street from us that is wonderful. I think she is the janitor of the apartment house there. She's some kind of foreigner, probably a Czech, for she gabbles in some kind of a language that isn't German or Yid. She's quite stout, and she comes out in the early morning, just as we're getting up—believe it or not, we get up at six-thirty these days—and sweeps off the sidewalk and waylays the mailman and gets everybody's mail and reads what she can of it, postcards and so on. The first time I ever saw her, I happened to look out the window one morning, and here down in the doorway was the damndest thing you ever saw—looked like a great big pink fruit of some kind, and at first I couldn't dope out what it was. Then I took another look and saw it was this old lady standing on the top step and bending over to brush off the second step going down to the basement, and she had on pink woolies—you know, like mine. She sure loves to be outdoors and she keeps that apartment house sidewalk as clean as a whistle.

Well, I like to got the pants scared off of me a week or so ago. This section of the city we live in is fairly close to the lower East Side and there are quite a lot of bums and drunks go along singing and so on, but they never seem to bother anybody, so we don't worry. Well, this Saturday noon I came home and went upstairs—we live on the second floor—to get the shopping bag and see what we needed for over Sunday. I couldn't have been more than ten minutes doing it, and when I came downstairs and opened the front door, there was a man lying in the entry covered with blood. I let out a yip and took another look and sure enough, it was a man covered with blood. The entry floor looked like a pig killing. I couldn't tell whether he was dead or not, but he sure looked funny, so I beat it back upstairs and told the janitor of the house to call an ambulance. She wouldn't believe that it was anything but just a man drunk, and all of a sudden it made me so mad that I grabbed her right by the back of the neck. I says, "You take your lazy ass down over those stairs and look for yourself, and then if you won't call an ambulance, I will, if you'll unlock the door and let me get at your telephone." She was mad, but she went downstairs. I waited for her to come back and she didn't, so I tore down, and there she was, standing on the front steps gawping up and down the street. "God sake, what are you doing now?" I says. "Can't you see the poor man's bleeding to death?" "Naw," she says. "He ain't. He's just like I said—drunk." Well, I was beginning to guess that she was right, but I hated to give in. He *looked* dead or dying to me. So I flipped out to the corner and just as I turned into the Avenue, along came a great big fatherly-looking cop. Boy, I was glad to see him! So I collared him and told my tale, and he came back to the house and first thing he did he leaned over the man and gave him a poke and the man sat right up straight. He was plastered. He'd been drinking out of a bottle, and when he passed out in the entry, he'd dropped the bottle and fallen on it and cut the side off of his hand. It wasn't an awful bad cut, but it had bled all over him and all over the entry floor. I felt kind of foolish. But heck, he might have been dying, so I was glad I got the cop.

It's awful nice to know that you are getting better all the time—the best news I've had this year. Some of that pill-medicine they prescribe is awful expensive. I wonder what the doc is giving you—sounds like a thyroid mixture of some kind. Well, you keep on, dear, and feel flippy as the divil. Are you still on a diet, and are you sticking to it? You better.

Too bad Harve had such bad luck with his car, but all anyone can say is that things like that will happen no matter what you can do sometimes, and I'm sure glad that no one got hurt any worse. That new insurance law is hellish, I don't know what benefit they think that can be to anyone except the insurance companies. Of course what they are trying to do is to get the cars off the roads to save rubber. But it makes it kind of hard for people who do have to use their cars, as we all do when we live in a place like McKinley and Bernard. Give Harve and Steve my love when you see them and tell them I'm glad they didn't break their necks.

Seems like an awful ways offshore for the fellows to go to get fish, doesn't it? And this time of year, too, so disagreeable on the water. I bet Orville was proud of that $81 day's work. I'll never forget as long as I live the day he and Tug got home after they caught the halibut. Well, I guess he earned it, going off to Clay Bank. I bet the baby is cute as a pickle seed, and I'd love to see her. I'm so glad they are all back home again. In some ways, it is hard for two families to live together, but it more than makes up for anything that doesn't scrape along smooth to have company and a baby in the house. It never seemed right to me to have Tug and Orville living up the road anyway. I'm damn glad they're back, and I bet you are, too.

You tell Sonny that the blade better be back in my saw by the time I get home, or I'll take what's left and saw his neck off with it. That's a promise. That was the best saw in Hancock County, and one day I was all set to kill a moose with it and would have, if the moose had come at me.

Well, well, well, so Junior has joined the navy! Oh, boy, I sure would like to be a mouse in the wall the first day the lieutenant finds him with his clothes not picked up. It sure would be worth all the labor that's gone into picking up bedrooms at our house. ...

Well, I must close now and see if I can get a couple of pages done on the novel before I tuck away for the night. Be a good girl and write when you can. I look forward so to your letters. Tell that Tink, for me, that it wouldn't break his darn wrist to write me a letter. Wish I could see them all. I'm so glad Pearl is doing so well, he's had such a run of tough breaks for the last few years. It sure must seem good to them to be getting their pusses above water.

Lots of love, dear, and don't pee out over the side of the pot.

Uppy

P.S. Do you suppose you could send down that Red Cross First Aid Book that I left home?

TO LOVINA MOORE

April 26, 1942

Dear Mommer,

Got your nice letter last week and was sure glad to get one at last. You know it seems kind of funny, and I wonder if you are not getting all the letters I write you, because I have written twice since I heard from you last, and your letter says that you haven't heard from me. Also, Eleanor had a letter from her mother and Mrs. Mayo said Esther was over one day to visit and happened to mention that you never heard from me. Who gets the mail, anyway? I don't know as I'd make any bones of letting it be known to the young fry in the house that I wasn't getting all the letters I was supposed to. I watched out pretty careful last summer, you know, and even so I think I lost one or two out of the mailbox. Well, maybe there's no reason to worry, but if I were you and Tug and Orville, I'd make sure that one of us got the mail ourselves.

Spring has really come down here. Today is as warm as summer, and I ought to have picked up my lazy bones and gone out in the country somewhere instead of sticking around the house. But it did seem kind of nice to sleep late—you know me. Eleanor has got a cold in her schnozzle—she got it from me—I had one last week—so we thought we'd just be lazy. I just would have liked to see that snowstorm you had. We had a couple of spit-storms last week, but the snow melted as fast as it struck the ground. Have you had any warm weather at all yet? I expect it will be time to get the plowing done pretty soon. I will try to send you something to help pay for it. Do you know yet who you are going to get to do it? I wish I could come up, but I don't know yet. It's all a matter of getting enough dough, and you know what that is. So far, Eleanor and I just about manage to break even week by week. Everything is so high down here and you can't breathe without paying for it. I suppose that is so in war-times. I would like to get some kind of defense job, but there does not seem to be much doing here in the city along those lines. There is a big long waiting list for every defense job which comes up, which seems strange, considering how much ballyhoo is in the paper about defense work. I don't quite know how to figure it. Well, I can probably make more money by sticking to my own profession, and I guess I will do that unless something special turns up.

I have got my book done and an agent has it. I don't know yet what is going to come of it—if anything. It may be offered to a publisher and it may not.

That's the way with such things, and it seems to take forever until you find out. It's a screwy field, and you may wake up to find yourself poor or rich, as the case may be. I hope to hear something next week, but I don't count on anything. Best way is just to keep your fingers crossed, I guess.

I got the notice of the interest on the mortgage and will take care of it. The old bank never forgets, does it? Well, someday we'll get the darn thing paid off and then we won't have to worry any more about it. I wish I was down on the island today. I'll bet it's a lovely day down there. Mrs. Mayo sent Eleanor a copy of the Bangor Daily the other day and there was a notice in it that Bernard was organizing a credit union, with one of the officers Ted Holmes, so I gather Ted hasn't been hung for a spy yet. Of all the crazy stories to get started, that one certainly took the cake, didn't it? I wonder if Ted knew it. Wouldn't he be some mad if he did!

Everybody here got jittery for a few days after the American flyers bombed Tokyo, thinking that New York would be bombed out of retaliation, but nothing happened, so I guess old Hitler must be too busy. I don't believe we'll have any trouble here anyway, in spite of all the precautions people are taking. There's too much going on on the Russian front right now for Hitler to want to spare any of his air force over here. We hardly ever even think about it—just go about our business and don't worry.

I bought myself a new blue suit that looks kind of kippy. Golly, if I hadn't, I would have been out in the breezes. Everything started to wear out at once, the way things do if you don't get any new clothes for a year or so. A lot of people down around here are wearing slacks, on the street and to business. I haven't tried that yet, because I work up off Park Avenue, and I guess nobody would like it much. However, the only ones who seem to make any objections to seeing women on the street in slacks are the Jews down on the lower East side. (Somebody ought to tell Mrs. Mayo that.) But of course, most of the Jew boys are in the coat and skirt business, and that makes a difference. Eleanor and I and a girl who lives in the same house we do went out on Second Avenue in slacks the other night, and a great big fat old Jew stopped right in front of us and waved his hands around and yelled, "Vell, vell, you soitnly are looking vonderful!" and Rose, the girl who was with us, said, "Vell, you aren't any raving beauty yourself." He couldn't think of one thing to say back, and boy, was he mad! But I don't think I ever saw a time here in New York when so many women appeared out on the street in slacks. It's kind of nice. ...

Golly, I'll bet it will be something down there on the island this summer, with everybody pulling and hauling to see who gets who and what. I suppose the next thing will be that somebody will want to buy Jennie Harding's house, and then we'll have a worse mess in our front dooryard. Poor old Jennie, doesn't seem possible that she won't be around any more. I'd give a pretty penny to know how much dough she left and who got it, but that is something that probably will never be known. She must have had quite a wugget saved up in addition to her legacy. Of course, it isn't any of my business, but I'm an inquisitive old gossip, and I'd like to know out of curiosity. Well, it will probably be one continual fight down there this summer, if last summer was any indication. I don't know what they would have done to each other if the summer hadn't ended. …

I've been feeling swell this winter, except for one cold which I had last week, and that didn't last long. I guess I must be a lot healthier than I was when I lived in New York five years ago and had a cold about every other month. Maybe the California climate did something for me after all. I guess the Hobarts have given me up as a bad job. Along about March, I got a notice from him as to the amount of salary they paid me in 1941, so that I could figure my income tax. Well, I already had my income tax figured, and according to my figures on what they paid me from January to May, 1941, I stood to pay an income tax of about five bucks, because I had no income at all from May to December of last year. According to the sum he said he'd paid me in salary, I stood to pay about forty bucks to the government. Well, he pulled that trick on me last year and I stood for it. The whole point of the matter was, of course, the way it figured, if I paid the forty bucks on my income tax, it meant forty bucks he wouldn't have to pay on his. I was mad, and rightly so, I think. So I wrote him and sent him my own figures, and said I was paying an income tax of five dollars this year, and he'd better revise his figures before he sent them in to the income tax people, otherwise he might be in for trouble with them. She wrote me back an awful mad letter, but they hauled in their horns and I paid five dollars. I hate like poison to have a thing like that happen, because for a lot of the time I was with them I had a nice time and we got along swell together. But I'd probably be right there now if they hadn't kept on being so funny about money. Well, it's too bad, but what can you do? The more I see of people who have a little dough, the more I realize that most of them are perfectly nice folks until it comes down to the old pocketbook, and then it's a different story. I guess I sound like a sorehead about it, but I do feel awful bad that it had to end that way. And I know in all reason, that if I hadn't been right about the income tax, they would have stuck to it like burdocks and I'd have had to pay the forty dollars. Shit!

Well, I hope by the next time I write you to have some news about the book. It's awful sitting around and waiting for either something or nothing to come of it. When I get to thinking about it, I get to sweating and thinking the darn thing is so lousy that no publisher would touch it with a ten foot pole, but if I don't think about it much, then sometimes I think maybe it may not be bad. Well, you never know. By golly, it would be nice to have something go, for once, though.

Be a good girl and keep an eye on the mailbox. Lots and lots of love to you and all the clan. Tell Tug that now she doesn't have to boil out so many milk bottles, she might have time to write me a letter or so. By the way, if I can get time to get down to Stump and Walter, I'll send you some seeds. What are you going to need this year, and is there any particular brand of pea or bean you want? If the book goes, I'll bring 'em home myself, and we'll grow another garden together this year, dear.

Uppy

Dr. Coffin was Ernest Coffin, one of the three Coffin brothers, all doctors on Mount Desert Island for many years. Silas Coffin had his office in Bar Harbor, Raymond in Southwest Harbor, and Ernest in Northeast Harbor. Richard Black is a fisherman in Bass Harbor. George Trask is Orville Trask's father. Father Coughlin was the notorious religious leader and Fascist.

TO LOVINA MOORE

June 21, 1942

Dear Marm,

Well, the summer heat has hit us and it feels like living inside an old horse blanket that has been soaked in pea soup. After the California heat, though, it doesn't seem so bad, and so far I haven't felt so uncomfortable as I did out there sometimes. I suppose it'll get worse before it gets better.

About coming home, I don't quite know yet how the cards will fall. If I get some breaks and round up a little extra dough, I expect you will see me someday. But I can't make any plans yet. The job I was working on I finished up last Saturday, and I have this week off until another one starts, but I don't dare to leave the city in case somebody else gets in ahead of me. I am holding my breath, but I have a chance at a job with the *Reader's Digest,* out in Pleasantville. It is in their Public Relations department, handling correspondence and relations with subscribers and what-not. They interviewed a lot of people for it and yesterday they telephoned me not to take another job until I heard from them. Well, that sounds pretty good, and I'll let you know what develops. I've got my fingers crossed. If that doesn't break, there's another one with United Airlines organizing a library of books on aviation. It pays a little better than the *Reader's Digest* job, but I'd rather have the *Reader's Digest* job because it's more along my line. I ought to know by next Tuesday and will write just as soon as I find out what goes on.

Macmillan still has my book I wrote last summer, and I guess they are still trying to decide whether to publish it or not. I wish they'd make up their minds, but there's no hurrying a publisher. I think they spend their time soaking their feet, and once or twice every year they read a book. However, that's on God's lap, too. I'm getting to the stage where if something doesn't happen, I feel as if I'd go off like a firecracker. Well, I suppose either things break or they don't. If they don't, I'll rootle around in something else. I feel quite chipper, as a matter of fact. I always like a lot of things going on—either one way or the other.

Oh—there's one nice thing. The story I wrote last summer is coming out in Mrs. Stoddard's July issue, and I'll send you a copy as soon as it's off the press. Guess it isn't much to brag about, but at least it's one step in the right direction.

You make things sound awful nice up there. I wish I could see your bouquet of trees around the house. I expect that old syringa is out too, isn't it? That old house always looks like a darn old garden this time of year. I sure do hate to miss seeing it. Aren't you the old divil—got your garden all planted and peas big enough to hoe and stick! You must have been able to get things done early this year. How was the ground—as easy to work as it was last year? It was in lovely condition when we planted it last year—remember how nice and crumbly it was?

I sure was glad to hear about Harve's good luck with the pollock. Gosh, it's about time that kid got a break. I hope they keep right on and make a million. That's about the best news I've heard for a long time. Too bad Steve's asthma has come back on her. I was hoping that was all over after Bill was born, but I guess it's tricky stuff to get rid of. Maybe after this time of year gets along she'll feel better. How are the kids? Full of beans, I'll bet, now that school is done.

* * *

You sound as if you were busy, as usual. How is the lameness? Has Dr. Coffin done you any good? You haven't mentioned it for a long time, and I'm hoping it's better, though I suppose you'd be less likely to mention it if it was worse. Come across now, and let me know how you are. Did you plant the garden yourself?

I bet the feethearter is something now and I'd like to see her taking those first few steps. I bet she makes the rest of you take up. I was thinking the other day, it doesn't seem a minute since Tug was down among the daisies on the hill down to Gott's Island with her doll carriage, and you could hardly tell which was Tug and which was a daisy. They were all about the same height and Tug's hair was about the color of one.

Most everybody I know is either going to the war or doing war work. I expect a lot of the men we know around there are going, aren't they? Did Richard Black go, or hasn't his number come up? They have got the air-raid sirens installed all over the city, and every Saturday noon they try them out. There is one on the elevated, just about a block away from our apartment, and poor old Eleanor was home the other Saturday noon when they first tried them out, and the one near us let go and like to scared the well-known s__t out of her. I guess they are just being well prepared, for we have had no sight or sound of an air raid yet, and I don't think we will. I suppose if I get the job in Pleasantville, I'll be out of N.Y. anyway, by next week. Pleasantville is quite a ways out—about twenty-four miles north of N.Y. City.

It is in lovely country—just a little town, about the size of Southwest, and the *Reader's Digest* offices are about a mile out from the town. They have a great big building that covers about an acre of land. I was interviewed once in New York, and then they sent for me to come out there for another interview, and while I was there, they showed me all over the building. It was awfully interesting, and the people would be nice to work with. Keep your fingers crossed for me, won't you?

It must seem nice for Pearl and Louise to have him doing so well again after all the cussed time he has had to get set. I hope Louise won't go to work in the factory again, though the extra dough would be nice, and I guess she kind of likes it. For two cents, if this job I'm after doesn't break, I'd come on up and get a job there myself. You better not tell Miss Weea I said that, because she'd probably laugh at me, after the way I didn't go to work there last summer. Well, you never know—and I guess I don't either. It seems terrible in a way to think that there has to be a war to make enough jobs for everybody, but I guess that's the way it is. They say Roosevelt has a program on to fix things so that people will have jobs when the war is over, and I wouldn't be surprised if he did.

What does George think of the way they up and arrested Father Coughlin? There was an awful lot of talk about it down here, but I guess most people figured he got about what was coming to him.

Well, I guess my newsbag is flat. Tell any of that lazy outfit up there that they might write to me—they *might* get an answer. That Tug, she could take a little time off and drop me a line, the bum, and Aunt Weea, she hasn't written to me since I was in California. Just because I'm a mean wicked girl about writing letters, doesn't signify that everybody else has to be just as bad. That's following a bad example, and I don't believe they ought to do that, do you?

Lots of love, dear, and write again when you can. *Uppy*

The following letters were written from 110 Bedford Road, Pleasantville, NY.

TO LOVINA MOORE

June 1942? (no date)

Dear Mum,

Somebody ought to crown me. I've had that letter I wrote to you in my pocketbook for a week. I'm so sorry, dear, for I wanted you to have it right away. I thought I'd mailed it, and then I looked for a paper today in my pocketbook, and there it was.

Well, anyway, I can tell you now that I got the job on the *Reader's Digest* and start work there on the 1st of July. It's about the best job I ever had, and it looks as if there'd be a future to it. It's so much better than the Hobart job, that I guess I can put down this past five months to profit and loss. Boy, I'm glad I came back East. I still can't believe it's happened. Strange as it may seem, I don't know yet what they're going to pay me, but I know it will be quite good. Maybe I can get somewhere now. About time, isn't it?

Eleanor and I are busy packing. The place is all tore out and looks as if the big wind had hit it. She is going to commute from Pleasantville to her job in New York. My new address will be 110 Bedford Road, Pleasantville, N.Y. I was out there all day looking for an apartment and I finally found quite a nice one—three rooms—bedroom, living room and bathroom and kitchen. Kind of a fuddy-duddy old lady runs the place, but she seems very nice. I only hope she isn't going to be the nosy kind, but I've got my fingers crossed. Pat me on the back, old dear. I done good.

We are moving tomorrow, so when you write, you had better use the new address. I'll write again as soon as I'm settled and tell you more about what the job is like. It's a lovely little country town—Pleasantville—about the size of Ellsworth on the main street, but not so big as Ellsworth in population.

Lots of love and whoopee, *Uppy*

TO LOVINA MOORE

July 10, 1942

Dear Marm,

Got your nice letter this morning and am going to break some kind of record by answering it. You'll probably be hearing from me more often now, because I have a lot more time than I ever had on a job before. This week and last we had a four-day week—quit work on Thursday night until Monday morning. It sure makes it awfully nice, especially when I've been working week in and week out from Monday morning till Saturday noon. It sure is a nice job. I still can't believe I had the good luck to get it. They're giving me a ten-dollar raise already, and I've only been there two weeks! They sure do beat the devil. Maybe in a little while I can get squared around and send you some dough. I've tried to manage it all winter, but we scraped by, and that was all. Kind of tough going, once in a while, but that's all over now, at least, I hope so, for a while. Well, I had an idea that thing would be kind of hard sledding after I came back to New York. I guess they would have been worse, if it hadn't been for the war and so many people needed. But I've got the kind of job now that I've wanted as long as I can remember. It isn't a terribly important one, but there's plenty of future in it, if you get the breaks. Right now I'm in what they call the Editorial Correspondence office—we handle the incoming letters and answer them. It sounds simple, but you have to know just what kind of letters to write to different people. What seems too wonderful to me is that I'm my own boss, practically, and don't have to be on the jump at somebody's beck and call.

About selling the punt, I kind of hate to. I don't believe Myron would want to pay what I paid for her—$14, and if he did, I'd feel that I ought to see that George got part of it for his time and trouble and paint in fixing her up. I know he wouldn't want to take anything, but I wouldn't feel right unless he did. So by that time, I don't believe it would be worth my while to sell her. After all, I expect to come home *sometime*, and I'd kind of like to have a boat when I do. If she isn't any use to Orv, and he doesn't need her, I wonder if Tinky wouldn't take the responsibility of her, look after her, and keep her nice for me until I get home. He's old enough to have a punt to use now, and if he'd take good care of her, I'd like him to have her to use when he needs a punt. Tell him to write to me if he wants to do that. I expect Orville would kind of like to get her off of his hands, wouldn't he? I think it's kind of foolish to sell a boat right now, when it would be so hard to get another. I don't believe I'd take any less than $20 for her, and she isn't worth that. You tell Tink to write me if he wants to make a deal about handling her for me. I may not get home this summer, but these *Reader's Digest* people are so decent about things like vacations, they might offer me a week or so this fall. I'm not counting on it, but you never can tell.

Well, that Tug! If she and that sprout of hers don't beat all! Tell her to eat lots of vitamins and have another one as nice as the fee-tarter. Maybe I'll get a chance to drop her a line one of these days, now that I'm not rushed to death every minute. I sure haven't distinguished myself for keeping in touch with anybody, either this year or last, have I?

Too bad it's been so wet this year—just the opposite of last, I guess, isn't it? Maybe the peas and the rest of the garden will pull out of it. We have had shower after shower here, and the hay in the field next to the house here is almost as tall as I am—or was before they cut it yesterday. I guess most of the vegetable growers around here are hoping for dry weather, too.

Eleanor and I moved up here bag and baggage at the end of June. We have quite a nice apartment—kitchen, bathroom, bedroom and big living room. It sure is different from that hole in the wall we lived in all winter. The kitchen is a real one—icebox and gas stove, too, and all kinds of cupboards and a sink. Gosh, I washed dishes in the bathroom so long that it doesn't seem right to have a real sink that works. I guess living in New York is over for me—for a while at least. It seems wonderful to be in the country again. Pleasantville is probably about the size of Ellsworth in population, but it seems smaller because there aren't very many stores. It is more a residential district than anything else. A lot of people commute to their jobs in New York. That's what Eleanor does. We're 35 miles from the city. She has to catch a ten minutes to eight train every morning and I have to go to work to be there at eight-thirty, so we get up, believe it or not, at half past six. The *Reader's Digest* plant is at Chappaqua, or outside of Chappaqua, right out in the open country, about five miles from here. The people who work there all go in buses or cars from the various little towns around where they live—Pleasantville, White Plains, Katonah, Mt. Kisco, and so on. Almost nobody lives near enough to do the job to walk there, although a few do ride bicycles. It sure is funny to see that great big brick building, sticking up out of the middle of the fields and woods, and only a house or tow for miles around it. But it makes a very nice arrangement with the buses. They go right to the door. I go to work at eight-thirty, have half an hour for lunch, and am all through for the day at half past three. Then, of course, so far we've had only a four-day week, though I understand that sometimes we work Fridays near the last of the month when they close the books. Pretty soft, what?

So dear old Sonny has left! Well, thank God! You better burn some sulphur. Honestly, when I think of what everybody has had to put up with from that poor soul, I wonder we stood him as long as we did. Are you going to try another boy, or are you too discouraged? I'm really surprised that Sonny lived to go away—I thought sure he'd be dead by this time from his tiers of wood falling over on him. If he has gone to work for a good stout man in Portland, I'll bet ten dollars that it won't be a week—sad as it may seem—until he gets that fresh ass of his tanned with a hoe handle or something. Not that I'd like to see him abused, but he sure could take some straightening out.

We had quite a number of air-raid test alarms before I left New York. They have got a siren up on top of the RCA building that will kill bedbugs in Brooklyn, as well as little sirens all over the city. They test them out at noon on Saturdays and the din is enough to make the hair sprout on the bottoms of your feet. I'm glad I'm out of it. I don't think they really expect an honest-to-God raid, but you never can tell, and if those things ever went off in the night, the whole city would be in a panic. Not much lying in bed and letting her toot down there, I guess.

Hope Louise has got a satisfactory housekeeper at last. She and Pearl must be doing swell now, with both of them working. I've been kind of homesick to come home for a while, but I guess I'll have to live it down for a few months at least. Would be good, though, wouldn't it? I haven't had any news of my book yet, except that Macmillan is still considering it. That's a fairly good sign, I understand. If they aren't going to use it, they usually bounce a book right back to the agent. I'm keeping my fingers crossed, though. Tell Harve he's still got to read it for me to see if I've pulled any boners with my haddock drag, but I don't want to go to all the trouble of mailing it to him unless it's going to be published.

Well, I've run on for quite a while. Give my love to Gram and tell her I'd love to have a letter from her. The same goes for all and sundry.

Lots of love, dear, *Uppy*

TO ESTHER AND ORVILLE TRASK

Sunday, 1942? (no date)

Dear Tug and Orv:

I guess you'll both probably drop over in a faint at the idea of a letter from me, but it's about time, isn't it? (About time I wrote, I mean.) I've been meaning to all this winter, but down in New York I didn't have a red minute that I didn't feel like going to bed, and that's a fact. Now I have more time, maybe I'll do better.

Of course you've read mom's letters, so you know all about my new job and that I like it and that I have untold time off to sit on my tail and chew my cud if I want to. Nobody knows just why the *Digest* treats its help so well, but I guess the editor has progressive ideas about how much time he wants people to work for him. If I were one of the bosses, why nobody'd think anything of it, but everybody works on the same time schedule, and the office just quits for the week half the time on Thursday night, even the low men on the totem pole, like me. Oh, I'm about a third of the way up the scale, I guess, with promise of more to come if I'm a good girl. Anyway, I sure do like the job and was tickled to death to get it. After last winter, it sure seems like paradise. Things got kind of low there, for a while, and I wasn't sure just how they'd turn out. This scrimping along on $25 rotten bucks a week in the city isn't all it's cracked up to be, as I guess you can tell about, too, Orv. Well, them days is gone forever, I hope. Of course $25 bucks is good pay, anywhere but in New

York or Chicago. I'd admire to have a job up home that paid that much, and I sure wish I did.

Orv, I meant to write some time ago and thank you and your father for taking such good care of the punt. It was sure nice of George to red her up, and thank him for me, will you? If he laid out anything for paint, and I expect he did, let me know, will you, too? Not that you could ever force him to take anything for it, if you hit him over the head and shoved it in his pocket while he was out. But I sure appreciate it, just the same. If you or he still want to use her, go ahead and do it. Mother wrote that you thought the best thing to do was to anchor her off in the creek, and that is all right with me, if she isn't being used. If I get a chance to get home this fall, and chances are I will, for a week or so, I can wangle somehow to get her up under cover—in the barn, or something. I thought maybe the responsibility of her might be kind of good for Tink, if he wanted to take it, but I don't know as she really is much of a boat for a boy to have, seeing she's kind of cranky. I'd really rather not sell her for the little I could get for her. Nobody'd want to pay what the darn thing is worth to me.

I sure was tickled to hear about the addition to the family that's coming along. I'm crazy to see the fee-tarter, too. I'll bet she is something by now. Does she still grin all over the lot at people? She's probably forgotten all about me now, but you might remind her that we were on pretty good terms when I left last fall. Walking all over the farm, I know, and it might be INTO THINGS. Well, I hope she gets a nice little brother, or sister, it'll be all right with me, either way. Which do you hope it will be? A boy this time?

Tug, are you having any steno business this summer, or are the summer people all dug in, in air raid shelters in Iowa, or other points inland? I can't see but what Westchester is doing all right—the cars seem to keep rolling on the roads around here. I know there are some summer people around Southwest—Eleanor's mother let drop some news about them every once in a while in her letters. Are you going to have any kind of sailing job, Orv? Or is the gas rationing hitting that business, too? Last letter I had from marm, you were slaying the fish, when you could get a chance for a trip.

Have you been down on the island at all this year? I understand Alice and Helen have taken over. Did they get the truck down there all right, and has Jane killed Alice yet, or vice versa? If there's any such throat scratching as went on down there last summer, I'll bet it's just a lovely place to be. Are they running any kind of summer business, or is it just a VACATION? I understand Helen decided not to go into aviation. Well, there, now, I believe I'm being catty.

Tug, I wish you kids would write me a nice long letter and tell me all the news you can think of. Along about this time of year, when I don't get home, I begin to get homesick. How do you feel, old dear, and is the new arrival-to-be behaving him-her-itself? Don't you be too flippy; eat lots of good greens and have as slick a one as you had before. One thing about us and our connections, we sure can make good babies, if I do say so as shouldn't.

I'm still waiting to hear whether I'm an author or not. Macmillan has had my manuscript now for two months, and my agent in New York says to keep my shirt on. So I'm keeping it on, but one of these days I expect to speak my mind. Of course, it's a bad time, summer, with all the editors away on vacation; but I sure could do with some word as to yes or no. Well, live and learn. It'll probably come bouncing back one of these days. The agent says it will sell; I suspect her of optimism, but you never know. They don't undertake a book, though, unless they think they can place it, so maybe she does think so.

Be a good lass, and write me, sometime. Now that I have two minutes or so during the week, maybe I might answer it, you never know.

Lots of love to you both, give the fee-tarter a smacker and the youngest a pat.

Uppy

Berl was Berlin Gott, the Gott's Island mailman.

TO LOVINA MOORE

July 13, 1942

Dear Marm,

It has been a nasty stormy day for Sunday and it hasn't cleared off yet. Looks as if it was hauling back to let go a few more tons of rain. Except for the last winter I was in California, I don't remember a season anywhere when it's rained more than it has here in Pleasantville. Everything is as green as a sarpint's back, as Berl says, and even the second crop of hay is almost as high now as the first one was before they cut it. One day it'll rain and the next be as hot as blazes. No wonder the fields and woods look like a jungle.

Well, the job goes along just as nice as ever. I sure do like it. Had three days off this week—Friday, Saturday and Sunday. Sure makes a nice long weekend, two and sometimes three times a month. They don't dock you for your time off, either. I guess the magazine is making lots of dough, and the editors feel that the people who do some of the work ought to cut in on it. Well, the more they cut me in on it, the happier I'll be. Sure is nice to work for people who don't demand every minute of your time. Four days a week isn't bad at all.

How are things with you? Have you had as much rain as we have? I've been wondering if the garden dried out enough so that the things got a chance to grow. That is an awful damp place in a damp season for a garden, and I wish there was some way to drain it a little better. maybe a ditch along the lower end of it would do some good, but it would be kind of a job to dig. Wish I could have got home this summer to help you out on the garden. Doesn't seem right, does it, a summer when I can't get home while the garden's on? Well, perhaps if I get a fall vacation I can help get the stuff in, who knows? I was glad to hear that the apples kept so well. I do believe that it saves them to pick them that way. Darn it, I didn't get very far with pruning the trees, though, did I? Next summer I will have a whole month's vacation, but that doesn't help us out much this summer, does it?

Tink didn't write me about the punt. I take it he figured he'd rather not have her, and I don't know as I blame him much. I really don't see much reason why he shouldn't, if he wants her, though I expect there is something in the argument that he might go out too far in her. If I get home this fall, maybe I can get someone to help me drag her up and put her in the barn. I don't know that it'll do her much good to stay anchored out in the creek, if nobody wants to use her. Probably I ought to sell her, but somehow I can't seem to make up my mind to. I hate to let her go, when sometime I might be wanting to use her again.

Has anybody been down on the island since we left? I've been wondering how the house is and if there's anything come loose again. That keg of salt mackerel I left in the store ought to be pretty fairly ripe by now. If you want it, why don't you ask one of the boys to stop by and bring it off? I should think the mackerel would still be good, and they ought to go kind of good, unless you've got a lot left still. It will be a month or so before the fresh ones strike, won't it? Doggone it, with I could be there to go mackereling again this year. Well, maybe I will, if it turns out that I get a chance to. If I get a long week-end with a day on either end of it, I'm darned well going to make a stab at it anyway, whether I get a fall vacation or not.

Is Harve still slaying the fish, out seining? I sure do hope his good streak kept on for a while. I don't suppose there is much summer sailing this year, is there? There isn't supposed to be very much gas around here, but I notice that people go out driving on Sunday just about as much as they ever did, although most of the cars you see are big shiny ones. I suppose that means that people with dough can work it somehow. Do you hear very much about the war, up around there? Eleanor's mother wrote that she was spending a few hours every so often up on top of the McKinley factory airplane spotting. I should think she'd sunburn her complexion, if you know what I mean. She also wrote that they're building another radio station down at Seawall, and that you can't drive around there any more. We don't hear quite so much talk about war since we moved up here, but down in New York, I guess they are getting jittery all the time for fear of an air raid. They say they've got antiaircraft guns plastered all over the city. Well, it doesn't surprise me much. I'm only glad I'm out of there. Up here, there isn't anything to bomb except a power line, and that runs from here to the city, so I guess they'd bomb it, if they were going to, somewhere below us here.

I had a letter from the bank asking me to put War Damage insurance on the house down on the island. I don't think that means very much, except they want their investment covered just in case. The government has been carrying it on all private property up to now. It only costs $3, so I guess they don't think it's much of a hazard. Do you and Tug remember what the company is that carries the fire insurance? The bank people said we could get the War Damage insurance from the same company, and I can't remember the name of the company. If you'll find out for me what it is, I'll send them the three bucks and have them put the insurance on. Also, will you find out how much taxes are due? Sometime pretty soon I can pay the taxes, if I know how much to send.

Is Gram still with you, or has she got homesick again? Poor old soul, it's too bad for her not to be contented in a place for a while. Give her my love, if she's still there and tell her to write to me.

Well, I guess my newsbag's empty, for now. I haven't told you very much, at that, I guess. The book is still on the fire—Macmillan hasn't made up its mind yet. I wish somebody would build a fire under them. They've had it for two months now. MacIntosh, the agent in New York, says that's a good sign, but I still keep my fingers crossed.

Lots of love, dear, and write, *Uppy*

Evidently, *Cry Discontent* was one of the first titles suggested for *The Weir*. Muriel is Esther's daughter. Eddie is Eddie Hamblin, the husband of Orville's sister Millicent.

TO LOVINA MOORE

Friday, Sept. 13, 1942

Dear Marmar,

Your nice long letter just came—just as I was starting in to write to you! I guess we must have read each other's minds. Your letters are so good to get—tell me all the news, and I don't know what I'd do without them.

I thought for awhile I was going to get home over Labor Day, I had four days off, but when I went to get train or bus reservations I couldn't get anything for love nor money. I waited too long. There was a big troop movement around Labor Day, and they carried the Army first. Well, that was all right with me, but I was kind of disappointed. I ought not to tell you, because you will be disappointed, too, to know how close I came. They haven't said any more yet about giving me a week off, and I don't like to ask, because I've only been there three months. But there may be some time off Thanksgiving, and if there is I won't get caught again. I didn't realize you had to get your tickets so far ahead, but by golly, I know now. Blast it!

Well, Macmillan turned down my book, finally, but it wasn't too discouraging, for the agent in New York who is handling it said they had a terrible time making up their minds. They kept it for three months, and according to the letter they wrote, they spent a lot of time reading it. Miss McIntosh, the agent, told me that they missed taking it by only one vote. Well, shucks, that was close, and it isn't as if they'd chucked it out first thing, I suppose. Houghton Mifflin in Boston has it now, and so far I haven't heard anything. Miss McIntosh seems to think she's going to sell it, but I keep my fingers crossed until I sign on the dotted line. I've got another one started now, and I've got so interested in doing it that I've almost forgotten what the first one was about. Maybe *Cry Discontent* will sell sometime. Apparently you can't hurry the process any. Personally I think the title is a lot of crap, but the agent seemed to think it was a good one.

My job gets more interesting every day. This is the big week up there, the week the magazine goes to press—"putting the baby to bed," they call it—so we've all had to work overtime. Most weeks, so far, we've been all through on Thursday nights, that is all except the third week of the month. I've got to work tomorrow from nine to one, only, but some of the kids have got to work right through the weekend. DeWitt Wallace, the boss, has been away on his vacation, and while he was gone, the boys got a little behind with their work. When he's here, he puts things through, and nobody has to work overtime. A lot of the men up there, incidentally, are going into the Army, and it looks as though some of us might get promoted, but we're all keeping our fingers crossed. Personally, I like the job I have now, but if they wanted to offer me more money to do something else, I wouldn't say no.

I don't know when I've heard such good news as that you've at last got rid of that old black cow and got another one that won't pull your arms out towing you around the field, unless it's that Dr. Coffin says you're getting along all right. That sure sounds good to me, too. Too bad we've got to lose Dr. Coffin. I guess he's a mighty fine doctor and knows his business. Has Millstein gone, or will Tug have him for the big event? Tug mustn't worry though. They say if the first baby isn't troublesome coming, the second won't be either, and from what she told me about Muriel, having the doctor was just an afterthought, anyway. Tell her to drop me a line when she feels like writing. I'll try to get one off to her sometime this week.

Isn't it good Harve's had such a good season's work? Boy, I'm sure glad to hear it. It's certainly nice for him; I'll bet his house looks nice with the new coat of paint and the new shutters. It must be a satisfaction, by golly, and I hope he makes twice as much before the year's over.

We've had the darndest week of hot weather here. September started out to be cold, and we like to froze to death in the house here, because the landlady said she was economizing on coal and the government said nobody was to start a furnace fire before Oct. 1. Well, we knew that there was something besides the government in it and we had the satisfaction of knowing that she was as cold as we were. But this last week has been hot and muggy—you can't get your breath, and the sweat just drops off in puddles. Today's a little cooler, and I guess probably it's the last hot spell of the year. Hope so. I've lost five pounds, but I'll probably get it all back.

Too bad you can't get the radio to working. If anyone wants to take it over to Bar Harbor or Ellsworth and get a new battery for it and send the bill to me, I'll be glad to pay it, for I think it would be nice for you to have a radio going, and it's too bad to have a radio in the house and not be able to use it. I don't imagine a new battery would cost over two or three dollars, and it would be worth it to me to know you had it to use. I don't suppose anybody goes to Bar Harbor or Ellsworth very often, but maybe if Harve or Orville or Eddie went, they'd just as soon take it along. Or if you can't get the battery there, ask the radio man to tell you what kind of a battery it takes, specifications and all, and I will send one.

I heard a naughty story the other day, maybe I ought not to tell it to you. There was a man came to live in a small town and he made a great hit with all the girls because he was so tall and good-looking. But he'd go around awhile with a girl for a while, and then she'd leave him, and then he'd go around with another, and she'd leave him, and so on. Finally the girls got to comparing notes about him. One of them said, "Why, he put his arm around me one night, and I said to him, what makes your arm feel so funny? And he said, It's a wooden arm. And he just unscrewed it and took it off and it like to scare me to death. My, I wouldn't marry him!" And the next one said, "I sat down on his knee one night, and I said, 'My, your knee feels funny!' And he said, 'I've got a wooden leg,' and he unscrewed his leg and handed it right over to me. My, I wouldn't marry him!" The next night, all the girls were at a dance, and they saw this fellow go out and sit down behind a tree with another girl. One of them said, "I'll bet he's out there showing her how his head comes off. I wouldn't be surprised if he had a wooden head." So they sneaked around though the bushes and peeked, and sure enough, there he was screwing his head off.

There, now, I ought to be ashamed of myself, don't you think so?

We had a murder out here two days ago—maybe you read about it in the papers. Bedford Village isn't far from us—I live on Bedford Road, as you know. A boy of seventeen did a nasty job on two little girls—killed them both. Our landlady's mother hasn't dared to put foot out of the house since. She's kind of a nice old lady, but awful foolish. Last night Eleanor and I came in and Eleanor kind of banged the screen door and the old lady came right out of her chair. "My God!" she says, "What you want to go and scare anybody like that for? If I hadn't of had my teeth out, they'd of fell out!"

I suppose before the cold weather really comes I'd better have you send down my blankets I've got packed away in that old trunk. There's quite a lot of things I'd like to have—a couple of rugs would come in handy, and I sure could use the phonograph and some of the records. But I've been holding off, because I didn't know but I might get home myself and bring what I want back with me. Don't send anything yet, because I may make it. Do you suppose, though, you could hang some of that woolen stuff, like blankets and rugs, out doors in the sun someday, so the moths won't get in them? Or maybe just have a look at them to see if they're all right. Probably you have anyway, but I just thought I'd mention it to be sure. Don't you or Tug try to do any lugging, at least until Tug gets over what ails her just now. There isn't any hurry about it, and maybe Louise or Steve would help someday when they're over. I don't imagine it would be much of a job, really, just getting them up and downstairs, though the rugs might be hard to handle.

Well, I must close now, dear, and mail this before the last collection. How are the apples this year? Did the garden pick up as well as you thought it was going to?

Lots of love, *Uppy*

The Pied Piper was a novel by Nevil Shute, and the movie version, written by Nunnally Johnson, was released in 1942. Esther's "new fee-tarter," George (a.k.a. Bud), was born two days after this letter was written, on October 31, 1942.

TO LOVINA MOORE

Oct. 29, 1942

Dear Marmar,

Well, what you t'ink? I've sold the book. Company by the name of William Morrow and Son in New York have bought it and they are going to publish it in January. It isn't a big publishing house but it's a good one—they published *Pied Piper*,—maybe you saw the movie. Well, that's that. Kind of good, ain't it? I'm still sort of stunned, or I'd probably sound excited about it. It only happened today. Probably by tomorrow I'll be screaming, seeing I've waited so long for it. Morrow wants a few revisions and they don't like the title, so I've got to change that.

Look, mom, they want some snapshots of me and some of the island. I don't know whether there are any good ones of me around, but could you look over the photographs you have and sent them on down as soon as you can?

That one you have on your mantelpiece might be a good one, if you could spare it for a little while—I'll see you get it back, as soon as they've made me a copy. Don't send anything but snapshots of me—photographers' shots aren't want they want. You know that book with all the blue pictures of the island in it, that I brought of last summer? It's got some good pictures of the old weir in it—if you wouldn't mind sending that whole bookful down, I'd see you got that back, too. What they want to do is to set an artist to work right away on a jacket for the book, and they want some photographs of the country up around there and of the weir for him to work from If you and Tug would also go through the collection and pick out what you think are pretty good of the island, I'd appreciate it.

I got your nice letter today and will answer it pretty soon. I'm so tired tonight I can't creep—I had to get the day off from the office and go into New York to talk with the publisher, and they about talked my ear off. I wonder how you're getting along up there, and Tug, how she is, and all. Wouldn't it be exciting if her new fee-tarter should come today, too? She and I giving forth on the same day, so to speak. Well, the Lord love her, and you, too. I guess this is a screwy letter, but I feel screwy. It doesn't seem possible the book is sold, but I guess it is.

Oh, hon, if you could send the pictures as soon as possible—I hate to ask you to hurry, seeing I don't know just how things are up there—but they want them the first of next week, if possible, so they can put the artist to work.

Lots of love, *Uppy*

Oh, and that old calendar (1910) with the picture of the weir on it—could you send that, too?

The Coconut Grove fire in Boston was the second most deadly fire in American history, killing 491 people on Nov. 28, 1942.

TO LOVINA MOORE

Dec. 14, 1942

Dear Mom,

I would have written before, but I've been into work up over my neck. We had to catch up for the time we had off over Thanksgiving, and then the galley proofs of the book began coming through, and they had to be read and sent right back, so my evenings were pretty much gone. However, today's a snowy Sunday, and I hope nothing bothers me till I get a nice long letter off to you.

We woke up this morning to a good old-fashioned snowstorm, and it's been coming down thick all day. There must be about eight inches on the ground now, and a while ago it looked as if it might be letting up, but now it's at it again. I hope it snows three feet. It's the first real snow to amount to anything I've seen since 1935. Maybe I can't be blamed if it looks good, can I? I'd be out in it if I didn't have a snotty nose. I had a cold come on day before yesterday and today I'm tooting like a good one. It isn't a very bad one—just juicy.

We had a real good trip back—no hitches. Got the eight o'clock bus out of Boston, which gave us time to have breakfast and stretch our legs. That Coconut Grove night club that burned was only a block from the bus station, and the fire had happened in the night. We saw crowds of people over there in the street, but we didn't go near it. It was an awful thing, I guess. We didn't realize how awful, until we saw the papers the next day. When we got into New York, it was raining pouring, and we had a tough time getting across town to Grand Central, because we had those suitcases and stuff, and there wasn't a taxi to be had. We finally found one and caught the 6:30 train by the skin of our teeth. We had planned to have some supper before we went out to Pleasantville, but there wasn't time. So we had some at the Pleasantville station, and it sure tasted good. We got home about eight o'clock and went right to bed and slept like pigs. Bed did feel some good, now I can tell you. Took us about a week to get caught up on sleep, but it was worth it. I felt as if I hadn't had but a glimpse of you, and I guess that was right, but it was a lot better than nothing, wasn't it? All the way back on the bus I kept thinking of things I had meant to talk over with you, and hadn't. But we'll do it next summer. It'll keep. Anyway, we got the peasticks burnt, didn't we? Gosh darn, though, it wasn't long enough. And I guess I was half asleep most of the time, wasn't I?

The first proofs of the book have been coming through all this week, and it sure does look weird to see it in print. They are doing an awful nice job on it, too. Everything is just as spick and span as can be. I wish I could send you a proof of the jacket, but they only sent me one so far, and I may have to send that back. They got an artist to do a picture in color of the shore of the Pool, from some of those photographs you sent down, and he's done a good job—

two old dories and a punt, with part of the weir showing off to the left, and some old ledges and spruce trees. It isn't an actual copy of the place—I wouldn't want it to be—but it's near enough so anybody'd know where it was if they'd ever been there. It sure is nice. As soon as I get an extra copy, I'll send you one. They'd had to postpone publication date from January to February on account of priorities—paper, I guess, or the government wants some printing done. I don't much care—I guess it'll be out soon enough.

I had a letter from Steve, when she and Harve sent back the carbon copy. She said they both liked the book, and that Harve didn't find any boners in it. I was glad of that. I wish, in some ways, I didn't have had to let anyone read that copy, as it isn't anywhere near as good a job as the finished one, but it was the best I could do, since there was only one copy of the finished one, and the printer had that.

Poor old Eleanor has had all her teeth out but four, and she's having those out tomorrow. She says to tell you that right now she isn't giving anyone any of her lip. Her puss has been pretty sore and she's still not eating anything but liquids, but I was surprised that she didn't have a worse time. I know I'm glad it isn't me.

We have decided to move out of this apartment to a better one—we hope—a little farther down Bedford Road. The people that run this one are being pretty hopeless about heating it—one minute it's boiling hot and the next it's down to freezing. I guess that's why I've got such a cold. We asked them a while ago if they couldn't give us better heat, and they were real snooty about it, so I gave notice for Jan. 1. As soon as they found out that we really meant it, they came down off the high horse and have like to roasted us out for the past few days. The new apartment is quite nice—bedroom, living room, kitchenette and bathroom. It's in an apartment house, too, not a private house, and that is a lot nicer, because you don't have everybody around underfoot. Our landlady has been kind of snooping around, too, I'm afraid. So I guess it's a good idea to move. As soon as we get under way, I'll send you the new address. I forgot to notice the number the last time I was down there.

The *American Magazine* editor wrote me a letter and said he had seen a notice of my book in the *Times* and would I like to write some short stories for the *American*. What d'y'know! After all these years. Let 'em come to me! So I've got one or two started, and I hope I'll have some time to work on them. The weeks before Christmas are the busiest up at *The Digest*, and I'm like the old woman who lived in the shoe, or maybe it was the "old sailor my grandfather knew, Who had so many things that he wanted to do, That when it came time and he had to begin, He couldn't because of the state he was in."

By the way, there'll be room for you in the new apartment, just in case you decide to pay me a visit this winter. How about it, a little later on? Say in February and March? You see if you can't farm the cow out for a couple months, and come down here till April or May. Oh, gosh, marm, would I like to have you! You might be a little lonesome during the day, but I get home around quarter to four in the afternoon. Well, you think it over, and if you want to come, I'll send you the dough.

Well, I guess the snow's letting up. I'll go mail this and then I'll have to go and sharpen up my old nose on the grindstone some more. If I keep on, I'll be able to peel potatoes with it.

Lots of love to you and everybody. Tell Tug she now owes me a letter. How's the pie-face-poo-baby and the feetarter?

Uppy

George and Emily Trask were Esther's in-laws. *The Just and the Unjust* was written by James Gould Cozzens. *The Seventh Cross* was written by Anna Segherf. The following letters were written from 181 Bedford Road, Pleasantville, NY.

TO LOVINA MOORE

Dec. 28, 1942

Dear Mum,

Got your nice letter today, and was so glad to hear from you I about cut a pidgin-wing. I was beginning to wonder if everything was all right. Why, you scamp, I hadn't heard a word from you since I got back after Thanksgiving! I was about ready to come home and spank your tail.

Did you have a nice Christmas? I thought of you all day long and wished I was there. Eleanor and I hunted high and low for a Christmas tree, but there was a shortage on account of transportation, so we finally gave up and had our presents on a table with some red candles lighted and fixed up pretty. Santy was quite good to me. I got a swell fountain pen, two books, *The Just and the Unjust* and *The Seventh Cross* from two girls in the office, a pair of panties, an egg-beater (I've been keeping house without one all these months), Mrs. Mayo sent me a box of writing paper; (!) some candy; at the office everybody got a great big red wooden bucket all packed and nailed up and in it was three quarts of real maple syrup from Vermont. It made a nice present. The bucket you're supposed to use to put sand in to put out bombs, in case any fall on you. So far I've used mine for a wastebasket. Your package hasn't arrived yet, but it'll probably be along Monday, and I think it's all the nicer to have Christmas stretched out a little. It will be lovely to have some new mittens, and I know they'll be good ones, too. The ones I have have sure had some breezes go through them this cold weather. And the pajamas sure will come in handy for mine have all gone to pot. I guess that white outing flannel I got in Ellsworth wasn't a very good quality, but you can't tell much about that, because when I was in New York last winter I sent them to the laundry quite a lot, and that sure does wear out even good quality cloth. I guess they use pretty strong soap.

As usual, I didn't do an awful lot for Christmas. I sent you a small package, which I hope you got all right, and renewed your subscription to the *Digest* for a year after your subscription runs out in April, or whenever it is. I sent subscriptions to Harve's and Louise's family, too. I didn't send one to Tug and Orville, because I thought it would be kind of silly to have two subs. of the same magazine coming to the same house, so if Tug will let me know what magazine she and Orville would like to have, I'll send it along...maybe *Life* or the *Saturday Evening Post*. I sent their subscription to the *Digest* to George and Emily, thought they might enjoy it. So I guess I didn't do very much all in all. I meant to, but I waited too long to do my shopping. I planned to shop on the Saturday before Christmas, and then on Friday night word came through the department that we had to work Saturday morning. So by the time I got into town on Saturday afternoon the stores were so crowded that we couldn't do a thing. I have never in all my life seen such a crowd as was in Macy's department store that day. I wanted to go up to the sixth floor, and it took us just one hour and ten minutes to get from the main floor to the escalators and up the five stories. People were packed in so close on the main floor that you couldn't go ahead, just had to move with the crowd. So we just gave up after that and came home. They say that there never has been such a record of Christmas sales in the stores—that 1929 was nothing compared with this. Well, I guess a lot of people are getting good pay and they aren't putting it all into war bonds. Not that I blame them a lot, after the hard times we have gone through. But it scares you a little to see people going after things like that.

I hope the shears won't be too heavy for your hand. I had to get a fairly heavy pair, because I wanted to be sure the hand grip would be comfortable for your fingers. They are the best pair I could buy and maybe they'll solve the problem of your rug shearing. I tried them out myself and they seemed nice and sharp. They come with lots of love, dear.

Well, we have moved out of our old apartment and into a new one, as you see by the new address at the head of this letter. We were awfully lucky and we found a swell place. It has a big bedroom and living room and bathroom and a small kitchen. If you come out to see me, you sure are going to laugh at that kitchen. It's just about five feet square, and it has an electric refrigerator, a gas stove, a sink and cupboard and a small shelf to cook on, in it. The living room has five big windows—kind of a bay window, and the landlady has furnished it with some quite nice pieces of furniture—a day bed, rocking chair, easy chair, lamps and tables. It looks nice. I am going to have to get curtains for the living room, because she only had enough for the bedroom. She had rugs, too, so I won't need mine for a while, but the lady that owns the rugs will want them around Easter, I understand, so I'll have to have mine then. So don't hurry about sending the rugs. I would like to have that plaid blanket I left home, though, and do you think I could have that quilt that we worked on that winter and that you finished up for me? I only had two blankets, so I bought two, and that plaid blanket and the quilt will make it just about right for the two beds. Don't hurry about sending them, just sometime when you get time. I hate to get too much stuff down here—you know me. If the book sells enough so I dare to, I'm coming home and camp out and write another one. Can't count the chickens before they're hatched, though. Maybe it won't sell at all, and in that case I'll be dang glad I've got my good job.

So far, things seem to be going along fine with the book. They send me advance proofs of the first advertising, which I'll tuck into the letter. "Stark and hardy realism!" Gleeps! Well, nobody knows what will happen. The publisher seems to be cheerful, and the publication date is February 24. Keep your fingers crossed, and don't be disappointed if the darn thing flops flatter than a fritter.

By the way, the new apartment has got three beds—a nice daybed in the living room, just in case you make up your mind to come down. I didn't think it was much use to think of your starting out before February, because the trains and buses are so crowded—at least, I read in the paper that the New York Central was sold out till January 30, and I expect that means the other lines are too. But maybe it won't be such cold weather later on—these cold snaps don't last all winter, you know, dear, and along about February, if you feel like starting out all on your lonesome, you better come on down and go sporting with me for a while. You think it over. It'd be a swell time for both of us.

Our nice snow is almost all gone now. We had quite a thaw this week that lasted over Christmas day. Last week it was fourteen below, the coldest day, and I tell you people down around here did some shivering and shaking. They aren't used to that cold weather, you know. I stood it like a major, myself, it felt darned good to me. I blossomed right out and went out and breathed down deep. A lot of people suffered scandalous, I guess, because of the fuel oil rationing, which didn't allow enough to heat the houses really warm. The *Digest* building was pretty chilly—they heat with oil, and I guess they were afraid of running out altogether. We kept our coats on one day, but except for that it wasn't any more than anyone could stand.

I read Eleanor the part of your letter about the doughnuts, and she let out a yip and said, "You tell your mama that if she sends me down some doughnuts, I'll eat em teeth or no teeth, by golly!" She is much better now, her mouth is all healed and isn't sore any more, but she sure was a sick kid for a few days. Her poor old gums looked like somebody's old ragged drawers-leg. She took it pretty well, though. I thought her tail would be dragging on the ground when she saw how she looked without any teeth, but she makes quite light of it and doesn't seem to mind. She can make up the most hideous faces I ever saw in my life. Says to tell you "hi" and Merry Christmas, and that if you were here she bet she could scare the be-jeezus out of you by touching her nose with her chin.

I don't know just when copies of the book will begin to come through. I ought to have some by the last of January if the paper shortage doesn't hold them up, and the first one I get I'll send to you. I'm awful glad you didn't want to read the copy Harve read, because I'd a lot rather you read the finished copy. It's much nicer and a much better story; but of course in that first draft of it the parts I wanted Harve to check on specially were all complete. I hope he'll like it better when he reads the whole thing.

Well, I guess that's all the news with me. Write when you can, won't you, dear? And do think hard about coming down, so when you start out it won't be so tough jerking yourself away.

Lots of love *Uppy*

TO LOVINA MOORE

Jan. 25, 1943

Dear Mum,

Seemed like the last letter I wrote you was so short it didn't count for much, and I guess I was in kind of a hurry. Maybe this one will fill the bill better. I'm so busy these days I don't know whether I'm me or whether I'm a pea on a hot spider. But I guess the worst of the rush is about over; at least the book's now on the press, and they tell me advance copies will be in by the end of next week. I will send you one just as soon as I get my hands on it. It will seem kind of funny to see it in print at last and I don't know even then whether or not I'll believe it when I see it.

Well, the latest thing is they want me to broadcast over the radio a couple of days after the book comes out, which is on Feb. 24—that is, Feb. 24 is the publication date, but I'll have my advance copies before that—I hope. The idea of broadcasting just about scares the pants off of me, but I guess I've got to do it. Anyway, the publisher puts it on the basis of look what he's done, and now it's up to me to do my share. Shucks, I wrote the book, di'n I? What more's he want? Well, anyhow, I go on the Mary Margaret McBride program over WEAF, from 1:00 to 1:45 p.m., on Friday, February 26. I guess you can listen if you want to, but I won't recommend it, because the Lord knows what they'll get me to say, and it probably won't sound the least like me. It isn't a talk—it's an interview. They ask questions about whether I thought up the book while I was standing on my head in a haystack, or did it just come to me, and I say, no, a little bird let drop on my hat one day and it just knocked the idea out of me, and all that. You get the idea. Maybe it'll fall through, the broadcasting, I mean, and I hope so, for I'd rather take a good licking. Makes me feel like a cussed fool. And probably I'll sound like one. Or I'll have the jitters so hard I'll sound like a machine gun.

I guess I'll have to go to town and buy me a new dress for it, because if I appeared at the National Broadcasting Co. in my old suit, they'd probably throw me out. Doggone, just when I was planning to invest my savings in the government, too, because the way it looks now, on March 15 the p'lice are coming around to put us all in the cooler. Nobody seems to know just how much Uncle Sam is going to bite out of the old pay check. I figured mine up to $195 last week, and then I got dizzy and quit. The lord knows how much it will be, by the time they get having it over, down there in Washington. I'll be all right, because I ought to get some dough for the book on the day it comes out—Feb. 24—just in time, by gosh. You know, I *would*, wouldn't I? Just my darn luck to put off making any money until the year when income taxes go up. Well, I don't know as I grudge it to Uncle Sam, with things the way they are, but just in passing, I kind of wish I could have cashed in a couple of years ago. I guess we're lucky, though, even as it is. It's awful to have all this ballyhoo going on, like the broadcast, and all, and not know for the life of you whether the book will be a success, or whether it will flop flatter than a cowflap. I'm so dizzy right now, I don't know as I care. I wish I was down on the island sitting on a nice rock.

We sure have had some queer weather here these last few days. Last Monday morning when I started out for work there was an inch of glare ice in the roads. I got a ride, luckily, so I didn't have to go on the bus—they said that old bus was just like a merry-go-round all the way up to the office. (I guess I've told you before, the *Digest* building is in the country, five miles out of Pleasantville.) It was icy all day, and then about five o'clock it began to melt, and the next day it was just like spring. The ice went as if somebody'd built a fire under it. About five o'clock that night, the wind began to blow, and in less than two hours the thermometer was down to 5 above. I never saw it cool off so fast in my life. Eleanor and I had gone down to White Plains to the movies and supper—we left here about 5 o'clock, and went into a restaurant down there and ate; and came out of the restaurant with our coats unbuttoned, expecting it to be as balmy as it was when we went in. Golly, that wind hit me in the gizzard, and I practically froze still in about five seconds. Felt as if all the nice hot dinner I'd eaten had gone into an icecake just the shape of my stomach. Was I surprised!

Everybody in the world got a cold that night but us, and so far we've got by without getting any. Up at the office everybody has been hacking and sneezing around, so I'll probably have my turn any minute. We've had an awful time keeping warm in the office anyway, becaue they heat the building with oil, and half the time they haven't had any oil. I guess it's been quite a crisis, the oil shortage around here. I know on three or four days in the past week or so, we've worked all day with our coats on and our fingers have been almost too cold to type. I think it will be better from now on, though, as I guess they've got the rationing arranged better.

Did you get your January number of the *Digest,* all right and has *Life* started to come yet for Tug and Orville? They wrote me that the *Life* subscription might be delayed a little, on account of the paper shortage, but it ought to be coming by now, and if it doesn't tell Tug to let me know and I'll jack 'em up a little.

How's the weather up there with you? We never know down here any more how the cold is anywhere else, because the papers don't print weather reports any more. I guess from what Eleanor's mother writes that it's been plenty cold, and you wrote me that there was plenty of snow. Seems a long time till spring, doesn't it. Have you really made up your mind about coming down, dear, and if you have, when would you like to come? I know it seems like an awful jerk to pull loose, even for a few weeks—or months, however long you'd like to stay. Anytime now, though, is all right with me; or if you'd rather wait till the going gets better. Let me know in plenty of time ahead, won't you, so I can be sure you have enough money and we can plan out how you'll come, so I can be sure to meet you in New York. You think it over, and whatever you decide will be all right with me.

Golly, I wish I was right up there with you now. If my life gets much more public, I'm not going to like it one bit. Be a good gal and write when you can, and I love you.

Uppy

I almost forgot to tell you how swell the pajamas are. They are just right—fit to a T, and that is a grand pattern you made them by. I do like that yoke pattern—seems to make em fit better somehow. I cuddled into the new pair last night and I was as cozy as a bug in a rug. You always know just what I like, don't you, dear.

By the way, I had a very cordial Christmas card from Bessie, hoping among other things, that the book would sell a million. My Lord, I haven't heard from her in years. Why now, I wonder? It wouldn't, just possibly, be the book, would it? There, I'm a nasty, suspicious-mindedb___h. What do you hear from Gram?

Hope you got the check o.k. before the town books closed. Hadn't been for you, we'd been on the delinquent list, sure as the lord made little apples. I don't know why I always put off things like that, but I do, I guess.

TO LOVINA MOORE

Feb. 21, 1943

Dear Marm,

Got your nice letter Friday and was so glad to hear that you enjoyed the book, and that Tug did too. I'll be glad to hear what Tink made of it—maybe he liked it, and I hope he did. Tell him I wish he'd write to me and let me know what he thought of it. Well, publication date is this week, and I suppose I'll know by Thursday whether it'll be a flop or not. There isn't any way of telling now. By the way, the broadcast date has been changed from Feb. 26 to March 12, so don't get your mouth puckered up for next Friday. Miss McBride had a sick spell, I understand, and it put her off on her program. Anyway, it'll be March 12, Friday, and the idea of it gives me the creeps. I've got to go to the National Broadcasting studios next Friday, though, and listen to the program so I'll know what to do, and get brushed up for my turn. The Lord knows what I'll make of it. Miss McBride invited me to eat lunch with her that day and I said I would, but I wish it was over. To hell with all this fuss. Makes me tired, and all it is anyway is some screwy idea of the publisher's that it'll make the book sell more copies. Well, I suppose that ought to be all right with me.

I had a letter from Miss Ovington wanting a free copy of the book, and I guess I was mean, for I wrote back that I didn't have any now—I haven't, either, except one or two that I want to send home. So I told her that I was awful sorry, but I guessed she'd have to buy one. Seems like everybody I know wants a free copy, and I think it would be swell to give them away if I didn't have to buy them myself, but on account of the paper shortage, the publishers all over New York have cut down on the number they give away to even the writers of the books. I guess I sound kind of mean. I do want to send some copies home, but when it comes to "old friends" I haven't heard a word from for ten years, I guess they'll have to put out the two-fifty. Too bad. I get meaner as I grow older, too.

I'm trying to get my vacation through June—begin last week in May if I can. I want to get home in time to help you put in a darned good garden. The way it looks now—and I'm pretty sure of it—people who don't have a garden this summer and put up a lot of home-canned stuff, are going to be damn well out of luck. You probably know as much as I do about it, but I met a man the other night who had pretty straight dope from Washington, and he said that the food situation by next winter might be serious. He didn't say it was anything to be scared over, but he did say that anyone who had a piece of land would be awful sorry if they didn't grow it for all it was worth. If you'll have that extra piece of land plowed up, out back of the barn this year, I'll pay for the expenses of it, and we maybe can all turn to and pay for the expenses of it, and we maybe can all turn to and plant it when I get home. I don't know how it will grow, and it probably ought to have been plowed up last fall, if we were going to use it. But maybe we can do a little something with it the first year. I've practically turned New York upside down trying to find a pressure cooker, but there isn't one to be had, not that it's so awful important, but it would be nice to have one. You think over about that extra piece of land being plowed up, and talk it over with Orville and Tug, because it's going to mean an awful lot next winter, particularly to people with children who'll need vegetables and stuff through the cold weather. Maybe you better pass the word along to Louise and Harve's families, too, that if they can raise any extra garden stuff this summer they better do it. Sounds as if I was trying to stick into people's business, but I thought I ought to pass the word along, seeing I got it so straight. I'll be home all through June so as to help out with getting it off to a good start.

Golly, this is such a lovely day I'd almost go out and stick in a seed this morning if I had the seed. Three days ago we had it 25 below zero and a foot of snow on the ground. Today the snow is all gone but a mess of puddles and slush, and it's so warm that I sat out on the upstairs porch in my pajamas for quite a while. This sure has been an up and down winter down here. I hope you're getting these two days or so of sunshine, for from your letter you were getting the same cold snap we were.

The box of grub arrived Friday and was it swell. Everything came out of the wrapping paper just as lovely as if it had just been packed. Eleanor and I had a chicken dinner that night with gravy and mashed potatoes and cramb'ry jelly and the fixings. And then we had another one last night. That poor old hen sure did look swell, but you ought to see her now! Gosh, it tasted good, marm, and I'd give an awful lot if I could roast a hen to taste as good as that. The doughnuts are every one all gone, and we've dipped into the cookies pretty hard. I almost got homesick, too, when I stuck my old tooth into one of those pickles. You were a bessy-darlin' to think of it, and I wish I was right there to tell you so. Eleanor says thanks, too, and to tell you that her new teeth didn't know what they were for till they hooked over one of those doughnuts.

I'm glad *Life* has started to come all right. I was afraid for a while there they wouldn't take the subscription, but I got a notice from the yesterday saying they'd sent it.

Well, whatever happens to the book, I may get a better job at the *Digest* out of it. Mr. Henderson, one of the senior editors, asked me to come in and see him the other day, and he said that they needed some new blood on the staff downstairs, and would I like to be it. Said he hadn't read the book yet, but some of the other editors had and they thought it was a pretty good job. He said nothing would probably happen for two or three weeks, and for me not to count on it, as nothing had been decided yet; but I'm sure he wouldn't have told me about it, if he wasn't pretty sure. So I'm sitting in a kind of daze, waiting for something to happen, and wondering if it will. I shan't be too disappointed if nothing does, because I like what I'm doing all right, and the more dough you make the more income tax you pay; but the job he mentioned was "Staff Reader." There are four or five doing that work, and keep it under your hat, but they get $5000 a year. It may not happen at all, so keep your fingers crossed. Me, I am. (I'll say I am.)

Who do you suppose I had a letter from yesterday? Old Dr. John Haynes Holmes! He said he had read the book and was I the same Ruth Moore who used to be his secretary. What do you know about that? Somebody said once that "the nice thing about success was that it put you in touch with your friends so easily." (Maybe I better wait a week or so before I call it "success" though.)

Eleanor has got a swell job in New York with the British Ministry of Supply Commission—that's the people from England who are handling the business side of lend-lease in this country. She's tickled pink about it—says she never could have landed it without her new teeth. It's a dandy job, and she did awfully well to get it. I sure am glad for it's about time she got a little credit. She's had to hang off until she got her teeth fixed and then until she got used to them, but I guess she's all set now. She's doing confidential paper work with ship-loadings and sailings, and I'll say the British were some pickers if they wanted somebody close-mouthed. It's essential war-work, too, so she won't have to be shifted around to another job, in case women are drafted. By the way, you'll be glad to know that people on *The Digest*—me, for instance—are now considered essential war workers. They call it "communications service"—publishing essential information and morale-builder-uppers, or something. So I guess I won't be shifted around either.

Well, my old newsbag is getting empty, too. I do wish I could get a vacation before June, for what with all this excitement, hard work and foofaraw, I'm getting awful tired, and the old gal isn't so young as she was once. I've got three white hairs right up on the edge of my forehead, and what do you know! But I guess I'll make it through all right—I don't seem to get thin any. The *Digest* offices have been cold, like all other offices this winter, and I haven't had a cold since November, though most of the others have and have breathed germs all over me. Maybe it's the vitamin tablets—they've been issuing vitamin tablets to the office-workers up there all winter. I took a lot of them at first, but one day I broke out with the darndest case of hives you ever saw—gee, was I a sight! All over, too. So I quit the vitamin tablets, and the hives went away, and now I only take two a week.

I guess I better stop, or this letter will be too long for Muriel to read. Lots of love to you all,

Uppy

P.S. I've got copies of the book all wrapped to send to Weese and Harve, but I didn't get to the post office with them, because we had to work all day Saturday. We thought we were going to have to work Washington's Birthday, too, on account of it was closing time for the April issue, but the boys downstairs caught up with themselves, so we didn't. I had had kind of a skinny idea that we might get a four-day week-end, but I was afraid we wouldn't, because it came right in the middle of the month when they "put the new issue to bed." Well, better luck with the next holiday.

TO LOVINA MOORE

March 15, 1943

Dear Marm:

It's a quiet Saturday afternoon, without much stirring, thank the Lord. I meant to write to you before as soon as I heard about Gram.

Poor old Gram, I'm glad she didn't have a bad time of it at the last. I guess we've all been expecting her to go for the last year or so, and seeing it had to happen pretty soon, I'm glad it happened the way it did. I guess we can't expect to keep people when it's time for them to go, and I hope there's a heaven for the ones who believe in it. She had a long, long, life—longer than most, and I think it was a good life, too. Hardscrabble, the way most lives are, with a good rest at the end of it for a tired old lady.

Yesterday was a lovely spring day with song-sparrows whooping it up and a regular Congress of crows down in the field back of the office building. There was even a little heat to the sun. But this morning it began to snow again, and it has snowed all day, turning to rain tonight, so I guess it won't last long.

I went downtown this morning to see if I could round up a little piece of meat for Sunday dinner. Getting even a little piece is like wringing blood out of a turnip, these days, and the meat men are so snotty you feel like wringing their necks. I did manage to round up a chicken, and the butcher hauled it out of the showcase and started to wrap it up and said, "I hope you know how to clean it." I said, "Sure, I can dress a chicken. But what's the matter with you doing it? Aren't you supposed to before you sell it?" "Oh," he said, kind of bored, "We don't do that now." It made me kind of mad, because they aren't supposed to sell chickens without dressing them, anyway, and the Lord knows, he wasn't busy. So I said, "What *do* you do to earn your dough? You sure aren't overworked selling meat." He said, "Lady, I don't have to sell you this chicken, you know." I said, "Mister, you can take your chicken and wrap it up in ten dollar bills and stick it wherever you've got a mind to. But you remember that roast I bought in here the other night? I noticed specially it didn't have any government stamp on it." Lord, you ought to have seen the way he shut up! He unwrapped the chicken, dressed it, wrapped it up again and charged me $1.50 for it; and I'm sure he said $1.80 when I first asked him how much it was. It was only a four pounder at that.

Well, they get you coming and going, don't they? When it's hard times and things are cheap, you don't have any dough; when you've got a little ahead and times are better, prices go up like a hen over a bunch of firecrackers. Of course, I *would* wait to publish a book the very year when the government is taking the most dough away from people. But, heck, I don't care. I'll do all right out of it, as it is, I guess, and nobody wants all the dough in the world.

I'm enclosing some of the reviews, so you can see them. They're pretty good ones, if I do say it as shouldn't.

The book went into a third large printing less than a week after publication, and the reports are that it's a very fast seller, though slowing down a little this week, while people get over the jolt of the income tax. I haven't any idea how many copies have sold or how much I will make, it's hard to estimate. But it will be a lot better than most first novels do, so they tell me. I do know that paper stock for a fourth printing is ordered, and they are going ahead with it as soon as the third begins to peter out. It's tantalizing not to know just how much it's going to amount to. I don't think we'll get rich out of it, dear, but we'll get us a nest egg. We won't really get rich anyway, probably, and I don't know as I want to, considering. We might get a little wugget from selling the book to the movies, though. I've got my fingers crossed and I don't take a deep breath over it, but Annie Laurie Williams says she has got a nibble from Warner Brothers. Three movie companies turned it down flat, but they (Warner Bros.) are interested, and said they'd wait a few weeks to see if the book was a good seller. Well, it's being a good seller, all right. So hold your breath, old dear. I probably shouldn't mention it, for it may be just a dud, but I figure you might just as well enjoy thinking about it the way I am. If it doesn't go through, why, what the hell, Archy, we didn't expect it would anyway.

So that's that. I'm glad you heard the broadcast, though I guess you wouldn't have missed much if you hadn't. I was too scared to do very much talking—I'm not very good at things like that. I had an idea I was making an awful fool of myself, anyway. I may have to do it again, but I hope not.

Yes, I've waited a long while for it, and you know, marm, now that it's happened, it doesn't seem the least bit real? I guess that sounds funny, but if I should wake up this minute and find it was something that had happened in my sleep, I shouldn't be a bit surprised.

Well, old dear, June isn't so very far off, and when I come home we'll gabble it all over. I'm dying to see you and tell you all the things that won't go in a letter, no matter how hard I try to get them across. I was hoping we wouldn't have to give up the idea of your coming down, it came kind of hard to have to, but I made inquiries about trains and busses, and there's standing room only on them for weeks to come. Don't that beat the deuce? But they are making big troop movements all over the east, they say, and the army gets priorities. I expect they ought to have it, but it's kind of dinktoed my plans. Well, June won't be long in coming, dear—2 months and a half now.

You're right about having a big garden—you mustn't fail to, even if we have to hire the help. We may be able to get somebody to hoe it for us. The food situation, while most people don't realize it now, is much more critical than we imagine—and it will be worse next winter, especially in places far away from the cities. People with little children mustn't fail to make plans, just in case the supplies go lower than is expected. I don't know how to put that serious enough. If you possibly can, you have the piece out back of the barn broken up, and if the menfolks have too much on their hands to be able to plant it, we'll shove it full of potatoes and beans when I get home the first week in June. I'll make it the last week in May if I possibly can. Are you sure you've got enough Mason jars to put up a winter's supply of stuff? If you think you haven't, you better lay in some more with part of the enclosed check. I know I sound like an old calamity howler, but I don't think we ought to take any chances. I've got pretty straight information. Not that I want to scare anyone, because that would be foolish, but I do think we ought to look at it in the eye.

Well, I must saw off now, and write to some of the darn people who have written me about the book. I guess I'm ungrateful, but it sure is a headache answering all these letters.

Lots of love, and tell Tug to write. I had a swell letter from Wee—sounded just like her and made me homesick to see the old scamp and all the kids. I sure am glad Tink liked the book. I'm glad you did, too, dear.

Lots of love *Uppy*

The Harlem Riot of 1943 was a major U.S. race riot. The *Bataan* movie was released in 1943.

TO LOVINA MOORE

Aug. 17, 1943

Dear Mum,

I meant to write you right after the doughnuts came how good they were, and I guess you'd have thought we liked them, if you could have seen the way I went and broke out the coffee pot and made a big batch of coffee. We sat right down with one container apiece and waded right through. You were a dear to think of it, and you ought to have had a letter before this. It's been so miserable here, though, that I've just gone to bed evenings, when I couldn't get my breath sitting up. We had about three weeks of this humid hot weather and I'll bet if the drops I sweat were laid end to end they'd make a brook big enough to catch suckers in. Then, to top everything, this is the week the magazine goes to press and we had to work Saturday.

I wish you could have had some of the drought that we've had. Except for a few thunder showers, we haven't had a rainstorm since the first of July. The farmers thought every once in a while that all the gardens were dried up, but then there'd be a thunder shower with just enough rain to keep things going. Night before last we had a good rain, and I guess now things will be all right, but it was nip and tuck there for a while. I do hope that you have some decent weather now and that the gardens will dry out. It would be a damn shame after all the trouble we went through—at least, I did a little of the worrying when I was home, if not much else—to have them rot out now. Maybe by this time you've had some nice sunshine and drying weather. And I do hope you didn't lose your hay. That would be lousy luck. How's the new cow working out? Sounds as though she might be easier to handle than the other two were.

My vacation doesn't start until September 20, but then I'll be home for a couple weeks as quick as the Lord and what transportation I can find, will let me travel. I've been something awful homesick this summer—more than I was when I was in California, even. Maybe it's because I'm so near and yet so far. Seems almost as if I got home oftener when I was farther away, doesn't it? Well, we sure will enjoy the two weeks when I get there, and talk everything over, won't we?

If you have trouble getting the shoes you want, why don't you send me your coupon and your foot measurements? I feel quite sure I can get you some "Minute Woman" shoes in the Coward New York store, if you want that kind. They had an ad in the paper tonight, with a picture—the same ad I sent you,—and saying the sizes were to 11. So if you can't get them in Boston, you do that, and I'll have a go at it in New York. Let me know, too, if the ones they send you are not satisfactory.

It seems odd to hear you talk about the peas and beans being in blossom, for down here the season is so far ahead. Most of the peas and beans have gone by, and everywhere you look you see gardens with big ripe red tomatoes hanging down. But of course we were late in getting our garden in, and then, in any year, the season's about a month behind the season down here. I bought some corn, yesterday, at a roadside stand, that had just been picked, and it was good, but it never seems to me that vegetables taste the same down here as they do up home. I really do think they have a better flavor up there, and I don't believe it's my imagination.

Sounds as if the fishermen up there had been having quite a time with the OPA ceilings, and it does seem as if they could have set ceilings a little higher, especially since it didn't make the slightest difference to the consumers down here. I've tried a couple of times to get some fish for a chowder, and the only thing I could get was a little piece of halibut that I paid $.68 a pound for. The prices down here haven't gone down a bit, ceilings or no ceilings, they've gone up, if anything.

I have worked my fool head off for the past two weeks, doing a condensation of what, I'm pretty sure, is to be the *Digest* book supplement for October. It's a swell book, called *Paris Underground,* about a little old American widow who helped refugee English soldiers from Dunkirk to get out of France. She lived in Paris and she was, apparently, just the kind of fool female you'd see around the stores in any American town—not very much sense, and so on—but the chances she took would curdle your blood. The German Secret Police caught up with her after a while, and she was arrested and put in prison. But before they got her, she and a friend of hers had helped about 150 English soldiers to escape from France. I got it down from about 350 pages to 70 typed pages—which will fill about 30 *Digest* pages, and boy, was it a job to cut it that much and still keep all the essential story. It was a lot of fun, though, and I guess they're going to use it. I hope so, anyway. I worked hard and put a lot of time on it, and it—as well as the hot weather—is one reason why I've been so late in writing.

You've heard me speak, I guess, of Annie Laurie Williams, who is the head of the agency in New York that handled my book? Her husband, Maurice Crain, was the belly gunner in a Flying Fortress, and she just got word the other day that he had been shot down over Germany and is a prisoner in a concentration camp. That must be kind of hard to take. She seems to feel pretty bad about it, but feels comforted—if that's the word—because he wasn't killed. When I hear about something like that, it makes me feel as if I ought to shut up griping about my income tax, though the Lord knows I do plenty. It is a worry sometimes wondering how to break even with 20 per cent of the old pay check gone, but I guess none of us ought to mind too much, when some of us have gone through what Annie Laurie's going through now, not to speak of Maurice, the poor devil. I knew him quite well—he used to take me out sometimes when I was in New York.

I can't wait for the weeks to pass until I come home. It seems like a longer time than I thought it would. I thought up until a week ago, that I could come August 20th, and then it turned out that a girl was sick and had to leave, and I couldn't be spared. However, she'll have to be a lot sicker than she is now to hold me in September. We've waited long enough, by gosh. And won't it be slick to get together again, old dear? Yes, I guess there are quite a lot of things to talk over.

We are still having quite a time here getting meat to eat, and fish, of course, is few and far between, to say nothing of the price being way up in the pictures. But there are plenty of fresh vegetables and fruit, and I'm getting to be quite a vegetarian. There's been a lot of ham around lately, and you can almost always get a slice of ham when you want it; but we're kind of sick of it now and don't care whether we have it or not. Eleanor was lucky a couple of nights ago, and she got a pound of hamburg. We had one of the girls who works up at the magazine in to help us eat it. It was an occasion—like having someone in to Christmas Dinner, or something. You never saw a pound of hamburg disappear so quick in your life as that one did, and my, didn't it taste good! I had baked potatoes and stewed tomatoes to go with it, and an apple pie from the bakery. The pie wasn't very good—the pastry tasted like flour paste, but we felt as if we'd had quite a feed, at that. It doesn't seem possible, does it, to be so short of good things to eat, when we've always had plenty here in this country.

So far, we've had quite a nice time with our bicycles, and I've got so I can ride quite a ways without poohing out. Yesterday we rode 8 miles to a lake and went fishing and then 8 miles back. I was pretty tired, but darned if I was so tired as Eleanor was. (She was getting the curse, so maybe that isn't quite fair.) We tied our fishing rods to the handle bars and took along a lunch in the northwest wind—the first cool day we've had in weeks. We did enjoy it and the cool seemed like heaven. I got sunburnt good and plenty but I guess I'm not going to peel.

Our doorbell rang last Sunday—a week ago—and who do you think turned up? Cousin Helen, all dolled up in her WAVE uniform. She had leave from her job in Washington and came up to New York, and tried to telephone me, but she couldn't seem to get a message through, so she came on out. She looks swell, and seems quite pleased with herself, her job and the world in general. She's lost about 20 pounds, which is becoming to her, and I guess she's done quite well at her job,—at least, she says so. We went back in to New York with her and had dinner with Stanley and Mollie Smith—you know, the Smiths that just built the house down on the island. They seem like quite pleasant people—have a nice apartment in uptown New York, overlooking the Hudson River. To get to it, we had to taxi through Harlem where the riots were a week or so ago—you probably read about it in the paper. I guess from the looks of the plate glass windows along 125th Street, that the cullud folks went on a real rampage, for there wasn't a store window, hardly, that wasn't boarded up. You know, I honestly don't blame them much. They live in dirty, hot slums, one on top of another in this blistering weather, for one thing; and for another, almost all the stores in Harlem are owned by white people who sock the prices onto the colored people, ceiling or no ceiling. They just got sick of being cheated and overcharged, so they smashed out the store windows and helped themselves to the goods. Of course you can't egg on a riot like that or say that it was the right thing to do; but at least you can see why it happened. I saw one awfully funny newspaper picture—or it would have been funny if it hadn't been pathetic. A cop was hustling along this skinny little colored woman whom he'd arrested for looting, and apparently one of the things she'd stolen was a white enamel slopjar. The cop had her by one arm and the slop jar in his other hand, and if you ever saw a man looking foolish in the face, it was that cop.

I guess that's about all the news, and I'd better saw off pretty soon, or you'll go to sleep on me. We went to the movies the other night and saw a show called *Bataan*. It was a pretty good show, but awfully grim, about the last stand that some U.S. troops made in the Philippines. I guess it happened about like that, but it sure made you feel bad. So long, dear, and write.

Lots of love, *Uppy*

TO LOVINA MOORE

Nov. 6, 1943

Dear Mum,

If I was you, I'd be put out, but there, I guess you're too used to me, or if you ever did, you wouldn't stay that way very long. The way it is with me, I keep waiting for a chance to sit down and write a good long letter, and that chance seems to take a hell of a long while to come. All the time I know you'd rather have a short one than none at all. By now there's so much to say that I don't know how to begin, except to start by saying that I'm a low-down heel for not writing before. I *have* been kind of gummed up with business, but that isn't much of an excuse, I guess. I got your two lovely letters and they sure were welcome, but I don't believe I'd have blamed you if you had given me a dishful of my own sauce and not written until I did.

I've been buried up to my neck ever since I got back, both at the office and at home. Things piled up while I was away for those two weeks, and then Christmas time is the busiest time of the year, beginning in October and lasting into January. The publishers got up on their hind legs and howled because they weren't getting my new book as soon as they thought they ought to have it, so I've been working at home evenings, trying to get that in some kind of shape. They want it for spring publication, but I don't know whether they'll get it or not. What with one thing and another, I'm about as busy as I've ever been in my life. I wish I had the next four or five months to do nothing but write that book, but I don't see how I can take 'em. Since I got back, the job has got more and more interesting, and I think the raise in pay is going to go through pretty soon. At least, it sounds that way now, though they sure are slower than cold molasses about it. I hope and pray, as the feller said. But Mr. Lynch, the personnel manager, told me this morning that the memo had gone through, and I could probably expect some action on it pretty soon. I better, or it'll be a long cold winter for somebody.

I suppose all the pretty-colored leaves are gone now and you are buttoning in for the winter. Most of the leaves are off down here now, all except for a few old die-hard maple trees that seem to hang on to theirs longer. We haven't had any cold to speak of here, just a few frosty mornings that warmed up later in the day. I wish it would be winter, doggone it, and we get some weather with some guts to it. We had a big no'theaster that started up people's ideas—

boy, it sure did rain for about three days. Washed out some highways and railroads and about swamped the New Jersey coast, I hear. I liked it first rate, but except for that, the weather just wambles along from day to day, not warm and not cold. Nuts to it.

I sure did have the dog-ail after I got back. As near as I could make out from your letter, I was having it just about the same time you were and just about the same thing. Had to pee all the time, and patter-patter to the bathroom for more serious reasons. Eleanor had it some, but not quite so bad. I wonder if we didn't pick up maybe a bug or something down to the island—both Eleanor and I got a swig of that Jennie's well water that was so bad, and maybe it was so bad. Well, I'm all over my trots now, and I hope you are, dear. It sure was an athletic disease while it lasted.

Guess who was to see me Sunday? Newman and Helen, all togged out in their uniforms. They both looked swell, and do they know it! Just the same, though, the Navy is doing a lot for both of them, especially Newman. He's put on quite a lot of weight and he's quite interesting to talk to now. He's stationed at Long Beach waiting to be shipped out somewhere, he thinks, though of course he doesn't know where or when. Helen, she let on to know all about it—being an "officer," of course she knows all about what goes on in the Admirals' minds. Boy, does she rub it in that she's an officer in the Navy and Newman isn't! If I were him, I'd hang a black eye on her, just for the fun of it. But, there, I suppose she can't help it. She sure never did have much to brag about before. She's a decent enough kid, but that continual blowhard sure does get tiresome. They're planning to come again a week from Sunday, if Newk doesn't get shipped out before, and Helen can get up from Washington.

We have another girl living with us in the apartment now—Jane Seely. I guess I probably mentioned her when I was home. She works up at the *Digest*, and her home is in Philadelphia. She's kind of nice and pleasant to have around, and of course, having three in the place cuts the rent three ways instead of two. Also, the other expenses, and makes things a lot cheaper all around. It's nice to have the pressure slacked off a little, so far as expenses go, and we all three feel it's a pretty nice arrangement. The apartment is a little small for three, but I guess we'll shake down after we get used to it. Eleanor got a job up at the *Digest*, too, just after she got back, quite a good one in the mail department. It makes it a lot better for her not to have to commute to New

York. She seems to like it pretty well, and it's a lot easier about meals now since we all three have about the same hours.

I'm still waiting to hear from some places I wrote to about that "ertron" treatment for arthritis. Have you had a chance to see Millstein about it, and does he know how to give it? Apparently their tongue's in their cheek about it. You probably read the article in the last *Digest,* the one I was telling about. People are writing in from all over the country to the magazine for information as to where they can get the treatment, and they'll probably be told in time, but it seems kind of slow. As soon as I find out more about it, I'll let you know. Like all new things, I guess it's slow getting before the public, especially in war time, when everything's slowed up. Seems a shame, when so many need it, doesn't it? Especially when it could do so much good for so many people. What I'm hoping to do is to find out some more about it and see if we can't try it, provided it won't do any harm, and I hope I'll have word pretty soon about it.

The boss, Mr. Wallace, is giving a party Monday afternoon to the editorial staff to meet, of all people, the Duke and Duchess of Windsor. Everybody is in a flutter wondering what to wear and how to act. Me, I don't know how to say hello to a duke or a duchess, and I guess nobody else does. Guess we'll all have to say, "Hi ya, Duke," and let it go at that. Sure does make me wish I was down on the island these days, digging clams or something. I'd a whole lot rather, and it wouldn't surprise me if I'd have more fun. Lord, sometimes I don't know myself, the way things are. For anyone who would rather eat a dish of haddock smother off an oilcloth, I sure do seem to get myself royally involved. Well, I guess I'll live through it, but just the same, I'll take vanilla.

The pajamas you fixed turned out swell—just right now and I use them every night. All they needed was to be lengthened and widened in just the right places. Eleanor bought her some in town the other day, and I didn't say so, but mine are a lot nicer.

I suppose you and Tug have got the apples all picked by now. Did Tug have any luck using the old apple-picker? Golly, don't I wish I could have been there to get a crick in my neck, too. You must have had any lord's legions of Spies and sweet apples, and I bet they make the cellar smell nice. Makes me homesick just to think of it.

Yes, I remember the day Pa brought that old boat home when she was new, and how proud he was of her. She was a dandy boat in her day. It's too bad

Harve is even a little disappointed in his new one, for when you have such a thing as a boat built, you want her to be just about perfect. Maybe he'll get a chance to sell the new one, if he wants to, and have another one like he wants. I sure would like to see her and was sorry to miss it when I was home.

We had such a nice supper tonight and I wish you could have had some—not that it was anything like so good as what you can dish up—but it did taste all right. Baked beans and brown bread and lettuce salad with cheese dressing, and baked apples. The stores have got a new kind of beans—pre-cooked, they call them, but I guess they're really dehydrated. You fix them up just the same as you do for baked beans, with salt pork and molasses and so on—no soaking—put them in the oven and bake for three-quarters of an hour. They aren't quite as good as home baked, but they're better than the canned and frozen beans. We had quite a feed.

How are you getting along, dear? I hope you've got over your dog-ail or whatever it was. Have you started going to Dr. Millstein again? I wish you would, for I think you ought at least to have a supply of your medicine. I'll send some dough just as soon as mine comes,—it ought to be along any day now—so you won't feel too short, in case you want to go to the doctor, or something. I feel kind of mean not sending any all summer, but, there, it couldn't be helped, and I'll send it when I can, and I guess you know I will.

I'm so glad to know Tink is doing well in school. It's foolish for anyone to think he can't, because we all know he's got a darned good head on him—as a matter of fact, you don't see many kids nowadays with as good a set of brains as he's got. Of course he'll do all right if he has a teacher who has any sense and knows how to teach. Too darned bad he got off to such a slow start, but I've never believed it was his fault, and I bet now you'll see him go places. He could do two grades' work in one year without turning his hand over if they'll let him try it. Golly, it don't seem possible he'll be ready for high school before we know it.

Well, dear, I guess I'll saw off for now, and I'll try to do better about writing. I feel awful mean not writing for so long, and my gosh, looking back, I don't see how I could have let the time get away from me so. It just goes rattling by, and I don't seem to stop three seconds in any day you could name. Give my love to all the babies and folks. Tell Muriel I get lonesome to see her and she'd better write me a letter.

Lots of love, dear, *Uppy*

TO LOVINA MOORE

Dec. 2, 1943

Dear Mum,

You certainly hit it right on the nose with that Thanksgiving box. It arrived the night before, and everything had kept just lovely. I put the old biddy in the oven and warmed her up and warmed up the gravy and cooked the potatoes and turnips and carrots and if we didn't have a nice Thanksgiving dinner I don't know who did. It's all gone now, all except some of the jelly and a little tiny bit of the mustard pickles. You are a bessy-darlin' for thinking of it and when I was eating of it, I thought about you and Tug packing it up and sending it and if I hadn't been so hungry I would have howled with homesickness. Goodness knows how we manage it staying apart the way we have to. I guess if that's the way it has to be, why, that's the way, but I don't think much of it, darned if I do. It was lovely of you dear and I do thank you.

I'm sending you a little something to put in your stocking. There aren't any strings to it, but I wish you'd use it, some of it, anyway, for a trip to Boston to see Dr. Brown, and see if maybe we couldn't get your knees more comfortable. You don't suppose you could go up and stay a week or so with Aunt Gertie and go in and see him, do you? He could take some X-rays and find out what is wrong with your knees and feet, and there isn't another doctor in the country who could tell you better what to do about it. The trip would be a tough one for you, but I don't know but it would do you good in more ways than just one—you'd get some vacation and it might be that Dr. Brown could straighten out what's wrong with the knees. If you'll do it, I'll take care of the doctor's bill, in addition to this check, and I'll write Dr. Brown and make an appointment for you and if you could plan to be there on a week-end, I'll come to Boston and stay over Sunday so we can see each other. I don't want to persuade you, if you don't want to, but you know, I've always had in mind your doing that as soon as we could swing the money part. You think it over and let me know. In a way I hate to think of you starting off alone, because the trip would be an undertaking, where it's so hard for you to get around, but maybe we could wangle someone into taking the trip with you? How about Harve, if he could take a day or so off and come right back, if he felt he couldn't leave his work for very long, and it isn't as if Boston were more than a day's trip away. The trip would do the old son good, I bet. Well, you mull it over a while and see how you feel about it, and if you think you'd like to try it, we'll set the ball a-rolling. I wish I could be there to do the whole thing with you, but I can make arrangements by letter for you with Dr. Brown and be there for over a week-end. Let me know, dear.

I see by the papers that a good old snowstorm hit the Maine coast last week, and I suppose the going is bad now, if it is still snowy. Maybe you'd rather wait till spring, if you were going to make a trip like that, and that's up to you, dear. But I have always said the minute I had the money I was going to do something about those knees of yours, and how long we wait now is up to you. But there, I won't talk any more about it. You decide, h'm?

Things roll along about the same here. So far we've had a couple of spits of snow, not enough to whiten the ground, that melted as it fell. I'm up to my neck in work, all day at the office and trying to write my book evenings, and it's about a 24-hour job. I guess I always squawk a lot about how busy I am, but there it is, darn it, I *am*. I haven't got very much done on the book, but it's in the stage where I know where I'm going with it, and that's at least something. I get tired, but, there, I guess everybody else does, too.

Oh, I heard a lovely funny story, not a very nice one, but sometimes they're all the better for that, shame on me! There was a soldier home on leave who hadn't seen any ladies for a long time and he was 'bout dead, so he went to a place where there was ladies to hire. He inquired about the price and the lady said it was ten dollars and ten points. The soldier said, "Gee! What'll I do? You know soldiers don't have any ration books." She said, "Well, take it or leave it. Ten dollars and ten points." So he went to another place that was cheaper, and there the lady said it was five dollars and five points. So the poor lad went out along the streets and ran into a nice little colored girl. He asked her and she said okay, so he said how much and she said, "Two dollars." He said, "You mean to say you don't want any points, sister?" And she said, "Mm-*mmm!* Dis de black market youse tradin' on now."

How's all the famblies? You tell Muriel I've got a bone to pick with her. She didn't answer my letter. Old Uncle Tink, he hasn't written to me either to tell me how he's getting along with saving up the money for his boat. That dough I've got waiting for him is sure getting mouldy. Of course, I write so many letters myself I'm all the time expecting folks to write to me, I guess.

I suppose Sonny is on his way to the Navy by now, and I'm wondering how you're making out with the barn-work. You be careful not to take a header into a snowbank, won't you? Gosh, I wonder what Sonny will make of the

Navy and what it will make of him. Poor old soul, I bet he has a tough time coming. Well, I suppose we'll never know, but I'd like to be a mouse on the wall, wouldn't you? Did you finally get the Spies picked, and boy, would I like to set my teeth into one of them right now! We get New York apples out here and they sure don't seem to have much taste. Speaking of tasting things, you ought to have seen me smelling of those turnips and carrots. I bet you'd have laughed, but honest, they smelt so good to me I almost took one to the office with me so I could sniff of it all day. I guess I'm an old fool, but that's the way I feel about things from up our way.

Well, dear, this isn't a very newsy letter, because my old brain's worn to a frazzle, but I'll try to write again pretty soon. Give my love to everybody and lots to you. By the way, there's enough in the check for you to get some new duds for the trip, if you decide to go to Boston.

Toodle, oodle, dear, *Up*

Marion was Newman Moore's wife.

TO LOVINA MOORE

Jan. 7, 1944

Mum, dear,

Got your nice letter yesterday, and I guess I've neglected you, too, though I didn't mean to. I guess about everybody has had this darn dog-ail. I had a couple of goes at it, one the week before Christmas and the other the week after. Knocked all my plans into a cocked hat, for I'd planned to do some Christmas shopping the Saturday before Christmas, and I was flat on my back with the flu. Darn it, it was the only day I had, for the magazine has its closing date the week of the 25th and we didn't get our usual extra day off before a holiday. I felt kind of mean just sending the magazine subscriptions, but maybe I can have a little private shopping-bee of my own later on. I'm all right now and feeling fine again. Almost everybody in town had the darn stuff, but I guess it's over now. Lots of people were out up at the *Digest*, and I guess they just about squeaked by in their Christmas rush.

You and Tug must have had a pretty hectic time with the kiddies sick and you all must have been worried out of your lives about poor little Bud. I thought when I didn't hear for so long that something was going on. I'm sure glad the little feller is feeling better. It sounds as if he had been pretty sick. I do wish I could have been around to help out. I don't know as there could be anything quite so frightening to everyone concerned as to have something the matter with the baby in the house. Well, I'm glad it's all over and wasn't worse. Has Tug got over her own cold, and how is the old gal?

We had a nice Christmas, considering everybody was either getting over or just coming down with the flu. Eleanor and I decided that since neither of us could go home and since we hadn't had a Christmas tree for 4 years, we'd have one this year if we had to use the clothes-tree off the wall. (The last one we had was that darn tumble-weed out in California—remember? I think I wrote you about it at the time.) So we bought one down in the super-market and trimmed it all up pretty with colored lights and tinsel, and put our packages from home under it and had us a real Christmas. It was kind of lonesome, I will admit, but a lot better than just letting the day go by, the way we usually have in the past year or so. I got your nice present, and thank you, dear, it was lovely of you. Just as soon as I get a day off to go to town, you'll get one from me. Maybe you could call it delayed action. Serves me right for leaving everything to the last minute, but I hadn't planned on the flu.

Newman was here to have Christmas Eve with us. I felt kind of sorry for him, I guess he is pretty lonesome, though he doesn't say much about it. He wanted to go home, but he couldn't get a leave long enough to take him clear to Maine and back. He said Marion could have brought the baby down to Portland and he could have met them there, but she preferred to spend Christmas at home with her father. ... It seems a shame, for he may get shipped out to God-knows-where any day now, and the lord knows when he'll get a chance to see his boy again. ... Newman seems a lot different—I think the Navy has done him a lot of good. He's pleasant to have around, and I invite him out whenever he can get an overnight leave. He seems glad just to get away from the camp and be around with the folks he knows.

You know that raise I was talking about when I was home, lamb-pie? Well, I got it. Nuff said, but it's going to make a lot of difference to us, dear. The good old government takes $72 of it away from me every month, and every time I think of the many long years when any of us hardly had 72 bucks a month to live on. But there's enough left to keep us in chiclets, and please God I can sock enough of it away to get caught up on all the things we need to get caught up on. Ain't that good, though!

I don't blame you for not wanting to traipse off to Boston in winter weather and with winter going. I do wish, though, that you could see Dr. Brown. I guess I better leave it up to you when you go. Why don't you use whatever you want to of the check I sent you, and whenever you decide to go, I'll send you some more. I didn't mean for you to keep the money just for that. If you need coal or to send a little on the rent, why not go ahead and do it, because any time you need it I can send you a driblet, God love you.

I *have* been as busy as all get-out, trying to catch up with my work, and I'm afraid I haven't done much lately on the new book. The job may be a good one, but it sure takes my time and energy to run it. I guess I am now probably what they call an assistant editor of the magazine—that's not so important as an associate editor. When you get to be an associate editor, you get your name on the list in the front of the book, and I haven't been around near long enough for that yet. Probably I ought to tell you, because if I don't nobody else will, and I expect you'd like to know that I'm the only one they ever had on the staff who got to be an assistant editor in less than five years. Sounds a lot like bragging, but I kind of wanted you to know. There, that's enough about me.

We had our first snow of the season here yesterday and today. What with rain and hail and sleet and god-knows-what, I shouldn't be surprised if some of it were frogs and tadpoles, we got quite a collection of goo on the ground. All of five inches, I guess, of good old ripe rosy slush. The going is something awful, and I tell you when you get 1800 people in cars and buses all going out at once to the *Digest* Buildings five miles outside of Pleasantville to get there at 8:30 A.M., you've got, what I mean, a *mess!* One party landed in three different ditches from three different cars yesterday morning, and if you ever saw a drubbled and drabbled bunch of people, it was them. We got along all right, because the girl we drive with is a swell driver, but most of the people around here don't act as if they ever saw slippery going before. Golly, the cars were going by today with smashed fenders, and one car had half of somebody's bumper draped across the front of the radiator. I guess it will be better tomorrow morning, for it is warm tonight and melting. I was glad to see some snow, darn it, though, even if it was only one of these illegitimate Westchester heavy dews. What I'd really admire to see is about five feet of good dry snow on the level. By gosh, I'd go out and roll in it!

The poor old lady who lives downstairs is getting so nosy that I don't know but we'll have to move. Poor old soul, she's 85 and her daughter and son-in-law go out to work so she's alone all day, and she's got so she cruises around the apartments poking among people's things. Honest, it was amusing when the Christmas mail started coming. You'd have died to see her. She tried to check up on all the Christmas cards and bundles that everybody got, and poor old soul, she got all mixed up and so nervous she like to flew. When the mailman started up the walk, she'd meet him at the door before anybody else could get there, and she'd take all the mail into her bedroom, she said "to sort it out." Any of the Christmas cards that had folded flaps, the way they do for a-cent-and-a-half, she'd open and read, and the bundles she about wore out feeling of before she'd give them up. Golly, we finally had to complain to the landlady, and I guess the landlady gave her an awful going over, not that it did much good. I felt so sorry for her I finally went down and wrote out about twenty Christmas cards with a lot of fine hard-to-read writing on them and addressed them all to her. They said she had a wonderful time for about three days, trying to figure out who they were from and what it said on them.

I already saw that letter from the A.M.A. Journal that Millstein gave you, as there have been some copies around up at the office. Well, it's hard to know who's in the right, because that is what happens every time Paul de Kruif prints one of his articles in the *Digest* about new discoveries in medicine. There's always a towse about it for one reason or another. There's a good many reasons for it, I guess. Sometimes it is because he tells about simple remedies that people can take themselves without going to a doctor, and that, of course, makes the doctors mad; and sometimes it's because the doctors feel that he hasn't waited until enough research has been done before publishing the material. Anyway, it's probably six of one and half-a-dozen of the other. I swear, I don't myself know the rights and wrongs of the Ertron business. I guess we'll just have to wait and see. Maybe Dr. Brown will know the answer. I do wish you could go to see him, but in the meantime, I think you ought to keep going to Millstein.

Well, I guess my old news-bag is just about empty. I'll try to do a little better, now I've caught up with myself. Oh, I almost forgot to tell you what I had for Christmas. Some of the girls at the office got together and bought me a lovely Bulova wristwatch, and Eleanor gave me a set of oil paints, and I had some books and handkerchiefs also from the office, Mrs. Mayo sent a pair of stockings, and I guess you probably saw all the nice things I had from home. That picture of the kids almost made me cry, they looked so cunning and natural and made me want to see them. Little Miss Muffet looked as though she were into something special, and Uncle Bud looked thoughtful as if he were trying to dope it out. Tell Tug I'll write her pretty soon . . . she knows me. Anyway it was a lovely Christmas and you are all a bunch of dears. All my love to all, and specially to you,

Uppy

TO LOVINA MOORE

Jan. 30, 1944

Dear Momma,

Guess it's about time I bust loose again, for I think I owe you two letters. The box of apples and doughnuts came and what do you think? It was here when we got home from work and we up and made a great big pot of coffee and sat down and ate four doughnuts apiece. Golly, they did taste good, and just as nice and fresh as could be. Both they and the apples are all gone now. It was lovely of you to think of it, dear, and I do thank you. So does Eleanor, for I don't think there is anything she likes so well as she does doughnuts.

Did you have a warm spell? We had a regular old January thaw, cleaned off the ground in good shape. It was just like spring for about five days. Cold again tonight, though, good and snappy. We had a nice ice pond from down back of our house, must be about forty feet across it, and big enough to skate on, and we were just waiting for it to freeze hard enough, when today along came three or four little kids and smashed the ice all to hell-and-gone, the little brats. So now I guess we'll have to wait till it rains again. I wish if they want to throw rocks, they'd throw them at each other.

How are you, anyway, old dear? Seems an age since I've seen you. I was thinking today how I wish I could run in and have Sunday dinner and have a good old chew with you. Gets lonesome, being away so long. Time sure seems to go awful slow, this time of year, but I suppose we can't complain. We're up over the hump of the winter, and the rest of it will be downhill and only two months now to spring. When you look back though, it seems as though the winter's gone awful fast.

Things are about the same with me. I don't know when I've gone through a winter without having more colds, but the flu around Christmas time was the only snotty time I've had so far. Things have slacked off a little at the office. The busy time is over for the year, and we've stopped to take a breathing spell. We had a three-day week-end this week—Friday, Saturday and Sunday. I wish we'd have a four-day, I don't know but I'd make a flying trip home. It's a little too long a trip for just the three days, though. I wish you didn't live any farther away than Jane's folk's do—that's the girl who lives with us, I think I've mentioned her before—her family lives in Philadelphia and she pops home for a week-end quite often.

Oh, by the way, one of the girls up at the office had a black fur coat—lapin, I think it is—that she didn't want, as it had got too small for her. It's quite a nice coat, lovely and warm, and I thought I'd send it home, maybe somebody can get some good of it. It has a little rip on the shoulder, but I think it can be mended without much trouble. Darned if I wouldn't like to have it myself, but it's too small for me. Tug might be able to wear it, and if she can't, why, she can pass it along to somebody who can. It's almost a new coat—this girl bought it last year, and this year she's put on about 20 pounds and can't wear it. So her loss is our gain, or maybe I should say her gain is our advantage. I'll try to get it done up tonight. I was going to send it to a furrier and have it mended, but I made some inquiries around, and it seems that the labor shortage is bad with the furriers, and they aren't taking any new customers. I suppose I could have taken it in to New York, but the Lord knows when I'll get another chance to go in, and by that time the winter'll be about over. Anyway, I thought I'd send it along. I don't believe it'll be much of a job to mend that little rip.

I can't tell you how good those Spy apples tasted. I don't know when I've had one. They don't seem to be in the market out here. Why, I don't believe I've tasted one since that fall I was home and helped gather them. I sure did have the juice running down my chin for a while there.

Have you heard from Sonny? Wonder how he's making it in the Navy, or maybe I better say wonder what the Navy is making of him. Poor old Sonny, I'll bet that keeping his bunk neat is pretty gowelling for him. Have you ever been able to get that room cleaned up? I'll bet it was some job.

Well, our nice long week-end is about over and tomorrow it's back to work. Gee whiz, I don't know how I'll ever manage to take a year off again. All the other jobs I've had, I used to think, well, shoot, they don't amount to much and if I quit I can probably find a better one. Since I got my raise, I keep thinking, well, guess I'm stuck for life this time. Well, I guess it's about time I settled down to one thing, but gosh, it comes hard. Still, it isn't do bad as working for next to nothing, the way I did for so many years. Maybe I can save up some dough now and we can have a few of the things we want. I hope so, but Uncle Sam is sure taking his cut, these days. By the way, will you find out for me what the tax bill is on the place down on the island? Might as well get it off out minds and get the discount, if there is one. I sent Omar Tapley the fire insurance premium, the other day, too, so that ought to take care of that for another three years. When I think of all the dough we've paid out on that poor old house, it does seem too bad that we can't get more good of it, and be down there more often, doesn't it? I know everybody thinks I'm crazy, but I wish I were down there right now, and could spend the rest of the winter there. There isn't a better place in the world to be, if anyone is contented without a lot of people around, and I am. Well, maybe, someday. Meantime, we can keep the expenses paid on it, and perhaps have a little work done on it, come summer, if we can get anyone to do it. The poor old thing is about falling down as it is, I guess.

Well, dear, this is kind of a short letter, and doesn't say half what I wish I could say, but letters are kind of a poor substitute anyway, aren't they? Maybe I'll be able to get home before the hens set again. I wish I could. How's all the famblies? Give them my love and be a good little peep your own self.

Uppy

Cliff was Orville's uncle, Cliff Rich, a renowned boat builder.

TO LOVINA MOORE

March 20, 1944

Dear Mom,

I guess you will think I have passed on for sure this time. But the last I knew I was doing business at the same old stand with—I guess—the same old bad habits. How is you, and how does it seem to be halfway up over old March hill? We have had two or three lovely spring days, but mostly it has been rain. There's a regular lake down over the hill back of the house, and it looks real pretty. Yesterday I heard a song sparrow and somebody at the office said she saw a robin. So I guess spring is on the way, though not yet for you folks, and time to be thinking a little bit about vacation.

I thought first I'd wait till September so as to be home for the mackerel run, but darn the mackerel, it's too long a drag. That was last fall when I thought that, anyway. So I'm kind of making plans to come for the month of July. I suppose I might split it up and take two weeks to a jump, the way I did last year; but that really wasn't a long enough time to be away at once, and somehow, when I got back and it was all over, I kind of felt as if I hadn't been away. So I guess, the way it looks now, it will be July. I can't get away so early as June, and August looks far off, too. Gosh, talking about vacation makes me wish it was right now. It's been a hard old winter and am I tired! All in all, it's been quite an interesting one on the job, but you have to keep on your toes and it's quite a lot of responsibility. The competition is, what I mean, terrific, as it always is when a woman gets to be more than a stenog in an office. So far I've managed to nose out the men—and boy, do they watch me! But I can't say it makes for what you'd call a restful existence. However, I'm having a pretty good time, and all in all, I guess I don't have to take any more than a man would take in the same job. If you go into a man's world, you have to put up with it, I guess; but I'll sure be able to use my vacation.

We have got kind of tired of living in Pleasantville, and I guess at the end of this month we'll go in to New York to live for a while—maybe until the hot weather begins. We'll commute to work, it isn't much of a chore, and at least, it will be something different. Eleanor wants to take some evening courses at the University, and I'll be kind of glad to go back for a while. I guess I'm an old drifter, for I can't seem to be happy living in one place very long. I had to laugh the other day—just for the curiosity of it, I counted up the number of places I'd hung up my hat since I left the island to go to high school, and there are 42 of them! I guess that must be pretty close to a record. We've got a room at the Murray Hill Hotel, 112 Park Avenue, for a month, just until we can look around and find a little apartment, and after the first of April, that'll be my address. Park Avenue sounds as if it might be kind of swell, but woe is me, it's the end of Park Avenue that's one the wrong side of Grand Central Station—of the railroad tracks, you might say. It's the corner of 42nd Street, and is about the first hotel built in NYC, I'd say.

Well, Uncle Sam certainly did make us dig down, didn't he? I thought when I shelled out 230 bucks for the December payment that he and I'd be square in March, but not a bit of it. I got an income tax man to make out my blank, for the devil on a pair of stilts with a fountain pen couldn't make head nor tail of the one we had to fill out this year; and he made it that I still owed the government 99 dollars. So just for the hell of it, I thought I'd check his figures, and I wish to God I hadn't, because I found he had made three mistakes in adding and it came out $120. So that makes it just under $800 I have paid in income taxes since last March, and I don't mind saying it has just about cleaned me out. I thought I was all set, because a while ago the boss sent around word that we were all going to get bonuses and I figured mine and it came to $600. And then, by gosh, the War Labor Board refused to let the *Digest* grant any bonuses to the Editorial Department, and all I got now is a mouth full of drool. The WLB may relent a little later, but nobody knows.

Well, I see the point all right, that if there's too much money floating around loose, as they say there is, prices will go up higher and nobody will benefit, but darn it, I'm not used to having things like 600 smackers handed out cold to me, and it is a disappointment. Well, cheer up, I guess I never will get used to it. There I go squawking again, but it *does* seem bitter, doesn't it?

I had a swell letter from Tink. He says he's going to get his boat about June, he thinks, which may be a little later than he wanted, but will give him a couple of months before school starts. He seemed quite tickled, and I hope he gets him a good one. I know it will be a good one, too, if Cliff builds it. Like to have a new one myself, by golly, but I guess the old one will do me, all the use I have for one now. I wish I could ever live around some place where there's water, for I get so homesick for water and boats that sometimes it seems as if I'd bust. Maybe someday I will be able to save enough so I can. But they sure do seem to dream up a lot of ways to take money away from people these days. Well, the war can't last forever, and there are quite a lot who seem to think that it will be over before too long. I sure do hope so, and, come to think of it, paying out dough is about the least anybody like me can do, for goodness knows, I'm not doing very much else to help out. But someday, marm, you and I are going to have us a place and live together again.

How are you, anyway? It sure was good news to hear that you aren't quite so lame, and I do hope you'll keep on going to the doctor, if it helps that much. Why don't you let him fit you to a good substantial pair of corsets? You can't tell how much support like that might help, and after all, $12 isn't an awful lot to pay for a pair of corsets like that, that really fit you and are comfortable. You go ahead and have it done, and by the way, I meant to tell you before, but if you want to you can ask him to send the bill to me. I'll send you some more dough, anyway, as soon as I get squared around from paying off the income tax. You scamp, you ought to have let me take care of the island taxes.

That dough I sent you was for your own use. But it was awful nice of you, and I appreciate it, honey.

How are all the babies and Tug and company? I'm glad the coat was a fit. I expect it comes in handy in the cold breezes, of which you've probably had a many, and it looked as if it might be nice and warm. If I hadn't got to be such a fat old thing, I don't know but I'd have hung onto it myself. I don't think I've put on any weight since last summer, but you remember then I was getting quite plump. Well, dang it, I can't get enough exercise to save my life, sitting on my can all day long.

By the way, that reminds me of a story I saw in one of the papers the other day. A grocer who had been collecting waste fat got too many cans of it on hand and couldn't handle any more for a few days, so he put a sign up in his window:

DO NOT BRING YOUR FAT CANS IN HERE.

Well, I guess my old news bag is getting kind of flat. It always seems to me that I never have very much new to tell you, for one day is a good deal like the next one to me. I spend my daytimes reading books and magazines and trying to root out some good stuff for the mag., and my old head is so full of reading matter that sometimes I wonder if there's anything else in it. I had pretty good luck on the May issue—found two articles and a joke which were used. The first one in the book, "What is an American?" and the one about the woman in the lifeboat with 34 men, were suggestions of mine, and the joke about the man socking the boss on the nose. You can tell when you read them which they are, when the new issue comes along.

Be a good gal and write me soon and give my best love to all and sundry. Love to you, too,

Uppy

Philly Dow, one of Louise Moore Dow's twins, hurt his eye in an accident and had to have plastic surgery.

TO LOVINA MOORE

April 17, 1944

Dear Marm,

Just a line to let you know we arrived back safely, if tired. We had a nice quick trip, or would have if the train had got in on time. It sat in the station in New Haven, God knows why, from 5:30 to 7:30 this morning, and as a result we were nearly three hours late. We caught the 10:20 to Pleasantville and got home at about 11:30. Eleanor is still snoozing, but I had my nap and feel rested, and I thought I'd just use up the time till suppertime by writing you a letter. If you are as lonesome as I am, you will be glad to get it.

I don't think I've ever hated to go away so bad as I did this time. The time seemed so short, I didn't get half the things done I wanted to do, and I suppose leaving you alone, as well as Philly being in the hospital, had something to do with it. It seems to me, and still does, that I ought to sit down up there and stay for good. Well, dear, perhaps I can sometime, but maybe not this year as things are. I'll have to save up a wugget—enough for what we planned and some over—and then, by gosh, you watch me!

It rained hard all the way from Portland on, last night. I slept some, but it was kind of noisy. At Worcester, a whole troop of Negro soldiers got on and about took over the car. They were perfectly nice fellows and didn't act up, but they were on week-end leave and out for a good time, so they didn't soft-pedal any. They wore out towards morning, though, and I slept all the way from New Haven into New York.

There isn't much news, as you've heard all of it too soon ago. I thought of our nice coal fire when I got back into this clammy apartment. Golly, that sure was a comfortable fire! Seeing it's a rainy day, but not very cold, the landlady has let the fire go out, I guess, and the apartment feels like the inside of somebody's casket. I guess it will warm up when they build up the fire this evening. I hope so, anyway. I guess you'll think I'm not writing you a thing but loud and sorrowful complaints. Well, I guess that's the way I feel, but I'll get over it. Darn this lousy town, anyway. I wish I was out in the woods with my ax.

We opened up the doughnuts and had some and some coffee as soon as we got home. They were sure swell. That little pat of butter you tucked in was a surprise and you were a dear to think of it, as a thing like that is sure a gift. We're going to enjoy it, I know. Jane had got in some eggs and milk and bread, so we won't go hungry, but I'd a lot rather have one of our breakfasts together. There, now, listen to me! I guess I must be homesick, and I better make no bones of it, I am. Probably you are just as lonesome, too, and I hope some of the family lugged you off for Sunday dinner, so you didn't have the day alone. I expect they did. Write me when you can, dear, and be sure to let me know how Philly is, and how you are and if you need anything. We sure did have a good time together, didn't we?

Love, *Uppy*

Hinkley's is the famous boatbuilding company on Mt. Desert Island. Bobby Rich was a boatbuilder in Bernard, and the son of Cliff Rich. Fred Mayo was Eleanor's father and Lawrence, her brother. The following letters were written from 36 w. 56th Street, New York City, NY.

TO LOVINA MOORE

Aug. 3, 1944

Dear Mum,

It's a rainy night, praise be, and cool for a change, and I thought I would settle down and have a good long gossip with you. It's been pretty hot—kind of a nasty, muggy, can't-get-your-breath-down heat, but the rain's cooled it off for tonight, at least, and I can tell you it feels good. We haven't had a chance to get out of it, for it's been hotter in Pleasantville this summer than it has in New York. I am getting along all right and don't seem to mind it much, but I will be glad when this month is over. It has seemed like a long time between vacations, but it won't seem too long now, will it, dear? The middle of September doesn't seem so far off as it did a while ago. And, oh, won't we have a good time and am I looking forward to it.

It's the old story with me—busy as a bee all day long and tired at night. Things are going pretty well, though. I've managed to get in some good licks on the new book, and I hope to finish it when I'm home on vacation. The publisher wants it to publish this fall, but I don't think I can get it to him in time. More like, it will come out in February, the way the other one did. But I'm not counting any chickens, for I shall have to finish it first, and the lord knows, I get little enough time to work on it. The job goes along about the same, except some people are away on vacations, which makes it a little harder and along about the 20th of the month when the magazine goes to press, I and some others have to hustle my old stumps around. But next month won't be so bad, because everybody—or most everybody—will be back. Oh, yes, there is some news. Last week the boss called me into his office and made with the compliments, and said that while they couldn't do anything about raises until after the war, he wanted me to know that I had a future there and that sometime soon I would be made an associate editor. He didn't say when it would be, but from the way it operates, I think probably sometime in the spring. That's when promotions usually go through. That, my good mama, will be a really nice job. Ain't that good, though?

I think about you a lot these days and wonder how you are getting along. The garden sounds like a big job—and I should know it is, for I've taken care of it often enough. I wish I could be there to have some of the new vegetables. I'll bet they are lish. Makes my old drool run. Vegetables here this summer are scarce, poor and high. Anything you touch makes the old pennies fly, I can tell you. Golly, if prices were only the way they used to be, we'd all be rich, wouldn't we? I saw some blueberries the other day in the market—59 cents for a basket that holds just a little over a pint—and I thought to myself of all the blueberries I have picked in my life for 12 cents a quart. Enough to make your blood run cold, isn't it? Strawberries this spring were 80 cents for the same amount. Well, maybe someday the war will be over and we will all go back to where we left off when it started. It looks as though it wouldn't be long. Too bad that feller that tried to blow up old Hit hadn't got him, wasn't it? They say here that it's only a question of time till somebody gets him, and that when they do Germany will collapse like a house of cards. I sure do hope that that is so, for it will mean so much to almost everybody you know or ever heard about. I guess Newman has been shipped, for he was in here two weeks ago and said that when he got back to camp he was going to be alerted; which means that he probably went out sometime soon after.

You are awful good about writing, even when I don't, and I do so enjoy getting your letters. I look for one when I get home every night, even though I have just got one the day before. Isn't that foolish?

We're looking for a place to settle down in the first of September, and hope to find an apartment in White Plains. I think that will be the solution of it, for Pleasantville is too far to commute from or to, and Eleanor expects to be working in New York this fall. She has finished another book, and this time the agent is pretty enthusiastic over it and thinks she may be able to sell it to a publisher. I hope it does sell, for Eleanor has worked like a dog over it, and it will be a big disappointment to her if it doesn't. Personally, I think it will, for I read it and thought it was a swell job. Apartments anywhere are darned hard to find, even in the country; and it's just about impossible to find one here in New York for the fall. I know I thought some about living in New York this fall and winter but I've made up my mind not to. It's too far to commute for one thing, and for another, all the apartment houses have waiting lists for their apartments—you can't even get your name on a waiting list, let alone rent a place. And my gosh, they want $75 a month for places that they ought to pay you to live in. White Plains is about as bad. We haven't looked much there yet, but I think we'll be able to find something in time. I thought some of renting a small house somewhere for the winter and putting it to you to come on down and keep house for me. How about that? So far I haven't been able to find a house, as people who have houses are trying to sell them, not rent them. But just suppos'n I should, how would you feel about it? Say the plan that you and I've got hatched up should come along all right? We'll talk it over, want to, when I come home in September.

I ought to write Louise, because I know she wants to hear from me, and I don't know what under the sun to tell her about bringing Philly down. So far I still haven't been able to find a plastic surgeon—one that I can be sure is good, anyway—who will take on an out of town case that he hasn't seen. And another thing that has come up, there is quite a lot of infantile paralysis around down here. They aren't saying much about it, but enough to let you know there's a lot more than usual. So I am still kind of holding off, to see if there is an increase in the cases of infantile. They have had a bad epidemic in North Carolina—are still having it, I guess—and it seems to be working north. There have been quite a lot of cases in New York and some in Westchester. I got to thinking about it, and maybe I'm being foolish, but I sure hate to take any chances. The hot weather will be over pretty soon, anyway, and that disease always goes away with it. If you see Louise, tell her I'll write her in a day or so. I was going to tonight, but I guess I've got to give up and go to bed. I mostly put it off, I guess, because I don't know quite how to advise her.

Too bad the shipyard has shut down. I guess from what Mrs. Mayo wrote Eleanor, though, that it was Hinckley's own fault he didn't get his contracts from the government. It seems he used the men and materials to do work on his own house and farm and charged the expenses up to the government. It's hard to tell just how much of that is gossip, though there's probably a little something in it. But it sure is hard on the men who might as well be working and still have their jobs. If that old devil did that, he ought to have his neck wrung, and it's a wonder he didn't land in Federal jail. I do hope Pearl has a nice job with Bobby Rich and that it will last. It sure is tough to have a job give out on you, just when you were getting along so well. Fred Mayo has gone to Boothbay Harbor to work—it's too bad to have to go away from home like that, though, isn't it? Mrs. Mayo wrote Eleanor that he looked better than he had for years, though, and had taken on a new lease on life. Heck, I wouldn't wonder. Lawrence is in Virginia, taking the last of his Navy training. He is with the Amphibious service, which probably means a landing boat, though he hasn't said. He's at an advanced training base, which means he'll probably go to sea pretty soon. It doesn't seem possible, those little kids, does it?

I love the way I send you all the news about people up there, but Eleanor just got this letter from her mother today, and I guess you probably haven't heard some of it.

What do you hear from Sonny? Is he still in Providence?

I just about *drool* to get home and see you all again. It seems like a long time, doesn't it? Seems as though when I do I'll want to lie down and sleep for a week; but I know when I get there I'll feel so good I won't be still a minute. There are always so many things to do, and things that I love to do, too, that I hate to waste a minute of time. It's wicked I can't be up there more, feeling the way I do about it and about you and all the folks; maybe when the war is over and things back to normal again, and I write a book that sells a million, I can come up and stay, and wouldn't that be kippy, dear?

I heard a lovely story, not very nice, but I bet you'll like it. I did.

There were two little mice scurrying around under the table picking up crumbs at the ladies' bridge club meeting, and all of a sudden one of the little mice stood right up on the end of his tail and spun around and around. "Oh, my, my, my!" he says. "Isn't that *lovely!*"

The other one says, kind of grumpy, "What's lovely?"

"Why," says the first little mouse, "all those beautiful legs."

"Huh!" says the second little mouse. "I don't like legs. I'm a titmouse."

There was another one, too, (and I ought to be ashamed) about a young man who met a young lady on the street and says to her, "Hi, hollyhock!" So she says, "Why did you call me a hollyhock?" "Aw," he says, "go look it up." So she went and looked up "hollyhock" in the dictionary, and it says it's "a tall stately flower." So the next time she saw the young man, she blushed and she says, "Thanks for the nice compliment." "What compliment?" says he. "Why," she says, you called me a hollyhock, and the dictionary says it's a tall stately flower." "Aw," he says. "Go look it up in the seed catalog." So she looks it up in the seed catalog and it says: *Hollyhock:* A tall stately flower. No good in beds, but better against barns and outhouses."

Oh, my, my. You didn't bring me up right. You just drug me up, or I wouldn't tell such horrid stories.

Well, dear, I guess that's enough for tonight. Write me when you can, and lots of love,

Uppy

TO GEORGE CLARK

Mr. George F. Clark
1105 B & O Building
Baltimore, Maryland

Aug. 27, 1944

Dear Mr. Clark:

My mother, Vina Moore, of McKinley, has sent along to me your letter of the 18th, about the house. I'm sorry I didn't get it in time to answer it before the 23rd.

She and I planned to close up the matter of buying the house from you when I go home in September. I thought she had written you to that effect, but apparently she thought there wasn't any hurry, or something—or perhaps she thought I had. In any case, you've been very patient, and we appreciated it.

If you will take a down payment of $500 and two yearly payments of $500 each for the house, we will buy it. I may be able to take care of the two $500 yearly payments in a shorter time and will if I can; but frankly, like everybody else, I don't know what the income tax situation will be next year, and I don't like to commit myself for more until I do.

If this kind of arrangement is agreeable to you, will you let me know? I'll be at McKinley on my vacation from September 1 to the 17th, and perhaps we can put the matter through then. Perhaps you had better write me there, as I won't be at the above address after next week.

With deep appreciation for your kindness through the years, I am,

Yours sincerely,
Ruth Moore

TO LOVINA MOORE

August 27, 1944

Dear Marm,

Got your letter last night, and wrote right away to Mr. Clark, and here's a copy of the letter which speaks for itself. It would be a shame if someone got in ahead of us now, and I wish the devil or the Draft Board would fly away with Richard Black.

Yesterday I got my vacation dates settled at last—I thought it would be the 25th but praise be it's the 1st to the 17th. So when you get this on Monday, dust off the doorstep, because I'll be home Friday morning. We leave New York next Thursday afternoon, the 31st, get into Bangor at 4:00 A.M. and will come down on the early morning bus from Ellsworth.

I thought I had better write Mr. Clark, as it would be quicker from here than to have my letter go all the way to you and then back to him. Hang onto the carbon copy, as we'll possibly need it later on.

I won't try to write more now, as I've got to fly this morning. Lots of love, dear, and see you soon,

Uppy

Barbara is Eleanor Mayo's sister. The following letters were written from 210 Martine Avenue, White Plains, NY.

TO LOVINA MOORE

Oct. 10, 1944

Dear Mummer,

Got your nice letter tonight when I got home from work, and it sure was a load off my mind to find that you could have Ralph's house, and had a place to go when you move out. I hope you will be contented there for a while, and if I know you, you will, for you never were a one to sit around and mourn over what can't be helped. I think perhaps we can get squared around by next spring—anyway, find you a place where you can have a garden and some chickens and a cow if you want them. It all happened so quick that we didn't have time to think this fall. You be keeping your eyes open for a place we could get, and in the meantime maybe you'll have some fun settling into a new house, where you'll have lights and running water. I can't say I don't worry about you, dear, for I know it is hard to pull up roots when they are down good and solid. And it isn't any use for you to belittle that old horse chestnut tree, for I know you loved it, and I did, too. There, that's enough of looking back and from now on we will look forward. If you get your eye on a piece of land that is nice, with some woods on it and good growing ground, you let me know, and we will buy it to build on after the war. We'll both look forward to that and to having the kind of house we've always dreamed about, all new, with no old gunk-holes; though, as to that, I don't know but I have kind of a feeling about gunk-holes. They're kind of fun, after all, aren't they?

The trunks got here all right—both of them on the same day, along with the bicycles. They must have hustled right down here. The express charges were enough to kill you—$18 for the lot; but it's like everything else nowadays, and we're glad to have our things, so we don't complain. Everything traveled fine, and there wasn't even a broken record in all that lot. I recognized that piece of old cow's rope the trunk was tied up with, and by golly, I went and got homesick over it. Now wasn't that damn sentimental?

The pillows were lovely, dear, just exactly what I wanted, and I don't know how to thank you. I know you did them at a time when you probably had more to do than you could manage, and when you were all harrowed up, so I guess I can't thank you. They look so nice in the room, and the hooked rugs go with them just grand.

By the way, people are crazy over that ship rug you made and I could probably sell all you could turn out at $15 apiece. I don't think, even at that, that that's enough for all the work that goes into them, but it's a pretty good price for a rug, the way prices are. I have got an order for two—one a ship rug, 42 inches by 2 feet, with a dark blue or black border, and the other the same size with the same kind of border, hooked in a herring bone pattern. There isn't any hurry—anytime this fall or winter will do, if you would like to make them. So when you get settled, if you feel like it, you might let me know. And while we're on the subject of close work, have you ever gone to see Dr. Clement about your eyes? If you haven't, you do it right away, or I'll come home there and wallop the sides of you.

We have moved into the new apartment and have got pretty well settled. We have had a darned busy time of it, trying to shop for furniture with everything so scarce, and both of us so rushed for spare time that we were about crazy. My desk at the office was piled up with work, and Eleanor was going through all the rush and excitement of signing the contract for her book, seeing the agent and the publisher, and doing a few last-minute revisions on her manuscript. She seems quite stunned by her luck, and I know just how she feels. I actually think I'm getting more fun out of her book than I did out of mine, for mine never seemed quite real to me; and I can tell by the way she talks that hers doesn't to her. But anyway, we finally got most of our stuff second-hand—there is an auction room here in White Plains, where you can do pretty well if you don't go during an auction—when the auction's on people are so crazy to buy things that they'll bid a second-hand p—s pot up to ten dollars. We skinned in there one night after work and bought a nice table lamp, a coffee table, and a real snazzy maple dining room table, all for $25—which is going some when you realize what prices are on things today.

They were all more or less worn, but we got us some sandpaper and some maple stain and some wax, and by golly now you couldn't tell those tables from new ones. The lamp we washed with soap and water and an old toothbrush, and got a new shade for it, and it turns out to be pretty slick. We like it fine, especially since now ones like it are priced even in the department stores for $35. Isn't that awful? I guess I sound smug, going to all that trouble and getting stuff second-hand; but it sure does grizzle me to have to pay triple what things are worth, and that's what you have to do when you buy them new. I suppose if I wasn't such an old tinkerer and didn't enjoy rebuilding things, I wouldn't have bothered; but I don't have to tell you what fun it is to gonjer up something nice out of an old relic. Not but what I guess you'd be glad not to have to for a change, wouldn't you?

Then we went to an unpainted furniture place and bought a dresser and two straight chairs, and we stained them maple and waxed them, and we're going to go to the lumber yard as soon as we have time and get lumber cut to make low bookcases to go all around the room, except in the space where the day beds are. I think we'll have a nice place when we get through, and I guess it won't cost as much as it might have. I'm glad of that, because I'm stashing away every cent I can to build our house after the war. So there.

The apartment itself is quite a nice one, and we were lucky to get it. The rent's only $52. 50, which doesn't make it too bad, with two to pay it. We have a big living room and a hall, a fair-sized kitchen with a set-tub, Frigidaire, sink, gas stove and lots of cupboards, all nice new stuff in good shape; a small bedroom, which we're going to turn into a kind of work-room and place to go to hang yourself; and a nice bathroom. I bought a flossy peach-colored bathmat for it and a shower curtain to match, so we can sit in the tub and hang our feet out on the mat if we want to. Oh, yes, we bought a set of plain gold band dishes, because they reminded us of you and of the island.

There, now, I've told you all about my new house, and I wish you'd write me all about yours, as soon as you get into it and find out what it's like. I hope it is as nice as they say, and I expect it is, but I am crazy to know all the details. Too bad he doesn't want you to use the bathroom, but I expect it would be hard to heat up the whole house just on account of it, and when it comes to that, I guess you and I both could get along if we never saw one.

By the way, those old navigation and fishermen's books that were in the hall closet, will you stick those away somewhere for me? I saved them out of the mess that Uncle Bert threw away from the old place, down home, and I kind of like them. I guess you probably know I do, anyway, but I thought I'd mention them, for they look kind of old and worn out and somebody might think so and heave them away. I meant to stick em in my trunk and forgot about it. You must be having a heck of a job, and I do wish I could be there, I'd feel a lot better about it. I may be able to get up for Thanksgiving if we have a four day week-end, but not before, I guess. If you need anything, dear, let me know.

How is everybody in my dear families? You know, I had to laugh, but I was so harrowed up the day Louise and Pearl were there that I forgot to say good-bye to them, and I guess they thought I must be out of my mind. I was, about. I will write Louise soon; she must be busy now getting herself set to go to Boston. I want to help her out some, whatever she needs, and maybe I better get a move on and do it.

I think you did a grand stroke of business with your cow and hay. And I think Ralph is being real nice about the rent. Things seem to be turning out better than we hoped or expected, don't they? Don't get rid of too many of your tools, for we may need them some day again. But there, I guess if and when we do, we can get some others. You better just go ahead and do as you think best about such things. Old Clark is a fart. He sounds as if he didn't know the difference between today and next week, but maybe he is an old man and doesn't. I was pretty mad at him, but what's the use?

I probably haven't said half of what I want to say, but I can put it into another letter as I think of it. I'm kinda weary tonight and guess I'll tool off to bed. I have got some drapes to make and some couch covers, too, and I sure wish you were here with your old sewing machine. For the drapes I got some dark red—really, I guess, wine colored—sail cloth; and for the couch covers some tan-gold monk's cloth. I think they'll be nice if we can ever get some time to sew on them.

Lots of love *Uppy*

P.S. I hope Friend Richard gets a nice, wet, sloppy cellar from the swamp, if he builds on that lot in front of Barbara's; but being him, probably the birds will fly in and drink it dry for him.

P.P.S. Be sure you address my letters 210 Martine, not 216. I guess your pen slipped.

Bill Worthington was a summer person.

TO LOVINA MOORE

Oct. 16, 1944

Dear Marm,

I had to chuckle over this letter to Mr. Clark, for it is right to the point and doesn't say a word too much. I think the bill is all right, too, if you're sure you can't think of anything else to stick on. Out here, if you had to have a room painted and papered, it would cost $30, but I guess we can't charge him that. I wish we could, darn his tripe. I'm copying the bill on the typewriter for you, and will keep a copy myself, so we will have one handy if he makes a fuss, as he probably will.

Are you sure your calculations on the rent bill are right? It was paid up to March, 1941, counting the $30 you sent him last spring—is that right? Your figures are probably O.K., but I worked it out and this is what I get:

March, 1941–March, 1942	$120.00
Mar., 1942–Mar., 1943	120.00
Mar., 1943–Mar., 1944	120.00
Apr., May, June, July, Aug. Sept., 1944	$60.00
	420.00
Less.	164.53
	$255.47

I hate to think that we owe the old son $255.47, but if we do, I guess we'll have to pay it sometime. I shan't be in any hurry, and if he fusses, I'll send him ten cents a month. No, I don't suppose I will, but I'd like to.

You probably have heard about Miss Lucia, by this time. She had a stroke last week and lived about a week without regaining consciousness. That's too bad, isn't it? I feel sorry, and I guess a lot of people will miss her. The island won't be the same, will it? Bill Worthington called me up to let me know on Friday, and I guess he feels pretty cut up. She was 78, and last summer, she was flipping around as lively as ever. These clippings are from the New York papers.

Oh, I've thought up some things to say to Mr. Clark, and if you think best, I will send the letter. I wish we could put our heads together over it, but we can't, so if you think it's a good thing, slide it in an envelope and mail it along to him. If you don't, just tear it up, and we'll forget about it. Send yours along first and wait until you get an answer, why don't you?

I suppose you're busy moving in this week, and haven't a minute. Don't do too much and get laid up, will you, dear? Just take it slow and easy as you can, though I suppose I might as well hoot at the wind as to tell you that. Anyway, be careful, won't you? I wish I could be there to help move in, for in spite of all the work and worry, it's fun to move to a new place and get holed in there for a while. I've moved forty or fifty times, myself, I guess, so I'm an old hand. But then, most always I could move in my suitcase which is different.

This is just a short note, as I've got to do an ironing, and I'll try to write you a longer one before the week's out. I thought you ought to have your letter back, though, and thought I'd hustle it along. Lots of luck dear, in the moving, and don't let it get you down.

Uppy

Leonard Mayo is Eleanor's brother.

TO LOVINA MOORE

Nov. 28, 1944

Dear Marm:

I guess you must be wondering, too, why no letters pass, and if I'm up to my old tricks. Golly, these days are just hustling by, and sometimes I wonder if it's worth it to work so hard. Spoils your life in a way, but I don't suppose I'd want to be without it.

Well, it sure was nice to see Louise and Pearl and Philly. As you know, I planned to go the next week-end, and then we had to work, though I think I would have skipped work if I hadn't caught a cold. I was kind of leary of going up and being around Philly where he'd just had ether—thought he might catch the cold. But I had a lovely time the week-end I was there, and it sure is a shame we all can't see each other oftener. That's another thing that spoils my life, by gosh, stuck off down here and can't get home when I want to. I guess you were kind of disappointed Thanksgiving and I was, too. We got all ready to come and then we found out that the War Travel Board had slapped a fifty-mile limit on travel for civilians unless you could prove that your trip was necessary. So we thought we'd better give it up. Wasn't that the downright hell? Well, Christmas comes on a Monday and we may get another four day week-end then, and if we do, I am going to try to make it then.

I'm so glad you had such a nice time up to Louise's while she was away. A thing like that makes a change when you're living alone, I guess. The house sounds kind of homey and cozy where you are, and it must be nice not to have to lug wood and water. But you know, and I guess everybody would think I'm crazy, but I always kind of enjoyed doing the chores around like that, getting snugged in for the night with your woodbox full. I suppose if I had a big family like the others all have, and a lot of people to do for, I get merrily sick of it quick; but when you're living alone, it's nice to have things like that to do. That's one reason I kind of worry about you living in a place like that, dear—sounds foolish, doesn't it? But I know you miss your work.

No, I guess there isn't any place that will ever seem the same to us as the island. Maybe we can do something about next summer, if all goes well. I want to have the house fixed as soon as I can, especially that store roof that leaks so. I just won't have it go all to rack and ruin, that's all. Maybe we can have us a kind of summer home down there and go down while I'm home in the summer. I wish I could make my fortune so I could come home and live for good. Then we could spend a lot of time down there, couldn't we?

One reason I've been kind of slow about writing is that I've been putting in about every minute I could on my new book. I hope to have it done now by next spring, and maybe it will sell. I do wish it would sell a lot. Maybe someday I could get enough that way to retire on, and then wouldn't we have the high old time!

We have had some snow, which didn't linger long, and a lot of rain this month. I guess the bad weather is pretty widespread. It has poured all day today—come down in steady streams. I will sure be glad when we get back to normal time in the winter again, for if there is anything I hate to do it is get up before daylight, and, of course, now, at seven in the morning it is as dark as a pocket. We get to work at half-past eight, usually just as the sun is beginning to peek out—when there is any sun. And these wet mornings it sure has been uncomfortable on the bus. I have about a ten mile bus ride to get to work, and usually I enjoy it, but now we have so many extra workers on up at the plant that the bus is a nightmare. Usually we have 800 steady workers at the *Digest*, but each year around Christmas time they put on more to help handle the Christmas subscriptions, and this year we have around 3000. I tell you to get on the bus you have to be a good football player, and I guess to get a seat you'd have to be God.

We had quite a nice Thanksgiving party—two girls from the office and Eleanor and I, and then later in the afternoon, another friend came in and brought her two little girls—8 and 2 years old. They are sure some cute. I sure do miss having children around, and it's nice to see some every once in a while. We had a roast chicken, mashed potatoes, baked squash, cranberry sauce and plum pudding. We couldn't get a fresh chicken—I guess there wasn't one in town—or a turkey. So we got a frozen one from the frozen food center, and you know, it was swell. They advertised a five pound chicken for $1.99.

Leonard Mayo has been spending week-ends with us for the last three weeks. He was down at the U.S. Maritime Service School at Sheepshead Bay. Now he's gone to Boston, so I guess we won't see him again for awhile.

We have got our apartment pretty well fixed up now, and it looks nice. The rugs are really pretty—you can't beat homemade rugs, can you? By the way, you never wrote me whether you wanted to make those two ship rugs, I wrote you about. Can I tell the people it's okay, or would you rather not undertake it this winter? Ship rugs are kind of hard to do. If you'd like to have some burlap, I think I could get you some. There isn't any hurry, though.

Well, dear, I guess I'll saw off and go to bed. I hope you are getting along all right, and are feeling well. Louise said you had a boil on your arm that was awful sore and that you wouldn't see the doctor. If it is sore and hasn't healed up, you see the doctor—see? Also, did you get your eyes tended to? You don't ever write me any of these things, you bitch, so I have to guess at whether you ever get them done. But I like to hear how you are, and how you're doing. Did you hear from Clark after we sent him that nasty letter? The old son, I hope he was mad.

Good night, dear, and don't get lonesome.

Love, *Uppy*

The "spy scare" Ruth refers to involved two Nazi spies who landed at Hancock Point by U-Boat in November 1944. The story wasn't reported until January 1945 when the spies were apprehended.

TO LOVINA MOORE

Monday, Jan. 9, 1945

Dear Mum,

It seems dreadful that this is the first chance I've had to write you since I got back, but there it is, the darned work was piled up, as you can guess, and I've just begun to get my head above water. I can't stop to pee but some kind of a darned job comes up, and to be away almost a week just about stopped the clock. But I can see up over it now, thank goodness.

We got back all in good shape early that Thursday morning. As usual, it was a pretty tiring trip, and instead of going to work as I should have, I came home and went to bed. We slept until late in the afternoon, and needed it. The Maine train was an hour late getting into Boston, and by the time we got to the 9 P.M. train it was so crowded we couldn't get onto it. It was a through train to Washington anyway, and the poor soldiers and sailors were jam-packed in the seats and sitting on their suitcases in the aisles. So we gave up and went over to Betty Holmes's for the evening, and took the 11 o'clock train. That was crowded, too, but we got there early and so got seats. We ran into that blizzard just outside of Boston, on the way down, which was one reason why the Maine train was late. It was one of the prettiest snowstorms I've seen—the kind we used to have up home, with the air so full of flakes that you could hardly get your breath. Betty said they had eleven inches in Boston; when we got down here we found they'd had two, just enough to make the road slimy. Since then, we've had another one—about six inches, I should guess, but it took all day to make it. I just wish it would let go down here for once and snow the damn gutters full. With those little spits we get, it just makes the road icy, and it sure was some slippery today. I got a ride down from the *RD* with one of the editors in his car, and boy, that old Buick sure did some skating. The bus, usually, is so heavy it doesn't skid much, but once in a while they take a slide.

Who do you suppose turned up here the day before New Year's? Newman, as big as life and twice as natural. He'd got home from France and he was headed to Washington to see Helen, and then out to California to see if he could find his wife and kid. Honestly, that must be pretty dismal, mustn't it, to get home from a thing like that and all the welcome you get is a kick in the peep. Even if she didn't think anything of him, she could have stuck around where he could see the baby. He seemed fine, but pretty tired and worn out. I guess he has been through some hard times, but he didn't talk very much about it, only just how glad he was to get home. He slept a lot the first day or so, but maybe that was because Eleanor and I tooted him to a New Year's Party in Ossining, and we didn't get home until 4 A.M. I suppose it was kind of mean, where he was so tired, but he seemed to want to go and had a good time. I cooked up some good meals for him and I never saw anybody eat so much or enjoy it the way he did. He said he'd had plenty to eat over there, but it wasn't very good. He brought us home some French perfume, which smells nice, only I don't use any kind, though I didn't tell him so; and he brought a German Mauser rifle, picked up on a battlefield, for Tinky. I've got it here in the apartment, and it sure is a wicked looking thing. Still smells of gunpowder and the stock of it is a bit rubbed up. I plan to send it along as soon as I can get a box for it, but I thought I'd write to Pearl first and tell him what was on the way. I guess it is okay for Tink to have; anyway I thought I'd write Pearl first. He can't get any ammunition for it anyway until after the war, so I don't know that I need to worry.

That was quite a spy scare they had up to Hancock Point, wasn't it? It was splashed all over the New York papers, with pictures of the place and everything. Maybe the Germans'll learn after a while that any stranger who is seen in a small town is the middle of the winter is something to ask questions about. I know if I saw anybody I didn't know walking through the streets of Bernard with a suitcase, I'd call up the FBI and ask who it was afterward.

There are a lot of scares around, but I don't think a lot of them are much to worry about. We had a report this afternoon that the Navy expected the Germans would try out some robot bombs on New York or Washington; but just after the report came out in the paper, another one came in over the radio that the danger wasn't any greater now then it was two months ago. So I didn't worry then, and I shan't now. There's no need of broadcasting those reports until something happens. I don't know why they do it, for it only makes people feel worse than they do, and that's bad enough.

I'm mailing you the burlap with the ships traced on it for two rugs. I don't think you'll want to make them as big as the margins indicates, but Eleanor drew them—since I was so busy I didn't have time—and she wasn't sure just how big to make them. If I were you, I'd stop the border where the margin begins and turn that margin under. It would be too much of a job to make such big rugs, and besides people sometimes like to hang them on the wall and the smaller ones are better for that. But you make them how you think they will look best. I think Eleanor did quite a nice job putting the ships on, don't you? She copied pictures of the "Young America," a clipper ship that made some records in the China trade in the old days.

She had a letter from Lawrence, today, which kind of took a weight off her mind. I guess none of them knew where he was. He is in San Diego, California, now, but doesn't know just how long he will be there. He wrote that he got engaged in Chicago, to a Chicago girl, and I guess Mrs. Mayo about had a juicy accident in her pants, when she heard about it. As Lawrence said in his letter, "she hasn't stopped talking about it yet." That will be the day, when one of those boys brings a wife home.

Well, dear, we sure did have a lovely time Christmas. It was so nice to be with you for a Christmas again. I thought of you taking the tree out, and I knew without you telling me that it would be a lonesome job. It's funny, you thinking about how near we are to each other, for before I got your letter, I was thinking that, too, and how I'd never realized it before. Oh, I know it, of course, but there was something about those few days, in the new place maybe, that kind of brought it home. I've always felt that there was something special between you and me, over and beyond the relationship of mother and daughter. I don't know just what it is, except it seems to be an understanding of each other without having to put it into words. Maybe as I grow older, I get to be nearer your age, for I don't think you grow any such thing as that, that means as much, into words, and of course, we don't need to, really, except it's nice to try to and nail it down once or twice in a lifetime.

I know, without your saying anything about it, that moving into a new place has been a pretty hard thing. I would have given anything to have been able to prevent it, but we couldn't, and so we did the next best thing. I miss the house, too, and all the things outdoors we had there, and I wasn't there much of the time either, not to compare with you. It's easier for me to adjust, because all my life I've moved around a lot, though I always felt I had that to come back to. Well, now I have another place to come back to, as long as you are in it. You mustn't get to worrying about where we'll all be next year, or things like that, for that isn't good. If you are too lonesome where you are, you'll have to come down here with me, and I mean it. I know you haven't said one word of complaint, but somehow I got to reading between the lines of your letter, and it made me wonder a little just how you *were* making out. I don't think you'd not let me know if you did get discouraged, but I want to make sure you would. You will, won't you, dear?

I talked quite a lot when I was home about you taking better care of yourself and I guess I don't have to say again for you to be sure you get the right things to eat. That sore throat and mouth I'm sure is from lack of greens and milk and stuff, and surely you don't need to get any thinner. I hope by this time you've seen the doctor and found out about that. Also, you have to *get* your new glasses. I hate to keep deviling you about it, but you *do* put off so everything that has to do with taking care of yourself. And seriously, mum, you mustn't do that any longer. Neither you nor I can afford to have you do it. If you should get sick, I should just about die, that's all, away down here where I can't take care of you. I worry awfully about that, about your not taking care of yourself, I mean; for I know you so well. You take all the pains in the world for your children or grandchildren, but when it comes to Vina, you give her the shit end of the stick. When you write to me again, will you tell me that you *have* been to see Millstein, and that you've taken some steps to get new glasses? And don't tell me a yarn, either—I wouldn't put it past you, you scamp. If you don't, pretty soon I'm going to write to Harve and Audrey and ask them if they'll scc that you do.

There, dear, I've read you a riot act, but your last letter kind of worried me.

I don't worry much—I don't really see how I escaped being a "worrier,"—but that is one thing I think about; for as I say, I know you so well. And be sure to sleep with that window open a crack, will you?

Now I must stop, and drop a line to Pearl about that awful rifle. Probably Tink will be thrilled to his teeth with it, but there's something about such a thing that gives me the crawls. Write me about all you do to keep busy and happy—yes, *happy*, dear. I know it isn't much fun to live alone, I've done a lot of it. But most always there's things anyone can find to do, as you've always said, that are real interesting. Let me know if the burlap for the rugs is all right. I'll write when I can; and I'll have another vacation before you know it, the time will go so fast. If there's anything you need, or anything that worries you, let me know, won't you? Be sure, for I know that whatever it is, I could do something to help it.

Lots of love, *Uppy*

Eleanor sends her love, and says she'd like to be going to that beautiful john of yours right now. Personally, I don't believe I could do much more than pee in it, but maybe she could.

The story sold to *Harper's Bazaar was "The Ladies from Philadelphia", August, 1945.*

TO LOVINA MOORE

Feb. 12, 1945

Dear Marm,

I guess it is about time—and how—that I sat down and had a little chatterbox with you. You must be wondering what the hell's the matter now, though you're so darned good about it when I don't write that I feel as if I ought to be shot.

Well, I have got some good news. My agent in New York has just sold a short story of mine to *Harper's Bazaar* for $200. Ain't that good, though! She has got five or six more on hand which she is sending around, and she thinks she may be able to sell them, too; though I'm keeping my fingers crossed. Of course, what with the taxes and her commission, I'll only collect about $140 of the $200, but even so, that's so much velvet, by golly. What I'm hoping for, is that in time I can save up some kind of a backlog to pull and haul on, and then, if my stuff still sells, make my living doing that and come home and live with you—if you'll have me. Golly, wouldn't that be kippy, marm! It sure is nice to find out that maybe, just possibly, it *could* happen.

So you see, if I haven't written you as often as I might—and I'm ashamed of it, too—it's because I've been putting in every spare minute I could getting those darn stories ready. I'll try to do better, now that I have a breathing spell, old dear.

How are you doing for money? I was thinking the other day that you must be about ready to cash that $250 check, and I wonder if you wouldn't like to have me write you out ten checks for $25 each, and then use a $25 check whenever you needed one, and keep the others on hand. Let me know if that would be a more convenient way than cashing the $250 one all at once. You could date them as you used them. If you're low on ready cash, perhaps that would be the way to do it, and then you wouldn't have to keep all that cash in the house. Anyway, let me know.

I haven't sent Clark his $200 yet, but will do it this month, as soon as I get a chance to get to the bank. Somehow, I feel as if I'd like to make the old bugger wait for his dough, but I expect I mustn't, as he is just the one to get nasty about it, and I sure am sick of hearing from his in any shape or form. So I'll send it this month. There, that's about all the business, I guess.

You are sure going right ahead on that rug. Louise wrote me that she guessed you had it about done, and she didn't see how on earth you had done it so quick. Well, I don't either, except you probably feel that because you don't have a lot of outdoors work to do, you can put a lot more time on sewing and rug-making. I guess you think it's a kind of a poor substitute for outdoors, I know I would; but maybe it's just as well, through the winter. It has been a pretty tough old cold one, hasn't it, and if you had been saddled with a cow and hens, I know I would have been worried out of my life, these icy mornings. Did you get the big snowstorm down there that we had and that they had in Boston? We had 8 inches, which is mostly gone now; but I understand they had 17 inches in Boston and that the rest of New England is still digging out. So, maybe it's a good idea that you weren't over there alone on the Eaton place this winter, with all the shoveling there would have been to do. Come spring, when it gets fit to be out and around, perhaps the place where Ralph's garden is will raise just as good vegetables and stuff as the one over there. Anyway, I hope we can plan to have a nice garden, just as we always did. I guess you do plan to have one, don't you? It's such a lovely day here, today, just like spring, that I got to thinking about gardens. I wish I could get some time off to come home and help you plant it, and perhaps I can. It depends on so many things. Right now the head of my department is away taking a winter vacation, and it makes things hard for me. Doesn't seem as if I'd ever get up over the pile of work on my desk.

It sure is some sloppy underfoot today though—slush six inches deep. I'd like to go out for a walk, for it is the first warm sunny day, seems like, that we have had all winter. Perhaps I will, later on, but right now it looks as if anyone would go in over his knees. And it's the wrong time of the month for me to go slushing, if you get what I mean. This last snow storm we had here was the kind of one I love—the kind you're always writing to me about and that makes me homesick. It stuck to the trees and telephone wires, and that morning when I went to work on the bus the ride was some pretty. I haven't seen a snowstorm like that in I don't know when—not since 1931, that year I spent at home, I guess, for after that I was in the city and then in California, and here in Westchester it isn't very often that the snow sticks like that. Usually it starts in to snow and maybe snows six inches and turns to rain. So I got quite homesick looking at it, and all the way to work I thought about you and what a good time we're going to have if I can ever make enough money to settle us down.

Louise wrote me that Tink was some pleased of the gun. I guess you have probably seen it by now. It sure is a murderous looking thing, isn't it? I'm glad it arrived all right. We sure had a funny looking packing case on it. We had to build it out of some slats we had, for it's just impossible to get any work like that done around here. I don't know what has become of Newky. He left here to go to Washington and see Helen and then he was bound to the West Coast to hunt up his wife and kid, poor guy. It does seem as if she might have stayed put until he got home from the war, doesn't it? Anyway, I haven't heard a word from him, so don't know how he made out.

Say, when I was home Christmas, did I leave my cigarette roller? When I got back, I couldn't find it in the suitcase, and I need it like the deuce. You can only get one or two packs of cigarettes out here a week, and the rest of the time Eleanor and I roll them with our fingers and I wish you could see them. Eleanor calls them "Camels" because they have a big hump in the middle. If you can't find the one I had around anywhere, will you look in my trunk and find the one that is in there and send it as soon as you can? I know there is one in there, for I saw it when I was at home Christmas. You may have to plow around among the old junk I've got piled in there—you know when I was home and got to poking around in that trunk, I had to chuckle at myself, for talk about the old treasures and keepsakes and old tools and stuff I've got laid away there! Honestly, anybody didn't know me would think I was crazy. Anyway, if you'll round up a cigarette roller and send it along, I'll bless you.

Eleanor has got the advance copies of her book and it is real nice. She is so tickled about it she can't talk. She is going to send you one tomorrow or the next day, as soon as she can get a chance to do it up, and some paper and string to wrap it in. We save every scrid of paper and string we can get our hands on, but even at that it is awfully hard to find enough to do up as many as ten books in. I had to laugh at Eleanor. I told her I was going to buy a copy of her book to send to you, and she almost hit me. She said her mother and father were going to get the first copy and you were going to get the second one, and did I want to make something of it? So I guess you'll get one pretty soon.

The box of eats arrived, and oh, marm, was it lovely! We did what we always do when we get one from you—made ourselves a good big pot of coffee and sat right down to the doughnuts. They were all gone the first day, and there isn't a thing left now but a little jelly and some mustard pickles. It did taste so good, particularly since it's hard now to get hold of anything that eats good. We have had an awful shortage of everything here this winter. Vegetables have held up pretty well, but no meat, except once in a while, and then it is pretty poor stuff. We have been able to get sausage once in a while, and then occasionally pork chops. No beef, no bacon and ham, and they say that this summer it is going to be worse. We have had quite a lot of baked beans—we bake our own when we can get salt pork, but there has been a big shortage of that. We've had enough, of course, to eat, but there hasn't been very much variety. So your box came in good, and we did enjoy it, you old darling.

That was quite a to-do in the papers over those two Nazi spies who landed at Hancock Point, wasn't it? Their trial is going on now over on Governor's Island in New York Harbor, and I guess they are going to give them the works. My soul, that gets pretty close to home, doesn't it? Well, the darned devils, they sure are taking a licking from the Russians this month, and I hope they don't stop running till the year 3000.

We have been quite lucky in our apartment house this winter so far as heat is concerned. The shebang heats with both coal and oil, and when they can't get one, they turn on the other. We haven't been too hot, but we haven't been cold. Many's the time, though, I have thought of sticking my old back up against your sitting-room heater. We have been looking for some kind of a little house out in the country somewhere, within jumping distance of work, where we could have a garden this spring, but so far we haven't had any luck. All the houses that are for rent are rented; and most people want to sell, and won't rent, so I guess we're out of luck. We're going on looking though, for I'd kind of like to have a place like that, with an extra bedroom, just in case I wanted my ma to come visit me.

I had to go out on an assignment for the *Digest* the other day to Eastern Air Lines in New York, and while I was there I met Eddie Rickenbacker, you know, the flier that was lost so long after his plane crashed. There was a lot about it in the papers at the time. He seems quite a nice man, but kind of knows he is a national hero, I guess. It was interesting, but tell Orville I'd rather help him cut wood.

How is Tug and her brood? Louise writes to me every once in a while, but do I ever hear from that Tug? Well, I know, of course she's awful busy, and what time she does have, I guess she feels like resting, not writing letters. I know just how she feels. But give her my love, the old so-and-so, and tell her I think about her once in a while. I'm so glad you're nearby, where the kiddies can run in and out. It must be lots of company, and I don't hold with people being lonesome.

I guess from what Louise writes the twins were quite pleased of their coats. I had a time getting just the kind I wanted, and finally had to order ski-pants special, which just came Friday and have been sent along. I guess they thought they'd get them to wear this summer, I was so slow; but you wouldn't believe it if I told you how short the stores here are of all kinds of goods. Oh, they have enough on hand to make the shelves look full, but all of it so sleazy that you wouldn't want the gift of it, let alone paying money down for it.

Eleanor and I are about dead from staying in the house so much—I guess we know just how you feel. It has been such bad weather for the past month that most people have just holed-up; we have, I know, and I feel as if I looked like something that has just crawled out from under a log in the swamp. We have both had colds, like everybody else, and the backdoor trots, like everybody else, this winter, and what with one thing and another, we'll be glad when it's spring.

I guess my old newsbag is about empty, so I'll stop for now and go get me some lunch. Write when you can dear, and let me know if there's anything you need and how you're making it. Give my love to all and sundry and tell Tug and Steve that if they have a spare moment sometime, I always like to get letters, even if I'm not very good about writing them.

Love, *Uppy*

The "Mary" mentioned in this letter is Mary Steyn (later Mary Dillon), Ruth's co-worker at *The Reader's Digest.*

TO LOVINA MOORE

Feb. 18, 1945

Dear Marm,

You will fall flat on your face getting so many letters from me in so short a time. I have had the grippe and have been home for a couple of days—not very sick, just wambly-cropped—but I am okay now and find myself with some blessed time free. Also I wanted to answer your letter, particularly the part about Gertie's gang going down on the island.

I think it is up to you, dear, whether we let them have the house or not. I know I consider that the house is yours, and I guess Tug feels the same. If you want to let them go down there, it is for you to say. … The way I look at the island, it is the only place I have got to be private in, when I want to go off by myself and work, or whatever. I guess I look at it as about as selfishly as it is possible to look at it, don't I? But somehow, it grizzles me like the devil to think of all those people going in there. And besides, I don't know when my vacation will be, and it might come just the month in the summer when I would want to be there with you for part of the time. So as far as I'm concerned the answer is NO. But I want you to do what you want to about it, and if you want them to have it, why, I'll understand. So far as the roof is concerned, I think I will be able to hire part of it done this summer, if I can find a man to do it. Anyway, I want to be there when it is done, to see that it is done okay. It has gone this long, and a few more months won't hurt it, I feel sure.

* * *

I love the way I say go ahead and do what you want to, and then say for gosh sake, don't do it. But that doesn't mean you can't let them have the house if you want to. If you do, I won't be mad, and I won't be upset about it, dear. You do just what you want to.

The *Harper's Bazaar* people are planning to put my story into a summer issue, as it is a story about summer people. When it comes out, I'll see you get a copy.

Yes, I was pretty tickled to hear it had sold. I hope I have as good luck with the others—the agent has five more, as I guess I wrote you. She has sent them to the *Atlantic Monthly* now, and I haven't heard. Will let you know, dear, as soon as I do hear.

I had a letter finally from Newman. He is at Camp Parks in California, I think it is San Diego, though I'm not sure. His address is Newman L. Moore, MM 2/C; T.T.U. 1—K 3, Camp Parks, California. I think he is pretty lonesome and perhaps some of the family would like to write to him. I will send his address to Pearl and Tink, and maybe they would like to—I know Tink will want to thank him for the gun. I thought Tink would be pretty pleased to have it.

* * *

I guess you have probably got Eleanor's book by this time. She sent it along last week. I hope you enjoy it as much as I did, and I guess you will.

Go ahead and cash the check, dear, as soon as you want to. I thought maybe if you had ten small checks instead of one big one, you could cash them as you needed them, and not have the worry of having cash around the house. If you want to, you can put the money in the bank and have yourself a check book. But you do it any way you feel is best. The money is there in the Pleasantville bank for you to use as you want to, and there'll be more when that is gone, thank the Lord. It wouldn't be any trouble for me to send you the small checks, if you want them.

People up at *The Digest* are still talking about your rug. I hope you didn't mind what I did with it. It was good business, I guess, for now I can sell all you can make. Only I don't want you to go at it too hard. There is no need for you to work so hard over the rugs that you blister your hands. You have blistered them often enough working hard in the past, and now you don't have to, dear. The only thing is for you to have something to do so you'll be happy—for, you old worker you, I know you won't be unless you're doing something. Of course, with your rugs, you have got a business there that will bring in some money every so often, and that, it goes without saying, is a tremendous help, these days. I guess what I'm trying to say is that we could get by all right now if you didn't do anything, but so long as you have something you can do, and that you like to do to bring in some odd dollars, why it certainly is worth while both to you and to me. And those rugs certainly are lovely. I was so glad that Mary exhibited hers at the *Digest*, for it did bring pleasure to a lot of people. You can buy hooked rugs at the department store, but they are never so pretty nor so well made. I don't think the colors were a bit too dark for either the sky or the water. I think they were just right, and so does everybody who has seen the rug. You're a dabster at it. Golly, I wish I could be home so we could make some together. I've never forgotten that one winter we had, have you? We did some fancy rug-cutting, then, didn't we?

Our snow is all gone but a few dirty dabs. We had a grandfather of a thaw, and for a few days it was just like spring. It is cold again today though, and gray-looking now, though it was lovely bright sun this morning. It wouldn't surprise me if we got another storm. I was surprised to hear that you hadn't had as much snow as we did. The papers have been full of New England digging itself out of all these blizzards, but I guess they must have meant around Boston. We've been lucky in Maine, haven't we, about hurricanes and blizzards.

I have got some pictures painted and ready to send home if I can ever find time to do them up. It is a wonder I find time to breathe, the way I talk, isn't it? One or two of them came out pretty well. That's the way it is, I find—sometimes you will gave good luck and get a pretty one, and most of the time the canvas looks as though the cat had been walking on it. How is Ann making out with her paints? I wish she would write me once in a while and let me know? Ask her if she needs any colors, and if she does, to let me know, for there is a paint shop right down the street and it's no trouble to drop by and pick up a few tubes. I would love to hear from some of Harve's folks once in a while and from Tug's, too, but I guess the way is to write them once in a while. I have managed to pry a few letters out of Louise, the old dear, I know she is so busy with her brood that it's hard to find time to write. But she has written me some lovely letters in the last few months, lord love her. I know I am awful bad myself about writing, and I make out as if I were the only one in the world that was busy.

Well, dear, write when you can. If you have already started the herringbone rug, just go ahead and finish it, there isn't really any hurry about the other one. But I would like to have the other ship rug for the lady when you can get time to do it.

Lots of love, and keep your pecker up, *Uppy*

TO LOVINA MOORE

Feb. 24, 1945

Dear Marm,

Got your nice letter this morning, same time Eleanor got hers. We were both pretty tickled. Eleanor said she was going to hurry up and write another book, so she could get another letter from you. Her book is already doing pretty well—it has gone into a second printing from advance sales only—it doesn't go on sale in the bookstores until March 12. Isn't that slick!

Here are the checks. I think it is probably the easiest way for you to handle it, and as for me, why, it certainly is for me. All you have to do is to put the date on each one before you cash it, and cash them according to number. That is, cash No. 339 first, 340 second and so on. Be sure the date is on each one when you cash it, otherwise it won't be any good.

There isn't much news. I done wrote out my news bag to you I guess in that last letter. We had the 23rd off from work for our holiday instead of the 22nd, which gave us a three-day week end, so I was home yesterday and am getting a nice rest. My cold is all gone except for a slight cough, and that is going fast.

About the rugs, I can get the burlap and Eleanor or I can draw the patterns for you if you want us to. Don't work your foolish head off, though, will you, dear? Just do them along as you get time. My lord, I don't see how you get them done so fast, all that shearing must be tough. Take it easy, won't you? There's no terrible hurry. We can sell them as you get them done, and nobody is in a hurry.

We had a terrific sleet storm here Wednesday night. I'll bet there was an inch of clear ice over everything. It turned to rain before morning and cleared it up some, but I'll tell you there was some skating around done. It so happened that that night I had gone up to see a friend of mine who lives back of Pleasantville on top of a steep hill, about a mile from the bus station. I took a taxi up and just before dark, why, of course, the sun was out and the ground was practically bare. We had dinner and sat around talking until about ten o'clock, and then I thought I'd better take the ten-thirty bus to White Plains, so I called up the taxi man. He said, "Nothin stirrin! I couldn't get up that hill." I said, "Why, the hill's all right. We came up just before dark." He said, "Lady, you crazy?" and hung up on me. So I looked out the door, and here was everything covered with this glare of ice. So they lent me an umbrella, and I started to walk down to the bus station. Well, boy oh boy! I made it all right until I got to the steep part of the hill, and then there was the road just like a smooth river of ice down the hill. I tried to walk on it, and I saw I couldn't, and for a minute I thought I'd have to park under a culvert until morning, or go back up the hill. Then I thought I'd try to slide, so I squat down on my heels and used the umbrella for a tiller, and by golly, I bet I slid a quarter of mile without stopping. Darned if it wasn't fun. There wasn't any traffic, luckily, because if I had met any all I could have done was holler out, "No brakes!" and *they'd* have had to get out of the way. I got down to the bus station just in time to get the bus, but it took us nearly until eleven-thirty to get to White Plains. Talk about Waltzing Matilda! That bus did everything except turn over on its top and slide along on that. We made it, but the bus driver said his hair had turned white and that he was going to join the Marines.

Well, I must stop now, and wait till my newsbag fills up again.

Lots of love, dear, Uppy

Carlton is Louise's second son; he is also called "David" in earlier letters.

TO LOVINA MOORE

Mar. 26, 1945

Dear Mumma,

Well, here we are, almost up over March hill, and isn't that lovely? It is a swell day here today, warm as summer, and all the little buds just popping. The leaves on the shrub outside our window look quite green, poor little things, they're taken a beating, for a week ago we had it warm and they began to stick their heads out, and then it turned cold enough to freeze off a lamb's wiggle and a lot of them got nipped. But I guess spring is here to stay. Anyway, I hope so. It's been a long dismal winter, in some ways, what with all the snow and cold and dark days, but it's gone quite fast.

I'm enclosing a check for your two rugs. I collected the money for both of them. I have got one more order for another shop one, and Eleanor says she will draw the pattern; but if you are tired of them, and the lord knows, I should think you would be, maybe you'd rather not make any more now that the long winter evenings are about over. This lady who lives in Asbury Park, New Jersey, wants one and will pay the usual $15 for it. You don't have to do it dear, if you are fed up, you know, but if you want to make another one, let me know, and Eleanor and I will draw and send along the pattern.

Well, I guess I have rented the house down on the island for the month of July, if you think it is a good thing. This very good friend of mine, Mary Steyn—the one who got your first rug, and who wrote you a letter about it, wants to come with her husband and two little girls. I told her the shape the house was in, and she says she doesn't care, so I told her I'd write you about it and see what you said. I have been thinking some about having the house fixed up a little this spring, if I could find someone to do it; anyway, have it given a good cleaning and maybe the chimneys fixed. What do you think? Anyway, this is what I thought we might do, and you write me and tell me your ideas on it.

Eleanor is going to take her vacation early and come up sometime this spring—I sure do wish I could get away to come along with her, but we are so short-handed at the office that I guess I can't. She has made a pretty good wugget on her book. and I shouldn't be surprised if she gave up her job entirely and spent all her time writing. At least, for a while. Anyway, she plans to go home in April or May, she hasn't decided just when yet. She says she would be glad to help clean the house, and I wondered how you would feel about going down on the island with her for a week, or less, or whatever time it took. I thought first that maybe Weeza would like to go, too, and help, but I wondered if she could get away, what with the boys at school and nobody to keep house. Of course, it would be out of the question for Tug to go, with her little fellers. The house hasn't been cleaned in such a long time that it is going to be a terrible job, and I don't want you to do too much of it, of course. Another plan I thought of was this, but I don't know what you would think of it. If you don't think it's a good idea, dear, say so, won't you? Eleanor's mother is a great hand to clean—she does a lot of summer cottages, you know, and Fred isn't working now, and I thought maybe we could get them both to go down the chimneys and perhaps give me some kind of an estimate on what it would cost to have the roofs fixed. He is very good at that, you know, has done that kind of work all his life. he has some arthritis this winter, and hasn't been doing much, but he might be willing and able to take on that kind of a job. I haven't written him anything about it yet, or her either; because I wanted to find out what you thought of the idea. He would be a grand hand to do the work, if we could get him, and I don't know of anybody else, do you? Everybody else is too darned busy, and I don't think Fred would charge me quite so much as somebody like Sylvester Dorr, because he thinks I've done quite a lot for Eleanor. If you felt like going down with them, and could stand the old lady for a week or a few days, I don't know but it would be a good way to get it done. I thought for a while of getting Blanche, but she is always so busy. And of course, if we got the Mayos, Fred could do some of the repair work. Anyway, you write and let me know what you think.

Somewhere, this year, I think I will have to get a new kitchen stove for the place, for that old one is sure a mess. We could make do with it, I guess, but I would kind of like to get a new one, if I could, or a good second hand one. If you hear of anybody with a good one to sell, will you kind of keep an eye out? I think the new ones are rationed, and I doubt if I could get one on that basis, but there ought to be a good second-hand one somewhere, if we could lay hands on it. Eleanor says she will help hunt one up when she comes up, but I thought you might hear of one in the meantime.

I thought what I would do this year is to have the chimneys fixed and have the house cleaned, and maybe the worst of the leaks in the roof patched. I guess I can't have it done all at once, especially not in war time, because everything costs so much now. But I don't dare to let it go very much longer, or the whole house will be gone. I didn't think I would try to get any wallpapering done this year, because it isn't much use to paper until we get the leaks fixed.

I don't know yet for sure when my vacation will be. I hope I can get it set for July, for it would be fun to be there when Mary was there. She is sure one swell gal and her little family is awfully nice. One little girl is ten and the other one three. Her husband is a Lieutenant in the Coast Guard, stationed in Washington, and he thinks he can get his two weeks leave in July. I doubt if I can manage my vacation much before July, because a lot of our people at the office have left either to go into the Army or into the Red Cross, and we are just that much busier, being so short-handed. What I would like to do is for you and me to spend the whole month of July at the island and let the Steyns have one part of the house and we have the other. That is what Mary wants to do, so it will be all right with them and we could be by ourselves all we wanted. Would you like to do that? If you would, will you plan for it, honey? They will do their own cooking and work, of course, and we won't need to bother with them or wait on them. I think it would be a lot of fun, and would like to do it. I hope you will like the idea, too. Of course that wouldn't mean that we'd stay on the island all the time and not see the families, because I wouldn't like that, not one bit, for I have to see all my kids. Maybe they could come over some, too. Anyway, we will see what we can do in the way of plans after we've decided.

I had to go to Boston Friday and yesterday to see Dr. Brown—there wasn't anything wrong to speak of, but I had been having a pain in my side and thought I better have it checked up on. So I went up Friday—we had a long week-end—and saw the old boy, and came back yesterday. He said it was a nerve that led from my back to my stomach which had got cramped up from sitting at a desk too much, and he gave me some exercises to do and said I was in fine health and okay. So that took a load off my mind. Darn it, sometimes I wish I had never seen an office or an office desk. They sure are woman-killers, but I guess I will have to see a lot of both before I get through. I guess I'm no worse off than anyone else though, and a lot better off than some. I sure wish I could give up the darn job and come home and live with you. Perhaps someday I can.

It sure was awful hard when I got to Boston not to keep right on coming. For ten cents and a leather button I would have, too. It was lovely spring weather—just the kind when Maine looks awful good to me, and I like to died yesterday taking the train back here. Well, July, if that is when it is to be, isn't too far away, and then I will be home for a full month. Boy, oh, boy!

I wish you could hear people take on about your rugs. I could probably sell a dozen of them if I had them, but I tell people the rug-making season is about over now and they'll have to wait until next winter. That herringbone one is a dandy and I sure did like it a lot myself.

The Weir has finally been published in England. My agent sent me three copies of the British edition, and a check for $80 which is an advance payment on sales. I will get some more dough as time goes on. The English are pretty careful, I guess, how they pay out money. When I come home I will bring a copy of the book so you can see it. It is the funniest looking thing you ever saw—printed on what looks like toilet paper, and about a half an inch thick—

the book is a half an inch thick, I mean. They have a terrible paper shortage over there, of course, and it is a wonder they printed it at all this year. I get a big bang out of it, for I guess it is quite something to have a book printed in England in wartime.

Eleanor's book is going like a house afire. So far it has outsold mine by quite a lot—darn her tripe! Well, I am awfully glad for her, because it is about time she had a little success. I hope it keeps right on and sells a lot more. She didn't get quite as good reviews in the papers as I did, so we kid each other a lot and say we're about even.

I have been about breaking my neck trying to find a decent jacket for Carlton, as I promised him, but so far I haven't had any luck. I guess I will have to send him a leather one, after all, and let it go at that. The shortages down here are enough to kill you. You can't buy one thing you want, and what there is is made out of mosquito netting, about. I hate to keep him waiting so long, but I also hate to send him one that isn't a good one. So if you see him, tell him to keep his shirt on, and the coat to cover it will be along in time.

I guess that about empties my old newsbag. Write again when you can, dear, and let me know what you think about all these plans of mine. I want us to have a bang-up vacation together this year, and by golly it'll be worth a little planning. Lots of love to you and all,

Uppy

Bump Galley was a Bernard boy who was killed in World War II.

TO LOVINA MOORE

May 21, 1945

Marm, dear,

I guess you will think you've lost me for good, for I am up to my old tricks; but here is time tonight and now for a nice long letter. As usual, or a little more than usual, I've been up to my ears at the office and for about three weeks haven't known which end I was on we've been so busy. The head of the department had gone away and one of the people left, and that left just two of us to do the work of the whole shebang, me and this man who is about as much good as two poops in the wind. So I've been dragging home from work anywhere from six to seven o'clock at night just about pooped out, and going to bed early. Things are better now, though. Fergy, the head of the dept. is back, and he always does a heck of a lot of work, so I feel as if the weight of the world had lifted. Boy, will I be ready for my vacation when it comes, and that will be in about a month, because it starts the 25th officially, and I think the Friday before is a holiday for us, so I can start home June 21st. And then we will have the holy old good time, won't we, dear. Seems too long since I have seen you, though it was only December, and I can only go just so long, you know. Well, it will be pretty soon, thank God.

I'm sorry you've been sick, dear. I guess you don't take as good care of yourself as you might. Though I know how tough it is for you not to go ahead and tear into the housecleaning. Please be a good girl and don't go at it quite so hard. It looks as if you'd have to coddle that knee a little for a while, doesn't it? Is your inflammation all cleared up now? Write as soon as you can and tell me how you are. Maybe you'd better go ahead and have a few of those heat treatments, until you can be sure whether they're going to help. I sure wish I could be there to take care of you when you cut up like that, you smart-aleck, you! Boy, would I slap you down!

I don't think you better plan to do any of the housecleaning down on the island, do you? I would a whole lot rather hire somebody to do it than have you over-do, and I know you won't hold back much, once you get started. I'm glad you and Eleanor didn't try to go down when it was wet and mizzly, and it wasn't a good idea at all, what with your bad cold. Perhaps we can hire the housecleaning done, and later on, if you feel like it, and it isn't too much of a jaunt, you could go too and kind of oversee the job. But I don't know as I want you to go before I come home. I'd kind of like to be along to look after you. Mrs. Mayo said she'd be glad to go later on, and she is a whizz at housecleaning, so you might get in touch with her. Maybe we could get her and Blanche Gott to go, what would you think of that? I know that both Louise and Tug would be glad to help me out if they could, but I hate to ask them, or Audrey, for I know that they have got their hands full. You might do a little asking around about Blanche, if you think that's a good idea. If you don't, why, then let it go. Eleanor and I will get up there three or four days before the company comes, and we can go down and air the house out and clean up the worst places. So don't worry about things, if you can't get anyone to go. But you mind me, now, dear, and don't go yourself, if you don't feel like it, and darn ya, don't you do any of that housecleaning!

I paid Eleanor for the stove, and she said she told the man to leave it in Fred's garage (Fred Mayo, that is) until we could get Abner or somebody to haul it over in his truck. I would kind of like to get it down there, to the island, before I get home, and set up, but I know how hard it is to get someone and how the menfolks hate to frig with a stove. I wonder if Mont still has a horse down there? If he hasn't, I will be in a tough row of stumps, I guess, for I can't ask anybody to lug a stove halfway across the island and up those hills. However, maybe just better leave it until I get home, for I know how hard it is for you to get in touch with people, with no phone, and how busy everybody is. And I don't suppose there's any terrific hurry anyway, except maybe we could get the mess cleared away before we start to clean house.

How do you feel, anyway, dear? Do you think you'll feel like spending July down at the island? If you don't, we don't have to, you know, and I would spend most of the time with you, wherever we are. What I mean is, if you're still feeling kind of morger, why I don't want you to do anything you ought not to do, though I know of course you feel the same way I do about the island. Well, we will talk it over when I get home—and doesn't that have a sweet sound to it!

Well, a lot of water has gone over the mill in the last few weeks, hasn't it? V-E Day, and all, and old Hit and old Musso passed in their checks. I guess there isn't much doubt about Musso, but I wouldn't be a bit surprised if old Hit was stashed away somewhere waiting for another chance. They say the Secret Service and the Intelligence and the Ogpu are doing some high old hunting, British and American and Russian Intelligence are hot on his trail, if he left any, which I doubt. They seem to have rounded up most of the rest of that gang of packrats, and it is too bad they don't line the lot of them up against a wall. I didn't see much celebrating on V-E day—as a matter of fact, I worked all day. The office was closed, but I had a lot to do, and three or four others were working, so I did, too. Nobody felt much like celebrating—that is, going out and getting hip, hip, hooray-ish, because too many of our people have menfolks in the Pacific. A lot of the men from around here are at Okinawa, and that, from all we hear, is no picnic. Most people were quietly glad that the Germans were beat, but nobody did much celebrating.

What a shame about Tinky's friend, Bump Galley. He thought an awful lot of him, I know, and it is a sin that such a young fellow should have to be lost, and so near to V-E Day, too. It must be awful hard on his family, and I know Tink must feel bad.

I felt so bad about the President that I bawled, and I guess a lot of people did, too; but there were some who didn't, from all I hear. It was a terrible loss to the country that he had to go at just that time, for he was the only one of the lot that knew enough to pilot us through for awhile; but I guess we will make out without him. Lord, the country's got to, and here's hoping they will wangle out a peace that will stick. I guess everybody feels the same way, and anyone who is old enough to remember the last war is wondering his head off.

Eleanor got back feeling like a million and I was glad to see her, but I was sure jealous. It made me feel bad to think of somebody else doing my jobs around the house, but I'm glad you got them done. Only I wish I could have been around to help. I had a rotten cold while she was away and was out of the office for a few days, but nothing serious, except I got to thinking about all of you up there and got kind of homesick. Darn it, I guess I never will make enough money so I can retire and come home to live, but maybe I will—you never know.

I have been doing a lot of thinking about buying the house, and I guess I will wait before making up my mind until I can get home and talk with you. How do you really feel about it? I hate to think of your having to move again so soon, and I don't want you to. If you really want that house, I will try to get it for you, dear. The way I feel about it, it is conveniently placed, near to everybody, and has a lot of the things to make you comfortable. The big drawback as far as I can see is that it hasn't any land with it; but it will be for you, and you don't want to go stramming around a woodlot. On the other hand, it is a rotten time to buy a house or land of any description, for anyone who has anything to sell in times like these wants all get out for it, and I don't know as I could meet anything like the price Ralph would want—and can probably get—for his house. I want to have a talk with Harve and see if he thinks it is a good buy and what I should offer for it, if we decide to buy. So do you think we can wait till I get home? I should have to borrow most of the money, or get some help from the F.H.A. on a mortgage, I guess, for income taxes this year have just about taken my overflow, outside of living expenses and a little wigget I've put by; and according to government ruling, we don't get any June bonus this year; but I shouldn't mind an F.H.A. loan. They make it easy for you, and you have a long time to pay it back. The only thing is, I hate to have to pay a lot more for a piece of property than it is really worth—which is what I should have to do if I bought one now. Well, we will talk it over. It would be worth it to have you settled down in a place where you want to be, if that is what you want, and to have some peace of mind about your home.

Eleanor hasn't heard any further word about selling her book to the movies, but she hasn't given up hope, for it usually takes quite a long time to close a deal like that. So she (and I) are sitting around with our fingers crossed. It would be too bad if it didn't go through now, what with hopes up, and all, though she is pretty sensible about it and says what the hell, if it does, it does, and if it doesn't, it doesn't. If it was me, I'd be quivering, but she doesn't seem to be.

How is everybody? Babies all over their colds? I expect they are all looking forward to school closing and vacation. How is Phil's eye coming along? Eleanor gave an awful good report of it, says it is healing up the scars and looks as if in time it would be okay. I sure was relieved to hear it—it was about the first thing I asked her when she got back. Louise and Tug, the little scamps, both owe me letters, and I will take it out of their hides when I get home. I owe Ann a letter, and Muriel one, too, and will try to answer them before I get home or they will skin me, I guess. Is Muriel taking good care of you? She promised me she would, and I guess from what Eleanor says, she is keeping her promise.

Oh, gosh, it sure will be good to get home. I guess from the way the week-ends will fall that I will be home for nearly five weeks. Won't that be kippy? It sure will seem strange not to do any office work for that long, and can't I stand it! It has been an awful hard year, in a good many ways, for we have been so short-handed at the office—a good many of our best people have left to go into war work or the service or abroad.

Helen wrote and offered me the use of her house for the summer, and I would have taken it for my company, but she also offered me Aunt Alice as an inducement. Said Alice wanted to spend July on the island with us. I haven't answered the letter yet. I thought I'd leave it up to you, since you're the one who'd see the most of her. What do you think? My own answer would be a flat No, with an exclamation point. Although I feel kind of mean. I guess we can make out with our own house, can't we? I will wait till I hear from you before answering Helen's letter. It is kind of embarrassing to have to say no, but I can put it on the basis that I don't want to take the responsibility of looking after her things and equipment, especially since Mary has got two children, aged three and nine. They are awful cute kids, incidentally, and nicely behaved, but I don't need to tell Helen that.

I think you will like Mary. I guess I told you who she is. But just in case I didn't, she is the girl who is head of the department where I first worked when I went to the *Digest*, and she is the one who saw that I got pushed along as fast as she could manage it, into my nice job I've got now. I've always wanted to do something to pay her back for that, and it looks as if I've got the chance this summer. We won't need to wait on them, or be mixed up much, the two families, I mean. The last two weeks in July, her husband is coming up, and she says she wants to entertain herself, so I don't feel very much responsibility for that. It's a good thing, too, for me I don't want to have the responsibility for anything. I just want to rest and to see you and the rest of my family.

Well, I guess that about empties my old bag for the time being. Give my love to everybody, and tell everybody to write. Lots of love, dear, and write and tell me how you are.

Uppy

The UNO was the United Nations Organization.

TO LOVINA MOORE

Feb. 11, 1946

Dear Marm,

Got your lovely long letter and was sure glad to have it—you do write a nice letter to me, and you always tell me all the things I want to hear about and all the news. I am feeling all right again now. My trouble was mostly a snotty nose anyway. One of those sinus infections, they say, is awful hard to break up once it gets a good hold, and I guess it is so, but all those jabs of penicillin certainly did the trick for me. Now I wouldn't know I had a nose.

Did you get the coat I had sent you, and was it o.k.? When I came to buy it, I found I couldn't remember very much about your size, except you wanted a 46, and that's what I had sent. The saleslady put it on to show me how it looked, and it seemed to me she was about your size. She looked swell in it, and it seemed like a nice warm one, too. They had some in dark green, but I thought the black one looked a lot nicer, and the green ones weren't so warm, and I wasn't sure you'd like the green—it was kind of an off shade. Anyway, I hope it fits all right and that you like it. If you don't, send it back, and we'll see what else we can do. The only thing I was afraid of was it might be too short, but the coats I saw were all short—this, as a matter of fact, was the longest one of any I saw. I had them send it from the store, and I hope you got it all right.

You sure have been having a taste of winter up there, I guess. That sounded like some old snowstorm. We haven't had snow down here, but we have had a lot of cold rain and sleet storms, and the weather's been raw and uncomfortable. I'd a lot rather have it real cold and get it over with. That wet cold wind goes right through you down here, and the going has been something awful. The old bus that I take to work has done some waltzing around, I can tell you. So far though, we have been able to make the trip, though one morning after an ice-storm we made most of it at three miles an hour, following along behind the County sand-truck.

I'm so sorry to hear Steve has had another asthma spell since they moved down to the shore. Gosh, that must be discouraging. I wish she could find something that would clear that cussed stuff up for her. I hope they will find something and get settled back down before too long, for it must be nerve-racking as the deuce not to know what you're going to do, or where you're going to be able to find a place to live. I guess the land-boom is the same all over the country. Here people are going wild trying to buy land, and it is pathetic. The dealers want anywhere from three to five thousand an acre for Westchester land, and people are practically mortgaging their teeth to rake up the money for a home. I think it is disgusting to charge so much for the things people have to have, and sometimes I wonder if it wouldn't be a good thing for the government to take over and put a price ceiling on such things as land, so that anyone who needed it could buy it at a reasonable price.

One of the funniest things that I have ever seen in my life is the way the wealthy estate owners here in Westchester are squawking out, because the UNO has decided to settle in the county. You have probably read something about it in the papers, as it has been getting quite a lot of publicity. The site for the UNO is right near the *Reader's Digest* buildings, so we all know the countryside around pretty well. A good deal of it is wild land, all belonging to big estates, acres and acres of it where nobody lives, and all plastered with "No Trespassing" signs in three languages, for godsake, so if "foreigners" happen by they won't be able to stop. I know, because when we lived in Pleasantville, Eleanor and I used to go biking around through the area, and it was hard to find a place to eat your lunch unless you ate it under a "no trespassing" sign. Well, to hear the owners squawk about the UNO, you'd think they were going to turn thousands and thousands of people out of their happy homes, when, as a matter of fact, the UNO committee couldn't have picked on a place in the country, unless they went out in the desert somewhere, where there are fewer people. Golly, I have to laugh. I always remember that time you and I and Tug went to Castine and couldn't find a place down by the shore to eat, on account of so many summer people's places.

To hear people talk, you'd think the UNO was some kind of a "foreign" bunch of gangsters, come in to steal their property and burn up their houses without paying a cent; when as a matter of fact, the UNO is about the only hope the world has got now to settle international squabbles and prevent a third World War. I get so mad, I could spit. If the Organization does choose the site, finally, they will pay for the land at the going price, and don't you forget it, the owners of it will make plenty.

Somehow it seems pretty sad, when, for once, an attempt is made to settle the world's fights by some other method than war, that there should be so much lying done about the very Committee that's been appointed to try it. Of course the answer to that is that some people always make a lot of money out of a war, and would be glad to see another one. It makes your blood run cold. The thing that's horrifying about it is that quite a lot of the newspapers and radio stations in the country are owned by that kind of people. So you can read a lot of news, right now, and hear a lot of broadcasts about the UNO not being a good thing. Quite a lot of people believe most of what they read in the newspapers and hear over the radio, too.

You certainly have been turning out the pajama suits and things. My own pajamas are swell, that nice blue color, too, and I cuddled into them last night and slept like a good one. The mittens arrived just in the nick of time—my old ones were beginning to give out. Thanks lots, dear. They're lovely.

Have you been to that clinic yet, to see about your tongue? I don't want you to let that go, old dear. It must be uncomfortable as the deuce to put up with, and there's no reason why you shouldn't have it cleared up. Also, if you need new teeth, and I guess you do all right, you go straight and have some made, and have the dentist send me the bill. Mind, now.

How are you off for money, anyway? I guess you must be all right, but if by any chance you get low, you let me know. I'll send some more soon, anyhow.

I haven't been able to get any burlap. I guess they aren't making any now. I've tried two or three places lately, and they look as they'd never heard of it. We are in a very tough spot out here as regards stockings, these days. You can't buy them anywhere, and haven't been able to for a month. Most people are going around with runs. I have just one pair left and they have a run an inch wide down the side, but I wear them because if I didn't I'd have to go bare-legged. Nobody pays any attention to runs anymore, though. They're just something that everybody has in their stockings.

Eleanor has been using up her spare time making a carved chest out of pine and it has come out swell. She carved a ship under full sail on the front panel and a flying hawk on one side panel and a seagull on the other, and it looks awful pretty. I guess she must have inherited something from her pop along those lines.

I haven't given up looking for the twin's skates, but it is a thankless job. They just don't have any. I went all over New York a week ago Saturday trying to find some, and the only thing I saw was one pair of double-runners for what appeared to be a baby. I'm sorry, I expect they would like to have them, but what can you do? When you see them, you might tell them that I haven't had any luck.

It is a nasty, wet, cold day here, sloppy as all get-out. I was glad it was a Saturday and I didn't have to go to work this morning. I'm a lazy girl, I've cuddled down on the couch and stayed here almost all day. Just got up to eat. Seems like a fine thing to do, on a day when it's so nasty outside. There isn't much to do here anyway in weather like this, so I just keep on being lazy and it does me good.

Give my love to all the folks and lots of love to you, dear.

Uppy

1950s & 1960s

Dorothy Lobrano (later Dorothy Lobrano Guth) was Ruth's early editor at Morrow & Company. As E. B. White's godchild, she edited *The Letters of E. B. White*. Louise Dickinson Rich, author of *We Took to the Woods* and other Maine books, was a contemporary and friend of Ruth's who lived nearby at "The Sands" in Corea. Wes and Helen Mary Lawrence were summer people; Wes Lawrence wrote for the *Cleveland Plain Dealer*. Adlai Stevenson was the Democratic Party candidate for President of the U.S. in 1956. "Clement" was Frank Clement, Governor of Tennessee, who made the keynote address at the Democratic National Convention in Chicago. Clement was a Fundamentalist "Bible-Toter." "Chenny" is Chenoweth Hall, artist, and friend of Ruth's from Prospect Harbor. Ruth Lawrence was Lawrence's sister. The following letters were written from Bass Harbor Head Road, McKinley, Maine.

TO DOROTHY LOBRANO

August 17, 1956

Dear Dotty,

The poem is super. Out of this world. I particularly like the part about Furry Purry being contented with her lot.

We were saying that we thought it would be nice if Morrow made you a sort of Roving Editor, a la the *Reader's Digest,* so you could maybe make a headquarters here in Maine and pick books out of the brains of all the Maine authors. There's lots, you know, and one could well make a career of that, make lots of money for the firm, and you could live with us. Louise Rich, now there could well be a life work for somebody. Put it up to Thayer, why don't you? We miss you. Louise, incidentally, who you must've heard when you were here, recently occupied Corea, is going to review Speak for the Sat. Review. Chenny wrote me, also, that Louise is "ecstatic." May God forgive me, I can hardly wait. John Gould, I understand, is going to do the *Times* review, and that I like; because John always gives me a nice review, though (and this is between you and me) I sometimes wonder if he ever reads the book. There. Nasty girl.

We had another shell heap dig last Sunday; missed you then, too. The Lawrences, Eleanor and I, and John Gould and family, all went. Had steaks, this time. I have found two ancient and aged little harpoons, beautifully worked out of bone. I even got Eleanor to say (she who is a little p.o.ed with scrapers,) that they are something.

No. Don't ask me to fly. Getting off the ground looks bad enough; to think of not being able to get back down for two hours flying in circles—oh, oh. Those who can do it must have bosoms cased in brass; which mine is not.

Fly those who will, or those who must
Get quickly out of town,
The going up looks bad enough,
But oh! The coming down!

Oh, well. It's a hot day.

It is hot, too. New York must be blistering. I can't see why, for what reason, as it used to say in the Latin books, you ever left us.

We went last night over to Ruth Lawrence's to the television and watched the Boys nominate Stevenson, and watched him, smiling every now and then as if somebody had pinched him from behind, (him, smiling, I mean, not us) put out the little speech about how the vice president ought to be (implied, he isn't) of first-class presidential material; so he for one (Stevenson) was going to stand aside and let the Convention nominate the country's best, etc., all by themselves. A very smart cooky. I expect I'll vote for him, if I can get the taste of Clement out of my nostrils.

This place is crawling with people. Thousands of cars up and down the road, people riding around and around. The cats have given up. They are all in the house today, sprawled disgustedly over all the chairs. Mike went off last week and stayed three days, scared us, too, because we thought better of it and came home. Yesterday I took the boat and went to Placentia again after mackerel; no fish but lots of lovely solitude. Sometimes I wonder why we don't all, cats and everybody, just go nuts and have it over with. A sample, for example, is the night we got back from the island dig, having the Goulds and the Lawrences for supper, and just as we got sat down with long cool ones, a knock came on the door and it's a woman and her husband claiming to be from the *Worcester Telegram;* she wants an interview. So I went out to talk to her, figuring that was simplest since I had a houseful of guests; but the husband went barging into the house without invitation, introduced himself all around; and the guests, figuring he must be a friend of mine, politely introduced themselves; whereupon the husband went tearing out to his wife, yelling that there were two more authors "in there"; so she deserted Eleanor and me, and *she* went barging in, announcing in a loud voice that she'd hit the jackpot, and poor Wes and John must forthwith come out and be interviewed, too, and have pictures taken; which they did like the pleasant lambs they are; and in the meantime, the husband, on the strength of the fact that he was the *Telegram*'s Garden Page Editor, took two baskets and went and picked all our cultivated raspberries, which might have been ripe, yes, but we were cherishing them and didn't wish them picked; and then he came back into the kitchen, waving the raspberries, said to Eleanor in a loud tone, not even "Please," "Gin and tonic!" and went into the living room and sat down among the guests.

But that's not all. Helen Mary, who, to look at her, you wouldn't think she was peppery, is; so she marched into the living room, and laid hands on Wes and John and said, "Come on, it's time to go home!" thinking that if they all went up to the cottage Eleanor and I could somehow get rid of the unholy two; and John, who had had a good stiff drink, looked at her and said, "Oh, do I have to go home yet?" (He and Wes, who hit it off mightily, were discoursing between themselves, letting the rest of the chips fall where they would, with a dull thud, I might say); and Helen Mary said firmly, "Yes, you do. Come on, now." So, somewhat dazedly, John and Wes and Dotty went off up to the cottage, leaving Eleanor and me alone with the interviewers; and the woman's first question went something like this: "They say if you get Book of the Month Club, you get $25,000, and the Literary Guild is just as much. Is that right?" I suppose I looked as if somebody had hit me in the face with a dead fish, for she went on, "Well, come, is it?" By that time I'd recovered a little, so I said, "I haven't the slightest idea. I've never had a Book of the Month Club." Then I heard a little sort of yip out of young Kathy Gould, John's daughter, who had made her exit early on, and was in on Eleanor's bed reading a book; and I realized that the creep of a husband was gone from the living room, and I looked around, and there, sure enough, he was, in the bedroom, pawing around among the private papers and things on Eleanor's desk. Well, that did it. I got up, marched in. "Look," I said, "I'm sorry, but this is after all a bedroom. You get out of it." He started to say something, but went. Fast, I might add. So then I told the wife that I was sorry, but I had guests and please to go; and she said, "Oh, of course," if I wouldn't let her stay and chat with me and get an interview, she'd have to make something up herself, and *you won't like that,* said she. I said I didn't think I liked any part of it, anyway, and would she please go?

After they'd gone, young Kathy came out of the bedroom with eyes like saucers, big and black. Seems the first thing she knew, "Why the old goat, he was right behind me, looking down over my shoulder, and then, when I jumped, he went over and started to claw over the stuff on the desk. Why … why, the old goat!" says Kathy. Well, he was a creepy sort, and older girls than Kathy, who is thirteen, might have done some jumping, I expect.

So then the guests came back, irate as could be, and we had a good old indignation meeting; and Wes has done a humdinger of a column which he is going to send to his paper about some of the things that writers have to put up with; and what's more, he swears he's going to send a copy of it to the Editor of the *Worcester Telegram*. I think, maybe, better to let it slide, but he says no, by golly, he's going to.

So you can see, we all had quite a time, and I do wish you'd been here, Dotty, if for no other reason than we wish you were here.

Do plan a week-end—why not Labor Day week-end, if that is a long one for you?

Love from us both *Ruth*

P.S. I suppose the moral of that sad tale is don't go barging in if there is a columnist present.

Dorothy Lobrano worked as an editor for William Morrow from 1950 to 1961.

TO DOROTHY LOBRANO

January 8, 1957

Dear Dotty,

There's always odds and ends of slimpsy paper lying around after somebody finishes a book—all those left-overs from the carbons, which some poor devil has to read, at least you jokers always tell me to make four copies, though I don't really believe you ever use more than two of them. So you get a letter on *this*, and I hope it holds together till you get it to read.

Any time suits us—if you and your ma like winter weather, you won't miss any if you come soon. This morning it was three below zero, clouds of snow blowing around from the northeaster yesterday which left us something like seven inches of what the radio liltingly calls "the white stuff," and the bay smoking like a pot from the cold. So we leave it up to you. We have two snow-shovels, incidentally; and Eleanor should be through with the Town Report by the fifteenth. Incidentally, also, when you come, do no, I repeat, do not, mention the phrase, "twelve cents" to Eleanor. Unless the occasion arises to be very bitchy, when, look her in the eye and say loudly, "TWELVE CENTS." And see what happens.

Let us know what to lay in—cold tea, cold soup, Bourbon, rum or Scotch. I know your tipple pretty well but not Mrs. Lobrano's. I do hope she will come, even with the above seemingly cold comfort offered, which c.c. is mentioned only to show that the scope is wide and covers everything. We might even rake up bloody marys or sake, if she has acquired any exotic preferences from Asia. Or that white drink which tastes so, and makes you see horses jumping over the bed—what is it, the name escapes me; begins with "p."

Pernod.

Does she like lobster? I hesitate to mention this—it makes me feel like the Maine Publicity Bureau, tolling everybody into the State for the sake of that old beat-up crustacean. At least, they don't offer lobster and pernod.

My God! What would happen to you?

Be a good girl, now, and don't abandon the trip for the sake of business commitments, sidewalks cleaned off by a Disposal Department, plain cold feet or the New York gentlemen. The first two items don't matter deeply, we can supply the third, and the fourth, if you want to, you can bring with you, and I wouldn't say it wouldn't be appreciated, in a mild way.

Take care, *Ruth*

TO DOROTHY LOBRANO

March 21, 1957

Dear Dotty,

At dawn, at dawn,
On Monday morn,
Nous
(The long-haired bearded hermits)
Arrivon.
At 7:35
J'arrive,
Avec
She.

We.
Whee!
Prothalamion!
Salutations
Et
Merci,
Mille fois.

The State of Maine Express
Is
7:30
I
guess;
But 7:35
Rhymes with
J'arrive.
    (It does if you say seven-thirty feeve)
    So Sharrup!
We'll go
To the ho-
tel
And call
As soon as rosy-fingered Aurora has washed her face and had
coffee
And all,
And cleared up the sinus and the cigarette cough,
Rauf!

Indeed bang the timbrel, (what is a *timbrel?* For Godsakes?)
Indeed beat the drum,
(I object to that word "eftsoon")
But thanks anyway for the lovely progrum.
It is the most.
Host-
Ess.
Yes.
Amour

Amour
Amour
RMoore
RMoore , or where are my marbles?

Honey in the Horn is the popular novel by H. L. Davis. George was George Richardson of Tremont who plowed the roads for years. Miles is Miles McIntire, who still lives in Seal Cove. Tom was Tom Kelly, Eleanor's mentor. Ruth was an amateur archaeologist who loved to go on digs on Gott's Island and around the area. She eventually donated her collection of arrowheads and other Indian artifacts to the Abbe Museum in Acadia National Park; and on Gott's Island there is now a Ruth Moore site. Ruth was working on her novel *Walk Down Main Street. The Witch Diggers* was written by Jessamyn West.

TO DOROTHY LOBRANO

April 23, 1957

Dear Dotty,

I'm late as usual with my bread-and-butter letter, but there's an excuse for it this time ... I know I generally don't have one ... I got stuck with jury duty and have been pining away the days in the county court house, just in case you've wondered. We were up there quite a while and tried one case, the consensus being that attorneys and criminals took one look at the jury, decided they were a bunch of tough old cookies and preferred to have the cases referred by the judge. I learned some fascinating new card games, made seventy bucks, and met Mrs. Mace who runs a sporting goods store up on the Air Line in Aurora. She wears wonderful hats; when the judge complimented the jury on its impeccable conduct of our one case and referred to us as "men and women of affairs," Mrs. Mace remarked with some asperity that "accordin' to the looks of that judge, he's had considerable many more affairs than any of us has." The best card game was of the solitaire type and is known as "Smudge." I will teach you to play it when you come for Memorial Day week-end. I also made the acquaintance of the First Selectman of Castine, who found the skull and bones of an Indian in his gravelpit and has invited me to come fetch them. His wife doesn't like them lying around the table on the back porch, and each day she fixes him with an eye and says, "What do you want me to do with your uncle?" So I can have them to go with my arrowheads; as well, I have an invitation to go dig in the gravelpit.

Apr. 30. (I got side-tracked)

We have been remodeling the hen-house, which is to be a workroom, and I've spent the day on the roof laying roofing paper and tarring it. The tar-pot I had was too small for the size of the brush I had, so I had to use a rag; spreading tar with a rag takes training and skill, of which I have neither; so most of the tar was on me. Turpentine takes it off; lard takes off the turpentine; so far, I have not discovered anything that takes off the lard.

The hen-house will be nice, I think, when it's finished; Eleanor is putting in long windows and re-siding it with some pine boards we got; scrubbing, so far, hasn't taken away the smell of hen, but painting will, when we get around to that. Of course, a skunk lives under it, who seems not to approve the activities. Occasionally he lets off, so that we have to go away and do something else for a while; but I expect he will get used to us as time goes on.

All the spring work piled up while I was either on the jury or going fishing—first things first, I always say. We still have to go down to the island and finish up laying in a wood supply for the summer. We were down a day in March with the power saw and whacked down some trees and trimmed them up; but they still have to be cut up into stove-lengths. Then, George is coming tomorrow to plow, so that after that all the seeds have to be planted; and then, it is wonderful fishing weather. All my nephews have found out that I am saving rocks—for whatever eccentric purpose it doesn't signify—so they are helping; you take five or six active youngsters from six to twenty all helping to save rocks, and the end product piles up. Rocks is one thing they is plenty of; looks as though my collection will be a match for the Natural History Museum's, if things keep on. That's all right, though; you can always use a good rock.

Today, on the hen-house roof, I was dive-bombed by a fish hawk—osprey, to you—I saw this terrific shadow on the roof beside me and looked up, and here was this bird, checking about ten feet over my head. I let out a yell, waved arms, grabbed hammers and so on, and it flew away. It came back twice, however. Nerve-racking. The only thing I can think of, we put up a synthetic chimney, made oh, out of all sorts of plastic and imitation brick, which isn't quite finished yet, and might, conceivably, in its present state, look like a fish-hawk's nest, if you were a fish-hawk; or perhaps it was my hair. I do need a do. Maybe he thought it was raw material. After the third time, he went away and didn't come back; so of course I spent a lot of time watching the sky; didn't get much done; never do. Doesn't always take fish-hawks.

I have had to do a little reconstruction on the over-all plan for the novel; just in time, I happened to read *The Witch Diggers*, which I hadn't read before; happened I was nosing along something like that same trail. Fortunately, I hadn't got a lot laid out; things are mostly in the bumbling stage as yet. I find this always happens to me at least three times before I finally get under way; in a way, it's salutary, I suppose—the idea was much too easy-come-by not to have been thought of before by someone. Always some conspiracy, dammit, to make people work harder than they thought they were going to have to ....

Got *Honey in the Horn*, and thanks a million. We're delighted to have it. Eleanor took it over to the town office for Tom to read—Tom, you remember, is the First Selectman—and Tom got to reading it in the middle of a busy afternoon; Lord knows what they were doing, computing everybody's real estate taxes and putting them down in the valuation book, or whatever; and Tom got to reading *Honey in the Horn* aloud and roaring over it, parts like about the chittim bark that had to be stripped down the tree for constipation, because if you stripped it up you got the opposite effect; with the result that Eleanor and Miles (the Third) didn't get anything done for the rest of the day; they had put it up between them that if they got Tom a good book to read it would keep him out of their hair while they computed taxes; but not at all, it just made him all the more sociable. Did them all good, E. said, including Tom, who was feeling his age that day. Well, no wonder, it's a great book, better than Mark Twain or any of them; nobody's ever done anything to come near it of its kind; I've always said Davis should have had the Nobel for it, and would have, if those Swedes weren't so taken with people getting eaten up in pig pens all over the Deep South.

How about it—you going to make it for Memorial Day week-end? We're hoping. If we get the hen house done, you can sleep in it ... or I will ... if we get it done ....

Love, *Ruth*

P.S.: Except for MY MISTAKE, our letters would have crossed, so now I don't know who owes whom. Only I'll have to write you to say thanks for Dough, Ray, and Me, and you'll have to write me to say about Memorial Day week-end. Never get anywhere with these things ... Don't know why I wrote 72nd, never had any assignations there ....

John Coffin Willey, a native of Cherryfield, Maine, was Ruth Moore's editor for many years at William Morrow & Company. Ruth's first book of poetry, *Cold as a Dog and the Wind Northeast,* was published in 1958. "Dotty" is Dorothy Lobrano. Ruth's novel *Jeb Ellis of Candlemas Bay* was published by Morrow in 1952. Dan Wickenden was a friend of the Lawrences, summer people who were friends of Ruth's. Thayer Hobson co-founded the Morrow Company with William C. Morrow in 1926.

TO JOHN C. WILLEY

July 29, 1958

Dear John:

Thanks for your letter of the 23rd about the contract on *Cold as a Dog*. Your suggestions sound all right to me—how about if we had the same kind of deal we had with *Jeb Ellis*—ten per cent until you get your seed back, if ever; and then if the thing has unexpected sales, we go back to terms of regular contracts? This is, of course, a Yankee-get-rich scheme to nick your profits in case the thing sells a million. Also, I am dealing now with a Maine man turned into a city slicker, so maybe we had just better have a word-of-mouth contract and see how we all make out. In that case, I'd better go on picking strawberries.

(We have taken 400 quarts of berries off of our small patch, and the take shows no sign of slackening off. After a week of fog and rain the damn things have not rotted; they hang there sleek and fat, half the size of a coffee cup. If you see Dan Wickenden, tell him it is his father's fault. Last year, I raised four pumpkins following the recipe of Henry David Thoreau and they weighed eighty pounds apiece; we did the strawberry patch according to "Gardening with Nature" and this year we are swamped, inundated, as you might say, berried. Ask Dotty if she won't come up and stomp on the rest of the blasted crop.)

According to Dotty, and to you, a good job has been done on *Cold as a Dog*, and of course, I'm very keen to see it. I suppose when I do, I will have some feelings of reality about it; I suppose I still feel too astonished (and grateful, too) at your being willing to do it in these roaring times of science. I told Thayer this in the historic letter that went astray—God knows what happened to it, but it is the only letter I ever wrote that I wish had not gone astray.

You should probably have some report on the progress of the new novel. I have a competent working draft finished, and am letting it sull for a while before I start working out the bugs. There is still a good deal to be done. I was, for a while, under the impression that this draft would be the final one; but I don't think so now, having got it to the stage where it's beginning to be fun to work on it.

Regards to all, *Ruth*

The new novel Ruth was working on in 1958 must have been *The Walk Down Main Street,* which was published in 1960. Fern was John Willey's wife and the guest cottage, which was built by Ruth and Eleanor, used to be across the road from the main house, but has since been sold and moved. Bass Harbor used to be part of McKinley, Maine. "Uncle" is what Ruth called the U.S. Government.

TO JOHN C. WILLEY

April Fool's Day (no year date)

Dear John,

Good. That gives me plenty of time and you plenty of time and nobody has to hurry. If you and Fern can make it in June, you can have the cottage. It's rented for July and August, I'm sorry to say, but we'll find a place. Any time.

I need $800 for Uncle by the 15th. Okay?

This is just a note, I'll really answer your letter later ....

Affectionately *Ruth*

Ruth and Eleanor went to England on the R.M.S. *Mauretania* in 1956, the year of the Suez Crisis, which caused them to return home sooner than expected. *Island MacKenzie* was written by Ursula Moray Williams. By 1961, Dorothy Lobrano had changed jobs from William Morrow Company to *The New Yorker,* where her father Gus Lobrano had worked for years. Ruth calls Dorothy "Mehitabel" (from Don Marquis' *archy and mehitabel*) because Mehitabel was an alley cat and Dottie was dating around at the time. Clementina was the name Ruth had given to her old Jeep. Eleanor's "rugged day" is probably in reference to Eleanor's being town tax assessor and selectman.

TO DOROTHY LOBRANO

December 28, 1961

Dear Dottie,

I don't know that I ever had such a glorious, magnificent long letter before, it seems almost a shame to answer it, because you had all that done, and now to do again (I hope). We both enjoyed it, because we got into that Dorset mud too when we were there; and Eleanor got bitten on the bottom by a nettle—of course we were willing to pay a penny, however contemptuous of the British double standard; but in all those towns the Place to Go was hidden carefully away behind vines, and if you asked where it was, you had to realize that all the English were under the impression that Americans never Went; it was out of line with national policy. So poor Eleanor, rather than disturb anybody, found a bush in Dorset; and was nailed by nettle, which, for a while, from what went on, I was positive must have been at least an adder.

We loved Dorset. We hunted for Corfe Castle and for the Cerne Abbas Giant and couldn't find either one; this was our own fault. We had traveled a lot of miles by then and were both hen-minded. I'm sure it would have done us both good to have looked upon the Giant, from whom as one of our books said "even the Wife of Bath would have averted her eyes." We found lots of other things though. Your letter made me think back; I dug out my English jottings to see where we *did* go; it seems we went the same way you did and had the same weather.

Like:

Oct. 30. Came onto Dorchester, in Dorset. Saw Judge Jeffries' Inn. The wind blew a gale, cold enough to sting ears; great masses of black cloud were scudding down from the North. Went South to Maiden Castle, which we saw from a distance as a series of layered green hills. Walked about a mile up a country cart track through mud to get to it. A vast fort, a quadruple-or-more line of earthwork entrenchments, once a fortification, and "iron age Camp." All clipped green grass, vast emerald-colored humps; we went up to the first moat, were turned back by a herd of cattle, part of whom were bulls. I think it very thrifty of the English to keep their Ancient Monuments in shape by pasturing cattle all over them; but it poses a problem for the innocent visitor who does not wish to be disembowelled. So we did not explore Maiden Castle beyond the first moat, but drove on to Weymouth, from which town my ancestor, Charles Gott, sailed for America in the early 1600s; had a queer feeling of having come full circle after 300 years. An old town with narrow streets; stone and brick houses, many built of the soft almost lemon-colored Portland Stone. A fine, fancy painted clock on the Esplanade; white cliffs to the east across the harbor which was green and blue in the gale that was blowing. Many of the square-sterned varnished lap-streak boats.

If you went to Portland, you saw the Chesil Beach. Oh, that I did love! Like:

Oct. 30. At first as you approach the Chesil Bank, you think it looks like sand; but you soon see that it is pebbles. The stones are polished, some translucent; many pieces of flint; Portland stone with fossils; the book says the sea brings some stones from as far away as Cornwall. The beach is in places 20-30 feet high and very steep, climbing down you slipped and skidded. Surprisingly little drift of any kind—a few strands of weed, some white cuttle, and occasional piece of wormeaten wood, but that was all. It was pebbles; mostly small; some colored like very good candy. I have never seen such beautiful pebbles.

The Isle of Portland is all little towns, castles, quarries and stone walls; we went all the way across and out to the end where the lighthouse is at Portland Bill. It is a very neat, tall sturdy lighthouse, painted a sort of yellow with a wide pink-red band. Found myself standing on a grille, under which was the Channel busily eating at the limestone cliff. limestone, s'I to myself, and got off of there. In this field, clipped neat and green—sheep, again—the big cubes and rectangles of soft quarried stone were standing about, full of fossils ... one great block of the soft pale stone was covered along its sides with almost perfect fossilized oyster and scallop shells ... Rode North to Lyme Regis and put up at the Three Cups Inn ... Spent next morning picking fossils out of the Blue Lias at Charmouth, under the lee of the high blue cliffs out of the wind, which has blown cruelly from the northeast for the last four days...

... Drove North all afternoon, coming in the early evening to Salisbury Plain, with far off over the rolling country, Stonehenge. By the time we got there it was dusk on Hallowe'en; we were just as glad the gatekeeper had locked up and gone, for Stonehenge on All Hallows is not for people, the grass very green, the stones very black and brooding; we drove on into Amesbury and spent the night.

Nov. 1. Went back this morning and found the gatekeeper huddling in his hut out of the wind, for November's come to England and the gale whipped up over Salisbury Plain, whistled around the trilithons, so we had to get our backs against the stones and stand in the lee of them, even to get breath. We were the only ones there, in the weather; a pox upon all Britons who say us Yankees is soft...

Well, I don't know why for godsake I afflict you with a diary; it's worse than showing slides; but your letter made me homesick for Dorset. Why it should I can't imagine, unless it's something in the genes. And there may be something in that, too, because at Knole, at Sevenoaks, in Kent (part of the temptation, of course, is to repeat those names), there were rows of pictures of ancient Earls of Dorset who were all blond and pink-cheeked and stout, and the spitting image of my fat niece, Ann Rich. Oh, what a bar sinister I could rake up there, I betcha! The wrong side of the blanket would be worn threadbare, I betcha.

Oh, before I get off of all this: have they restored Stonehenge? Because it was mostly tumbled down when we were there; well, not mostly, you could sure see what it used to be, but a lot of the big fellows were on their sides. Eleanor says she wouldn't like it so well, restored; I'm of two minds. I tried hard when I was there to imagine what it might have been when the circle was complete.

Fleece-lined shoes, okay; but *high-heeled* fleece-lined shoes ...? Oh, my Dottie, who else? Keep them, I want sometime to see.

We had a nice Christmas, though not placid. In the first place, it snew. We had to bust out through three feet of it at the edge of the driveway where the snowplow had gone along, and in through three feet of it to get at Clementina's jeep, before we could disperse to our various families for the morning Christmas trees. Eleanor had a rugged day, because the Road Commissioner was being airy-fairy lillian about plowing the roads out; seems it was his day for plowing out the back roads where nobody lived, while on the main highways people were, let's say, struggling and complaining, and everybody in town was stuck on Crockett's Hill. Such a balls-up always means our telephone wears out by noon; we weren't home all day, which meant that all the things to say backed up until evening and the next day; when she is here she always answers politely, but it is lovely when she isn't here, and they get *me*. Of course, all I do is wish them a Merry Christmas, in a nice way, but it seldom suffices.

I can see how there can't be much to do at the *New Yorker* after the

Christmas issues, *et al;* I always thought when the skimpy ones began to come, it was because everybody there was exhausted, but apparently not, they're all just sitting on their hands. You can tell E. B. White and A. J. Liebling and all the rest of them, that they could at least review a book; when there is no book section, I, for one, do not read the goddamn paper.

You sent me *Island MacKenzie* a long time ago—it's one of my favorite books. I feel I ought to give it to a child, and have wavered on the brink, but I can't bear to part with it.

I am glad, Mehitabel, that your love life is resolving itself and that you will, after all, 'ave a 'appy. The candlesticks from London are very beautiful indeed and we like them very tremendously and thank you. Eleanor, when she can break away from the weather forecast long enough (if it snows again on top of this, with the roads not plowed, everybody will have nothing to do but call her up, until spring) sends love, and I do too, and all the best for what's to come.

Up the bowl, *Ruth*

Eliza is the character (played by Lillian Gish) in the film *Way Down East* who is on the run down a river fleeing in the winter by jumping from one ice cake to another.

TO DOROTHY LOBRANO

Nov. 10, 1962

Dear Dottie,

I know I am very bad; awful; but you are used to it, and besides, we'd much rather talk to you, for which happy and unprecedented occasion I have been waiting like a spider in a bush …

John and Fern are coming to eat Thanksgiving with us; could you come, too? And visit with us while they visit their mother in Cherryfield? Think of the lovely long ride through the ice cakes, Eliza. Or snowballs, as the case may be. (We are having nice snow this morning.) If you can, I bet John and Fern would shove over and make a place under a corner of the laprobe …

Oh, hell, you probably can't; but you have to admit, it's a good idea.

We have got all kinds of things to show you; much better seen than written about; this fall we built a camp down by the shore—you know, the utopia of child-mind, a playhouse in the woods; and E. has made lovely jewels.

These and other wonders …

I haven't yet mentioned this to John; he will be amazed if (and when, I hope) you call him. (You could say I'm just trying to get out of writing another letter.)

Maybe?

Love, *Ruth*

After William C. Morrow died in 1931, Thayer Hobson, former partner, bought Mrs. Morrow's equity in the company, and essentially took over, running the concern for the next 30 years. A wealthy Yale graduate from the class of 1921, Mr. Hobson started out as a young salesman for the Dodd, Mead & Co. He married five times, and the third of his wives was Laura Z. Hobson, the author of *Gentleman's Agreement*. Mr. Hobson was gassed in the First World War, and he smoked; thus, by 1960, he wished to retire and move from New York and move to a warmer climate that would be more conducive to his health. He moved with his fourth wife Isabel to Arizona, where she died. Subsequently, Mr. Hobson married Bettie Davis, the widow of Morrow novelist H. L. Davis, who was from San Antonio. Hobson moved with her to Texas, where he died in 1968.

As for his final relations with the publishing world, before he left New York, Hobson arranged to have John T. "Sam" Lawrence and a group of Morrow employees buy the company. Sam Lawrence served as President and Chief Executive from 1960 to 1965 when he stepped down and Lawrence Hughes took over from 1965 to 1985 at which time the Hearst Corporation bought the business.

TO THAYER HOBSON

February 20, 1964

Dear Thayer,

It is to Wm. Morrow and Company's good that I've been so long answering your very nice letter. Since I got it, I have finished fifty pages of the new ms. and am now on page 170. (And don't think I have ever before told any officer of aforesaid co. what page I am on, either. In case of popping out of the woodwork, which you might have once but now have no fear.) (And it isn't that I like to leap full-blown like Minerva from the head of Jove, but only in case I poop out and can't finish the damn thing.)

Your letter was both pleasant and reassuring. It has been years since anybody has called me "child." And I was beginning to wonder if you had vanished over the Wall of Texas forever. I am sorry to hear about your wonderful horse. On a smaller scale, I went through much the same last summer when my old cat (15 years) went from home on a walkabout, and was, we thought, gone forever. He came back after eleven days, looking like a little ghost; but in the meantime, much repining, because I know of PEOPLE I could spare better than I could Griget. He not only understands English, at times he speaks it.

I would, of course, be honored if the University of Texas wants my manuscripts. It sounds like a wonderful thing they're doing. The University of Maine where I once studied for 1/2 of a Master's degree and which once gave me an LL.D. (I think it was, nobody ever believes this but I have the damndest looking hood you ever saw in your life, to prove it)—where was I? Oh, the U. of M.'s librarian casually asked my sister last summer what I was going to do with my mss., but I haven't heard anything else, so sucks to them. Owing to not knowing anything about the procedure, I have to bother you with it, and I'm sorry. But I do thank you. What I would like is the tax relief arrangement—shoot, anyone can always dig up cash, and what's that, anyway?

I enclosed a list of what I have. Frances suggested listing all editions I own, so I have; but this may not be necessary. Anyway, I have; just to make it look good, if nothing else.

Thanks, I would love to come, and perhaps, someday, will. Texas, of course, scares the bej—s out of me; the worst skid I ever took in my life was crossing the Panhandle out of Amarillo when we fishtailed 19 times on an icy road. (In Maine, you only fishtail three times.)

Regards to Bettie.

Affectionately *Ruth*

The book Ruth must have been working on when these letters were written was *The Sea Flower,* published in 1965.

TO THAYER HOBSON

March 9, 1964

Dear Thayer,

Here is your letter back from Mr. Roberts of the University of Texas; I can't think how to thank you and him.

Yes, do please proceed along the lines suggested, which I understand are as follows:

(1) That they get my manuscripts and books as listed on the sheets I sent you (letter of Feb. 20) together with ms of *Second Growth,* which Morrow must have.
(2) That they appraise them.
(3) That item you refer to as "the gift" be spread out over a period of years, for tax relief.

Is this correct? If it isn't, proceed as you think best. Item No. 3 above, I expect, is the gimmick. For me, that is.

Oh, yes, and (4) I think I would prefer to send the lot to the University as soon as arrangements have been made; because what if the house should burn down? I really don't have any way—vault, etc.—here, and it looks like a dry season coming up. (Have to think of these things if you live in the woods.) Also, I have taken ms. of *F. Balloon* out from under the cat. There wouldn't be any advantage in my keeping them, would there? When if I took emoluments and still had the responsibility and it would give me a nervous breakdown?

Bless you. And thanks again. I am now on page 270 and have got the damndest thing going.

Affectionately *Ruth*

Arvid is a character in *The Sea Flower*. Paul McGettigan of W. C. Heston and Company of New York was Ruth's accountant.

TO JOHN T. LAWRENCE

June 8, 1964

Dear Sam,

After Frances's letter and your telegram and phone call, I'm still reeling a little bit, naturally. I thought I had a whole, fine lovely long year to lie in the daisies and cuddle in the snowbanks without a brain in my head; and now, bang, we go into production for October. In case you think that sounds querulous, it isn't; I think this is all very wonderful indeed. I'm delighted that you all like old Arvid; I do, too, and I don't think I've ever had so much fun doing a book.

I wish I could say I've come up with a sensible title; I haven't. My brains seem to be curdled. Nothing spontaneous occurs; I've been battling Bartlett and bumbling around in the Bible, as all title-costive authors do, and the only thing I've got is *Burning Bright,* which is of course no good for this book, in addition to which it sounds like the Chicago fire. We really need John for this, I expect. He comes up here with a list which he hands over dead-pan and waits like a coon under a bush while I discover the one he's planted along toward the middle and which turns out to be exactly right. I'll think some more, if any of us could call it thinking.

With regard to Paragraph TWELFTH in the contract, I would, of course, be most grateful for advice. Paul McGettigan over at W. C. Heston has been doing my income tax return for me ever since *Spoonhandle;* I look upon him as God in these matters, since I myself can't add two and two. He could tell you my taxable income from 1959-63 better than I could, since his files are, without doubt, in better shape than mine. If we do turn out to have another book club income from the *Digest,* and there's a more advantageous way for me to take it without wronging Uncle, I'd be happy to know; and this letter will authorize you and your tax people (who are Heston, anyway, aren't they—or have you changed since Thayer's retirement?) to secure any information you need. And I'm very grateful for this, Sam. I am a financial idiot.

In case we do change Paragraph TWELFTH, do you want me to go ahead and sign the contract as is? I'll wait till I hear from you on this. (But will sign it, in case you're worried.)

Burning Bright. That's something about Van Gogh, isn't it? Well, anyway. You can't say I didn't try.

Thanks again, and I feel like the old lady with seventeen fingers, all crossed at once.

Affectionately *Ruth*

The Appaloosas were horses owned by Thayer Hobson. *The Rockweed Tree* title was eventually changed to *The Sea Flower.*

TO THAYER HOBSON

July 4, 1964

Dear Thayer,

I've received the enclosed letters from Dr. Roberts and am astounded. Perhaps it was the cat sleeping on them all these years that's put up the value. They must have found a few cat-hairs. In any case, this is eminently all right with me, if you agree it should be; I'll wait to hear from you before I write Dr. Roberts accepting with acclaim. My goodness, throw money around like that!

I'm a little hazy about what to do next, or what the procedure is so that I will do Uncle no wrong and end up in jail. I expect I had better talk this over with Paul McGettigan, hadn't I? Or what? As I understand the thing (from Frances) you make this donation to the University and then you can have the amount of the appraised mss. deducted from income tax, spread over a period of years? Right? For example, I could have a deduction of $1000 a year for twelve and a half years, if that's the way it still works. I don't want to bother you any more than I have to, you've gone to a great deal of trouble already, for which I can't tell you how grateful I am; but I'll wait till I hear from you before writing Mr. McGettigan. He's done my yearly return for me since *Spoonhandle,* and thank God he has, or I should have been doing time years ago. Because nobody can ballsup a mess of figures as thoroughly and as quickly as I can.

I was delighted to hear from all the Appaloosas, all their achievements; they do sound like wonderful fun and I am so glad you are having it. Do you know Odetta's song, "All the Pretty Little Horses"? We have it on our new hi-fi, it drives the cats crazy.

John and Fern were here last month, overnight, not long enough, but we were lucky to get them, even for that. We had a wonderful time, gossiped about everybody. Wished they could stay longer, and they wished so, too. John says they really do like *The Rockwood Tree*. I was a little unsure about the title; it doesn't seem to mean much with regard to this particular book, but who am I to quibble, I couldn't think up anything better because my brain's dead.

Thanks again for everything and best to you both,

Affectionately *Ruth*

TO THAYER HOBSON

January 22, 1965

Dear Thayer,

Oh, damnation, I suppose you fell off of one of those emulsified horses. I would gladly shed ap, if (1) I did not most sincerely wish to know how you are and (2) if I were not slowly going nuts re. all the communications I have suddenly received about those emulsified manuscripts and (3) if I knew where else to turn. If you are still under the weather, please fire back this unhealthy mass of enclosures and I will deal individually with Roberts,

McGettigan and Gotlieb, settling matters as best I can; because I would rather donate the whole mss. to Gorham State Teachers College for nothing, than have you pestered by it further, if you are still sick. I would not have pressed matters now, if McGettigan hadn't said that since the donation was made in 1964 it should be listed in the 1964 return with all required data, and he and I are already beginning the annual amassment of material.

But first, how are you? And for no other reason than that I am affectionately concerned. And the hell with Roberts, Ransom, McGettigan and Gotlieb.

Gotlieb? Well, see enclosure No. I. What do I do now? I'm naturally pleased and impressed, already beginning to feel like an archive. In some ways, it might be more logical to stay in New England, where, very likely, I belong; but when I think of all our correspondence and the mighty amount of work done at Texas (because it must have been a colossal job to appraise that gob of papers). I don't really feel I can change now. However, I won't answer Dr. Gotlieb until I hear from you, beyond acknowledging his letter and asking for time to consider.

I note that both Dr. Roberts and Paul McGettigan warn about "overevaluation" in case of objections by the Treasury Dept., and I truly don't want to get involved with Uncle because I'm starting back to work, and anyway, who wants to get involved with Uncle, period, if it isn't necessary? I'll, of course, abide by your advice on this. I suppose I worry. Too much? I suppose I feel that $12,500 is a large appraisal for a mess of old papers the cat has slept on, cheap skate that I am. But I am no match for mathematicians, and if investigated, would probably say anything and end up in jail.

As for "smarming, buttering-up, old," et cetera, I believe I also noted in my letter that such was YOUR phraseology, and that personally I liked Dr. Roberts. So sucks to you.

Best to Bettie. We have snow and below zero temperatures, and all goes as merry as a marriage bell.

Affectionately, *Ruth*

TO DR. F. W. ROBERTS

January 25, 1965

Dear Dr. Roberts:

If Thayer Hobson is building fires under you, I, as a fellow sufferer of many years standing, send sympathy. Actually, I suppose I should have written you, but have seen no real reason to press matters until recently. (I also avoid writing letters if I can- they have always seemed to me a fretful way to communicate)

But now I suppose I must get under way somehow in the matter (1) because of the exigency of putting together 1964 tax material for Uncle and (2) Boston University seems very much to want these same manuscripts and papers for their new library, and I have to send some kind of answer. I have written Thayer about this and he will doubtless really burst into flames, I warn you.

I am beginning to feel wonderfully like an archive.

Thanking you again, I am

Sincerely *Ruth Moore*

TO THAYER HOBSON

January 29, 1965

Dear Thayer,

So after 25 years of slanging matches, I should misunderstand you. Such a smarming, buttering-up performance I have NEVER seen in my life! I AM patient, I, too, am having a ball and only if you are sick do you get calves' foot jelly.

I realize that I must misled McGettigan and will let him know. I suppose I thought that we were going to donate the opuses to Texas—knowing that, without doubt, you'll eventually get around Dr. Roberts—and that if we did, then they got the mss. in 1964. Go ahead. Call me "stupid."

Enclosed is a copy of letter to Gotlieb, written as practically dictated. If I know Boston, that word "appraisal" will scare them into the next thicket.

I'm delighted to see pictures of the Appaloosas. I have to admit they are beautiful beyond the dreams of man and I take back that ill-considered word "emulsified." Eleanor says don't you want to hire a hand—she will shovel stables and consider it a privilege. WE only feed the overflow tame rabbits from Wildwood Park (the roadside zoo up the road), a flock of 300 grosbeaks, 20 chickadees, 100 juncos, three cows and a seagull.

Who was really fascinated, though, was our old friend, Oz Tolman, who dropped by yesterday. Oz is ninety, an old Maine race track man, whose Bible is what he calls his "hoss magazine". His first comment was, "Them hosses has got Arabian in 'em," and then he said that Flint McCulloch who used to be on "Wagon Train" always rode one, and that there's a lady here in Maine who raises them. He then went over the photographs one by one, pointing out withers and hocks, et cetera,—said that one, I'm not sure which, had "blocky withers" and he wouldn't care for him; but when he got to Texas Blue Norther he fell truly in love, you could see; remarked that that was about the best horse he ever saw in his life, that was a dandy. Didn't read the text, either, because he didn't have on his reading glasses. When we pointed out that this was the No. 1 Champion, he said he certainly wasn't surprised to hear it.

Affectionately, *Ruth*

TO HOWARD B. GOTLIEB

January 29, 1965

Dear Dr. Gotlieb:

May I thank you for your letter of Jaunary 15 with regard to my manuscripts and papers, which makes me feel wonderfully like an archive and gives me great pleasure.

I have for some time planned to donate my material to some university library, and last fall, with that in mind, I placed the matter in the hands of Mr. Thayer Hobson, my publisher. He now has much more information than I have as to what is being done—I do know that he has been discussing the matter with another university, but do not think anything has been concluded, as he has so far been dissatisfied with the appraisal which has been made.

For details, would you get in touch with him? His address, at present, is Deer Ledge Ranch, Comfort, Texas.

Thanking you again for your pleasant letter, I am,

Sincerely Yours, *RUTH MOORE*

It was decided by all parties finally that Ruth's papers would go to the University of Texas. Who the "Author in Residence" was is anyone's conjecture (Katherine Anne Porter, perhaps, whose big novel *Ship of Fools* was published in the early sixties). Frank Sullivan, author of *A Rock in Every Snowball,* was the famous American humorist who used to compose the annual Christmas poem in *The New Yorker;* Ruth called Thayer Hobson "Frank Sullivan" in jest.

TO THAYER HOBSON

February 28, 1965

Dear Thayer,

OK, with cream. I don't ask for better, and anyway, if Uncle is jumpy in these matters, I'm more than satisfied. Maybe we didn't win, Ma, but it was a darn good try, and many types of thanks are due. As a matter of fact, I'm not sure we didn't come off with a few laurels, you know; enough, anyway, to inflate my ego, if not yours. I once saw the Author in Residence sweep into Grand Central Station with attendant royalty and it was a glorious sight in mink, or maybe sable, I wouldn't know. Don't kid yourself, she'll have a bigger tomb than I will. Bet you she does, with a telephone. (This is catty.)

If you've had fun, I have, too; among other things, it's been a delight to swap correspondence on a literary project again; a pleasure which I won't say I haven't missed since you vanished into the sagebrush. The *vin du pays* here is Old Hickory; if you and Dr. Roberts can stand being drunk to in it, I will root out that old half-empty decanter as soon as I hear the operation is closed. (At least, I say "half-empty" and not "half-full".)

So far as reputation-status, I believe it is now-is concerned, you know perfectly well I've written the same old book ten times and have coasted along on it gloriously (and financially) for twenty-eight years. I should at least have done a book on the Bible or something personal about my ancestors to sweeten the literary pot, and if I haven't, it's because I've been having too much fun doing what I'm doing. I'm a darned good professional, but that's no real reason for anyone's offering me thousands for the cat's bed—which he didn't even sleep on all the time, only when he wanted a change. (He misses it.) He's old, poor lamb, and hates change, too.

Today, on the last day of February, the ice in the inlets is breaking up and great floes of it are coming down the bay. In sunlight, it's a lovely sight to see and maybe means early spring break-up. I would be happier if I didn't have to review Herman Wouk's new book, *Don't Stop the Carnival,* which I said I would do before I read it. It is another regional book about Madison Avenue and The Great Dream of retiring to a tropical island forever, which doesn't work out; and a sad book because of the spectacle of a most competent writer trying very hard to be interested in his characters and showing it all over the drip-dry.

So: the front of my hand to you, Frank Sullivan, and love to the horses.

Affectionately, *Ruth*

TO PAUL K. MCGETTIGAN

March 16, 1965

Dear Mr. McGettigan:

Thanks for your letter of March 11.

Checking back my correspondence with you, I find I did tell you that "I had donated my mss. and papers to Texas"; but Thayer tells me that this was not so, at the time, that there WERE strings attached, and that there's no obligation to take this deduction in 1964 tax. As a matter of fact, he has been in contact with Boston University, which wanted the papers, SINCE I sent them to Texas for appraisal; and had B.U.'s appraisal exceeded that of Texas, we would have sent them to Boston. On his advice, I decided to let Texas have them; but the final decision was made in 1965. So my feeling is that we had better make the first deduction on '65 tax. Isn't this right? Maybe we could pre-date a letter as Dr. Roberts suggests, and get away with it, but I'd rather not.

Since Thayer tells me in accents dire not to sign anything "without first checking with McGettigan," I am enclosing my letter to Dr. Roberts, which states, finally, that Texas can have the bloody things, under date of March 16, 1965. If this is the proper way to do, will you mail the letter on to Dr. Roberts? As you may guess, by this time, I am good and well sick of the transaction, which has been going on since last June; except it has been fun being in correspondence with Thayer again since he vanished into the sagebrush. I do have to say that I feel he thinks more highly of my literary reputation than I possibly can.

Under the circumstances, shall we go ahead with the same type of tax return we made last year? As soon as I hear from you, I'll send along the figures.

I shall be 62, God help me, the 21st of July, this year. Isn't 62 the age for Social Security for females? Should I do anything about that, or let Uncle keep the money? He apparently needs it the way he goes on with rockets.

Thanking you again, I am,

Sincerely, *Ruth Moore*

Annie Laurie Williams was Ruth's motion picture agent in New York in 1965 and she had written Ruth that James Gregory, an actor, was interested in Ruth's novel *Second Growth* as a possible property for a movie. Maurice was Maurice Crain, a New York literary agent who was Annie Laurie Williams' husband.

TO ANNIE LAURIE WILLIAMS

March 25, 1965

Dear Annie Laurie,

Thanks for your letter of March 18 re Mr. James Gregory. His name did seem in a way familiar, but I've been out of touch so long with what goes on in the Theater, I might not even remember Eva Le Gallienne, or like of what. Shame on me, for knowing more now about chickadees and grosbeaks! It would really be nice, wouldn't it, if something came of Mr. Gregory.

It tickles me, in a way, that I have had more fan letters about *Sea Flower* than any of the books I've ever written. With the others, I busted a gusset and got in all kinds of SIGNIFICANCE, but *Sea Flower* was written off the top of my head, easily, and I had great fun with it. It's gone into a second printing, too, which is encouraging, John writes me. Well, you never know. But I do think that this field of professional writing is about as exciting as any—with the possibility of yours, I might say.

We are fine and busy as bees. No use, I suppose, to wonder if you and Maurice will get to Maine on a trip. I honestly don't know when we'll get to New York again. Not this spring, I expect, maybe next fall.

Best to you both,

Affectionately, *Ruth*

TO JOHN C. WILLEY

April 2, 1965

Dear John,

Can I have a thousand dollars for Uncle? Soon, if convenient, as the 15th approaches and Mr. McGettigan and I have been nipping it fine. Though we aren't either of us to blame; we've been waiting for the U. of Texas and Thayer to utter final benediction to the Gift. It has finally been bestowed, as of 1965, so as usual I've no deductions to speak of, can't even claim depreciation on myself.

We seem to be up over March hill and the days are glorious, but cold. Our rabbits, coons and skunks have come through the winter flying; all fat, from the bird seed. We now have an animal show each evening-tell Fern. Six coons, four rabbits, two skunks, all amiable feeding together; though I will say the skunks don't like cats. One of them let go on our long-haired black and white female the other night, thereby causing great difficulty and excursions. For tomato juice.

How do things go? It would seem from this end, well; I'm puzzled by the number of fan letters about *Sea Flower;* usually I get some, but this is more than usual, I think, though probably not enough to stop the world for. Anyway, I'm pleased.

Best from us both to you and Fern,

Affectionately, Ruth

Mason Trowbridge was a doctor in Ellsworth, Maine, during the 1950s and '60s. Britt's was a department store in the then-new Ellsworth Shopping Center on High Street. It's now the IGA store.

TO MASON TROWBRIDGE

January 4, 1966

Dear Mason,

I am not beginning this letter "Dear Dr. Iactogenic," according to my impulse, because while sometimes you have a terrific sense of humor, at other times you do not; though I understand from your own words that when you do not it is to raise (or lower, as the case may be) the patient's blood pressure. This makes me feel that I am entitled to be as fresh as I like. With reservations.

This letter is to ask advice and to eat some crow.

Eleanor and I both have new glasses; we are in a bind with them. We are not calling any names and however boiling mad we are, we are interested now only in what to do about our eyesight.

This is the case history.

We went to an ophthalmologist. We were one month and one-half getting an appointment with him. We waited in his office an hour and a half before we could see him; whereupon he gave us from half an hour to forty minutes of HIS time. When the glasses arrived, he handed them to us without checking as to whether or not they fitted. His office girl collected, one-half on the day we were examined, and the other half on the day we got the glasses, a total of $126. We found we were not permitted to leave the office with the glasses until we paid in full. Eleanor found her close-up vision was slightly better; her distance vision was sadly impaired. I found that (1) overhead lights made me dizzy; I nearly passed out in Britt's. All I could think of was O God, to die like this in Britt's. (2) Everything on my right was distorted: objects on my right were eight inches higher than on my left; the kitchen sink ran all its water uphill, the typewriter keyboard was tilted, the piano keyboard rose in a great surge to the right, giving me a tremendous forte in the treble. A thing like a book, for example, on my right, was an oblong instead of a rectangle and two inches shorter than I know it was. Also, I was all but blind in my right eye.

We called the doctor. He said all this was normal. He told me I just had to get used to trifocals and seemed put out when I told him-as I already had-that I had already worn trifocals for ten years. He said, just wear the glasses. So we did. At the end of ten days, approximately, I called again and said some of the distortion had straightened out, but I still couldn't see out of my right eye. He said, it was very strange. He had said that he would see me before he went away on a short New Year's recess, but it seems he could not. Just wear the glasses, he said. I wore them for three weeks, with no more change. During that time, I haven't dared to drive a car because of the distortion on the right. I have tried to call his office. Apparently it is closed. We have both, out of necessity, had to go back to our old glasses. With my old glasses, my right eye sees perfectly, as it did in the beginning.

We don't actually know what to do about this. My wish is to send the glasses back and ask for my money. We know what would happen if I did this; or what would be likely to happen. We would doubtless get no where. We hate to lose all this. On the other hand, if we do go back, what will happen to our eyesight? We need it. I believe, at this point, we're ready to ask for, and to take, some top-notch medical advice.

I hope you will understand that the reason we didn't go to Bangor in the first place was because it's too damn long a trip to keep running on; and after all, we do have this terrific medical complex nearer home ... All right. The same to you.

It was pleasant to get yours and Mrs. T's Christmas news letter, and I congratulate you on those tremendous children. The Letter also contained some deathless words, which I now quote:

"When I have taken all the crap I can take ..."

Sincerely *Ruth Moore*

Dr. Osler is Dr. Jay Osler, an ophthalmologist from Bangor, who summered for many years, and now lives year-round, on Hancock Point.

TO MASON TROWBRIDGE

January 14, 1966

Dear Mason,

It seems a mistake was indeed made.

Somebody wrote 100 when he should have written 10 on the prescription, so that the lens was in kitty-cornered or upside down; if I could have worn the glasses perpendicular, pinned, probably by a thumbtack to my right eyebrow, I would have had right-side vision. If I could have known this a month ago, I would have bought a thumbtack.

We are both deeply grateful to you and Dr. Osler, who has the matter in hand and says everything can be fixed up without anybody's losing any face. My bad temper having been ground down to 10 instead of 100, I'll probably go back to the source, as Dr. Osler recommends. I might even wish the guy a Merry Christmas.

In other words, thanks a million. I can't tell you the load that's been lifted off both our minds.

Sincerely, Ruth

P.S. Eleanor says, "Don't we have fun—in a noisy way?"

Emily Louise Trask is Ruth's niece and in 1966 she was a music major at Bard College. "Mods" referred to moderation. At the end of the sophomore year, all students had to go through a testing process in a major field in order to pass to the "Upper College." Those who failed were not allowed to continue at Bard.

TO EMILY LOUISE TRASK

June 10, 1966

Dear Emmy,

Congratulations, a million. I myself hadn't any doubt about your passing your mods, but I could see from your letter that you had, and why I have waited a while before answering is because I had a notion that after you'd passed, your feelings would change some. Haven't they? Anyway, you done good, dear, and I don't believe you need too much advice from me now. However, you asked for some, and I'll do the best I can with what I have, operating always on the premise that older people who give advice to the young are almost always prigs. Even when the advice is offered with love and with respect for the minds and abilities of the young. As mine is.

You have, I've always found, an innate ability to rise to occasions, a thing which not too many people have, or if they do have it, they aren't able to use it very well. Which I think you can. Know you can, as a matter of fact. Your trouble, of course, is worry, inherited from a family of worriers with palm. Your father, my father—all of us, Lord God, worry like fools, losing sight of the fairly self-evident fact that when the dreaded thing happens, or doesn't happen, as the case may be, it's never so bad as the anticipation of it. In the meantime, good energy's been used up, which might better be used for almost anything but gibbering with worry. However, I guess this can't be helped, with us, anyway. To be able to meet whatever it is when it comes is the thing, and to meet it head on, which I have seen you do quite a number of times.

About your trip to France, I think you should go. (1) Because going on a journey is like exploding a firecracker in the brain, changes attitudes, often wipes out formless fears and somehow, perhaps by breaking up a boring routine, shines up a lot of edges that need honing. Travel makes your soul turn green again; it's like a kind of springtime after winter. (2) I think that going abroad is worth a year's education in school to any young person, or any person at all; because it seems to me that education is becoming a citizen of the world, not just a citizen of a college or a town. So far as the money goes, you will have to budget; and it won't hurt you at all, my good lass, to learn to budget. Now will it? I don't think you should feel that going to France to study, even for a short time, is the action of a "crazy kid having one last fling." The last thing you are, it seems to me, is a crazy kid, only at times an insecure one, so don't insult your excellent courage by feeling like a failure. You can behave, and have, in your time, behaved like a flibbertigibbet, but, hell, who hasn't? I once spent my last ten dollars, jobless in New York, for a mess of dahlia bulbs sent home to your mother and Nanny. But that was in another country, and besides the wench is dead. Or is she? Anyway, this trip to France is not foolish.

If you came home, after all these sparkling plans, there's no doubt you would be stricken dead with boredom after a week. Not that we don't want you, we do. We miss you. This I don't need to say, but I'm a saying it all the same.

About changing your major, this, of course, is up to you. You know better than anyone else what you want to do. Music is very tough and takes unlimited time; considered seriously, it tales almost more time than almost anyone has or is willing to give. Writing is much the same way; it took me twenty years to learn to write even a passable book and I still have a long way to go. However, after farting around half my life at business and editorial jobs in New York, I found out the one thing I could do and do halfway well. You will, of course eventually want to marry; and what will become of any creative work you do will depend on the attitude of your husband. If he feels that music—which will take a great deal of time and attention away from him (if you do it well) detracts from your marriage; if he isn't interested in it and thinks, as many do, that all creative work, any work of the mind, stinks, then the jig's up. You might as well stop now. On the other hand, music, I think, is what you do best. You are a long way from scratch with it; but with languages, you will have a longer way to go, starting from a lesser beginning. You mustn't think that a summer in France is going to teach you to speak French fluently; it takes longer. Even with good brains like yours and an aptitude for linguistics. Have you got one, incidentally, or does tongue twisting come hard?

This is a question you'll have to decide for yourself, lamb. Nobody can advise you about your career. No one will think less of you if you marry and give it up for a happy husband and children, which is what many do. The ideal, of course, is to have both. Perhaps you can.

I have the feeling that I've written you a very dull letter. But advice is always so. I always feel like a hen pregnant with a turkey egg, when any of you ask me what to do, partly I suppose because we're a whole damn generation apart. And anyway, affection and faith in you darn little gobbets of protoplasm is worth more than a lot of this-is-what-I'd-do-if-I-were-yous.

So, shed your jitters, old gal. If you go, go with the conviction that it's an invaluable addition to your education, an essential part of it, and not to be traded for a year in a classroom. Having a good time is nothing to feel guilty about.

All my love and bon voyage, Up

John T. McClintock was Ruth's stockbroker with whom she had corresponded in 1962 about her stock certificates in American Gas and Electric and Socony Vacuum, which had changed their names to American Electric Power and Socony Mobil, respectively.

TO JOHN T. MCCLINTOCK

August 16, 1966

Dear Mr. McClintock,

(Please note that my address had been changed from "McKinley" to the above, "Bass Harbor". The name of our town's post office has been readjusted to attract tourists, none of whom, of course, recall the poor sad old slaughtered Republican president. For the present, however, it is perhaps wise to include the name "McKinley", since it seems to be taking the Post Office Department a little while to realize.)

Since our last correspondence was in March, 1962, perhaps you will want to refer to it.

Mobil Oil, as you of course know, recently split their stock two for one, so that I now hold 1020 shares. I would like to transfer one half of these shares (510) to my heir, Eleanor Mayo. Can you handle the transaction for me? I have no idea what the procedure might be. As soon as I hear from you, I'll send along whatever is required-the stock certificate, I suppose, and whatever the company needs to make the transfer.

Thanking you, I am,

Sincerely, *Ruth Moore*

TO MRS. RUTH GREENLAW STODDARD

June 20, 1967

Dear Mrs. Stoddard,

Thank you for your pleasant letter.

I sorry I can't read your novel. It's partly a matter of time—there's only so much available before my deadline in the fall and I'm working all out to meet it; partly because I'm a writer, not a critic; and mostly because it's a waste of time for one writer to try to criticize another writer's work. Perhaps what you need is good professional advice; perhaps you don't. I can't give it, critically; but I can put you in touch with people who can. A New York literary agent is your best bet: one of those will go all out to market your book if it is marketable, and there's certainly a market for good novels, particularly good ones about Maine, right now.

Maurice Crain, 18 East 41st Street, New York, 10017, is an excellent agent, whose business it is to market manuscripts. He may charge you a fee for reading if he doesn't think he can sell your work; how much, I don't know, but if you write him, you could ask.

So, good luck.

Sincerely yours, *Ruth Moore*

TO JOHN C. WILLEY

March 5, 1968

Dear John,

I've recovered, hope you have, and how was Florida? We are still cold as a dog, and by the way, can I order 10 copies of *Cold as a Dog?* I'm all out. So, perhaps, are you, I can't remember. There are some other books I'd like, a copy of *Winter Beach,* one of *Gabriel Hounds,* and oddly enough, *Price Guide to American Cut Glass.* Is this okay? I always feel like a bum, but you say not to. If this privilege extends to the new Morris West, that would be nice, too.

We had a zinger of a town meeting. As an old town meeting buff, you'll realize what happened when the selectmen insisted on appointing the town manager town clerk. To most, this was creeping fascism, though not called by that name. The citizens went ahead, on the premise that the town had been electing a town clerk for 100 years and expected to go on doing so. The last we knew, the town manager and the selectmen were taking the matter to court. It has caused a hassle—you have to be careful whom you speak to, if you want a nice answer back. It will blow over.

I feel wonderful, free as air (can't even type, as you see); all this lovely time to spend for a while, not working on anything except the woodpile. This, of course, is always the best time—the ms. is out of my hands, the publisher says he likes it, and no reviews out yet to clobber the glory. That, I expect, will come, it always does, and he who expects nothing shall not be disappointed. I have been at this a long time. And don't grow thinner because of it, I must say.

Love to Fern, and I suppose you and she won't be up at all now that I can't drag the carrot in front of your noses.

Aff, *Ruth*

Martin Levin reviewed a number of Ruth's books for *The New York Times.* On January 3, 1965, for instance, he wrote of *The Sea Flower:* "The odyssey of these two innocents beset by hostile natives, homosexual police officers, the cruel sea and sundry devilment will enthrall anyone who is enthrallable." His review of *The Gold and Silver Hooks* on February 9, 1969 concluded: "Most of this Down East Lynne takes place on the rugged New England coast Miss Moore knows so well—but the motivation of her characters, especially the males, is thinner than the salty air they breathe."

With such comments about her work, it's easy to see why Ruth would be both sad and mad.

TO JOHN C. WILLEY

1968? 1969? (no date)

Dear John,

This will confirm the word I left on Friday at your office, re. Annie Laurie Williams. (Forgot it was Friday and that you might not be in.)

She phoned me early in the week—wants a copy of the new ms. I can let her have my extra copy if this is all right with Morrow. Word has apparently got around. At any rate, it has got to Martin Levin as see the enclosed, which, if it is merely coincidence, is surely a dandy, and makes me not only very mad but very sad. I'm afraid "the significance of the last remark" certainly doesn't escape me.

However, things get into the air sometimes and the public domain is the public domain.

Shall I send Annie Laurie my copy, or do you have Xerox?

Yours, in considerable pain, *Ruth*

TO ROBERT S. CONNOR

May 2, 1968

Dear Mr. Connor,

Thank you for your informative and helpful letter with regard to my application for benefits under social security. I have been getting records together, but would like to talk to you or to your representative before completing the application. Could you let me know when said representative comes to Bar Harbor? It would be convienent for me to see him there if possible; otherwise, I'll call on you at the Federal Building at your convenience.

My difficulties in filling out the application are not great; but I'm a writer, not yet retired, my income being mostly from royalties on books written over a period of some twenty years, and it is hard to estimate just when I am at work earning, and when I am not. For example, I have just finished a book and now will have to rest for a year or so before undertaking another ... if I ever do, for that is a question also. For another thing, my book was finished in January, this year, and I signed a contract for it in February, receiving a royalty (advance) of $2000. I'm not sure how to enter this on the application, since it's part payment for nearly three year's work, previous to 1968—or is it? So I expect an application.

Thanking you again, I am,

Sincerely yours, *Ruth Moore*

TO JOHN C. WILLEY

August 16, 1968

Dear John,

Herewith the corrected galleys, Air Mail because I've taken longer than I should to read them. Mostly because of all that broken type, which always puts me out because it's not my doing. But then, probably the printers have had a long, hot summer. (See Gals, 45 and 46 for sample.)

All in all, I think it goes quite well. I'm glad to have had all this time to get a perspective; it helps. The first part in spots I now see is inclined to be pedestrian, but it picks up when Jos gets clobbered. If readers can get that far.

I haven't made any changes to speak of, except a couple that I'd like your advice on.

(1) Re. the spots for Parts Four and Five. Part Four, I think now, ought to begin on Gal. 95 as indicated and be titled JULIE.

Part Five, on Gal. 113, titled ABIGAIL.

I have also indicated some spots where I think space markers should go in, because the quick transition is a little confusing without them.

(2) On Gal. 125, last para. and Gal. 126, first two lines.

Transition here seems quick and awkward. I would like this to read as follows:

What is a good man? Larry Cartwright asked the tall slate stone. You could read A GOOD MAN IS and that was all. Heaped-up, fallen leaves hid all but the first four words of the final inscription. What was a good man in the days when John Constant Randall's stone was cut? (I haven't made the change on the galley, pending your opinion.)

I wish, in a way, we could have brought this book out before the national elections; I hopefully timed it that way, but of course you have your problems, too. Not that it would have made all that difference except to me, trying to put in my two cents. You always (1) feel that your own personal Word of God is going to (1) change, (2) benefit the scene, or at least jog some consciences in time; but, shoot it never does and I ought to know that by this time. I never seem to learn anything, do I? Someday I am going to destroy my image by sending you a flock of poems—serious ones, not flapdoodle; I've always threatened to, you know, and you can squawk all you like and Longmans can throw a wingding; but you DID print Thomas Hornsby Ferril and I'm quite good, honestly.

(Of course, if you don't want any such foolishness, that's all right, too, probably better in the long run.)

I've been frivoling since I got the book done, collecting old bottles from old dumps, getting stung by hornets while digging up history. To our astonishment, Eleanor and I have now resurrected a collection of antique glass containers of one kind or another, which according to dealers' catalogs, is worth quite a sum; turns out there's a tremendous hobby-kick in the country at large for old bottles, particularly bitters bottles. If your relatives in Cherryfield have any ancient dumps, we will gladly dig them and make a mess on the premises.

How are you both? We were disappointed that you and Fern didn't get up. Perhaps sometime. So welcome, when.

I have had a royal time with the Dept. of Health and Welfare who jogged my memory last June (or was it May?) about applying for Social Security and Medicare—seemed they had had a paternal eye on me for years and couldn't wait until they heard. So I applied. Then we ran into sad times over my 1966 Income Tax—seems the records showed I hadn't paid the last installment. Well, I had—I had the cancelled check. So they wanted to see all my checks for 1966. So I had them all photocopied, back and front, sent them along. This they said, wouldn't do. They had to have the original checks. Nossir! s'I. If some dope in the Collector's office has made a mistake and failed to enter that last check on my record and ther'es to be the Man coming around, I want those checks right here under my blotter to show him. So I called up Albert Cunningham—he's the Pres. of the Bar Harbor Banking and Trust, and asked him to certify all five 1966 checks from his ledgers. Which he did. Albert was in high school with me so there was no problem; anyway he had the records. I sent his letter off to the Dept. of H and W, and heard nothing for weeks. So I wrote and said, Do I go on paying Blue Cross and Blue Shield or have I got Medicare? And got a printed notice back saying that "necessary development re. your 1966 Self Employment Income was forwarded to San Francisco Payment Center on 7/9/68." And please to let them know if I haven't received first payment by Aug. 23.

So here I sit on Butternut Hill. With the mails the way they are, I'll be lucky if I hear from San Francisco before 7/9/69.

Nice about the Norwegian sale of *Sea Flower*, and we can always sell the bottles.

Give my love to Fern. Tell her, just in case, not to let you come to Maine until after Labor Day. We are crawling with tourists, the worst year we've ever had. My God, they're coming through the floor.

Aff. *Ruth*

On November 8, 1968, Annie Laurie Williams wrote Ruth about the possibility of yet another movie deal, this time for *The Gold and Silver Hooks,* in which Saul Cohen, the Eastern Story Editor for Walt Disney Studios, was initially interested. Mr. Cohen later wrote back to Miss Williams: "*The Gold and Silver Hooks* was an excellent book. It reminded us of *Giant* in its theme, scope, and treatment. However, for Disney purposes, the time span and the involvement of the characters in Prohibition and Depression activities mitigates against our considering it as a possibility for a Disney film. This was a fine book, and a marvelous read. Many thanks for letting me see it."

Despite the Disney rejection, Miss Williams told Ruth she'd be sending the galley proofs of *The Gold and Silver Hooks* around to other motion picture producers.

TO ANNIE LAURIE WILLIAMS

December 2, 1968

Dear Annie Laurie,

Thanks for your letter of November 8, which I should have answered before, if I hadn't been galavanting around, having what's known in these parts as a vacation. It's always an occasion for rejoicing when a letter comes from you. We don't get down to New York much these days, perhaps I would be more truthful if I said we don't get down at all; but if and when we do, we'll be by, and hope for a dinner date with you and Maurice.

I don't think, myself, that *The Gold and Silver Hooks* is really a movie unless it could be slaughtered to make a Hollywood holiday, the way *Spoonhandle* was; but one thing I do know, that if it's saleable at all, you will sell it. I'm glad you like it; it's one I've always wanted to write about the integrity which many people nowadays cannot afford, and now it's off my chest, I'm glad it is. The conclusion it forced itself to come to isn't pleasant to face; but there it is, the fight and the logical ending.

I hope you and Maurice and all are well and prosperous, and that we shall see you someday. Perhaps you, too, would like to see the Never-never land which most people seem to feel Maine is, and which, except for the scenery, my new book belies, but you can't write too many books about the stomach rising and falling with the tide because of too many clams; now, can you?

We are well and chirky; have been, for some time past, both of us learning to play the piano. I'm terrible; have rhythm trouble; can't count.

Nonetheless, I am having a lovely time with it, playing only for myself; and the piano is known in this household as "Miss Chickering, Mr. Darling."

All our best wishes

Affectionately *Ruth*

Chenoweth Hall, Ruth's friend, is the author of a Maine novel *The Crow on the Spruce* published in 1946, the same year as *Spoonhandle*. Chenoweth, however, is best-known for her painting and sculpture. For many years she has lived in Prospect Harbor with her friend Miriam Colwell, the novelist, and author of *Wind Off the Water,* published in 1945. Chenoweth is also a musician. Eleanor Mayo, too, had published her second novel, *Loom of the Land,* in 1946. Harold Davis was H. L. Davis, popular author, also published by Morrow, of *Honey in the Horn, Beulah Land,* and other books. Mr. Zanuck, of course, was Darryl Zanuck, the legendary head of 20th Century Fox, the movie studio that filmed *Deep Waters* based on Ruth's novel *Spoonhandle,* in 1948. Emmy is Ruth's niece, Emily Trask Eaton, a musician; and "The Hang-Downs" is one of Ruth's poems published in *The Tired Apple Tree*. Charlie Riggs was a good friend of John and Fern Willey. Ruth called John Willey "Frank Sullivan," too, presumably for the same reason she called Thayer Hobson that.

TO JOHN C. WILLEY

December 2, 1968

Dear John,

I've had a letter with regard to musical settings for *Cold as a Dog*, copy of which I enclose together with copy of my reply. The settings mentioned were done some years ago by a friend of mine, Chenoweth Hall, who's nervous about letting them go anywhere before they are copyrighted. The Lord knows what they're like, I myself don't, having heard only one of them played from a tape over the telephone shortly after *Cold as a Dog* was published. Composers are funny. Just in case, how DO you get music copyrighted? I've no notion, and neither does she. Anyway, what do you think I should do?

Incidentally, regarding copyright, Eleanor wanted me to ask you how one renews copyright—would her various publishers do it now, automatically, or would she have to take steps herself about her books? I ought to know more about the copyright law, and perhaps would if I hadn't been rotten spoiled by Wm. Morrow, who does this automatically for me—right? I think Thayer told me once that this was what happened. When DOES a book go into the public domain—how long after publication?

I haven't thanked you for the books, which I do now. *Galapagos* is wonderful. You don't know that amazing story about Dr. Frederick Ritter and Dore Strauch, and the Baroness Eloise Bosquet von Wagner and her lovers? On Floreana Island? My, what a tale that was in the '30's! It's all in a book called *Satan Came to Eden* by Dore Strauch, as told to somebody, and in old copies of *Liberty Mag.* and the newspapers of the period. What material for a novel, oh boy! I must say, I've often thought about it, but never could discover how quite to disguise the plot well enough. Ritter, of course, is dead, as is the Baroness and two at least of her numberless boy friends. Dore, though, is probably still living, in Germany. The Lord knows. And, of course, I couldn't do Galapagos, never having been there; but I do know lots of desolated and haunted islands.

So far the Soch' Security hasn't demanded its checks back, so I guess I'm afloat, so far as old age is concerned. I still haven't dared to spend any of them; my savings account for the first time in my life is quite fat.

Wonderful about the Harold Davis letters. I do so hope they turn out to be publishable. Both Eleanor and I, when we run out of reading, as we do in these benighted parts—benighted at the library after the summer people are gone—we dig up H. L. and reread him.

Annie Laurie Williams wrote me that Walt Disney Enterprises insisted on reading *Hooks* but weren't in the end interested, which didn't surprise me. After all, after my one experience with movies, I'm not terribly interested either, and besides, for all I know I'm blacklisted because of the unregenerate way I treated poor Mr. Zanuck in 1947. So the back of my hand to THEM, Frank Sullivan. If they never forget, as Annie Laurie once told me they didn't, well, hell, I don't either.

I am working on my fabulous bandersnatch, the book of poetry, which I still don't know as I am going to cram down your throat. (I have spells of being deeply embarrassed by it.) I say cram down your throat, because of an utterance by a connection of W. W. Norton who was summering here—I believe she was publicity for them, or something, who after trying with certain sweet blandishments to winkle me away from Morrow and not succeeding, said nastily that of course you HAD to publish *Cold as a Dog* or risk losing me to another publisher. I was mildly astonished at the idea, it never having entered my head, so I just said, "It's a tough world, isn't it?" and thought, Some do, Some do not. All the same, I may not send it to you, for other reasons, mostly because it may not be worth the paper it's typed on, which is for you to say, if I do not send it. Novels I turn out like a potato peeler. Writers, like composers, are funny. Or poets, perhaps.

I recall my twenties, when in a brash moment, I submitted a full ms. for a book of poems to Scribners, and got back all of it with a rejection slip and the reader's comment, inadvertently (I hope) enclosed with it. "THIS POET IS LIKE A YOUNG PUMPKIN IN THE FIELD, LIGHTLY TOUCHED WITH FROST." God damn it, at least she called me a poet.

I hope you and Fern had the best possible twenty-fifth in Portugal. Give my love to the old gal, and tell her that one of the highlights of my life, as she must know, was the night she and Emmy performed "The Hang-Downs" to the fascinated audience of you and Charley and I and Eleanor. It was a gasser.

Aff. *Ruth*

Dorothy Lobrano married Raymond C. Guth on August 31, 1963.

TO DOROTHY LOBRANO GUTH

December 13, 1968

Dear Dotty,

Hi. Holiday smoosh and all that. How are you?

The enclosed is a portrait of our tough cat, Tofy. (If you see Frances, you will know that I can be accused to writing both of you the same news; so, if you see Frances, hide this communication, please.) This cat is leather-lined. Last November, about three weeks ago, he got shot by some pinheaded pilgarlic who was wandering around the woods shooting anything that moved, apparently. He (Tofy, not the hunter, though I would have been glad to return his bullets likewise if I could have caught up with him) had five 12-guage double-ought buckshot holes in him; we thought he was a goner and rushed him to the vet, expecting to come home with a corpse; but the vet is a good one and Tofy tough. This is not his corpse; he is merely resting a while from climbing trees. We thought such stamina deserved commemoration.

We have had a plague of hunters-poachers, really, because Mount Desert Island is of course protected, out of limits, because of the National Park. Every November, everybody who lives in the woods is beleaguered in the house. I've been shot at in the vegetable garden and our nextdoor neighbor down the road nearly got shot at her own back door. Eleanor has dreamed up two solutions to this crazy situation; and it really is one. Somebody shot a dog riding in the front seat of a car with his owner, and a man who put a stuffed deer on his lawn, just for a joke, made $22. 50 selling the lead he took out of it at the end of the season. The vet told us that the shot cats, dogs, horses, ponies, cows and even pigs and goats he sees are a horror. Altogether, this season, eight hunters were shot dead and some 27 wounded. So, Eleanor says, set off a large acreage of Maine's waste land, put the hunters in there and let them hunt each other; or, arm all the animals with high powered rifles, thereby making the carnage a true sport.

Goodness, how I have carried on! You'll think I feel strongly about this.

We saw "Marat/Sade" on the TV the other night. It had a great build-up by the ETV gentleman who always tells you what you may expect; but who, having watched it, apparently was somewhat daunted. At the end he said, in a dazed way, "Well, that was a tough show to follow." I'm probably a barbarian from having lived in the wilderness for 23 years, but one thing I learned in Drama was that too much tragedy is funny; that two buckets of blood don't carry more of a wallop than one bucket of blood, particularly if the second bucket of blood has cake icing poured on it. (We still have a black and white TV.) Realistic and horrible, as the man said, but so might be the inside of an ox.

We bustle along about as usual. I am deep in a book, but have had to come out of it because all my grandnieces and nephews got worried I wouldn't for Christmas.

Winter's with us; nice. We miss you; I never get my galleys back without feeling a great sense of loss, though John is, of course, wonderful, and I love him dearly, he's a vice-president now and I don't dare slambang at him the way I used to at you. How about a nice letter, saying "I'm here"? And this reminds me of old George Kelly, who, at 90, was living off in the woods by himself and got snowbound in a bad storm and wasn't heard from for three weeks, until the selectmen of the town waded in through six feet of snow to check on him. There was his house, no tracks around the door, no smoke coming out of the chimney, no response to knocks and the door locked on the inside.

"I guess," the first selectman said, "that old George is a goner. We'd better break down the door."

"Well, now," the second said, "I know George pretty well. Let's just walk back into the trees a piece and then come back."

So they did, and sure enough, there was a note pinned to the door panel. "I AM IN HERE AND I AM ALL RIGHT. OR I WOULD BE IF YOU LAZY BASTARDS WOULD PLOW THE GODDAMNED ROAD."

So, okay, sweetie.

Love, *Ruth*

The following poem came with the above letter. Ruth had a habit at Christmas time, especially, of sending one of her poems with her cards. Pat is a reference to Pat Nixon.

It is a consolation that
The country at last is standing Pat.

All our troubles will soon be fixed
When everything is nicely Nixed.

Hickel
Schmickel.

Our Christmas here has been somewhat spastic,
The stores were full of good old plastic.

Plastic love seats and plastic spanners
Plastic beans and ditto bananners.

Plastic novels, nice and strong,
Like an old piece of tripe which has hung too long.

For heaven's sake, if they want to do it
Let 'em go and do it—why all the fuss?
Writing it down is a poor substitute,
And very revolting to all of us.

Trash
Schmash.

Well, we're not married, not so far,
But we've heard rumors, nasy pas?
So more and more and more and more
Is getting to be one hell of a bore.
Let 'em buy a bicycle, write a letter,
Or read Dostoievsky.
He did it better.
And if *War and Peace* turns out too sad, (Tolstoi)
The Wind in the Willows is not so bad,
Since Toady and Ratty and Moley and all
Were all boys together in old Toad Hall.

So what?
Schmut.

So little Willy in his pretty sash,
Prints unmitigated trash.
(Sorry to use trash twice, it's fated.
Indicated.
Cut for Mr. Beecroft.)
(As an old editor of mine used to say and—
sometimes—make it stick.)

So ring the bells out,
Happy or not.

It's enough that the goose is in the pot
And old acquaintance
Not
Forgot.

Ruth's sister Esther was with Helen Moore, their cousin, on a visit to England in 1969 when Ruth was working on her novel *"Lizzie" and Caroline*. Bud Trask is Esther's son and Jackie is his wife. Muriel is Esther's daughter and Mulligan was Muriel's dog. Jennie Grindle was a local woman from whom Ruth and Eleanor bought a manure pile for their garden. The manure pile had evidently been used as a dump, too, because they found all kinds of things in it when beginning the planting. Larry and Mary Lou are Eleanor's brother Larry Mayo and his wife. Tofy was Ruth's cat and Grammie and Mit were Orville Trask's mother Emily Trask and sister Millicent (nicknamed Mit) Hamblen. Spider Lewis was a local Tremont man.

TO ESTHER TRASK AND HELEN MOORE

Aug. 4, 1969

Dear Tug and Helen,

I meant to write before this, but all kinds of hideous contretemps to use up time turn up from day to day. Like people you know forty years ago and never liked much anyway turning up as nearest and dearest and visiting for six hours or so. By the time I have thought of something to say to them, I'm so weakened that I can't think of anything to say to my honest-to-God nearest and dearest and have to go to bed.

Well, "August, go she must."

This makes me out a witch, with either a "w" or a "b"; ;if someday I produce broom and fly off on it, you will know witch.

We had a fun sail on the Hannah with the kids and Mulligan. Mully was a real gentleman only objecting to boarding and leaving the boat, when he flinched. We went to the back side of Black Island for a picnic, then sailed out around B.I., through the Pasture and home. Bud put up the genoa jib for the last part of the sail and it was a beautiful sight, blue sky and white sails, like an old-time popular song. I think Bud does a tremendous job handling the boat. We all felt we should act as crew, but nobody but Jackie knew what to do so we all sat on our fat. They started out for Jonesport, I understand, but Muriel said a day or so ago they were fogbound in Northeast Harbor, and no jeasly wonder—we have had fog for days. Thick and wet—you know the kind. Wring out your clothes in the morning before you put them on, and the rug in front of the bed squelches.

If I had known Jennie Grindle's pigyard was so potent, I would not have bought so much of it. My garden is a jungle, squashes tangled up with beans, tomatoes with corn. I struggle to get this unprecedented harvest into the freezer, which is again plugged up with mackerel. We didn't intend to have so many this year, but Larry and Mary Lou came, complete with kids and son-in-law; they caught a plethora, put them in our freezer, because they wanted to get dry ice and take them back to Chicago, and then couldn't get any dry ice. As for Jennie Grindle's pigyard, I am about to have a lawn sale with all the lovelies I have found in it. Not only old bottles, but horse collars, dolls heads, stainless steel forks and many other priceless, but unidentifiable objects, including a poker chip. Personal possessions of the Grindles' Saturnalia up there on moonlight nights, during which they danced in the pigyard and threw things around.

The special town meeting, designed to conclude what to do with the $20,000 State subsidy, was held last Thursday. Approximately 25 people were there, fortunately a quorum. I might add, a quorum of all the soreheads. But for once all were unanimous; they voted to use the subsidy to abate this year's taxes. Don't get your hopes up, it won't be much. Arthur Silver was there, along with a gentleman named Sontis, I think it is—he's the one who bought the Ernest Joyce place in Goose Cove. They had the effrontery to SPEAK. I could see Lurlene start to twitchel and zero in; finally she got out the list of qualified voters and with this in hand, told these intruders that they were SUMMER PEOPLE. Arthur said, "Yes, we are, and this is something the town is going to have to face." A holy silence ensued. "Silence remained and everyone resum'd his Human Majesty. And many conversed on these things as they labour'd at the furrow … Labour well the Minute Particulars, attend to the Little-ones, And those who are in misery cannot remain so long, If we but do our duty …" William Blake

Eleanor got up and remarked peaceably that the meeting would be glad to hear what the non-residents had to say, but there was a State law; it would be a simple matter to recess the meeting temporarily to prevent its being disqualified, in case the non-residents wished to say more. The meeting was not disqualified, nor recessed.

Before the meeting, our household was waited upon by a synod of those who wanted to know what the right thing was, re. the subsidy; Eleanor was in the bath, washing off the day's discolorations, and our bathroom door, due to the dampness, won't close. I thought she did very well conducting a lecture through it, her words received* well except by Spider Lewis, who, I don't think, heard a word, being overcome and fascinated by the fact that the bathroom door wouldn't close.

Tofy, the little murderer, has taken to eating hummingbirds. He waits until they sit and then leaps crashing into the delphiniums. Seldom misses. I am not quite sure whether he's a cat or a devil.

I am toiling away; we both are. Nobody has any mental energy left; a senile sort of condition. I am on page 79, second draft; Eleanor is on page 138, first draft. We are spuck-eyed. Raspberries are ripe. Grammie and Mit went sailing with Bud and both wore their Sunday hats. Yesterday we declared a holiday and went to an auction in Blue Hill. It was a gasser. People paid untold sums for trash, especially if somebody else started bidding. A cracked sugarbowl, which we bid a dollar on, went to a dealer for four dollars. There was an 1890 living room set, in s-brindle plush, complete with love seat which somebody bought for $40. The people were—avid, I believe the word is, and faces showed it. E. took innumerable pictures. Your cats are fine, so far as I know. I wish I had more in my newsbag. (News, not cats.)

I have read your letter to Muriel, et. al. It sounds like a lovely time. Take care, have fun, hurry back, we miss you. E. sends love. I do too. Here it is:

LOVE, *Uppy*

* *"received," a hangover from the Town Report*

TO MRS. CRAWFORD D. PATON

October 12, 1969

Mrs. Crawford D. Paton President
The Killingworth Library
Killingworth, Conn. 06417

Dear Mrs. Paton,

My mother's "Clam Cake" had no clams in it—it was simply quite a nice spice cake made with sour milk or buttermilk, which my father dearly loved. He hated, however, to dig clams and seldom did, unless bribed with a "Clam" Cake. So whenever we had clam chowder, we also had:

VINA MOORE'S CLAM CAKE

1 cup sugar	1 teaspoon soda
1/2 cup butter	1 teaspoon cinnamon
1 cup sour or buttermilk	1 teaspoon cloves
2 cups flour	1 cup raisins or currents

Cream butter and sugar. Add sour milk. Sift soda and spices with flour and lastly add raisins, floured.

Sincerely *Ruth Moore*

1970s

TO JAY OSLER

June 23, 1970

Dear Dr. Osler,

Can you fill this State Vision Screening test out without seeing me? I can't detect any change at all since I saw you last. If it isn't legal, can I have an appointment? If possible, before July 21?

Thanking you,
Sincerely, *Ruth Moore*

TO JOHN C. WILLEY

March 23, 1971

Dear John,

I've got a problem with the Social Security Administration, which I'm sorry to have to bother you with, but I do need advice and information and perhaps your legal department can help.

I've been trying since 1968 to find out how to report royalties properly. Twice I've consulted the representatives of the Social Security people in Bangor who, apparently, haven't told me accurately what I should do, so I have been going along supposing that you should report on earnings from work done in a current year. No mention was made by them in either case of the fact that the copyright date of a book makes a difference, and of course the copyright date of *G. & S. Hooks* is 1969.

Now, I was careful about this. My 1969 report was made out for me by the S.S. Representative whom I consulted. I told him I had worked in 1969, but the work was scrapped; therefore in 1969 I hadn't any earnings. He rather browbeat me into letting him put down that I had worked for two months, over my protest that I hadn't received any pay for the work. I told him that my latest book was written in 1966 and '67, before I applied for Social Security, that it was submitted to the publisher in 1968 and published in February, 1969. He didn't inform me that the 1969 copyright date of the book was what counted, or that I should have reported 1969 royalties as earnings, and I went on supposing that since the work was done in '66 and '67 the income was as of those two years. He also insisted that I put down an estimated income for 1970. I said if I finished a book and the publisher accepted it and it was published in 1970, I couldn't possibly estimate royalties, but gave him a tentative figure of $4,000. But of course, any work I did in 1970 was also scrapped—no earnings from it.

Then I got a letter from the San Francisco office (my checks come from there, since I was living in Calif. when I began payments in '36) saying that they'd overpaid me $310.40 in 1969, so please pay it back. They also said I'd reported I would earn $4,000 in 1970, so they were withholding checks.!!!!

So, I wrote down the above, whatever was pertinent, including information about my delayed payment contract with Morrow, saying that undoubtedly royalties from my latest book were paid into my account in New York in 1969, but that the work was done in '66 and '67. I asked for a review of my "case," and sent copies of all the correspondence to the Bangor office, as well as the originals to San Francisco.

I heard nothing for months. I heard nothing from Bangor for nearly six months. I got a letter recently from San Francisco, saying they would review my case, but it would take time.

Then, on Saturday last, I got a letter from Bangor, asking if I would call them. I did so, on Monday. A lady there, Miss Tremble, said that income from books, no matter when written, should be reported as earnings in a current year. I asked, "As far back as 1942?" and she said "Yes." And she insisted on it.

Well, I might not know much, but I'd been all through that with the first representative I consulted in 1968, when I applied for benefits. He had had all the information at that time, including information about the $2,000 advance which I'd received in '68 when I signed the contract. I told him then that I didn't think I was entitled to any benefits in '68, because that was over the allowed $1,680, and he said my business expenses would bring it down to well under that limit. He didn't give me any information about copyright date, either. So far as I know, and have known, I've been reporting earnings properly.

So then I began rooting around in my file and found a little 1968 booklet which I hadn't referred to because I thought I had all the pertinent information, and there it was about royalties. Earnings on books copyrighted before I applied for Soc. Sec. weren't concerned, so she was wrong about that. But there was the item about the copyrights on books after I applied, which, for the Lord's sake, I hadn't had an inkling of.

I called the lady back and read her the whole passage; she said she would check and be in touch. A half hour later she phoned again and said she had read further now and realized that the past books weren't to be reported as current earnings; but when was the copyright on my latest book?

By that time I had been around the barn, around and around, so I told her that I would check the date and the amount of royalties paid on my latest book in 1969 and let her know, and please, could we get this straightened out?

Now. How do we disentangle the royalties? If Morrow paid me more than $1,680 for 1969, and also for 1970, I shall probably have to return 24 months' worth of Social Security payments, and it will be a blow. The above sums, of course, are on *G. & S. Hooks* only. I don't know enough about our delayed payment contract to know whether this can legally be worked out proportionately—part payment of back royalties, say, and part on the 1969 copyright book. If not, I will need to know exactly what the royalties on *G. & S. Hooks* were for 1969 and 1970, so that I can report them correctly.

And God help the mariner.

I'm sorry to trouble you with this long letter, but I do need help, of a legal sort. My work schedule has gone to grass and I'm slowly going crazy, mostly because even the experts do not seem too well informed. I wrote Mr. McGettigan (of Heston) last year, and this year I have written Mr. N. Jerry Palumberi, who has taken McGettigan's place there since he retired. (They are Lester Witte & Co., now). I haven't heard from Mr. Palumberi yet.

A wonderful time with you and Fern and Charley. Will write a real letter when I have a brain.

Affectionately, *Ruth*

In 1972, Morrow published both Ruth's second book of poetry *Time's Web* and the novel she was then working on, *"Lizzie" and Caroline*. "Lizzie" was the name of a boat.

TO JOHN C. WILLEY

April 12, 1971

Dear John,

I hope you and Fern had a marvelous vacation, that the laryngitis is gone with the sun. I thought I'd wait until I was sure your date of return was past before I wrote. Otherwise, I should have been on the telegraph or the telephone or the certified special delivery air mail, to say how wonderful it is that you like the poems well enough to publish them. They are a long-time thing with me, and it's going to be a fulfillment. The five per cent royalty on the first 2000 copies is all right with me. As to the arrangement, please suggest. I have copies of all the poems but not copies of how I arranged them. Because I wasn't quite sure that I'd have the courage to submit them to you, and then, when you all arrived, Fern and Charley, I had a drink and ker-whango! I shoved it at you.

The Social Security people in Bangor (represented still by Miss Helen Tremble) won't accept the arrangement as described in your letter. They say that if earnings from a book with a 1969 copyright were paid into my account with you in 1969, then these must be declared as earnings for that year, regardless of whether I received the money or not. So they demand to know the figures for 1969 and 1970. I'm not quite sure from my royalty slips which year the returns (of books) should go on. I judge I went in the hole on *G. & S. Hooks* for 1970 because of returns—right? I have every confidence that your "legal Eagle" can come up with the proper answer to the S.S. people's objection, but I guess I had better cooperate with them on the figures for 1969 & '70. They are getting quite shirty. F.B.I. next?

I'm sorry to have to bother you with this gloomy business, and wouldn't if I knew what else to do. You must be busy as a bird dog.

The new book goes merry as a marriage bell, and I've a large fat pile of ms. Incidentally, now with Xerox, do you need as many copies as of old? Last time I made the original and three carbons, and had two carbons left. So fi what's convenient?

I could go on with amenities about our snow being gone and crocuses out, and the damned old spring gravel pit on my right being activated again, so that all my work is done to a stink of diesel fumes, eleven-wheeled trucks cavorting by like spring lambkins and the roaring engine of the loader. However, I won't. You have too much to read as it is.

Best affection from us both to you and Fern and Chas.

Ruth

TO JOHN C. WILLEY

May 7, 1971

Dear John,

Well, after all, it's a contract for a book of poetry, and with poetry, the author naturally expects fifty per cent on the first 2000 and seventy-five if it sells a million. However, I'm delighted to sign this one; in a way (except for the first one), it's the most satisfactory and exciting one I ever signed.

Thanks for all the briefing on the Social Security matter. I am very mad with them. After all, I have been trying for two years to get information from them on how to report royalties properly; I called their attention to the 1969 contract, with attendant difficulties for myself (they hadn't known about this); so of all the cussed, shin-kicking, et cetera, who has tried to defraud the government?

I am warned, ominously, that all the correspondence and material has now been sent to San Francisco for scanning. Well, maybe to God somebody out there will read it. I don't think they do read anybody's letters. At least, mine, asking for information, never got any answers. I think it's an unjust law, sloppily administered; will result in an inert mass of able elderly people on Welfare who are penalized for doing their thing; and if ever any politician would set himself to reform the whole mess, he would receive for his earthly reward an accolade of votes—hell, he could be President. I think I'll write this to Muskie.

Did you know that if I so much as touch a typewriter for as little as 15 hours a month, and then scrap the work, not even submit it to a publisher, but burn it, I am performing "substantial services" in my business and cannot receive S.S. checks? I don't honestly believe this can be true, but I am informed by the Bangor office that it is. Well, I might as well stop sputtering. Bwaw! This year, my tax-payment to them was $265. Had I made coffins, I might have lived singing to four-score and ten. (Well, skip the ten.)

How are you and Fern? We (except for my temper at the moment) are fine. I ought to be out planting corn, but instead am swotting away on the final draft, which should be finished by June. When it's done, I'd be glad to get it at last out of the house, so do you want it then? In my present mood, I would like to title it:

LIFE, LIBERTY AND THE PURSUIT

Not that I shall. Definitely not, when I shall have heard your opinion on the matter.

Aff. *Ruth*

Throughout the summer of 1971, Ruth was busy finishing both her book of poetry *Time's Web* and her novel *"Lizzie" and Caroline*.

TO JOHN C. WILLEY

August 9, 1971

Dear John,

I hope you have gone on vacation.

I have been doing some brain-beating as you may have guessed. You are a great one for blowing the mind.

1. About the novel: It seemed to me, myself, that I was forever getting the Macomber under way. I can do something about this, and will. I have the carbon and can work from it. I haven't come up with a title, but hope and pray.

2. Re. the poems: I find your suggestions excellent and I agree, basically. Since the poems are, collectively, one concept of Time, and counting "Phebe Bunker" and "The Indian Shell Heap," cover its passing for a thousand years or so, I'd like to suggest the following:

A. For title and title page:

Time's Web

Look to see no end
And no beginning,
But Time, the immortal spider,
The orb-weaver
Forever spinning.

I would put "Phebe Bunker," undated, at the beginning, and "The Indian Shell Heap," undated, at the end. This closes the circle of the orb (I express this badly) and emphasizes what I think is the point of the book—the return of human events, not to begin, but to happen in the same fumbling way, all over again.

I'm unhappy about using The Mountain of Snow *and Other Poems,* for the title. First, not long ago, I recall reading in the *N.Y. Times* a review of a book of poems with a similar title—I've racked my brains trying to remember what it was. This can, of course, be checked. But it was near enough to make me wonder if I shouldn't abandon this title for the sonnets and find something else.

Second, these sonnets are from a very young pen; they're somewhat derivative (of Millay and David Morton).

Third, they were written in the early thirties, and if we use them, they belong there. With early poems, which they certainly are.

Fourth, to give their title to the title of the book, gives them an importance which they don't deserve and impairs the Time unity which you suggested.

Fifth, people who have seen them have liked them, and possibly people nowadays would, since the notion of true love seems to be creeping back into books. So I don't say don't use them. Just put them into perspective, back in the thirties where they belong. Nowadays, you either have to be Rod McKuen, or somebody unintelligible which nobody can read. So I don't know. I'll leave it to you.

3. I have made some minor changes here and there—nothing drastic, only tightening up where needed. See pp. 23 and 24 of "Phebe Bunker." I have removed "Inscription for an Atom Bomb," which is corny. I have also removed "On a Morning After a Death," which is too damn glum, and reminds me of something somebody, I think Charles Lamb, once said: "Put a sidesaddle on Pegasus and he heads for the Graveyard." The Lord knows, there's plenty of graveyard. As a matter of fact, I've thought of lightening things up by including a set of poems from the New York period, entitled "Songs and Sonnets to a German Bartender," which begins, "Put by, put by that little glass of gin."

I've replaced "On a Morning, etc." with a recent poem called "Tourist," which, if you don't care for, file in the wastebasket.

4. I've included a tentative index, which, except for the above suggested changes, follows your outline.

5. I'd like a dedication page: FOR ELEANOR MAYO

I think this covers everything. If not, let me know. Enclosed the contract (three copies) for the novel, signed and witnessed ....

Affectionately *Ruth*

TO JOHN C. WILLEY

August 12, 1971

Dear John,

How nice to hear from you in the middle of all these tourists. The poor devils have just gone through a tornado-watch. I MUST tell Eleanor to take that curse off the weather. We got everything else, why not a tornado?

I expect the enclosed would fit in dated 1938, due to the reference to Munich in No. V.

Gezundheit, *Ruth*

P.S. No, definitely not the South Seas. Look what happened to poor Gauguin. Leprosy.

Ruth is in reference below to the poem "Songs and Sonnets for a German Bartender—1938," which appears in *Time's Web*. Number 5, or Part 5, of the poem is entitled "Song for New Year's Eve." "Herman" is the German bartender from the poem, which comes just before "The Mountain of Snow" in the collection. Evidently, one of the titles being considered originally for the novel *"Lizzie" and Caroline* was *The Separate Struggles*.

TO JOHN C. WILLEY

August 28, 1971

Dear John,

Herewith, revisions for *The Separate Struggles*.

I have cut out the first hospital scene in Part III and the entire scene of young Ned Macomber and the Point Milton relatives. This cuts Part III by twelve pages and causes it to move much faster. Any essential exposition or whatever in the eliminated parts has been incorporated where needed. Since there was so much revision, it seemed simpler to re-type all of Part III, which I did. So pps. 89–126 can be removed in toto from the original ms., and the new Part III substituted. I think there's only one other change—on page 143, line 6, change Ned's House to Mrs. McKlosky's.

I have done my best to come up with a substitute title and so far, simply haven't. At the moment, I seem to have very little brain left, but hope for recovery.

I'm delighted you liked Herman, who, I pray, will take the cuss off of *The Mountain of Snow*. You must know how happy I am, after all these years, to have a book of poems in the works. I was discouraged early on about poetry by a reader at Charles Scribners' Sons, whose criticism was "This writer is like a young pumpkin in the Field, slightly touched with Frost." I prayed she would marry a ghost and bear him a kitten, and threw away all the current works, which was probably a fine thing for all concerned, in 1927.

Speaking of curses, we are now awaiting Hurricane Gloria, Eleanor's latest creation. The Tent City is now empty, all its inhabitants having fled inland. As Maurice Crain once said of Annie Laurie, it is something, living with a witch. How is Annie Laurie, incidentally? Do you ever have news of her? I had a sad letter months ago from her, saying Maurice had died and she was closing her office.

Thanks for the check.

Regards from all.
Affectionately Ruth

At the end of 1971, Ruth was still working on her two books. The Bodoni she mentions is the type of print used in *Time's Web*. Roy Macomber is a character in *"Lizzie" and Caroline*. Morris West is the popular novelist also published by Morrow.

TO JOHN C. WILLEY

October 10, 1971

Dear John,

These do look nice, and I'm delighted with the Bordoni. Poems being the edgy things they are, you couldn't have done better. I am, of course, in that state of seeing them in print for the first time, and have not yet begun to squirm at the content of some—not all—only able to look at the lovely print. This is unprofessional of me.

Only two things, which I have noted on the galleys, not really very much. On Galleys 2 and 3—of "E Equals MC-Square." Did I write it this way or did somebody change it from MC^2? I don't know that this makes a great lot of difference, but MC^2 seems more authentic to me; "MC-Square" sounds almost as if we were talking down to somebody.

On Galley 17, as I've indicated: The half-stanza marked should read:

And you've had
Munich-on-the-rocks.

Munich, dash, on-the-rocks isn't right. Please be sure?

Otherwise, outside of a few normal proof corrections, the thing is a masterpiece of printing.

Have you decided on a format, and, if possible, could I see it before it goes to press?

I'm glad you approve of the cut version of Part III of the novel. I do, myself. It should amuse you to know that I almost did this before I sent the ms. Phooey on a lot of characters who appear once and then vanish forever. I expect this aberration was created by a bit-in-the-teeth determination to get in Roy Macomber's tape somewhere.

About the title. What's bugging me ... Part I is long. Unless the reader expects Caroline, she is going to come with something of a jolt. This would make ME mad, if I were reading it for the first time. So, in the title, something has to be done to make the reader expect Caroline. Who is she, where is she? Also, the theme of the book is struggle for survival in the midst of stupidity, greed, cruelty, power over this-one-and-that-thing—well, say forces of evil we all, in our time, have to fight. And, the two struggles are separate. So? Two books? I've racked a brain that isn't a masterpiece at the moment, being slightly unhinged from between works, and so far haven't come up with anything that fits better than *The Separate Struggles for Survival of "Lizzie" and Caroline.*

Cumbersome, yes. I agree. But no worse than the full title of *The Compleat Angler, or Sailing Directions for the Coast of North America Between Cape Canso in Nova Scotia and New York Compiled Principally from the Surveys Made by Order of the British and United States Governments.*

I'm still trying, however.

Sure, I know. It's a gasser.

Eleanor's had a magnificent poem published in the *Maine Times* which we're happy over, and we are building with our own lily hands, a new garage across the road from the house. Today we are putting up rafters. With lame backs.

On the 20th we are breaking loose from the cocoon and going to Cape Hatteras for ten days. With our luck, there will probably be a hurricane, which we look forward to. We're not coming anywhere near New York, God forbid, except it would be nice to see you and Fern somewhere.

Our regards to you both, and congratulations to the company on the new Morris West which seems to have "had legs" regardless of Martin Levin's lousy review in the *Times.* (Somebody ought to clobber that guy.)

Affectionately, *Ruth*

Franny and Zooey is the novel by J. D. Salinger and *Bob and Carol and Ted and Alice* is the title of a popular movie that came out in 1969. Brian is Ruth's nephew Brian Trask.

TO JOHN C. WILLEY

Fall 1971? (no date)

Dear John,

I thought I'd wait until you got the post-vacation tons of whatever cleaned off your desk top; so look at me—three weeks late! However, it's not too late to say how pleased I am with the specimen pages and specifications for *Time's Web.* I think they are just right and do thank you. I return them herewith just in case, finding it a little difficult to part with even three pages of the printed word. Silly, isn't it?

Thanks also for fixing up Munich-on-the-rocks and the Einstein bit.

We-ell, *"Lizzie" and Caroline.* But not *Struggling for Survival.* Makes it sound like an ecological study of wild animals fleeing a freeway, doesn't it? I wish I could think of something better; so far, I haven't, and anyway, if you and your people like *"Lizzie" and Caroline,* I expect I won't find it difficult to go along. After all, *Franny and Zooey* and *Bob and Carol and Ted and Alice*—it could be a gasser, and you've come up with some excellent titles in your time. I'm not about to worry at this late date.

Where did you and Fern go? We went to Hatteras and puddled about in the rain. They had a cloud burst on the Outer Banks added to fifteen inches of rain left by one of the hurricanes—Ginger?—the streets in Nag's Head were under eight inches of water and likewise the highway down to Hatteras. Tell Fern the Volvo did beautifully. She plugged along, making a splendid bow-wave and did not falter, even though we could barely make out the white lines on the hardtop shimmering under all that flood. It really blew the mind. At Nag's Head we walked on the sand beach and found that we weren't allowed to re-enter the motel until we had washed the tar off the soles of our shoes—tar removal stations were set up at intervals along the beaches, with kerosene rags for the purpose. Made you wish that all captains of tankers who pump bilges off the coast had to eat the mess on strawberries. Along with feathers. Hatteras was better, though, and Brian and his wife came along from Washington and met us there—he is now a Lieutenant in the Coast Guard, working out his draft.

We came back and finished our new jeep-garage across the road which we had done except for shingles and window frames. Local carpenters tell us grudgingly that it is "a nice little building," but their wives really compliment us—they ride by and shout up that they would like to live in it.

Eleanor says she wishes we could have a publication party this winter—same crowd as last February. ... Tell Fern and Charley to persuade you. Regards to them both; lobsters are just beginning to get good in Feb. or March.

Aff. *Ruth*

Eleanor had taken a wonderful black-and-white photograph of a spider's web that wasn't used for the cover of *Time's Web;* but the original photo Ruth taped into the front of her own copy of the book.

TO JOHN C. WILLEY

Jan. 2, 1972

Dear John,

Herewith, your page notes with as much abandon as I could manage—they are later than I meant to be, but two things: (1) The Post Office closed for the weekend, so this won't go out until Monday, and (2), I'm flattened out by the flu, with a brain that rings like for whom the bell tolls. Generally, I go along with your notes, as you will see by the enclosed.

Let us now cease and desist with any more titles. *"Lizzie" and Caroline* let it be, once and forever. Whistle Island, I cannot and will not—you talk like a tree fell on you.

I might have known that you'd have found something absolutely stunning for the *Time's Web* jacket. It is, you know. Beautiful, and chosen with the impeccable taste and sense of what's right which I've grown to rely on in the years we have worked together. Thank you, and I wish my darn head weren't so thick at the moment, so I could say it better.

I liked the write-up in the Spring catalog for *T. W.* Only, please, please, DON'T SAY AGAIN ON THE BOOK JACKET WHERE I LIVE. I can't emphasize this enough. Over two million tourists go past our back door each July and August now; the "tent city" is 200 yards up the highway from us. We are sitting ducks now and if there is any more publicity than already, we'll surely have to move. Last summer was simply awful.

I hope I've managed to cover everything. A better letter will follow as soon as my affliction clears up.

Best regards to Fern and do manage to rake up Charley from wherever he is, for a Feb. or March trip north.

Affectionately, *Ruth*

John Lyons of Los Angeles was trying to purchase the film rights to *"Lizzie" and Caroline* through Ruth's agent in New York, Annie Laurie Williams. Warren Bakeley was actually Warren Bayless, a literary agent.

TO JOHN C. WILLEY

January 13, 1972

Dear John,

Here is the John Lyons correspondence, what there is of it, and please tell Mr. Bakeley (is it? I hope I didn't misunderstand his name over the phone) how much I appreciate his generosity.

Annie Laurie's sister Lee says in her letter, (I quote):

"We doubt that she can ever be active again," and "My sisters and I think that all negotiations should be between you and Mr. Lyons."

For written confirmation of our telephone conversation:

Until Mr. Lyons phoned me from Los Angeles, I had had no word whatever from Annie Laurie about her negotiations with Mr. Lyons, and do not know what (if any) the "good and valuable consideration" mentioned in his option contract might be. I don't believe we ought to sign anything until we find out.

Annie Laurie's sister, Lee, is Mrs. Leone Dehn, 240 First Avenue, NYC 10009. She is at present going through what she calls "the mountains of papers" in A.L.'s hotel rooms, and tells me that if she finds a carbon of a letter to me or any sign of a check (in consideration of), she will let me know. She's a little shirty about this, I don't know why, except the poor girl's probably going crazy with documents.

I'm not sure I want to sign off TV and allied rights to Mr. Lyons at this stage. However, I'll take Warren Bakeley's advice.

Annie Laurie's sister's telephone number is 212-OR7-3671. She, apparently, works part time at the Hotel Bedford where A. L. lived before her accident.

This might amount to just peanuts, then again it might not. I do seem to be swamped these days with young entrepreneurs who are conspiring against my having time enough to write another book. However, it's exciting and fun. If bewildering. I may have to get a bigger truck.

Affectionately, *Ruth*

TO ANNIE LAURIE WILLIAMS

February 3, 1972

Dear Annie Laurie,

My dear, how are you?

I thought you might like to know that my new novel, "Lizzie" and Caroline, is to be published in August, and Morrow will, of course, send you a galley if you'd like to see one.

We would so much like to hear from you.

Sincerely, *Ruth*

Hal Siegel designed the cover for *Time's Web*. McIntosh and Otis were Ruth's literary agents in New York.

TO JOHN C. WILLEY

February 3, 1972

Dear John,

Time's Web is a beautiful job of bookmaking and I do thank you. You would have heard from me before, but I have been creeping out from under the flu and stopping smoking, which have seemingly addled my brain. But now that I've decided to live, I can appreciate how lucky I am and what pains have been taken. Things have come to a pretty pass when I can't find anything at all to gripe about, except what I always do gripe about, the price of the book. Will anyone pay $6.00 for a thin book of poems? Apparently, you couldn't make it $4.50 in spite of the royalty cut I took; but all prices are weird now and what use even to wonder? It is a lovely job, cooperatively speaking, yours and the company's part in it as much as mine. And do tell Hal Siegel how much I like his jacket.

One or two items: A. The enclosed communications from McIntosh and Otis puzzle me. Why their noses in, now? I haven't had anything to do with them for years. I thought Morrow automatically attended to the renewal of copyrights when necessary. Or am I mistaken? I'm sure we had a conversation about it when you were here last year. Is it any of M. and O.'s business, now? If it is, I'd rather it wasn't. They're being busy, busy, busy, if you ask me. (I probably wouldn't be this cross about it, if I had a cigarette handy. I don't imagine it amounts to much, does it?)

B. I'm glad we've finally settled on *"Lizzie" and Caroline*. After I've got used to it, it doesn't seem too bad. But come, now, I wasn't born on Mt. Desert Island, you know, and the jacket mustn't say so.

Our local librarian in Southwest Harbor told me yesterday that she'd seen a "review" of *Time's Web*. This turned out to be the item in the Morrow spring catalog. She said, "People are going to be some old disappointed that this new book isn't going to be a novel." Ayvay! Why do I try to write literature? Why does anybody?

We are still having an extraordinary winter of no snow, and not really too much cold weather. Everybody in town has the flu. Dropping, as you say, like flies. But we are both better, if a trifle wobbly.

Love to Fern. We do thank you for the Christmas box. That grapefruit juice probably saved our lives.

Aff. *Ruth*

TO JOHN C. WILLEY

February 8, 1972

Dear John,

I had a phone call from Annie Laurie Williams last evening—she wants to see a galley of *"Lizzie" and Caroline*, and I told her I'd ask you to send one, when available. She has given up her offices on 41st Street and is now located at the Bedford Hotel.

I hadn't heard from her for a couple of years, maybe longer, and was surprised—thought she retired after Maurice died, but apparently not. It's early, perhaps, to send out galleys? Anyway, I leave it up to you. She seems a trifle vague, but says she's still doing lots of business, more power to her.

Regards, as always *Ruth*

archy and mehitabel by Don Marquis featured a cockroach named Archy who was always saying "Wotthehell."

TO JOHN C. WILLEY

February 24, 1972

Dear John, Returned herewith, as requested, three copies of your letter of February 18, 1972, countersigned by me, said letter being with regard to reversion of rights of *Jeb Ellis of Candlemas Bay*. The whole matter is still a mystery—why, for instance, did M. & O. pick out that particular contract?

If the copyright reverts to me, does this mean that they have a say and pickings, when I haven't had anything to do with them for years? I don't think I even know any of the people there now, except possibly Elizabeth Otis, (if she's still there). Do you think they'll be likely to frig around with other contracts?

We are fine, here, buried under seasonable weather at last—northeasters with heavy snow, one after the other, and the flu is over and forgotten. I'm receptive to galleys, (not yet arrived) but lazy as the devil about working. (Social Security has got to reward me for this.) I'll be found out on snowshoes.

Regards, *Ruth*

P.S. Sorry we aren't going to be made wealthy by the R. Digest, *but, I tell myself, wotthehell, archie, there's always the Welfare. Speaking of Archie, do you think Phebe Bunker will be looked on as a relative of his?*

TO JOHN C. WILLEY

March 3, 1972

Dear John,

Herewith the galleys. Nice clean ones they are, too. I found very few corrections to make, and those, simple. I finally got through my thick head what you meant about when Lewis sold his house. You were right; I must've had the flu. So, on Galley 14, 4th Para. down from the top, I've changed lls. 1 and 2 to read: Her owner, who had bought the house through Lewis Wyman's agent (etc.). It'll mean re-setting the paragraph, I guess, but it does eliminate the difficulty.

The book goes quite well, I feel, and I'm compatible with *"Lizzie" and Caroline* now, although I still feel that if I hadn't stopped smoking, hadn't had the flu, and had had any brain, I might have come up with something better.

Don't risk coming near New England until the weather gets normal, for heaven's sake, even if Chas. is back. We are having storm after storm, heavy snows, and this morning an ice storm such as we've never seen, with, actually, quite a snappy thunder shower, and apparently more to come. This is fantastic—ice is so heavy that it's breaking down trees—we've lost one beautiful birch, and shall probably lose more, to say nothing of the Bangor Hydro and Electric's power, which left us at 6:10 this A.M. So, if these galleys are delayed, you'll have to blame God.

Aff. *Ruth*

TO R. H. SHUMWAY

March 16, 1972

R. H. Shumway, Seedsman
Rockford, Illinois 61101

Dear Sirs,

I am sorry to have to say that the onion plants (Red Burgundy, Sweet Spanish) which you sent me arrived in a very bad condition. I managed to salvage about fifteen Sweet Spanish and perhaps 25 of the Red Burgundy. Also, the plants themselves, outside of the rot, are not good, being too tiny and woody-stemmed to spend time pruning and planting. I ordered these in March, as you will recall, but Maine spring planting is late and I had no way of keeping plants sent earlier than May.

I've been a Shumway customer for a good many years and this is the first time I've received anything in the way of seeds or plants which hasn't been superb. Perhaps some conditions out of your control were responsible; I'd be tempted to think so, because of our past customer relations. However, I feel you should know, since a dissatisfied customer gets unhappy.

If, by this late date, you can replace this order with satisfactory plants, could you send them Air Mail? And bill me for the postage.

Sincerely *Ruth Moore*

Gabriel Fielding was one of Ruth's favorite authors, who wrote *Eight Days, Through Streets Broad and Narrow,* and other books. Ruth's idea for "a sort of school text-book" titled *Lyrics to Make Up Tunes For* was never published. Lydia Rosier designed the cover for *"Lizzie" and Caroline.*

TO JOHN C. WILLEY

May 27, 1972

Dear John,

We've been gadding around; also trying to get the garden planted in a year that's a month late. But you would know, I think, without a letter, how much I like the jacket for *"Lizzie" and Caroline*. Except for the *Speak to the Winds* jacket I really think this is the best one I've had. So thanks a million; and perhaps you'll mention to Lydia Rosier how admirable I think it is. You'd think she'd seen, somewhere, an old tired vessel going on the rocks.

What a rotten time for you and Fern! We're so tremendously sorry that she's had such a go-round; for a dancer, too, to have had to go through such an ordeal with knees and legs. I think of the night here when she and Emmy sang "The Hang-Downs," and went whizzling around together all over the premises. We give her our best love and wishes—according to your letter she should be at home now and nearly well again. What I feel like saying is come and have our house and look at the wild pear in blossom. It is quiet—at least, now, even though on Friday night a drunk came barrelling down the Lighthouse Road, plowed through a fringe of trees and took the whole corner out of our new, just finished, jeep-garage. This happened around midnight and the crash was so tremendous that I thought a car had exploded in the road by the house. Then, realizing, we went out expecting to find a dead man (or more than one); but it was just one man, sitting in the field unhurt, saying over and over, "I am so embarrassed, I am so embarrassed." Well, I was lucky, at that, because a small twist of his steering wheel and he, his car, and various cans of beer would have been slap into the bed with me. So perhaps, delighted as we would be to see her, Fern would think twice about a quieter place. Tell her that our cat hasn't been out of the house since, poor little duffer, he got so scared. Times change, and civilization creeps up, doesn't it? What with these amenities of it, sometimes I feel as one who flew over the cuckoo's nest.

I do want some of the books in the new catalog and will write again, but Gabriel Fielding's sounds very good to me at the moment. We have all his others.

I have an idea for a sort of school text-book which you may or may not take to; or it might go to music clubs or batches of young people studying music. I have some lyrics lying around the house, and recently have been doing more. The "Hang-Downs," which you've heard, is a sample.

It could be a paperback, or perhaps even a loose-leaf notebook kind of thing, with the lyric on the right hand page and blank music paper on the left, or vice-versa, and the title I think of is *Lyrics to Make Up Tunes For*.

I know that at the U. of M. at Machias there's a music club which meets periodically, bringing their own instruments and their own compositions to play and sing, and I understand that good lyrics are hard to find. There could be and probably are comparable groups in other colleges.

Maybe the thing's been done—I wouldn't know. Anyway, if you don't cotton to the idea, I shan't die of disappointment. The lyrics are a lot of fun to do, and I can't seem to stop doing it. Like peanuts, I'm enclosing a recent one, "Little River," which Emmy is at the moment trying her hand on.

Best to Charley, and tell Fern to start whizzling around again as soon as she can.

Aff. *Ruth*

TO JOHN C. WILLEY

August 14, 1972

Dear John,

I thought you were probably on vacation, as one who must desperately need to be, and have put off writing so as not to add to your weight of mail when you got back. Needless to say, I was relieved and glad to get your letter of August 1. So thanks for the letter and for sending the reviews, some of which are stinkers, aren't they?

There is a lovely book called *Every Little Crook and Nanny* which really does a fine job on some of the English-seminar-book-reviewing-smart-asses, naming names, among them Martin Levin. It did me some good to read, but I am still jumping up and down mad, as well as puzzled. Why on earth all this venom and out-and-out lying, as if deliberately trying to destroy what has been an, let's say, adequate reputation? I suppose it's no use to get mad or even protest. If somebody lies about you in print behind your back, says you're a drunken souse and go around town whoring, you can go to law, but in this screwball profession—what? Power corrupts, and as somebody, not I, once said, absolute power is a lot of fun. I suppose these reviews are responsible for no ad in the Sunday *Times?* Or is Morrow trying to tell me something?

Some nice things have been happening here, if it's any comfort to me. The *Bangor Daily News* gave me a swell review, well in advance of publication date. (Baloo has noticed us.) *Down East Magazine* is doing a Profile, with photographs, for later publication—at least, I've been lavishly interviewed. Part of *Cold as a Dog* got on national TV, in a program called "A Fresh Breeze Down East" and I've had letters from as far West as Wisconsin asking where copies of the book can be got. I've had to recommend second-hand bookstores, my own copies being few and far between now. Local bookstores have been wailing because the book's out of print. It might be a fortuitous occasion for Morrow to do a paperback?

It's beginning to seem, after all these years of protest, that I'm being finally and irrevocably pinpointed as "regional." I believe I once swore at Thayer about this.

This is about all. My next letter will probably be nicer.

We have been thinking of you all summer.

Affectionately, *Ruth*

Martin Levin's negative reviews in *The New York Times* continued to upset Ruth.

Hancock is Hancock, Maine, a small town jutting out into Frenchman's Bay across from Mount Desert Island. The Dillons eventually retired to Hancock.

TO JOHN C. WILLEY

September 5, 1972

Dear John,

Well, I was good and mad, also frustrated. I have cooled off. The Author's Guild tells me that many other authors suffer from this kind of irresponsible reviewing, but that they would rather put up with it than curb free expression of opinion. True, so would I. If it is opinion based upon honest appraisal of work, no one could scream bloody murder, and I have probably had as many unfavorable reviews as anybody in the profession. However, what I got this time was neither honest nor an appraisal. Which really dumped me. Then, too, after waiting a year and a quarter for publication, a lady develops a cold. Your letter was a tremendous help; because I hadn't heard a damned word.

Before I forget, I'd like ten copies of *"Lizzie" and Caroline* and ten copies of *Time's Web*. Also, did you ever see a letter I wrote you about an idea I had for a kind of text book of lyrics to make up tunes for? I shouldn't be surprised if you didn't, because I sent it at the time of your worst trouble, before I knew what was happening. I thought the idea might be a good one; but if it seems not, to you, never mind. If you think not, would you send back the copy of a sample lyric I enclosed, which has probably been filed with the letter? I do understand why you might not have seen it or, considering, not registered if you had.

I'd like a copy of the new Fielding (Gabriel), too, if one is handy. We do like his books so much.

I spent a recent afternoon with Mary Dillon, with whom I worked at the *Digest* and with her husband, now a retired senior editor. They brought me up to date with all that's going on there, which seems more interesting, in a way, than it used to be. They actually have five women senior editors on the masthead now (of whom Mary is one). I understand they went to bat, along with Women's Lib, pounded fists on desks and so on before being listened to. It's amazing, really, because women were not too often listened to, before. The Dillons have bought land in Hancock and will build there, first for summers, then for retirement. It'll be nice to be in touch, and especially nice that the new women editors are smart and liberal. Three of them I know well.

I expect to go to work again after the first of the year. I can't relax now about working because of the continual wrangle with the Social Security people. I shall keep a log of working hours, a nuisance, of course, but I never know what will happen. The Bangor office will say one thing and be very uppity; the San Francisco office not long ago, sent me a check for $3000. Yes, no mistake. $3000. If they want it back in 1973, it will go back to them, intact. Or perhaps I've convinced them that my deferred contract of royalty payment from Morrow is indeed a deferred contract on a first-in-first-out basis and that current book royalties will not be due me until 1978 or 9; we'll slog along comfortably until I am 72. However, I never know when or whether there'll be a crackdown. Keeps me young, really. Bangor is always ominously wanting copies of 1966 or '67 income tax returns, with the implication that, by gum, they're not through with me yet.

September, thank God. The campground's closing and sweet corn is ready. I wish I could send you and Charley some, it's good this year, but by the time you got it, supermarket produce. Our garden was more or less looted this summer by the campground denizens, but we got some of almost everything except beans, which somebody stole on a wet night, so that the vines rusted and rotted. I put my cuss on the thieves, so maybe they had bellyaches or strangled.

On second thought, I'd like a copy of *Sir Francis Drake*, too; but oh dear, it's a ten dollar book! So use judgement.

I hope things go as well with you as you say. We were so sorry to hear about Fern's mother, poor lady, but perhaps she is better now.

Affectionately, *Ruth.*

During 1972, when the Post Office initiated its change in having all the mail go first to Bangor as Ruth mentions below, James Russell Wiggins, the publisher of *The Ellsworth American,* enlisted the assistance of the likes of E. B. White and others who helped show in the paper for a few weeks running how much faster a letter could be delivered locally by ox cart, canoe, on horseback, and bicycle than it could by the new Post Office way.

1. The view of the inner and outer pools of Gott's Island from the Philip Moore house. (courtesy of Esther Trask)

2. *Bass Harbor Head Light. (courtesy of Esther Trask)*

3. *Gott's Island weir; Philip Moore on the left and friend. (courtesy of Esther Trask)*

4. Philip and Lovina Moore and children: L to R: Ruth, Louise, Esther, and Harvey. (courtesy of Esther Trask)

5. Gott's Island, 1912–1913: L to R: Laura (Mrs. Enoch) Moore and her daughter-in-law Lovina (Mrs. Philip) Moore with Esther and Louise. (courtesy of Esther Trask)

6. The Philip Moore family, before their house on Gott's Island, probably about 1919–1920. L to R: Viny Moore, Louise, Philip, Esther, Ruth, and Harvey. (courtesy of Ted Holmes)

7. Lovina Joyce Moore. (courtesy of Esther Trask)

8. Ted Holmes and Ruth Moore going swimming. (courtesy of Ted Holmes)

9. Ruth at college at Albany, New York (at left, with unidentified classmates). (courtesy of Esther Trask)

10. Louise Moore Dow. (courtesy of Louise Dow)

11. Harvey Tink Dow, Louise's first son. (courtesy of Louise Dow)

12. Harvey Moore. (courtesy of Esther Trask)

13. Harvey Moore's children: L to R: Ann, Mary Lee, John, and Bill. (courtesy of Esther Trask)

14. Ruth Moore, Berlin Gott (Gott's Island mailman), and Esther Moore Trask. (courtesy of Esther Trask)

15. Ruth Moore. (courtesy of Esther Trask)

16. The picture of Ruth Moore (taken by Edle Sand, 1949) that appeared on the jackets of several of her books. (courtesy of Esther Trask)

17. Dinner with the Willeys. L to R: Eleanor Mayo, John Willey, Ruth Moore, and Fern Willey. (courtesy of Esther Trask)

18. Ruth Moore and Eleanor Mayo building their new house in Bass Harbor. (courtesy of Esther Trask)

19. Eleanor Mayo and Ruth Moore just before setting sail on the Mauretania. (courtesy of Esther Trask)

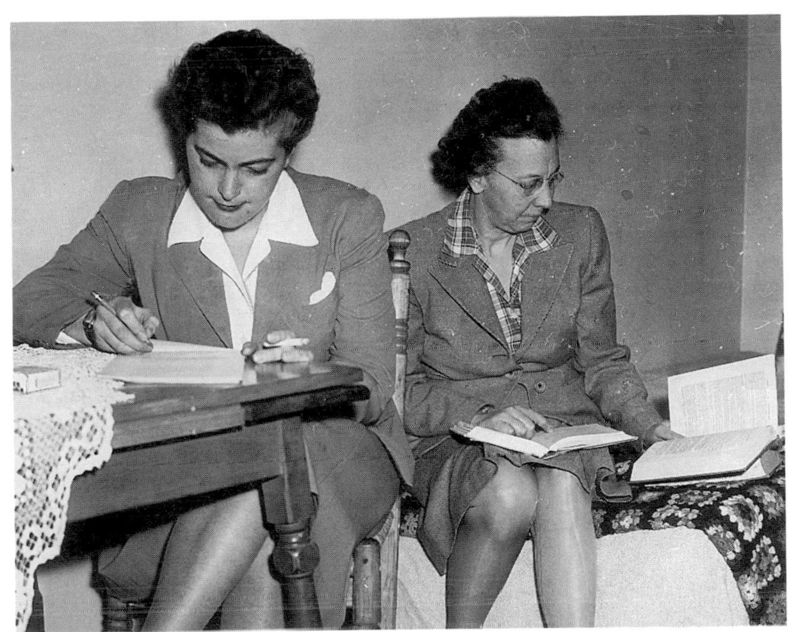

20. *Eleanor and Ruth at work on their books. (courtesy of Esther Trask)*

21. *Eleanor, Ruth, and Miriam Colwell at Miriam's house in Prospect Harbor, 1959. (courtesy of Miriam Colwell)*

22. *Eleanor and Ruth. (courtesy of Esther Trask)*

23. Ruth Moore. (picture taken by Eleanor Mayo; courtesy of Esther Trask)

24. Eleanor and Ruth with Harvey's step-son, Lester Radcliffe on Gott's Island. (courtesy of Esther Trask)

25. Ruth seated in front of her relatives: Front Row, L to R: Aaron Trask, Colleen Trask, Jennie Trask; Second Row, L to R: Amy Trask, Jackie Doughty Trask, Marilyn Adams Trask, Esther Trask, Emily Trask-Eaton, Katherine Eaton; Third Row, L to R: Muriel Davisson, Farrell Davisson, Bud Trask, Brian Trask, Jim Eaton, Phil Trask, Donna Trask, Sven Davisson. (courtesy of Esther Trask)

26. *Louise Dow's children. (courtesy of Louise Dow)*

27. *Eleanor Mayo. (courtesy of W. W. Norton Co.)*

28. John Willey, Ruth's long-time editor. (courtesy of the University of Maine)

29. Mont Gott of Gott's Island.

TO JOHN C. WILLEY

Dear John,

Many thanks for the new books. I have got into *Drake* and he is terrific. Fielding comes later and we're looking forward to him.

I'm a little concerned over the shipment of *Time's Web* and *"Lizzie" and Caroline*, which hasn't come. The concern is because we've been having difficulty with our mail, since the sorting was taken from Ellsworth and moved to Bangor over the wails of the Ellsworth P.O. What goes on in Bangor nobody knows, but mail's either late or sent to the wrong places; one day Bass Harbor had no mail delivery at all and nobody knows where it went. Some of ours has been sent to Bar Harbor. The Ellsworth people, in protest, have instituted an ox team route between Ellsworth and Surry because it takes two days or more to get letters delivered down Surry way, since everything has now to go to Bangor and be—what? recycled?—there. If you shipped UPS it'll probably be all right, and the books, anyway, will doubtless come tomorrow and I'll wish I hadn't written you. The new Federal P.O. is really a gas in these parts. The ox team game is nice clean fun, but once we really did feel the P.O. was one thing we could trust.

All here is quiet and nice now that the campground is closed. Our cat goes in and out of the house normally now, not chased by any screaming little children, and so do we. It's heaven. Blackberries are ripe.

All our best, *Ruth*

In 1972, folksinger Gordon Bok bought the rights to reprint Ruth's first book of poetry *Cold as a Dog and the Wind Northeast*. He had already read some of her ballads on the MPBN television series "Down East Smile In." Marshall Dodge was the famous comic who, along with Robert Bryan, created the *Bert and I* series. Mrs. Conrad's bookshop The Owl and the Turtle is in Camden.

TO GORDON BOK

October 12, 1972

Dear Mr. Bok,

Thank you for your extremely pleasant letter. If I could feel any prouder after listening to your reading from *Cold as a Dog* on television, this letter would probably burst me. I would have written you long ago if I had known how to get in touch with you, and I was very sorry not to be able to accept the invitation to the readings at the Penobscot Valley Country Club. But I was up to the eyes at the time.

I like your suggestion for a reprint very much. For one thing, it'll shut up all the people who keep bugging me for copies of the book and for another, if people want a book of poems that badly, the Lord knows somebody ought to do something.

I've no idea in the world about the business end of it—surely you should have some sort of commission and money should be returned to Mrs. Conrad's bookshop to compensate for any donation. But these matters can be talked over, I expect, later. So far as I'm concerned, a paperback would be satisfactory, or a magazine-bound sort of thing. And I've not notion as to what such reprints cost. However, this too, is a matter for discussion.

I have written John Willey of Morrow asking about the plates of the book, but I think he told me some time ago that books are printed nowadays by some sort of offset process. In any case, by this time, the plates have doubtless been melted down, or eaten, whatever printers do with them. When I hear from John, I'll be in touch again.

As you probably know, Marshall Dodge was in touch with me last fall about taping *C. as a D.* for a record to go with his *Bert and I* series, but I have not heard from him about it, and no commitment was made, so I judge he has given the matter up. Possibly he ought to be written to about this reprint—I don't know. In any case, I would not think of trying to compete with the magnificent voice I heard on television. I am a lousy reader of my own works, anyway.

Thanks again.

Sincerely, *Ruth*

TO JOHN C. WILLEY

October 12, 1972

Dear John,

The enclosed letter from Gordon Bok (copy) is self-explanatory, mostly. He is a folk singer and reader of folk material, pretty well known over New England and to a certain extent nationally—several of his programs, including his *Cold as a Dog* readings have been on national TV. He does a magnificent job, incidentally—listening to his concerts, I've felt as proud as a peacock. No one could ask for a more artistic and skillful reading of works. I'd like to know your thoughts on his suggestions.

I know Morrow doesn't want to do another reprint of *Cold as a Dog* and now, knowing from the enclosed letter from you to Mrs. Conrad, I can understand why. You know, I never did know what actually happened to that reprint. At the time, the letter I got, whether from you or the warehouse people I can't remember, stated that they were clearing out the warehouse to make room for new inventory and since there were only 40 copies of *Cold as a Dog* left, they were being sent to me for possible disposal in local bookshops. So I have gone all this time, in a fool's paradise, supposing that the second printing was all sold out. However, that's over the mill and now Bok wants to do what, I suppose, would have to be a private printing.

I rather like the idea, myself. For one thing, it'll shut up all the people who keep bugging me for copies of the book, and for another (see Bok's letter) if it's done, "it'll be a pretty thing." And, God knows, if people want a book of poems that bad, someone ought to do something.

Now, do tell whoever types the letters going out to bookstores and individuals (if there are any) what the actual title of *Cold as a Dog* is; because if the publisher can't remember, it's a sad commentary. Ain't? I wouldn't be picky over a typing error, either, only, I feel a little belittled, if that's the word.

I think you told me once that books now aren't done from plates, but from some kind of an offset process, right? In that case there wouldn't be any plates, and in any case, they would probably by now be melted down, or eaten, or whatever printers do. But if there are any, what would they cost to buy? I've got to answer Bok's letter fairly soon.

Thanks for your pleasant letter, which I'll answer sometime. That Charley! Isn't it grand about his pictures?

Affectionately, as always *Ruth*

TO GORDON BOK

October 27, 1972

Dear Mr. Bok,

I'm sending you Morrow & Co.'s reaction to your proposition about *Cold as a Dog*, a favorable one, I'm delighted to say. If you will let me know yours, I'll write John Willey about the reversion of rights to me, and we can take it from there on, whatever the next step may be. I could wish they'd be a little less rigid about the price for the flats, and perhaps I can wriggle around pathetically and get them to reduce it, since they don't plan to use them again. I might say that I, myself, will have to absorb one-third of the price for said flats, which might start them thinking.

Perhaps you and Mrs. Conrad will foregather on this and let me know what you think about John's suggestions. I think, myself, that a paperback, printed from the flats, would make the best-looking book, but I haven't an idea in the world about costs, and I don't want anybody to have to take a financial beating on this. Which, considering your reports and letters I have had since you began including *C. as a D.* in your concerts, isn't likely to happen.

With all good wishes *Ruth Moore*

P.S. Have you made a record which includes the Isle au Haut ballad and does Mrs. Conrad have it? Would you ask her to send it to me and bill me?

Mary Beth was a typist and proofreader at William Morrow.

TO JOHN C. WILLEY

October 31, 1972

Dear John,

I am probably driving you nuts.

Well, I'm not all up the wall myself. Only halfway. Dammit, I don't know anything about production.

This, yesterday, from a man in Saratoga Springs, N.Y.; can he have the name and address of my "Canadian publisher" since he can't find any copies of *Cold as a Dog* in the U.S. and wants some for Christmas gifts. Seems to me I remember that we don't have a Canadian publisher, but work through a representative news agency, right? However, I'm not sure, so have to pester you again before I can answer his letter. Anyway, I can tell him I'll put his name on the list. If this keeps on, I'm going to call it the S-list.

Thanks for your good letter of October 23. I should say it covers very adequately all the information this new publishing firm needs. I have sent a copy of all essential points of it to Bok, but it's too early to hear from him, since I gather he's out on the trail doing his thing. At least, he must have been in Saratoga Springs around October 27. When he gets back, I expect you'll hear from him, or me, re. what plans will be about buying the flats of *C. as a D*. and the reversion of rights to me. My own feeling is that we should buy the films outright; unless, since Morrow isn't going to use them again and they'll eventually be destroyed, they might be given to me for Christmas, as a monument to pure serendipity. I know, I know, I'm not asking. You should at least get your seed back. I'm not sure I want another publisher, either; but you "birds" have got your heels dug in. Not without reason.

Thanks for the reviews of *"L." and C*. Harmless, my foot!

Well, I tell myself, stop bellyaching, and do some work for a change.

Please do make up for me with Mary Beth about the typo. I should have guessed that it wasn't her fault, only your mumble. I'll bet she's thinking right now, "Damn that old bat, anyway." Besides, you probably work the poor girl to death, anyhow.

We're settling in for the winter and it's very fine weather today. The campground's closed, tenters all gone. What we have now is poachers of one kind or another—hunters after deer, and three small migrating hawks, young smart-alecks and ineffective. Like some book reviewers. The hawks have set up tent and the crows chase them, turnabout and a game; about every half hour they dive bomb the flock of bluejays which explodes with such a rachet as might take place if some hoodlum threw rocks into the middle of a Ladies' Aid meeting. The deer hunters are something else again. We have (or had) two young does who have slurked around all fall, eating our apples and, oddly enough, exotic feed from the herb garden, like marjoram and sometimes a mess of catnip. We've never bothered them nor they us—got used to each other, all of us tame as cows. Some slob shot one of them practically under our windows the other morning, no doubt resting his telescopically-fitted rifle on a NO HUNTING (or perhaps it was a NO TRESPASSING) sign. She died nastily and bloodily. We called the Park rangers and the game warden. Nobody, so far, has come but they are busy men. Now the same slob is after the other doe, but we begin watching at dawn, and when we hear his car come by, we turn on every light in the house. So far, he's got the message and has made tracks fast, but we know it's only a matter of time.

Civilization does have a knack of catching up with private places. At this time of year, we get a sense of terrible wildness in the woods, and not from the animals, and can practically smell the blood-lust.

Don't bother to answer all this chat, only the business things. I just felt like running on.

We hope things are getting better for you now, and E. and I think of you often.

Affectionately *Ruth*

Miss Isabel Currier was a free-lance writer who wrote a number of articles for *Down East* magazine. The following letter has been cut because Ruth wrote Isabel the same things she wrote John Willey about settling in for the winter, having trouble with poachers, and civilization sneaking up on private places.

TO ISABEL CURRIER

November 3, 1972

Dear Isabel,

This is a beautiful job, and I'm delighted with it. How you did it, with only the sketchy notes you took, is something I can't fathom. I haven't done too much damage—only corrected a few dates and names, and one or two facts on which I'm sure I misled you. I've added a few clarifying details, which use or not, just as you wish.

It's a great occasion when a (any) writer finds a perceptive and articulate reader. I was so pleased to find that your profile recognizes sociological significance in my books. It's true that I've been yattering on for years about pollution and the slobs who butcher woodlands, etc., egged on no doubt by the fact that we personally now live on a mesa, with gravel pits on two sides of us, a gravel pit and a tenters' campground on the third, and on the fourth, the harbor, which is polluted. Up until recently, it's been like what Don Marquis once said about publishing a book of poetry: "Like dropping a rose petal into the Grand Canyon and waiting for the echo." So, thank you.

I wouldn't want to seem an elbow-jogger, so I haven't written you. It struck me that you were having troubles enough. Of course, I've been interested, but there's been plenty of time; and the piece you've written has been well worth waiting for. When D.E. publishes it is up to them, of course. I feel that you and I have done our part well.

We hope you are feeling better.

Best, from both of us.

Ruth Moore

"Peter Kagan" and "Isle au Haut" are songs and records by Gordon Bok. The College of the Atlantic is in Bar Harbor and Captain Morse is folksinger and storyteller Kendall Morse. Gordon Bok had the reprinting of *Cold as a Dog and the Wind Northeast* done by the Camden Herald Publishing Co.

TO GORDON BOK

November 10, 1972

Dear Mr. Bok,

You can't have "Peter Kagan" back, so please let me have "Isle au Haut" and for goodness sake, let me pay. And thank you.

No, I don't suppose we know what we're doing, but for amateurs we seem to be starting out pretty well. Good and businesslike, and I like that. I have your check for $248.00 for the flats of *Cold as a Dog* which I'll endorse to William Morrow & Co. and send along to them as soon as they assure me that said flats are in good condition. I have just been on the phone to John Willey who says he doesn't know but will check. He says they are bulky, look rather like a section of culvert (mysterious, the things they have). In that case, do you want them shipped direct to you or to The Owl and the Turtle? Somebody's going to have to fall over them until they go to the printer's, and the bookstore probably has a storeroom.

John says he will send at once the reversion of rights to me.

When I wrote him on the 31st, I told him it would be nice of Morrow to give me the flats for Christmas as a monument to pure serendipity, but no soap. They have to get their seed back, I guess, though goodness knows they got it with the first edition of *C. as a D.* And, I must admit, so did I. But I find, through long experience, that if publishers are Scrooges, it's because they have to be.

Answering your suggestions:

1. Printers' information, yes. Between $1 and $2 sounds about right to me, but price will have to be based on cost, right? We should also find out from the printer we choose if he's equipped to handle "Flats", such as ours.

2. Of course, talk to your lawyer. Perhaps a straight-ahead publisher-author contract would do it—never having had any other kind, I wouldn't know, but your lawyer should.

Or, if you and the Conrads would like it, we could split costs three ways, nobody to get rich until the costs were paid up, and then profits split three ways. This, of course, is up to you, as publisher: what you decide, I'll go along with. I'd like, in any case, to send you my check for $82.77, one-third of the cost of the flats. Okay?

Now, I'm in a bind about coming to your concert at Bar Harbor on the 18th, much as I'd like to. I've just refused an invitation to read at the Univ. of Maine in Machias—the head of the Arts Dept. there, Chenoweth Hall, is a good friend of mine—and if I show up in any guise but a ghost's at the College of the Atlantic—well, she'll surely be there, too. ... I'm no-account in a crowd anyway—if recognized, my tongue swells up. So how about you and Mrs. Bok and Captain Morse (if he's with you) starting out a little early on Saturday afternoon and dropping by Bass Harbor for early dinner? Whatever you eat before a concert—crackers and milk, fish chowder, roast beef—Mrs. Bok will have to let me know. We are 17 miles from Bar Harbor—instead of turning east for Bar Harbor at the Mount Desert Island bridge, you drive straight south, through Somesville and Southwest Harbor. Once through Southwest Harbor, the road forks left and right; either way will do, the road makes a loop which is marked with a Coast Guard Light Station sign. We could arrange time so that you could easily drive to Bar Harbor by eight o'clock, if we don't make you tipsy with before dinner cocktails, that is.

If all this sounds too complicated before your concert, as it well may, don't think twice about saying no.

Failing to get you on yesterday, I called The Owl and the Turtle and had a very pleasant chat with Mrs. Conrad, who has undoubtedly been in touch with you before now, at least, she said she would be. I needed to know for Morrow the proper shipping address for the flats, mainly; but it was nice, also, getting acquainted.

What else? If there's anything I haven't covered, let me know. And thank you again for "Peter Kagan." He is a very beautiful job.

Sincerely, *Ruth Moore*

TO MRS. E. C. THERIAULT

November 11, 1972

Dear Mrs. Theriault,

Thank you for your interest in my book, *Cold as a Dog and the Wind Northeast*.

The book is indeed out of print and copies are extremely hard to find, but we are negotiating a paperback reprint, to be published in the not-too-distant future and if you don't mind waiting, we'll put your name on the list.

Sincerely *Ruth Moore*

TO GORDON BOK

November 14, 1972

Dear Mr. Bok,

Don't blame you—if I had to do a concert I wouldn't want to see anybody for a month ....

Drop around any time on Sunday. We can talk things over then, much the best way. Let me say now, though, that whichever way you wish to handle things will be all right with me and I don't in the least feel yarded into anything except a lot of fun.

Looking forward to meeting you,
Sincerely *Ruth Moore*

Philip P. Mason, the Director of the Archives of Labor History and Urban Affairs at Wayne State University in Detroit, had written Ruth on September 25, 1972 about her work for Mary White Ovington, one of the early founders of the NAACP (the National Association for the Advancement of Colored People). Mr. Mason wanted to know if Ruth had any of Miss Ovington's correspondence that they could have for their files. Theodore Ovington Kingsbury was Miss Ovington's nephew whom Mr. Mason had visited in Maine.

TO PHILIP P. MASON

November 15, 1972

Dear Mr. Mason,

I am so sorry to be late in answering your letter about Miss Ovington, but I have been gadding and things have piled up somewhat.

I was, around 1927, Miss Ovington's secretary, living in her home on East 86th Street, New York, so that very few letters passed between us, and unfortunately I did not keep any of them. The only written material of possible use which I have been able to find in my files, is part of the carbon copy of a manuscript—a detective story never published—which I typed for her at that time. I sent this on to Theodore Kingsbury, who possibly may be in touch with you about it.

Miss Ovington belonged to the old Civic Club on East 10th St., N.Y., I believe; my memory is faulty. I don't know whether it still exists, since I've been out of New York for years; but I think Roy Wilkins, now head of the NAACP, would remember it. Most of the then Civil Rights people belonged to it—John Haynes Holmes, Babette Deutsch, Paul Robeson and many others, and Miss Ovington was a very active member. Records might exist, if you could find them.

I wish this information weren't so scanty, because I feel that this is a great project you are undertaking and I wish you very well with it.

Sincerely, *Ruth Moore*

TO MR. KIMBERLY RAY

November 15, 1972

Dear Mr. Ray,

Thanks for your interest in my book, *Cold as a Dog and the Wind Northeast.*

The book is indeed out of print now and no easier to find in Canada than it is in the U.S. But we are negotiating a reprint paperback, which we expect to publish in the not-too-distant future, and if you don't mind waiting, we'll put your name on the list. I can't guarantee it will be out before Christmas, but it might be.

Sincerely *Ruth Moore*

Isabel Currier's profile on Ruth never appeared in *Down East.*

TO ISABEL CURRIER

November 20, 1972

Dear Isabel,

The final draft is fine— a very good job and I pass it A+, with all your editorial suggestions.

Down East is certainly a beautiful magazine graphically, and I do go along with your editor if he doesn't like purple prose and airy-fairy-Lillian stuff. Keep it simple—I always try to, much the best way. A perennial argument goes on in this house about Faulkner; E. likes him and so do I, but she doesn't mind a sentence forty-two pages long and I do. She doesn't have to keep looking back to see where-the-hell the thing started to tell where it's going, and I do—I don't have that kind of mind. I also say that the Reader's part of the action, so why make it harder for him than you have to; she says, Let him stretch his mind. We have a lot of fun with this argument; nobody ever wins it.

We are having the grandfather and grandmother of a southeaster today. The house buckles and the cat is scared. It's rain, though, taking off the snow cover of a few days ago. If it changes to snow, according to the forecast, we are out of luck, because the man who does our plowing has got caught with his plow down.

Paper is paper, my friend. I myself have made notes in the john on what is available there.

Take care and keep your leg up. I hope it feels better by now. You are more cheerful about your long siege than I should be.

Sincerely *Ruth*

Folk Legacy is the record label for which Gordon Bok records. In their catalog for 1984, they also listed books such as Ruth's *Cold as a Dog and the Wind Northeast* as available from them.

TO GORDON BOK

(no date)

Dear Gordon,

I have just sent John Willey of Wm. Morrow & Co. a copy of our publishing enterprise and told him, on a note of triumph, that while we might not be getting rich we aren't wilting on the vine, by gum, either. I also sent him one of your Folk Legacy cards. I expect him to wriggle a little. Or drool. All that publicity, my! (Free!)

Most of my early books are out of print—I began publishing in '42, but a good many libraries still seem to have them on the active list. Here are the titles, for what it's worth:

The Weir
Spoonhandle
The Fire Balloon
A Fair Wind Home
Candlemas Bay
Jeb Ellis of Candlemas Bay
Speak to the Winds
The Walk Down Main Street
Second Growth
The Sea Flower
The Gold and Silver Hooks
"Lizzie" and Caroline

The two books of verse, *C as a D* and *Time's Web* you have.

All suggestions in your letters are okay with me.

If, by some unexpected chance, you don't get your seed back, I hope you'll let me know. I've been feeling guilty ever since you sent me that thunderous check.

Good luck to your current tour, wherever it may be.*Ruth*

TO GORDON BOK

December 27, 1972

Dear Gordon,

I do thank you for the records. I would like to say simply how beautiful and moving they are.

Seals come along our shore in the summer, nosy and mysterious and endearing; when I was a youngster and my father had his herring weir at the Island, I was pretty much a Clerk of the Works helping him tend it; we'd go down, early mornings, and if we found any fish at all, there'd generally be a full, fat seal, round as a keg. My father would fly into a rage, forget about me, and swear something awful at the seal. He would talk to it. "Raisin' hell with the herrin' again," he'd roar, with appropriate adjectives, and I'd always think he'd kill the seal, but he never did. He'd open the outer weir gate—a hard job, too, without losing the fish—and let the seal go. "Same damn one, every time," he'd say.

Two local bookstores are very much interested in our reprint, Sherman's Bookstore in Bar Harbor (Michael Curtis) and The Bookstore, High Street, Ellsworth (Scott Lamb). Both stores were bedevilled for copies of *C. as a D.* after your two concerts and for your records, also. And I have a sheaf of letters asking, which I've answered, mentioning the reprint, but unable, of course, to say when. I feel, in a way, I'm not pulling my weight in this project—if there is anything I can do, please let me know.

I haven't embezzled your check, but am still holding it until the printer has passed on the flats and has found them okay. I do have to send it soon, because the Morrow boys are getting a little edgy, the Scrooges.

Have good holidays.

Sincerely *Ruth*

Walden Two, published in 1961, is the most famous book by behaviorist B. F. Skinner. *The Hessian,* by Howard Fast, was published in 1972. The biography of Harry Truman was the one written by his daughter, Margaret Truman Daniel.

TO JOHN C. WILLEY

January 3, 1973

Dear John,

We were disappointed, but did understand. I hope you slept for seventy-two hours straight. Times, this is the only thing, and we do hope you got good and rested.

Herewith, at last, Gordon Bok's check for the flats of *Cold as a Dog*. They've been checked and are in fine condition. So, all right, we were silly; only it wasn't me. I've trusted Wm. Morrow, God rest him, for a good many years, as you know.

We are starting out with a thousand copies and doubtless will lose our shirts, but never mind, it is very good fun. Gordon Bok has been very careful about choosing a printer. Which is what took so long. Also, holidays intervened, I understand.

I heard quite a good story about amateur entrepreneurs, not on reprints but on Christmas trees. Two fellows took a truckload of trees from northern Maine to Boston, paying the producer of the trees a dollar apiece for them. In Boston, they sold them for a dollar apiece. Then they got to figuring why, how, they'd got into such a horrible hole. What to do next time? "Why, said one to the other, "Next time we'll have to get a bigger truck."

We both thank you for the books. I have read *The Hessian* and think it's terrific, but haven't got to Harry Truman as yet. The holidays were strenuous; besides I've started work again. It was thoughtful of you to choose books you knew we would like. Along with other millions, we loved and respected Harry. His death is surely the end of an era and we surely need someone like him now.

It's good news about *"Lizzie" and Caroline*, and some of the nice reviews have smoothed down a somewhat grimpsy ego, I'm sure. The book seems to be going well here in local bookstores, too.

Best from both of us, and do stop busting a gusset over work. Maybe we should all of us read *Walden Two*.

Affectionately *Ruth*

TO JOHN H. LYONS

January 13, 1973

Dear Mr. Lyons,

We have been shocked and saddened by the news of Annie Laurie William's accident. She has been a great figure in the motion picture world for many years, and for the same time has been my very good friend. Her sister tells me that it is doubtful if she will ever be active again.

I regret extremely that your project has been so held up. Until your phone call, I hadn't heard a word about the matter from Miss Williams and was pretty much surprised and bewildered. It has taken me some time to get in touch with her family and even so, I haven't been able to get much information. I still don't know what the "good and valuable consideration" mentioned in your option contract may be.

Mr. John C. Willey, William Morrow & Company, 105 Madison Avenue, New York, 10016, (my publishers), (Tel. 212-889-3050) has been in the process of locating a New York agent, a friend of Annie Laurie's, who will take over, at least temporarily, the matter of *"Lizzie" and Caroline*, and you will doubtless soon be hearing from him.

What's holding us up, both you and me, is lack of adequate information, understandable under the circumstances, which I hope will soon be rectified. In the meantime, your project sounds exciting and very good fun, and I wish you all luck with it.

Sincerely *Ruth Moore*

Lee was Mrs. Leone Dehn, Annie Laurie William's sister. The Fern mentioned below was not John Willey's wife.

TO ANNIE LAURIE WILLIAMS

January 15, 1973

Dear Annie Laurie,

We were both so sorry to hear about your accident. As soon as I heard, I got in touch with Lee by phone and she told me what a bad time you have had and how painful your injury was; she also told me that you were soon going to Mt. Vernon to be with Fern, which means you are better, and we thank God for it.

Don't, for goodness sake, worry about business affairs of mine, or have them on your mind until you are really better.

I'm a flubdub about business negotiations, as you know, but never mind about that. I heard a good story not long ago about two people who really were just that—they were two young entrepreneurs who bought a truckload of Christmas trees from a Maine dealer and hauled them down to Boston. They paid the dealer a dollar apiece, and, in Boston, they sold them for a dollar apiece. Then they put their heads together to try and figure out how they could have ended up in such a dreadful hole. Finally, one said to the other, "Now, what'll we do?" and the other said, "Well, we'll just have to get a bigger truck." I'm afraid I'm inclined at times to buy a bigger truck; so get well fast, honey.

Affectionately *Ruth*

Mr. Warren Bayless was a literary agent in New York who wrote to Ruth requesting that he replace Miss Williams as Ruth's agent in negotiations with John Lyons in Hollywood about the film rights to *"Lizzie" and Caroline.*

TO WARREN BAYLESS

January 22, 1973

Dear Mr. Bayless,

This is to confirm our telephone conversation of today's date, with regard to Mr. John H. Lyon's request for a 90-day option on the motion picture rights of my book, *"Lizzie" and Caroline*, and I hereby authorize you to proceed with negotiations to that effect.

I enclose, also, Mr. Lyon's latest letter to me.

I was very glad to have your letter of January 19. I have been sitting here like a bird in the wilderness—possibly, a hoopoe—and about as helpless as one without Annie Laurie Williams.

The first I heard about this option, was when Mr. Lyons sent it to me to sign. I didn't know about Annie Laurie's accident or her illness. the wording of the option troubled me, particularly the part about "For good and valuable consideration, the receipt of which you hereby acknowledge." I don't even know what "allied rights" may be, and I'm not at all sure I want to tie up television rights in connection with a movie. This was done in connection with the 20th Century Fox movie of my book, *Spoonhandle*, which as *Deep Waters* has been shown many times on TV without any remuneration to me. Possibly it is customary, however, to include TV rights in connection with movie options and contracts; I expect you will know how best to handle the matter. (If I say "in connection" again, I am going to scream. Don't you.)

I sent one copy of Mr. Lyon's option contract to John Willey—if he has handed our correspondence over to you, probably you have it on your desk. The other copy I kept for my file.

I don't doubt for a moment that Annie Laurie either intended or tried to get in touch with me. For one thing, we have been having trouble getting our mail—the Post Office seems to have gone to hell, at least in these parts. One lady here sent a parcel to her daughter in New Jersey, which ended up in West Germany; our letters have been forwarded from Bar Harbor, and for some idiot reason, Brooksville. The only thing about Annie Laurie, I could put my head back and howl like a wolf because of what's happened to her.

Thanking you again for your immense favor to me, I am,

Sincerely *Ruth Moore*

TO JOHN GOULD

April 27th, 1973

Dear John,

We went gadding to Boston and breathed there, so came home with a bronchial something which did us both in for a week. So I'm late answering your letter, but how pleasant to hear from you again. It's hard to imagine the Farmer Taking his Wife to Friendship, i.e. away from the Farm; and I expect you miss it, all those magnificent acres; but times do change, as the air changes and as the taxes on acreage do; we have 30 acres with 800 or so feet of shore front; our first tax on it was $15 and now is nearly $1200. It's a hard life for a gal on the Gut.

It's heartbreaking to me to have to tell you that Gott's Island has also changed, is almost all now owned by an uptight little group of summer people who frown on picnickers. The last local people who went there for a Sunday outing, I understand were ordered off, since even shorelines now are mostly private. If we could get transportation for a party of ten, we could probably go, but for that I honestly wouldn't know where to turn. The fishermen aren't equipped—they don't carry passenger gear—not that many life preservers, for example, and restrictions are Coast Guard strict. My brother and brother-in-law, whose boats we used to depend on are both dead and our young people all flew off to college and are now distributed over the U.S. from Augusta to

Illinois. There's a mail service, beginning in June, but the fellow hasn't got a ship-to-shore telephone and can't carry more than five passengers. We sold our house on the island years ago—too bad, if we hadn't we would now be rich.

I don't blame John for wanting to come back after his memories. It was a magical time and a magical place we had and I've never forgotten that party either. But we go back only on Memorial Day, my sisters and I, to pull the weeds out of what we have left there, the family lot and put a pansy or two on top of Ma, who loved pansies. One time we, unfortunately, took a walk in the woods and were pursued by a lady-owner, who carried on about dropped cigarettes and setting the island on fire, until at last my younger sister, who is outspoken in the manner of her heritage, said: "Madam, we were born and brought up on this island and the only time it has ever been set on fire was by summer people. Aren't you the lady who poured the fireplace ashes down the backhouse hole and burnt up not only the backhouse but the cat and kittens? Then for Christ sake, go home and tie a rag on your tongue."

She was, and she did.

The devil damn black the cream-faced developers, who are driving us all up the wall.

We would most dearly love to see you, and our 800 feet of shoreline, with a shore came on it—while it isn't magical, involves no boat-ride and has no Indian shellmound, is still a nice place to picnic.

I wish you could plan your party for May or perhaps late October when the neo-islanders aren't there. I couldn't guarantee to bludgeon one of the local boys with a sizeable fishing boat to take us down for a day, but I could try it, and I would.

I realize I have been hard on the people now at the island—I suppose we, too, feel the same way about privacy, Acadia National Park, jammed with three million people a summer, being practically in our back dooryard; but we EXPECT to be overrun, to find backpackers sleeping in our buildings and looting our vegetable gardens. And who are we to be better than backpackers? Leave us not be prissy and prigs.

So what was the Frenchman fishing for and did he catch anything? First things first, for heavens sakes.

There was a big potato-grower in Aroostook (tic?) who got in a bind for help, one time, and came down to the U.S. Employment Bureau in Bangor.

Asked the lady at the desk if she could supply him with twenty-five hoers. "Sir!" she said. "Do you mean prostitutes?" "Well," he said. "I d'no's I care what their religion is, long's they can hoe potatoes."

We are yours, as always, *Ruth*

TO MRS. HOPKINS

June 24, 1973

Dear Mrs. Hopkins,

The enclosed snapshot is of your great-grandmother, Nell Joyce, taken in 1913. If you'd like to have it copied, I'd be pleased to have it back, as it's a part of my childhood memories of Gott's Island. She was a wonderful woman, old even when I was a child—a great story-teller; I can hear her now telling about General Israel Putman and the wolf, holding all the island kids spellbound as the General crawled into the Wolf's den. "He went down four feet perpendicular and four feet horizontal, and then he looked into the glaring eyeballs of the wolf." I remember her with deep affection, though I was pretty small when she died.

Gott's Island is owned now by summer people, mostly. They are not very hospitable to visitors. But a relative of yours, at least I think she's a relative, Flavilla Reed, has a house there and I suggest you get into touch with her. Her address is Mrs. Lyle Reed, Bass Harbor, Maine, 04653. Her mother, Emma Gott, was, I think, a sister to your grandmother. I'm a little shaky on this, but I believe if you write to Flavilla, she'll set you straight and will give you the information you need about seeing Gott's Island.

I think I am also a relative of yours—my mother Lovina Joyce Moore, was a niece of James Oliver Joyce, Aunt Nell's husband. I remember Herman very well—he was in the Gott's Island grade school with me, and his younger sister, Myrtle, was my contemporary. She died some years ago, to my sorrow. She, too, was a wonderful woman, with a magnificent growth of flaming red hair, and I loved her dearly.

Do, please, get in touch with Flavilla. She can tell you anything you want to know about Gott's Island and your family history there.

Sincerely, *Ruth Moore*

"Little River" is a poem of Ruth's that appears in her last book of poetry *The Tired Apple Tree*.

TO GORDON BOK

October 13, 1973

Dear Gordon,

Well, here's old *Dog* come home again after fifteen years in a new overcoat, looking as crisp and exciting as he did in 1958, and I don't know but, more beautiful. I'm tickled to death and feel very very lucky, because not every writer gets a reprint handled by artists. Please say so to the Camden Herald Pub. Co., who really have done a tremendous job, haven't they. As for your part in it, you already know what I think, but perhaps you won't mind all my thanks to add to that.

What can I say about your music for "Little River" except that it's exactly right? I always thought Charles Dickens was a stuffy creep, bursting into sobs when he heard his own work read; I didn't do that, but I did what my grandmother used to call "puddling up"—got some gulps which I had to swallow. Eleanor did, too, when we played your tape and she is harder boiled. I said, above, all my thanks, but there are plenty left over for "Little River," and for the good professional talk about lyric-writing, of which I can certainly see the point. My sister's kids and I have been batting out these things for years, not exactly haphazard, but mostly for fun; music runs out of their fingertips and once in a while they need a lyric. So far, we've only got four that we felt worth putting on tape. I felt somewhat guilty offering you "Little River" and wondered later if you didn't feel as if you'd been bitten in the eye by a black fly. But it's come out so well, I take that back.

Herewith, what's left of the list of orders I had. A few diehards. Some got put out with waiting and cancelled, one or two nagged me until I sent them personal copies to shut them up. I'm sorry about this. If I hadn't been so walled-up inside the job at hand—I worry for about a year when I start something new—I might have coddled some of them along, but Ken Morse stopped by and said you were having a rugged summer, and I wasn't sure what to tell people. However, Mrs. Scott Lamb, The Bookstore, High Street, Ellsworth, will take some copies; she said, "Whatever it is, bring it in," but she didn't say how many because we weren't then sure of the price. Ditto, Michael Curtis, Sherman's Bookstore, Bar Harbor. I can't help much here, because you'll have to figure wholesale and retail prices first; whether or not to operate on a contingency basis—bookstores always want to return what they don't sell, if any. I know you don't want to be involved in a lot of letter-writing, so skip the bookstores if you'd rather.

As for royalties: Send me ten copies and hold back royalties until they're paid for and you've got your seed back. When the cost of publication is paid for, I'll accept royalties gratefully, but not until then. After all, you know this project is serendipity for me.

Good hunting. And thanks, yourself.

Ruth Moore

TO KIMBERLY RAY

November 15, 1973

Dear Ms. Ray,

I'm terribly sorry that the publication of the edition of *Cold as a Dog* has taken so long, but I'm truly not responsible for your letters not being answered. The book is out and Gordon Bok, the publisher, is handling orders for it. I sent your correspondence to him long ago. He has been, I understand, on extended tour, which perhaps is why you haven't heard from him. His address is:

Gordon Bok
Box 840 Camden,
Maine 04843

If he is still on tour and there is more delay, I suggest you get in touch with "The Owl and Turtle Bookstore," also in Camden. Mrs. Conrad there will surely see that you get your six copies, before Christmas-time.

If you have any more difficulty, let me know and I will jump up and down on somebody.

Sincerely *Ruth Moore*

TO GORDON BOK

November 15, 1973

Dear Gordon,

I'm profoundly impressed and pleased by the check you sent, and what's to be rubbed raw about? If this way is all right with you, it's all right with me.

I'm still puzzled about what to do about people like the lady (see enclosed postcard) whose correspondence I've already sent you, since I don't know whether you've sent out copies, or what, and we'd be silly to duplicate.

I know how you feel about the bookkeeping—the same way I do, both of us being too busy with work in progress to think about much of anything else. I wonder if Mrs. Conrad at the Owl and the Turtle would be willing to handle these occasional orders for us? For example, Mrs. Scott Lamb, The Bookstore, High Street, Ellsworth, wants 15 copies, but she wants to be sure for her customers' sake that she can get more copies quickly if she needs them, and Mrs. Conrad could probably lay hands on extra copies more quickly than I could, or you could if you were on tour.

One thing you and I can be pleased about (above other things)—the people who've heard you do these ballads 'fore God want the book and are willing to bug us for it. I might say, over and over again.

Also, people who have heard the tape of "Little River" are crazy about it. I am, too.

Good luck with all your doings; let me know if I can help further with "Dog."

Sincerely, *Ruth*

By late 1973, Ruth must have been working on her novel *The Dinosaur Bite,* which was published in 1976. *The Letters of E. B. White,* in which there's a letter E. B. White wrote about Ruth, was also published in 1976.

TO JOHN C. WILLEY

Dec. 6, 1973

Dear John,

We like the result of our joint publishing enterprise, copy enclosed. I think Gordon Bok and I and the Camden Herald Pub. Co. did a very slick job, credit of course to Morrow's original format. The thing's going well. Gordon is plugging it on his country-wide concert tours, Folk Legacy is handling sales, and I've had, so far, two hundred bucks royalties, free and clear. Gordon is very strong on campuses and goes on tour for two or three weeks each month. He travels, not only Maine, but many States outside; he says that people, particularly the young, really go for Charley and his herring weir and for "Little River," a song for which I wrote the lyric and he the music. (I think I sent you a copy of that; the lyric I mean, some time ago.)

Well, not to get rich, not really, but not wilting on the vine either, by gum, and wow, man, have we all had a ball! I'm in the wrong end of this business, right?

How are you? Seems like a long time I've owed you a letter, but in the first year of agony on a new book I always go underground, as you know. And here it is Christmas again! Now I'm about done with thinking and ready to start work; on January 1, not to upset the Social Security Administration for '73. Thinking, per se, seems not to be performing "substantial services" for which you lose your monthly check. No one in said Adm. seems to be able to understand my royalty arrangement with Morrow—it's as if a little man, a different one each year, goes through my file and starts jumping up and down screaming. Two years ago, I wrote demanding a full investigation of my "case" which I got, documented, so now I keep Xeroxed copies of the documents which I send out each year when the demands for explanation arrive. So far it's worked. Simple.

This was the year we had baseboard heating put in the house. Not the right year. At any moment, we may start heating with the fireplace. Eleanor got on the conservation Planning Board for the town—she's Chairman—and is now in the middle of hell-breaking-loose, now that the town's found out that if we don't zone, the State will do it for us. The "By-God,-I'll-do-what-I-want-to-with-my-own-property" mail is very heavy.

Dottie Lobrano Guth was in Maine last week, helping E. B. White prepare his letters for publication. She was in Brooklin, across the bay from us, but couldn't get to see us, blast her, so she called us up. It was wonderful to hear her voice—that laconic crawl—after all these years.

I need ten copies of *"Lizzie" and Caroline* and ten of *Time's Web*. If I could have them before Christmas, why, fine, if not, people will have to wait for Santy Claus.

I had a nice surprise not long ago—three copies of *Abigail's Hus,* the Norwegian edition of *G and S Hooks*. I didn't even know there had been such an edition: if your office notified me of it, as I don't doubt it did as is usual last summer. I understand. Anyway, it was a nice surprise. The P.O. Dept. has gone to hell along with the rest of the—shall I say, country?

If you have the books sent United Parcel, I think I would have more chance of getting them before next summer.

We're having spring in November here—green grass, birds still, a green leaf coming out on the rosebush.

All the best for Christmas,

Affectionately *Ruth*

Mary Grahn was one of Ruth's college friends with whom she stayed in touch. Anwar Sadat was the Egyptian leader. "The inhabitant on the enclosed card" may have been Anwar Sadat, who was much involved in trying to make peace with Israel in the Middle East. "Little Willie" is a satire on the once-popular verses of 19th century poets like Julia Moore. "Man will survive" is a reference to Faulkner's Nobel Prize acceptance speech in 1950.

TO MARY GRAHN

December 11, 1973

Mary Grahn
Drama School Library
Yale University
New Haven, Connecticut

Dear Mary,

The world's got so pretty to look at these days that just the sight of the inhabitant on the enclosed card made us feel better, so we're willing to share. But Merry Christmas is as far as we'll go.

Item: PROJECT THE MAKING OF A STATESMAN

Emissaries have ransacked 19th Century warehouses in Britain and have at last found Dr. Frankenstein's original machinery. Techniques for developing the perfect man from his flawed formula are being researched as rapidly as possible due to shortages, but while work is in progress the factories are playing soul-music, just in hopes.

Item: Little Willie in the best of sashes
Went to Egypt to ease the clashes;
Found the frontiers all a-smolder,
And no one wanting to stir up Golda.

Item: Man will survive. He will not only survive, he will endure. End quote.

Comment: And how.

Item: God is trying. We had a rainy summer, not fit for lizards, but October was lush; sunny day after sunny day, and November and December, so far, have been warm. Bird feeders are still full of birds who haven't left. (I would, if I were them.) And some green leaves which will later be sorry have come out on the rosebush. We were thinking that this was not the year to put in baseboard heating, which we did, but that was before the b.s. (Before Sadat) in case you have other thoughts. However, with the warm weather, we find that the kitchen stove and the fireplace keep the house at a nice warm 68. I help, with an occasional hot flash. The only one who suffers is Tophet, the cat, who's rotten spoilt and now determined to sleep with the people. We have had to ask him not to throw up his mice on the bed.

Winter is nice here. We're settling back into privacy with the campground groupie, the deer hunters and the fool-iage crowd all gone home. Seven pigeons from uptown, three mourning doves from the forest come calling. It's pleasant to hear their wings whistling on a frosty morning. I have got my nose on the grindstone again, underground, but have come up for the holidays: daylight looks nice. The first year, when I start a book, my conversation consists of "Shut up," which seems to mean to everybody, "I don't love you any more," but only means, "I don't love you at the moment." Few understand this. One might suspect that our Christmas card is a photo of me at my best.

How are you and what does? Did you travel this summer? Do give my regards to Ted and Rosl. I realize that this letter is a gasser, but have no brains.

Ruth

The letter from E. B. White that Ruth refers to below is included in Appendix A. In *A Fair Wind Home,* the character's name is Lizabeth, not Elizabeth, as Ruth refers to her.

TO DOROTHY LOBRANO GUTH

April 8, 1974

Dear Dottie,

Here's Mr. White's letter. Eleanor doesn't think it would Xerox very well, in fact, looks like Xerox already. So use it, by all means, and return it when you're finished, okay? It says splendid things about me, anyway.

I still don't agree that 800 feet was too far for Elizabeth to dog paddle, with the wind under her hat as under a parachute and blowing her toward Carnavon's skiff. She was modeled after my grandmother, who was formidable, unstoppable and unsinkable even by the forces of nature, though I will admit that my grandmother couldn't have done it without her hat. As a sailing man, Mr. White of course was right.

We, too, had a splendid time. After all these years, I thought, there's Dottie and she hasn't changed, which, I expect, says it. Your kids are wonderful, slick as leprechauns and charming to be with. As this same grandmother once said to a hen which produced fourteen chicks out of thirteen eggs, "Didn't you and that rooster do good, dear." Please come again and bring everybody. We'll promise Ray always lobster, unless the supply fails. If I were you, after I finish with E.B.'s letters, I'd start another book called "Letters by my Children." Tell them the cat wouldn't let the bird-grave be, so we had to transfer it to a place Tofy doesn't know about.

This is short because I have to go to work, God help me.

All our love, *Ruth*

TO LEONA E. QUIGLEY

July 30, 1974

Dear Miss Quigley,

Thanks for your very pleasant letter. I do appreciate your kindness in letting me know how much you've enjoyed my books.

I wish I knew where you could find, now, either of the books you mention. I , myself, have one copy of *The Weir*—it belonged to my mother who died in '56 and I can't part with that. *The Weir* has been out of print for a long time; it was published in, as I recall, 1943, and being my first book, was a small printing. *Jeb Ellis of Candlemas Bay* was an edited-for-young-people reprint of the original *Candlemas Bay,* mostly the same material, and I don't even have a copy of it.

I think your only hope is a second-hand bookstore—perhaps F. M. O'Brien, Antiquarian Bookseller, 33 High Street, Portland, Maine, 04401, who advertises a free search service for rare books. This is the best I can do and I'm almightily sorry.

When I lived in California, what I missed most was snow. I recall weeping salt tears one February morning at the sight of, far away across the Reliez Valley, Mount Diablo with a snowcap on him. So I can truly understand how you feel.

I am, incidentally, a graduate of SUNY, but at the time, it was New York State College for Teachers, at Albany. I understand that times have changed vastly in its rotunda which has, probably long since, withered and gone; but that was a long time ago. My Litt. D. was from the University of Maine.

Thanks again, and good luck with your search.

Sincerely, *Ruth Moore*

In 1974, Gordon Bok was appointed Artist in Residence at the College of the Atlantic (COA) in Bar Harbor. His wife's name is Pat.

TO GORDON BOK

July 30th, 1974

Dear Gordon,

Enclosed is my check for $3 for copyright of "Little River." Little enough. My cucumbers are not yet even in bloom, due to a late season. You and Ken Morse can have some, in time, if you pick them yourselves—but not a damn cucumber if you come to Bass Harbor again and don't stop by to see E and me, you skunks.

We envy your nice, broad-beamed converted rowboat. We're without a boat this year, because when we went to put ours into the water, the man who was helping us said, "For godsake, don't step off the floorboards or you'll go right through the side of her."

Well, she's old. You can't expect too much. We had her built in 1945 by Cliff Rich, now dead, who was famous for his skiffs and punts and who put his—what?—essence? into her because he liked us. She's the smoothest-rowing boat I ever saw, lovely in the water—not much good with an outboard because she wasn't built for one. Actually, she hates outboards and tries to drive her stern under and let the ocean come in on to the stern seat. The only one she's ever tolerated was a Seagull, 3-horse power. But that's all right with us. We'd rather row or sail, and she sails something beautiful with a spritsail. Cliff, just before he died, (he was in his 90s) reinforced the stern-board for us and wouldn't take any pay for his work: "Because," he said, "anybody that'll take as good care of a boat as you girls have, don't deserve to pay for repairs on her." He also gave us his mast and spritsail, he being too old to sail his own skiff any longer.

We had her overhauled last year, but the fellow who did it only caulked a few seams and painted her, charged us $105 and didn't trouble to tell us that the timbers were rotten. Cliff's grandson, now, wants $800 for retimbering her and other boatyards are only interested in selling us a fiberglass job. Which we spit on. While reflecting that times have changed.

You might have fun at COA. They're nice young people over there, doing all kinds of interesting and progressive things, and very hot on music, particularly yours. You might have to demand privacy, but I guess you could do that. I don't really know what an Artist in Residence does. We have a friend, Chenoweth Hall, who is A. in R. at Machias U of M, a sculptor and painter, who teaches. Do you teach? Or like to? I couldn't, I would go all to jelly in such a traumatic situation, and run like a rabbit if confronted with a roomful of bright young faces. Or any faces. You nem them, I run.

Regards to Pat. We did so enjoy meeting her that day you slopped the coffee on your ankle. I'm not too sure I didn't joggle you, but not on purpose.

Have fun, *Ruth*

TO GORDON BOK

November 14, 1974

Dear Gordon,

We also tilled. I got a monumental lame back from (1) shoveling compost and (2) splitting fireplace logs out of an old apple tree. It seems to be a year for cutting down trees and our neighbors let us know, instead of carting the wood to the dump. This tree, according to rings, was over a hundred years old; had a robin's nest in it. It gave up hard. Having fought every inch of the way for a century, it wasn't about to take much from wedges and a maul. I didn't do well in the lumbar vertebrae, but much better now.

You'll surely have fun at COA. It's a good place for you and they'll like you, too.

I haven't copyrighted "The Old Men of the Bay," never thought of it. Why don't you, or perhaps jointly as we did "Little River"? This might be the way, especially if we do do another book—which I think would be lovely and a lot of fun, as *C. as a D.* has been. Whichever you do would be all right with me—remember I said "no strings" when I gave "The Old Men" to you. Probably what I am doing is wiggling out of looking up how to copyright and writing a letter to Washington, which isn't fair since you're doing all the work now and are without doubt as busy as I am. Incidentally, you've never cashed the check I sent you for my share of the "Little River" copyright bill. Poor old Eleanor's been carrying this along in the checkbook and cussing every time she comes to it. You're as bad as I am. After all, three bucks is three bucks—it'll buy a pound of sugar.

Are you really serious about doing another book? I take it you didn't lose your shirt on *C. as a D.* as at first I was afraid you might. Being under contract to Morrow and Co., I'd have to arrange with them, ask them if they cared and all that—I don't think they would. Some years ago, I sent them a suggestion for a college textbook, *Words to Make Up Tunes For* or some such, but what they want from me is fiction, period. I have a limited backlog of material scattered around; I would have to get it together and edit it. I don't think there's enough for a book. Not yet. Some of it's in ms., some's tape-recorded. Some probably wouldn't be worth considering, but there could be fresh material, given time. So?

Good luck with your January project. Be glad to see you and Pat any time.

As usual, but gimpy *Ruth*

Charles B. McLane is the author of *Islands of the Mid-Maine Coast* (1982), in which a history (with map) of Gott's Island and Ruth's family appears.

TO CHARLES B. MCLANE

November 14, 1974

Professor Charles B. McLane
Department of Government
Dartmouth College
Hanover, New Hampshire 03755

Dear Professor McLane,

I have your letter with enclosed questionnaire with regard to your interesting and, I might say, man-sized, historical project concerning the Maine islands. The scope of it staggers me.

Certainly you, with three hundred islands on your plate, wouldn't thank me for duplication of material which I gather from your letter you already possess.

I can give you some sources which I don't doubt have already been suggested to you:

Daniel Gott, Mount Desert Pioneer, by William O. Sawtelle (Pamphlet)

The History of Swans Island, by Dr. H. B. Small, which contains a chapter on Gott's Island, with anecdotes; (recently privately reprinted)

Back issues of the Bangor Historical Society's magazine, available for examination at the Maine State Library in Augusta.

These should take care of pioneer background sources. There is a good deal of duplication, since original sources must have been necessarily skimpy.

I have a photostatic copy of the original deed to Gott's Island, inherited from my father's people, made out to Daniel Gott and dated 1789—I wonder where the old boy got 18 pounds, but apparently he had it. The original deed, I understand, is now in Washington.

I also have a copy of what I am told is the original map of the Gott's Island area, made by officers (map-makers?) of a British man-of-war which apparently cruised the coast in 1776. Its legend reads "Published according to Act of Parliament July 15, 1776, by J. F. W. Des Barres, Esq." This is interesting for one detail (at least to me) because the long chesilbeach which now encloses the tidal pool at Gott's Island is missing. Either they didn't bother to put it in or it wasn't there in 1776; and if it wasn't, one wonders what cataclysm in Blue Hill Bay threw up what's there now.

I expect I haven't helped you much. My fiction, as you say, is fiction and I do thank you for your pleasant remarks about it.

Sincerely, *Ruth Moore*

"The Lower Lights" song that Ruth mentions below is actually titled "Let the Lower Lights Be Burning," and Kendall Morse recorded it on his album Kendall Morse: *Lights Along the Shore* (Folk Legacy, 1976).

TO GORDON BOK

November 15, 1974

Dear Gordon,

The first day I met you I told you who I thought should record those ballads. So go ahead with my blessing, I'd be honored. As an author should be by any work of hers spoken or sung in that voice of yours.

And many times thanks for the rest of your letter. If we had picked up our mail an hour earlier, I'd have been able to include this in the letter posted to you this morning. Nobody has ever, repeat ever, got two letters from me on the same day.

If Kendall sings "The Lower Lights" I want to be in that number who hears him.

Aff. *Ruth*

James Longley was governor of Maine from 1974 to 1978. Gore Vidal, of course, is the famous American novelist and critic.

TO MARY AND LOU DILLON

December 23, 1974

Dear Mary and Lou and whoever has surfaced for the holidays,

The third day of winter. The first two got completely by me. Only realized since I have surfaced for Christmas. it is a pretty day, with a dusting of snow and green grass showing through, and robins still around with white-throated sparrows. I suppose summer's lease will hath too short a date, but it's a pretty day and to hell with a full graveyard.

God help a lady who has always been hen-minded who is over seventy. Only He knows what I'll do THIS year. Last year, I stuck the postage stamps on the back of the Christmas card envelopes, under the impression that they were tuberculosis seals. I gave up trying to learn to play the piano, not because a basketball hit me on the end of my ring-finger in 1924, rendering it intransigent, but because I couldn't learn to count. The music teacher and I would sit solidly (sic), she being also stout, on the piano bench, and she would say, "Count." So I would begin: 1-2-3-4. 5-6-7-8. Etc. After the sixth year, she got so she would turn on me a sick look without compassion. So, finally, I told her the story about the music student who made the same mistake 99 times and when he made it 100, the teacher committed suicide. Oh, wow! Laid myself wide open. She said, "I have no intention of committing suicide," and left it lie where it was. So I bought some Bartok records for the stereo and said goodby with all goodwill. (She hates Bartok.) It's still a pretty day. Sing *cucu.*

Maine elected an Independent Governor. How about that? Of course Mr. Longley rode into office on the front end of the pure white horse of not putting up the state income tax; now he says, "It is going to be tougher than I thought." Undoubtedly. We also, after twenty years of the same cruddy old law, have elected a new Hancock County Sheriff. It is about time somebody made a change. I suppose you read in the paper how some racy boys—nobody yet knows whom—who?—shot out most of the street lights in Tremont one euphoric midnight and put two bullets through the front windows of Ronald Gott's market. We hope we don't win anything in the Maine State Lottery, we live too near the road. As for National politics, I have only one comment: That I have fallen in love with Mr. Gore Vidal who mentioned in public "the jack o' lantern Nixon left on the White House doorstep."

We plug along, doing what we can with what we have. Eleanor is up to her ears in the Planning Board, riding, occasionally, a high cloud of flak, since the word "zoning" has been dirty in Tremont for generations. But the Shorelands Zoning is finished and accepted over several dead bodies at Town Meeting, and the Board is now girding to produce the Comprehensive Plan for the whole town. Don't laugh, men, the poor devils are dying. As for me, all I can say is, I've surfaced for Christmas.

Best season's and love *Ruth*

Into 1975, Ruth continued to have trouble communicating with the Social Security people both in Maine and in California. A number of her letters that have survived deal with Social Security.

TO THE SOCIAL SECURITY ADMINISTRATION

April 11, 1975

Dear Sirs:

I became 72 on July 21, 1975.

I am self-employed—Occupation: Writer.

In 1974, I worked on a book during January, February and November and December. I was unable to finish the book because I felt the work unsatisfactory. I had no earnings from it.

In 1975, I have worked through January, February and March. I do not know when this second book will be finished, since I am somewhat slowed down because of eyestrain. It is certainly not ready to be offered to a publisher, and I have had no earnings from it in 1975; and do not yet know whether there will be any.

For your convenience, please refer to my letter of April 11, 1972, together with its reply from Mr. Paul Quandt, explaining the status of my claim.

Sincerely yours *Ruth Moore*

Jaws, the famous movie, was released in 1975. John's wife Fern died in 1972.

TO JOHN C. WILLEY

April 19, 1975

Dear John,

It's ridiculous that I haven't written you. I've meant to, but I suppose I'm on what hell is paved with. I look at the date on your letter and I SWOON with guilt. But I have had my nose to the well-known you-know-what since January, and no brains outside of what grinds off. Thayer used to jaw at me for being so "coy" he called it, God bless his soul. But I never know what I have until it is nearly finished, as it is now. I have got possibly 50 pages of top copy still to do, and a few ends to tie up, as always, and I expect you can have it, well, let's say, tentatively (?) sometime in May. Eleanor hasn't read it yet and she always picks up the bloopers, like, on the same night the moon is full and the tide is high in one place and no moon and tide low in another.

I am never very good at synopses, especially when I've written the book. They always look so naked. I would rather have you see the book itself first. If I had written you beforehand about the ms. I wrote last year and got sick of on page 200-or-so, and scrapped, where would we both be now? This one I'm much happier about and you will be, too, I think—it has two love stories in it; three, if you count a happily married couple. This is quite some doing for me, who would usually be content if I could just say "Joe loves Josephine," or something like that. As you know.

I do have a title which I shrink from sending to you, in case you want to change it. This time, I might really fight.

It is: *The Dinosaur Bite*

"The way to be safe from dinosaur bites is to be little, fast, furry, warm-blooded and smart . . ."

This comes from *The Last Whole Earth Catalog,* and is a quote from its Editor, Stewart Brand. He wrote this in his review of a book called *Patterns of Survival,* by Lorus and Margery Milne. The rest of the quote goes this way:

"(The way to be in hazard of dinosaur bites is to be another dinosaur.) We're talking about education in the school of survival, which every school is, despite pastel walls."

Not that I thought of using the second half of the quote, makes things a little too long and I don't ever like to dot the i's and cross t's. But it does come close to the theme of my book, which is about survival in our times—a city-man, a teacher, takes his children away from what is happening to them in the city, in civilization, to a safe and quiet place. Let me know what you think when you've read the ms.

My book isn't about hippies, or Swiss Family Robinson. And do not come at me about *Jaws,* which I am aware of.

I knew you were in Florida at Christmas time—some cronies of Frances's saw you there. (The eyes that watch you from the underbrush.)

And I haven't yet been in touch with Gordon Bok about the new book of ballads. I have been too damn busy to be in touch with anyone. Besides, he hops like a grasshopper from place to place, on concert tours—the last I knew, he was on the West Coast. But we'll probably get together when he comes back to Camden. Thanks for your approval of this. Our first effort with *Cold as a Dog* has been quite successful, I understand is sold out. I made Two Hundred Bucks. Sucks to you, can't sell ballads! See how rich I am.

I went back to smoking when I found I couldn't work without. My blood pressure went up, I ran a temperature, my brain was a sog full of dumplings. So I said to the damn doctor, "I would rather enjoy my life now than live to be 90."

I hope you are feeling better. Spring perhaps has helped. I don't like to think of you not feeling well. I worry. Not because you are MY EDITOR, but because you are John.

Regards to Charley.

Affectionately *Ruth*

TO JOHN C. WILLEY

April 27, 1975

Dear John,

I got finished up earlier than I thought I would—things toward the end fell quite nicely into place. Perhaps your encouraging and very pleasant letter helped. So get the thing out of the house. I thought—It's come to the point where it ought to be somewhere else. I'm so very much pleased and relieved that you like the title.

It came out a little longer than I anticipated. 293 pages in all. The numbers go to 291, but when I checked I found pp. 34 and 94 had to have 34-A and 94-A following them—a mistake in numbering.

There's a carbon, if you need it. All the carbon paper I could get is plastic and juicy, but the copy's clear enough to read.

Now I am going to start the garden. If the darn spring would ever get rolling, that is. Today we have had snow squalls all day, grimpsy weather.

Aff. *Ruth*

In the following letter, there's no hint as to whether Mrs. Friedman was a classmate of Ruth's at Albany or not, but, obviously, she had written to Ruth about attending the 50th reunion of the Class of 1925. By 1975, a whole new campus had been built at Albany.

TO MRS. FRIEDMAN

April 28, 1975

Dear Mrs. Friedman,

Thank you for your pleasant letter and for the photographs and information about what has taken place at N.Y.S.C.T. since 1925. A happening, certainly. The new buildings look impressive and beautiful. I suppose they have completely snowed under the old peristyles and the rotunda in which Minerva stood. Whatever has happened to Minerva? She was always there, a kind of Educational Mother with a yellowish complexion, which acquired rouged cheeks and a mustache, whenever the freshmen and sophomores had a bash and stole banners. As I recall, she had a bulletin board attached somewhere, for personal messages, which made the whole rotunda homey and nice. To me, at 18, she was impressive and beautiful, too.

What I remember chiefly about the college is the education I got there and an Indian Ladder hike. I had four magnificent teachers. Agnes Futterer, who did her best with my Maine accent in her Drama classes; Edith Wallace, who taught me the sense and sounds of the Odes of Horace; Dr. Thompson, who let me, a freshman, into his Poetry course limited to upperclassmen—(God knows why he did, except he was man of goodwill); and Dr. Hastings who taught Literature by reading it aloud. I remember how he curdled the blood of the entire class simply by reading, in his dry voice, Coleridge's Christabel. My God, the woman turned out to be a snake!

The Indian Ladder Hike—do they still do this?—was the time some of us put up tents and stayed all night. About twelve o'clock, a terrific thunderstorm came up—in those mountains thunderstorms bounce from peak to peak; that one would have scared Rip Van Winkle. I remember lying shivering on the ground; I was, and still am, an awful coward in thunderstorms. The tents collapsed; we got rained on and soaked; Miss Scotland, Biology, had for some reason worn a new and expensive corset; it was ruined. Dr. Croasdale, who had no use for corsets, said to her, "I've always told you I don't believe in the spirit of those things." To which, Ms. S. said, "But, you know, it isn't the spirit, it's the flesh that's weak."

As for me, the best I can say is I've been busy. After I found out that I wasn't a very good teacher, I did secretarial and publicity work in New York. For awhile, I managed a nut and fruit ranch in California. Here in the East, we'd call it a farm—it was only 18 acres, not very impressive, but fun. Back

East, I did magazine work for five years or so, and then wrote books. The list of titles which you asked for is attached.

I wish I could come to Albany for Class Reunion, but I'm really snowed under with commitments here. I'm sorry. But goodwill to my classmates and congratulations for surviving as long as we have.

Sincerely *Ruth Moore, '25*

My respect for Ruth Moore was such that I never thought of writing her or calling her, even though we lived in the same area and knew many of the same people. I had grown up reading her books and making book reports in English classes on them. When *Spoonhandle* was made into the movie *Deep Waters,* everyone went to see it. As a teenager, I was in love with the game of basketball, and I read Ruth's basketball novel *The Walk Down Main Street* with great interest in both the *Reader's Digest* Condensed Book version and the original Morrow edition.

When I went to college at the University of Maine and became a student of Edward M. "Ted" Holmes's, I heard more stories about Ted's good and lifelong friend Ruth. He read to us from her work, encouraged me to try and write my Maine stories the way Ruth did. To the local people of Hancock County unfamiliar with the works of E. B. White and other famous writers from away, Ruth Moore was Hancock County's most famous and beloved author. She was ours, after all, one of us.

But it wasn't until I left Maine and was teaching in Central New York and writing my "Letters from Liverpool" and "Maine Book Review" columns for the now defunct *Tuesday Weekly* paper of Ellsworth, 1973–75, that I dared write Ruth and ask her for an interview. I was writing from Liverpool, a suburb of Syracuse, at the end of the school year thinking I could come see her as soon as I got home for the summer.

TO SANFORD PHIPPEN

May 31, 1975

Dear Mr. Phippen,

Thanks for your pleasant letter. Which I honestly don't know how to answer. Regarding interviews for publication, I have a problem—I live too near the highway, and not far from Acadia National Park. Past the house, starting in April and ending at the close of hunting season in November, goes a procession of three million people, including a minority, let's say, of Celebrity-Snatchers and some of the finest hoodlums in the world. If you get your name in the paper and become one of the Sights to See While in the

Vicinity, you might better be dead. Because your privacy is. And I am always thunderously busy and need it.

I'm sorry if this sounds stuffy; I don't mean it to. Of course I like recognition as much as any writer does, but the Decade of the Winnebago and the back-packers has really got me on the run. Down East has been cooking an interview with me taken some two-three?—years ago, and I pray God they don't use it until I am done. For an obituary, maybe.

Look, you don't need to chomp around interviewing other writers. I've known about your work for quite a while—first, from Ted Holmes, and lately from what you are doing in the Tuesday. Why not do your own thing, which you obviously have plenty of? Interviews, for publication or not, are a load of old codwallop. They use up time which might be better put in on something else.

Good luck and thanks very much.

Sincerely *Ruth Moore*

Leafy Piper and Rosie are characters from *The Dinosaur Bite,* which was published in 1976.

TO JOHN C. WILLEY

June 17, 1975

Dear John,

Herewith is the contract, signed, initialled and witnessed, as requested. It looks all right to me—contracts do. One thing, I haven't procured from Steward Brand permission to use the quote from the *Last Whole Earth Catalog*. Your side has always done this kind of thing for me—will you still do it? The address is *Whole Earth Catalog,* 558 Santa Cruz Avenue, Menlo Park, California, 94025. Random House is the publisher, near to you by phone.

I'm delighted that you like the book. Your letter didn't make the garden grow any faster—it sits there in the fog looking very gruntled and yellow, but I am pink and twice my natural size. I didn't think I'd be able to finish so soon—thought it might mean months more work; then suddenly pieces fell into place with a clatter that surprised me. I suppose I could have prolonged suspense by letting Leafy Piper tote Rosie into the back country with him and that was what I was trying to do; but the thing bothered me. To do that would have flawed the whole conception of Leafy's character; he is, after all, a limited sex-pot, his margins close together, bounded by the budding and maturing of maple leaves. Confronted by the reality of his ancies, could he do anything else but run?

On second thought, I don't really care if you publish in '76—at least, I won't have to read the thing through again until time has passed and I can bear to look at proofs of it. So please don't hassle your already-set-up schedule, in case you are trying to. At the moment, I haven't a brain in my head and am into the gardening, though with this weather, all I can grow is onions. They look spiffy, but the rest of it looks as if it had been trodden on by an army of bullocks. After all, nearly five inches of rain in a week ... And FOG, you wouldn't believe!

I don't know how to say thank you for your letter except to repeat. In August, I'll send you and Charley some onions to express my deep sense of creative accomplishment—ephemeral, perhaps, but nice as long as it lasts.

Eleanor sends her regards and mine are infinite.

Affectionately *Ruth*

The "other Ruth Moore" was Ruth E. Moore, a journalist who specialized in scientific articles and books like *Man, Time and Fossils: The Story of Evolution* (1953) and *Earth We Live On* (1956).

TO JOHN C. WILLEY

July 7, 1975

Dear John,

Thanks for your letter of July 3, plus contract. I take it you didn't find anything in the ms. you want worked over, thank God. I really will send you some onions.

About book clubs, I have, as always, my fingers crossed. I'm too ancient a pro to worry about it, but it would be nice again, if some large, wealthy conglomerate got bit by a dinosaur. But if this should happen, please don't let anybody, carried away by publicity, mention where I live, especially if it turns out to be a summer publication. This year—and doubtless next—every crudhead in the United States seems to have headed for Maine, and I've already had to furnish a cave in the woods. Thing is, they get here and find there's nothing really to DO except look at scenery—no Coney Island, no Disneyland, only nature walks at Acadia Park, so to speak, so they wander around looking bored and tired, poor souls, hunting for Sights to See While in the Vicinity. I don't mind if the backpackers sleep and have assignations in our woods and fields, or wouldn't, if they didn't leave such messes. Eleanor suggests that we put an ad in the Bar Harbor Times, such as, "Will the lady who left the pink Kleenex and the flattened down roll of chicken wire beside our lilac bush, please come and get her pantyhose. We have picked up the beer bottles."

What the chicken wire was all about, we don't know. I had it beside the garden fence, ready to put us to stop skunks. I suppose it made some sort of foundation.

Thanks for everything, including relieving my mind about the Stewart Brand quote.

As always, *Ruth*

P.S. The other Ruth Moore, as she always seems to when I do, is bringing out a book this year—I can always tell—I begin to get odds and ends of her mail.

Mary Dillon says that her new house in Hancock was finished by 1975, so I'm assuming the following letter was from that year, because Ruth left off the year on the date; but she does repeat the same story about placing the ad in the *Bar Harbor Times* that she mentioned in the July 7 letter to John Willey. Ruthie is Mary Dillon's daughter.

TO MARY DILLON

July 9, 1975

Dear Mary,

But I don't raise dahlias—I raise peonies, which, E. says, when in full bloom look like prostitutes in church. So let that be the end of the matter.

We'd love to come over, of course, but for us too later on will be better. Right now, and I hate to say this or even believe it, we hardly care to leave the place by itself, and this is no old maids' jitters, either. This year's tourist crowd includes some very pleasant and decent people, the majority perhaps; but it can't be gainsaid that past these doors go some of the finest hoodlums in the world. This seems to be the gist, let's say, of the July vacation crowd, which may change toward the end of the month when this batch goes home.

* * *

Our old cat, who is a eunuch, has got ideas from somewhere. He is pursuing a lady-cat, rambling nights and coming home in the mornings absolutely beat-out. We have seen his performance and it is pitiful, poor lamb.

Building a house is wonderful fun, isn't it? I know you and your batch of kids are having a ball. We always did. Our last effort was the new jeep garage across the road. Of course two days after it was finished a drunk came barreling down the road, lost control of his Consol and took the northeast corner out of it. (The building, I mean. My antecedents get funny sometimes.) Missed the jeep by an inch and knocked the building three inches off its foundations. We took one look, pooped out and called in professionals to make repairs. After all, fun's fun.

Of course we want to see your new house, and will, with pleasure. And Ruthie, my friend, who, if she reads this letter will think I have turned into more of an old monster than ever. I don't suppose I have—I just get put out at times.

Love, *Ruth*

The article about Mary Dillon that Ruth mentions appeared in the *Tuesday Weekly* newspaper on August 26, 1975. Since the letter that follows has no date, I'm guessing it was written right after the article appeared.

TO MARY AND LOU DILLON

August 27, 1975? (no date)

Dear Mary and Lou,

I saw the picture in the *Tuesday* and thought, that is one hell of a terrific face, before I realized that I'd always thought so.

In the second one, you and Lou are finding scorpions—or is it earwigs?—in the cucumbers, no?

When can you come over? I will build a fish chowder for lunch if I can find anything but sculpins at the fish wharf. Failing that, maybe a hard-boiled egg accompanied by vegetables, which as my Uncle Grover Cleveland Dunham used to say, will come "Rateoutthegarden." Something edible, anyway.

We have a couple of friends we think you might enjoy meeting—Martha and Joe Hubbard, who live in Brooklin across the bay from us. They're agreeable and pleasant and fun to be with. Martha's an artist working in stained glass and Joe, now retired, was for years head of the Economics Dept. at Bryn Mawr. Joe's a very remarkable man—he's been totally blind since he was 21, and got his education from being read to or from tapes and such, retaining everything in his mind without reference to anything visual, such as notes, and so on, which to me, with my flipping mental equipment is miraculous. They live much as we do, except we don't have hens, we gave them up years ago when we found out that the eggs cost us $5 a dozen—organic garden, loving the winters, wouldn't go back to Bryn Mawr if dragged by horses. Joe, incidentally, cuts up all their firewood, using wedges and maul and bucksaw, and he built the henhouse, from sills to shingles.

This lunch date is all tentative—maybe you and Lou would rather come be by yourselves with us, if so, no sweat. Martha says they can't come until week after next, Monday or Friday, and I can't remember when you said Lou was going back. If we can't mesh joints, you and Lou come Monday or Friday this coming week, ok? Call us or drop a line?

I hope your garden is getting this rain. It's running down our drainpipes like a river, thank God.

Love, *Ruth*

Ruth crossed out the Mondays above and added this note:

Tues. or Thurs. This letter won't go out till Monday, I suddenly realize. Flipping mental equipment.

TO ASHER TREAT

September 9, 1975

Dear Mr. Treat,

I thank you so much for your beautiful and moving letter.

Ever since my first book, *The Weir*, came out in 1943 I have been trying to write as you say I have, simply, as a friend and neighbor. Readers write me, but no one has ever pinpointed so clearly—almost as one might facet a diamond—what has been in my own mind for so many years.

Thank you again, and my very best wishes to you and Mrs. Treat.

Man in the Environment was written by Ruth E. Moore (the "other Ruth Moore").

TO JOHN C. WILLEY

Sept. 9, 1975

Dear John,

I do wish somebody would tell the Authors' Guild once and for all that I didn't write *Man in the Environment*, that my publisher isn't Knopf and that they surely have something struck crossways in their computer. Of course, I've always received some of Chicago Ruth Moore's mail, and once, long in the past, my picture was used in the B. of the M.'s club bulletin, announcing *Man, Time and Fossils*, or some such, thereby getting me in dreadful wrong with my mother, who to the day of her death believed I'd written a book and had never shown it to HER. A rugged time for us all.

The Guild keeps sending me a questionnaire re. my royalties and publisher relations, saying please, please answer; but all I tell them is that while I have every sympathy with what they are trying to do, I haven't a clue to my namesake's royalties and my own relations with my publisher, who is William Morrow, are excellent, dammit. I enclose latest copy of said questionnaire.

I have also a copy of a fan letter to send along. It's very moving and says so clearly what I have been trying to do ever since *The Weir*, that I thought you and maybe some of the other people at Morrow who've been coddling me along for decades, might like to see it. A book, as I've always told you, being a cooperative venture.

We're getting along well; summer's over, thank God, and the 3 million tourists have mostly gone home. They have been over us like a tent; don't tell us that Winnebago has gone bankrupt. They SMELL so awful, the monsters; it takes a week for their fumes to blow away. Most of the harvest is in; the onions are curing beautifully. We bought a small greenhouse "kit" which Eleanor is putting up with prayers and curses. I have one tomato plant in a tub to put into it when it is finished.

As always *Ruth*

TO JOHN C. WILLEY

October 26, 1975

Dear John,

Herewith the galleys for *Dinosaur Bite*—nice clean galleys they are, too; only a few typos and no changes whatever. Please compliment the printer.

I'm glad you gave me plenty of time—for some days I couldn't either write or type, having in a state of euphoria slammed the car door on my thumb and had to have ten stitches. Two good things came of it, however. The number of stitches impressed my grandnephews no end—"Wow, ten stitches!" —and not able to do much else, we took off on a needed vacation, went to Canada, joined the fooliage crowd and drove 1800 miles around and across Nova Scotia and Cape Breton. Had a wonderful time, slept and healed.

Thanks to you I got a magnificent apology from the Authors' Guild; I am, after all, "their own Ruth Moore"—the other one doesn't even belong, it seems. I shouldn't have bothered you with it, busy as you are; but I thought a real stern publisher's letter might do some good. Of course it's a natural mistake, made by many. I wished at the time that I could have got you involved in the war we've been having with the *New York Times's* computer, which has insisted on sending us two copies of the *Sunday Times,* merely because we renewed our subscription. For a while, we practically had to use the jeep to haul home the mail. This, however, has been fixed—perhaps they destroyed the computer.

I don't know who Asher Treat and Joy Gilder may be, but it was a good fan letter. I get quite a few still about past books, but kept and answered this one. They come from all sorts, from kids to the lady who appeared in person from Brooklyn, this summer—said when her husband asked her where she wanted to spend their vacation, she'd like to go to Maine and hunt up me. They'd both read everything from *The Weir* on; seemed to know the books practically by heart. It was pleasant. He was a mechanic, she a school teacher, both young, and not celebrity collecting, only interested in saying thank you.

We send you and Charley some onions, to Norwalk—I hope the great P.O. Dept. doesn't bang them around till they come apart and stink up your mail.

Affectionately *Ruth*

"Old Men of the Bay" remains one of Ruth's uncollected poems.

TO GORDON BOK

December 6, 1975

Dear Gordon,

I can't think where your letter has been—it was postmarked Nov. 29, but in it you said you were going on tour and would be back by Thanksgiving ...? Never mind—I'm sorry to be so long in answering it.

I'm delighted to hear you want to do another printing of *Cold as a Dog,* so go ahead with my blessing. The old *Dog* seems to be indestructible, thanks to you. He seems, still, to have legs. You mention "This last batch of books"—have you done two printings already, or did you mean the last batch of the first one? If two, I think you have done marvelously with it. Marvelously anyway, really.

I wish, in a way, we could include part, at least, of the "Old Men of the Bay," but I know it would shoot up the costs, probably out of all reason, since you already have the *Cold as a Dog* plates.

Some time ago, you suggested our doing another little book together—are you still interested? I would be, if I could larrup my creeping brain out of its jog-trot and do some more ballads. I always go into a coma when I finish a novel, which I have just done—*The Dinosaur Bite*, due to come out next May. So I'm free of commitments for this winter and might go back to work after the holidays. I have some beginnings which need revision, but I think I'd need at least six new ballads to make a book of any size at all. Possibly more. But this is all for future consideration on both sides—gives us both plenty of time to think it over. If you've lost the impulse, I won't repine too much.

Our best to you both, and have a good Christmas.

Ruth

Frances Phillips was the editor-in-chief of Morrow and a friend of Ruth's from the New York days. *Ragtime* is the famous novel by E. L. Doctorow that was published in 1975.

TO FRANCES PHILLIPS

Dec. 6, 1975

Dear Frances,

It was no use writing anybody so close to a holiday—they all go off to spas and play for days. So I waited for a well-omened date halfway between Thanksgiving and Christmas. There is a conference sometime in December at which some of us writers are going to be discussed and I hope to hit it close to the nose. They will all say, "How come SHE is asking all these intelligent (impertinent) questions? How come she knows enough to ask them?"

I am scared of those queens, having known some in my time. Annie Laurie Williams (an Empress) briefed me, years ago. I wish I had her around now. She smote upon hips, and was a witch with second sight. When accused of making $30,000 a week, she replied, pie-faced, "Oh, my no, I don't make that in a month." I think she is dead. Her blasted sisters haven't seen fit to let me know. Tails to her comet, they were, now feeling oats. God stiffen them.

I don't need to tell you how invaluable your professional advice is to me, but I do need to say thank you, with diamonds. I'll let you know what wasps come out of the nest. If any. If when.

Hope things are going well for you. We and the Ladies' Asses will be glad to see you back.

Yours *Ruth*

We haven't read Ragtime, *but will do, as soon as we can round up a copy.*

Mr. Paperback is the name of a chain of Maine bookstores owned and operated by Magazines, Inc. of Bangor. Barbara Adams worked for Morrow.

TO JOHN C. WILLEY

December 7, 1975

Dear John,

The top of the season to you and Charles. Up till this morning, we were having spring here, and then the cat came in iced up like a sundae.

Our private printings of *Cold as a Dog* are now sold out and there's still demand for it, so we are printing another edition. It seems to have legs (your phrase, if I recall). Mr. Paperback has been querying me as to why my books aren't in paperback, and I've also had other queries from people who say they can't afford to buy hardcover, but would like to own my books. All I can say is that the Pocket Books editions are out of print. Of course they must be. It's got me thinking a little.

Would you ask Barbara Adams to send me a history of submissions to paperback houses on my last two books? To whom were they submitted and when? What is Morrow doing about making a paperback sale for *Dinosaur Bite?*

What does our contract with Pocket Books say about rights when their edition goes out of print? Do the rights revert to us so that we can sell them to another paperback house? I'm thinking of some Young Adult paperback lines done by both paperback publishers and juvenile departments of book publishers.

I suppose the Walt Disney Productions nibble has sunk without a trace, or you'd have let me know. (Nice mixed metaphor, that.) Or not, if you consider the size of the fish. Unless he's dead.

I'm coming out of my post-natal coma which always seems to follow the finish of a novel, and my mind has started to, well, jog-trot, at least. I'm starting in on a set of new ballads, sort of a companion book to *Cold as a Dog,* which we may publish if we don't lose our shirts on the present printing. We have had and are having a lot of fun with this.

I'm sorry about the delay with the galleys. It was my fault, really, but I'm putting your name on this.

Aff. *Ruth*

TO GORDON BOK

December 14, 1975

Dear Gordon,

Mercy, man, don't send me any files, books, or figures—they would scare me out of the County. Let me go on record, here and now, that I have no criticism whatsoever of the way you have handled the re-publishing of *Cold as a Dog* and have been delighted with what you have done every step of the way. Something in the first of your recent letters made me wonder if you'd done a second printing; my only thought, honest to God, was pride in our joint accomplishment and hope that you'd made enough money out of it to make it worth your while. Good Lord, you did all the work, paid all the expenses and sent me $200. All this, in addition to having rescued a book I was proud of from the publisher's limbo. I would be a picky, grasping old hag wearing the chains of Scrooge if I felt differently about this. Rest your mind, for heaven's sake.

You should certainly not have had to check through 1000 copies for upside-down binding, as in the sample you sent me. Aren't you entitled to take these back to the printer and get proper compensation? A mistake like that's unforgivable, even in a small printing, and you should call his attention to it, I believe. If he won't do anything about it, tear the maimed copies up and jam them into his press. With my blessing.

Let's put off the idea of a new book of ballads until later and then see if we both feel like doing it. It will take me months, anyway, to produce satisfactory material; ballad-making comes to me by fits and starts anyway. When you suggested the project some time ago, I wrote my publisher about it and got back an enthusiastic response—John Willey says he will sign any sort of release we need. It seems they are pleased with you, too, thinking in terms of publicity for one of their authors. Apparently, there has been some which they are aware of, Lord help us all. The Eyes that Watch You from the Underbrush sort of thing? Well, we shouldn't mind that, I expect, though that wasn't our original intention. I thought I wrote you about this release on their part, but probably didn't. At the time I had no brain for anything but my new novel, *The Dinosaur Bite*, scheduled now to be published next May, and was having pre-natal pains because the damned thing wouldn't jell.

So I send you my Christmas felicity and my thanks with all my heart.

Affectionately Ruth

TO JOHN C. WILLEY

December 19, 1975

Dear John,

Folk-Legacy Records, Inc., is sending you from me a phonograph record, which I think you'll like to hear. It's very nice indeed.

The grapefruit were splendid, large as the breasts of Venus and sweet as a honey-bee tree. Eleanor and I both thank you with all our hearts. You notice I say "were."

This is not to butter you up. If I don't get an answer pretty soon to my letter of December 7, I am, dammit, going to send you another onion. One only.

Yours (slightly huffered up) *Ruth*

The reference to "Jairmany calling" is Germany.

TO MARY AND LOU DILLON

December 21, 1975

Dear Mary and Lou,

Winter solstice and right on the nose, snow. Lou, you'd be delighted and so are we. Up to last week, we had Indian summer, warm, sleepy days with the sun silvery in the south. Then, last week, we thought we had it. Our wind indicator registered 70 knots an hour in one puff. But no snow. Not like today. Up to now we've had eight inches and the forecast is for snow today, tonight, and tomorrow. Whee-O!

I am mad at the UN. I won't even use the postage stamps with UN on them. After "Jairmany calling," you'd think the world would see justice done and let the Jews alone. I know the children UNICEF helps aren't to blame for what their elders do, but I'll bet it's the kids in the third world who get most of the help. I went so far as to haul T. E. Lawrence's *Seven Pillars of Wisdom* down off the shelf, but replaced it soon. In the thirties, when I first read it, the Three Worlds seemed so far away; now they are on top of us, and I wasn't about to curdle and chill my blood with Lawrence's record of cruelty and sadism—which he seems, at times, to go along quite gaily with—against the black backdrop of what's going on now.

What a hell of a way to start a Christmas letter. With chauvinism. Of course you can't hate whole nationsfull of people, and I don't. I'm only scared to death of them.

Eleanor and my sister Tug finally weevilled me off Bass Harbor Head this fall—shut the door of the house and locked it before I could get back in. We drove 1800 miles around and about in Nova Scotia—went up to Pleasant Bay on Cape Breton's northern tip, where my grandmother came from. In her time, the only ways to get to Pleasant Bay were either by boat or by a foot-trail across the mountains, and she had a gruesome tale to tell about it which we kids used to listen to with our hair on end. Seems one night in the cold winter, her father, old Sam Hinckley, brought home from the town tavern a lady named BlackBet, and turned his wife and eleven children out into the snow. They walked thirteen miles over the mountains to Chetticamp, the older kids carrying the younger ones. "And none of us had any drawers." I can hear her now. Seeing those mountains, which the Cabot Trail, a thruway, goes over now, all I can say is "Oh, Grammaw!" Because I think what she remembered was the trauma or something, not the facts. Old Sam went to work and got another tremendous family out of Betsey—I think, twelve. Pure Dostoievsky.

We thought we might run into some relatives up there, but all we found was Jack Hinckley, Sam's grandson, aged 87, slightly vague, but sprightly and composed, who greeted us with "My! What large ladies!" Then, realizing he'd been less than tactful, he added, "Well, all the Hinckley women WERE big." It's certainly true that all the women in our family in their time developed ample fat cans, a heritage that our flesh is heir to. Nobody mentioned old Sam or my grandmother's horror story. I did ask if Jack knew where she was born—if the house was still standing, and he said, "Motel and gift shop there now. Put up smack-dab on the foundation."

Eleanor is still wound up with the Planning Board, trying hard to get the town zoned. It ain't easy. The yowl of course is, "It ain't right that a man can't do what he wants to with his own property." With this, in a way, I sympathize; but now that urban sprawl is creeping up, something's got to slow down the man from putting a row of camps around Seal Cove Pond, which is part of the local water supply. Or from letting his toilet empty direct into the harbor where the fishermen's lobster cars are. I went to one meeting (only) and came away unpopular because I said that what the town needed was a nice case of cholera. I am seldom so civic-minded.

My book, *The Dinosaur Bite*, has gone to press and is scheduled for publication next May. *R. D. Condensed* turned it down, said "it wasn't their sort of thing." Apropos of that review I told you about last summer, now where does that leave me? Between two stools, ha, ha, ha. Smack-dab.

The hammer of God surely did hit the raccoons last summer and fall. In this area, they are all gone, the game wardens say wiped out by whatever distemper it was. We haven't seen one since early September, and this was the first year since the cornpatch. They were reprobates, the coons, but there are none left now and we miss the slyblack masks and the little bright dishonest eyes peering out from under the bird-feeders where they used to congregate nightly to pick up the birds' castoff sunflower seeds. Distemper—what is it and what on earth caused it? You might wish it would hit a less defenseless bunch of critters, like, say, politicians, whom we could better spare.

My typing, as you can see, has gone to absolute pot, ever since I slammed the car door on my thumb. For a while I had to four-finger, but it is better now, only a little lumpy and stiff, wanting to leave out a letter here and there. Very frustrating, especially when finishing off a ms.

If I were a business woman and could add two and two for the State and Federal tax-boys, I could make a fortune selling Pet Rocks. This fall we had to move our collection to make way for a small, lean-to greenhouse which we put up against the Mad House wall. I think there are about four tons of specimens, collected from Nova Scotia to California. Some are really spectacular, and some are even radioactive—the ones from Black Mountain in the western part of Maine particularly so. Seems it would be as status-making to carry a nice cancer-causing radioactive rock as to carry around any rock at all, in a pet-carrier, I mean. Our pet, the cat, has just come in out of the weather iced up like a sundae. I have to go dry him off, so Christmas greetings and all, and let us know when you're turning up in Hancock in the spring.

Love, *Ruth*

Polly Street worked at Morrow for many years, and had retired by 1976.

TO JOHN C. WILLEY

January 4, 1976

Dear John,

Thanks for your letter of December 23, which gives me exactly the information I asked for and some besides. I'm happy to have it and your spring catalog; both give me a comprehensive idea of what Morrow, or perhaps I should say the reading public, has become. Actually, you know, I haven't had a Morrow catalog since the publication of *Sea Flower*, and the difference is overwhelming. I do realize how busy you must be, full and over-time, which is why I don't really write too often, even after a book comes out and I'm perishing to know how things are going. (This undoubtedly is a hangover from the many years when I was rotten spoilt by Polly Street, God rest her.)

My sudden interest in paperback editions was brought on by people writing or asking me about them—not only recent books but the old ones, for heaven's sake. You go into a paperback store and you find the shelves loaded with fiction trash that no paperback publisher ever in God's world paid a million dollars for, and every contemporary writer who ever piddled a title is represented. Except me. Which circumstance made me wonder, so I asked you. Not intending to be querulous or critical, but sobered and thoughtful.

I think the jacket for *Dinosaur Bite* is terrific, and it's a pleasant change to have a photograph instead of the usual boat-going-on-the-rocks painting. Please congratulate the photographer for me.

Well, trends are trends, and the next great one, so some recent thoughts I read on the matter tell me, will be science-fiction. Poor old fiction, battling to keep its head above water! And I can't write a *Reader's Digest* "sort of thing"; or about the beautiful people or TV passion plots; and as for the theme of Mr. Rochester-and-his-housekeeper, the original of that was handled too superbly for me even to think of rehashing it. I think I'll try again to write literature. God knows where that will land us all.

My printing-connection with Gordon Bok concerns only lyrics to put tunes to and ballads for reciting at his concerts. Doesn't stretch to fiction paperbacks. I'd be on my own with that, I expect.

This one doesn't need answering—it's a sort of tie-up-loose-ender. If I think twice about a do-it-yourself paperback, I'll be in touch.

As ever, affectionately, *Ruth*

Emmy is Ruth's niece Emily Trask Eaton, then living in Illinois where Emily's mother Esther Trask came to visit. Bri is Brian Trask, Emily's brother, and Alison is Emily's daughter.

TO EMILY TRASK EATON

January 13, 1976

Dear Emmy,

Well, apparently, nobody gets rich, as you can see from the enclosed letter from Folk-Legacy. But we have got an "in" at last which has taken a long time to get, and what'll follow knows God. The Folk-Legacy people are cordial and are showing a good deal of interest; I guess we'll have to wait and see. One thing, we would be nowhere without Gordon Bok, because we need a professional singer to perform anything we do, and he, of course, has been the prime mover in getting "Little River" published, and he sure does a beautiful job singing it, as you'll see from the enclosed record.

So far, I haven't shown anyone "The Hang-downs" or "Fair Andy" or any of the other songs you and I and Bri have written. If—and when—I do, I am going to insist that they be used as written, with the original music. I don't think "The Hang-downs" can be better done; besides, we're all too fond of the tune to accept anything else. Okay? It's been a tough field to crack, but we've made a beginning after the long wait, and the beginning may stop where it is, I don't know. But … we know we've got something on the ball at last. (I expect we knew that anyway.) Iffy, now, but wait and see.

I'm glad ma arrived safely, having skidded past all the near airplane crashes and train wrecks, to your doorstep. She thinks I worry too much, and I'm sure I do; but she and Eleanor got me to Nova Scotia this fall—actually, they tolled me outdoors and locked the door so I couldn't get back in. Just a matter of getting started it was, I had a fine time. They got jumpy, of course, expecting me to want to start back home at any time, which was hard to put up with, since I was enjoying myself as much as anybody. We ALL had a ball. Give her my love and tell her that, now she's there, I'm glad she went. She needed to. Also, I miss her. Selfish about it, I guess.

Roaring old winter is on us, 12 below yesterday morning, zero today with snow. That time of year when nobody can get outdoors without falling down, and the cat gets bored and throws up all over the nice clean rug. Snow spoiled the skating—for awhile we had lots of kids swarming over the gravel pit pond.

We miss the screeching and yelling and hell-raising up and down the Lighthouse Road, lots of company. There was a small character in red pants down there the other day I'd say less than two years old, who apparently hadn't ever seen ice before, and of all the pratfalls and yells of joy—it was swell to watch. He'd go down ka-whango on his fat stern and then stick it up in the air getting up, laughing like crazy all the time. Everybody was fascinated.

Give my love to all your crew, especially to Alison, who does me the honor of remembering me each time she comes. And return the Folk-Legacy letter which I need for my records, okay?

Love, *Uppy*

The *Kirkus Review* had reviewed *The Dinosaur Bite*. Paul Shields was a summer person who retired in Bass Harbor. Now deceased, he ran the old movie theater in Southwest Harbor.

TO JOHN C. WILLEY

March 25, 1976

Dear John,

I've been flattened out with the flu (as who hasn't?) or you would have had this letter sooner. I wouldn't send you a germ.

The books are here and very nice they are and thank you with oak leaves. Oak leaves? Or is it palm? My head is still a trifle muzzy. The jacket I think is one of the best we've produced, and I'm not picky because the blurb does me out of two novels. I myself never can remember how many books I've written. At the moment, it seems like a lot . . . just enough words left to let you know how very pleased I am with our finished product.

I don't suppose this cockiness will last long—only until I worm into the thing and realize what I could have done and didn't do with the plot. But right now, it's comforting.

Mercy, who do they have reviewing books at *Kirkus* now? Leprechauns?

Fame, which as you know, hasn't heretofore caught up with me in my home town, seems to be stirring around a little now, at least peering through the keyhole. The local Theatre group plans to open its season in May with, of all things, *Deep Waters*, and to make a Thing over the Memorial Day weekend—whether this is because everybody thought I might die of the flu or not, I don't know, but it seemed to be pushing things a little. I've told them that it's a terrible movie, sepia and drear, but with no results. I've also said I'd help in any way I could that didn't entail public appearances, also with no effect. Does Morrow have, say, a *Spoonhandle* poster from the muddy old archives, if any, which could be sent to Paul Shields, West Tremont, Maine? I don't dare to hope that any such thing exists, but it's all I could think of—being helpful, so to speak.

On second thought, Memorial Day week-end would be an opportunity for you and Charley to drive up. Then Charley could make a speech, if anyone got called upon and we could all go home and gorge upon lobsters, which would give us a much less dreadful case of indigestion than sitting through that awful movie. I wish people wouldn't DO things like this. (The above suggestion I realize is preposterous considering the work-load you carry, and when all we have to offer is salt air and seafood. I don't imagine the Thing will be much more than the showing of the movie.)

We are well, considering the circumstances, and spring has sprung in the shape of a white-throated sparrow whose pipe is hoarse and scrannel.

Aff. *Ruth*

Thanks to the efforts of English professor Donald F. Mortland of Unity College, Ruth was awarded an Honorary Doctor of New England Literature degree on June 26, 1976. Because she couldn't be there, the award was made in absentia and Professor Mortland read the citation at the graduation ceremonies.

TO ALLAN B. KARSTETTER

April 19, 1976

President Allan B. Karstetter
Unity College
Unity, Maine 04653

Dear President Karstetter:

Unity's award of the honorary degree of Doctor of New England Literature is indeed a tremendous compliment to me and I accept its intent with both humility and pride.

The trouble is, I shall have to be away traveling in June on a working trip—research and material-gathering for a new book, commitments for which were made as far back as last fall. Try as I may to reorganize plans, I can see no possible chance of getting back by June 26 or even later. This bad luck comes from being a continual nose-to-the-grindstone working fool, which I've had the occasion to regret in the past and surely do now. Under the circumstances, I feel it is only fair to you and your Board to mention that I would thoroughly understand should you wish to withdraw the award since I cannot be on hand in person to receive it. I'm very sorry about this.

With deep appreciation and thanks, I am

Regretfully yours *Ruth Moore*

Richard Rostron was in the Art Department at Morrow. *PW* is *Publishers' Weekly*.

TO JOHN C. WILLEY

April 19, 1976

Dear John,

I flop around between getting letters answered and doing the outside spring work which has arrived too early for comfort this year—not that hot weather in April here is to be sneezed at. We rake and rake and pile up dry leaves and old grass for compost and sonder why we were so darn lazy last fall and let it accumulate.

How nice of you and Richard Rostron to devise a special poster. Please tell him how much I appreciate it, and thank him and his busy department for taking this trouble. I didn't even hope that anything would be left in your Cain's warehouse of *Spoonhandle*, but thought I ought to do SOMETHING. I don't think this "fracas" (your word) will amount to much but a showing of the movie and maybe free popcorn—haven't heard a word since from the theatre people, so goodness knows what deviltry they're up to.

I've weasled out of Unity College's commencement—they've awarded me an honorary degree, Doctor of New England Literature, which I must say floored me, this title seeming very toplofty to me for a competent hack. Am I a competent hack, do you think, or do I write literature? I've begun to wonder, late years. Anyway, their commencement is on June 26, and I can't be there, because I'll be on a working trip—research and material gathering for the new book. Last fall, on Cape Breton Island and in various Canadian fishing ports, I began thinking and getting stuff together, and made some commitments then to be back in June. So first things first. I'm too damned old and rickety to face crowds of people and publicity—perhaps I always was. So I get out of it whenever, trying not to tell polite fibs or hurt people's feelings. I think I must be related to Lulu Webtoe, of Mother Goose fame: "Oho, oho, cried Lulu Webtoe, I don't like my hat and I don't like my bow. I was asked out to tea and I just wouldn't go."

All the leprechauns I've known personally were endearing, yes, at times when they wanted to be; but they could make bad mischief, yes, when so inclined. Thanks for the *PW* review. It helped to take the nasty taste out.

I'd like ten more copies of *Dinosaur Bite*, when you get around to it, please.

I had a mystery in the mail the other day, a copy of *Dinosaur* forwarded from Morrow, from Ziegler Associates in Los Angeles, enclosing a slip printed: Memo. Nancy Hardin. And no other message. I'm at sea about what to do with it. Ziegler Associates, I read in Time, is Ron Ziegler, and he, of course, is Nixon. Now, do they want an autograph, or has Somebody got mad and returned the book?

(the conclusion to this letter is missing)

TO ALLAN B. KARSTETTER

April 26, 1976

Dear President Karstetter,

Thank you for your understanding letter of the 21st. I sense between its lines the mind of a man who comprehends personally how demanding creative work is and how selfishly it limits time away from it. Where mine is concerned, I suppose I am a troglodyte. I don't know where I shall be or at what stage my present project will be in June, 1977. It's like being on a roller-coaster—until it stops, you can't get off.

I enclose this letter in a copy of my new book, *The Dinosaur Bite* (out in May), with thanks and deep appreciation to you, your Board of Trustees and Professor Mortland. Its successor will have to be blamed for my absence from your Commencement ceremonies both this year and next. If, as you suggest, you still wish to confer the degree IN ABSENTIA, I shall be more grateful (if undeserving) than I can easily say.

Again, regretfully, *Ruth Moore*

TO JOHN T. MCCLINTOCK

June 28, 1976

Dear Mr. McClintock,

The last time I wrote you was on August 16, 1966—perhaps I'd better identify myself. Your former partner, Mr. Mitchell, advised me in 1946 to invest in Mobil Oil stock, which I did. The 1966 letter was with regard to my transfer of 510 shares to my heir, Eleanor Mayo, on which transaction you very kindly advised me.

I am now in need of more professional advice.

We now hold 510 shares each. We have received from Mobil the enclosed letter, which is self-explanatory. Also somewhat frightening. What, if anything, would be the sensible thing to do, under these circumstances—sell the shares and invest in something else or take a chance and wait to see what Congress does in July? It seems likely, at least possible, that some shareholders on receiving this letter would sell, thus causing the stock to go down in value, does it not? I should hate to sell—this has been a very good investment for 30 years, the kind Mr. Mitchell (rest him) was famous for, not a large income of course but a safe and steady one. But at 72, I'm not inclined to wait "ten or twenty years of litigation to sort out the rights of security holders."

I'd be grateful if you would advise us about this, if you can, and you will, of course, bill me for any professional information you are able to send.

Sincerely yours *Ruth Moore*

In gratitude to Professor Donald Mortland, Ruth sent him a copy of her poetry book *Time's Web.*

TO DONALD MORTLAND

July 12, 1976

Dear Professor Mortland,

Because of my travels, the answer to your letter comes later than I'd wish it to, but not so late that I can't say now how much I appreciate it.

I wondered why your name seemed so familiar. My sister, Esther Trask, remembered it at once. "He is the best English teacher I ever saw," she said without preamble. "I'm delighted to know where he is now." I don't know how many of her youngsters you taught, but I suspect most of them—they all got tremendous basic English from someone. The one you mention, Muriel, is now Muriel Davisson, Ph.D. in Genetics, doing research at Jackson Lab. George got his degree in Math from Bowdoin; he is teaching in Bath. Brian chased his subject, Geology, after his graduation from Amherst, to Yale, the University of Texas and Syracuse, and now has his Ph.D. also. I will now stop bragging about our kids, but I thought you might like to know. Also, I can reciprocate a little by championing your work, too. I do thank you for championing mine. Your citation is probably more than I deserve, but it is beautiful and after reading it, I am not about to make any gestures of modesty now.

Years ago, after the publication of my second book, *Spoonhandle*, the University of Maine gave me a D.Litt., to my great surprise and bedazzlement. I could only think that that year they must have run out of celebrities. But now, after the fifteenth book, a lifetime of work, I feel that Doctor of New England Literature is more for me, an adequate recognition of what I have tried to do; I am proud and happy to have it. Also, if I am ever called upon to appear in public (which I pray I never will be) capped, gowned and hooded, I can wear blue on the back and orange on the front, and thus astound the academicians.

The accompanying small book is a part of gratitude. I doubt if you ever heard of it—it didn't splash around much. I think it was Don Marquis who said that publishing a book of poems is like dropping a rose petal into the Grand Canyon and waiting to hear an echo.

With best wishes, *Ruth Moore*

TO JOHN C. WILLEY

July 21, 1976

Dear John,

I'm not surprised. Can't win 'em all, don't expect to, never did; and I've known, of course, about the changes in the publishing business which you mention in your letter. The *Author's Guild Bulletin,* March–May, has on p. 26 the report which you doubtless know about. It ain't comforting. And the fact does remain that owing to increased costs of production, which I understand, the majority of people who like and read my books can't afford to pay $7.95, plus tax, for one of them. This is why I flapped at you about a paperback. People wrote me, asking. It takes little reading of reviews and best seller lists to advise that science and porn, also, have their fingers in the till.

I don't know that I have very much more to say. It's a good book, I think, took a long time and a lot of work to write. Not that this signifies much. Only to me. The local librarian had a hell of a time getting copies from Eastern Book, but the two she finally got are on reserve for weeks ahead. And I've had some very nice letters about it.

I used to bitch about being pinpointed as a regional writer; Thayer had harsh words from me about this, and I don't recall, but I suspect you have had some too. The citation which accompanied my honorary degree has just come through—I wasn't there, but the college did it just the same. I enclose a copy for your personal file. You may think I'm bragging and perhaps I am; but I thought that you might like a reminder of what Thayer and you and Frances and Polly Street and I did in the days before the market went to hell. A cooperative effort from the beginning, and remembering it, I am not bitching about anything now.

Affectionately *Ruth*

The article that Ruth refers to below is probably "Author Wants to Be Just a Neighbor" by Riva Berman, which appeared in the *Maine Sunday Telegram* on Sept. 26, 1976. The Dickey-Lincoln dam project involved the flooding of part of the St. John Valley; the Furbish Lousewort is a plant that grows only along the banks of the St. John River, and its "endangered" status was one of the reasons the Dickey-Lincoln dam was never built.

TO JOHN C. WILLEY

November 26, 1976

Dear John,

I've been working and haven't looked up for weeks, so everybody thinks I'm dead, praise the Lord. No interruptions, except I got written up in the Portland paper, which masterpiece you have probably seen already. It was published along with a snapshot of me, taken in situ, which makes me look like my own mother, only slightly lewd, which I am and she wasn't.

I'd like 15 copies of *Dinosaur Bite*, if you have any left, which I expect you do. I would also like some Morrow books, if convenient, as follows:

Cat Astrology by Mary Daniels The book about rare plants on the verge of extinction, which was reviewed not long ago in the *N. Y. Times*, and which I can't remember the name nor the author of. (Not the Jack Kramer book.) The new Mary Stewart And: *Exposure*, by the Art Gallery of Ontario. Now, this one is very expensive, and I will be happy to pay for it, if you feel this list bulges too much. An editor friend of mine from McKay says, "Go on, sting 'em for it. They've made a lot of money off of you." Note: She said that, I didn't. I don't feel it's polite. Not for the season.

See enclosed clippings. This is the best news I have had since *Second Growth.* We have all been appalled by the idea of Dickey-Lincoln.

We are having a pleasant fall—no snow as yet, though some of us would prefer it. We had a great thing happen the other evening at dusk—a tremendous buck led his harem of four does and three lambs into our apple orchard, where they ate all the windfalls and played games with each other. A lovely sight and not often seen.

Well, praise the God who seems at last to be looking after one of his own—the Furbish Lousewort, and have good holidays.

Affectionately *Ruth*

TO MARY DILLON

December 13, 1976

Dear Mary, et. al,

If you never hear from us again, put it that we have blown into the sea. Wild gales from all directions, registering 86, 76, 61 knots per hr. on our wind indicator, one after the other; and today's northwester's already up to 52 and showing promise. If you are still in Hancock, which I don't expect you are, you know about all this; but don't mention to any fishermen that you like windy weather, or you'll get ridden out of town on a rail. At least, we would. But (whisper) it's really been glorious.

We were damn sorry not to see more of you while you were here. Let's remedy that next summer, or the next time you come. Both of us all wound up being busy—I've started working again after taking a year off. Nose to the grindstone for weeks, not looking up except to swear, having hell and brimstone's own time with plot, as usual, because, as you have reason to know, I am hen-, not plot-minded. So everyone thinks I'm dead, but not so.

What did you think of the election? I believe we all agreed that we would like a statesman for President, but where was (or is) the statesman? At least, we didn't get Reagan, which is something. We've decided to play wait-and-see before moving to Canada; besides, here in Maine we have the Furbish Lousewort, Pedicularis gravi. Some comfort, in spite of all.

Perhaps you know about the Furbish Lousewort. In case you don't: It is a wild snapdragon of great rarity on the edge of extinction, which grows in the St. John Valley in northern Maine and nowhere else. Also growing in the St. John Valley are plans for the Dickey-Lincoln dam, a 600 million dollar hydroelectric project which would flood 100,000 acres of the Valley, part of Canada, and the habitat of the Furbish Lousewort. And, lo, there turns up a Federal law which prohibits trifling with the habitat of a rare species on the edge of extinction. It seems that, temporarily at least, (oh, they'll doubtless get around it somehow), the great project has been brought to a grinding halt. So we are going to let national affairs drop where they may and think about flower power versus the hapless state of the stout boots of the Army Engineers.

Last year's spikehorn buck (portrait enclosed) has changed since then. Looks fragile and lonesome, doesn't he? You should see him now. He came thundering into our orchard one late afternoon at the head of a harem—four does, three last spring lambs—and with a rack of antler on his head you wouldn't believe. We think it must be the same buck, because he's so tame. We'd never seen so large a herd together before, nor had we seen deer at play. The does were doing a rock-and-roll all over the orchard, and the lambs were bugging Big Daddy, snatching his apples, bumping him behind, and ducking fast when he shook his antlers at them. It was a lovely sight, very exciting to watch. I don't know whether he survived bloody November or not. Poachers have carried on a shooting war all over our woods for weeks, mostly at night, we hear the rifle-shots. The last time I saw him, he was in E's herb garden where the yellow delicious tree had dumped bushels of apples. It was early daylight, still gray, but light enough to see him, and also see a car backing, creep, creep, into our driveway, for no other reason than to get a shot at him. We have told the poachers that what they do in the woods is none of our business, but if there is any shooting around our house by God the Game Warden's going to get called. So I banged up the bedroom window with a crash, the car took off like a bat and the buck went over the herb garden fence in a lovely, soaring, fluid leap. So goodby. He made it through last year; perhaps he will this.

So Merry Christmas and Happy New Year and see you next year.

Love *Ruth and Eleanor*

TO JOHN C. WILLEY

January 20, 1977

Dear John,

There was no hurry about the books. They were, if Christmas at all, presents for me—one I wanted to own, myself, and very nice they all are and I do thank you for them. The plant book wasn't the one I had in mind—I must've seen it advertised in another company's ad, I guess—but I'm pleased to have yours all the same.

Thanks, too, for the *Down East* review. Their reviews of my books always tickle me a little—usually good, but a bit wry, on account of I don't make the dear old State sound like a fairyland. Re. *Dinosaur Bite*—well ... Their magazine is more than half real estate ads. So I think they did quite well this time, considering. ...

There's no news about the Furbish Lousewort, but the Dickey-Lincoln is in other trouble—Canada is taking great umbrage over having 100,000 acres of their forest land flooded so now where it will end knows God.

This seems to be really a thank-you letter. We are enjoying tremendously the maple syrup you sent us for Christmas and have been eating more pancakes than we should, on account of calories. I have had to go out and cut fireplace logs to work some of it off.

Have you seen E. B. White's letters, and didn't Dottie do a job!

Winter's rough, as you say—we were hit blunt-and-foremost by a tornadium which sent our wind indicator up to 79 knots an hour; but even so, we aren't having it as bad as west and south of here, and I'll bet you wish you'd stayed in California.

Affectionately *Ruth*

The Shiver Mountain Press of Washington Depot, Connecticut had contacted Ruth about re-publishing *Speak to the Winds* as a paperback.

TO JOHN C. WILLEY

January 26, 1977

Dear John,

What should I do about the enclosed?

Me, I haven't the faintest, never having heard of the Shiver Mountain Press.

Re. the date on the heading of this enclosure, if said Press wants to wait that long, *Speak to the Winds* will undoubtedly be in the public domain. …

I don't know. My mail is full of fast-buck ripoffs, these days, and my Yankee caution feels prickly.

Sorry to bother you—I doubt if this proposal amounts to much.

Aff. *Ruth*

In the letter below, Edith Hutchinson, whom Ruth called "Hutch," was the Librarian at *The Reader's Digest*. Rosemary was Edith's daughter.

TO MARY DILLON

January 26, 1977

Dear Mary,

Thank you for letting me know about Edith. As you say, she was dear to us both in the old days and we had very good times together. She is still dear. Would you tell Rosemary I said so? Except through you, I was out of touch with Hutch for all these years after I vanished into the hinterland; but there are whole avenues of things about her, neither gone nor forgotten. That old Ford that so many times she scared the bejeezus out of me with—would it hold together and which tree would she pick … and never did pick one. And that brew of coffee which never left the burner, only got added to. I mustn't rake up, I'll harrow us both. I'm so terribly sorry, Mary.

You sound as though you wouldn't be getting to Hancock now before February. I was looking forward. You're wise not to come, though. Driving conditions are hellish, or have been; we had snow which turned to rain and then back to snow again. The rain went straight to bottom and froze, so that highways were sheets of ice and are only now getting cleared to what you could still skate on, if you came to skate. I fell down, tail over budget, in the woodlot, carrying in one hand a bucksaw and in the other two axes. All landed about six feet apart—the axes didn't get nicked and the bucksaw was all right, but I got a lame back out of it and was laid up for a few days, but better now. E. has rooted out an ancient pair of "creepers" which she insists that I wear. "If you don't," she says, "and you break a hip out there, I swear I'll leave you in the woodlot."

You sound busy with your book, and happy with it, too, which I wish I could say about mine. I'm fossicking around getting material together out of unconsidered trifles picked up over a period of years, and it's rugged. Always is, beginning, when one's not over the sharpening-the-pencils period.

Prejudice is a bad thing. I suppose we all have some, more or less serious. I grew up with it—my father and my brother wallowed in a great mire of opinion against higher education for women, who should be potwallopers in the kitchen and available for sex whenever; they sounded off during my short stays at home for college vacations. It was hell, hell, hell, hell, hell. My father once told me that I was "no good," meaning what you may suppose he meant. Poor old Pop, he died before I either got married or wrote a book. He went to his grave seeing only the worst of me. But I think now, that due to this exposure to it, my prejudices now are concerned with such things as big fat Winnebagos, whose owners stop by our local grocery and buy their supplies with Food Stamps. There may be others—as you know, I have to struggle sometimes to be tolerant of things I don't agree with.

Let us know when you come—we'll give-a you candy.

Love *Ruth*

Susan Tibbetts had a radio show called "Roots and Branches" on MPBN.

TO KENDALL MORSE

February 22, 1977

Dear Kendall,

Your request for a radio tape interview is hard to say no to and normally I'd accept with pleasure, but right now I'm laid up and can't. A while ago I fell down on the ice and am still trying to joggle various points of contact back into place—not a serious injury but a painful one. So I not only have cabin fever but am unbearable—mean and ugly, waiting it out.

My advice to any sensible person who falls down on the ice, the way it is now, is just to lie there until something melts.

I'm really sorry. Thanks just the same and thanks to Susan Tibbetts, who is nice to want me on her program. Good luck with yours.

Sincerely *Ruth*

TO MRS. WILLIAM HUNTER MOORE

March 23, 1977

Dear Mrs. Moore,

Thank you for your letter.

I can't imagine what Hancock Bar is, or was, unless the term "Bar" refers to the then legal bar of Hancock County. Was W. C. Moore, perhaps, a lawyer? Herbert Silsby, a lawyer of Ellsworth, who is a well-informed historian of the area, might help you with this.

Moores, of course, have always been schooling around these parts. The pioneer, so far as I know, was Samuel, who was lost at sea, leaving four sons. These boys were brought up by Philip Langley, who married the widow, Margaret Welch Moore, owned Greenings Island and a farm at Seawall. I think it likely that one of these four boys (and Samuel) is your ancestor. They stayed at Seawall and spread around—to Sutton Island, Cranberry Island, Gott's Island, Bass Harbor, Prospect Harbor; my own line, (from Samuel) reads Welch, Philip, Enoch, Philip, Harvey. The last four, Gott's Islanders. Welch apparently stayed at Seawall; he is buried there in an abandoned cemetery off the Seawall road; but there is also a Welch Moore buried at Prospect Harbor. It is very confusing. Joseph Moore and members of his family are buried in a private (or once private) cemetery, in back of the mobile home concentration just off the Seawall road. He must have a lively time of it.

William Moore lived on Sutton Island; he kept sheep on Bear Island and later moved to Bear to live. He was the first keeper of Bear Island lighthouse. I suspect he is the ancestor you are looking for. From here on, my information is somewhat shaky and facts should be checked—perhaps at the county Courthouse? Benjamin Moore built a house in Manset in 1828. His descendants were Peter, whose son was Herbert, buried in Mt. Height cemetery, Southwest Harbor. And I have found a record of a William Moore who built "a large set of buildings on this road (the Manset road) and went to the far west to live with his sons." Is this the W. C. Moore you mention?

This is the best I can do, unfortunately. I wish I could be more helpful. Do you know about the Genealogical Library in Salt Lake City, maintained by the Mormon Church? It is a fantastic undertaking, the purpose of which is to trace the family lines of practically everyone in the U.S. and beyond. I know for a fact that they have already done a great deal of research of this Mt. Desert Island area—a niece of mine visited there last summer and was astonished to find detailed information about our family. She even came up with a transcribed interview with our other grandfather, Edwin Joyce's physician, who was treating grandfather for cancer. Salt Lake isn't far from you, and they have miles of microfilm. You might find there exactly the records you want.

Good luck. *Ruth Moore*

Ruth was reading *The Letters of E. B. White,* edited by her old friend Dorothy Lobrano Guth.

TO DOROTHY LOBRANO GUTH

March 23, 1977

Dear Dottie,

What a mean time you and Ray and the kids had—everybody sick. I hope you're all well again and soaking up sun in Florida where you certainly belong to be after breathing in NYC. The main reason I don't come there any more is that I can't breathe it, though I might as well do that, I suppose, as fall down in the woodlot flat as a fritter and get laid up with a lame back for the entire month of Feb. One thing, though, I got sucked in on the swine flu program—shots for the elderly, by God—and swam gaily around all winter all full of swine juice and Victoria-A, without a smidgin of a cold, flu or piglet. You ought all to be elderly, that's your solution. Don't hurry about it, though—there's other complications here and there.

Old *Cold as a Dog and the Wind Northeast* has come to life with a clatter. I thought you'd like to know since most of it, including title, was your doing. The Maine Folk Lore crowd have got hold of it, using the paperback reprint which Gordon Bok and I financed and put out some years ago—Wm. Morrow turned up its hairy nose at republishing it then. All they did was to send me the remainders—forty copies of the first and only edition they did, which same I have in my closet roosting as a back-up against poverty, since available copies are now selling at fifteen bucks a throw in the rare book stores. We did well with the paperback and have reprinted it twice.

So now I have been asked to be featured poet at the Maine Festival at Bowdoin in July, which I have declined to be, since my poetic volume is so skinny, resting only on *Cold as a Dog* and a thin book of poems called *Time's Web,* published by Morrow, and which so far as I'm able to find out, no one in God's living world has ever heard of. So I told the Maine Festival that, said no, and let them make what they will out of it. I'm told I ought to get up off my duff and go lecturing to ladies' organizations, et. al., but I don't agree. I couldn't do it without blushing; I'm too damn old; my whole philosophy these days is Lulu Webtoe's.

"Oho, oho," cried Lulu Webtoe. "I don't like my hat and I don't like my bow. I was asked out to tea and I Just wouldn't go."

Love from us both, *Ruth and Eleanor*

P.S. I finally relaxed my New England niggardliness and bought a copy of your Letters, *and am having a wonderful time with it.*

TO MIRIAM DYAK

March 23, 1977

Dear Ms. Dyak,

Thank you for your pleasant and enthusiastic letter of March 14.

I think a Maine Festival for the creative arts is a wonderful idea, and I am sorry that I must decline your invitation to join it. I don't really believe my work as poet merits such an honor as you suggest; its volume is skinny—*Cold as a Dog,* which you mention, and one thin book called *Time's Web,* which so far as I am able to find out, no one in the living world has ever heard of. There are other Maine poets who deserve this honor more than I do, and I don't believe you'll have to hunt to find one.

Thank you, all the same. I am touched and most appreciative, and sorry I can't come.

Sincerely *Ruth Moore*

In the *Letters of E. B. White,* there is a letter that Mr. White wrote to Dorothy Lobrano (as she was then) on May 16, 1953 after he had finished reading Ruth's *A Fair Wind Home.*

TO E. B. WHITE

March 24, 1977

Dear Mr. White,

I am into your letters and find, to my delight, the one you wrote to Dotty re. the rescue of the lady in my book *A Fair Wind Home*. I have owned and cherished the original of this letter since Dotty sent it to me, years back.

I think it is only fair to me to let you know that this episode stems from an apocryphal tale about a vague ancestor of mine whose hat blew off in a gale off Cape Horn. It was a good hat, so he jumped overboard after it, got it, held it up to catch the wind, sailed after the vessel and climbed back aboard. With this murmuring in the background, what more? Why, the lady was sailing the crests sustained only by her hat.

Please don't trouble to reply. I would say, from this magnificent book of letters, that you have enough on your plate. I have one original E. B. White letter and deserve no more.

Yours, with admiration, *Ruth Moore*

E. B. WHITE TO RUTH MOORE

April 1, 1977

Dear Miss Moore:

You are lucky to have an ancestor whose hat blew off in a gale off Cape Horn. My ancestors' hats blew off, but usually in the subway—the draught from the A train.

It's possible that Dotty and family will be paying us a short visit this spring, to remove the cork from a bottle of champagne. I hope so. Have not enjoyed good health this winter and perhaps a reunion with my goddaughter would work a cure. Thank you for your letter.

Sincerely, *E. B. White*

TO BERTRAM READ

March 29, 1977

Mr. Bertram Read
Shiver Mountain Press
Washington Depot, Connecticut 06794

Dear Mr. Read,

I am sorry that you have had so long to wait for a definite reply to your letter of January 20. I have found that trying to move a monumental New York publishing company into action is a little like trying to move a monument.

I am delighted that you are going ahead with motions to make a paperback reprint of *Speak to the Winds*. I wish you all good luck with it.

About film rights, I am still in touch with Morrow and Company, and will write you immediately as soon as I hear from them. I hope it will not be so long this time. I have put a buzzer under them.

I see no reason why I can't grant you permission to go ahead with negotiations for a film, but would like things to be a little more definite before I commit myself to anything. With what film company are you negotiating? I'd be interested to know.

Sincerely *Ruth Moore*

TO JOHN C. WILLEY

March 29, 1977

Dear John,

The Shiver Mountain Press writes that Morrow has made arrangements with them for a paperback reprint of *Speak to the Winds*. What arrangements, and shouldn't there be some sort of contract mentioning royalties, and shouldn't I know about terms? Or sign the contract?

They also want film rights. They ask would I be interested in granting the right to make a film on a royalty basis on gross receipts from the final product. They say they are in cooperation with another company which makes films. What company? They don't say. They want my permission to go ahead with it.

The whole matter seems iffy and doubtless won't amount to a great deal, as most of these matters seem not to. I checked the Speak to the Winds contract—Morrow gets 10% of sales on film rights, as you of course know. I think I'd better have word from you on how to proceed, under the circumstances.

I can grant permission to them to go ahead negotiating for a film, but I don't want to commit myself to a sale of film rights until things are a little more definite. Is this proper? About a royalty deal based on gross receipts, am I interested? What is good business in this case? I surely don't know.

I'm sorry to bother you with these (probably peanuts, I know you're busy), but I do need information.

Spring is lovely here. Sun in and out of rain, enough of both to be out in.

Affectionately *Ruth*

P.S. I'm busy as a birddog.

Dr. R. H. Kirtland was Ruth's college English professor.

TO KATHLEEN [SURNAME UNKNOWN]

June 5, 1977

Dear Kathleen,

Thanks a lot for your pleasant letter. Of course I remember you, and well. It's always nice to hear from someone who likes my books, doubly so if it's an old classmate.

I believe there've been four since *Second Growth*—of fiction, that is, and one of poetry:

The Gold and Silver Hooks
"Lizzie" and Caroline
The Sea Flower
The Dinosaur Bite
Poetry: *Time's Web*

These all should be available at your local public library; or they could be ordered from the publisher if they aren't at your bookstore. The publisher is:

William Morrow & Co. 105 Madison Avenue New York, N.Y. 10016

My editor, John Willey, should be able to help you there.

I don't know what's become of Olga Hampel. I'm terribly out of touch these days, of course, having turned into an old work-horse with my nose to the grindstone—Prof. Kirtland would have a word to say about that mixed metaphor, wouldn't he?

Your own productions sound pretty distinctive, all those youngsters and a daughter at the Sorbonne.

Thanks again—

Sincerely yours, *Ruth Moore*

TO GERALD JOYCE

June 6, 1977

Dear Gerald,

I surely did get a surprise opening your letter. I suppose I must have seen you in the days when I used to visit Gramp and Gram Joyce—Ed and Mary, to you, but I was pretty small then, though I remember Herman Joyce and Uncle Levi and Aunt Matilda were dear friends. I used to go up there a lot when I was in Atlantic. Yes, my mother, Vinie, died in 1956, and Aunt Delie was a neighbor around the harbor at Bernard for many years. Bessie Dunham lives in Southwest Harbor, near her son Wilfred. I see her now and again. Do write her; she'd love it.

Your record of the Joyce family background astonished me. I've been interested in it, but knew nothing about it beyond James, Senior, and what's in Dr. Small's *History*. Aunt Bessie told me that the Joyces came from Gloucestershire, England, but that was about all the information I had; and I didn't know anything at all about the Staples connection. Amos Staples lived on Gott's Island when I was a child growing up there; he married Belle, a daughter of Uncle Jimmie Joyce, who was also our neighbor—she was, of course, a cousin to Ma, Uncle Jimmie being Ma's uncle. All dead now. My, we were all mixed up, relatively, as you might say, about everybody, everybody else's second, third, fourth and so on, cousin. Quite recently, a man named Philip Gott undertook to trace the Gott lineage, and came up with a fat volume an inch or more thick, 8 x 11! All full of Gotts—descendants of Charles Gott who came over from Weymouth, England, in 1624, on the, I believe, Abigail. It staggers the mind. To think how we've populated a whole country is awesome.

Thanks again for the fascinating information, and double thanks for liking my books.

Yours, relatively, *Ruth*

P.S. Incidentally, you probably do know about the genealogical records researched and kept by the Mormons in Salt Lake City. Apparently, they are trying to trace the backgrounds of everyone in the world, and to some extent are succeeding. My niece, Muriel Trask Davisson, was there last year and found (of all things) a written-down interview with the Doctor who treated Gramp Joyce's cancer for one thing. Those young men they send around everywhere do the research, which is taken back to Salt Lake City and microfilmed. Amazing, isn't it?

TO JOHN C. WILLEY

June 22, 1977

Dear John,

No, we haven't thought much about titles during all these years—unless it was a slight difference of opinion over the title of a book. I think you know how I feel about our relationship as author to editor and you must also know that no change of title on your part could possibly alter it.

It may be a very good thing that you're freed from the vast overburden of work, which, for a long time, I've sensed in your letters. And it gives me a lift to know—as I should think it would give you—that it's going to take two strong men to carry what you have carried so brilliantly and so well for the past twenty years.

If I sound a little choked up, it's because I am; and because I can't help but think of the way big business devours its best and its young. Perhaps the slow erosion of my own career has something to do with this.

Take care, and all the best, as ever,
Ruth

John C. Willey retired from William Morrow in 1980 and the company was taken over by Hearst Corporation in 1985.

TO FRED BURRILL

August 20, 1977

Dear Mr. Burrill,

I expect you have been trying to get in touch with me by telephone and haven't found me at home. Since I think I can answer at least three of your questions, I thought perhaps you might like written information.

I have been ransacking a box of old letters which my mother kept and have found correspondence as follows:

1. A letter from my father to me, dated July 5, 1936 in which he says, I quote:
   "Tena gave her part of the old place to Edith, so Edith owns 16/45 of the whole place."
2. A letter from Tena A. Ford to me, dated June 3, 1936, in which she says, I quote:
   "Your letter was forwarded to me today. And while I was not sure which place on the Island you were going to sell or rent or possibly both, I trust however that whatever you do will be for the best of all parties concerned. I am reducting this number by one by giving Edith my interest in the old homestead."
3. The Philip Moore you mention, whose residence was Southwest Harbor was, perhaps, a distant relation, but to my knowledge had no interests in the Gott's Island property under discussion.

My father, Philip Moore, who died at Gott's Island in early 1937, was Enoch N. Moore's second son, mentioned in the list of heirs. In 1932, he deeded his Gott's Island properties to my sister, Esther (now Esther Trask of Bernard, Maine) and to me.

I don't know anything positive about the heirs of Mary E. Moore. So far as I know, Philip, (my great-grandfather) had only one son, Enoch N. On page 150 of H. D. Small's *History of Swan's Island* is a note which might be helpful. I quote:

"Mrs. Trask afterwards became the wife of Philip Moore of Gott's Island, by whom she had three children, none of whom reached adult age."

I hope this is helpful. I'm not much on ancestors, and they've all been dead so long.

Sincerely, *Ruth Moore*

TO SALLY MORONG

December 2, 1977

Dear Ms. Morong,

Thanks very much for your pleasant letter.

For "Little River" see the Coast Guard Light List, Vol. 1, Atlantic Coast: page 26, No. 203:

LITTLE RIVER LIGHTED WHISTLE BUOY, Ln 280 feet, Red. 44 37.5 67 09.8

Listed next to it is Machias Seal Island Light, so I expect it's the one you want, all right. So finish painting your ghost and the best of luck to you.

Sincerely, *Ruth Moore*

TO JAN MILLER

December 12, 1977

Dear Jan Miller,

Your subscription blank in the *New York Times Book Review* isn't large enough to list the four gift subscriptions I would like sent, so I'm listing the names and information you need below. I hope this won't be a bother or fuss your computer.

Please send gift subscriptions of *Cricket* to:

Colleen Trask, age 7; niece 1409 West Healy Champaign, Illinois 61820

Laura Trask, age 6; niece R.F.D. 3, Box 105 Wiscasset, Maine 04578

Alison Eaton, age 7; niece Box 27 Waldoboro, Maine 04572

Sven Davisson, age 7; nephew Bernard, Maine 04612

My name is Ruth Moore Address as above.

My check for $51 is enclosed.

Thank you, *Ruth Moore*

Mary Dillon, after her retirement from the *Reader's Digest,* wrote a little book on magazine article writing for *Writer's Market*. After the Dillons retired and came to live in their Hancock house year-round, several of their children followed suit.

TO MARY AND LOU DILLON

December 21, 1977

Dear Mary and Lou,

I've been working my head off, as you say, and I didn't call you in November which I meant to do. The thing is, there are times now when we know we can, so that's all right. I've had trouble getting my nose away from the grindstone, but was reminded of the season by a partridge in an apple tree outside the window. Nevertheless, my Christmas letter's late, but I suppose you'll get it sometime, if the leprechauns in the Post Office don't manipulate themselves into bankruptcy before then.

Congratulations on your book. There must be some place I can buy it, and I mean that, too. Don't worry your head. Who's the publisher? I think you told me, but my memory these days is usually in the place where the dead crabs go.

I find, to my astonishment, that I am a witch. I didn't know this, I thought Eleanor was the one. She can call whales from the vasty deep and they do come when she does call for them. At least she did it once.

The entrepreneur who has re-opened the gravel pit on our south line has been raising merry hell down there, hauling away Bass Harbor Head in huge truckloads all summer and digging great holes so close to the line that our trees are dying from exposed roots. This summer, being a wet one, the pit flooded, so he rigged up a pump that threw a six-inch stream of water and pumped the water over the line into our back woodlot, which adjoins our vegetable garden. We kept hearing the pump—it ran day and night for weeks—but didn't realize where the water was going until our potatoes put forth vines six feet long and all the dry beans turned black and died and the turnips refused to grow at all. It was a wet summer, anyway. But one day I caught a glint of water over behind the garden where none had ever been before; we located the pump and found three feet of oily, muddy water spread all over the place. We complained and got the pump stopped. There's a Maine Law which reads: "Any person who collects water artificially on his land and pumps it back over his neighbor's land is liable for damages." This is under MISCELLANEOUS NUISANCES. So we thought about suing the SOB but the roadfill business is really big in Maine—all our roads take a beating from three million tourists each year, takes a lot of sand and gravel to fix up for next—and it carries a lot more clout than two mad old maids with a few dead beans and some thalidomide potatoes.

I was sitting in the jeep house one morning, thinking all this over, and considering Malicious Animal Magnetism, when I saw a heavy-duty truck loaded with about fifteen yards of Bass Harbor Head come charging up the road, and I said to myself, "I wish that damn thing would break down."

My God, it did. About ten feet from where I was sitting.

There was a screeching crash and a horrid sound of busted-up metal and pieces of iron flew all over the road. I was absolutely appalled.

I ran out to see if the driver was all right. He was. He was on his hands and knees with his stern up in the air, peering under the truck. I said, "Looks as if you'd had a breakdown."

He said, "Yeah."

I said, "I guess there isn't anything I can do to help, but would you like to come back to the house and telephone?"

He said, "No, another truck's coming right along. He'll push me off into the field."

It came and it did. The poor wounded thing sat in the field hors de combat for a week, load and all.

I was talking this over with my cousin, Elsie Lunt, and she said, "You good and well know that anyone brought up on Gott's Island is a witch. You remember how Uncle Mont cussed the eelgrass and the whore's eggs, that time?"

You may remember Uncle Mont. He was there the summer you visited. He went out one morning to haul up the anchor to his skiff, and found it so wovelled up in eelgrass that he couldn't budge it. He put back his head, and with no thought in his mind of profanity, addressed the Heavens. "Go-ud Almighty! I want you to do something about this damn eelgrass." It's a matter of record that the eelgrass all along the coast died and didn't even begin to come back until a few summers ago. Same way with the sea-urchins. He hauled up a lobster trap and found it so covered with them that he couldn't see the trap, so he cursed the sea-urchins, and not one of them was seen along the coast for years. Anyone here can tell you that.

Elsie said, "Uncle Mont may be dead now, but there's no way to know what he might've passed along to us."

Do you have anybody or anything that you would like me to cuss?

It seems we do not live very far from Salem, after all.

Wonderful that your kids are making it here, have jobs and a good time all around. More power to them.

Have good holidays, and forgive my running on so.

Love, *Ruth and Eleanor*

P.S. Put salt on this letter before you read it.

TO G. TEN BRINK

January 27, 1978

Dear Ms. Ten Brink,

I am sorry to have been so long in answering your letter.

Jeb Ellis of Candlemas Bay was condensed from the original *Candlemas Bay* and published separately as a book for children. The printing, I believe—this was years ago—was very small comparatively; the book would not be available now except in second hand stores, if that. I don't myself own a copy now.

But since you've read *Candlemas Bay*, you've already read *Jeb Ellis* etc.

Thank you for your interest.

Sincerely, *Ruth Moore*

TO CAROLINE CONSTANTIN

February 3, 1978

Dear Ms. Constantin,

I honestly do not know how to advise you with regard to publishing your book, because I'm not in touch with the needs of the present market.

I would suggest, however, that you pick up a copy of *Writer's Magazine*, which I think would give you information beginning writers need to know. Most news stands carry this, and I think it's professionally very good.

Good luck.

Sincerely *Ruth Moore*

In the letter below, Ruth is telling about the plot of *Sarah Walked Over the Mountain*, a story based on a supposedly true life incident featuring Ruth's grandmother from Cape Breton.

TO JOHN C. WILLEY

March 29, 1978

Dear John,

Yes, you're very nice about what you call prying, and I do and always have, appreciated it. I have to hermit up, as you know, and can't write about work until it, at least, stops tooling off in all directions at once. I always feel guilty about that because I know your schedule has to be made up ahead of time. If I could say definitely that I'd have a finished manuscript by June, I could be forgiven all. I can't. Because I never know.

I am over half and have a tentative working first draft. I have a title—*Sarah Walked Over the Mountain.* If you, or anybody among that swarm of strangers down there, want to change it, I will personally send cyanide.

It has been a wonderful winter. For most of it, we have had snow up to the meeting-rails on our windows, but we have snowshoes. We had two old god-wallopers of storms—the one on Feb. 9 tore the whole coast of Maine to ribbons; our wind indicator clocked seventy-six miles an hour. The walkway on the Town float went down to Swan's Island all by itself, and one of the wharves in the harbor was ripped off and tossed over into the ice-cubes of which the whole works was foul and seething. You miss a great deal by frowsting up in New York City, boy, when your abandoned state is where the action is.

Well, she did walk over the mountain. She walked twenty miles in the dead of winter, with her six children, two of them babies and with her goods piled on a dogsled hauled by an old cow. The big ones carried the little ones and none of them had any underdrawers. There was also a bear who wasn't there to see what he could see—he was after the cow.

Now, you'll have to put that in your pipe and smoke it, because it's all you're going to get for now. Peace.

This morning, I scared up two woodcock out in the edge of the woods. Magnificent.

Affectionately *Ruth*

TO JUDITH SCHWARTZ

April 18, 1978

Ms. Judith Schwartz
College of the Atlantic
Bar Harbor, Maine 04609

Dear Ms. Schwartz,

I appreciate deeply your invitation to speak at your Summer Forum. I'm sorry I can't. I'm not a very public person and a ridiculously poor speaker, and the last time I appeared on a platform was at a college debate some fifty years ago. So thanks for the honor, but no.

I would like to take the chance to tell you what a great job I think your people are doing, particularly in the field of Land Use and Conservation. I expect your Mr. MacArthur in his research study has seen Bass Harbor Head as it is now, with its gravel pits along the roads and its development. I only wish he could have seen it thirty years ago when it was wilderness—before the tree with the osprey nest was bulldozed down to make a test pit for gravel. Before the three million tourists who drive down each summer to view the lighthouse or the gravel pit—which, I'm unable to say.

Yours, with all good wishes,
Ruth Moore

TO JOHN C. WILLEY

May 10, 1978

Dear John,

I'm not going to wail to you about the snows of yesteryear—we both know they were damn fine snowstorms.

And I'm not going to drivel about changes hard to take, such as the thick black pencils swiped from English seminars and used now, apparently, to write reviews, because some unkind person might say the grapes are hanging low and they are sour.

I can't think of you as even nearing the age of retirement, though I look at the date and suppose you are. God knows I'm so far past it that I've forgotten when it was.

I'm jolted to the bottom rock of my foundation—to know that in something over a year you won't be any longer at Morrow.

We have done some good books together.

So, my prized and long-standing friend, we have one more to do. I will make haste with all deliberate speed, as usual, to get you the manuscript, and if you can winkle some publicity out of the company, it shouldn't be too bad of a swan-song.

Affectionately *Ruth*

Mary is Mary Clarke, a longtime friend, who once worked at the *Reader's Digest* with Ruth. She and her sister Cynthia used to summer at New Harbor.

TO MARY CLARKE

August 9, 1978

Dear Mary,

This letter's late and I'm sorry, because there's nobody I'd rather see. One thing and another, I've had to put off. Eleanor's mother, over in the nursing home in Bar Harbor, has had some bad turns—she's 89, has been there for two years, and we thought this might be terminal. It's meant almost daily trips to Bar Harbor, but she has settled down and now we know we won't likely be called on for emergency.

So, why don't you and Cynthia shoot for next Wednesday? That would be the 16th. I suggest the middle of the week, because the traffic is terrible on weekends, Winnebagos bumper to bumper. My sister used to teach school in Bristol and she used to allow three hours to get from there to here and perhaps you'd better plan that or a little over, because I can't promise that the Winnebagos will stay home, even if it's Wednesday. The island, at the moment, is jampacked and it always gets worse toward the end of August. We'd be better off at Broadway and 42nd.

Now, look, honeybun, if you don't want to fight that traffic twice in the same day, I think you'd better plan to spend the night and start out fresh. We don't have a guest room, which seems miserably inhospitable, and this is one of the times when I wish we did. So it would have to be a motel, and you'd have to make reservations ahead of time. There are two in Southwest Harbor:

Harbor View Motel, Main Street, S.W. Harbor, 244-5031
This is on the water and it's nice down there.
Southwest Harbor Motor Inn—244-5057
Can't miss it as you drive into town.
The Moorings at Manset, a couple of miles farther down on the road toward us. 244-5523

Our phone number is 244-5826. Let us know if you have any difficulty, and we'll see what we can do. We have it on good authority from the weather man that this streak of fog and humidity should break soon. It's been bugging us since June. When the forecast comes on the TV in the morning and starts with "The weather is next," the only possible comment has been, "And that's all you can say for it."

It'll be lovely to see you and we'll look forward.

Affectionately *Ruth*

TO JOHN C. WILLEY

November 13, 1978

Dear John,

I sent off the manuscript a week ago today, via United Parcel. Probably I should have let you know then, but we were somewhat uptight, what with

Eleanor getting home from the hospital, and one post-thing or another. She is fine—a lucky girl, no complications.

You will find, as I did, that I have written a whole novel and ended it with a preposition.

Affectionately *Ruth*

Mrs. Lillian Eleanor Mayo died on January 1, 1979. Ruth's last novel, *Sarah Walked Over the Mountain,* is dedicated to John Willey.

TO JOHN C. WILLEY

January 12, 1979

Dear John,

I took for granted that you'd gone gadding over the holidays ... thought it a good idea and am glad you had a nice time.

Here's the copyright form for the Contracts Department, duly signed and approved. Sorry it's taken so long, but we have been pretty much occupied by the death of Eleanor's mother and attendant circumstances ... Poor old lady, she had been a vegetable in a nursing home for two years and a half, so that her passing was a blessing for her and all concerned. But it was a complicated time, of course.

Yes, I'd like the $3000 advance at any time and at your convenience.

Thanks for your advice about the Swan's Island material. I'll abide by it. But I do think that the other scene I mentioned to you in my letter should be edited. Possibly as I indicated in the carbon sheet sent to you. The subconscious is odd, certainly—to let me do that and then telegraph a warning, thank goodness.

We are having the Lord's own whimsy of a winter—no snow to speak of, but if a good storm shows signs of settling in it turns to rain and floods the country, and then gets bare-ground-colder than the Scandinavian hell. We are both fine, though, enjoying what there is.

I'm glad you're pleased with the dedication ...

Happy New Year to you, too.

Affectionately *Ruth*

Kendall Morse was hosting the TV show "Down East Smile-In" on MPBN-TV.

TO KENDALL MORSE

January 23, 1979

Dear Ken,

Congratulations on your hosting job—this is really something, and it's nice to hear how you're getting along. I wish I could help out, but you know I can't. For one thing Willie off the Pickle Boat couldn't do worse with an interview than I do, and it isn't that I've got to be an indescribable old hermit, either. The main thing is, our house is too near the road, which is one of Acadia Park's main drags for tourists; three million people went by our windows last summer, going to see either the gravel pit or the lighthouse, which, I haven't been able to decide. We've no way to avoid visitors if either of us gets to be too public a person; and while most of the passers-by are pleasant and nice, we do get quite a few weirdos. And, as you know, we've no close neighbors. It is sad to have to say that this is a problem, but since we moved here, times have changed. So I lie low as I can so far as publicity is concerned.

Thanks a lot for asking me, and good luck with your show.

Sincerely *Ruth*

TO F. C. MORRONE

March 2, 1979

Dear Dr. Morrone,

I am interested to read your letter of Feb. 24, asking for information about the Cates family at Gott's Island, and Harrington. I really don't have "a great deal" of information about them; but there is certainly a Judith Cates buried in the Moore family plot at Gott's Island. So far as I'm able to tell, she was a sister to my great-grandmother, Asenath Gott Moore; but this doesn't agree with your records and I wonder why. It would be interesting to track this down.

My sources are two: A pamphlet entitled "Daniel Gott, Mount Desert Pioneer—His Ancestors and Descendants," and *History of Swan's Island*, by H. W. Smith, M.D., published in 1898 and recently re-published—that is, within the last few years. The pamphlet is far out of print now but a few copies exist. It was done by William Otis Sawtelle, founder and curator of the Islesford, Maine, Museum, and is an excellent research job, or so it seems to me. He is long dead, but his daughter lives in Northeast Harbor (ME), and might have a copy to spare, if you're interested. I don't, at the moment, have her name handy, but can get it, and will add it to the end of this letter as soon as I do.

According to Sawtelle's pamphlet (page 15) the children of Nathaniel Gott and his wife, Elizabeth Gott Richardson numbered thirteen, twelve daughters and one son. Judith is listed as the seventh child, briefly, as follows:

7. Judith: m. Sept. 25, 1821, Edward Cates.

She was, apparently, an older sister to my G. grandmother, Asenath, the ninth child, whose listing is:

9. Asenath, b. Nov. 20, 1802; m. Nov. 7, 1826, Philip, son of Welch and Sarah Spurling Moore, b. Feb. 19, 1802. Res. Gott's Island. Asenath d. July 29, 1852. G.s. Gott's Island.

The date of her death, July 29, 1852, matches up with the date in the diary Mary McLean has—obviously a first-hand account of the date-death of Judith Cates (whoever she was) who died a few days later in 1852, and whose gravestone is near here in the Moore plot at Gott's Island.

The eleventh child was Clarissa, whom you mention:

11. Clarissa, b. Nov. 6, 1808; m. 1st. Feb. 26, 1826 (Gilley Bible record) William, s. of John and Mary Woods Gilley. William lost on the *Minerva* in the Artic (sic), March 1829. Clarissa m. 2nd, David Cates, his 2nd wife.

Who in the world was DAVID Cates? Do you have any record of him?

Now, as to the *History of Swan's Island,* which contains a short history, also of Gott's Island:

Page 167.

II. Nathaniel Gott was born Feb. 11, 1765. His wife was Betsy Richardson, who was born April 14, 1767. He settled on Gott's Island. They were the parents of twelve (?) children—one son and eleven daughters, all of whom but one married and reared large families. Mr. Gott died January 27, 1841. His wife died March 15, 1844.

The following were their children: Asenath, wife of Philip Moore, of Gott's Island; Jane, wife of James Greening, of Southwest Harbor; Lucinda, wife of Thomas Stanley, of Little Cranberry Isle; Esther, wife of Philip Longley, of Southwest Harbor; Clarissa, wife of William Gilley, of Cranberry Isles; after his death she became the wife of David Cates, of the same town; Hannah, died, unmarried; Deborah, was the wife of John Clark of Beech Hill; Nathaniel, Jr., married Huldah Hadlock and settled at Gott's Island; Rhoda, wife of Daniel Hemblen of Bass Harbor; Betsey, wife of

Nicholas Tinker of Southwest Harbor; Mary, wife of Benjamin Richardson of Somerville; Judith, who was the first wife of Mr. Cates.

I'm sorry that this is all the Cates material I've, so far, been able to come up with. There might be more in the Cranberry Island records—it would be interesting to take a look at the Gilley Bible Record mentioned in Sawtelle's pamphlet. There is a book entitled *John Gilley,* written by Charles Eliot, a former president of Harvard and sponsor of the famous Five-foot Shelf of Books; it might just possibly mention William, his son—if William WAS his son; they all named their children after their ancestors, so that would be hard to pinpoint, I'm afraid. Also, Rachel Field in one of her books told the story of the *Minerva* disaster in the Arctic.

I wonder if the Gott's Island Judith Cates might have been Edward (David's?) daughter, but tht's only a guess, yours as good as mine. If I can come up with anything more, I'll drop you a line.

The name of William Sawtelle's daughter is Mrs. Louise Libby, Northeast Harbor, Maine, 04662. She, I understand, was in charge of Sawtelle's records at the Islesford Museum, after his death. Her son, Robert Pyle, is librarian at Northeast Harbor. Either one might be able to help you.

Sincerely *Ruth Moore*

TO F. C. MORRONE

(no date, but the guess is March, 1979)

Dear Dr. Morrone,

Some months ago, *Maine Life* magazine carried a short piece entitled *The Decease of Judith Cates, From an Island Diary—1852,* edited by Mary McLean.

Mary McLean (Mrs. Harris McLean, Jr.) lives in Sullivan Harbor, Maine, took this excerpt from a diary handed down in her husband's family, who were Gott's Island people, as my own family were.

The piece contains some items which I'm sure might be helpful to you in your search for the elusive Judith. I quote:

"June 18—It is a dull rainy morning the wind is S.E. Miss Judith Cates seems fast failing and Mr. Moore has not yet returned with the Doctor.

"June 19—It is a foggy morning the wind is in the West. Poor Judith continues to fail. The doctor has not yet arrived.

"July 7— It continues pleasant the wind is S.W. Miss Cates is a little better. Her sister, Captain White's wife of Harrington, has come to see her and will probably stay with her until the decease of Judith.

"Aug. 2— It is a pleasant morning the wind is in the West. Mrs. Moore died last Thursday and was buried Saturday." (This Mrs. Moore was my own great-grandmother, Asenath.)

Mrs. McLean has the complete diary, written, I understand, by the contemporary school teacher. If you write her, she might be willing to rummage in it for further facts about Judith Cates, if any. The last item in the *Maine Life* article is as follows:

"Aug. 8—It is a beautiful day the wind is in the West. Poor Judith is no better."

Maine Life Magazine, (Sedgwick, Me., River Road) would undoubtedly send you a copy of their issue with the piece in it.

At least, this information pinpoints the 1852 date and almost exactly in August that year when she died.

Now, rest in peace, my good man.

Sincerely *Ruth Moore*

TO GERALD E. WEILER

March 20, 1979

Dear Mr. Weiler,

It is too early days for me to be interested in discussing motion picture and/or television rights of my book, *Sarah Walked Over the Mountain*.

I have not, myself, yet seen galleys for proof-reading, and I have no spare manuscript copy.

Thank you, however, for your interest.

Sincerely *Ruth Moore*
(without an s*)

TO JOHN C. WILLEY

March 20, 1979

Dear John,

I never know what to do with these fishing expeditions, which come along every so often, and from which I seldom hear a second time, regardless of whether I answer them or not. Since you must have suggested that he write me, doubtless you know something about him and his company; I, myself, am somewhat puzzled about his interest in my "property" since he obviously hasn't read it and doesn't even know how to spell my name.

If you think this answer to him is adequate, would you drop the envelope in the mail? If otherwise, drop it into your wastebasket. (Save the stamp.) I expect I'd better have his letter back for my records.

How are you doing? Eleanor and I have both got the cabin fever which happens at times in March. But tomorrow will be the first day of spring, so it isn't serious.

As ever *Ruth*

P.S. galleys?

TO JOHN C. WILLEY

March 26, 1979

Dear John,

Thanks for mailing my letter to Mr. Weiler. He had a nerve, and next time should bait a better hook than one to catch suckers with. I loved Annie Laurie, miss her with all my heart; but they don't make two.

Herewith the corrected proofs. They arrived on the day after I mailed my moderate query about them, as I might have known they would have; but I don't trust the P.O. much either.

They are very nice clean galleys and I caught only a few typos which might very well have been my own. I'm not truly taken with the large, black Roman numerals marking the chapter sections; but won't weep if they remain as is. Likely the book designer had something in mind. Anyhow, having been wovelled up with *Sarah* for some three years, I doubt if I shall ever read her through again, and will never know.

Oh, yes. What with three beautiful spring days and the crocuses up, our cabin fever has gone where the dead crabs go.

Could I see the blurb before it goes irrevocably to press?

Affectionately *Ruth*

TO RAY BRIDGES

April 5, 1979

Dear Mr. Bridges,

Thank you for your letter, which I have read with a great deal of interest. The Gott family certainly got around, didn't it?

I am sorry I have no very helpful information about the Gott's Island Appletons. I know that they lived there, at one time long ago, but when, where they went, or whether they were William Appletons, I don't know.

All I have is this: I once found on Gott's Island Neck, growing toward the light in a thicket of catspruce, a small plot of tiger lilies which had round black seeds, and gathered some. There seemed to be no old house foundation that I could find, but it was hard to tell, the big trees had grown over everything. So I asked around, "Who lived there?" and Berlin Gott, an old man long dead now, said "That was where Marm Appleton lived, and those are Marm Appleton's tiger lilies." I add below, a sketch of Gott's Island, with the place marked X. I don't suppose it will help you very much. This was thirty years ago, and all the Gott's Island older people who might remember are, of course, now dead.

If I can round up any further information, I'll let you know.

Sincerely *Ruth Moore*

Professor Donald Mortland published an essay, "Ruth Moore: Maine Coast Writer" in the *Colby Library Quarterly*, Colby College, Waterville, Maine, March 1979. In the article Ruth is compared to Sarah Orne Jewett, Mary Ellen Chase, and Herman Melville.

TO JOHN C. WILLEY

April 5, 1979

Dear John,

The most tiresome people are the ones who answer letters the same day they arrive—you don't, thank God, and I don't, usually. But I do want to make clear at once that I've always whole-heartedly liked and enjoyed your jacket copy and have had no fault to find with it. This time, I only wanted to make sure that nobody pinpointed where I live, because if the name of Bass Harbor is so much as breathed, I am mortally wounded by visits from hordes of tourists from Acadia Park who seem to be obsessed with calling upon anything or anybody which might be considered a "point of interest." Three million people ride by here twenty feet from our back door—so far, they don't all stop.

The catalog is great—I couldn't ask for better, and thanks for sending it along.

I thought you might like to see the enclosed copy of the *Colby College Library Quarterly*. Pretty fancy company I'm traveling in, unbeknownst to you and to me, too, for heb'm sakes. I was astonished. I wrote thanks to Professor Mortland and almost addressed him as "Dr. Livingstone, I presume," but stopped myself in time.

About crocuses, we once had a splendid bed of color, about six by seven feet. We now have seven crocuses. Damned chipmunks.

As ever, *Ruth*

TO DONALD MORTLAND

April 7, 1979

Dear Professor Mortland,

Thank you. More than I know how to say.

I have been writing fiction for almost forty years and have had some success at it—at least have made my living doing it—but have always been somewhat surprised at how many of the pieces written about my work have stressed what I do BESIDES writing. I puzzle over being told that I garden, that my car is a jeep, that I cut my own firewood; years ago, when I was helping to build the house I now live in, I thought, well, if I go down to posterity at all, it will be as a lady-carpenter.

But you have not only put me in distinguished company, you've written a concise and literate evaluation of what, all these years, I've been trying to do; if I could separate myself from it—if I read it about somebody else's work—I would look on it as a brilliant piece of literary criticism, as it, of course, is. I'm most deeply appreciative of your Speak to the Winds analysis. I have always known that its underlying point has been there for a perceptive mind to find.

About profanity, I think you are quite right. Realistically, it's a part of local speech—I grew up with accomplished swearers. I'll never forget the time Frank Babbidge ran his lobster boat aground on the Foreshore Ledge down at Gott's Island. His thoughts on his situation were Homeric—in thunderous hexameters. I wouldn't have missed it. Mostly, swearing's automatic hereabouts; isn't noticed or even considered profane. Like when my first book, *The Weir*, came out, a young fisherman friend of mine read me out good and proper for using bad language in it, and ended up saying, "Jesus Christ, Ruth, we don't never swear like that in front of the womenfolks." The point is, and

I've been years learning it—the spoken word is flavoring, but in print it shows up as exactly what it is—profane, and to many people, offensive.

Again, all my thanks and appreciation.

Ruth Moore

TO KENDALL MORSE

May 20, 1979

Dear Ken,

Sorry about the delay—but you didn't include your address on your post card and I couldn't remember it.

It's all right with me if you want to read *Cold as a Dog* on your program, but I think you should get in touch with Gordon about it. Perhaps you already have. But since he undertook the reprint and handles the sales of it, we have been in the thing sort of together. If it's okay with him, it's okay with me.

Good luck, anyway, and peace yourself.

Sincerely *Ruth*

TO LYNNE ALBRIGHT

June 23, 1979

Dear Ms. Albright,

I am sorry to have been so long in answering your letter and phone call.

Since the death of Annie Laurie Williams I have had no agent and have relied on the counsel of my publisher, whose advice is, in short, to make no commitments without firm financial offers. Money up front, they say, which seems like a tough policy but is nonetheless sensible.

Another thing—the motion picture rights to *Spoonhandle* were sold years ago—I believe in 1946—to Twentieth Century Fox, whose production entitled *Deep Waters* is still kicking around among the artifacts of that, shall I say, era. At least, it occasionally turns up on television, and not long ago the film was shown here in a local movie theater. I expect that you, with your experience in the field, must know about this. I mention it just in case.

Frankly, I don't know how else to answer you. All I can suggest which may be helpful, is that you write to my editor, John Willey, at William Morrow & Co. for his opinion.

I do appreciate heartily your interest in my work and thank you for the pleasant things you say about it.

Sincerely *Ruth Moore*

TO JOHN C. WILLEY

June 23, 1979

Dear John,

I've been gadding about and trying to get my garden planted—in one of the muddiest and dog and frizzle seasons I've ever seen. Fourteen days of steady rain and, in May, only three days of sunshine. So no reply to your letter, which deserved better.

I'm tickled to death with *Sarah's* jacket—if I'd designed it myself I couldn't have done half so well. So thanks again—I might say, for many beautiful jackets.

The catalog's very impressive. E and I would like a copy of *The Last Voyage of Captain James Cook,* by Richard Hough, when it's out. And thanks for that, too.

Professor Mortland will be pleased, I think, because you are quoting him. Will Morrow send him a copy of the book? Or I will, whatever.

The enclosed correspondence with McIntosh and Otis and a Hollywood entrepreneur named Lynne Albright and me is probably only another headache. I don't like to dump it on you, but I really don't know what else to do. Albright is very gung ho—she's telephoned here—fortunately I wasn't home—and left her number to call collect, which I haven't done; and I haven't written McIntosh and Otis either, not wanting especially to get involved with them. Pound me on the head, if you want to.

Aff., as ever, *Ruth*

The following excerpt from Donald F. Mortland's article in the *Colby College Library Quarterly* was reprinted on the back cover of *Sarah Walked Over the Mountain.*

"Among all those writing today, one way or another, about the Maine coast, surely Ruth Moore is outstanding. She has thirteen novels to her credit, all of which deal with Maine settings and Maine characters. She has also published two books of poetry. She is now at work on another novel (*Sarah Walked Over the Mountain*). It is the quality of her writing, however, not the quantity, that places her, in my judgment, at the head of the group of living Maine writers. Although different from her predecessors Mary Ellen Chase and Sarah Orne Jewett, she is of their caliber.

"Piles of books have been written about the Maine Coast and its people, some of which are sentimental slush, some simply wrong ... Ruth Moore does not idolize either the place or its people, nor does she see them as quaint, nor does she patronize them.

"In the process of preserving a way of life, Miss Moore also preserves a way of speaking that television and formal education will probably soon expunge. Many writers try and fail to reproduce the speech of the Maine coast, the speech of the man on the street there, or the man at the oar or throttle. Miss Moore invariably succeeds. ...

"She has the most extraordinary knowledge of THINGS, and of the exact terms that apply to them. She can describe accurately and minutely the lace on a lady's nightgown or the process of getting about from a ledge. She knows both a man's world and a woman's world, and possesses an astonishing accuracy of vocabulary for describing either ...

"In a recent newspaper interview, Miss Moore said, 'My object is to interpret this region realistically. After all, I grew up in it.' She has succeeded marvelously well."

TO JOHN C. WILLEY

July 16, 1979

Dear John,

Could you let me know the name of an editor at Harper & Row to whom Eleanor might submit a manuscript?

As you doubtless know, H & R merged with Crowell who published her *October Fire,* but her editor there was Lois Cole, and we neither of us know how editors might be scrambled around by now. I guess it's practical to have a name—you recall how my galleys landed in the unsolicited bin because I inadvertently forgot to write, for once, John C. Willey, on the bundle.

She thought she'd try H & R first, because she's not without a background with Crowell—they wrote recently wanting to renew the copyright for *October Fire,* but all the name she has is somebody in their copyright department. If you could do this, why, bless you.

This letter may smell of "ozone" and the Bermuda High, which have been over us for, it seems like, weeks. Fog and stink from the industrial cities west of here.

Foggily, but affectionately, *Ruth*

P.S. I think it would be nice since Time's Web *is headed for the shredder, if the company sent me five copies for free; but if this is too mingy on my part, would you tell them to send them and deduct the cost from the kitty?*

TO JOHN C. WILLEY

August 7, 1979

Dear John,

So far, two copies of *Sarah* have arrived and I don't know how to tell you how pleased I am with it. It is, as you say, "trim-looking," but the best thing about it is that the artist has got into the jacket picture what I tried to get into the book—how shall I say??—the mysterious secrecy of wilderness and its un-humanity, which *Sarah* had to cope with. Thank you all, very much. You've done a great job, and I'm grateful.

Dr. Mortland's address is Unity College, Unity, Maine, Zip—04988—I don't have his home address.

I don't wonder you've sent the books piecemeal. Our mail, particularly first-class, seems to be scattered all over the works by the Post Office. Some of it has ended up in Lubec, some in Bath, some I doubt if we get at all. The plague seems to be general around here. I hope you got my letter re. a movie agent. Some time ago, if you'll recall, you suggested that one of your office people would find one for me. This was after Annie Laurie died, and the circumstances for *Dinosaur Bite* were something the same. Nothing came of that, and I can't remember the agent's name, but I know I wasn't committed to him by contract.

We fared poorly in the hot weather which also brought "ozone" from the industrial cities to the west of us. Both of us felt fuzzy-headed and downspent for weeks. But yesterday and today are beautiful and clear and we can get our breath down. Take care.

Affectionately *Ruth*

TO JOHN C. WILLEY

August 10, 1979

Dear John,

I think your suggestion is a good one, that I assign motion picture/television rights on *Sarah Walked Over the Mountain* to William Morrow and Company, proceeds therefrom split 85% for me, 15% for Morrow. Please consider this letter authorization for same.

Best to you, Aff. *Ruth*

TO JOHN C. WILLEY

October 15, 1979

Dear John,

I am sorry to have been so long in writing you, but we have had a very bad time here since August, when Eleanor began having cobalt treatments for brain tumor. In a world knocked cockeyed, I haven't had either the energy or the brains to handle business or personal relationships; through September it was mostly almost daily trips to the hospital in Bangor where Eleanor was; besides she wasn't willing to let me harrow our friends until we knew how things were coming out. They have come out well—the treatments have been successful. We have every reason now to know she will get well. She is at home now, still weak, but still, by God, fighting.

Now. About *Sarah*. Publication date slid by here without any more notice than it, apparently, was noticed by William Morrow and Company. I've had no news and no reports. I am not asking anyone to temper the wind to my personal misfortunes; I'm too old a pro for that. But I'm also too old a pro to sit on my duff and see Sarah drop into the abyss the way *"Lizzie" and Caroline* and *The Dinosaur Bite* did. Sarah started out too well for that. I want to know what's being done. I would also like to call attention to the items in my contract dealing with my money going back into the Company in return for adequate publicity and advertising. (Incidentally, *Dinosaur Bite*, remaindered, seems to be doing quite well locally, now that it is offered at a price which people who want to read and own it can afford to pay.)

September 18, I suppose, WAS publication date? I have reason to think *Sarah*'s now on the market. I've had some very nice fan mail about it, so some people have certainly had access to it. I enclose one letter from an acquaintance, a lady now retired, who has spent her working years in advertising and who has done a great deal of television advertising. Perhaps the suggestion she makes will be of some use to the Morrow department which is handling my movie and television rights now. In some ways, I wish I had gone ahead and got hold of an outside agent; but I have always trusted your advice which has been generally good. Perhaps you've already retired? But I understood you'd be at Morrow until the end of the year.

I wish you would show part of your letter dealing with *Sarah* to Larry Hughes, if he is still around.

If I were able at the moment to end this tirade with

Affectionately, I would *Ruth*

TO JOHN SEXTON

November 3, 1979

Dear Mr. Sexton,

I don't know why your letter took so long to reach me—perhaps it's been wandering around in the caverns of the Post Office as some mail does. But I have it now and do want to thank you for all the pleasant things you write about my books. I'm sorry it's taken so long. The Chicago Ruth Moore and I in years past used to get mail mixed up, but it hasn't happened for a long time until now. Ruth Moore isn't an unusual name, I know. There were two others in college with me, and at one time, nine in the New York telephone book. But here, at last, are my thanks for your letter.

Yes, I went to college. English courses there helped me a great deal. But what helped most was actual practice writing. Since I don't know you, I can't advise you about college; but I can say, "Write and write and write about everything you see or know about." If you are really serious about it, you will find, if you do that, that technique and your own personal style, etc., will develop as time goes on. Get to know grammar thoroughly. You might read *Strictly Speaking* by Edwin Newman, or his *A Civil Tongue*.

My books are fiction, except for the region I write about and know best; it doesn't do to put in people one knows, neighbors and such. Besides, it's more fun to make up your own characters, you'll find.

I'm not writing at the moment—on vacation, as I'm all written out temporarily. My latest book, *Sarah Walked Over the Mountain,* came out in September. It took me three years of hard work to do, and, as yet, I haven't an idea in my head.

I enclose the autographs you want.

Good luck *Ruth Moore*

TO JOHN C. WILLEY

November 14, 1979

Dear John,

It seemed like old times to talk with you on the phone, and it's been reassuring to know what's being done. Please thank Bob Spizer for his comprehensive memo—there do seem to be few places that *Sarah* hasn't at least visited. Bad news I can always take, and good news as it comes. No news at all drives me up the wall. So I flipped; but I don't doubt that your European vacation was sadly needed, and I don't grudge you it.

Reviews, well. I never can make up my mind whether I like, or don't like, to get them. Times, they make one's own work sound incomprehensible; other times, they tell all the plot; sometimes they're venomous, for no reason I can see except the reviewer has a bellyache or has to establish his own slickness in panning a book. The *Kirkus* review tickled me a good deal—that guy there is undoubtedly either a disgruntled Maine tourist who's heard the definitive remark, going the rounds this summer, that they come here with one clean shirt and a five-dollar bill and don't change either one for the duration; or he's a hunter, who objects to my snide passes about the blood-must-flow boys. Speaking of that, the *Ellsworth American* hasn't reviewed *Sarah,* but has recently published a long editorial on deer hunting, in which the writer, Dale Coman, points out that hunting is a religion, as I did in Sarah, not mentioning her or me and not using quotes; which seems to mean that she's being read around, or that Dale and I gave birth to the same idea, only I published it first. Don't know; don't much care, as long as somebody gets a point I've been trying to make. As for the *New York Times,* I recall that one of my books which came out in September, wasn't reviewed by them until just before Christmas. That was *Speak to the Winds* which did all right without that particular holy laying on of hands.

Thanks for returning Beth Egan's letter. I enclose one herewith (which doesn't need to be returned), because it's a sample of what I've been getting about *Sarah* and bears out what Frances Lamb, who runs The Bookstore in Ellsworth says about fiction: That she can no longer sell "dirty" books, her clients won't buy them, so she doesn't bother any longer to put them on her shelves.

We are getting along fine. We spent yesterday afternoon at the Tumor Clinic in Bangor, where Eleanor's doctor told her that she is "over the hump." They say there that they have been lucky with this one.

Please give my regards to Larry Hughes and thank him for me for the trouble he has taken.

Affectionately *Ruth*

TO JOHN C. WILLEY

November 29, 1979

Dear John,

Local reviews have begun to come through and I enclose two of them—

from *Down East* magazine and Maine Life. Also a fan letter, which doesn't need to be returned, as I have answered it.

Did it slip your mind to have ten copies of *Sarah* sent me? Or are they cowering somewhere in the caverns of the Post Office? Best to use UPS, if convenient, and then things won't end up in West Texas or East Germany, such as isn't beyond the bounds of possibility and has been known to happen.

We're fine, getting along well, though our hands are still pretty full.

Aff. *Ruth*

Burying Island is off the eastern shore of the Hancock peninsula in Taunton Bay; Jay Dillon was involved at the time in protesting nuclear plants and military facilities where nuclear missiles were stored.

TO MARY AND LOU DILLON

December 19, 1979

Dear Mary and Lou,

Our news is good. The Tumor Clinic doctors have told Eleanor that she is "over the hump"—their words; no more cobalt treatments and, now, a fine chance for full recovery. I believe them, and if you get a chance to come and see us, I think you will, too, for she is like herself again—the person you saw when you were last here is no longer with us. She's now doing most of the housework, helps me with the outside chores, whichever ones aren't too heavy, no longer needs the walker or the cane, and best of all her wit is back and used and her brain, fuzzy so long, is sharp as a gimlet. Now she's recovering from the treatment, which will take a while. We are both beginning to forget the hell of the last 15 months and are laughing together from time to time.

As you must know, I have admired Jay since the day on Burying Island when we all dug around in the Indian shellheap—I think he was six (?) then. I think he is doing a great job, one which takes guts to do, and I think he should have full support from the country's entire population; and that the yobbos who don't think it's important to turn off the air-conditioner, et al., ought to be sent to Iran to take the place of the hostages there. I'm sorry I've had my hands too full to help him in what he's doing, but I'm glad I thought to offer him a hot bath, the day he bicycled over from Hancock (or was it Ellsworth?) and arrived speechless with exhaustion. Do tell him this. I have just read your piece about him which came this morning, and it does my heart good to know that you are both now on his side, too, as you goddam well better be, and every other United States citizen who, so far, is walking around healthy.

My book, *Sarah Walked Over the Mountain,* is doing well—much better than the previous two books. It's had some excellent reviews, though the *New York Times* hasn't uttered and probably won't; their *Book Review* is much too full already, reviewing books that, so far as I can tell, nobody in the God's world would ever want to read. You can say if you like that my grapes are sour and hanging low and perhaps they are; but I recall one of my books which came out in a September and wasn't reviewed by the *Times* until past Christmas of that year, by which time it was Literary Guild—That was *Speak to the Winds* which did all right without any of their holy laying on of hands.

If you're in Hancock now, you probably arrived blunt-end-foremost in the middle of our cold "snap" which has fluttered the dovecots all over this town at least, we not being ready for it after the mild, green fall. Just the kind of welcome you need, Lou—you should have come two weeks earlier when everything was still green in 50 degree temperatures.

All the best, love and Merry Christmas

Ruth

TO DOROTHY LOBRANO GUTH

December, '79 and January, '80

Dear Dottie, et al,

1980! Where did the time go?

I started my Christmas letter, but it turned out to be New Year's, because, simply, I have had my hands full. Eleanor has fought a long and gallant battle against cancer, which, the doctors now tell us, she has won—they say they have been lucky with this one, that she is "over the hump"—their words—and will get well. I find that after a year of sitting on top of this volcano, we both find it hard to talk about it. And I won't, except to say that our news at last is good and the winter ahead doesn't look to be so long and cold. As it did, earlier on.

My book, *Sarah Walked Over the Mountain,* came out this fall and appears to be doing quite well; I have had some good mail about it, one or two nibbles from movie and television people, and some excellent reviews. True, the *Times Book Review* hasn't uttered, but that's not too surprising since it seems mostly to be written these days by some woman named Oates, ad infinitum reviewing books by an old Jewish gentleman named Singer. I peruse it each week trying to find something that anyone in the God's world would ever care to read. My mail is grateful to me because *Sarah* isn't "dirty," and perhaps we are going to live to see an upturn, becausc Mrs. Lamb, who runs a nicely sophisticated bookstore in Ellsworth, tells me that she will no longer order "dirty" books or stock them on her shelves—her customers will not buy them. Another lady, who wrote me from New Jersey, announced, "Sex is here to stay—why write about it?" This tickles me some, because as you know, I never in my life could.

I've just finished Maxwell Perkins' letters, which makes me realize how lucky I have always been in editors at Morrow, who left me alone to go my own way. I know he was a great editor, no doubt of it, and did great wonders, too, for the scintillating names of his clientele of that day, which names he dropped all over the place until you began to wish that "Hem," for godsake, would stay put in Cuba; which names, you wonder, might not have skintled so brightly without the masses of Perkins criticism poured over them like molasses. Oh, the best molasses, without doubt. If I had ever got one of those eight-ten pages of creeping analysis, I would have flung up the sponge—preferably at him, thc affable old son, and given up and gone back to putting away pieces of paper in New York offices. But nothing like that from Thayer or from you, and John never utters unless there's a blooper. Thank God. Which there was—a beautiful blooper in *Sarah,* when I got the dates of the French Revolution ten years out of place. Wow! as you used to say.

All the best from us, for Happy and Merry, and Love,

Ruth and Eleanor

1980s

TO JOHN C. WILLEY

March 18, 1980

Dear John,

Thanks for sending along the reviews from the two local papers, which I'd already seen, since we get both the Bangor and Bar Harbor offerings. I've often speculated on who writes their reviews—nice ladies, I suspect, possibly the publishers' wives. Lit'ry ladies. *The Bar Harbor Times* has recently been sold—to a Saltonstall gentleman from Mass. who specializes in the coy and the cozy—bitkins which local minds will be able to take in, like wild animals behaving like humans and cats up a telephone pole. His own column, longish, is called "Under Uncle Dick's Hill." The "raw realism in silhouette against a stark Maine setting," which you mention, tickled me, too. I bet that lady thought she'd said a mouthful.

We're getting along fine. Eleanor is driving the car again—for short distances—and is walking upwards of a mile a day. We are breathing again, and I'm putting back the 20 pounds I lost. I wish I wasn't. I looked elegant for a while, having been temporarily the only woman in my family on my mother's side who didn't have a fat can. The winter goes fast and we are nearly up over March Hill.

I hope things go well for you.

Aff. *Ruth*

"The Washerwoman" reference in the letter below is to Elizabeth Hardwick's novel, *Sleepless Nights,* wherein she describes her Maine washerwoman. Mary Ellen Chase is the noted Maine author, a contemporary of Ruth's.

My editor at the *Tuesday Weekly* in Ellsworth was Wayne Mayo, whose aunt was Eleanor, and Wayne was always telling me stories about them. He even said he'd take me down to Bass Harbor sometime so I could meet Ruth; but he never did. Ruth's and my correspondence continued, however, especially when I began to branch out and publish articles like the one I did for *Puckerbrush Review,* published in spring 1980, entitled "Missing from the Books: My Maine." The article caused a bit of a stir about The Pine Tree State, and thanks to Virgil Bisset and MPBN-FM, the article became the basis of a 1981 radio series called "The Maine That's Missing." Here's how Ruth reacted to the article.

TO SANFORD PHIPPEN

August 1, 1980

Dear Sanford,

For heaven's sake, man. Your piece, "My Maine," doesn't need any discussion from me, or anyone now, and didn't before it was written. It's a truthful, gravely considered and simply-written analysis with which, if this matters, I'm in almost total agreement. My opinion can be expressed in two words: well done.

I don't go along with any regional writer who does an excellent job of describing a local "washerwoman," but, it seems to me, without compassion. "Her" washerwoman? Huh.

I don't go along with another extreme, Miss Mary Ellen Chase appearing in one of the coastal sardine factories and lecturing to the women packers on "The Dignity of Labor." A friend of mine who was elbow-deep in oil, or tomato sauce, mustard or whatever, told me that the occasion was one of outward politeness and deep inner glee and much was made of it later.

You mention Miriam Colwell's *Wind Off the Water*. Have you read her *Young?* Dedicated to: TO WHOM IT MAY CONCERN, it details a situation which might be called typical, in a small Maine village. In a quiet, dead-pan kind of way that curdles blood and freezes marrow. One hell of a good job on what you call My Maine.

I don't go along with writers who have fed on honeydew and drunk the milk of Paradise flowing from publicity bureaus. This goes a long way back, to the 1880s, when some feudal-minded old totty discovered Maine's pretty scenery and (also feudal-minded) local citizenry. It's not to be wondered at—a man has to make a living, doesn't he? So you can catch more flies with honeydew than you can with vinegar; lay it on, and eventually you get "Bert and I," etc., a split society, and not much to be done about it; and "regional" writers, whether summer or winter people, catch it like a disease and not to be blamed too much, considering?

I have two words in my vocabulary I think of as obscene. One is "regional," the other "interview." "Regional," because I believe Maine is a microcosm of anywhere else; "interview," because I have seldom had contact with the press which may quote me verbatim, but slants what I say toward sensationalism or eccentricity, and sets me to sulking in my tent for weeks. This is why, no other reason, I said no to your first letter to me.

So PLEASE, don't quote me on any of this, okay?

You can tell Ted Holmes that some of my best friends are summer people.

Sincerely *Ruth*

On January 30, 1981, Eleanor Mayo, who was 60, died from cancer in the Maine Coast Memorial Hospital in Ellsworth.

If Ruth wrote any letters in 1981, they can't be found. From 1980 through 1985, there are only 22. However, from 1986 to 1989, when the "real Maine" movement was catching on, and Ruth's works were re-discovered and began to be re-printed in paperback by Gary Lawless and The Blackberry Press, she wrote more letters than ever. One hundred fifty were found, and most of them are re-printed here.

TO JOHN AND DOROTHY GOULD

January 18, 1982

Dear Dotty and John,

For two years, going on three, Eleanor fought a brave and valiant battle against cancer, which she lost. For a while, in the summer of '80, we thought she would be all right, but things happened very quickly in the fall. I should have written you then, certainly answered your letter of last June, but it's been hard to join the world again, which I have now. My sister Esther has come to live with me so I'm not alone, and have been able to go back to work again.

What is the "Perry Mason" book you mention in your letter? I hadn't heard of it, much less read it. I don't know any of the people at Morrow now except Larry Hughes, who, the last I knew, was Chairman of the company. Apparently, a clean sweep was made after Morrow was sold, or the people we knew are all dead or retired now. Avon Paperbacks owns the company now, and who owns Avon? I heard it was some tremendous publishing house in West Germany, but this may have been gossip, though I wouldn't be surprised. John Willey was my contact there for years, my editor, and he was great, but he's retired and gone to live in Vancouver, Washington—I wrote him that he reminds me of John Gould's squash vines that foretold a long cold winter by growing twice as long, so as to get as far away as possible, and I don't blame him, laving his feet in the Pacific Ocean.

Best to you both.

Affectionately *Ruth*

"Old boy trying to get to West Quacko" refers to one of Gordon Bok's records.

TO GORDON BOK

January 25, 1982

Dear Gordon,

Thank you for the 10 *Cold Dogs* and for the new records. The old boy trying to get to West Quacko is right down my alley, one of your best, I think. I got Folk-Legacy to send out four of him to various family connections, who have kids, and he got a great reception. One youngster said, "HE thinks HE'S got Hogans—he ought to look into my arithmetic book." She's no part of a math expert, poor lamb.

About the folk opera—so far I haven't come up with anything that doesn't seem like something an elementary school teacher wrote and produced at a school "time." I'm beginning to see what you're up to, though, and it's not to do with "The Hangdowns." I thought of that because it has a good, rousing tune and is based on authentic folk-legends about what scares people in the woods; "hang-downs" were the worst of the lot—sometimes a big owl would mistake a man's hat for a skunk or rabbit and swoop down into the black dark along the woods-path, in complete silence, too, and either knock the hat off or fly away with it. So WHAT was that? Uh-huh, a hangdown, guaranteed to scare a man silly. Good comic opera, maybe; but not what you have in mind.

You must know that you don't have to ask me about recording *Cold as a Dog*. I'd be delighted and if you do, I hope you'll find a place for "Sam."

I'm still fussing around with the two new ballads. One, I think, is quite good; the other needs work. I'm supposed to be working on a new novel and would be, if I didn't get maddened because that damn second ballad won't come right.

I hope you haven't frozen in your solar-heated studio. It's surely a winter, isn't it? I don't dare to say I enjoy it, because everyone thinks I'm crazy if I do, including my old cat. He's going on for sixteen and despises having to dig and bury in deep snow, thinks it's not neat. Two winters ago, when we had some snow, he was horrified when spring came to find his entire winter's product on bare ground—he spent days digging and covering until every last evidence was safely under ground. Not a sign left to say Tophey fecit.

Best to you both.

Affectionately *Ruth*

TO SUSAN WOLF

(no date) 1982

Miss Susan Wolf
Maine Public Broadcasting Service

Dear Miss Wolf,

Mr. Gordon Bok is welcome to use my ballad, "The Night Charley Tended Weir," on the television program, "A Fresh Breeze Blows Down East," provided he does not edit or change it in any way.

Perhaps you would let me know when the program is to be, as I'd like to see it.

Sincerely *Ruth Moore*

When my first book, *The Police Know Everything,* was published in August 1982, I wrote to Ruth to let her know.

TO SANFORD PHIPPEN

August 8, 1982

Dear Sandy,

This is good news about your new book and of course I want a copy, check is enclosed.

You've taken your time. I've wondered when the world of literature would hear from you. I look forward now to seeing what I know will be a—well, let's see—literate piece of work, written in English, which doesn't depend on pornography or horrors and supernatural monsters scaring young children to take it screaming to the top of best-seller lists designed to catch the TV-scraped minds of those who like such things. What a sentence!

So more power to you, and good luck with it.

Sincerely *Ruth*

P.S. A smashing title, too.

When it was clear that there was to be a second printing of *The Police Know Everything* in 1982, I wrote again to Ruth to see if she'd consider giving me an endorsement for the new back cover.

The earliest reviews of *The Police* that I must have sent Ruth were the one by Pat Flagg of *The Ellsworth American,* which was a rave, and the "Searing Maine blood-letting" one by Robert H. Newall in the *Bangor Daily News.* I'm not sure what the third one was; but I did ask Ruth for her "Pope's blessing."

TO SANFORD PHIPPEN

September 29, 1982

Dear Sandy,

My dear man, the Pope?!!! I'm overcome, but here's a blessing, for whatever it's worth. And thanks.

I'm delighted to hear that you're heading into a second printing. Two of the reviews you sent me are excellent, written by intelligent people who have got your point and who hold up your hands. The third has some unpleasant and ugly adjectives, it's true, but the word "bloodletting" will sell you a lot of copies, don't you think? I had this happen to me when I wrote *The Walk Down Main Street,* which attacked the sanctified institution of B-ball in the schools. People who are jumping up and down and clashing their heels together with rage always want to know what you have to say. You'll very likely get some letters, not exactly and not all fan letters, only concerned with what has hit the fan. (I don't think you had better quote me on this—the Pope wouldn't say it, would he?)

I appreciate being asked to put an opinion on the back cover of your new edition. Most of what I would like to say has already been expressed better than I can in two of your reviews. But if the following pleases you, you are welcome to use it.

Good luck, and rest you merry, *Ruth*

> Many readers will enjoy *The Police Know Everything* for Mr. Phippen's subtle humor and his clear-spring-water style. Others who have swallowed the Maine myths, established back in the 1880s when the first tourists discovered our pretty scenery, will not care for it, nor will those who make profit out of Old Salts and lovable eccentrics. But there is, surely, among us, a majority which will welcome this honest and deeply concerned attempt to sweep reality out from under the rug.

TO JOHN GOULD, JR.

September 30, 1982

Dear John, Jr.,

I'd love to come to the Golden Wedding Celebration, and will, if I can manage it. My health, after some 80 years of banging around, is a little wabbly now, so that long drives are a little chancy for me, but this is one party I'd hate to miss, and will try.

Give John and Dottie my love and tell him that my squash vines are all over the field, so maybe I WILL try to get as far away as possible.

Sincerely *Ruth*

TO JOHN GOULD

December 7, 1982

Dear John,

I was sorry to miss your anniversary party; it sounded like a good one. But around that time, I went innocently to the eye-doctor to have my glasses checked and he discovered a small cyst that had to be removed; so there I sat at home, regretting, with my right eye spouting what I thought might be crocodile tears, since the cyst wasn't anything to worry about, really.

I can't remember whether it was you or James Thurber who remarked once, "They aim these things at me."

I look forward to reading your book about the Jesuit priest who smuggled. What did he smuggle and aren't you going to be in trouble with the Pope?

I haven't done any real work—except for research, and all that, for a couple of years, but I'm back at it again, now. It's time the public got offered something besides horrors and monsters which go shrieking to the top of the best-seller list. God help us all.

Have you run into a book called *The Police Know Everything*, by Sanford Phippen? It's about what he calls the "true Maine" and really racks open some dusty old glory-holes. He's not only a fine writer, but he has a kind of wry, sideways humor that's a pleasure to read. His relatives in Hancock are all very mad at him because he's used some of them, without disguising persons and places. One of his old aunts, outraged, told him, "Sandy, this time you've gone too far." It's a paperback, brought out by the Puckerbrush Press in Orono, and has already gone into a second printing, seeing it's fluttered some other dovecots outside of his own home town.

My best, as always, to you and Dot.

Ruth

TO GORDON BOK

December 7, 1982

Dear Gordon,

I think that the last time I wrote you—IF I wrote you—I was on the verge of illness—a nasty type of virus pneumonia which didn't respond too well to antibiotics and which plagued me all summer and practically wiped out my brains, so that some things I don't remember. But I'm okay now and have gone back to work, thank God. Being without work was worst.

How are you? Did you get along with the opera, and is there a record of it? Have you any new records? Folk-Legacy hasn't sent me its current list and I need one, because I always give your records for Christmas. Is their address still Sharon, CT, or have they moved? Have I ever told you how much I love "Another Land Made of Water"?

Can you spare me ten copies of *Cold as a Dog?* Five will do if you're low.

I'm working on a couple of new ballads not yet finished, that is not yet polished up to my satisfaction, but will be.

Best to you and yours—

Sincerely *Ruth*

I had sent Ruth what Louise Dickinson Rich, author of *We Took to the Woods* and a friend of mine since 1960, had written about *The Police,* and I also asked her if *The Walk Down Main Street* was based on Pemetic or Mount Desert High School (now combined with Bar Harbor High to create MDI High School) and their basketball teams.

TO SANFORD PHIPPEN

December 9, 1982

Dear Sanford,

Thanks for your letter and for sharing with me some of your endorsements and reviews ... You've had some pretty nice ones, and deserved them, too. I've been interested and tickled to see who's been jumping on your bandwagon. I'm late writing you because I've been all wovelled up in trying to get my mind off work in progress and onto preparations for Christmas for probably one of the largest families in the State of Maine. Speaking of families, incidentally, I've always been accused by mine of putting this one or that one in a book, and when I deny it and point out characteristics which show convincingly that I haven't, then they get sore because I didn't. They get over it and so will yours—if that's any comfort to you now.

Walk Down Main Street wasn't either Pemetic or Mt. Desert, just any B-ball crazy town anywhere, and I got flak, most of it from Indiana, in spots quite obscene. Mercy, you'd have thought they were all running "to hide their dates and bread, and cluck their children in about their knees."

I knew Louise Rich very well for years and was sorry to hear she'd left Prospect Harbor and had gone to live in Boston. I found her wonderful company and a superb round-house cook. There are few enough of those, and I've missed her. Her approval of Police is characteristic—exactly what she would say and think.

I'll bet Ted Holmes has never told you that I taught him to swim when he was eight years old.

Now, look. Always when you've wanted to see me, you've also wanted an "Interview," and all I could possibly say was No. I keep my head down, these days, so far as publicity is concerned; I have tourists all summer for one thing, all headed for the Bass Harbor Head Lighthouse, which is one of the publicized sights on MDI. Some are nice and some not so nice and I have no near neighbors. Such are the uses of publicity—if I stick up, I have visitors. It's not that I don't like them, I do, but it's hell on working hours, and also, even at this time of year OUR local police tell us to keep our doors locked and not to let in strangers. You, of course, would not be a stranger. But I gave up "interviews" a number of years ago. Okay?

All the best *Ruth*

Gary Lawless had written an article for *Downeast Libraries,* the Maine State Library magazine, trying to stir up renewed interest in Ruth Moore's works. When he couldn't get any of Maine's small presses interested in re-printing any Moore, he decided to do it himself.

TO GARY LAWLESS

April 26, 1983

Dear Mr. Lawless,

Your letter to me has been held up somewhere—possibly in the maw of a computer which has a habit of devouring its young. I have had this happen too many times to my mail not to suspect something of the kind. Late or not,

I am very pleased to have your letter and to read what you have to say about my books. It was a pleasant and thoughtful thing for you to do and I appreciate it. Was this written for me, or for some publication? I should be glad to have my publishers, William Morrow & Co., 105 Madison Avenue, 10016, NYC, see a copy of it. Intelligent evaluation, particularly of fiction, is hard to come by these days, and Lawrence Hughes, President of the Company, just might be glad to listen to some.

My latest book, *Sarah Walked Over the Mountain,* came out in 1979, I believe, and since then I have been up to my ears doing another. It usually takes me three years to write a book; and the current one is difficult. So I'm happy to retire from the world until the job's done, and to get forgotten about is splendid.

Many thanks for a bang-up job on your part, too.

Sincerely *Ruth*

TO MARY DILLON

July 27, 1983

Dear Mary,

I'm really sorry, hon. It sounds like a pleasant party. But Esther's youngest son, Phil and his wife, will be here on that Sunday, for one thing; but mostly, I, honestly, am not up to the drive and the traffic, since I do have to spend most afternoons flattened out in bed. The summer traffic is howling hell even down our back road. Esther says she might be able to manage getting off Mt. Desert Island, but she wouldn't guarantee getting back on in the bumper-to-bumper stuff of late afternoon, on a Sunday. I wish that ratty old lighthouse would break off and fall into the sea, carrying with it the Maine Publicity Bureau entire. We had ten million go past our house, Turnpike Tommy and Turnpike Tilly, at eighty an hour, going down to view that poor old remnant which isn't even activated any more. The ten million was last year's count; God only knows what this season's will be. Seeing that we've just outlived good weather and a full moon, maybe things will settle down a bit. A good fog mull would help, too. Last night, they were oo-ing and ah-ing all over the road ALL NIGHT. There was some screaming, down along, so possibly we had a touch of rape put on to make them feel at home.

Being a semi-invalid increases my persecution complex, as you might guess from the above.

It was lovely to see you and Ruthie the other day; perhaps we can get together later on when I don't wobble quite so much.

Love, *Ruth*

I was thrilled to receive from Ruth an original signed copy of *The Walk Down Main Street*. I had told her previously how I'd love to have another copy since my first one had been lost.

TO SANFORD PHIPPEN

April 23, 1984

Dear Sandy,

This copy of *The Walk Down Main Street* was looted from a friend who had two. The shelf was dusty, so she won't miss it—I feel you'll make better use of it.

I can add a postscript to the remark made by the summer person in *Police*—"We wouldn't want to be buried up among all those Maine natives."

When the Black Island Quarries were in full blast, the owners shipped in quite a number of Italian and Scottish stone cutters, the most skilled to be found. (Black Island down the Bay is next south from Little Gott's); there's another Black Island up the Bay.

These foreigners all had to be ferried out to Black in I don't know what kind of boat, probably a small sloop. Over-loaded, perhaps, because on the way across it capsized and twenty foreigners were drowned. Only one who got away was the skipper of the vessel, a local man. How, I don't know.

Bodies kept washing ashore on neighboring islands, a good many of them on Gott's. Whenever one was found, it was buried in the Gott's Island cemetery; most were in bad shape with no identification left, and each grave was marked with a granite boulder.

Then, after a time, another lot of foreign workmen came, and exactly the same thing happened again. You can read it, above—only the skipper of the boat got away.

That's practically all the facts I have, except that the last body was in such shape that the Gott's Island men had to bury it on the shore where it lay. The boulder-markers can still be found—they are in an open space in the middle of the cemetery with local people buried all around them. Some of the locals' graves, too, are marked only with granite boulders.

Fairly recently, three or four years ago, a summer man died, who had wished to be buried in the cemetery. His wife asked a "native"—one who was always ready to favor the summer people with whatever they wished, just so they were pleased—where in the cemetery her husband could be buried, and he told her, "Oh, any place where there looks to be room." So his smashing great marble monument is smack in the middle, right on top of the foreign stoneworkers. That cemetery has been full for years.

I don't suppose they mind; if they do they won't say anything.

Yours, *Ruth*

TO MARY AND LOU DILLON

Dec. 24, 1984

Dear Mary and Lou,

Time zings by so fast that it's hard to realize that Christmas has rolled around again. Being busy working and occupied also with what's known in this household as the week-end gremlins, (which I'll go into later as briefly as possible) I almost forgot it and this letter's late. My memory's not much good—for past things, fine, but what I had for breakfast yesterday is still a mystery. I now quote what I believe is the biggest lie in English literature. "Grow old along with me, The best is yet to be, etc." Though I wouldn't doubt at all that the bouncy boy who wrote that is in some splendid Victorian Heaven, cuddled up to Elizabeth Barrett.

I've told you before what I think of Jay and how much I admire him for what he is doing. He has the integrity and courage to stand up for the cause he believes in. And I believe that he and the people he works with have already succeeded in getting across many facts and home truths to the public who needs to know them. Because Seabrook is certainly wobbling and there are many more eyes than there used to be watching from the underbrush.

About the week-end gremlins, we seem to have them in our plumbing, et al. I am not actually falling to pieces but it seems my house is determined to. First, the furnace had to have a new transformer, then a leak in the water-pipe under the sink, then the bathtub refused to hold water. Bathroom faucet began to drip large fat tears. Element in the electric oven burned through, had to be replaced, took a week because new one had to be ordered. Don't give up, the worst is yet to be. Two weeks ago, our well went dry. The expert on wells promised to be here last Friday. He hasn't shown up. Probably won't now until the Christmas chaos is over. All of these discombobulations took place on week-ends. All I can say is, with (I think) James Thurber, "They aim these things at me."

Esther took off to spend Christmas and New Years with her various children downstate, confidently expecting what my other sister, Louise, would come and stay with me, but Louise came down with a cold and can't come. (She got the cold last Saturday.) I drink bottled water, wash fingertips and cheeks in it; no dishwashing, no laundry, NO BATHS. Primitive-like. If you smell anything, likely it's me. I don't mind being alone, though. Rather enjoy it. Nice solitude to work in. I'm busy revising and adding to my first book of poems, *Time's Web,* which I've never been too pleased with—it has some good poems but quite a lot of lousy ones, which I wince at now. That wasn't entirely my fault; the editors at Morrow edited the hell out of the original ms. Too "gloomy" they said, so would I send them something to "lighten" it. After a savage editorial battle, I gave in. I wouldn't do that now. I can get mad, at 81. Speaking of Morrow, the man to write there is Lawrence Hughes, Wm. Morrow & Co., 105 Madison Ave., 10016. I haven't read the Caldicott book, but would like to, later.

Speaking of getting mad, I am very sore at Television commercials which cut off people like Victor Borge before he's quite finished playing; smear *The Sound of Music* with six commercials every fifteen minutes; use the good old Christmas carols for background music for some silly piece of junk that no one in his right mind could possibly want to own. Water-beds for dogs, heated underneath by electric wires ... My god, what if the poor beast chews it? Dead dog.

One thing, I don't discuss politics anymore. Someone wrote me that the country preferred a mountebank to a wimp, but I don't go along with that. I think Cabbage Patch dolls did it.

Love to both, *Ruth*

In 1985, I was editing *The Best Maine Stories;* and I had written to Ruth to ask if she had any short stories. She sent me three; and of the three, we published "A Soldier Shows His Medal," which appeared first in *The New Yorker* in 1945. Dr. Andrew Gay of Belfast, along with his colleague Dr. Euclid Hanberry, had started a series on monthly programs called The Bay Poets for which they had convinced me to act as M.C. and to which they invited all kinds of writers and musicians. Carolyn

Chute's story "Ollie, Oh ..." was also published in *The Best Maine Stories* (1986). Chute's first novel, *The Beans of Egypt, Maine,* had appeared in 1984. Edgar Allan Beem did finally do a major article in the *Maine Times* on Ruth on October 24, 1986.

TO SANFORD PHIPPEN

April 26, 1985

Dear Sandy,

The New Yorker published "The Soldier Shows His Medal," October 27, 1945. It is probably the best I've done, the only one I've at hand which got published. "The Lonely of Heart" and "The Gargoyle" went the rounds in the early days, but nobody bought them. I got tired of rejection slips early on and chucked everything into an old chest where they came in handy for material in novels, now and again. Just looking in that chest gives me a cold grue.

"Step-Over Toe-Hold" by Sanford Phippen is at the top of my list so far as liking short stories goes. One of Ted Holmes's stories—the one which has in it a drumbeat re. the death of a fisherman comes next, I think.

Margaret Dickson did write me—tell her not to give up hope—I've been sweeping up odds and ends and writing new for a second book of poems, and my sister says if I lived here once I will probably live here again. Margaret's letter will be answered. I don't neglect nice letters like hers unless I am crazy temporarily.

To add to the glories of a Maine winter, our well went dry last December 11. The well-digger promised to come in two weeks. We lugged drinking water in bottles all winter, took sponge baths in the few dribbles we could get from our pump. It was hell, hell, hell, hell, hell, until the first of April, when the well was finished, with a damned queer taste, but it was water. "They aim these things at me," J. Thurber, I think. A fine critique could be written of lying workmen.

Sounds like a pleasant and interesting job you've got to do, editing the short stories. Good luck to you.

Ruth

TO SANFORD PHIPPEN

June 6, 1985

Dear Sandy,

I appreciate what you're doing with those ancient short stories. Goodness knows, I haven't thought about them for years—haven't a clue as to what's in that old chest, but don't think there's very much publishable stuff. Anyhow, if you want to take trouble, why, thanks, and go ahead. It's nice of you.

I'm really sorry. I can't accept Dr. Gay's invitation to read because of throat trouble and an unstable voice; and I can't travel anywhere just now because of a lame foot and leg which is keeping me from doing very much walking. You will probably think I made all this up; but now, I really do have some very nasty large pink pills to cure all this which I'll guarantee to feed you some if you insist. Please tell Dr. Gay how much I appreciate his invitation, and would help out if I could.

Ed Beem of the *Maine Times* phoned me last night. He seemed quite interested in whether or not I felt overlooked by the world of modern fiction—neglected, that is, and I don't think he understood that I don't, and please no publicity because I live too near the road with no fence between me and five million tourists.

I'm fascinated by Carolyn Chute's work—she really took off like a rocket, more power to her. "Ollie, Oh ..." is a heart-breaker, at least it temporarily broke mine, which is tough, and somewhat scarred up already by the reality of Egyptians, over many years. Lord, whose family isn't aware of a few Egyptians of Maine among their sacred pasts?

Take care, and keep on leaving tall footprints behind you.

Affection, et al, *Ruth*

Inside Vacationland: New Fiction from the Real Maine was published in 1985. My story included is "The Maine Food Plan" and Carolyn Chute's is "Crowe Bovey's Burning-Cold," which later became a chapter of her second novel *Letourneau's Used Auto Parts.*

TO SANFORD PHIPPEN

Labor Day 1985

Dear Sandy,

It is time I wrote to you and have been meaning to, but steamy and sweaty August isn't a time to write anyone. So I haven't.

Two items need some explanation to you, I think. Number one, about Dr. Gay's invitation. I actually have been laid up with a bum foot and at that time I wasn't walking anywhere. I am better now, walking, but not very far—from the house to my garden over in the field is as far as I get without sitting down.

So I stay home, not that I don't appreciate. Number two, when Ed Beem called me on the phone, all I thought was how pleasant of him to call. He said nothing about an "interview," didn't mention publication of any kind or ask permission to quote me. I should have known better, as an experienced publicity-ducker. We simply chatted pleasantly for about ten minutes. That was all. I was astonished when someone said, Hey, you've got your name in the paper. If I'd been going to hand out an interview, it would have, of course, been to you.

Sometimes I wish that that lighthouse, the sweetheart of the Maine Publicity Bureau, would crack off and sink in the sea along with all the celebrity-hunting tourists who go by my house to see it.

This sounds very grungy, doesn't it. Well, it is.

This business about the "real" Maine, Sandy. I have read *Inside Vacationland* and have found in it some good high school and college days writing, some jump-on-the-wagon material and, unhappily, have to say that without you and Carolyn Chute, it's not very interesting. You will, perhaps, not cast me into outer chaos for saying so. After all, it's only one person's opinion.

So I thought, I'll think further. It got me to rummage in a book published in 1967 by Hal Borland, "Hill Country Harvest." He lived in New Hampshire, hence the title. A retired reporter living on a farm he wrote columns for local newspapers, mostly Nature stuff, but stuck his nose into about everything going on at the time. He's a little old-fashioned, ends sentences sometimes with "as it were," and such, but his Nature columns are beautiful and believable and his opinions of other matters sensible. I quote from one column which concerns the American people.

"In the beginning, as colonists, Americans dreamed of freedom from political, religious, and economic tyranny. They were not reaching for absolute security, but for a place and a way of life that would allow them to go as far as they humanly could toward a peaceful life of achievement and satisfaction. They wanted justice in their own courts, their own religion and representatives and a chance to earn a competence and a decent start for their children."

Now this is all out of whack and one-sided and reads like some good, good man making a speech to the Rotary Club and you start to squawk because he hasn't mentioned in all this generality, any of the villainy, religious hypocrisy, crime, skullduggery that all took place in those high and piping times. As we all now know. But wait. He's just setting out basics. He goes on:

"Fundamentally, it seems to me that is still true of us, as a people. Cynics will deny this and they will point to the headlines and the stories behind them. I would point to the ten thousand unwritten stories of peaceful, hopeful, honest people for every story of crime and violence and corruption.

"True, we are guilty of many failures, injustices, many wrongs of every kind. But chiefly we are guilty of belonging to the human race, which is both good and bad, worthy and worthless, damnable and exalted. Even so, never before in the history of the world has any people done so much to ease pain and suffering, more to alleviate want, more to ease the troubles of the helpless and the aged, more to help other people all over the earth to achieve freedom and physical comfort than we have done and are still doing day by day. We even dream of making this a world where there will be no more war. Perhaps we will never succeed in all these efforts, but that is characteristic of the dream to keep hoping, trying and reaching for success in a purpose beyond our present reach."

Neither you nor Carolyn Chute is a regional writer. You are both, of course, pinpointing a staked-out area, the State of Maine, but none the less pinpointing every state, city, town and village which has bigotry, slum poverty and a hopeless, neglected class of people. You are gentler than she is—in some ways I feel that your quiet voice is more effective. She goes for the guts and explodes in blood, incest and scenes—like a pickup truck body loaded with slaughtered and decaying crows. Both of you outspoken and speaking truth which needs to be told. If you like crows, you cry. As I did. Who was to blame for that? It's unspoken, but it's there. And if you hate bigotry and snobbery and sugared slavery, you spit. As I have done for years.

What you are writing about is the "real" everywhere. And the real everywhere is a rag-and-bobtail-dream, half achieved and at present floundering. So I thought you might like to read Hal Borland's piece.

As ever, *Ruth*

About the letter which follows, Dorothy Lobrano Guth writes, "Ruth refers to the death of our son the preceding spring. The visit she refers to was after the death of my dad (Gus Lobrano) in 1956."

TO DOROTHY LOBRANO GUTH

October 27, 1985

Dear Dottie,

These are sad days for you, I know. Sad and very tough. Of course nothing I can say will help, and I shan't try. But my memory, which is not much use to me now because it is full of great gaps and holes, suddenly brought back to me the long visit you made to Eleanor and me, so many years ago. Details of that wonderful time came into focus, clear as springwater; I even remembered you and Eleanor persuading me not to wear shorts. And we comforted you then, without saying anything, not even that we loved you, too.

Loss of memory is a devilish thing for anyone. For a writer, it's torture. Try and remember the exact word you want... It won't come and you can't look it up because you don't know what the word is. I began to have it after I lost Eleanor. I took care of her for the better part of three years while we tried to fight the cancer together; we thought, her last year, that we'd won. Then it turned to brain tumor and she was paralyzed. I nursed her, day and night, until her last month, when she had to go to the hospital. My sister Esther moved in and helped at the last of it, but even both of us couldn't give her what she needed. We were both worn out and I drooped into a kind of coma of exhaustion which laid me wide open to a number of nasty conditions, including pneumonia, which I won't go into further. It was a long illness which I fought as soon as I had guts enough to fight anything. Being a tough old bird I won eventually, but for many months I couldn't work, couldn't drive a car and couldn't communicate with anyone. I don't even remember if I wrote you about Eleanor. Probably didn't. Couldn't write anything. I now plug around on a bum leg, but this year, at last, planted my garden.

I read a lot, and this fall, oddly enough, I went through all of E. B. White's books, which I, of course, own. (I can't call him Andy because I never met him. The closest I came, I sat down beside him, accidentally, at the restaurant in Britt's in Ellsworth. Fortunately, he didn't look up and I quickly and unobtrusively moved away to another seat, because I was afraid he might think I was there because I was going to claim acquaintance with his books and spoil his lunch. This has happened to me many times in Ellsworth, because I went to high school in Ellsworth and my ugly mug is quite well known in these parts anyway. It always spoils lunch.) I'm finicky myself about it.

In the *Letters* (and what a job you did there) my memory loss was considerably helped, because in the letters from 1926 to 1936 were the years I lived in New York and loved it, he mentions places and people whom I admired or knew, such as Dr. Devol, the high irrigationist, who once gave me a high irrigation. Then, of course, the '40s and on, when I was in touch with some of the publishing crowd.

All my love, which I don't need to remember

Ruth

Ruth added the following poem:

Sleep well, my love, under your quilt of snow,
The world you left us is a silent place.
Your cat and I have now nowhere to go
To hear your voice again, to see your face.
Daily he hunts, patrols the rooms, the shop,
Pricks up his ears inside the garden gate,
Races the path, comes to a sudden stop
Breathless, beside me, and sits down to wait.
He's an old cat, beginning to get lame
His age sneaked on him this short time ago,
I offer him my lap, I say his name.
"That's the wrong lap, my friend.
You ought to know."
I cannot reach his trouble, knowing only
That whom the gods destroy, they first make lonely.

This is a sample of the work I'm now being able to do. A book of poems seems simpler than a longer work like a novel, for which you do need to have a clear and shining memory. This poem will be included in a section called *Last Letters* which is nearly finished.

Ruth's book of poems was published posthumously, but is entitled *The Tired Apple Tree,* a title that she chose, according to publisher Gary Lawless.

"DeVoto" is Bernard DeVoto, a well-known critic and book reviewer. Gene Stratton Porter was a popular novelist who wrote *The Girl of the Limberlost* and other romantic novels. The chapbook mentioned below was never published, but served as the genesis of *The Tired Apple Tree,* Ruth's third book of poetry.

TO GARY LAWLESS

October 30, 1985

Dear Mr. Lawless,

Thanks for your pleasant letter. I'm well aware of the campaign you have been carrying on during the past two years for me and for my books and I can't find words to tell you how much I appreciate what you're doing. If I have seemed unresponsive, it has been because of a long illness which has prevented me from doing much work and cut down communications. We won't go into that, because I am all right now and, besides, who wants to hear about someone's acting-up tripes, anyhow.

I'm very much interested in your chapbook project, think it's exactly the right thing to fit in with the "real Maine" movement which is blossoming out with new writers and fresh material. Some of these younger people are going places—Sandy Phippen certainly is and Carolyn Chute, of course, is already there. Speaking of the "real Maine," though, there's a long-ago anecdote which, I believe, first mentions the term. Bennet Cerf, or perhaps it was DeVoto, anyway, one of New York's literary trotties, drove up to Maine along Route 1, and later published a piece, full of outrage and horror, about the mess of billboards, hamburger joints, et al, which he saw along the highway. He pulled no punches, and of course he was right. It didn't stir up much of a wave except for the sturdy old *Ellsworth American* who published an answer, very polite, which ended, "Please come back sometime and let us show you the 'real Maine.'" At the bottom of this was an Editor's Note: Since this invitation was issued, the gentleman mentioned has died. Ha! Real Maine, plus humor.

I'm delighted to have the chance to pay you back a little. I am working, just now on a book of poems. I enclose two poems for your chapbook, if you would like to use them. They are old-fashioned in that they rhyme and their meaning isn't obscure. They may not be read by anyone except old ladies, not in tennis shoes but in an era leading back to high-button boots, and to Gene Stratton-Porter who is still their goddess, and who come into our local library often nowadays. Asking, "Aren't you ever going to have a new book by her?"

I haven't any larger work in process, except a half-finished novel which I've put aside for a while because I don't like it.

Sincerely *Ruth*

TO SHERRY ARDEN

November 21, 1985

Mrs. Sherry Arden
President of William Morrow and Company
105 Madison Avenue
New York, New York 10016

Dear Mrs. Arden,

I have been a Morrow author since the early '40s, but due to personal complications, have not produced anything since 1979, when my last Morrow novel was published.

Also, and it's not surprising considering the stretch of time over so many years, that all my friends and associates at Morrow have long since gone—either dead or retired or moved on. Even in '79 Lawrence Hughes was my last contact there. My novels are all out of print now, and I think you'll agree with me that it's time I moved on, too.

The contract for the '79 book, *Sarah Walked Over the Mountain,* contains an option clause on my next novel, but I have no next novel and no plans for one. Will you cancel this option and effectively release me from it?

Please let me know.

Sincerely *Ruth Moore*

TO ED STEINER, JR.

January 30, 1986

Mr. Ed F. Steiner, Jr.
Steiner Cheese Factory
Baltic, Ohio 43804

Dear Ed,

Goings on at Bass Harbor aren't dramatic, I'm afraid—I spent the holidays gadding around down-state, visiting my nephews and family and have just got back. But one of the nicest goings on has been the arrival of word from you and your nice package, as of old, at Christmas time. Recalls old times, so it does, and I remember so well the good time the four of us had at Gott's Island on that pleasant day. I'll never forget that.

Your Swiss Cheese is the work of art it always has been and so is the trail bologna. This is to say thank you for the treat—to say also that I wish we could get such Swiss Cheese in this part of the world; but more than anything to thank you for the remembrance.

Yours, always *Ruth Moore*

TO MARY KAMENOFF

Dec. 19, 1986

Dear Mary,

It isn't that I'm too stingy to buy a Christmas card; it's a matter of getting out to the stores to buy one. I have a bum leg. If I walk more than 400 feet, it's likely to drop me flat on my face. Otherwise, I'm fine. Regardless of what the flesh is heir to. So let's hear no more of that. The goose is in the pot and old acquaintance not forgot. How are you?

This has been a strange, bewildering, but lucky year. Last June I gave my New York publisher the boot, William Morrow and Co., who've been bringing out my books since 1943, was subsumed (nice word that, I had to look it up to find it means "sucked in") by Hearst, for one thing, and I be dag if I was going to move from bad to Hearst. So I told them to git. Lucky I did. For the Blackberry Press, which is a Maine publisher, wrote me, saying they wanted to bring all my books out in paperback and they are now starting to. My first book, *The Weir* is already off the press and doing well, and they are now working on *Spoonhandle*. Ironical, because I've always fought like a lion against being called a "regional" writer. Which I now am. But getting real nice royalties, I will say. And some very pleasant publicity.

I don't know where the Maine Publishers & Writers dug up the picture of me they printed on their enclosed brochure. But don't I look like a sweet-tempered (and tongued) old lady though. Ha ha.

Poor Mr. Reagan. He has a prostate, now. My heart bleeds.

I'm working on a new book of poems now, and it's nice to get back to work. I haven't written a stitch since my friend Eleanor died in 1981. You wrote me in one of your Christmas letters that you couldn't read *Time's Web* and I was sorry, because you were one of the people I wrote it for. Surely, you have, by now. If you haven't, please do. You didn't tell me why you couldn't read it then. It's got some good things in it, outside of the Dorothy Parkerized bunk, which was insisted on by my then publisher, who felt that it was too grim and needed lightening. Like, was it Charles Lamb? who said, "Put a sidesaddle on Pegasus and he always heads for the graveyard." Some grimpsy old chauvinist said that.

We've had no snow to speak of and the little we have had lies over green grass. I lost my old cat aged 19, Tophet, his name was. It was real lonesome without him.

Scrappy bits of news, but Love,
anyway *Ruth*

Katherine is Emily Trask-Eaton's daughter, Ruth's grand-niece, who had written a piece that she showed Ruth. Ruth usually hated to have work brought to her—but in Katherine's case, she made an exception.

TO KATHERINE EATON

January 16, 1987

Dear Katherine,

I'm sorry to have kept your piece of work for your novel for so long. I'd expected to talk with you about it while I was there with you, but it got mixed up with some papers I had in my suitcase; and what with Christmas and all, I didn't think about it until I was putting away my suitcase and found it in one of the pockets. And you hadn't mentioned it again.

Please forgive me for being so careless. Let me say now what I would have said then. I think you have done some very good organizing, which makes the work interesting, and you have certainly done some good writing. I hope you'll finish it, and let me see it again when you have.

Tell your Ma that I had a lovely time at her house. It was nice to see all of you for more than just a peekaboo time.

Love *Up*

TO JOHN GOULD

March 11, 1987

Dear John,

I look at the date on your letter and I feel like a skunk. This is an honest attempt to get rid of the white stripe down my conscience. But I can produce reasons.

Here I was, a comfortable and lazy hermit, enjoying growing my own vegetables, mowing the lawn once in a while so I could get into the house, shoving back the wilderness which kept creeping up—I won't say happy as a clam, because clams are very unhappy these days, having been dug into extinction, but happy, anyway. What I considered my last novel, *Sarah Walked Over the Mountain,* was published in 1979, and I wasn't pleased with the slapdash way William Morrow & Co. handled it. It may have been because John Willey, my editor there for some forty years, was retiring in that year; or maybe the book itself was to blame. Anyway, I got to thinking that I'd said about all I had to say about this region and was starting the same book over and over. So I called it a day. Then, later on, I learned, not from Morrow, but from an item in *The Author's Guild Bulletin,* which I subscribe to, that Morrow had been "subsumed" by Hearst, that all my friends there, except one man, Larry Hughes, had been got rid of. (Lovely word, that, "subsumed." I didn't know what it meant, looked it up, and found, with considerable glee, that one of its meanings was "sucked in.") So I wrote a nice polite letter booting Morrow for keeps. They didn't seem to shed any blood over that and neither did I. Seemed to me that one glance at the horrors and sex now called fiction justified my honest retirement.

Then, last fall, out of a clear sky, Gary Lawless, who owns the Gulf of Maine Bookstore and the Blackberry Press in Brunswick, started a campaign to get my books back into print, offering to republish them from the beginning. He brought out *The Weir* just before Christmas and *Spoonhandle* in January. They are paperbacks, very nicely done, with good paper and colored jackets, and, for goodness sake, there turned out to be a demand and the sales are excellent, so have been the reviews. Seems a lot of people thought I was dead and were glad I wasn't. So was I. Amazed, overwhelmed, yes, trying to get used to publicity again. At 83, it ain't funny, McGee. All the same, I'd be a dreadful prig if I denied being darned pleased about it.

Good to hear about you and Dot and your family. I would love to see you both, but this time of year isn't right for you to come. I wish I could put you up, but if you'll remember our house, you'll know we haven't a guest room. We are also in snow to our windowsills and hard to get at. After Eleanor died, my sister, Esther Trask, came to live with me so I'm not alone, and we manage quite well, except the town snowplow checks us last, seeing our location at the edge of town. She has a regular job—she's one of the town tax assessors, and while she doesn't threaten anyone, or even mention it, there seems to be an inherent nudge to the genes of the snowplow that taxes might go up if we don't get at least plowed out once. Why don't you wait until spring weather for the gam and the mug-up, when the path to our back steps gets over being a hip-breaker? But of course you'd be welcome at any time.

As ever *Ruth*

TO JOHN C. WILLEY

March 12, 1987

Mr. John C. Willey
6041 Northwest Kauffman Ave.
Vancouver, Washington

Dear John,

Well, it does seem that quite a lot of people have thought I was dead, and are glad I'm not. So am I. I have to say that getting used to publicity again ain't funny McGee, but I'd be a dreadful prig if I didn't admit I'm pleased, if astonished, at what's happening.

I thought, of course, when this re-publishing project began, that results would be regional, since Blackberry Press is a Maine publisher. A flash in the pan, sort of. But Gary Lawless has now got a national agency—I don't know who—working with him, and I'm getting letters from South Carolina, Ohio, Connecticut, etc. as well as the Maine ones. And these letters aren't the usual I-have-read-your-books, and so on. They are personal, almost as if the writers had recovered a lost friend. Some are affectionate, some have the intelligent appreciation that would make any writer want to spin and toe-dance. Except for a very few, I've never had anything like this before. So I answer letters now.

Take a fellow from Ohio who wanted more and rooted around till he found a copy of *The Sea Flower*. He writes:

"What moved me most to write is Arvid. I discovered Arvid. I recognize Arvid. He had me in tears. He had me in stitches. He is an absolute delight. He speaks to my condition."

I'm well, if snow-bound, still. We finally got our driveway plowed out and sanded, at least passably. Every man who owns a pick-up truck has put a snowplow on it, so that they have a monopoly on driveway plowing, and can charge what they like, but the Catch-22 is that they don't know how to do it, it not being their regular job. I just barely saved our outside well from being smashed over by one of these amateurs, and Esther and I got considerable amusement over the big lump of frozen snow left in the middle of the driveway—he sanded carefully around it and left it where it was. Our car was too low-slung over it, so we had to chop it up with a hatchet, it was practically solid ice. When he finally got what he judged was a clean-plowed driveway job, he sent us a bill for $84 bucks. Thank God it's already March. This story speaks to our condition.

Be well and comfortable.

Affectionately *Ruth*

TO SANFORD PHIPPEN

June 2, 1987

Dear Sandy,

Man, dear, I thought you must be dead, but only temporarily. I know how you whizz around. I, too, have been busy, trying to work while being bitten by the tartar-smudged teeth of Publicity. Once more. And again. Over and over. Please don't think I belittle this resurrection. I have been astonished and pleased; for a while, blown up with vanity, et. al. Like Lazarus, back from the dead. But my real life is cockroach-in-the-woodwork-eyes-that-watch-from-under-brush. Two great advantages—I have, thank God, at last kicked free from a New York publisher, and I do better work when a hermit. I told Hearst-Wm. Morrow, where they could shove it.

Of course you'll be welcome to visit, you know that, and I'll be delighted to meet Betsy Graves. Let's say June 9, at 4 o'clock, if this is ok with you. Let me know if you would rather come on the 11th. If I don't hear from you, I'll expect you on the 9th.

I haven't heard very much about a symposium at Searsport. Dennis Damon, who is to speak there, told me about it. So far, no one has invited me to come there and "read," as some organizations have. Thank God, I have as good and honest a reason for refusing as anyone could have—I've got a bum let which I can't stand or walk on for any very long length of time, so can't really go anywhere. Besides, in crowds of people, my wits go where the dead crabs go.

Cheers for your new job. Your high school kids are going to miss you (and need you) but university students need you more than they do. (I think.) You can undo a lot of the slapdash attitude toward writing and reading most—at least, some—of the high schools do, and you'll dig up some talent too, without a doubt. Most of the contemporary fiction, as you of course know, is complete trash. Try the *N.Y. Times Book Review* for samples—can you honestly find any fiction reviewed there, which you want to read?

As a choice between *Spoonhandle* and *The Weir, Spoonhandle* for your writing course. But I understand that Gary Lawless is planning to reprint *Speak to the Winds* this fall, and that one's better. Do you know Gary? He is a remarkable man, like you, into everything. I've met him once—he dropped by here with a couple of friends. If you go to Searsport, likely you'll run into him there. He owns the Gulf of Maine Bookstore in Brunswick, and if you do see the *Maine Writers & Publishers Alliance Monthly*—yes, I know you do, you'll find a list of his many reprints, etc.

I'd love to see a copy of *People Trying to Be Good.* Is it out yet?

I seem to run on; but there's always a lot to say.

Your Hancock brochure reminds me of what is going on in this town, Bass Harbor. Only our trouble is real estate developers. The whole village has or is being turned wrong side out. Two summer men, with apparently all the money in the world, have bought out the whole center of the town, for unbelievable prices. They now own practically all the business places—the General Store, the Powers and Robinson Machine Shop, now called the Little Island Marine, some of the fine old houses, one re-modeled into the Bass Harbor Inn, uncounted lots of local property. A Bangor developer is now fighting with our local planning board for permission to put up 14 condominiums along the shore front; Bass Harbor Marina, which will have summer people's yachts fighting the fishermen over who owns the boat moorings in the harbor. Across the Harbor, acreage has been sold, I believe 12 acres in one piece, for half a million dollars. Our annual town meeting is now composed of enough summer property owners to carry the votes.

Oh, hell. There's hardly a house in town now which doesn't have a For Sale sign on it.

Some of use remain, as always. We had a Newspaper Recycling hut up by the Town Hall. It was working well, until somebody used the hut for a water closet, and the man who put it there got mad and took it away.

Salaam, love, and keep at it. I'm trying to.

Ruth

Mr. Burr was Greg Burr, a student of Dr. Mortland's who lived in Northeast Harbor.

TO DONALD MORTLAND

June 23, 1987

Dear Professor Mortland,

What I must write you may seem a grudging return for what you have done in past years for me and my books; I am deeply aware of it. And I honestly feel that I should repay a part, at least, of my debt to you by saying yes to any favor you may ask of me. I'll do this, of course, but there are reasons why your student, Mr. Burr, can't possibly find in a talk with me what he finds in my books. He will find an old lady of 84, simple-minded and stiff, trying desperately to communicate with him in his own tongue. He will go away, I'm afraid, feeling let down, not very much liked, and bewildered. All of which isn't so, and for which I am to blame.

This I can't help. It's the result of so many years of being a solitary and a workaholic. I've always fought off publicity, have never "read" from my work for organizations, never had an autographing party, etc. The recent revival of my books by Gary Lawless has been, of course, wonderful and astonishing, but the publicity in connection with it, while fertilizing for vanity, has huddled me into a corner, from which I try to peer out not looking too much like a mouse. It's particularly hard to manage, now that the tourist season's started; strangers park in the driveway or bang on the door—if I'm not in evidence, they wait, peer around, and while waiting, pick my lilacs. So my work time goes to hell, hell, hell. There's a poem:

Summer is over
The old cow said
And they lock me up
In a draughty shed.
Milk me by moonlight
When it's cold
But I don't give much
Now I'm old.

Look. Why don't you drive up to Northeast Harbor, collect Mr. Burr and both come to see me? You two could talk and I could listen. I'm an excellent listener. ?????

With gratitude and I might almost say with affection

Ruth Moore

TO WILLIAM SARGENT

July 23, 1987

Dear Bill,

Of course I remember you and Jean, and how sorry we were to have you move away—people we missed.

You've asked me to do something I can't do—I'm a writer, not a critic, and in most contracts I've had with publishers, I can't read or criticize manuscripts. Sorry about this, but what you ought to have is criticism from a publisher.

I suggest you write to Gary Lawless, RR1, Box 228, Nobleboro, ME, 04555, or go to see him at the Gulf of Maine Bookstore in Brunswick. He owns Blackberry Press, which is bringing out the reprints of my books and he is a reliable publisher, who does a very professional job. If I were you, I'd go to see him, show him a copy of what you have and ask him if he'd be interested in publishing it.

This is the best I can do, except to wish you luck.

Sincerely *Ruth Moore*

TO DENNIS DAMON

August 1, 1987

Dear Dennis,

Thanks for the pot of beautiful azealers.

As usual, I'm late thanking or anything else by letter, due, I guess, to being still somewhat groggy with getting out into the world after a long time of being a solitary.

The flowers are beautiful, and I can see them as I sit here.

Did I spell azealers right?

Yours, with affection *Ruth*

TO GARY LAWLESS

August 1, 1987

Dear Gary,

You are a great man. I've been struggling out from under a heap of what-there-is-to-do, or you'd have heard from me sooner. Thanks for the checks and for the notices of what you've been up to publicity-wise to bring those old dead books of mine back to life. It took a lot of doing. I'm aware of that, certainly. And I don't really know how to say thank you. But I say so, in the words that there are.

Sandy Phippen, whom you probably know, has a new job—he is now an Assistant Prof. of English at the Univ. of Maine, tells me that he is using my books in his classes, beginning this fall. I don't know whether or not he's ordered any from you yet, but I expect he will. Prof. Mortland of Unity came to see me and brought one of his students who wanted very much to come. Your publicity has certainly reached out-of-state—I've had letters from New York and New Jersey, and California, and an 8th grade batch of kids in Beloit, Wisconsin each wrote me a personal letter—some 25 letters in all, arrived in a fat envelope, all wanting personal answers. How do I handle that? I'm trying to work, in private, and there isn't enough time for the day. Oh, well. Sometime I'll catch up. Can't help it if things pile up.

By the way, from what I've been able to make out, various members of my family who live around the Waldoboro and Brunswick area, some known and some unknown to me, have been to call on you at your bookstore. I hope you haven't been bothered too much. My niece, Emmy Trask-Eaton, who owns and runs the Five and Dime Store in Waldoboro, tells me that a clutch of these are parading around claiming relationship with "Aunt Ruth." I've no idea who they may be. I'm glad though that my grand-nephew, Sven Davisson, came to see you. He's a very promising youngster, a senior in high school this fall. Wants to be a writer, and to my way of thinking has written, already, some very good stuff.

Have I answered everything? I'm still a little groggy with what's happening, but I'm sure not complaining about that, no way.

All the best *Ruth*

TO BETSY GRAVES

August 8, 1987

Dear Betsy,

I look at the date written above and I'm shame-faced. It's been so long since you sent me a copy of your excellent review for *Puckerbrush* of the reprints of *The Weir* and *Spoonhandle*. You certainly rated plus-A for it and a thank you from me for one of the most sensitive and intelligent reviews I have ever had for any book.

The thing is, I've been what my grandmother used to say at house-cleaning time, "all wovelled up." After some six years of being a solitary, with plenty of time for work and meditation, I find myself spinning in the middle of publicity which I can't avoid, because I've felt under obligation to Blackberry Press to help wherever I could. In my whole career, I've had two public appearances, one on a radio program, the other (which I blew) before the Women's Club in Pleasantville, N.Y. Crowds of people anywhere, anyhow, and my brains produce nothing but a kind of curdled pea soup. I'm better at the eyes-that-watch-from-the-underbrush position.

So, up to now, I've refused all interviews, but lately have forced myself into giving several, all to local papers. Sandy Phippen is probably mad at me, because I have always refused to give him one; but if he is, he'll probably get over it. I think he is a great man, a kind of jewel-in-the-crown, headed, no doubt, for the New York market, which he will probably detest, seeing how nearly all of the fine old publishers are now taken over by huge business corporations, whose editors, considering the fiction they're bringing out, can't tell a dangling participle from a split infinitive. There's a sentence for you! I, myself, politely resigned from William Morrow & Co. last year, after that company was taken over by Hearst, and all my friends there were dumped. I thought I'd rather find a Maine publisher and, with luck, one came to me.

Blackberry's first printing of *The Weir* is now sold out and they are reprinting; *Spoonhandle,* in one day, sold 216 copies. I'm wondering now what to do with some 20 fan letters in one bunch, from a 9th grade class in Wisconsin, each asking for a free book, or some money. How do you handle that?

So, forgive me, do for being so late with an answer.

Sincerely *Ruth*

Would it be possible for me to have a copy of the Puckerbrush *publication with your review in it? I'd like one for my file.*

Marion Stocking, the editor of the *Beloit Poetry Journal,* and retired professor from Beloit College, is friends with Ann Arbor, a teacher in Beloit who assigned *The Weir* for her students to read.

TO MARION STOCKING

August 11, 1987

Dear Ms. Stocking,

I apologize for being so long in writing you, but things do pile up, and I'm trying hard to get out from under what-there-is-to-do.

I do appreciate very much reading your note to Gary Lawless re. Ann Arbor's class of 9th graders. Some time ago, a fat envelope came, enclosing some 20 letters, one from each of those nice youngsters. A heart-warming experience for me from kids so far away, and each so enthusiastic, and I might add, with all my heart, so intelligent.

Thanks very much for letting me know.

Yours sincerely *Ruth Moore*

Douglas Savage did not interview me for the Preview! *cover story in 1987. The interview was done by Jane Smillie, a former writing student of Connie Hunting's at the University of Maine. The article appeared in the July 6–12 issue of* Preview! *My novel* Kitchen Boy *remains unpublished.*

TO SANFORD PHIPPEN

August 21, 1987

Dear Sandy,

God only knows when I wrote to you last, my over-all feeling is that I didn't. Memory failure caused by guilt. For a time, I've had to give in on interviews. Gary Lawless didn't ask me to—I felt under obligation to help him in whatever publicity I could manage to come up with. I found out pretty soon that he didn't need me, not that live wire of Blackberry Press. He's done a terrific job with those old dead books of mine—the first reprint of *The Weir* is sold out and being reprinted again; *Spoonhandle* is still selling over 200 a day. I haven't heard from Gary whether he has done Speak to the Winds yet, as he planned. He seldom writes a letter—just sends me an occasional royalty check. I told him in the beginning not to send any royalties until he'd got his printing, et al, expenses paid, got his seed back, but he certainly has done that. Meanwhile, I'm wriggling like a worm on a hook, trying to get answered fan letters, requests to come to bookstore autograph parties, come and read my work at Ladies Aid celebrations, etc., and at the same time trying to get back to work, which there isn't time enough in a day or even in a week to manage. I seem to be halfway between deep and honest appreciation for what is being done for me, and a nagging desire to get back my solitude and my eyes-that-watch-from-the-underbrush position where I function best, with what's left to work on.

Oh, well. Change position and scream. I seem to be screaming well.

Douglas Savage sent me your interview with him for *Preview!,* which I read with interest because it told me a lot of things about you that I didn't know. Not really snooping, but certainly affectionate interest, as from the beginning. Of course you won't remain a "regional" writer, it goes without saying. I don't think you'll have much trouble finding a New York publisher, if you want one. Most of the famous old ones, of course, have been snapped up by this-and-that big business outfits, whose intent seems to be the destruction of fiction and replacing it with over-priced descriptions of blow-by-blow sexual intercourse, child abuse and horrors, or whatever other choice based on jokes told in the locker room over the martinis. I have let fly with all this cranky snarling because I think there's a change coming, and that it will come head-on from the customers, the book-buyers themselves, who are going to demand that the word "literature" be hauled out of the wastebasket and set to work again, in fiction. Me, I haven't bought a novel in ages, because I always look at the beginning first and if there's porn on the first ten pages, I don't buy the book. Not at $18.50, by gum. I get a lot of information from the *N.Y. Times Book Review* and from the *Author's Guild Bulletin,* too. Also: We're a small town about 1100 after the summer residents go home. We have a small library with limited space and each year we have a library Book Sale, to get rid of the overflow. We price books from ten cents to a dollar. This year, with what we had, we made almost a thousand dollars; everything, except a few battered specimens went. Not only summer people, but local people bought. And if that isn't a bottom line, what isn't? Other libraries on Mt. Desert Island report the same results. We are a book-hungry people, is my guess.

I don't know what your plans are for *Kitchen Boy,* but if the above guesses are worth anything, and a change is coming, you might think this might be a time to try for a New York publisher. Please don't think I'm trying to advise you or recommend in any way, or meddle, which would be impertinent. After all, it's only one person's opinion, or guess, and so sweet are the uses of publicity, I may not be quite normal, temporarily.

Did I write you saying okay re. your putting my letters to you in with your things at the Fogler Library? Go ahead. I'm pleased to be put away in such distinguished company.

Congratulations on your new job. Best of luck with it. When am I going to see a copy of *Kitchen Boy?* Let me know and I'll buy the first copy that comes off of whatever press.

Yours, still ruffled but combed out, *Ruth*

The special program on Ruth Moore at the Penobscot Marine Museum in Searsport was held on Sept. 11–12, 1987. Gordon Bok and Dennis Damon were on the program, and the film *Deep Waters,* based on *Spoonhandle,* was shown.

TO ANN MOFFITT

August 27, 1987

Ann Moffitt
Penobscot Marine Museum
Searsport, Maine 04974

Dear Ann Moffitt,

I'm sorry. I wish I didn't have to write this letter. I have even put off writing it, for which I apologize, with honest and deep regret.

There's no possible way I can manage to come to the meetings at the museum on September 11 and 12. While it is true that I have always avoided public appearances and publicity of one kind and another, I certainly wouldn't let such personal preferences stand in my way on this occasion. This is no autograph party; this is more a gathering of old friends, as mentioned in your letter. The least I could do would be to stop for a while being eyes-that-watch-from-the-underbrush and show the appreciation and affection I feel toward those who are taking some much trouble to bring back to life my long out-of-print books. I would add, also, the respect and obligation I feel toward the publicity people, like yourself, who have done the work of setting up such a meeting. Your letter is a masterpiece of persuasion.

I can't come because I'm physically unable to. For some months back, I've been recovering from an illness which has left me lame. While not actually house-bound now, I can walk only a miserable ten feet or so without sitting down to rest. Traveling any distance is out of the question. So is sitting, for any length of time. I can't wear shoes. Poor Dennis must have been edified, each time he's dropped by, by the sight of my stocking-feet. I am, however, getting better and am promised graduation to bedroom slippers and eventually to shoes again.

Regretfully yours, *Ruth Moore*

The result of the successful Maine Literature Project for Middle Schools was the anthology *Maine Speaks,* published in both hard cover and paperback in 1989. There were also two special summer programs held at Bates College in 1988–89 for Maine teachers, librarians, and others interested in the project.

TO THE MAINE HUMANITIES COUNCIL

November 24, 1987

Dear Council Members:

I am writing to express my enthusiastic support of the Maine Literature Project for Middle Schools, a joint undertaking of the Maine Council for English Language Arts and the Maine Writers & Publishers Alliance.

As a Maine writer, I have long supported the efforts of young writers in our state and have long lamented the almost complete lack of emphasis on Maine literature in our schools. From what I understand, this omission is due in large measure to the lack of suitable materials for instruction. The Maine Literature Project for Middle Schools would address that deficiency, not only by producing an anthology of Maine literature for use in the schools, but also by offering guidance to the teachers who will be using it. This ambitious project is long overdue, and those who now seek to undertake it deserve all the financial support you can give to help see the project through.

What is perhaps most laudable to me about this endeavor is its stated goal of helping to build a literary consciousness among our young people by exposing them to literature that grew out of experiences they recognize and share. Surely there can be no better way of promoting an appreciation for Maine's literature and for its unique heritage. With the impressive group of scholars and teachers MCELA and MWPA have gathered to execute the project, I am confident that the work they produce will be of the highest quality. This project will be of lasting benefit to Maine's educational system and to the students in it, and I strongly urge you to give it the financial help it needs to succeed.

Sincerely yours, *Ruth Moore*

TO MARY AND LOU DILLON

Dec. 1987? (no date)

Dear Mary and Lou,

Late again, as usual, with everything. Only this time it isn't because I've ducked into the underbrush, to work and twiddle by myself. I've just got home from a ten-day stay at the Bangor Hospital, where the Vascular Center there fixed up my dead right foot. So I no longer have to walk a-side-and-a-half to a time, and could kick myself in the eye if I wanted to. After two years, this is NEWS. I know it's one hell of a bore to hear about somebody's operation, but mine was really fascinating. They used a contraption called a "doppler," which I understand was developed in World War II, to locate submarines with—it spots unseen noises from a distance. Using it on me, they could listen to the flow of blood through my body; it found a blood clot in my ankle, spotted an artery that could be used to substitute for the blocked vein, traced a route for the surgeon to follow. Fifteen minutes or so, and no X-rays. It found no submarines, fortunately.

I got home with great joy, thinking I was going to go to work at once and live like a hermit crab, as I've done for quite a while. But I found my desk piled up with a mountain of mail, most of which had to be answered. I'm slowly crawling through it. It is mostly invitations to speak at Women's Clubs, ladies Aids, hold autograph parties in various bookstores, et al. I've been completely astounded by the revival of my novels. My memory, these days, seems to want to live in a rocking chair, but I may have told you the day we met in Ellsworth, that I had fired my New York publisher. ...

I now have a Maine publisher, Blackberry Press, run by a wild man who is also a genius, a great man, really. And I'm glad to be published in Maine. You get honest treatment. The New York publishing companies, the old and dignified ones, have many of them been bought by big industrial firms, and the fiction they put out seems to be a kind of ragtag-and-bobtail mixture of horrors and pornography. Of course, after TV, such seems to be what people would like to read. (One person's opinion.)

There's a literary renaissance in Maine, known as the Real Maine movement, mostly carried on by the younger generation, and some middle-agers, who were sick of the sentimental clop put out by the Maine Publicity Bureau to attract tourists, and of course we have always had our popular novelists who have written about good-hearted "natives" and old-salts-of-the-earth and so on. Sandy Phippen—he says he has met you at the Library—is very active in the Real Maine movement and so am I. It has a considerable backing at the Univ. of Maine. Sandy, by the way, has a new job—he is now an Assistant Professor at the Univ. and Constance Hunting, also in the English Dept., owns and publishes the *Puckerbrush Review* which prints much material, short stories, poems, etc. along the Real Maine line. She is also famous for the many books she has published, her Puckerbrush Press giving many a beginner a boost and is well known for her own poems and writings.

Puckerbrush Review recently printed the enclosed review of my new books, which is probably the most understanding review I have ever had. This tickles me, because I could probably be the great-grandmother of the youngsters in the Real Maine movement.

All the best, as ever *Ruth*

TO GARY LAWLESS

December 7, 1987

Dear Gary,

I'm sure you've been wondering why I haven't been in touch for a while, but I'm just back from a ten-day stay at the Bangor Hospital, where I had a not serious but needed operation on my foot. I've recovered neatly, and the lameness that's been keeping me practically house-bound for a couple of years is now fixed.

Of course I'll be delighted to see you and Beth at any time it's convenient for you to come. The 16th would be a little better for me, but the 9th is all right if you want to come then.

Thank you for the check for $746.10 royalty payment for Sept. to Dec. 1 sales. You know you mustn't feel obligated to send royalties to me if you're having what you call "money worries" about any reprints. I leave that up to you to be sensible about it.

I think you've done a magnificent job, both of format in the reproductions of the books and the publicity. How you do it I don't know, but it certainly works. Even the nurses at the hospital knew who I was (not from me) and brought in copies of *Spoonhandle* to be autographed.

Looking forward to seeing you and *Beth.*

Ruth

Grendel is the novel by John Gardner.

TO KENDALL MORSE

December 8, 1987

Dear Kendall,

You'll wonder why you haven't heard from me re. *Grendel*. I'm sorry it's been so long, but I've been stuck in the Bangor hospital, where I've had a not too serious operation on my right foot, while everything piled up at home.

Anyway, thanks, belated, for sending me *Grendel*. It's not really my kind of thing, because I've given up reading about horrors, which fiction, these days seem to be specializing on them. But *Grendel* is different, and I can see why you like it. The satire is lovely.

Happy holidays, and all Christmas wishes.

Ruth

Betsy Graves, a former Orono High School student of mine who became a friend and fellow writer, went with me in the spring of 1987 to visit Ruth. Betsy asked Ruth to read *Past the Shallows,* her novella that was later published in *Puckerbrush Review*. Betsy, after graduating from Yale in 1985, was studying for her M.A. in English at the University of Maine where she was also teaching College Composition.

TO BETSY GRAVES

December 16, 1987

Dear Betsy,

I'm later than I meant to be in answering your letter of the 11th, and sending you my thanks for the excellent job you did in the reviews of *The Weir* and *Spoonhandle* in the *Puckerbrush Review*. And for the copy of the *Review* itself, which I've found most fascinating, along the lines of the Real Maine, which we are all rooting for. The freshmen are lucky to have you teaching them how to write.

Fact is, I have been roosting for a couple of weeks in the Bangor Hospital, where I had a minor operation on one of my feet, on which I've been gimping around for years, walking a side-and-a-half at a time. But that's all over now, all fixed up and I'm home again and well.

I appreciate your wanting me to read your story, and will do so with pleasure, but you mustn't expect me to criticize it because I'm no good at criticism, being not a critic but a writer. I can only send you one person's opinion, I like or I don't like. Okay? In other words, I wouldn't want to meddle or to influence you—you don't need that, for heaven's sake, you're already a professional.

Many thanks again, and have splendid holidays.

Sincerely, *Ruth*

TO SANFORD PHIPPEN

December 16, 1987

Dear Sandy,

Heaven knows when I wrote to you last. I know, anyway, that I owe you a letter. ...

How is your book going? Are you near finishing it? I don't in a way see how you can have enough time for your own work what with your new job and all the irons you seem to have in the fire. I thought I'd have time in the hospital and took along pen and paper—but my God, a semi-private ward is like a zoo with all the animals let loose. Nobody even goes to sleep there, let alone concentrates on anything. My ward-companion was an awful old woman to whom someone (certainly not me) whispered the word "celebrity"; she was always wandering around my bed yakking. If she couldn't find out what I had for breakfast she was there at lunchtime—"What are you having?" If I made-believe asleep, she would shake the bed up and down. If I went to the bathroom, she would come and open the door. I did manage to keep my cool, she was very old and I think very sick, and, anyway I didn't have anything to throw.

It was lovely to get home and quiet. A rousing snowstorm today, with three deer in the orchard outside my window, digging windfall apples out from the snow. And my mind back in my head and some honest work done, even while glancing up at the deer, whose coats were black against the white snow.

Take care, my dear, and please, not too many hostages to fortune.

As always *Ruth*

Ms. Mary C. Clarke, one of the many Marys in Ruth's life, was a friend who summered on the Maine coast; she and her sister Cynthia came to visit Ruth several times. Taos, New Mexico is the famous art colony which attracted such writers as D. H. Lawrence, painters such as John Marin, and a painter-writer from Ellsworth, Maine named Alfred Morang.

TO MARY C. CLARKE

December 22, 1987

Dear Mary,

As usual, I'm late. Seems as though at Christmas time THEY? aim these things at me. Last year I spent the holidays in Waldoboro with my sister's kids. Took along my Christmas card list only to find that I hadn't brought addresses. …

I got home with great joy, thinking I was going to be able to go to work again, and live like a hermit crab who creeps into his shell to twiddle by himself. But I found my desk piled high with unanswered mail which I've been trying to catch up with. There's a literary renaissance in Maine, known as The Real Maine movement, mostly carried on by the younger generation of writers who are sick of the sentimental crap put out by the Maine Publicity Bureau to attract tourists and of course we have had popular novelists who put out the same goo, about good-hearted natives and old-salts-of-the-earth and so on. Since in my novels I've always tried to tell the simple truth of what I saw and knew about, I've got quite popular with the Real Maine people, which tickles me, because I could be the great-grandmother of most of them. I think it's a healthy movement. In some ways it reminds me of Taos, where I stopped over on one of my cross-country wanderings, and no one on earth could translate some of their poetry into a logical meaning. But at any rate, it's different. And some of their work is very fine indeed. …

I lost my old cat Tofy, two years ago, and still see, when I got past the jeep in its garage two white feet hanging out over the top of it—where he used to spend a lot of time snoozing. Haunts you like a lost person, only more so, doesn't it?

Love, *Ruth*

TO JACKSON GILLMAN

December 30, 1987

Dear Jackson,

Well, I've survived the Merry Christmas Glee-o and the familyitis typhoon—my God, my folks are scattered from Dan to Beershebe and always expect attention, every one. So Merry, merry to them.

So now I'm able to tackle the piled up fan mail which is still driving me up the wall. The revival of my books.

So all holiday greetings to you are, first, love, and second a mention of all you've done for me this past year. Accept it like a lamb—you know perfectly well what I mean. I appreciate.

I have been to the Bangor hospital and had my lame foot fixed. I can walk on it now, tentatively, but it's not painful any more, and the doctor promises it will soon be back to normal. This is my good news. I have walked a-side-and-a-half to a time for the past two or three years. Don't tell anyone, because I can still use if for regretfully(?) refusing all invitations to read and autograph, to address this and that organization, to join clubs and send money. ...

Looking forward to seeing you in the spring, and best of luck with all your enterprises.

As always *Ruth*

TO BILL SARGENT

December 30, 1987

Dear Bill,

I'm sorry to have been so long in answering your letter with your poems, but my Goodness, I have got relatives scattered from Dan to Beershebe, all expecting me at once.

I'm sending you a copy of *This Month in Maine Literature,* put out by the Maine Writers and Publishers Alliance, which I think might be useful to you. If you'll look at the back page under "Submissions" you'll find some addresses you might try with your own poems. Some of the ads are out of date, but the addresses are there, and you can easily get an up-to-date copy of the paper, by writing to Maine Writers and Publishers Alliance, 19D Mason Street, Brunswick, ME 04011. You might even subscribe to the paper, it's not expensive, and it's helpful to beginning writers.

Good luck and good 1988 coming up.

Ruth

TO GAIL KOPPEN BUTLER

December 30, 1987

Dear Gail,

It's very pleasant to hear from you and have an address to write to. If I didn't let you know that Eleanor died in '81 that was the only reason. My memory has gone where the dead crabs go, and perhaps I did write.

As for me, I'm still cussing around at 84—don't like what I see in the world, as who does. I'm healthy and able, still working—on a book of poems now, instead of a novel, though I have a novel a quarter finished, only I want to let it curdle by itself, at least for a while. After all, I've done 14 novels and only two books of poetry (if I can call it that). One of these a book of ballads

(*Cold as a Dog and the Wind Northeast*) was published in 1958 and is still going strong; the other, *Time's Web*, dropped into the abyss and sent no seed back, as modern poetry is likely to do.

There's a literary renaissance going on in Maine, known as the Real Maine movement, mostly carried on by the younger and middle generations of writers who are sick of the sentimental glop put out by the Maine Publicity Bureau to attract tourists and developers, and the popular novelists and developers, and the popular novelists who have put out the same glop, about good-hearted natives and old-salts-of-the-earth and so on. Since I've always tried to tell the simple truth of what I saw and knew about, my stock is high with the Real Maine people which tickles me, because I could be the great grandmother of most of them. I think it's a healthy movement. In some ways, it reminds me of Taos, New Mexico, where I stopped over for awhile on one of my cross-country wanderings. No one on earth could translate some of their poetry into logical meanings. But also we have Sanford Phippen, whose wonderful book, *The Police Know Everything*, published by the Puckerbrush Press in Orono, is now in its 7th printing and still going strong. It's about his boyhood working for summer people and his attempts to make real friends with some of them. And don't condemn Carolyn Chute entirely—her book is shocking, but she's "telling it like it is" in almost any town in Maine, and doing it excellently well. And some others whose work is very fine indeed.

I'll bet my hair is whiter than yours is.

All the best *Ruth*

TO JENNIFER DURGIN

December 30, 1987

Miss Jennifer Durgin
Lewiston Junior High School, Room 210
Central Avenue
Lewiston, ME 04240

Dear Miss Durgin,

Sorry I can't help you with this questionnaire you have sent me. I've never done this kind of thing about myself. Surely your instructor, or whoever wrote this questionnaire, must realize how much private and personal material is asked for, stretching from my birth to the present day. Some of the questions I can't answer because they go too far back, and I don't remember and some

I literally don't know the answers for. The research would take much time, which I don't have.

I suggest you write the Maine State Library who must have a biographical file on me, and also *Maine Life Magazine*, which did a biographical sketch some months ago, which covered all the information needed; the Colby College Library has a long appraisal written some years ago, which I can approve.

With all good wishes *Ruth Moore*

TO ED STEINER

Jan. 14, 1988

Dear Ed,

Everybody runs out of time before Christmas, I know I did. I was away for ten days and got back to find your box of good eating—we can't buy Swiss cheese with the flavor of yours here and nowhere, of course, can Trail Bologna be duplicated. Many thanks for it and for your note. It was very good to hear from you.

No, I didn't know about Wes Lawrence—nobody told me, and I expect Helen Mary is in a hard way, both with his loss and her own health which was precarious last year. I heard from her then, but not this year, and I don't have any address for her now. Wes's sister still lives here—she has three nurses who take turns looking after her around the clock, and so far as I can find out she hasn't been told about Wes. Probably if she were told, she wouldn't be able to take it in. Makes anyone of us sad, doesn't it?

I, too, have never forgotten the day we had at Gott's Island. You wouldn't know the place now—most of it has been sold to out-of-state people who are overseeing the lands there now—somebody follows you around warning you not to drop lighted cigarette butts, or leave picnic messes. I haven't been there for years—I'm haunted by the magical place it once was and remember it like that, I guess. Besides, nearly everyone there owns a guard dog, which greet you en masse, barking and snapping; or they did when I was last there. So I said Hail and Farewell years ago.

Hope you will find your way here sometime. I'll be happy to see you.

With affection *Ruth*

TO JOHN GOULD

Jan. 14, 1988

Dear John,

I dunno, either. Here it is Jan. 14 and your letter's dated Dec. 6. I do have an excuse that'll hold water, though. I've been away at the Vascular Center and the Bangor Hospital, having surgery on my right foot, which up and died on me, so that I have been walking a side-and-a-half at a time for a couple of years. The final verdict was either have the surgery, or we'll have to take that foot off. So cussing and protesting, I went and had surgery. Operations are the bore of the world to have to hear about, but mine was fascinating. I watched most of it, up to the actual slicing. They used what they called a "doppler," which is sensitive to unseen noises ... With it they located a blood clot that had gone to roost just below my knee, also the track of an artery which could be used to take the place of the slogged-up vein. ...

I got home lusting to get back to work again, and found on my desk a mountain of mail. I've been stunned and astonished by the revival of my early novels, which I'd given up even thinking about. I'd already given William Morrow the boot when they had been "subsumed" by Hearst. ... *The Authors Guild Bulletin,* which I subscribe to, used it ("subsumed") first in its "new job" section. Also mentioned how everyone except Larry Hughes, the then President of Morrow, was the only one of the Morrow people who hadn't been tossed out. That was the only way I found out—nobody at MORROW notified me. So I said, politely, "God die." And nobody misses anybody.

I had a garden last summer but it came to grief when the half-witted fellow whom I hired to weed it for me decided all by himself that it would be easier to take his tiller into the garden and plow it all under, which he did, except for four rows of potatoes, at which I caught and stopped him. He obviously thought I was a woman, so was crazy. "Warn't nothin there," he said. "It was all weeds." My sister, Esther, who lives with me now, wanted to stone him off the place, since we had no gun with which to shoot him. Of course from June to Labor Day no local person can hire any help; everybody is yearning for a job with the summer people, which just possibly may mean a heaven on earth as a winter caretaker when one may sit with his feet in the oven and collect rocking-chair money. So we dug our own potatoes and they turned out well. And they aren't splattered with insecticides, either.

It was great to have your letter, with news about you and Dot and all your young people. Esther's grandchildren—my great-nieces and nephews,—seem to be all zeroed in on getting on to a TV program or going to Hollywood. They are bright kids, all A students, but that's not the first reality, apparently. When somebody in a conversation mentioned that I'd been to Hollywood, one of them, a girl, sixteen, stared at me with considerable unfriendly disbelief. Silence. Then she said, "What? You went to Hollywood? That's not fair!"

Well, it was long before she was born, so I left it at that.

Take care of yourself. All the best to you and Dot.

Never failing appreciation for your books *Ruth*

TO MR. AND MRS. SANFORD DOUGHTY

January 28, 1988

Dear Mabel and Sanford,

I was sorry not to come with Esther at Christmas-time. I expect Esther had explained why. However, I went to Bangor yesterday for a last viewing with the doctor, and I'm so much better, I can't believe it. I was pretty much housebound at Christmas time.

Sorry to have missed the festivities. Maybe next year??? And some more of Sanford's stories.

Sincerely, *Ruth*

Nan Lincoln is a reporter for the *Bar Harbor Times,* and a magazine writer.

TO MRS. CHANDLER L. NOYES

January 29, 1988

Dear Mrs. Noyes,

Thanks for your pleasant letter.

I remember well coming to your house with Eleanor when she returned the pictures you had lent her for copying.

When she died, in 1981, she left me her pictures. For a long time, I didn't know exactly what to do with them. She had planned to write a history of Tremont, but, as Nan Lincoln mentioned in her article, did not live to get any of the writing done. Then I found out that the Southwest Harbor library would be delighted to have them to add to their oral history, which seemed to me to be the very place for them, since Eleanor was brought up in SW Harbor, graduated from the High School there. I agree with you that Nan did an excellent job.

Muriel Davisson is my niece, and I have already mentioned to her that she write the history to accompany the pictures. She said she'd love to, but she doesn't know when she can find the time. She has her own lab at the Jackson Lab, for one thing, and travels a good deal to national and international conferences on Genetics ... Paris, London, Belgium, etc. and is now just back from Miami, where, I might say, she's missed most of the cold weather that is keeping most of us house-bound. My typing shows the effects of cold fingers.

Blackberry Press, who is reprinting my early books, has now donc *Speak to the Winds,* which is now on the market. I understand that another one will be re-printed next fall, but I don't know which one, yet.

Thanks again for remembering me as I have remembered you.

Sincerely *Ruth Moore*

"Mene, Menc, Tekel, Upharsin" was a "bit of silliness," as Ruth says, but Mary Kamenoff traces its origin to the Book of Daniel, Chapter 5, an Aramaic phrase meaning "numbered, numbered, weighed, divided." It refers to "the miraculous writing on the wall interpreted by Daniel as foretelling the destruction of Belshazzar and his kingdom" (*Random House Dictionary of the English Language*). Mary says, "I suppose we were being uncharitable about our sorority sisters!"

TO MARY KAMENOFF

January 30, 1988

Dear Mary,

To hell with the aging process. From the snapshot you sent, which many thanks for, you are neither worn nor rusted out, but so far as I can tell, unchanged from the Mary V. who helped me write "Mene, Mene, Teke, Upharsin" over the top of the closet door of our room in the sorority housc some 60 years ago. Admired, beloved, and of all things sensible. Why I remember that bit of silliness, I can't say, except I do recall that my priorities were out of joint certainly in those days, mostly displaced EGO. ...

Maybe with all this clatter about faulty education, we'll get some effective reform in the schools, but first they have got to educate some effective teachers, and a public that's interested in something besides sports and athaletics. My family is split down the middle—one of my sisters produced five grandsons, all practically seven feet tall, handsome, with shoulders a yard wide, who were the whole town's heroes because they knew everything that could be done with a ball, base-, foot-, basket-, etc. One of them got an athletic scholarship for college.... My other sister, Esther—you met her, remember?—her five kids sucked up whatever they could find in high school, did a lot of home reading, and then earned scholarships as they went along which took them to Mt. Holyoke, Yale, University of Texas, etc., from which they graduated cum laude, and now all have terrific jobs. They are all Ph.D.s. Her eldest girl has her own lab at the Jackson Laboratory in Bar Harbor, where she's doing original research in Genetics—she has a son who keeps winning honors for his writing, has published poems, and came out high up in the national examination—SAT, is it?—that high school seniors take. ...

As you can see, it doesn't take too much to make me sound off about education. Too bad we can't find an educated man to run for President. I have always voted, it's a way of life with me, but who is there, so far?

I send you a poem to finish off '87 with.

Love, much of *Ruth*

THE DAY AFTER

We should have sent the honesty of delphiniums,
The order of green fields,
The dignity of trees,
The first tentative footstep of springtime
The bright sliver of silver that was morning
The bright circle of gold that was afternoon.

Mankind deserved trustworthy emissaries,
Not wheelers and dealers, spies, traitors, What's-in-it-for-me
politicians,
With their left hands held out for peace on earth,
While their right hands behind their backs
Curled snugly around the bomb they carried in their hip pockets.

Ruth met David Caron in her doctor's office in Bangor and he sent her a model copy of a "pinkie" boat.

TO DAVID CARON

February 1, 1988

Dear Mr. Caron,

Have you in your researches done anything about the Chebacco (she-bak-o) boat? For some time I've been trying to get hold of historical material about this boat, and all, so far, I've been able to find only a dictionary record.

> "A fishing boat built mostly in Essex, Massachusetts, in the 18th and early 19th centuries. A pink-built stern, two masts, one mast in the eye of the boat."

I'm sure there must be more history about her somewhere—I've seen the Chebacco mentioned in various historical novels, dated much earlier than the 18th century. This may be just fiction, of course, but I would have guessed that she was around much earlier than that. Perhaps you have already made a model of her—if you have, I'd like to buy one and will send you a check.

Sincerely *Ruth Moore*

TO MRS. DONALD E. FOSTER

February 3, 1988

Dear Mrs. Foster,

I have no information that would be of use to you about Carl Foster. The last time I saw him we were children playing together; I haven't heard from him since, and I learned only recently that he had settled down, with his family, in Maine. I was not notified of his death in 1976 and knew about that only recently and by chance.

Sorry about this and wish I could help.

Sincerely *Ruth Moore*

TO JOHN C. WILLEY

February 13, 1988

Dear John,

The Lord only knows when I wrote to you last and I'm sorry about that. But civilized impulses, such as writing a letter to a beloved and practically life-time friend have to be fought for, it seems, these days of trumpeting publicity. Also, my memory at going on 86, isn't too reliable; so if I tell you anything I've told you already, please put up with it—it's not intended.

If you were to come back to the State of Maine now I don't think you'd recognize it—particularly the small towns on the coast where real estate developers have bought up the shore property and any acreage that has a view of the ocean. To get past Southwest Harbor now, you have to drive past three—shortly to be four—rows of the ugliest buildings I think I have ever seen—condominium units, built on the shore property and the foundation of a fine old 18th century house which was bulldozed down and its historic timbers trucked away somewhere—probably to the dump. If you didn't know what these buildings were—which you do know, with a clutch at your heart—you'd think they were a State's prison, which they look like. Well. There's no way to fight money, a mighty lot of which has changed hands in these deals. Bass Harbor will probably be next. Across the harbor from where I live a twelve-acre piece of shore property was sold not long ago for half a million dollars. So we have now not only pollution of air—we have pollution of history.

You were smart to move to the West coast, where you can dabble your toes in the warm Pacific. Or isn't the Vancouver Pacific warm? Whatever, take care of yourself. Sorry I have no Valentine Hallmark card to send you. …

Well, I wasn't exactly retired when this hurricane wind of publicity blew over me. I had a novel quarter part done which I wasn't particularly satisfied with. …

I seem to be running on, and other people's operations are boring to listen to. What I started to tell about was that word had certainly got around—no way from me—I was only aware of it when the nurses began to bring around their copies of *Spoonhandle* for me to autograph.

Thank God, the publicity has begun to dwindle some, and I've been able to get some of my own work done at last.

We've just got through with a howler of a snowstorm. Everything that isn't knee-deep in snow is six inches of ice.

How are you doing? I'd dearly love to hear.

Affectionately *Ruth*

Connie Hunting had asked Betsy Graves to interview Ruth for the *Puckerbrush Review*.

TO BETSY GRAVES

February 16, 1988

Dear Betsy,

I'm glad to know you're considering lengthening your story—Not that it doesn't stand by itself, and is a pleasure to read—but I did keep wondering what was going to happen next.

I'm sorry to have been so slow in answering your letters. As you know, we live off the main highway; side roads are the last to get plowed out and when we finally did, it snowed again and then rained. Our driveway and the road as far as we could see were both inches deep in glare ice. I suppose the Commander of the Coast Guard, who inhabits the lighthouse at the end of our road, got his mail every day. He has his legions and many big, fat trucks, with chains.

It was a beautiful storm. When the sun came out, everything sparkled and all the trees were loaded with snow.

Well, interviews. I duck them if I can, along with public appearances, etc. With strangers, I usually can wiggle out. But you're no stranger, and, in a way, Mrs. Hunting isn't either, for I've admired her work and what she is doing for a very long time. So set your own time, let me know when you will be coming. I'll look forward to seeing you.

(Sandy Phippen will probably never speak to me again.)

Sincerely *Ruth*

TO EDWARD M. "TED" HOLMES

Feb. 18, 1988

Dear Ted,

Your letter, signed "As in old times" hit me where I lived, because I've never forgotten what good times we all had on the Island, and how decent your family always was to me, and how I loved you all dearly. I can even recall the time you were all coming up the hill to supper (or dinner) and I yelled, "Stand by and repel boarders" and my mother was so mad about it that she didn't speak to me for a week. She felt it was bad manners. And when Ma didn't speak she didn't speak. A lot of up-and-down water's gone over wherever it goes to since those sunny summertimes.

For a while I was homesick for the Island, but for the way it was, not for what it's like now. Esther and I and Louise used to go down on Memorial Day each year to weed off the Moore lot in the cemetery, but the last time we did that, we took a walk and were dogged by some lady who kept yapping about us leaving a mess or smoking cigarettes in the woods because of fire. I didn't know who she was, but Louise, who keeps abreast of things, did, and finally she blew up. She said, "Look here, aren't you the woman who scraped the ashes from your fireplace down the backhouse hole and burnt up not only your backhouse, but your cat and kittens?" Seemed she was and she left us to start all the fires we wanted to. There were some other incidents—a batch of teenagers practically set their dog on me when I was walking alone up the Head Road; J[...] got after Bud's wife when she was harmlessly unpacking a picnic lunch on land that Bud still owns—"Don't leave a mess, etc." Shoot, I wouldn't be caught dead down there now. It almost seems as if the people down there now were afraid of something. I wouldn't know what. I know it seems haunted to me. Not without reason. The offshore islands are mysterious, anyway. I've been on some of them where there once were villages, even towns, where there's a definite atmosphere, almost in the air, that no one is welcome there—that the island belonged to itself and always did. And always will. Black Island is one, Orono Island another, regardless of boundary lines and deeds. Pretty silly? Probably.

I didn't know you were living alone. How come? Where are all your girls? I thought two of them were living with you. I thought I was going to have to, but was lucky when Esther decided to throw in with me. In the beginning we had some sibling disagreements, but we soon got over that, and now get along comfortably, just so we don't meddle with each other, or tell each other what to do.

Drop by when you feel like it.

Also, as in old times *Ruth*

TO J. CARY NICHOLS

February 20, 1988

Mr. J. Cary Nichols
State Librarian
Maine State Library
Cultural Building
Augusta, Maine 04333

Dear Mr. Nichols,

I am sorry I can't be with you on Maine Authors' Day. A pleasant and courteous invitation such as yours is difficult to refuse, but at present I am recovering from a not-too-serious, but unavoidable health problem, which keeps me house-bound, at least in wintry weather.

In any case, I wouldn't have many books to autograph or to sell, since most of them have been out of print for a very long time, so that the only copies I have of them are my file copies. The only ones available now are three of the early ones—*The Weir, Spoonhandle,* and *Speak to the Winds*—which have been re-printed by Gary Lawless, of the Blackberry Press, RR1, Box 228, Nobleboro, Maine, 04555, and are available from him, should anyone be interested.

Copies of *Cold as a Dog and the Wind Northeast* can be ordered from Gordon Bok who lives in Camden.

I wish I could think of some other way which might be helpful.

Sincerely, *Ruth Moore*

TO MRS. ROBERT BUB

February 23, 1988

Dear Mrs. Bub,

Thank you for your pleasant letter, of Feb. 17.

I appreciate your invitation to speak at your annual Maine Authors Series, in September, but I do not make any public appearances—I never have—and I am much too aged to start now. I cannot be with you, but I thank you again and wish you well.

Sincerely, *Ruth Moore*

The State of Maine Reader that Ruth refers to below is probably *The Maine Reader*, sub-titled *The Down East Experience, 1614 to the Present,* edited by Charles and Samuella Shain, and published in 1991. No writing of Ruth's appears in the book.

TO GARY LAWLESS

February 24, 1988

Dear Gary,

I enclose a couple of letters which I expect you ought to see. Do you know anything about these people and their anthology, *The State of Maine Reader?* I've never heard of them, have you? It does seem to me that the scope of their project, "from the 16th century to the present" is somewhat ambitious and that this particular kind of authorization from me is a little puzzling. What do you think? My first reaction was to say all right, but thinking it over, I think I'd rather say no. If you feel as I do, please return this copy of the letter to me, and I'll write to them and say so.

The other letter—from the American Association of University Women—I've already answered and politely refused, saying I don't make any public appearances and never have, and am too aged to start in. I imagine that the Owl and the Turtle Bookshop which in the past has sold many copies of my books now out of print, would already have sold copies of the three you've reprinted. What you have already done publicity-wise is terrific—I don't know how you do it. I couldn't ask for anything more, and I don't. But if you feel that sending a few copies of what you have available to the bookshop for AAUW's Maine Author Series, would be helpful, it's okay with me. I may as well say that I don't particularly care for AAUW's method of raising money for their Scholarship Fund—a 20% donation for each copy sold—to come out of publishers and authors. As I understand it, that is. I don't know whether or not it's sensible to send books with me not there to autograph (for heaven's sake), but you, of course, will know, and if you don't want to bother with it, I'll hold up your hands. And don't send me any royalties on anything you do send.

One more thing—can you send me the lump sum of what you've paid me in 1987? Income tax, blast 'em.

I've had fan letters, not only from Maine, but from New York, New Jersey, Indiana, and California, so far. I can't keep up with the mail. Thought you'd like to know.

You are a great man, as I think I have told you before.

Yours, stunned, *Ruth*

TO VIRGINIA HUGHES

February 26, 1988

Dear Ms. Hughes,

Thanks for your pleasant letter of Jan. 22.

The only copies of my novels in print, as of now, are *The Weir, Spoonhandle,* and *Speak to the Winds*. These three have been re-printed by Gary Lawless, Blackberry Press, RR 1, Box 228, Nobleboro, Maine, 04553, and may be ordered from him. I am sorry, but my own file copies of my books are all I have.

My book of ballads, *Cold as a Dog and the Wind Northeast* may be ordered from Gordon Bok, The Owl and Turtle Bookshop, Camden, Maine.

Thanks again, and with all good wishes,

Ruth Moore

TO PHILIP W. CONKLING

March 18, 1988

Mr. Philip W. Conkling
Island Institute
60 Ocean Street
Rockland, Maine 04841

Dear Mr. Conkling,

This is to confirm my conversation over the phone with Mr. George Putz re. my permission to use the sentences from my novel, *The Weir,* on the back cover of your magazine, the *Island Journal*. I am honored and pleased to have you use them.

I ask in return only that you send me a copy of the magazine when it comes off the press.

Sincerely *Ruth Moore*

At "The Maine Novel in the 20th Century" conference, held first in Portland on Sept 26–28, 1986, and later around the state in Bangor, Bar Harbor, and Farmington, Connie Hunting gave a talk entitled "Caliban's or Ariel's: Whose Maine Island?" in which she mentioned both Ruth and me. The Bar Harbor symposium was held on Nov. 8, 1986.

TO CONSTANCE HUNTING

March 31, 1988

Dear Mrs. Hunting,

This is the nice day which many people invite many other people to have—for me, it's a spring day, tomorrow we can say April. My grandmother used to say that the minute she could say April and get a storm window off so she could listen for the peepers, what she wanted to do was to go out and roll on the ground in her shape. No peepers yet, but I have two crocuses in bloom, some song-sparrows back and singing, and best of all, I have here a letter from Constance Hunting, telling me how she feels about the work I do. If I'm late in answering it, it's probably because it's been hard to find the words to tell you how much I appreciate and thank you for that.

I'm glad Betsy Graves enjoyed the interview. I did, too. We got so interested talking that neither of us noticed when the tape-recorder ran out of tape. I feel, as you do, that she is, first of all, a writer, and I think that we'll be hearing much more from her talent, and I hope, soon.

I'm glad to know that Sandy's second book will soon be on the market. I've been a fan of his ever since I first read *Police* and I'm looking forward now.

Yes, I did sneak in and out of the Conference at Bar Harbor. I was, at the time, in a state of shock because of the astonishing revival of what I thought of as my long-dead books and I didn't think anybody would know me, anyway, though I did wonder as I came away after hearing your talk, "Whose Maine Island," if somebody might recognize me as Caliban. This was because the early newspaper articles were accompanied by photographs that linked in with what the press-boys thought a "fisherman's daughter," should look like—at least, I couldn't think of any other reason. God in heaven only knows where they dug those pictures up, I certainly didn't pose for them. And I did sometimes comb my hair.

At the Conference, I hung around for awhile on the edges of the crowd, hoping to get near enough to say hello, and to tell you what a beautiful job I felt you'd done with "Whose Maine Island"; your sensible and truthful use of Prospero's magic to highlight what you were actually up to. But you were so surrounded that it would have taken more elbow work than I had.

Have a nice day, *Ruth Moore*

Diane Kopec is the director of the Abbe Museum in Acadia National Park.

TO DIANE KOPEC

April 1, 1988

Dear Diane,

I am very much interested, as are some of my Mt. Desert Island neighbors, in the Abbe Museum's on-going plan to salvage and professionally excavate Indian shell heaps and village sites in this area. Your people have already done tremendously important work, replacing some conjectures about the tribes who got here first with fact based on sound scientific research. And if we really want to know these facts about pre-history, where else is there to go for them but to the remains left by people whose place this was for some seven thousand years?

I think it's time and over-time that the archeologists stepped in. Their work already shows respect for the dignity of the first inhabitants—a respect which I haven't seen much of in amateur diggers, particularly in the case of Indian burial places, where much irrevocable damage has been done.

Good luck with the financing of your project.

Sincerely *Ruth Moore*

Catherine S. Baker is the author of *Island Girl*. Mrs. Beston was Elizabeth Coatsworth, and their farm where Gary Lawless lives now was called Chimney Farm.

TO CATHERINE S. BAKER

April 2, 1988

Dear Mrs. Baker,

It's always pleasant to get a letter like yours of March 11, and I haven't ignored it—It is only that I have been literally rushed off my feet, trying to keep up with the flow of mail which has flooded my desk since my old dead books started to be re-published. I hadn't published anything since 1979, but hadn't stopped working, and it's been difficult to handle everything at once. So will you please forgive this longish delay in telling you how much I enjoyed reading your appreciation and friendly discussion of work already finished and back on the market again with more to come. (My typewriter isn't co-operating very well this morning, as you might guess.)

For years I have admired the writings of both Henry and Elizabeth Beston and I wish with all my heart that they were both with us now. I am often reminded of them because Gary Lawless, the owner of Blackberry Press, has his headquarters in Nobleboro, where the Bestons lived.

My father and my brother were life-long lobster fishermen, and father owned and ran a weir, as well, at Gott's Island where I was born; at times, as you say in your letter, it was pretty much hand-to-mouth down there on the island. But nobody ever went hungry, and it was a beautiful place to be born and have your childhood there.

Thanks again, and with all good wishes,

Sincerely *Ruth Moore*

Betsy Graves' interview with Ruth took place in March, 1988, during Betsy's spring break from the University of Maine. As Betsy says now, "She was wonderful about it. I wrote thanking her and enclosed a copy of 'Telling Our Stories,' an article I wrote for the *Maine Mosaic* (a magazine published by the University's Franco-American Centre) in 1987."

TO BETSY GRAVES

April 2, 1988

Dear Betsy,

Please put up with me for being so late in answering your letter enclosing "Telling Our Stories" ... I'd have had a lot more fun writing you, my friend, than I've had batting out as politely as possible, answers to hither-and-yon requests to "Come to our autographing party and bring your books, you can sell them right at the desk." There are, of course, a couple or so answers to that: (1) "Sorry, but the only copies of my books I have are my field copies; the current reprints are all sold out," or (2) "Sorry, but I would rather be caught dead than caught peddling my own books." I admit it's a temptation, especially since the politer I am, the crosser people get. I sound NASTY, but it's only letting off steam, which, since we had our interview, I know I can do to you.

I find exactly how I feel in your "Telling Our Stories," and I quote, "As if I were leaving my more likeable self behind ... adopting instead a harsh, inflexible persona quite unlike me." I think you did a tremendous job with that, and I did enjoy reading it. May I keep this copy of it you sent me, or do you want it back? One thing, it'll keep me from boycotting the Post Office.

Come any time you like, any afternoon you have time and, by all means, bring cookies.

Sincerely *Ruth*

TO JOHN C. WILLEY

April 4, 1988

Dear John,

This is the nice day that many people invite many other people to have—oh, foggy, of course, but we haven't had a real old mull all winter and this is a wowser, can't see across the front yard, but it's also a sure sign of spring. My old grandmother used to say that when she could say April and get a storm window off so that she could stick out her head and listen for the peepers, it made her feel like going outside and rolling on the bare ground in her shape. When I was little, I used to hang around her to see if she'd do it. She never did, but she left the message. She was a grand old gal, and I loved her dearly. She died in 1915.

I'm relieved to know that you're all right, enjoying your retirement, reading a lot and "lazing around," which, by gum, you deserve. I wonder if you can find any good fiction to read—I can't. Horrors, slimy sex, child abuse seem to be what the big business interests which have taken over most of the fine old publishing houses feel worth printing. Most of it seems like trash to me—and I'd be about as interested in going to a Lion's Club party, where all the gentlemen watch with glee naked girls taking baths in big slippers full of wine. Or so I've been told.

And what on earth has become of experienced editors? Have they got them emptying wastebaskets now? Nobody, apparently, reads proofs now, and errors stick out uncorrected all over, sometimes two or three to a page.

I don't know how interested you are in what goes on in the New York market now. I, thank God, have no contact whatever there, since I kicked myself out of Morrow, but I do subscribe to the *Authors Guild Bulletin*, and occasionally find traces of old lang syne there. For example, and I quote: "Howard Kaminsky, whose dismissal as head of the Random House trade division shocked the publishing world last fall, has landed solidly on his feet as pres. of the Hearst trade book group, which includes Morrow, Avon, Arbor House, Greenwillow Books, Hearst Books, and Hearst Marine Books. Former pres. Lawrence Hughes has become chrmn."

And this choice bit: "Sherry Arden at Morrow is starting up her own imprint, Silver Arrow books after resigning as Morrow's president. James Landis has been appointed Morrow publisher and editor-in-chief. He has stated that the imprint will be maintained within Morrow."

If this water-over-the-mill stuff doesn't interest you or makes you feel like throwing up, let me know. But there's one more item under New Ventures which makes me wonder somewhat.

"Stephen King ... has started up a very small publishing company of his own, Philtrum Press, based in Bangor, Maine ..."

Why? Well, I wouldn't actually know how to guess, but it does seem to me that horror fiction and ghastly tales of unknown monsters popping out of the woodwork are lower down on the best-seller lists than they used to be.

We still have, God help us, murders and child abuse on TV and blow-by-blow divorce cases, not to speak of innocent little children speaking the commercials which are supposed to sell cereal, but you can always turn that off. I now eat old-fashioned oatmeal for breakfast and very nice it is. No additives, and no naked babies. Ugh!

Now, I have sounded off enough. There are other things more interesting to wonder about. Who, for example, will the Democrats find to nominate? Jesse Jackson is sweeping the country, it seems—he did here in Maine, certainly. But if he wins out, won't there be enough bigoted rednecks nation-wide to split the Democratic vote wide open? Racial prejudice, again, and worse? I don't know, I'm asking. The others, money-backed I can't see. Actually, the only one who makes sense is Paul Simon.

Me, I'm still sitting in a butter-tub. The first three books were snapped up and re-printed, especially *Spoonhandle* and that's to be re-printed again in June. The fourth one, I shudder to say, is going to be, Lord help me, *The Walk Down Main Street,* largely because it's being ordered in lots of classes in colleges and particularly the U. of M. Coming this fall just about when the basketball madness will start again. Keep a sofa in your parlor. I may have to leave town.

* * *

I thought for a while I'd boycott the Post Office—them and their three cents hike on postage! That, I find I can't do. Don't you either. I miss you.

Have a nice day. Affectionately *Ruth*

TO MRS. H. J. BUTLER

April 24, 1988

Dear Mrs. Butler,

This is the kind of day many people invite many other people to have a good one—whatever the weather may be doing—rain, snow, hail, fog, like today. But I have at hand your letter of April 24, telling me how much you like my work, as pleasant as any I have ever had, so let it thunder if it wants to, and I don't like thunderstorms. Thank you, very much.

Yes, great changes are taking place in Maine, as well, I suppose, as in many States who have pretty shore-fronts, with a view of the sea, or access to it. Some of our small towns here on Mt. Desert Island are already unrecognizable, with rows of condominiums overlooking the water, built on the foundations of fine old houses dating back to the seventeen-hundreds, now bulldozed down and the historic lumber hauled to dumps, or burned. In many ways, it's heartbreaking to think of the concrete slabs covering the good farmlands, too, some of them used and cared for for nearly three hundred years. Well times change, and they never move back. There's a surge of people coming in from the "westard" who are willing to pay the unbelievable prices set up by the real estate developers, which means that the towns will be re-valued, taxes will go sky high, and local people can't afford to live here any more; their young can't afford to buy property; they scatter, out of State.

Thanks again and, I hesitate, have a good day.

Sincerely *Ruth Moore*

The "Maine book" to which Ruth refers below is *The Best Maine Stories* published in 1986. The Ted Holmes non-fiction story based on the burning of Miss Peterson's house on Gott's Island is called "There Is an Island in My Life" from *Driftwood* (1972).

TO CONSTANCE HUNTING

May 2, 1988

Dear Mrs. Hunting,

Thanks for your pleasant letter.

Of course, I'd be delighted, not to say, honored, if you want to use my piece, "The Lonely of Heart" in *Puckerbrush Review*.

I've never done very much with short stories, and this wasn't actually written as one, but only as a factual report of a real tragedy that took place on Gott's Island (where I was born). It never occurred to me to offer it for sale anywhere, but I had to scurry around in old writings for short stories for the Maine book, and came across the one and sent it along. I also used some of the material, fictionalized, for Miss Greenwood in *Speak to the Winds.*

There have been various write-ups about the island—occasional newspaper pieces and so on, which nearly always zero in on the burning of Miss Peterson's house and she with it, not always accurate, I'm afraid, but there's a reason for that. One of the last locals to live there after the community moved away, was a wild old solitary who told horrendous lies to any "flatlander" who asked him for information. He was really an artist at it.

Also I have a vague memory from long ago that Ted Holmes used the Peterson story in one of his short story books. You might want to ask him about copyright, if necessary.

So far as I'm concerned, go ahead—print, edit, change title if you want to.

Sincerely *Ruth Moore*

TO GARY LAWLESS

May 20, 1988

Dear Gary,

I have copies of all of Eleanor Mayo's books which I'll gladly lend you, if you haven't already tracked them down. I know I can trust you to let me have them back when you're finished with them. There are five of them:

Turn Home, 1945, Wm. Morrow & Co., New York

Loom of the Land, Wm. Morrow & Co., New York, 1946

(These above two were also reprinted in London by T. B. Boardman, 14 Cockspur St., London, SW)

October Fire, 1951, T. Y. Crowell, New York

Swan's Harbor, 1953, T. Y. Crowell, New York

Forever Strangers, 1958, W. W. Norton, New York

Eleanor also left behind two finished manuscripts, *The Dark and the Daylight,* and *The Pleasure Dome.* I let Mark Melnicove take these, some time ago. He returned the first, but he has kept *The Pleasure Dome.* He'll probably send it to you if you want to see it. I haven't heard from him about it, so I don't think he wants to use it.

Since Eleanor left me her entire estate, I suppose I own copyrights. I've already sent the Anthology people (Mr. Fischer) my permission. This letter gives you permission from me.

At the time of her death, she was working on a photographic history of the Town of Tremont. Not only a writer, she was a professional photographer as well. Her method was to find old family photos, copy them and return the originals. She had a tremendous collection of these old photos, dating back for many years, complete with identifications and negatives, all labeled and filed. I couldn't see keeping these valuable records, not known, so I let the Southwest Harbor Library add them to their similar collection where they are available to the public. She had done very little actual writing on the project, but the pictures speak for themselves.

You'll find some biography in the dust jacket of *Forever Strangers*. I wish you and Beth could drop by and bring a tape recorder, I could tell you more, but considering what you are doing, I can't see how you could find time. For goodness sake, don't send me any more royalties, if money is tight. Remem ber, I told you not to? I want some more copies of *The Weir* and *Spoonhandle*—say five of each, and I'll pay for them at the going rate, if you'll let me. I'm not selling them, but I find that an occasional autographed gift gets around—shows up in sales at local bookstores, I'm told. Mr. Paperback in Ellsworth recently advertised *The Weir* and all bookstores around have been carrying them, or are just out,—Curtis in Ellsworth, and Bar Harbor, the larger ones, and, of course in Bangor.

Let me know which of Eleanor's books you haven't yet got, and I'll send them along—Unless you can drop by and pick them up. In that case, I won't have to do up a bundle.

I've been snowed under with fan letters, some as far away as Indiana and California, women's clubs from all over are still inviting me to come and read and bring along an armful of my books which I can sell while autographing. I try to answer all of them, politely and regretfully, and truthfully, too—because I have been house-bound all winter. I don't say that I'm better now, but I am. And I don't say that I'm a private, not a public, person, and would be embarrassed speechless if I had to peddle my own books. Which I don't. (Thanks to you.)

Thanks for sending along the *Journal Tribune* review of Speak to the Winds. It's a very nice one.

How you do it I don't know—it must be some kind of magic touch you have which brings these old otherwise dead books back to life again. It's a great work you are doing, and I love you for it.

I hope you'll be able to bring out *The Walk Down Main Street* before the basketball scramble begins next fall. When it first came out, I thought I was going to have to leave home, but the crowds of fans aren't as savage now as they were then, and we don't see fist fights between townies any more. It tickles me a little that the most furious readers of the book were in Indiana then—and now a lot of the fan letters I got on my revived books have come from Indiana!

I've covered everything, I hope, which you might wish to know. Now that the fan mail, etc. is slacking off, I have time to work on my own project and am up to my ears in it, which is why I've been so late in writing you.

With all my thanks, as ever, *Ruth*

Nicholas Sichterman is a Mr., not the Ms. or Miss that Ruth thought when she wrote the following note. Mr. Sichterman owns Blue Hill Books where he holds public readings and autograph parties.

TO NICHOLAS SICHTERMAN

Maine June 2, 1988

Dear Ms. Sichterman,

I am honored, of course, and pleased to be invited to one of your Thursday evening gatherings in August. I only wish I could accept, but matters of health keep me, while not exactly house-bound, still I can't accept any invitations which include long car rides, or public performances, of any kind.

Thank you very much, and with all best wishes for your project.

Sincerely *Ruth Moore*

Betsy Graves' novella *Past the Shallows* was published in two parts in *Puckerbrush Review*. Betsy sent Ruth news of an excerpt from her novel's winning a Grady Award at the University of Maine, and asked Ruth if she could come for another visit. As Betsy says, "Unfortunately, I never got there again."

TO BETSY GRAVES

June 29, 1988

Dear Betsy,

Happy 4th of July!

I'm late answering your very nice letter of the 14th and I'm sorry. My desk has been a mess and still is, but not such a mountain as when it began to be, and I'm beginning to be partly sane again. Thank God, what goes up must come down, eventually.

Glad to see you any time you, too, can find the time. Drop me a line first, if nobody answers the phone and set the date and time. I'm always here, but not all the time inside the house where I can hear the phone. I have to confess that for privacy's sake, I have bought myself a screen house which is set up in the bushes behind a big tree. Only a few know where it is, and I flee to it to get real work done. I know exactly how you feel, trying to write, with so many obligations which have to be tended to.

Congratulations on the success of your novel, and your prize for it. But we'll talk about things when you come. You are always welcome, and I'll look forward. …

Affectionately *Ruth*

Never mind cookies—what in the world is your address now?

TO GARY LAWLESS

June 29, 1988

Dear Gary,

Many thanks for the royalties (acknowledged $463.85). Considering the wonderful thing you've done for me, I almost feel guilty about taking any. But I do appreciate, as you must surely know.

I did enjoy so much seeing you and Beth—I wish you lived nearer, and could come more often.

If you do want to have a go at the book of poems I'm working on now, I'd be glad to have you do it—at least, look at it when it's finished, which will be a while yet. Next year, possibly. I haven't been able to work on it for some time, due to a piled up desk … I feel strongly about answering these requests, because I think that anyone who takes trouble to write me should get back a polite and decent reply, with an explanation why I cannot accept. One thing I have done to restore a little privacy, I have bought a screen-house which now sits secretly in the bushes behind a big tree. Only a few people know where it is. No phone, no drop-ins.

I'm really glad you are bringing out *The Walk Down Main Street* in July before the basketball scramble begins with the opening of schools. I don't think I'll have to leave home, anyway, because the sports fans at the games are not so savage now as they were when the book was first written, in 1960. In those days the fans would pile down on the floor, and fist fights between winners and losers were often pretty vicious, with bad injuries to some.

As I recall, the movie from *Spoonhandle* was made at Vinalhaven, so it isn't surprising that the people there might want copies of the book, sadly misnamed *Deep Waters*.

Don't think I'm complaining about this "privacy" business. I manage well, and you, as I've told you, are a great man, who has restored not only my career, but my spirits.

As ever *Ruth*

The Maineiac Express, "The World's Only Maine Comedy Newspaper," was produced by Mark Melnicove and Michael Kimball in two editions in 1987–88.

TO MARK MELNICOVE

August 8, 1988

Dear Mark,

Many thanks for sending me a copy of *A Caribou Alphabet*. I'm very pleased to own a copy. It's not only beautiful for its lovely water-color illustrations, but a splendid job of book making as well. Congratulations, too, on *The Maineiac Express*.

I'm sorry to have been slow in answering your letter, but I have in a way gone into hiding, trying to get some work done which I've been unable to do since the ghosts of my early books have risen from the dead. It's been hard to get caught up.

I'm working now on a book of "collected poems" which I hope to finish by the first of next year, though it may take longer than that. Gary Lawless will publish it when it's ready. I don't think I have anything in print that could be considered "Maine" poems, actually, unless *Cold as a Dog,* the ballads. Gordon Bok is now the publisher of these—he bought the original from William Morrow & Co. and now owns it, and publishes it in paperback. As for *Time's Web,* there's very little in that, I should think, that would qualify for a Maine anthology. Anyway, Gary Lawless can tell you what you need to know.

Thanks again for your nice letter. It's always pleasant to hear from you.

Sincerely *Ruth*

Over the years, Connie Hunting has reviewed many books, including Ruth Moore's on her old program "Small Press Review" on MPBN-FM radio, and on other programs. In 1989, Connie read all of Ruth's *The Walk Down Main Street* on "The Maine Reader" show.

TO CONSTANCE HUNTING

September 27, 1988

Dear Constance,

I blush at the date on your post card—Sept. 10. Please forgive the long delay. All I can say is, I've been hiding in the woods in a tent, and mail on my desk in my house where I usually work, has got ahead of me. You didn't mention a date or an hour when your radio talk would be, and if you've already made it, I've missed it. If you have a written copy of it which you could send along, I'd be more than pleased and honored to read it. Any contact with you is always a red-letter time for me.

Hiding in the woods in a tent isn't quite as silly as it sounds. The Maine Publicity people have recommended Bass Harbor Lighthouse as one of the sights tourists should see, and my house sits about twenty feet back from the highway that leads to it. All summer long we have bumper to bumper traffic going past mostly at sixty miles an hour; the word "celebrity" alas, has somehow gotten out and seems to be a donkey's carrot to tourists. If I'm there and have forgotten to lock the doors, they walk right in. Thus the tent, a desperate grab at solitude. I realize the compliment and am always polite, and then they tell me their life's history. Time is love and there's the will. If I'm not there, no problem.

Right now, my sister who lives with me, and I are harvesting for freezing and canning, our quite large vegetable garden. Our twelve apple trees have produced a crop you wouldn't believe unless you saw it.

What shall I do with ten tons of apples?

Faithfully yours *Ruth*

TO GEDDES SIMPSON

October 22, 1988

Mr. Geddes Simpson
Box 400, Bar Harbor Banking and Trust
Bar Harbor, Maine 04609

Dear Mr. Simpson,

Enclosed, my real estate tax bill for land and buildings—$205.87 for land with one building (Town Assessment Land Value, 15,000, Building Value 2,100, Total Value 17,300 as of 4-1-88, Account 454, Map 2, Lot 11. Also, $1623.16 for Land Value 87,000, Bldg. Value, 49,400, Total Value 136,400, which includes home, outbuildings, and 262 shore front, some 11 acres. This is on Town Map 455, Map 2, Lot 16.

All this information, of course, is on the accompanying bills on the Town assessment, but I'm keeping a carbon for my own information and files, so I won't have to bother you in case I need a reference. I do appreciate your handling this for me. I would have had to transfer the total sums from money market or agency accounts to my checking account anyway, as I did last fall when I was billed for $850, because the town changed its fiscal year from January to December to July 1 year to year; having the bank handle it for me seemed to me only sensible. So thank you again. I leave to your judgment which account to use.

As for John Strange, I think he's scarpered—I don't know. He doesn't answer letters. His divorced ? wife sailing into town and putting the land he owes me for into Gary Blanchette's hands for sale didn't see me, as you already know. Gary, whom I know well, is taking customers down, off and on, to show the land; as of yesterday, he said that the Stranges will have to come down on their price, which is $300,000, and that he'll never be able to sell it for that. No condominiums can be built down there, owing to a restriction in the deed I gave him, which forbids it; according to a town ordinance, recently passed, which limits building to family houses, restricts development. However, if somebody is a fool enough to pay Strange's price and he pays me all he owes me for interest plus the $28,000 still due, all in one lump, it'll scoot my income tax sky high, won't it? His yearly payment was due in March; we gave him three months; then another three months and we haven't heard from him. I don't have any record of his paying me anything for this year. Or am I mistaken?

Thanks again, for all your trouble taken.

Faithfully yours, *Ruth Moore*

TO TED L. SPURLING, SR.

November 1, 1988

Dear Capt. Spurling,

Thanks for your pleasant letter of Oct. 26. I've been rooting around trying to find (or remember) about Placentia Island and the names of families who lived there. Sorry to say I haven't come up with much. I think you'd get better factual records from the Ellsworth Court House, if you'd like to write there.

There was a Poor Farm there in the early days—I don't know when. My sister, Esther Trask, whom you, of course, know, recalls hearing the Poor Farm mentioned, but as of a very early date, almost of colonial times when Maine was a part of Massachusetts and emigrants were still coming to settle in. I found in an old atlas, pub. 1881, two names of families living on the island, G. Mitchell and A. Richardson. Gott's Island, at one time, was known as "Little placentia." According to an old diary kept by a Gott's Island woman, there was in the '80s a flourishing community on Placentia. Families from both islands knew each other well and had many fine times together. Harris McLean, Little Island Cove, Box 32, Sullivan Harbor, ME 04689, owns this diary. Undoubtedly, he would give you information about names mentioned in it. I think Charles Welch of Gott's Island and Boston owned land there, possibly the whole island and the Harding family, also of Gott's Island put up a big sheep barn and ran flocks of sheep there for a long time.

This is about all I can tell you, first hand. Good luck to your hunting.

Sincerely *Ruth Moore*

TO HARRIS L. MCLEAN

November 2, 1988

Dear Harris,

Thanks for your pleasant letter. I enclose herewith your Ancestor Charts. Thanks, also for letting me see them. It is, as you say, amazing, isn't it?

With regard to your questions, I'm sorry to say that I gave up, some years ago, trying to untangle the Philip Moores, who was No. 1, etc. According to Mrs. Thornton's book, *Traditions and Records of Southwest Harbor and Somesville*, Samuel Moore, who was lost at sea, left his wife, Margaret Welch Moore with four sons.

p. 25, William O. Sawtelle's *Daniel Gott, Mount Desert Pioneer, His Ancestors and Descendants:* "Esther, the third child of Nathaniel and Elizabeth Richardson Gott, of Gott's Island, was born Nov. 17, 1790; married

Philip Langley Sept. 18, 1818, his second wife. Philip's first wife was Margaret Welch Moore, widow of Samuel Moore, the founder of the Moore family of Southwest Harbor. Samuel Moore was lost at sea before 1790 and Philip made a good step-father to his four sons ... Descendants of Joseph, Samuel and Welch Moore owe him a large debt of gratitude for the paternal interest which he took in his step-sons."

At Seawall, there is a small, overgrown burial place, where other Moores lie. There must be a fourth son of Samuel. The names which can be read are: Betsey L., wife of Thomas Moore, died 1904. Capt. Benjamin Moore, died 1898. Rachel Moore, wife of Philip Moore, died 1825. Welch Moore, died Feb. 7, 1845, aged forty-two. Thomas Moore, died 1858, aged forty-seven. Samuel Moore, died 1839, aged sixty-eight. Sarah Moore, died 1861, aged eighty-eight. Gilbert H. Moore, May 16, 1861, died 23 (Civil War) on same monument. Ezekiel Moore, died 1899, His wife Mary, died 1887. Philip Moore, whose dates can't be made out, they are so old. I suspect this must be the fourth Samuel Moore son.

Asenath, born Nov. 20, 1802, was the 9th child of Nathaniel Gott, of Gott's Island. She married Nov. 7, 1826, Philip, son of Welch and Sarah Spurling Moore. She died July 29, 1852. They were my great-grandparents and their grave stones, with names and dates are in the Moore burial lot at Gott's Island.

This is about as far as I can take you. My nephew, George Trask, has much more complete records than I do. His address is Box 547, RFD 3, Wiscasset, ME, 04578, if you wish to get in touch with him.

Sincerely *Ruth*

TO GARY LAWLESS

December 6, 1988

Dear Gary,

I thought I'd better get word off to you re. your friends who want to turn *Spoonhandle* into a play. You ask three questions:

1. Am I interested in having this happen? Yes, of course I am, and this will confirm that they have my interest and permission, as far as that may go.
2. I don't need to see a rough draft—I leave that up to your judgment.
3. Are there any legal complications? Yes, I think there may be, since this involves turning the book into a play and producing it. As you'll recall,

> I got permission and passed it along to you from William Morrow & Co. But Morrow has been bought by Hearst & Co., and I now have nothing to do with them. However, this doesn't alter the permission I gave to you.

I should think your playwright friends wouldn't have any difficulty getting permission from the present owners of Morrow for the use of *Spoonhandle*, but they should do so. Also if they are interested in *A Fair Wind Home*, *The Sea Flower*, or *Second Growth*, all Pocket Books. 20th Century Fox made a movie out of *Spoonhandle*, which they called *Deep Waters*, for some silly reason.

Don't worry about royalties. You know what I told you about that.

You brought me a huge boxful of *The Walk Down Main Street*, which I haven't any use for and no place to keep so many. Why don't you and Beth take a trip north and take most of them back with you? Looks as if you could use them—according to your royalty account for December, *The Walk* is outselling any of the others, and I can't get out comfortably either to do readings or to peddle my own books.

Thanks a lot for what you're doing. I do appreciate, if not often heard from.

Faithfully, *Ruth*

Mr. Lance Tapley is the former publisher of Lance Tapley Books and Yankee Books.

TO LANCE TAPLEY

December 20, 1988

Dear Mr. Tapley,

I'm of course delighted to receive a copy of your new publication, *Best Stories of Sarah Orne Jewett*. It is a beautiful book and you and its editors deserve many a congratulation for the way you have produced it … a good job, well done.

I'm sorry I can't write you a review of it—I haven't done any reviewing for a good many years, and never was very good at it. I always did the best I could, but some questions kept poking in and bothering me—such as, "Who am I to pass judgment on this book? Isn't it only one person's opinion, anyway?" so what does that amount to?

I've owned *The Country of the Pointed Firs* since my school days; have read Sarah Orne Jewett's work wherever I've found any. Your *Best Stories* with new material should surely be welcomed—by people with long memories.

Thank you for letting me know about it.

Sincerely *Ruth Moore*

TO BETTY HOLMES BALDWIN

Jan. 5, 1989

Dear Betty,

I've been gadding all over Maine visiting relatives—left before Christmas and Esther and I are only recently back, which is why holiday cards are so late. Mail piled up and I look at it gasping. Glad to get home, though.

Of course I'd love to see you any time, but you mustn't ask me to go to the Island. I haven't been down there for years, and have no wish to go. It's no longer the magical place I knew and loved and grew up in and the changes made set too many ghosts walking. So why dig up heartbreak when you don't have to?

I guess you'll have to come and see me when you can.

Love *Ruth*

TO JOHN GOULD

January 6, 1989

Dear John,

... I just managed by the skin of my teeth getting to see you. I was thinking about leaping out of the woodwork and screaming "Surprise!" Our home-base was Waldoboro, where my sister Esther's daughter, Emmy Trask-Eaton, lives—she owns the Five and Dime store and lives a block from it. Friendship's not far, so why didn't we make it?

Talk about Moore and Gould together again! I could write you almost the exact same letter you wrote me with very little differences. It's a family tradition to drive over to Week's Mills on Christmas Eve and have a tree-unloading with Esther's youngest son, Phil, and usually everybody goes who can make it. We started out, but didn't make it. The going was what they call in this area too "greasy." The car hydroplaned off the road into the ditch and went on to take down a tree and telephone pole and yards of telephone wire. The car was totaled, nobody was hurt, except Esther bumped her head slightly and bent her glasses. I wasn't aboard that load, having gone on ahead with Jim, Emmy's husband, in a four wheel drive truck he uses in his volunteer work as an ambulance and accident group on call that night. He's a highly-trained driver, as he has to be to be a member of that voluntary group and he got me to Week's Mills with no effort at all. We had barely got to taking our coats off at Phil's when the phone call came about Emmy's accident, four or five miles behind us. Jim took off, helped the police, the wrecker, his Voluntary Corps substitute clean up the mess, get everyone back home again. Then he came back to Week's Mills and took me back to Waldoboro. Re. Mothers: Emmy was sitting with a state trooper in his car, waiting for transportation home, when the trooper practically jumped out of his skin. He said, "Oh, my God! See that car? That's my mother. She's been to church." The car was just passing, traveling fairly fast, but smoothly. It turned the curve up the road without slowing down, and went out of sight. The trooper said helplessly, "She's 92."

So that's why I didn't get to Friendship. No transportation. And I'm darn sorry I missed you.

I don't exactly boycott the Post Office, though I do feel that 25 cents is more than the long-suffering public ought to pay. But in a way, seems to me said public will have to pay more of the same when the newly elected President takes over. I don't know how it can be helped, unless God himself takes over.

Were you ever hugged by an IGA supermarket? I was. Talk about a freak accident! Esther and I went grocery shopping at our local IGA and were leaving by the regular entrance and exit doors. She was on ahead with the groc. cart and I was just behind her. She took the proper exit door, but the other door was wide open, so I took that. I was halfway out, when my door, which was the entrance door, closed up on me. I had to struggle to get out, and I was already hearing my ribs creaking. I managed by the skin of my teeth, but it was touch and go. All I could think of was the Mark Twain character who fell off the shot-tower and flattened himself so flat that they had to slide him between two barn doors and bury him edgeways.

Thanks for "Boats and Harbors" and many thanks for getting Moore and Gould together again. We shouldn't have lost each other in the first place.

As always *Ruth*

TO MARY KAMENOFF

January 9, 1989

Dear Mary,

... Don't say computers to me. I have a nephew who teaches computers at the Morse High School in Bath—has already supervised putting computers in nine schools in that area and I understand that this is going to keep on, even down into the kindergartens. This seems to mean that even small kids won't be taught reading, writing, and arithmetic any longer—the computer'll do the work for them. I'm too old-fashioned to swallow this easily. But the kids love it. I have so many grand, great-grandnieces and nephews now that it's hard to sort them out. They all delight in telling me how to think and how to make use of my time, which tickles me somewhat, because I'm up to my neck in putting together a book of collected poems and there never seems to be time enough.

Have another good year and many to come, and stick in, wherever there is room for it, my best love,

Ruth

TO ED STEINER

Jan. 9th, 1989

Dear Ed,

I've been gadding up and down the State of Maine, visiting family, and have only just returned, so my holiday cards are too late to be such. But thanks, just now, for a chunk of the best-tasting Swiss cheese in the U.S. of A, and for the trail bologna. Wouldn't have been Christmas-time without your remembrance.

Hope 1988 was as good a year to you as it has been for me and that 1989 will be better. To you and yours,

Affectionately *Ruth*

TO SANFORD PHIPPEN

Jan. 10, 1989

Dear Sandy,

... I have been gadding practically all over the State of Maine, visiting family, and have only recently got back, which is why all my holiday communications are so late. Also, I have been of several minds as to whether or not to boycott the Post Office. You can't, of course, but I can remember when two cents was all I needed to send a single letter; 25 cents, Boo! But why the fuss when what I actually want is to be let alone to do my work?

Well, I certainly got rid of that silly attitude and got shed of it quickly. I not only picked up a lot of new and fresh material, I got re-acquainted with four generations of kids that go back behind me. As soon as they found out that I wasn't doing an eyes-that-watched-from-the-underbrush job on them, they all, from about the fifth-grade to high school began to lecture me about my old-fashioned opinions and habits. One and all, they were TV and schoolroom conditioned about the horrors of smoking. I agreed; not mentioning that I've been smoking for some seventy years, and was still alive and kicking at 86; not mentioning, either, the years of Prohibition and what happened to the entire country then. It was all good stuff to know, and I was glad I'd gone.

... All good thoughts and luck for the coming year,

Sincerely *Ruth*

TO MARY DILLON

Jan. 12, 1989

Dear Mary,

... I expect I have written you about my dear old friend, Lenora Higgins, who was 92 the last time I saw her, and what she said to me was: "There's not a single thing wrong with me except old age and I guess I'll never get over that." I haven't caught up with her yet, but I'm headed that way. However, I've got both of my legs working now and don't walk with a limp any more. Last year I couldn't walk out in the snow, but if there is some I could go snowballing if I wanted to.

... 1988 has been a very good year for me, and I look forward to the same in 1989. You sound to me as if the same could be said of you. So bless you and

With affection *Ruth*

TO JOHN C. WILLEY

January 15, 1989

Dear John,

If you were to come back to the State of Maine now, I don't believe you'd ever recognize it as the place you left. I don't know about the Cherryfield area, not having seen it, but I can guess. Bar Harbor is like Coney Island now; Southwest Harbor has a row of condominiums you have to look at as you enter the town, together with a huge one on its shore. The long one looks like a jail or a barracks, very ugly. Our town, Tremont, which includes Bernard, Bass Harbor and several other small villages, has had the sense to pass an ordinance forbidding shore-front building, except for one-family houses, within a thousand feet of the shore-front. However the developer who was planning to put in fourteen condominiums along our harbor, was overheard to say, "We'll wait awhile. We'll get it. All we've got to do is make these people comfortable."

Well. I suppose he's probably right. Over across the harbor, in Bernard, a 20 acre of shore-front was recently sold for almost half a million dollars. Yesterday, three of our friends sold their houses and moved to Vermont. The big house where my brother used to live and bring up his family, has been sold three times, last price, over three hundred thousand dollars plus fourteen acres of land. So it goes, and none of it's going to come back. It's going to mean 50-foot lots and inadequate water. We've already had to have our well deepened.

Me, I have had a prosperous year. I think I wrote you that I bought a screen-house tent, which I've hidden in the woods back of my vegetable garden, where nobody can find me. I use it mostly in the summer, when the 10 million tourists, urged on by the Maine Publicity Bureau, go past my house to view the Bass Harbor Head Lighthouse. If my house doors aren't locked, there will always be some who will walk right in, not bothering to knock, breathing through the nose the all-permissive word, "Celebrity."

This kind of snotty behavior makes me, even myself, wonder who in hell I think I am, because after all this is part of my public, but my Maine publisher says don't worry about that, he'll take care of the publicity. And he certainly does. I don't know how he manages to get my revived books known in places like Hawaii, and Puerto Rico, and, of all places, Samoa, but he has received orders from all of these. I think he must work it by a kind of osmosis. Since I wasn't helping him any, I told him that I wouldn't want any royalties, but he sends me faithfully ten per cent every month. Last month's take, for me, was a little over eleven hundred dollars. That was just for December 1 to January 1, 1989.

It's good to know you are all right. I guess a good many people don't have "grim forebodings" for the national future, and aren't too dissatisfied with the present, since according to figures on the national election now being published, they show that less than half of the qualified voters didn't even bother to go vote.

... Well, Time does go. Sometimes I'm stunned to find that it goes so fast. I was looking through letters from you—I always keep all your letters—and found the one in which you mentioned what a pleasant time you had when Esther's "kids" came to call. Oh, my. They are all middle-aged now with grown up kids of their own and scattered all over the map. Our young folks don't stay here—no jobs. The only one here is Muriel, her eldest girl, who went to Mt. Holyoke and specialized in genetic research. She has her own lab at the Jackson Laboratory in Bar Harbor with a staff of 30 people. The others: Ohio, Augusta, Bath, Illinois, Wiscasset, Waldoboro. I can't resist bragging about all the PhDs. and thought you'd be interested, too.

So far, no snow. A brown winter. I'm working now on a book of poems, which will probably be published by Blackberry Press sometime in the spring. I have no contact at all with New York, and don't care. It's nothing to me, not with you not there.

With affection, as always *Ruth*

TO DIANE KOPEC

January 16, 1989

Dear Diane,

... I've been meaning to get in touch with you ever since I got the last of my vegetable garden out of the ground, last fall. It's a fairly big garden, about 100 x 70 feet, divided in the middle by an asparagus bed. For the last thirty years or so, I have had it tilled twice a year, once in spring, once in fall. The tiller was a big riding tractor, which went about a foot deep. It left hard pan, which needed to be broken up. So this last spring the man who owns the tiller brought a much bigger and heavier tractor, which not only broke up the hard-pan, but dug at least a foot below it, turning up soil which hadn't been tilled before.

In the section between the asparagus bed and the back end of the garden, I began to find pieces of what looked to me like worked stone, some of them unmistakably so. It didn't seem to me that these stones could be artifacts, because the work on them, if that is what it was, had no hard stone, like felsite, but were all of the soft stone which is local to the region, which is a medium gray stone, quite easily broken in your hands. But always, on each piece there was one smooth side, as if used to smooth something off. Some were pointed. Some were not. There were no arrowheads, the seemingly worked ones were all very rough, untouched, except for the one smooth side. Then I realized that in the section of the garden above the asparagus bed, there were no such stones at all. I picked up as many as I found, and have, now, a couple of boxes full of them.

I don't know if this would interest you at all. So say, if it doesn't. Outside the garden fence, in this edge of the woods, is a pit about six feet deep, which I had always taken as a dried up well belonging to the farmhouse which has left a foundation up by the road.

Thought it wouldn't hurt to let you know. Probably it's nothing at all.

Sincerely *Ruth Moore*

TO ELLEN SMITT-STROOPER

February 17, 1989

Ms. Ellen Smitt-Strooper De Waarden
171 7206 G.D. Zutphen
The Netherlands

Dear Ms. Smitt,

Thank you for your pleasant letter.

I'm delighted to send you a copy of my book of ballads, *Cold as a Dog and the Wind Northeast,* which is enclosed. This is a free gift from me to "my Dutch fan."

Additional copies can always be ordered from Gordon Bok, Box 840, Camden, Maine, 04843, who is now the publisher of this paperback.

I have written some other ballads. Not yet in print, but which will be included in my book of collected poems; I am now working on this, and hope to have it finished sometime within the next year.

Winter, which is a splendid time to work—below zero seems to stir around in the brain and there are few callers, all the neighbors being out of sight under blankets and boots.

Thanking you sincerely again, and with good wishes for the New Year.

Yours *Ruth Moore*

TO GARY LAWLESS

March 20, 1989

Dear Gary,

Never mind the royalties—you already know what I told you about them. You sound discouraged, and I'm really sorry about that. You've certainly kept me going.

So far as I'm concerned, I've never even thought of anyone but you as publisher of the new book of poems I've been working on all winter. I think I'm nearly finished with it—what it needs now is a good editor—I have what I think is a good title for it, as I suggested to you—*The Tired Apple Tree,* which is a longish narrative poem—can be taken as satire or as goody-goody sweet, depending on what the reader thinks of it, if he manages to get to the end of it. Then I've got "The Bay People," which takes up the bulk of the book. Then "Children's," some of which I can't stand myself; then a lot of new poems which can't be classified, but which drift around in what's left, including five or six Ballads which haven't been printed anywhere, but which are well-known because I've let them go to young performers like Jackson Gillman and Dennis Damon, etc. who come and ask if I've got anything new which they can use. Altogether, it's got more subjects than the Bible, though I can't attempt to quote.

I've half a mind to dump the whole thing onto you and let you and Beth have a go at organizing it. I do like Beth's jackets. I have a photograph of an ammonite, which might fit in as a frontispiece, if not too expensive a matter. You have my permission to use what royalties you have already on hand, if you want to.

Let me have a word, and as usual, bless you,

Ruth

TO SANFORD PHIPPEN

March 25, 1989

Dear Sandy,

Look, you great booby, in all the letters you have written to me, you've never sent me an address, home or otherwise. So the only way I can reach you with a letter has been to send it to the *Puckerbrush Review,* because I do know that you're on the masthead there. Fortunately, this time you did.

Of course I wrote you, right away, saying how much I liked *People Trying to Be Good* ... I think it's tremendous, and I've recommended it to a great many people, whenever I have had the chance to. What I'm looking forward to now is some new writing from you.

I've got my nose to the grindstone, trying to finish up a volume of *Collected Poems,* which Gary Lawless is going to publish as soon as I can get it finished ... it's been a job, because it goes back to 1927 ... a longish narrative poem published in the *Saturday Review* of those days, which of course is not now the same as it was when Christopher Morley ran it. What it needs now, is a good editor—what to include and what to throw out? I find my latitude-and-longitude is somewhat flaky now.

You know, of course, that I'd be delighted to see you at any time you have time to drop by.

As always, *Ruth*

As it turned out, the poem "Voyage" published in the *Saturday Review* in 1929 did not get included in *The Tired Apple Tree* collection.

TO GARY LAWLESS

April 5, 1989

Dear Gary,

Thanks for your letter, and your offer to help organize my poetry manuscript, which I most certainly need. My feeling, now that we are supposedly ducking winter and five days into spring which consists of snow, rain, fog and drizzle, is to drop the damn thing page by page down the john and flushing.

What do you think about my title, *The Tired Apple Tree?* Now that apples are being banned from markets because they are poisoned, and getting a great deal of publicity in the Press? Wouldn't a better title for the book be *Collected Poems?* It's almost as if I were riding along on this ready-made publicity. And no way of letting anyone know that I got there first.

I don't think, now, that dividing the book into parts, like "The Bay People," "Children's," etc. makes much sense.

I'll be happy to take your advice, and thank you for it.

I'll send the whole works to you, at Blackberry Books, Chimney Farm, Nobleboro, in a few days to come. I've still a few pieces to add to it.

Affectionately, *Ruth*

Apples were being banned at the time because of "alar," with which some apples were sprayed.

TO GARY LAWLESS

May 1, 1989

Dear Gary,

I'll be delighted to see you and Beth on May 10. Not only then, but any time, as you know, goes without saying.

Come to lunch if you'd like to, but before you decide, let me know if you both like lobster. It's easily got here and takes very little time to cook. The reason I mention this, is because of Sven, whom I never can ask to a meal because he's completely vegetarian, if that, and won't eat anything Esther and I can offer—local pesticides, Alar, and whatever. So be sure to let me know.

I can surely use the extra time to put on the poetry manuscript—it's practically finished, except for a few more pieces to work into it, and some copying to be made. To be able to talk to you face to face about it will be wonderful.

Love, as ever, *Ruth*

In June of 1989, Esther had to go to the hospital in Bangor for an operation. She was gone for six weeks, and during this time, Ruth's health began to degenerate. She neglected to take care of herself, wouldn't eat; and by the time Esther was home in July, she noticed Ruth wasn't well.

Ruth entered the Mount Desert Island Hospital where she was treated for dehydration; and in September, Ruth decided herself that she wanted to move to Summit House, a nursing home in Bar Harbor.

On November 29, Gary Lawless and Beth Leonard visited Ruth there, where they finalized plans for Ruth's last book, *The Tired Apple Tree*. Gary remembers that Ruth had a poem in her typewriter and the title was "I Have Seen Horizons."

On December 2, 1989, Ruth suffered from an aneurysm and she was moved back to the Mount Desert Island Hospital, where on December 3, she died. On her gravestone, there is a plaque that reads: "I have seen horizons."

Appendices

Appendix A

MIRIAM COLWELL

My acquaintance with Ruth and Eleanor began over forty years ago, when Eleanor wrote me a note soon after my first novel, *Wind Off the Water,* was published by Random House. Ruth was still working at *The Reader's Digest,* and they were living in the Pleasantville, New York area. The next time I came down to New York City Eleanor and I met for lunch at the member's restaurant on one of the upper floors of the Museum of Modern Art.

There seems to be a lapse of time after that, until Ruth had resigned her job, they had built their house at Bass Harbor on the road to the lighthouse (Eleanor and her father built it), and suddenly we were all good friends, Ruth, Eleanor, Chenoweth Hall, and I. Over the next twenty years or so we saw a good deal of each other.

There was a wonderful weekend on Gott's Island in the house where Ruth was born and grew up. There was an expedition together to visit Elisabeth Ogilvie and Dorothy Simpson, with an overnight stay on Elisabeth's Gay's Island below Thomaston.

We visited back and forth between Prospect Harbor and Bass Harbor (McKinley then) very often, getting splendidly oiled and argumentative over before dinner drinks, and gradually sobering with a big dinner before the fifty mile drive home. Those were years when we were all writing, Chenoweth was painting and carving wood and stone, and middle and old age were as far removed as the next century.

Ruth and Eleanor always had a big vegetable garden, and at one memorable meal when Chenoweth and I were exclaiming over the first lovely taste of spring asparagus, Ruth remarked airily, Oh, asparagus is a weed with us!

I remember their two big tiger cats, and a family of chipmunks who lived in the ground just outside their livingroom window.

Eleanor was very much involved in town affairs, and served a long term as Chairman of the Tremont Board of Selectmen.

One very cold Thanksgiving, we all had dinner at Eleanor's mother's house in Southwest Harbor, and on a walk afterward, our two Border Collies, one quite old, plunged into an icy pond for a swim, but without apparent harm to their health as they had raced themselves dry again before we got back to the house.

The warmth of our friendship never wavered, or our affection for each other, but as time went on, as often happens, we began to see each other less often, our widening interests were taking us all in different directions.

After Chenoweth retired form the Art Department, University of Maine at Machias, and I retired from the Prospect Harbor P.O., we began to spend half the year in Georgia, and were rarely in touch.

Ruth wrote a sad note to us at Jekyll Island when Eleanor died, not wanting us to learn of her death through the *Ellsworth American.* I think our last visit with Ruth, and her sister Tug (Esther), was over lunch at Annabelle's restaurant at Seawall. That day, with Eleanor gone, our lovely times together, those clamorous happy evenings, seemed very much in the past, along with our youth.

They were both wonderful warm and generous friends, and the years we shared so many happy hours together are precious memories.

ELISABETH OGILVIE

Ruth's first book, *The Weir,* came out just before my first book, *High Tide at Noon.* I was understandably apprehensive, wondering if my career was to be drowned at birth by this. I had thought until then that I had the whole coast of Maine to myself. Well, I bought and began the book—nervously and reluctantly—and one chapter into it had me hooked. She was GOOD.

I stopped worrying, because our styles were so different. There was plenty of room for both of us, and so it has always been.

I knew many of her books before I knew her. The meeting came about after I reviewed Miriam Colwell's first book, *Wind Off the Water,* and was so impressed by it I wrote her a letter. Miriam introduced us, and it seemed as if I had always known this peppery, no-nonsense witty woman.

I wish we had lived nearer to one another; work, and Life itself, made the distance much greater. But we got into correspondence again a few years ago, by happy accident when someone mixed up our addresses and I received a letter meant for her. Her letters were like herself as she had always been. She was working on a book but not hurrying, she said; modern publishing being what it is, one never knew what to expect from one month to the next.

It was a good time, though short. I'm glad I had that much contact with Ruth, and I wonder if she finished that book. And I miss her.

DOROTHY SIMPSON

I don't think I really knew much of Ruth Moore till I saw the movie *Deep Waters* being made in Rockland, particularly a scene in front of the court-house. I was amazed to see a supposedly modern sea captain dressed like somebody in the 1880s. Then Ruth Moore with some friends came to call at Tides' Way, Gay's Island, and by that time I knew she was a writer and I liked her style.

I began enjoying her personality at once, her wit and cheery way; and while we walked the wooded paths on the island, with every one joining in the varied conversations, I learned that Ruth and I had a lot in common. Especially about people from away.

My childhood island (Criehaven) is 25 miles at sea, and the people from away didn't look down their noses at you. They liked you, were really interested in you as a person and all you did and were.

In later years I left that island for one just a stone's throw from the mainland, and more people from away than I had ever imagined came walking up the path to the house where I now live. Many have been welcomed if they returned, but those who seem to have what I call wizened minds I never want to see again.

Ruth Moore had told me to wait before going into such glowing comments about those I had known so well, who had come from away. I learned the wisdom of her words.

I never met her many times, but it was always good fun and interesting conversation when she was close by. I always wished I could have seen more of her. She really entertained. She will never be forgotten.

GORDON BOK

Before I knew of Ruth's novels, I found the little hardbound book *Cold as a Dog and the Wind Northeast* and was astounded by it. Like a British dialect monologue, but our own!

I began to read these to my friends, realized I had memorized some, and, at my friends' suggestion, began to tell them in concert.

Soon my audience began to ask for the original, which I found was out-of-print. The publishers showed no inclination to reprint it, so I asked Sandy Ives (of Northeast Folklore) how to get permission to reprint. He said, "Ask Ruth," and told me where to find her.

When Ruth agreed to meet with me, I was unaware that she knew of my music. She said, "First of all, I feel it behooves me to come down on you severely for performing my work without my permission."

Eleanor leaned forward in her chair and said, "Oh yes, Ruth, come right down on him. I've got to see this." From then on it was second gear all the way.

I visited her rarely, but each time was a delight, especially introducing her to Kendall Morse, that great singer and storyteller (originally from Machias)—and watching those two go at it together. That was a grand old ride, and I hardly got my oars wet.

She was always encouraging of other writers, artists, performers. I have a lot to thank her for, there.

It seemed to me she was always more interested in the work of an artist, rather than the product, which is as sure a guarantee of sanity as an artist can find, these days.

And she seemed to well know (as Kendall is wont to say): "Life goes on—whether you're enjoying it or not."

JOHN GOULD

Back in the 1940s William Morrow (who published both Ruth Moore and me) sold my *Farmer Takes a Wife* to *Reader's Digest*, and I was dismayed.

Reader's Digest is the bathroom substitute for culture that takes living literature and decomposes it to the duration of a bowel movement, offering folks of fourth-grade ability a chance to amuse themselves while on the hopper—an article a day of lasting interest. It isn't all that much fun to be digested. An honest hack can toil mightily and bring forth something like: The place of our leaving was the breakfast shore of Serenity Cove, where poplar leaves were rustling in the dawn's first breeze at the lingering edge of darkness, and a timid doe, head up, was anxiously alert as her fawn had a drink.

Anything like that comes out in *Reader's Digest* as, Our point of departure was...

So I was dismayed. Then the good word came that Ruth Moore, then working at *Reader's Digest* but yearning to be free, would condense my book. I now had no qualms. I knew that once Ruth finished, the dozens of surgical editors at *Reader's Digest* would never dare to monkey with her version. Had they, the hullabaloo and ruckus would have been clearly visible back home at Bass Harbor Head in a fogmull. And about the time my digested book appeared in *Reader's Digest* Ruth came home to Bass Harbor and lived happily ever after. She never disputed my contention that her condensation of *Farmer Takes a Wife* was the only decent digestion the magazine ever printed. I loved Ruth Moore.

Ruth came to build her home on the Bass Harbor Head road. In the ceiling of her livingroom is an inadvertent hammer pockmark that I contributed while helping put up sheetrock. Ruth wouldn't let me plaster and conceal it. When there came visitors that Ruth cared enough about to ask them in, she would point to my dimple in the ceiling and make a snide remark about the ineptitude of cheap help from the mainland.

E. B. WHITE

On May 16, 1953, E.B. White wrote Dorothy Lobrano, his god-daughter, a letter about Ruth Moore. It is reproduced here:

Dear Dottie:

I've just finished *A Fair Wind Home* and it gave me a fine time. Thanks for sending it and for the other Ruth Moore book. She is certainly a natural story teller and when she gets her hooks in you, there is no escape. I think one reason she's so good is that she has such affection for the people she's writing about; there is just no substitute for that kind of emotion. Of course, like all historical novelists, she occasionally gives my credulity an awful shaking up. When Frank Carnavon throws Lizabeth into the sea from the deck of the *Turkey Feather*, climbs down a rope ladder, cuts the skiff free, and then finds Lizabeth dog-paddling her way to the boat, I began to tremble with disbelief. I even started to do a little quiet arithmetic on the side. The *Turkey Feather* was running before a gale, which means that she was probably doing about nine knots—but we will call it eight to be conservative. Eight knots is roughly 48,000 feet per hour, or 800 feet per minute. I figure that Frank Carnavon, a heavy man, must have taken at least a minute to scramble down the ladder and cut himself adrift, but we will give Miss Moore the benefit of the doubt and say that he was able to manage it in 45 seconds—a very credible performance in a gale. That means that when the skiff dropped free of the ship, Lizabeth was left approximately 600 feet behind, or more than six times the distance between third base and home. "God help all," thought Carnavon, and I echoed his thought. The woman had all her clothes on, presumably didn't know much about swimming, and was surrounded by cresting waves. Carnavon describes her as "a good, sweet woman, honest as the day," but I think she was far more than that, if she made it to the skiff. She was practically Esther Williams.

K and I had a flashy trip to Maine last week, carrying a dachshund puppy in a rented car. Now we are chewing our fingernails waiting to get back on June 1.

Lots of love, *Andy*

MARY DILLON

I met Ruth because she and Eleanor were in New York and she was looking for work and she hadn't found a job she liked the looks of; and she needed a job badly. She had written but hadn't sold *The Weir* yet. The war was on—this must have been 1942–43; and she had taken on the responsibility of Eleanor, who was nearly twenty years younger. Ruth had been working in California for Alice Tisdale Hobart, the author of *Oil for the Lamps of China*. Ruth was a private secretary for her, but she didn't like California. From the west coast, she came east and she and Eleanor were living in New York City where Ruth had some odd jobs. Somehow, she got the name of a guy named Pendleton Dudley, a long-time friend of the DeWitt Wallaces and PR man for the *Reader's Digest*. Mr. Dudley helped get the magazine going.

I was working at the *Digest* in the editorial correspondence department where we answered letters. I had been doing it for a few years, and it was thought that this was a good place to break Ruth in. They had a method of locating promising people, and Ruth was one. Ruth was not your ordinary applicant. They sent her in to me and I hired her. I had no choice under the circumstances. She was quite a little older than I. Also, I don't like people handed to me like that, and I could tell she was contrary, too. But in the end we got to be very good friends.

She worked there for a year, then shifted over to the book department. At that time the book department was concerned entirely with combing new books for material that could be used in shorter pieces or as supplements in the magazine—not the same as the later condensed book operation. Ruth was reading all the time and cutting then. She edited, but she never wrote for the *Digest*. They did, however, condense at least one of her books for the magazine and one for the condensed book series (*Walk Down Main Street*).

I knew Ruth didn't like much of what was published about Maine. She was edgy about Maine. She had her own view—highly prejudiced. The way Ruth could talk about summer people was unforgettable. Since I was then a summer person, our relationship could be edgy, too.

Ruth worked at the *Digest* for about three years; and she and Eleanor had an apartment in White Plains near Pleasantville where the *Digest* is.

Ruth knew my two daughters, Joanne and Ruthie, from my first marriage; and after I was married to Lou Dillon and had Jay and Mary, Ruth took quite an interest in all my children.

We went to stay with her once on Gott's Island—the summer of 1945 for two weeks. Ruth's mother was doing the cooking. Her mother was forceful, outspoken, and a very good cook. She didn't especially like strangers coming in. I had some of that feeling. It was strange to meet the people of *The Weir* in person. Mr. Gott, the man who ran the mailboat, could have stepped right out of her book. The speech was wonderful. I was new to Maine then, and I hadn't heard such talk. Ruth had captured it perfectly.

Ruth was a lot of fun to have in the office. Writing the letters, too, was always kind of fun. She got a kick out of it. She was also, of course, very far away from the *Reader's Digest*'s political posture. She had to hold in quite a lot of indignation about some of the stuff we published. Always my trouble, too, so we saw eye to eye in that area. We figured out a way to work with it.

They used to always have a Christmas party in the editorial department, and they got bigger and bigger. They finally made a change, so that one year there was a stag party for the men and a luncheon for the ladies. Mrs. Wallace presided over the latter and it was held in the magazine's cafeteria. There were place cards and I wasn't placed next to Ruth, but Mrs. Wallace was. When I went to get her that day, I found Ruth happily drinking martinis with a kindred spirit at twelve noon. They had been at it since 11 a.m., and were feeling no pain. At the luncheon, no one else was drinking and Ruth was at the point where she might say anything and get obnoxious. I was very nervous about her that afternoon, especially since she was sitting next to the boss's wife.

Ruth left the *Digest* and New York for Maine after the success of *Spoonhandle* in 1946; and after we bought the land in Hancock and had a house built, I'd usually drive over once a summer to Bass Harbor with my kids to visit. Eleanor and Ruth came to Hancock, too, for several visits.

DONALD MORTLAND

I met Ruth Moore only once, as I shall explain below, but I first encountered her novels in 1946. I was in the Army, stationed at Camp Atterbury, Indiana. There was a library on the base, not far from my barracks, and I spent some of my free time there. One day a new Maine book appeared called *Spoonhandle*. Somewhat homesick for Maine, I suppose, I read it with great pleasure that ripened into enthusiasm. I knew nothing of the author, Ruth Moore, except what the dust jacket said, but I remembered the book and the author's name and tried to get hold of each of her books as they came out thereafter.

That fall I was out of the Army, back home in Maine, and soon in college (Bowdoin), to prepare for life and for a career as an English teacher. After two years of teaching and a year at Yale for graduate study, I was again teaching, this time in the high school in Southwest Harbor. Ruth Moore's novels were always easy to sell to most students, but in Southwest many of the students knew the author, making her work of special interest. Indeed, several of my students were her nieces and nephews. One day after I had spoken to my seniors (who were studying American literature) about the excellence of her novels, one of the senior boys, a modest, quiet, clean-cut young fellow, said to me with quiet pride, "You know that Ruth Moore is my aunt." I assured him that I had guessed as much.

Living in Southwest Harbor, only minutes from her home in Bass Harbor, I learned of Ruth's love of privacy and made no attempt to meet her. I came to know and like her sister, Mrs. Trask, who at that time sometimes taught English with me as a substitute. I continued to admire Ruth's novels.

Two of my best students at Southwest Harbor were Kenneth Hutchins and Meredith Rich, later Mr. and Mrs. Kenneth Hutchins. In August of 1976, knowing of my keen interest in Ruth Moore's novels, Kenneth and Meredith kindly took my wife and me out to Black Island, where we picnicked, and back to Great Gott Island, Ruth Moore's birthplace and childhood home. As far as I can recall, no one was on the island that day except Mr. and Mrs. Ted Holmes. As Kenneth had some business to transact with Mr. Holmes, we made our way up to their house and spent a pleasant hour with them. Thus, although I still had not met Ruth Moore, she was responsible for my meeting Ted Holmes.

Oddly perhaps, the thing that I remember best about the afternoon, or the part spent on the island, was that as we were walking back down to the shore, Mr. Holmes stooped every now and then to pull something from the grass. Eventually I realized that he was pulling spruce seedlings as one would weeds, for indeed spruce trees grow like weeds on those offshore islands, and he was saving the view for future generations.

I don't think that Kenneth and Meredith knew Ruth Moore very well, but of course they knew of her, not only as a novelist, but almost as a fellow townsperson, as Bass Harbor is so close to Southwest Harbor. Meredith Hutchins is now becoming a new Maine writer, having reached a point in her life where she can devote full time to writing and having published recently in *Down East* and some other periodicals.

After three years at Southwest Harbor, I taught in a variety of schools in Maine and New Hampshire, and in 1966, when Unity College opened, I came home to teach here and have ever since that time. In 1976, I persuaded Unity College to confer upon Ruth Moore an honorary doctorate. This produced an exchange of letters (*q.v.*). She was in the midst of writing *The Dinosaur Bite* and so did not wish to come to Unity for the ceremony; therefore the degree was granted in absentia. I composed and read some introductory remarks and the citation [see Appendix B].

In 1977, I wrote a short article about her work and it was published in Maine Life. I'm not sure that Ruth ever saw it [see Appendix B].

In March of 1979, I published a longer article in the *Colby Library Quarterly*. (A copy is enclosed.) This brought another exchange of letters (*q.v.*). Her answer to my mild objection to the amount of profanity in her novels is a classic, I think. I have read it to numerous friends and to classes in which I have discussed her work. I have been teaching a course entitled Maine Writers for about fifteen years and have always used at least one of her novels in it, usually *Spoonhandle*. This year I decided to go all out, as it will be my last year of teaching, and I'm using two of her novels, *Spoonhandle* and *The Walk Down Main Street*.

On October 7, 1982, I gave a lecture on her works at the public library in Southwest Harbor, thanks to my friends Kenneth and Meredith Hutchins. Ruth didn't come, but her sister, Mrs. Trask, did. She urged me to come to see Ruth, but we both agreed that the timing was bad for that evening. The lecture was to begin in a few minutes, and afterwards it would be late for me to be making my way to Bass Harbor for the first time. Thus I narrowly missed meeting her then.

The summer of 1987 was a big Ruth Moore summer for me. At the end of the summer was the big Ruth Moore Week-end at the Penobscot Marine Museum in Searsport (my old home town). I attended with some of my students. After seeing *Deep Waters*, we knew what Ruth meant by saying that "They butchered it." But during the summer I taught the course as a directed study to one student. After completing it he wanted more, so we arranged an independent study for further study of Maine literature. This student was Greg Burr, who was living in Northeast Harbor at that time. He became especially enthusiastic about Ruth Moore's novels. The rest of this story is told in the letters, but perhaps I should add that the meeting went very well, despite Ruth's dire predictions. Also, Greg and I arrived in Bass Harbor with no trouble, as he knew the way, but we had a devil of a time finding her house. We asked three people (in Bass Harbor!) before we found one who knew where she lived—indeed, who had ever heard of her! We concluded that the others were recent arrivals—non-reading recent arrivals. When we did find the house, we were charmed by it and the location, as I suppose everyone is, but we didn't see any tourists skulking about, and her lilacs seemed to be intact!

My wife and I attended the memorial service for Ruth and felt that it was very appropriate and moving. I spoke briefly of her work and read the citation that I had read when the honorary degree was conferred.

I am most grateful to Gary Lawless for bringing Ruth's novels back into print.

KENDALL MORSE

I'm not sure when I first met Ruth Moore, but it must have been sometime in the late '70s. My good friend, Gordon Bok, had introduced me to a book of poems titled *Cold as a Dog and the Wind Northeast,* sometime in the early '70s. So, when he asked if I would like to meet her, I jumped at the chance. At about this same time, he also loaned me a copy of *Speak to the Winds*. That did it. I now have original hard cover copies of both works autographed by Ruth. Gordon can tell a very funny story about the scene he saw when I tried to pay her for *Cold as a Dog*. I didn't want to take it as a gift, but she felt that it had been taking up space in her back room for years, and that someone should get some use out of it. Finally, I reminded her of a line from Jack London's *Martin Eden,* in which he states, it is a work performed, even if it doesn't sell, and she stated that she was not Jack London! I wasn't about to pass up getting a copy of that book just to win an argument, so I gave in and walked away with a hard cover copy of *Cold as a Dog*. Autographed. I can't imagine anyone winning an argument with Ruth Moore.

After receiving an open invitation to visit her whenever I was in the area, I saw her a number of times in the following years. On one occasion, she and her friend Eleanor Mayo were out in the garden weeding. You can imagine how she was dressed for such dirty work. Having brought my camera, I asked Ruth if I might be allowed to take her picture. She asked what I was going to do with it, and I told her nothing. I just wanted a picture of one for whom I had great admiration. After a long silence, she said that it would be O.K. as long as I was not going to use it to make her famous! After taking the shot, I turned and saw Eleanor with her mouth wide open in disbelief. She said, I don't believe it. "No one takes her picture." I felt very special for that.

On another occasion, I stopped by and we were swapping stories and experiences. I had brought along my guitar, so I sang her a song about a boat which went down taking away the Captain's living and his friend. Ruth was in tears, and her only comment was, "You got me with that one, Mister."

One of the more humorous visits involved a true story which Eleanor told me:

In recent years, the people who owned the property next to Ruth had turned it into a campground, and it had become a real problem to Ruth and Eleanor, what with strangers wandering all over their property, picking berries and stealing fire wood. One night about two in the morning, they heard a hair-raising scream outside the house. They figured that a fox had caught a rabbit and it was making a dreadful noise in its last moments. (I've heard that sound myself, and you would not believe what a hideous racket they can make.) It sounded just like someone being murdered. Ruth grabbed the shotgun, stepped out onto the front steps, and let go with both barrels. The screaming stopped instantly, and the next morning that campground was totally empty! We had great fun speculating on what those city folks thought was happening in this savage wilderness!

After I got to know her better, I thought it was safe to make comments about her writing. One time, we were talking about her novel, *Speak to the Winds,* and I told her it was one of the best stories I had ever read. She commented that she wished that more people appreciated her work as much as I did. Sticking my neck out just a tad, I said, "Surely you know that your works lack two essential ingredients, SEX AND VIOLENCE! That's what sells on a grand scale these days." It didn't even faze her. She replied, "I only write what I know about, and I've never had any experience with either!"

I'm sad that she is gone but I will always have a small part of her in my memories, and those two books in my collection. I wouldn't trade either of them for a farm down east with a hog on it.

EDWARD M. HOLMES

When I first met Ruth Moore I was ten years old. That was in the summer of 1921, when an aunt of mine took me and my sisters (rusticators all) to Great Gott's Island, about a mile southwest of Mount Desert Island. For a month we boarded at the home of Ruth's parents there, a hilltop house with a wide view of Blue Hill Bay, of the silhouetted Camden Hills, and of the sunsets. It was where she, her brother, and her sisters had been born and brought up, her family sustaining themselves well with lobster fishing, with a garden, with cows, pigs, chickens, and a woodlot.

Ruth, as later also her sisters did, waited on the summer people's table then, and it was easy for her and me to become friends. She had just finished high school in Ellsworth that year, and went off to college in Albany, New York that fall.

My relatives, by then hooked on the Maine coast, as I was myself, returned to the island summer after summer for more than a decade, at first living at the Moores' home, and later, having bought a house, being summertime neighbors and, some years, boarders for the evening meal.

Ruth always claimed it was she who taught me to swim. I still don't believe it, though we never quarrelled over the matter. It's true I was slow to learn that art, but I know the first assuring strokes I experienced came at a goddamned Scout camp my parents ordered me into in New Jersey, when I knew from the depths of my being I should be on Gott's Island with Ruth Moore, Esther Moore, Louise Moore, their parents and their neighbors. True, summers, year after year, Ruth, Esther, Louise, I, and neighbors did swim a lot on Gott's Island's Inner Pool, a placid, sheltered tidal inlet, pure then, contaminated now.

After college, Ruth tried teaching, disliked it and quit. She moved to New York City, struggled with secretarial jobs, and in 1931 even came to the University of Maine to work toward a Master's Degree in English. One of my sisters, my college roommate, and I breezed in to Orono that fall and corralled Ruth to go down to the coast and to Gott's Island for a three-day weekend. By that time, the island village had disappeared, all of the fourteen island families having moved ashore about 1926, but we few all felt good about being there for a day or two in a non-vacation season; even my roommate had been contaminated by the Gott's Island virus a few months before.

Three months later, Ruth left academia (in the 1940s, the University of Maine awarded her an Honorary Master's Degree) and returned to New York City. There was a gap in seeing her at all when she went off to California to be manuscript typist and companion for Alice Tisdale Hobart, author of *Oil for the Lamps of China*, but for some years of the 1930s and into the 1940s she was in New York City in a small but comfortable apartment on Minetta

Lane, Greenwich Village. In the years of the Depression, years when I was around New York job hunting or working briefly here, there, and everywhere, Greenwich Village was a delightful place, especially Ruth Moore's residence where the modest but congenial parties, New Year's Eve or any other eve, were great fun. Also there were good times to talk about books, and about writing. Once Ruth suggested she and I collaborate on a novel. I felt complimented, thought about it, and declined. I doubted that we could go at writing quite the same way, or in ways that would harmonize. Probably, I believe, I was right. At all events, Ruth did extremely well without me.

She was working for *The Reader's Digest* in 1943 when her novel, *The Weir,* was accepted for publication by William Morrow and Company. Some time later came *Spoonhandle* and the sale of its movie rights, which enabled Ruth to desert New York and return to Maine; for a while, now and then, to Gott's Island, but essentially to a woodsy portion of the Town of Tremont on Mount Desert Island where she had someone build the house she wanted to live in and write in. Gott's Island, by then overflowing with far too many out-of-state summer people, no longer appealed to her. Indeed, she felt alienated from it.

As the decades passed and I and my wife and children moved from one to another of seven communities in Maine, we now and then saw Ruth, at first, for a time, on Gott's Island, where through a few full years we lived, but more often at her home in Bass Harbor, part of the Town of Tremont. I remember especially the pleasure of reporting to Ruth that her book of poetry, *Cold As a Dog and the Wind Northeast,* had become an assigned reading in an American literature course at the University of Maine.

Then, in her last year—no, her last month, December 1989—I drove to Bar Harbor to see Ruth at the nursing home where she was, by then, for sound reasons, living. She was up and around, though moving slowly. We had a good talk about her writing, about her writing in progress, about our mutual failures of memory. Ruth said she liked that mountain-top home from which, on high, one could look out over Frenchman's Bay, not really so far from, nor so different from the Blue Hill Bay beside which she had grown up. I believe she liked the place for other reasons too, for I noticed that the attendants kidded her in a friendly manner, and she kidded back. It was precisely what she would like, what she needed.

As I think back, I am strongly glad that she could see published, and some of them republished, the works she did, not just the ones mentioned here so far, but also *The Walk Down Main Street, Time's Web, Second Growth, The Fire Balloon,* and others. They are a valuable contribution, not just to Maine writing, but to literature.

BETTY HOLMES BALDWIN

I first went to Gott's Island in 1917 with family members, very much summer people all. I knew Ruth only casually; for instance, when her father or brother would take us on a trip to some neighboring island. It was when we started boarding at the Moores'—by that time Ted, 8 years my junior, had joined us—that the real acquaintance with Ruth began. Ted's memories and mine coincide—trying to learn to swim in the cold Inner Pool, sitting on the porch after competing in doing the dinner dishes, and watching the sun set over Blue Hill Bay with Camden Hills outlined in the distance. Other things I remember: Ruth rowed Ted and me over to Black Island the year it burned. In a dry year if a fire gets started on one of the Islands, it burns underground through the centuries of sprills dropped by the fir trees; that year the abandoned village burned house by house. We wandered about among the pathetic buildings and ruins and helped one house to meet its fate and felt very devilish. I got pictures of Ted and Ruth sitting among the cinders trying to act the part of the burned-out.

Ruth's flair for storytelling showed up in skits which we used to put on with or without an audience, scenes from *Alice in Wonderland:* the Mad Tea Party, the baby howling in the kitchen, the Frog Footman delivering the Letter to Play Croquet to the Queen (my sister Florence played the Frog Footman). Then we moved on to more and more elaborate Charades, which grew into social affairs held in the evening at various houses. I recall the walks through the woods at night with swinging lanterns—very scary—and refreshments at Miss Peterson's house at the Head. Daytimes we'd think of long words to use next time, and costumes could be anything.

Esther seems to have given me credit for starting Ruth toward college. I don't recall doing so, though Ruth being only one year my junior was ready for college. It was my aunt, Miss Caroline Holmes, who had bought and fixed up one of the empty farm houses, where we stayed after boarding at the

Moores', who loaned Ruth the money to go to college. I also recall that Ruth, when she finally got to earning money, repaid my Aunt in full, much to my Aunt's pleasure.

Ruth and I used to walk at night and have long talks; the moonlight nights of course, but I especially think of the clear "dark of the moon" nights when the Milky Way was like a carpet thrown across the sky. People speak of Ruth's edginess and I've heard her often enough, but to us her teasing and calling us "rusticators" was always said with a twinkle in the eye. Ruth had a big part in helping me to grow up, or, perhaps to learn not to be so scared of life, and although for several years we didn't see much of each other until the New York days that warmth continued.

Once in the '20s when I was teaching in the Berkshires, Ruth and I met at the cottage of Mary White Ovington for whom she was secretary in Miss O's work to help the Negro people. While I was there James Weldon Johnson and his wife drove up to talk business. Ruth had known Miss O. from her cottage at Gott's Island (the Fifth Avenue Ovingtons, though I don't recall the connection).

After five years teaching I went to California and got a job as a social worker; so in 1931 I returned East and enrolled at the New York School of Social Work in New York. Ruth by that time was secretary to John Haynes Holmes (no relation) who was then a well known preacher. Ruth had an apartment on Minetta Lane in Greenwich Village across from the music school whose vocal and instrumental students could clearly be heard through open windows. It was a two-room basement apartment with an area entrance right off the sidewalk. The front room contained a bed and a fireplace, the back room a bathtub and a two-burner gas plate—maybe a sink but I don't remember. Like most Village apartments this also had its share of cockroaches nearly as big as mice it seemed. We had a bootlegger (it was Prohibition) who brought Booth's gin which we mixed with orange juice, usually no ice. Friends brought friends. When the orange blossoms held sway we'd sing St. James Infirmary, or The Bastard King of England, or Frankie and Johnnie or some such, which of course I had learned from Ruth. Friends knew enough to bring along pieces of scrap wood or broken wooden boxes which they found in the gutter to keep the fire going—once someone brought the back of a broken cello. Ted came, on the edge of unemployment; Ralph Babbidge, who had grown up on Gott's Island near Ruth; and Ted Kingsbury, though I doubt he remembers. All were welcome. By that time I had gotten an apartment on Minetta Street two blocks away—no more commuting to New Jersey. Ruth was doing some writing then. Not novels, lyric poetry as I recall, but now I can't seem to find that type of writing in any of her more recent books. Probably she found poetry didn't sell as well as fiction. After my one year at School of Social Work I commuted to Long Island to work at the Red Cross, still living on Minetta Street two blocks from Ruth. Then suddenly in the summer of '33 my father died and things fell apart. I went home a lot and then in the winter was suddenly offered a job in Boston—child guidance—just what I wanted. So I moved to Boston in April 1934.

Once in New York when Ruth needed money for some medical expense, I loaned her $1000, since I had a bit of private income. After the War when I was without a car and too poor to buy one, Ruth suddenly sent me the $1000 with interest carefully computed over the years. She had just sold *Spoonhandle* to the movies. What a godsend! I went right out and bought a car.

What a marvellous person she was!—not only in her art and her imagination, but in her personal relationships as well!

HARRIS MCLEAN

My earliest recollection of Ruth was in the early 1930s when I went out to Gott's Island with my great-great uncle Charles Welch (he was the treasurer of the Christian Science Church in the U.S.). He lived and worked in Boston, but he used to come home for his annual pilgrimage back to Gott's Island. For some particular reason, my mother, Fannie Amanda Joyce, wasn't able to go. She suggested that perhaps I'd like to go. So, I went with my uncle in a lobster boat—he had hired someone to take us out—and we landed at the inner pool and walked up to the Moore house where we stayed overnight.

Getting there, there was a rip tide between Bass Harbor Head and Gott's Island and we were tossed around a bit.

By the inner pool, there were a few little shacks. One of them was Mont Gott's house. He was an island character and he had a little backhouse that was painted Gott's Island Blue. There was an apple tree just beyond the backhouse, and the story was how Mont got his deer every year by sitting in the backhouse and shot the deer grazing for apples from there. Mont always had toilet paper hanging out of his pocket.

Ruth's father was the postmaster and the post office was in their house. This was at the same time that Ruth was at the University of Maine getting her Master's. I was quite impressed because she was a good looking gal and her job was waiting on tables. She was the boss of the dining room. As a young fellow, I was amazed that a University of Maine graduate student would be actually waiting on tables! And felt quite privileged!

The room that I stayed in that night was a front room, a small bedroom. I could look out at the pool and see my grandmother's house across the path.

Now, being another generation, I wasn't as close to Ruth as my mother was. It wasn't until years later, after I came back home after World War II and started working in the Liberty National Bank in Ellsworth, that I had any interest in returning to Gott's Island. Unfortunately, my mother gave away the property that we had out there, so there wasn't any close contact. The reason she gave it away was because she thought nobody in the family would ever go back to the island. Then, with my interest, through my wife Mary, of getting into genealogy, I really began tracking down my ancestors and establishing that relationship.

One little story that might be of interest to you:

When Ruth and my mother were young girls, my grandfather had a big Friendship sloop, one of the last ones that was built down at Friendship Yard. In fact, he used to sail some summer people at Hancock Point summers and the rest of the time he used the boat for fishing—dragging scallops and ground fishing. This was my grandfather Clarence Joyce. One day, my mother Fannie Amanda and Ruth decided they would be stowaways, so they went down in the cabin and hid. My grandfather got out to sea a little ways, and up they popped! He was quite upset because he wasn't planning to come back right away, but, evidently, he decided, well, while they were there, they were going to have to make the best of it. As my mother told the story, they caught a big haddock and my grandfather made a fish chowder. The two young girls had quite an experience as stowaways.

My grandfather came from Swan's Island and my grandmother, Myra Mueller, came from Gott's. Her father, Heinrich Carsten Friedrich Müller, captain of a German whaling ship, was shipwrecked on Gott's Island. Parts of the remains of the wreck are still there. In fact, Ruth told me that she and her family used to go down to the wreck and get some of the ship's timbers to use as structural timbers on their house. Captain Müller liked what he saw on Gott's Island so he stayed and he married into the Moore family. Of course, the German crew couldn't speak any English, but they came up and knocked on the door of the Moore house and said, "Ve are castavamen. Let us in." I often wondered what my grandfather thought—being German and being (washed up) on Gott's Island, which in German would be "God's Island."

My mother, of course, read all of Ruth's books and she would say, "Oh, that character was so and so." All of Ruth's work was based on fact. That's why it's so good.

In later years, as my interest in genealogy became almost a disease, I went to visit Ruth to get a few things straight. She introduced me to Gerald Joyce's letters and our *Mayflower* ancestor.

She and Eleanor lived there at Bass Harbor. Later on, after Eleanor died, Esther came. Ruth was always such an interesting person to talk to—always smoking cigarettes. At one time, Ruth made notes from Susanna Gott's diary for my wife Mary. When Mary and I visited Ruth, we talked about family and island life.

A good source on Ruth might be Northwood Kenway. His family came to the island for years and lived right in the middle of the Moore property. There were some family connections way back. He now lives in Southwest Harbor and on Gott's Island in the summers. He has taken upon himself personally and financially (even though my uncle left a small trust fund) to maintain the Gott's Island cemetery. The railing which had some unusual turnings was repaired. Kenway now has the only generator on Gott's Island—so he can play his electric organ! He's a good fellow—a former summer resident and Harvard grad.

One more Gott's Island story: when Admiral Byrd used to live nearby, he used to sail out to Gott's Island. One day in the fog he ran aground on the ledges on the southside of the island. Since then, they are known as Byrd's Ledges.

CONSTANCE HUNTING

[Reprinted from *This Month in Maine Literature,* February 1990]

Last summer [1989] I had the privileged pleasure of reading aloud on MPBN, under the wise tutelage of Virgil Bisset, Ruth Moore's novel *The Walk Down Main Street,* in the radio series "The Maine Reader." Each

Monday for several weeks, we taped for six hours (with brief breaks) five or six sections of her novel, which would then be cut into half hour segments for daily radio presentation. To read at such length is to subject a work to the most severe kind of sense scrutiny. For to put the words of a novel, usually read silently to oneself, in air will expose any weakness of language and any faltering of style. Ruth Moore never let me down. Always as the hours of reading aloud progressed, exhilaration and admiration built—at the remarkable power of this quiet, impeccable style, never fantastic, always rooted in understandable and understanding prose. And that breath of the sentences and their elements was as humanly natural as that of … well, it reminded me of that consummate practitioner, Lewis Carroll.

What a modest mistress of her art and craft was Ruth Moore! Private in person, seeking not limelight but light for our language, she never lost sight of the primary integrity of words shaped and honed in the service of bringing her "characters," who under such unsparing and loving vigilance were brought live to her readers, fully into robust, if sometimes ornery and quirky and maddening being. And the place of these people: Maine. Nobody knew its granitic, romantic qualities better, no writer made us nod in amused and bemused agreement better. Yes, we say to ourselves, reading on, this is how Maine was and is.

Ruth Moore's work was written. Some readers still have its artistry to meet. All writers of and about Maine have her, whether they realize it or not, as tart and benign godmother; can learn from her as from Flannery O'Connor and Thoreau and Chekhov how to set forth in words the vicissitudes and small triumphs of what some would call ordinary existence. That extraordinary situation … so common, and so profound.

Thank you, Ruth Moore.

JACKSON GILLMAN

My first visit to Ruth Moore's home in Bass Harbor was made with a bit of trepidation. I had been forewarned that she could be fierce about her privacy. And how would she respond to my request for permission to perform her ballads? … Well, Ruth was polite though not particularly warm. She appreciated my courtesy and I was welcome to perform the ballads on the strict condition that I did not tell anyone where she lived.

I asked her if she ever presented the ballads herself, and if so, could I hear one? "Oh golly, no," she said, dismissing those old ballads that she wrote and shelved decades ago, "but I wouldn't mind hearing you tell one." I did. Ruth heartily approved of my treatment. Things warmed up considerably from then on. On subsequent visits a new story was expected and relished each time. Ruth liked hearing her stories brought to life and animated. But she was more eager to hear others in my repertoire, new to her. Over the last decade of her life, I tried to visit a couple of times each year, which was never as much as either of us would have liked. She, Esther and I got to share a lot of stories.

A couple of times I asked if I could bring a visiting friend.—By all means. I chose these friends very carefully ... Buckley Smith was a marine artist sailing in from Vinalhaven and signed her gift copy of *Moonsailors,* his illustrated sailing fantasy. Ruth showed off her own carving handywork ... Doug Elliott was a nature writer from North Carolina with copies of his *Woodslore and Wildwoods Wisdom* book and cassette. On arrival, Doug with a bouquet of Appalachian posies ("I never go courtin' without posies") pays his respects—"I've been a great fan and have been looking forward to meeting you for years." Ruth twinkles back—"Well if I'd have known of you before, I'm sure I'd be a fan of yours too." Generations apart, it seemed they were both smitten. Ruth would joke how much she enjoyed having all these nice young men coming to call on her.

One time she wanted to play a certain song for me on her hi-fi, but no, it wasn't working. How long had it not been working?—Oh, years. Gears churning, I schemed—Ah, this would be a nice gift for her, a new sound system. Later I learned that she and Eleanor built this hi-fi and cabinet themselves. A new stereo?—bad idea, I deduce. Ruth was very surprised and tickled by her gift that year of a repairman who still made house calls, resurrecting her antique and allowing her record collection some new turns on life.

I had never made any recordings myself but my impetus to finally do so, was to produce a recording of her ballads while she was still alive. I did this in 1986. Not only was she very much alive, but she was a welcome and vocal part of the process, nixing some of the interpretation, and sending me back for retaping, resulting in a final product that we were both very proud of. Oh, and Buckley's art work on the cover!

Ruth was not interested in remuneration for the project. I knew it would be years before (and if) I ever saw any profit, but I wanted to give her something. Hmm, what?—I had already given her a number of books. Then I learned that as she no longer drove, and Esther didn't drive at night any more, neither had seen a movie in years. Ah ha. Christmas that year brought "that nice, young repairman" again! (the same that fixed her hi-fi) delivering and installing a VCR in her living room.

A colorful anecdote that I recall that exhibited Ruth's devilish wit and tact, was how she relayed dealing with the Jehovah's Witnesses that came calling on her one afternoon.—"Oh, you're just in time for afternoon refreshment, come on in. ..." Whereupon Ruth graciously opens the cupboard underneath her sink, revealing her liquor cabinet. "What would you like?"—The callers decide that they have other homes they need to call upon. How deft.

My friend Doug reminded me of how some of her stories came out during visits. Doug was soliciting a corroboration of how there was often a young local girl, a female hellion character in her novels, and might there just be a parallel to a certain spunky islander that she once was? (and still was for that matter). "Oh no," she dismisses. "What do you mean?" pipes in Esther. "What about that time you bit that summer lady on the leg?" "Oh yes," confesses Ruth, and the truth and tale ensue ... Ruth as a young girl picking blackberries, whilst an annual summer dignitary promenades by with long dress, bonnet, parasol and all. "Oh, are you a little native girl?" prompting Ruth to sink her teeth into the woman's leg. Savage, you might say. "And mama spanked me for it too, but not too hard. ..."

Prized gifts from Ruth often arose out of her comment about a certain ballad which " ... I've shown you before." "Actually, no, you haven't," I'd correct her. Whereupon she'd hoist herself up out of her armchair, disappear into her room for a bit, rustle around and return with some yellowed papers holding a moldy-oldy. "Read this." I'd offer a cold reading. She'd been holding out on me, another classic. "Well, if you think you can do something with it, take it. No, wait, that's my only copy. I'll have Esther copy it at her office and you can come back and get it another time." This was how T*he Ballad of Sam, The Hard Luck of Ol' Randall,* the *Hang-Downs,* and many others were parcelled out to me one at a time over the years. Lucky and grateful me of course would return for another unpublished gem that I felt was smuggled out to me from her literary treasure trove.

All of these pieces were fortunately included in her last collection of poems and ballads which she had been working on ever since I'd known her. (And others too of course which still hadn't come up in passing.) Three days before her death, her final stamp of approval for that collection was made to Gary Lawless, another one of the privileged few who had earned her confidence and affection. He had already republished several of her out-of-print novels and *The Tired Apple Tree* was published posthumously later that year. Found in her typewriter when she died at 86 was a sheet of paper with four words: I have seen horizons … .

The woman's life and her passing was poetry, equal to that of her writing. Her memorial service was held in the small orchard behind her island home. Her stories were told once again there, with Ruth silently interred but perhaps for her gravelly laugh. A large boulder sitting under a particular tired apple tree served as her monument. Inscribed on it was written:

Ruth Moore 1903 – 1989
I have seen horizons …

DENNIS DAMON

I first met Ruth through her book, *Cold as a Dog and the Wind Northeast,* maybe in 1974. I was teaching a high school class on the topic of the Maine fisherman. This young man, Greg Dow, came up to me and said that his aunt had written a book and that he'd like to have me read it. I didn't do much reading at the time, but he gave it to me—the hard-cover edition—and I put it in my briefcase and there it stayed until a couple of weeks later when he asked me, Is there any chance I can get that book back?

I said, "Jees, Greg, I haven't quite finished it. If you'd just let me have another night …" So, I opened it for the first time and started to read the ballad "The Night Charley Tended Weir," and, well, I had never read anything before that grabbed me quite the way that did. And before I gave the book back to Greg, I shared it with the class, since it had to do with fishing. They really enjoyed it. High school kids can usually be a bit put off by these things, but they really enjoyed it.

So, from then on, every time I taught that class on fishing, I shared more and more of this book with my students. Greg, incidentally, is one of Ruth's grand-nephews.

A few years after that time, in 1979 or 1980, on Father's Day, my wife said to me, "I have a Father's Day present for you, but you'll have to come with me to get it." So, we went down to a place on Mount Desert Island in Bernard to a Dow's house—another Dow who used to play baseball for me—and I asked what are we doing here? They just kind of had Cheshire cat grins on their faces/ and in just a short time, this woman walked in and it was Ruth. At that time, she really wasn't a recluse, but she valued her privacy. She didn't invite people into her house or go out of her way to meet them. So, to have this woman sit down and carry on a conversation with me after all I had felt about her work was really quite a gift. We had a chat for about 15–20 minutes, and that was really it. It was a long time ago. She ended up signing my copy of the book which I have since lost.

In 1986, after I had left teaching at Mount Desert High School, I went to a lecture given by Gary Lawless in Bangor ("The Maine Novel"), after he had started re-publishing Ruth's works; and an awful lot of what he had to say seemed like I already knew (whether I did or didn't is immaterial); but what that evening did was put that bit of spark into me. When I got home from the lecture, I had a big dose of enthusiasm, and I called Ruth up on the phone. She answered and I introduced myself. She said, "Why, of course, I remember you."

After I built up enough nerve, I asked if I could come and visit her.

"I'd love to have you come visit," she said. "When can you come over?"

This was on a Wednesday, and not wanting to seem forward, I asked, "What about on Friday?"

"Oh, Friday isn't good, de-ah. I'm going to have to have this cussed foot checked out by the doctor. What about at one today?"

At one o'clock, I was on her doorstep. We sat down in her living room. I had no agenda. I just had to meet with her again.

She asked, "What do you want to talk about?" She still regarded this as a meeting which might be to pull something from her, and she hated interviews.

I said, "I don't know. I don't really know what to talk about. I just wanted to see you."

We hit it off and what I thought would be another 15-minute meeting turned into a three-hour treasure of a talk. She invited me back. I continued to go back; and from 1986 to 1989, just before she passed on, I had a chance to have some great times with her that will always stay with me. During these times, we'd sit and tell stories back and forth. I'd tell about my childhood and how the things she wrote about I had lived. And she would tell me stories.

One time I read the "Charley" ballad for her, and I never had an audience that responded to it the way she did. At the end she just clapped her hands and said, "That's the way I wrote it." We were sitting in her living room and she was chain smoking, wearing a red flannel shirt and dungarees. She looked at me with those crystal clear eyes of hers. I couldn't have gotten a much better compliment.

She said that it disturbed her that I wasn't still teaching. And that was kind of nice because one of the reasons I'd gotten out of teaching was that I felt I wasn't being appreciated. It was always curious to me what impetus compelled her to leave Gott's Island. If you've come from an island or small town, there's a fear associated with the big wide world. Yet she left there on her own to go to New York State Teachers College in Albany, because her true wish was to be a teacher. She claimed she tried to teach for a year and failed miserably at it. She held teachers and teaching in very high regard. She felt if there were people who could teach—and not everyone can—then they should.

I asked her, too, not only why she would go off the island to travel or go to school, but why she would go to teach, as I had done, too. It was curious to me why I had done so, since that wasn't something my family had done. There were these kinds of threads that bonded us together.

I said, "You know what's happened, Ruth? You've gotten me reading." And again, that night, she looked at me with those eyes and said, "You know, de-ah, that's not all bad."

LARUE SPIKER

"Your Summertime Comes Back Again ..."

I can't remember how I managed to wangle a first interview with Ruth. Later knowing her reluctance to open her privacy to public airing, I am still amazed that she consented. I was writing for the *Bar Harbor Times* then; so it was an interview, not just a social call in spite of a strong personal desire to meet her. Later the relationship developed into a warm and enriching friendship.

Early on, I was summer people. I came in the spring and absconded in the fall. So I had a couple of strikes before ever swinging the bat, but I think Ruth may have sensed a similarity of background, albeit in a different setting, and that led her to overlook the seasonal peregrinations.

Her antipathy for featherless birds of passage may have arisen from her early experiences with snubs. They were a strong element in the relationship between summer people and locals in the early years. I think, as relationships changed, Ruth recognized that incomers could have values for her, but she never forsook her very real respect and affection for the Maine ethos.

Somehow from her name, and Eleanor's, their literary achievement, and apparent remoteness, I had dreamed up an aristocratic couple of people reigning over professionally landscaped gardens and a house with flat white walls to set off carefully selected paintings and pedestals bearing vases of elegantly arranged flowers.

As a result, I donned my best suit, nylons, and heels, no less, for the interview. As soon as I got to the house I was decidedly uncomfortable, and I think Ruth was decidedly amused. She of course was wearing a faded shirt, blue jeans, and ancient sneakers and her big recliner in the corner formed by the windows on the southwest corner of the living room. The books, the brightness, the paneling, and the big rag rug created a warmth it was easy to relax in—had you been dressed for it. I can't remember just what transpired in the interview, but that hardly matters now.

Ruth worked out her tensions and discomforts through her writing. But Eleanor was basically an activist in spite of the novels to her credit; and she was deeply involved in town affairs at the time, holding several responsible positions over the years. Later she worked out some of her creative energy through photography. And she was good at it. Photography and writing must share a common gene; a lot of people have a knack for both.

Ruth's chair looked out on an old apple tree which must have been growing there when they built the house. It was pocked by woodpeckers, tunnelled by worms, and twisted by storm. It didn't produce much for the table (Ruth called them pig apples) due in part to its age and in part because poisons and sprays were anathema to Ruth. But it shone with pink and white in the spring and dropped knotty fruit in the fall. Deer came in to feast on the windfalls. Eleanor got a picture through the window of one of the animals, head raised and muscles tensed for flight.

Technically it was not among her best work because of the glassy barrier between camera and subject, but Ruth was inordinately proud of it, showing it frequently and later framing it for display on the mantel.

In the earlier years she frequently hopped from her chair to point out other examples of Eleanor's efforts—polished stones they had gathered together, jewelry or skill fully crafted furniture. I think that after Eleanor stopped writing novels Ruth felt her need for recognition. Eleanor was perceptive and sensitive as well as talented. She spent a great deal of time in the shop built along the north property line. Chuckling, Ruth called it the "mad house," but it was well equipped and Eleanor spent many productive hours there.

Part of Ruth's admiration for Eleanor's craftsmanship may have arisen from her own lack of manual dexterity. She claimed she couldn't even run the vacuum without getting tangled in the cord.

This may have been a disinclination as much as anything else, for she was a top notch gardener—organic to the core. The big vegetable garden on the rising field across the road prospered and produced prodigiously with Ruth's guidance and sweat. It poured forth the usual staples and each year something a little more exotic. One year they put in strawberries so people around here can afford to have some. Another year she planted poppies so deep in color they were almost black. They kept coming up year after year until I think Ruth was a little haunted by them, but she never grubbed them out, fascinated by their novelty and persistence perhaps. I've always been a bit surprised that a novel titled *The Black Poppy* never appeared, but it has a familiar ring and perhaps someone had already used it.

Ruth was appalled by anything that smacked of imitation. Once she bitterly criticized a well-known Maine writer because she felt one of his books was a development of a device used by Rod Serling in a story. As a matter of fact, her bent toward originality got me in trouble once.

She was full of amusing yarns about people and incidents in the past. I used one of them once as a slice of history in the *Bar Harbor Times* and got into deep doo with some overly sensitive descendants. The story had apparently been richly embroidered as it passed through Ruth's dancing imagination. After that I listened to the yarning with pleasure and let it go at that. Never mistake a novelist's extravaganza with in-depth history.

One of the things I have admired most about Ruth's work is the gusto that transmutes from her personality into her writing. Her style is as robust as was her own orientation toward life. Her characters leap straight from the pages wearing in full costume their blemishes and glories. As a matter of fact, if anything is missing in Ruth's writing it is a sense of mystery, a sense of something unprobed, just beyond reach.

Her style is fast moving, decisive and graphic, especially in its imagery:

> It was foggy. The moving gray wall circled the boat, seemed not more than ten or twenty feet away. (*The Gold and Silver Hooks*)
>
> He's even been known to blast an aged turtle asleep on the creek bank, to see the giblets fly. (*Second Growth*)
>
> At the foot of the boat ramp, the river water, sand colored and roily, splashed up in peaks six inches high. (*Sea Flower*)
>
> Where the ropes of rain drilled into it. (*Sea Flower*)
>
> The thick pencils of rain roared down. (*Sea Flower*)

Some of the best descriptive writing I have ever read occurs in *The Fire Balloon*. It depicts the first slow sigh of the onset of a storm, creating an ominous tension seldom encountered in American fiction.

Ruth had a strong sense of ethics, and if she ever violated it, I never observed the dereliction nor heard of it. Her characters seldom wander from their patterns of basic good or evil. Where there are faults they are the product of the virtues on which the character is based. Her villains are frequently without redeeming qualities in their evil, and somehow the reader experiences a sense of barren loss in their depravity.

One of the characters that sticks in my mind is a small girl, who appears in a number of the books. She is a proud youngster with keen sensitivities she keeps to herself and inner resources seldom recognized by others. She is quick of mind and determinedly independent. She is strictly her own person. I've often wondered where she came from and where she went.

A shelf in the little library across the Harbor from her home is dedicated to Ruth and contains a complete collection of her work. This would have pleased her.

MARGARET DICKSON

[Reprinted from *This Month in Maine Literature,* February 1990]

There is a poem of Ruth Moore's that I would like to find again. It includes or ends with lines like "we've got better things to do than stand here gawking over a graveyard fence."

For me, this is typical Ruth.

"Get going" is what I've always heard her saying, through all those vigorous, straight-out novels and poems. "Write literature. Don't dangle participles or split infinitives. *Illegitimi non carborundum!* And the orts go to the pigs."

She's laughing as she says it, but I know that in her work she has shaped delicate flying crystals of snow into kittens; she has disciplined children, built houses, fed crowds, and fished the ocean.

I see her developing so many kinds of characters and doing it with such care and enjoyment. I hear the rhythms of her words and feel her graciousness and good sense.

Here is her *Candlemas Bay*, and young Jeb, whose beloved grandfather, Jebron, has passed away. Ruth marks this simply and finely. The boy picks up a pen. On an old map aged soft as cloth he writes with a steady hand, "Jebron died."

That is grace at Candlemas.

MARILIS HORNIDGE

[Reprinted from "Bookview," *Maine Mountain Digest*, August/September 1990]

Mourn with me. Ruth Moore is dead.

There were no headlines, no front page articles. You may not have even noticed unless you are a devotee of the obituary column. I wouldn't have known it except for a good friend who sent me a small article from a Maine paper without a dateline or, for that matter, much information other than the basics. If that was due to the wishes of the Moore family, I won't cavil. If it was rather, as I strongly suspect, because no one in the media world remembered her work or valued it as it should be valued—if none of them thought her talent would be terribly missed, I intend to cavil at the top of my lungs. Ruth Moore wrote 14 books of fiction and two small volumes of haunting poetry. Every word in all of them says MAINE. Not the "new" Maine or the "traditional" Maine—not the "tourist" Maine or the "other" Maine. The real, genuine 48-carat article.

Her words ring like crystal, they scratch like diamonds. They are not glitzy or gritty or shocking-on-purpose. Her people are real people, the places are real places, not neatened-up. Her plots get under your skin…when you put the book down, you can't tune the story out. She doesn't duck or gloss over the hard times or the not-so-admirable sides of human nature, but she doesn't dwell on them either. That's life, she says, that's people. That's Maine. Ever and always, there is the unextinguished unextinguishable flickering flame of hope—that tomorrow will be better … or different … or at least interesting. And survivable.

My own two favorites are *The Weir* with its dark brooding sorrow and *Spoonhandle* with its upsurging hope. Maine Public Radio, to its everlasting credit, did a reading of *The Walk Down Main Street*, as applicable today as it was when it first came out. A real Ruth Moore devotee once told me her favorite is *Second Growth* to which she has always desired a sequel. The last book was *Sarah Walked Over the Mountain*. The fact that it is now referred to as the last book makes me want to howl at the moon. Many of her books have long been out of print and available only through antiquarian booksellers (at astronomical price). Recently Blackberry Press has been bringing them out in affordable paperback, may their name be blessed by readers who are discovering Moore late.

Biographical material on Ruth Moore is equally hard to come by—she was essentially a private person, although she never made a fetish out of it. Critical material on her work is tough to find as well. Real Live Critics are their sharp-and-clever best when blasting things, and Ruth Moore isn't blastable. Big Time Critics tend to get either lukewarm or sneery with writers like that, so those of us who write for readers (rather than critics or publishers or even writers) have an obligation to stand up and shout.

I'm shouting.

I wish that I had written this long ago so that she would have known how much she is still read and loved—and that we bring other readers along. I think it would have pleased, and maybe surprised her.

Somehow, thinking of the loss of Ruth Moore, I am reminded of a verse written by folksinger/songwriter Gordon Bok from his evocative "Turning Toward The Morning," which I would like to quote in valedictory farewell. Because of his love for her poetry, I don't think he'd mind.

It's a pity we don't know
What the little flowers know
They can't take the cold November
They can't face the wind and snow
They fold their glories all around them
Bow their heads and let it go
But you know they'll be there shining
In the morning.

It must indeed be a shining morning where she is. It's dimmer for a lot of us readers, though, now that she's gone.

GARY LAWLESS

[Reprinted from *This Month in Maine Literature,* February 1990]

On November 29, 1989, Beth Leonard and I went to Bar Harbor to visit Ruth Moore, and to finalize plans for a book of her selected poems to be called *The Tired Apple Tree*. We had been working on the manuscript for nearly a year. Ruth agreed that the manuscript was now ready to go. She did add that if she indeed wrote more poems, we would just have to publish another book. We talked also of reprinting another two of her novels, *Candlemas Bay* and *The Fire Balloon.* We had lunch together and then, as Ruth seemed to be tiring, we said good-bye. There was a poem in her typewriter. The title was "I have seen horizons."

Three days later, Ruth passed away at the age of 86. Her passing was briefly noted in local papers, but to Maine literature it is an event of considerable importance. Ruth published fourteen novels, a book of ballads, and a book of poems during her lifetime, and in the spring there will be a new book of poems. I feel that her novels were the best to come out of Maine yet. We have lost her voice but her spirit, her gift remain with us. We will always have her work, and through it, we have a record of life in Maine's coastal fishing communities, a life now lost to us.

My life has been honored by the opportunity to read Ruth's work, and by knowing her; participating in the republishing of her work, and the revival of interest in her has been a great gift. I like to think of Ruth in the context of a description of her character Roger in *Fire Balloon.* She says that "Roger came to feel an almost mystic relationship with the region of lakes and forests, the ocean shorelines and the windy islands off the coast, set with green and secret trees. He was aware at times of a deep inner homesickness for a place of mind which he had known as a young man trying to write poems, a place still and solitary where he had been able to listen and set down some part of what he heard." We are most fortunate that Ruth Moore set down some part of what she heard.

What follows the time of developers
no human voice can tell.
But the silent offshore islands know,
and they handle their mysteries well.

They speak with a voice that is all their own,
and this is what they say:
That they talk in terms of a billion years
That their now is not today.
And the ghosts they brought along with them
Have never gone away.

—from "The Offshore Islands"
by Ruth Moore

SVEN DAVISSON

"Blood of my Blood, Ancestors that have gone before, I thank you." So begins a modern Amer-Yoruban reverence for the mighty dead, the souls and intellects who have gone before and reside in a space where they look over those who remain. I am reminded of Ruth's poem "The Ghost of Phoebe Bunker," where she returns to survey the island cemetery. I can remember several times making this very pilgrimage with Ruth, Esther, and assorted family to the cemetery on Gott's Island—the plots of the island families and the unmarked graves of black island stone workers, lost at sea. I can remember Ruth, with her simple smile, discussing how the newcomers were arguing over these seemingly empty plots and the surprise they would find when it came time to bury old Uncle So-and-so.

As her grand nephew, I spent a great deal of time with Ruth during the last decade of her life—Sunday visits were almost a ritual. I can remember earlier, as a child, visiting her and Eleanor and playing in the midst of their living room with large stuffed animals that were always kept on hand for smaller visitors. During these early visits, I missed the significance of the boards upon which I played. It was only later, after Eleanor's death, that I realized what a monument to these two women this house truly was, the buildings and even most of the furniture built with their own hands. One of my fondest memories from this period are the times when we traipsed to the "mad house" together—an outbuilding erected to store their numerous collections when they outgrew the house. Once there she would unearth some small treasure that had come up during the conversation we had been having.

During later visits we would sit either in the living room or by her garden and discuss literature and writing. We often traded books, passing finds along across generations. Allen Ginsberg for Don Marquis' *archy and mehitabel,* which had remained one of her favorite works since it had been originally serialized in *The New Yorker.* We would trade stories—hers growing with each retelling. She would sometimes bring out something she was working on and read the draft to me—looking for comments and, also, sincere enjoyment.

I feel privileged knowing her for the relatively short time that I did. The exchange will always remain one of the most profound periods of my life. Though those conversations are over, I know strongly that she will never truly be far away from those she chose to allow within her domain. As she stares forth from Eleanor's portrait, I am drawn back to a sonnet from Ruth's "The Mountains of Snow":

> The rocks will never miss you, nor the sky.
> The sea will be unchanging, oh, my dear;
> Tomorrow by the water, only I
> Of all things else shall know you are not here. ...
> Somewhere in time, remote beyond belief,
> Compassionate summer leased to you and me
> A sheaf of days as beautiful and brief
> As bubbles, rising, breaking, in the sea.
> Remember them for me and help me bear
> Pitiless water and impassive air.

Appendix B

DEWITT WALLACE
EDITOR, *THE READER'S DIGEST*

The Reader's Digest
Pleasantville, N.Y.
August 28, 1947

Miss Ruth Moore Bernard Maine

Dear Ruth:

Could you take one moment only from the important manuscript before you to autograph our copy of *Spoonhandle*, being forwarded under separate cover? If so, Lila and I would be deeply obliged, for we are both Moore fans—literary and personal—from years back!

To say that we miss you is simply to express succinctly a feeling which might itself be expanded into a long narrative.

With cordial best wishes from us both,

Sincerely yours, *Wally*

P.S. Hearty felicitations upon the awe-full responsibility now yours, Doctor!

ARTHUR A. HAUCK
PRESIDENT, UNIVERSITY OF MAINE

May 16, 1947

Miss Ruth Moore
c/o *The Reader's Digest*
Pleasantville, New York

Dear Miss Moore:

At a meeting of the Board of Trustees of the University of Maine on May 15, it was voted to confer upon you the honorary degree of Doctor of Letters (Litt.D.). The Trustees wish to recognize your fine achievements in the field of letters.

We sincerely hope that you will accept this award at our Commencement Exercises to be held on Sunday afternoon, June 15, at 3 o'clock. Will you please let me know as soon as you possibly can whether we may expect you. If you plan to be with us, please return the enclosed card with the information requested so that we can make arrangements for the rental of a cap and gown for you.

No public announcement is made of honorary degree awards until Commencement day, so please regard this as confidential.

Sincerely yours,
Arthur A. Hauck
President

P.S. If this letter reaches you in California will you please send me your answer by telegram. A.A.H.

ALLAN B. KARSTETTER
PRESIDENT, UNITY COLLEGE

April 16, 1976

Miss Ruth Moore
Bass Harbor Maine 04653

Dear Miss Moore:

At the last quarterly meeting earlier this month, the Board of Trustees of Unity College voted unanimous approval of the Faculty's proposal to award you the honorary degree, Doctor of New England Literature, at our annual commencement on June 26.

Long an admirer of your work, Professor Donald Mortland of our Arts and Humanities faculty proposed and championed you as one deserving of the finest institutional compliment we know how to pay.

I hope you will honor Unity College by accepting our tribute to your talent and achievement. May I hear from you that you can indeed join us for our own rite of passage on June 26?

Sincerely,
Allan B. Karstetter
President

DONALD MORTLAND
PROFESSOR, UNITY COLLEGE
Introduction to Conferral of Doctoral Degree

As Miss Moore is not here in person today, it seemed to us fitting to read a brief passage from one of her novels. I shall do that before reading the citation.

Ruth Moore is a master in presenting human relationships. It appears to be human to have difficulty in getting along smoothly with someone different from oneself. On the coast of Maine in this century, the people who are natives of the region and people from away have found themselves living together, in varying degrees of harmony, for three or four months of every year. Love has brought them together, but it is the love that they all have for the Maine coast, not love for each other. Often, mutual affection does develop, even though the division remains, the division into people who belong here and people from away.

Sometimes a summer resident decides to stay all year.

I should like to read a passage from Miss Moore's novel entitled *Speak to the Winds,* which I think is her masterpiece, in which this has happened. Miss Roxindra Greenwood and her aged mother, who are from away, have decided to make a permanent home on the island where they have spent several summers. The events are told as Elbridge Gilman saw them, when Miss Greenwood hired Luther MacGimsey to build the house. Luther is an old man and very skillful, especially with stone, who has built many cottages for summer people, and has always told them how they wanted it done.

[Here Professor Mortland read pages 49–51 of *Speak to the Winds*.]

Citation

Two or three generations ago, Sarah Orne Jewett wrote this now-famous advice to Willa Cather: One must know the world so well before he can know the parish. Today we honor an American novelist who knows both. Ruth Moore writes of the parish but for the world.

Miss Moore is an author who has used her Maine heritage to create novels of enduring worth; who has recorded and used in her work the speech of the Maine coast fisherman with greater accuracy than any other writer that we know; who has created characters by the village-ful as memorable as those of Dickens; who has seen in her own people both the meanness and the grandeur of which man is capable; who has used her Maine coast people both to extol magnanimity and to condemn narrowness.

RUTH MOORE TO THE TOWN OF TREMONT

(no date)

After some twenty years of living unmolested on our property, we are now having to post and fence it. This seems a pity, because we believe that land anywhere should be free for people to walk on and enjoy, provided they do not do damage or create nuisances. But our woodlot is being pillaged for wood for campfires; finished two-by-fours intended for the construction of said fence have been carted off, as well as part of a winter's supply of cut wood seasoning in our back yard; our vegetable garden has been looted and an open-air privy made at the end of our field near the potato patch.

There seems to be little to do about this. A lady discovered heading for our woodpile with a basket said she was looking for mushrooms; two others caught digging in our potato patch said they were getting dirt for houseplants. We were left in wonder, because these two had nothing to carry dirt in except a used Kleenex, which they dropped for us to pick up. Now, wouldn't we have looked the fools of the world if we had hailed them into court for criminal trespass and they innocently doing no harm at all? They said they didn't see the No Trespassing signs, which, anyway, costs only a dollar in court.

After dark one evening, we came upon a lady and a gentleman carrying out of the woodlot a freshly-cut, twenty-foot tall green catspruce tree. I say cut—it was beavered down, the way President Theodore Roosevelt is said to have done when visiting a Maine lumber camp. A lumberman, reporting, said, I cut down two; Mr. Roosevelt beavered down fourteen. The lady and gentleman were panting and struggling; they had had a time and it seemed a shame to interrupt them. But when we pointed out that the woodlot is private land and posted as such, the lady cried out indignantly, But it's all falling down! Which broke our hearts, because our woodlot is a tended one, the dead wood cut out each winter and the green trees left to grow as green trees should do. So far, we have lost five nice ones.

Many don't, but we do, value a growing tree.

We have puzzled a good deal over this state of affairs, even asking the opinion of a friend of ours who runs a campground. He shrugged and said, City people are like that now.

Now, we don't believe that. We have talked with a good many campers and they seem, generally, to be decent, well-spoken people, and friendly. Well-heeled, too, considering the size and opulence of their camping equipment. We don't think they'd carry on this way except under some kind of duress of savage necessity. One mustn't judge too soon. What if a man might have spent too much on his Winnebago, so that now his children are starving? He has nothing to buy wood for the campfire with, so they are shivering and cold. He has spent too much on his vacation, perhaps, or his check hasn't caught up with him. It could be any of a number of things, circumstances beyond his control.

If this state of affairs is prevalent over the State of Maine as it is with us, I think we should get together and do something. We can't let anybody go hungry and cold. In our town surplus foods are available. Maine people are generous; we're sure that any needy family getting surplus foods would share it with needy out-of-State families. As for firewood, truckloads of refuse wood are hauled to our Town Dump almost daily for burning. It can be picked up free and some of it is green, if campers prefer it that way.

Or perhaps we could start a fund. Instead of contributing to CARE, why don't we all put in together enough to keep our summer visitors from being pushed beyond their moral endurance?

A gentleman asked me why we were putting up a fence around our vegetable garden. We said we'd been having trouble with skunks. Well, we were, so no need to take personal umbrage. A skunk broke under the wire and tarryhooted around among the vegetables. He might have eaten a few snap beans, but he didn't clean out the crop. If he did, he wore high-heeled shoes and did it on a rainy night when the vines were wet. Any Maine skunk would know better than to rust a whole patch of snap beans. Besides, he paid for the damage he did by cleaning out an entire hatching of white grubs in the grass near next year's strawberry patch.

Ruth Moore: Tongue of Granite, Tongue of Salt

by GARY LAWLESS

From *Killick Stones*

There is a quotation from a patriarch of Zen Buddhism: "To seek one's own true nature is a way to lead you to your long-lost home."

I speak of the work of the Maine novelist Ruth Moore. I do not speak as a critic, but as a writer responding to the work of another writer. I speak as a native, hearing the language of home. Reading Ruth Moore's work is, for me, a way of leading myself to a long-lost home.

She begins her first novel, *The Weir,* by saying, "That was the place you were homesick for, even when you were there." Moore's work creates (or re-creates) a community, a community of many lives, many rhythms and cycles, breath and life. Her work is a landscape, a geography. Her work is the voice of water against rock, a littoral voice. Tongues of granite, tongues of salt. Voices heard on the wind. I have come to believe that it is actually the land itself, the community of things speaking through Ruth Moore. Her writing gives voice to place, a quite specific place.

So let's begin with a quote from the poet William Stafford:

> All events and experiences are local, somewhere. And all human enhancements of events and experiences ... all the arts ... are regional in the sense that they derive from immediate relation to felt life.

It is this immediacy that distinguishes art. And paradoxically, the more local the feeling in art, the more all people can share it, for that vivid encounter with the stuff of the world is our common ground.

Artists, knowing this mutual enrichment that extends everywhere, can act, and praise, and criticize, as insiders—the means of art is the life of all people. And that life grows and improves by being shared. Hence, it is good to welcome any region you live in or come to think of, for that is where life happens to be: right where you are.

Stafford says that it is "good to welcome any region you live in." It is really important to emphasize the word "in",—to live "in" the region rather than on top of it, to be a part of the region's natural rhythms and cycles, the voices of place, and to welcome the place into your life, your work. To derive writing from the "immediate relation to felt life." Stafford feels that this encounter is our common ground. This is the common ground on which the reader meets Ruth Moore. She is giving voice to a very particular place. It is identifiable, locatable, imaginable. It feels real. *The New York Times* has said of her work, "It is doubtful if any American writer has ever done a better job of communicating a people, their talk, their thoughts, their geography, and their way of life."

Ruth Moore's books are rich with information, specific information given in a very precise, correct language, preserving a way of life in a particular community now lost to us. The place has changed, the people have changed, yet we can look to her books for accurate depictions of the lives lived within this place.

I want here to quote from an essay on Ruth Moore written by Donald F. Mortland and published in the *Colby Library Quarterly* (Vol. XV #1, March 1979):

> Piles of books have been written about the Maine coast and its people, some of which are sentimental slush, some simply wrong ... There are several ruinous rocks to be skirted in writing about the Maine coast. One is the danger of being sentimental. Another is the tendency to be folksy. A third is the danger of falling into ruts made by previous writers that lead into folksy stories about quaint people with hearts of gold who speak a peculiar dialect, mourn about the past, and spend their lives dealing with trivia over which the author makes them triumphant in some miniscule way. Ruth Moore avoids all of these.

Each place has its own rhythms and cycles, its own language. There are ways of living in a place that are in harmony with these rhythms, and there are ways of living in a place that are destructive to these rhythms. We can live in place, mindful of these rhythms, attempting to attune ourselves with them, or we can bring other ways of living, other ways of seeing and doing, from elsewhere and destroy the local, natural rhythms, changing the place forever.

As writers we can draw deeply on the spirit of place, tuning in to the cycles, plant and animal, air and water, and seeing how these cycles move in the depths of our own imaginations. In Ruth Moore's work we draw on five generations of living in place, a long-term devotion and attention to place, and a deep relationship between lives led, language and imagination. Action here is understood in relation to place, and the structure of the story involves the structures of life around it. A long-term residence in a specific place brings to the writer a deeper understanding of action in terms of consequence, the ripples, ppools, and long-term effects that are usually not obvious.

A place is a form and has its own influences on the literary form that is created within it. If we do things which are not in harmony with the place, we destroy the place or exile ourselves from it. We become lost because we cannot see where we are. We are uprooted, the strength of our vision is gone, and the reader follows our lead. We then speak as outsiders, and however well-intentioned, we do damage to the place with our images, our ideas and our representations.

I feel this happening here in Maine, that the language and literature are becoming gentrified and actually removed from the "Real Maine" while supposedly portraying it. One critic has said that "because of the cliché that 'dirty' facts are real, and imaginative perceptions and truths are 'unreal,' the best fiction talents of our time are reporting on less than half of our life—the lower half."

Ruth Moore has written that she has tried "to write, as truthfully and accurately as I could, about small communities and the life in them which I have known well." She told the *Bangor Daily News,* "My object is to interpret this region realistically. After all, I grew up in it."

She was recently quoted as enjoying Carolyn Chute and Sanford Phippen because "both of them are telling the truth about a segment of Maine life—a segment that isn't in accord with the fairyland view of Maine put out by the Maine Publicity Bureau."

The New York Times noted her "authentic feeling for place, for the true and ordinary values of every day, the meaningfulness of independence, of work, of honesty and kindness." Another reviewer called this her "beautiful explicitness of time and place and individuals."

I feel that there is a sense of healing in Ruth Moore's ficiton, a sense of balancing, the loss of balance and balance restored. Characters, emotions, community and the natural world are pictured in various states of balance and imbalance. Long before the "New Maine Fiction" we find the subjects of abuse, alcoholism, racism, sexism, family violence, and murder portrayed, but with a wonderful sense of balance, of being within a larger community. We are not rolled in the mud, nor flown to the heights of romanticism. All endings are not happy, but we are given full characters, rich characters—people we feel we have known, and communities we could call home.

In her novel *The Fire Balloon,* Moore writes that her character, Roger, "came to feel an almost mystic relationship with the region of lakes and forests, the ocean shorelines and the windy islands off the coast, set with their green and secret trees. He was aware at times of a deep inner homesickness for a place of mind which he had known as a young man trying to write poems, a place still and solitary where he had been able to listen and set down some part of what he heard." This is what I think Moore has done with her work, to listen and set down some part of what she has heard.

* * *

Ruth Moore was born on July 21, 1903, on Gott's Island (or Great Gott Island). Gott's Island had a steady population from the 1780s to the late 1920s. There are reports of French settlers there around 1680. Champlain called it Petit Plaisants. In 1789 the island was purchased by Daniel Gott and its name changed.

Moore's family lived on the island for five generations. Her father Philip Moore was the island's postmaster, in addition to running a small store and a herring weir. The Moores also boarded the schoolteacher. Ruth graduated from Ellsworth High School and went on to graduate from New York State College for Teachers in Albany in 1925. For the next 20 years she spent most of her time away from Maine, working as a teacher, as a secretary in both New York and California, and as an associate editor of *The Reader's Digest.*

A long poem, "The Voyage," was published in the *Saturday Review of Literature* in May of 1929. Several of her short stories appeared in *The New*

Yorker and *Harper's Bazaar*. She was 40 when her first novel went to a publisher. The first five had been set aside, but the sixth went out. She was living in San Francisco at the time "doing jobs I disliked. Further, the climate there simply didn't agree with me." Her first novel, *The Weir*, was published by William Morrow and Company in 1943.

When Ruth Moore was growing up, and while she was away, her home on Gott's Island was going through a transition. Most families were fishing and lobstering families, with small gardens and perhaps a cow. The attraction of the mainland was having a strong effect on the community. People were going there to sell fish and lobsters, to buy supplies, to go to school, and to have many of the conveniences which town life provided.

From the 1890s the summer visitors gradually discovered the island. The Moores were among the first to take in boarders. Summer homes were built, land changed hands, and the island economy changed. Moore writes about the process in Candlemas Bay:

> Jen and her kind were everywhere. To them the wonderful heritage of a house and land meant nothing but how they could use it to make money out of the summer people. Sell the land for summer cottages. Fill up the house with boarders for a season or so, remodel it into a hotel. Then would come a bad year when the summer trade didn't show up, and the hotel would fail. There it would stand, windows broken out, doors banging in the wind, paint scaling off, an eyesore to the countryside. No good to anyone. Like the Griswold house. ...
>
> And where were the Griswolds now? Their land was sold, the money spent. The womenfolks of the younger generation were working in the sardine factories, trying to keep their families' heads above water, or they were cooks and maids in the summer cottages. Their menfolks were caretakers or gardeners or deckhands on somebody's yacht. In the wintertime, none of them had any work. They lived on credit from the grocery stores, and during the Depression they'd had to take food from the government.

In 1927 the house and barn of Clarence Harding burned. Also in 1927 Washington decided to discontinue the post office on Gott's Island. These two events mark a finality in the history of the island, and almost all of the permanent residents had left by the end of the year, including the Moores.

The Weir chronicles this transitional period from the points of view of several characters, including Hardy, based on her father. Hardy is the last to fish with a weir but is torn by his longing for something else, perhaps to open a store on the mainland. He longs for the peace of mind and security which had been on the island but was no longer there. It was the same island, changed only by cleared fields and snug houses, which in the 1700s had meant home and harbor, an island wrapped around by water, set off from the world by a curtain of peaceful sound, which was the sound of water hanging in the air. Existence had been sweetened and protected here, but now people groped after that safety, feeling it lost. If it were not here, then it must be somewhere else—Hardy feels the island, gone to seed.

And yet once they have left the island, the land stays in their minds and hearts:

> Days in the fall, when the leaves were yellow and the sky that color it gets, and the air blew down over the town, cool and crisp and all but snapping, he felt like taking off for some place back of beyond, at a dead run—run and run until he got back that lean, limber feeling he'd had all his life, up to now. All at once, the island which he'd been so crazy to leave, had seemed like heaven to him.
>
> He'd wake up nights, thinking about it, sometimes the color of the water behind the breakwater, that deep green when it lay in the shadow, or the sound the ducks made as they scaled down into the pond in the swamp.

To digress for a moment, I have found that there is a special place in these novels for the swamp. In *Spoonhandle* Moore's character Mag has returned to the island and bought the swamp:

> [She] remembered the swamp of old. It was a secret and private place where nobody went. All her life she had thought of it, off and on ... There in the back of her mind would be lying, quiet and cool, a picture of the old Stilwell swamp, its ferns and its moss and its crooked tree roots, its black pools edged with green, the alders thick as a man's leg growing between the aisles of the spruces. She remembered the Salt Pond Water, emptying and filling twice a day, and the lookout from the footbridge, and the soft sound of the ebb and flood under it. Some days, she told herself, thinking about such things was about all that kept her a-goin.

And from *Speak to the Winds:*

> The swamp flowered all summer, no matter how dry the season. Above it, the granite crisped its lichens in the sun, baked as fiercely dry as if the heat had struck outward from its furnace fires within. But the growth around the pool stayed brilliant electric green. Alders grew thick as a man's thigh, and some of the old swamp birches were three feet through at the base. Tall trees and the hill kept away the wind, so that the air hung hot and still, full of rich jungle smells of muc and moss and lush, sunny leaves. Squirrels lived in the swamp, and deer and mink and beaver and muskrat. Hermit thrushes sang there all spring long. The trees were full of wing-flash and flutter and the four or five clear notes, repeated a thousand times, of the white-throated sparrow. Ducks gathered in the pond; at fall dusk it might be brimful of them, floating side by side. To these inhabitants, at any time of the year, the swamp offered shelter, either of shade or snow.

Moore's second novel, *Spoonhandle,* brought her home. Shortly after its publication in 1946, interest was shown in turning it into a play. Twentieth Century Fox offered more money and it instead became the movie *Deep Waters*, filmed on the Maine coast with Dana Andrews, Jean Peters, Dean Stockwell, and Ed Begley. The author feels that the movie butchered her book. She had been under contract to write the scenario but found that she hadn't developed the technique and passed the job along. The movie did allow her financially to return to Maine with the freedom to write.

In 1947 she returned to Maine and spent the summer on Gott's Island. She and Eleanor Mayo (who has also published novels based in the same region) built their own home and workshop in McKinley, on Mt. Desert just across from the island.

One of the central characters in *Spoonhandle* is Anne Freeman, a young woman who is returning to the island after spending some time in New York and publishing her first book. She has come to work on a second book.

As in *The Weir,* we see an island community in transition, to which Anne returns from the city:

> I had a lot of fine foolish rapture about living simply and doing good simple hard work ... I'm scared of this part of the country. It's bleak and unyielding. Here people start to go down for the third time and everybody knows it, but nobody does anything. In the city you've

made a place for yourself, you know your way around, you can go out and get a job. …

Yet she is looking for a chance to think without being driven. She wonders why she has returned to a place she fought to escape from—and if her work fails, where will she go, what will she do?

This place here, this countryside, was what she loved and wanted fiercely to be a part of, yet the way she was now, divided, it hadn't anything to offer her.

I guess I'd like to belong somewhere, she told herself forlornly, but I'd have to guess again to know for sure where. …

During the busy years, the wild and solitary beauty of the eastern shore had almost gone out of her mind—at least, it was still wild and solitary if she kept to the stretches of shore line that remained where summer cottages weren't under construction.

Wandering along the shore, she could feel no reality in the fact that everything was sold now, the acres which for so many generations had belonged to the Freeman family. The place was the same—except for the growth of the spruces and a few alder thickets which had sprung up here and there, she couldn't see any change. She told herself that she hadn't any right to feel at home here, but it didn't do any good. The sense of at-homeness, of belonging, almost a sense of possession, stayed automatically in the back of her mind. Even while she walked along saying to herself, in a few months there'll be a fat, ten- or fifteen-room house right here, probably showing a Georgian influence, and a tiled swimming pool dug into Apple Cove Beach—could be, with steampipes to heat the salt water, that was the kind of thing they did—even while her reason said this to her, the land, something else said, twas the Freeman land and always would be.

It seemed absurd; but there it was—not actually regret that the land was sold, but more a habit of thinking, as if a feeling for land might be hereditary, transmitted as naturally as the color of eyes and hair, through chromosomes. She hadn't realized, before, that she'd feel like that. She would have thought she'd been away from the eastern shore too long. But, apparently, it was something you didn't get over. …

Everything is so dull and drab. But don't you know it's full of marvels. …

It's natural, I guess, to want to see other places than the one you know. But people are the same anywhere, wonderful, tragic, and places.... They had to find out for themselves. No one could tell them.

It is Anne's need to write that brings her home, and that gives her more insight into the people around her:

She'd learned to write, concentrating on the impact, the effect of human beings on one another, for that, in essence, was what you tried to do. She'd begun to understand a little better the insecurities, the frustrations that made a man like her father act like he did. She learned to take the trouble to find out and understand the inner stresses and strains that made people need to interfere with other people, most often the ones they knew best and loved.

Out of this looking at the effect of human beings on one another Moore creates a complex community of characters. Anne's place within the community, as a writer and a woman, is tentative. People know that she has written a book, and seem pleased and proud, but few have actually read the book. In her short story, "The Soldier Shows His Medal," Moore explains:

The year I myself was 20, I published a poem in a little magazine, dead now these many years, both poem and magazine forgotten. It wasn't much ... but I remember how I wanted people to know. They never did, for whenever it was on my lips to tell, I kept hearing the neighbors: Guess she thinks she's something, bragging about her writing being printed, somewheres to the west'ard.

This leads us to another major theme in Ruth Moore's work—the roles of women within the community. In the first two novels we meet women who have gone away from the island and have returned with a wider view of themselves and the world.

Anne Freeman in *Spoonhandle* returns only to be met at the dock by insulting behavior from the local store owner:

The neat way in which with three words he had turned her into a silly interfering female had made her angry, but something else too. It had been a long time since she had encountered indifferent disregard of herself as a thinking human being—so long that she had almost forgotten how it felt.

She'd expected it. That was the way men here were to their womenfolk; you couldn't count on any change. She'd had it and fought

> it, all through her childhood and youth. What it had done was to make her try hard, discipline herself, train her mind into a tool that could give her back some self-respect. ...
>
> [Actions such as his made you] wonder if there weren't some common ground on which human beings could meet without trying to wrench each other out of shape. If you took the trouble, couldn't you find out and understand the inner stresses and strains that made people need to interfere with other people?
>
> The books in high school had never given her an idea of any work she could do, nor of how she could best go about doing it if she knew what it was. What they had given her was a restless craving energy, a determination not to let the worth she had be wasted. She didn't suppose she wanted everything in the world—only to live her life so that it made sense.

But when Anne returns to the island, there is a fisherman who wants to marry her. She questions what would happen to her if she were to marry him, as she looks around at the other women in the community:

> She knew well enough what it would mean if she got married and stayed here at the harbor. The tired, discouraged women and girls whom she saw every day were evidence enough. They kept house for the menfolk and children at night, and worked in the sardine factory in the daytime. The day's work most of them put in was too much for any woman to stand, and they showed it in the way they looked and the way they dragged around.
>
> Not that she minded hard work—she'd certainly done enough of it, but to struggle along like that, to know your menfolk expected it of you, would take the heart out of any woman.

She considers marrying the man, and wonders what would become of her own individuality:

> Would he make a companion of her, let her have a part in the important things of his life—she didn't think that he would. He'd look on her as something he possessed, to make love to, to keep his house and make him comfortable, something less than a person who had the same kind of brains and feelings he did. The men around here all felt that way about women.

Like Anne Freeman, many of the characters in Ruth Moore's community are trying to live a decent, quiet life. She says in *The Weir* that "most people would be OK, if other people would let them alone." In several novels central characters are children, many of them with bad childhood experiences—orphans, "state" children, runaways, and children of alcoholics. In Candlemas Bay she says, "You were all so beautiful when you began, before the world and your lives flowed up over you like the sea." The author has a great depth of sympathy for them. In *Sea Flower* she talks about not offending the little ones:

> That word offend. ... It meant to harm them inside in a way they never got over. How many people did you see, well, not all, but an awful lot of them, grown up, man-grown out of offended little ones, who might have been twice-three times what they were, if it hadn't been for the harm? They got it early and they kept it going, passed it along the way they passed the color of their hair and their eyes, so it never died out, but got to be as much a part of the human race as legs and fingers. Look at the way they mistreated everything that couldn't fight back, give a wound. Animals. Birds. Look, for Godsakes, at the way they mistreated trees. Offend—probably the real work on earth of the devill. ...
>
> Animals had no recourse against human beings: in the end, animals always lost. It did seem that mankind, so marvelous in many ways, and Nature's finest achievement through millions of centuries of trial and error, should know what itself was, without having to prove supremacy, again and again, with blood and terror, over organisms weaker and less fortunate.

The speaker goes on to say, "I am a solitary man for that reason. I haven't ever been able to stand it." And later he says that "what a man is used to is a cup of coffee and his own shoestrings and tomorrow, and standing on the beach looking at the water and saying 'God, ain't that pretty.'"

> In each of her books there are one or two characters who choose to live alone, apart, to separate themselves from the push and pull life of the community, "not because they are different from anyone else (and if you live apart, people begin to think that you are) but because they like to." Her character Willie, in *Spoonhandle*, is not a violent man but one who can't stand the "pull and haul between people" and chooses

to come away by himself. It is this "pull and haul," this "effect of human beings on one another" which lies at the core of each Moore novel. Another character, in *A Fair Wind Home*, considers the life apart:

> It might be lonesome for while. But a picture floated before his mind of small, solitary beaches, dreaming in the sun, silent woods, sun-spangled stretches of water. No people with their complications to burst in tangling up your life and your privacy, pressing their concerns, their wishes, their problems on you, until your own life seemed to dwindle, until you had no life at all you could call your own.
>
> For a man to live a simple, honest life, not breaking his neck to get money, not kicking his neighbors in the face for it—he admired that way of living. ...
>
> Their love of the countryside went back and back. It was hereditary, almost, like something in the genes, understandable since their people had wrestled a hard living for generations out of this rock. But if you knew so much, if you knew how to cope, to handle, to deal with, why should this not make you the more confident, why should you not the better enjoy?

Many of her plots revolve around small misunderstandings or quarrels which start innocently enough but soon have whole families and groups of islanders lines up against each other. Consider these excerpts:

> Sometimes I think it is not the forces of nature we have so much to fear, but the ill-will over little things that breaks out of even good Christian men.
>
> Not the place; there was nothing in places for a man to fear. The natural disasters—two storms meeting overhead and bashing it out together, lightning striking, the sea rolling up to drown—were land and sea and sky and weather, minding their own business. They were what a man coped with the best he could, but not afraid so much as watchful. Death in its own good time, but in between, breakfast and birds' nests, the birds on the trees, apples and sunsets, grass with dew on it, a winter overcoat, a man's wife and his children, spring coming and full-turned leaves, a hot buttered rum on a cold night, and clean spruce chips and clam chowder and snow. Not the place or the dark, or the nightmare of the bears' woods; but the malice, the ill-will, the rancor, running like pus out of the minds of men. ...

She knew what an island row meant. They started over trifles and snowballed on trifles until whole families took sides, down to the children, and for months, years sometimes, people didn't speak or have anything to do with each other.

People don't want to hear about using each other decent. They'd damn sight rather sit around and shake over the idea of a puddle of hell fire waiting for them, or for the world to come to an end. It's more fun. Besides, to be decent means a certain amount of give and take. Most people would rather see everything smashed up than give one goddamn inch.

No one would have to set his mind on finding a grudge or two to smolder over, the island being what it was, people living for years in each other's placket holes.

Town rows. Sometimes they got better, sometimes worse. The thing grew like a tumor. And when a row really got rolling and hate and violence took over, you couldn't stop it; it had to run its course. Usually, when it was over, you found more damage had been done than anybody could afford. …

People think, a good fight will help us get through the winter. That was just the trouble. Too many people, in the beginning, thought they might enjoy a fight, not figuring ahead to when it might end. …

Stick your nose in somebody's business, get just about what you asked for. A fight was like a teeter-board; you hurt somebody and you went up, they hurt you back and you went down. It got going faster and faster; winding up tighter and tighter, until what you saw everywhere was ill-will; and you no longer wished for things to be righted, but for yourself to be appeased, to be in the acknowledged right of it. … for the world to come on bended knee.

Good juicy venom of this kind was meat and drink to Flo. You know full and well, she told her friends, I speak no evil of anybody, but the only liveable, nameable thing in my mind always and forever is the good of this town. But. …

It was a decent town. … He didn't have many illusions about his neighbors. Some might think they weren't so tough and competent as the old-timers who had built the town, but he was a long ways from believing that. You had to take into consideration what worry and

> being in debt and scraping along on the skin of your teeth year in and year out would do to a man; three-quarters of the time, no work and no prospects, sandpapering away at him till he wore thin; until, if he didn't say to hell with it, he acted as if he might, any time, and the summer people, seeing how he was, wagged heads as if at a funeral, saying it was too bad, a fine old solid section of the country was petering out.
>
> But let some project come up where a man felt he was useful and needed, or an emergency. ... You would see the old toughness, the old competence, the old skills come out overnight, and none of them rickety, either, from lack of use. ...
>
> One town, this size, doesn't amount to much; but the world, after all, is only a mess of towns, some big, some small. The history of the world's nothing but town records, records of one kind or another, records of government. And government, when you boil it down, is decent people getting together and making decent laws for themselves to live decently by. If you have it, you've got the best there is so far; if you don't have it, you've got nothing—a mess of thieves and pirates.

To add to the quarrels, to the movement away from the islands to the mainland, the transition of the community, we have the advent of the Summer People. The summer people found Gott's Island late in the 1800s as they worked their way along the Maine coast. Ruth Moore's family was one of the first on the island to take in boarders.

The summer people signal a major shift. While changing the economy of the community, they also change the way the local people view themselves, their land and their community:

> They say there's quite a lot of summer people wants to buy places on this island. Be a wonderful thing for the town, if only they did start to come here more, wouldn't it?
>
> Would be if you like summer people.
>
> Well, of course nobody likes them. They have t'be waited on hand and foot, and frigged with, and they act like they was God Almighty. But they do bring a lot of money and work to a town. ...
>
> The summer people acted like royalty, with royalty's gracious, condescending manners, and the local people took it for granted. Why Colonel Swansley told me, she was saying with pride, that I was the only housekeeper he ever had whom he considered worthy to mingle

with his guests. Bellport, from a village of independent fishermen and farmers, their own men who took nothing from anybody, had become a townful of domestic servants.

One of the summer people in Moore's work thinks to himself:

What he wanted now, more than anything, was to be the center of some small world, where simple, kindly people looked up to him—not because of money or favors they could expect, but sincerely. Bellport was too full of his own kind, of too many who wished to be looked up to, some of them able to command more respect than he. The little place on the island was to be a kind of manor house, with himself in it, through the mellow summers of his declining years, dispensing jobs and advice.

Another summer visitor speaks:

I quarrel with Mr. Clawson about coming to these dead little towns but you know it's such a relief to be away from it all, where there isn't one thing to attract my attention and no so-called interests—except, of course, the natives. I'm always interested in them. You see, in a small way, I'm a sociologist. I hope someday to have enough material for a book on rural customs and the economic life of these people.

We've been in many of these coast towns, Mr. Clawson and I. I find their economic situation most interesting.... Here you have some of the oldest towns in the country falling into decay because, with changing conditions, there's not enough work to support their people. I understand this entire region was once farming and fishing communities. Now, of course, it's largely summer-resident property.

The solution would be so simple, if they only had a little gumption. ... Your local people have no place here any longer. If there are no jobs, they should pick up and go elsewhere, where they can find work. But will they? No.

They cling like limpets to their old way of life, the life their fathers set up here and which is now gone. They squabble like crows over the few paying jobs there are. And each year we come back, we see them still poorer, still nearer the—er—ragged edge than ever. They have only themselves to blame.

We're hospitable. We like to keep enough cooks and maids and chauffers around so that our summer visitors can be comfortable. A

> grocer, too. And one plumber and one electrician, so that lights and water in the cottages can be turned off in the fall and on in the spring.
>
> "Don't you think, Miss Ellis," she asked, fixing Candace with a narrowed, sociological eye, "that inbreeding in these coastal towns is responsible for so many feeble-minded children?"
>
> But let the subject come up at any time and the thought was automatic—someone would be sure to express it too—the summer people were helpless, they didn't know how to cook or wash or clean or any of those things that really capable people knew how to do—like anything said over and over often enough, people would believe it, no matter how much proof to the contrary stared them in the face. Like still thinking of Miss Roxina as summer people, an outsider. You did and she was, and would be, if she stayed forever.
>
> To Elbridge's way of thinking, if anybody lived in a place as an outsider, and looked, talked and acted different from everyone else, it was bound to have an effect. With anyone like that, ordinary things could be twisted around, quite easily, to look peculiar. Anybody who looked different, was different, was fair game.

In several of the novels we find these characters, outsiders who have chosen for various reasons to stay in the community. There is a Jewish schoolteacher, a Portugese family, and rumors of "Nigger/Wop/Indian" blood. At one point in *Speak to the Winds* one of the most spiteful characters forms a "Society of American Christians—No Foreigners or Niggers need apply."

But in the end, say from 1927 on Gott's Island, and in the finality of Ruth Moore's novels, it is the summer people who stay. The locals leave or their community, their culture, gradually disappears.

> Everybody here has been twizzling like a windmill, for years, hoping he can sell his land to the summer people. You know that. This is the loveliest place on God's Green Earth, and no better anywhere for folks to live, if they want to try to live and make something of it. Why, people from away come and pay thousands of dollars, just so they can stay three months out of the year. But it's like anything else in the world—if you've got something that's worth something and you don't value it or take care of it, someone'll take it away from you, legally or otherwise. ...

> Think what you would about the offshore islands, love them as you must, they were still an enigma, a mystery. There they were, peaceful and lovely, the black trees with moonlight on them—places for a man to find his soul when he had lost it. But pitiless, silent, saying nothing back to warm flesh and blood. Sufficient to themselves, take them or leave them. People came, built houses; lived there; died; went away. ...
>
> Places for a man to find his soul, when he had lost it. What remains is the islander's sense of a place that had been, a slow moving memory of a place, changed forever, lost forever. A place lovely as some place you might have made up in a daydream. Green, sleepy islands; little wooded coves, trees down to the water's edge; high granitc bluffs; black bull-backed ledges where the surf washed over; water stretching away forever, blue, whitecapped, shining in the sun.

"That was the place that you were homesick for, even when you were there."

Bibliography

A. BOOKS

1. Beston, Henry, Editor, *White Pines and Blue Water: A State of Maine Reader,* Farrar, Straus, and Giroux, New York, 1950. "The Catch of the Halibut" from *Spoonhandle,* pp. 357–362. Moore biography, p. 406. Reprinted by Down East Books, Camden, Maine.
2. Brechlin, Earl, "Ancient History: Unearthing an Island's Prehistoric Past," *Bar Harbor Times,* Sept. 24, 1992, Sect. B., pp. 1–3. Illustrated. An archaeological dig on the Ruth Moore Site on Gott's Island.
3. Fischer, Jeff, Editor, *Maine Speaks,* Maine Writers and Publishers Alliance, Brunswick, Maine, 1989. "The Night Charley Tended Weir," pp. 234–238; from *The Weir,* pp. 369–379; from *The Walk Down Main Street,* pp. 397–406; Moore biography, pp. 453–454.
4. Guth, Dorothy Lobrano, Editor, *The Letters of E. B. White,* Harper & Row, New York, 1976. Letter from E. B. White to Dorothy Lobrano Guth about Ruth Moore and *A Fair Wind Home,* pp. 377–378.
5. Holmes, Edward M. Ted, *Driftwood,* Puckerbrush Press, Orono, Maine, 1972. "There's an Island in my Life" (Gott's Island), pp. 9–15. Many of Ted Holmes' stories are about Gott's Island and its people.
6. Holmes, Edward M. Ted, *Mostly Maine: Short Stories and Other Writings,* U. of Maine Press, Orono, Maine, 1977.

7. Holmes, Edward M. Ted, *A Part of the Main: Short Stories of the Maine Coast,* U. of Maine Press, Orono, Maine, 1973. Re-printed by U. of Maine Press in 1990.

8. Kirtland, R. H., Editor. *A Book of Student Verse,* 1909–1926, State College for Teachers, Albany, New York, 1926. Ruth's student poems are included in this rare volume edited by her English professor.

9. Lawless, Gary, Editor, *Gulf of Maine: A Blackberry Reader,* Blackberry Press, Brunswick, Maine, 1977.

10. Mayo, Eleanor, *Forever Strangers,* W. W. Norton & Co., Inc., New York, 1958. A novel.

11. Mayo, Eleanor, *Loom of the Land,* William Morrow & Co., New York, 1946. A novel dedicated For Ruth.

12. Mayo, Eleanor, *October Fire,* Thomas Y. Crowell Co., New York, 1951. A novel based on the Bar Harbor Fire of 1947.

13. Mayo, Eleanor, *Swan's Harbor,* Thomas Y. Crowell Co., New York, 1953. A novel.

14. Mayo, Eleanor, *Turn Home,* William Morrow & Co., New York, 1945. A novel.

15. McLane, Charles B., *Islands of the Mid-Maine Coast: Blue Hill and Penobscot Bays,* The Kennebec River Press, Woolwich, Maine, 1982. Gott's Island and the Moore family, pp. 423–431.

16. Moore, Ruth, *Candlemas Bay,* William Morrow & Co., New York, 1950. A novel dedicated to Sarah Driscoll Capen, a great-granddaughter of Sam Gott who lived on Gott's Island and was a great friend of Ruth and Eleanor.

17. Moore, Ruth, *Cold as a Dog and the Wind Northeast,* William Morrow & Co., New York, 1958. Ballads. Re-published by Gordon Bok, Camden Herald Pub. Co., Camden, Maine, 1973.

18. Moore, Ruth, *The Dinosaur Bite,* William Morrow & Co., New York, 1976. A novel.

19. Moore, Ruth, *A Fair Wind Home,* William Morrow & Co., New York, 1953. A novel dedicated to Frances Phillips, editor at William Morrow.

20. Moore, Ruth, *The Fire Balloon,* William Morrow & Co., New York, 1948. A novel dedicated to Eleanor Mayo.

21. Moore, Ruth, *The Gold and Silver Hooks,* William Morrow & Co., New York, 1969. A novel.

22. Moore, Ruth, *Jeb Ellis of Candlemas Bay,* William Morrow & Co., New York, 1952. A novel for young people condensed from the adult version of *Candlemas Bay.*

23. Moore, Ruth, *"Lizzie" and Caroline,* William Morrow & Co., New York, 1972. A novel.

24. Moore, Ruth, *Sarah Walked Over the Mountain,* William Morrow & Co., New York, 1979. A novel dedicated to John C. Willey, Ruth's editor.

25. Moore, Ruth, *The Sea Flower,* William Morrow & Co., New York, 1965. A novel dedicated to Mimi and Cheni (Miriam Colwell and Chenoweth Hall).

26. Moore, Ruth, *Second Growth,* William Morrow & Co., New York, 1962. A novel.

27. Moore, Ruth, *Speak to the Winds,* William Morrow & Co., New York, 1956. A novel. Re-printed by Blackberry Press, Nobleboro, Maine, 1987.

28. Moore, Ruth, *Spoonhandle,* William Morrow & Co., New York, 1946. A novel dedicated to Any American Town. Re-printed by Blackberry Press, Nobleboro, Maine, 1986.

29. Moore, Ruth, *Time's Web,* William Morrow & Co., New York, 1972. Poetry.

30. Moore, Ruth, *The Tired Apple Tree,* Blackberry Press, Nobleboro, Maine, 1990. Poetry and ballads with cover photo by Eleanor Mayo.

31. Moore, Ruth, *The Walk Down Main Street,* William Morrow & Co., New York, 1960. A novel dedicated To Schoolteachers with Admiration. Re-printed by Blackberry Press, Nobleboro, Maine, 1988.

32. Moore, Ruth, *The Weir,* William Morrow & Co., New York, 1943. A novel dedicated To My Father and Mother. Re-printed by Blackberry Press, Nobleboro, Maine, 1987.

33. Phippen, Sanford, Editor, *The Best Maine Stories,* Yankee Books, Camden, Maine, 1986. "The Soldier Shows His Medal" (short story), pp. 287–293.

34. Putz, George and *Island Journal* staff, Editors, *Killick Stones: A Collection of Maine Island Writing,* Island Institute, Rockland, Maine, 1987. "Ruth Moore: Tongue of Granite, Tongue of Salt" by Gary Lawless, pp. 3–19; and "Whose Maine Island?" by Constance Hunting, pp. 108–117.

35. Small, H. W., *History of Swan's Island,* Maine, Hancock County Pub. Co., Ellsworth, Maine, 1898. Gott's Island, pp. 159–174.

B. SIGNED ARTICLES, REVIEWS, STORIES, AND POEMS

1. Atkinson, Oriana, review of *The Fire Balloon, Saturday Review of Literature,* Nov. 13, 1948, vol. 31, p. 17.

2. Beem, Edgar Allen, "The Weir Fisherman's Daughter," *Maine Times,* Oct. 24, 1986, pp. 20–23. Illustrated with pictures of Ruth and her home by Christopher Ayres.

3. Berman, Riva, "Author Wants to Be Just a Neighbor," *Maine Sunday Telegram,* Sept. 26, 1976, p. 1C. Illustrated.

4. Carruthers, Olive, review of *Candlemas Bay, Chicago Sunday Tribune,* March 25, 1951, p. 6.

5. Chase, Mary Ellen, review of *Candlemas Bay, Saturday Review of Literature,* March 24, 1951, p. 16.

6. Crosby, Katherine, "Mystery of Gotts Island," *Boston Globe,* Aug. 23, 1925. Sub-titled: "Summer Visitors Listen to Strange Tale of Tragic Passing of Lone Maine Character." Illustrated. Miss Elizabeth Peterson, a model for a character in *Speak to the Winds.*

7. Dangerfield, George, review of *Spoonhandle, Saturday Review of Literature,* June 22, 1946, vol. 29, p. 42.

8. de Belloy Williams, Patricia, "Life on the Maine Coast," *Bangor Daily News,* Jan. 17, 1980, p. 11. Review of *Sarah Walked Over the Mountain.*

9. Dickson, Margaret, "Remembering Ruth Moore," *This Month in Maine Literature,* MWPA Newsletter, Feb. 1990, p. 11.

10. E.M.B., "Toiling Islanders Drawn Honestly in *The Weir!"* Publication and date unknown. Sub-titled: "First Novel of Ruth Moore (of Gott's Island) Tells of the Tough and Tirred Fisher Folk Who Lack Security of Miss Field's and Miss Chase's Characters." Moore compared to Maine authors Rachel Field and Mary Ellen Chase. Article found among Ruth Moore's papers. A copy is included in Sanford Phippen's collection, Special Collections, Fogler Library, U. of Maine.

11. Feld, Rose, review of Spoonhandle, *Weekly Book Review,* June 16, 1946, p. 5.

12. Feld, Rose, review of *The Weir, The New York Times,* Feb. 28, 1943, p. 17.

13. Fournier, Norman, "Deserted Island Enchanting Setting for Moore Novel," *Maine Sunday Telegram,* Jan. 10, 1965, p. 40. Review of *The Sea Flower.*

14. Gould, John, review of *Candlemas Bay, The New York Times,* April 1, 1951, p. 28.

15. Gould, John, "That World Called Maine," *The New York Times,* Nov. 21, 1948, p. 6. Review of *The Fire Balloon.*

16. Graves, Betsy, "Getting By," *Puckerbrush Review,* Orono, Maine, vol. 8, no. 1, 1987, pp. 102–103. Review of *The Weir* and *Spoonhandle.*

17. Graves, Betsy, "An Interview with Ruth Moore," *Puckerbrush Review,* vol. 8, no. 2, 1989, pp. 12–14.

18. Henderson, R. W., review of *Candlemas Bay, Library Journal,* Oct. 15, 1950.

19. Higgins, A. Jay, "Sale of a Novel to Hollywood Set Writer Ruth Moore Free," *Bangor Daily News,* Sept. 9, 1987, p. 4.

20. Hornidge, Marilis, "Mourn With Me. Ruth Moore Is Dead," *Maine Mountain Digest,* Aug./Sept. 1990, p. 78.

21. Hughes, Riley, review of *Candlemas Bay, Catholic World,* June 1951.

22. Hunting, Constance, "Remembering Ruth Moore," *This Month in Maine Literature,* MWPA Newsletter, Brunswick, Maine, Feb. 1990, p. 1.

23. Joy, Hale G., "Island LIving Is Portrayed by Ruth Moore," *Ellsworth American,* March 31, 1988, Sect. III, p. 4. *Speak to the Winds* is reviewed.

24. Joy, Hale G., "The Weir Is Typical of Moore and Also of the Maine Coast," *Ellsworth American,* Oct. 9, 1986, Sect. III, p. 3.

25. Kelley, Elizabeth, review of *Spoonhandle, Library Journal,* June 1, 1946, vol. 71, p. 824.

26. Lawless, Gary, "Bring Ruth Moore's Books Back into Print!" *Downeast Libraries,* Vol. 9, No. 2, spring 1983, pp. 4–5.

27. Lawless, Gary, "Remembering Ruth Moore," *This Month in Maine Literature,* MWPA Newsletter, Feb. 1990, p. 1.

28. Lawless, Gary, "Ruth Moore Bibliography," *Island Journal,* vol. 3, 1986.

29. Levin, Martin, *The Dinosaur Bite,* review, *The New York Times Book Review,* May 9, 1976, p. 41.

30. Levin, Martin, *The Gold and Silver Hooks,* review, *The New York Times Book Review,* Feb. 9, 1969, p. 42 (section VII).

31. Levin, Martin, *"Lizzie" and Caroline,* review, *The New York Times Book Review,* July 23, 1972 (section VII), p. 20.

32. Lincoln, Nan, "Friends and Colleagues Remember Ruth Moore," *Bar Harbor Times,* May 31, 1990, p. 1. The memorial service for Moore.

33. Lincoln, Nan, "MDI Loses Respected Writer, Poet," *Bar Harbor Times,* Dec. 7, 1989, p. 1.

34. Little, Carl, "Collection Is Vintage Moore," *Bar Harbor Times,* July 19, 1990, p. C8. *Review of The Tired Apple Tree.*

35. Moore, Ruth, "The Ballad of the Three Green Waves," *Down East,* Sept. 1959, pp. 36–37. Illustrated.

36. Moore, Ruth, "Dry Farm," *The American Girl,* August 1938. A poem.

37. Moore, Ruth, "Farmer Takes a Newspaper," *The New Yorker,* July 3, 1948.

38. Moore, Ruth, "The First Christmas Spent in the House Ruth Built," *Boston Sunday Post,* Dec. 6, 1953. An article.

39. Moore, Ruth, "How Come You're Picking My Violets?" *Tuesday Weekly,* Ellsworth, Maine. No date. Found in Moore's papers. A copy is included in the Sanford Phippen collection, Special Collections, Fogler Library, University of Maine. An article.

40. Moore, Ruth, "It Don't Change Much," *The New Yorker,* vol. 21, Oct. 27, 1945, pp. 70–73. This same story was re-printed in *The Best Maine Stories* in 1986 under the title "The Soldier Shows His Medal."

41. Moore, Ruth, "Jeb Ellis of Candlemas Bay," *Compact: The Young People's Digest,* March 1954. Illustrated.

42. Moore, Ruth, "Ladies of Philadelphia," *Harper's Bazaar,* Aug. 1945.

43. Moore, Ruth, "The Lonely of Heart," *Puckerbrush Review,* vol. 8, no. 2, 1989, pp. 22–23. A story.

44. Moore, Ruth, "Pennies in the Water," *American Girl,* July 1942. A story.

45. Moore, Ruth, "The Soldier Shows His Medal," *The Best Maine Stories,* Yankee Books, Camden, Maine, 1986, pp. 287–293. A short story that originally appeared in *The New Yorker* under the title "It Don't Change Much" (Oct. 27, 1945).

46. Moore, Ruth, "Some Notes on Clerks of the Works," *Bar Harbor Times,* June 26, 1972. An article.

47. Moore, Ruth, "Voyage," *Saturday Review of Literature,* May 18, 1929. A poem.

48. Moore, Ruth, "The Walk Down Main Street" (condensed), *Ladies Home Journal,* Feb. 1960.

49. Moore, Ruth, "The Work of Alice Tisdale Hobart," Bobbs-Merrill Co., 1940. A 25-page brochure.

50. Mortland, Donald E., "Ruth Moore: Maine Coast Writer," *Colby Library Quarterly,* Colby College, Waterville, Maine, March 1979, pp. 48–57.

51. Mortland, Donald E., "Ruth Moore: Maine Novelist," *Maine Life,* Sept. 1977, pp. 46–47.

52. Newman, Eleanor, "New Novel by Maine Writer Gives Realistic Picture of Coast Life," *Bangor Daily News*, Nov. 8, 1948, p. 10. Review of *The Fire Balloon.*

53. Phillips, David E., *The Dinosaur Bite* review, *Down East,* Oct. 1976, p. 102.

54. Phillips, David E., *The Gold and Silver Hooks* review, *Down East,* July 1969, p. 110.

55. Phillips, David E., *"Lizzie" and Caroline* review, *Down East,* May 1973, p. 112.

56. Phillips, David E., "The Ruth Moore Revival," *Down East,* Jan. 1987, pp. 95–98. Sub-titled: "Echoes of the 'Real Maine'—a voice from the past tells it like it was—and is—down east." Illustrated.

57. Phillips, David E., *Sarah Walked Over the Mountain* review, *Down East,* Dec. 1979, p. 76.

58. Phillips, David E., *The Sea Flower* review, *Down East,* April 1965, p. 62.

59. Phillips, David E., *Second Growth* review, *Down East,* October 1962, p. 58.

60. Phillips, David E., *Speak to the Winds* review, *Down East,* October 1956, p. 48.

61. Phillips, David E., *The Walk Down Main Street* review, *Down East,* Aug. 1960, p. 64.

62. Phippen, Sanford, "Good Storyteller: Tedious 'Examples,'" *Maine Life,* Dec. 1979, p. 46. Review of *Sarah Walked Over the Mountain.*

63. Phippen, Sanford, "Great Poems Sometimes 'Happy Accidents,'" *Tuesday Weekly,* Ellsworth, Maine, April 29, 1975, p. 27. *Review of Cold as a Dog and the Wind Northeast.*

64. Phippen, Sanford, "Maine Book Review," *Maine Life,* Aug. 1976, pp. 40–41. Review of *The Dinosaur Bite.*

65. Phippen, Sanford, "Maine's Master Editor," *Maine Alumnus Magazine,* Fall 1992, pp. 23–25. Illustrated. An article about John C. Willey and his relationship with Ruth Moore.

66. Phippen, Sanford, "Remembering Ruth Moore," *This Month in Maine Literature*, MWPA Newsletter, p. 1. Picture of Moore taken by Phippen.

67. Phippen, Sanford, "A Tribute to Ruth Moore," *Puckerbrush Review*, vol. 10, no. 1, summer 1991, pp. 51–53.

68. Ross, Mary, review of *Candlemas Bay, The New York Herald-Tribune Weekly Book Review*, Nov. 14, 1948, p. 5.

69. Ross, Mary, review of *The Fire Balloon, The New York Herald-Tribune Weekly Book Review*, Nov. 14, 1948, p. 5.

70. Rugg, W. K., review of *Candlemas Bay, Christian Science Monitor*, March 30, 1951, p. 9.

71. Schreiber, Laurie, "Island Life: Rita Kenway Writes a History of Gotts Island," *Bar Harbor Times*, Sept. 3, 1992, Sect. B, pp. 1–3. Illustrated. Rita Kenway and her husband Northrup were neighbors of Ruth Moore.

72. Scoggin, M. C., review of *Candlemas Bay, Horn Book*, May 1951, p. 196.

73. Smith, Grace Cutler, "New Fiction from the Atlantic to the Pacific," *New York Herald-Tribune Weekly Book Review*, March 14, 1943, p. 10. *The Weir* reviewed.

74. Spiker, LaRue, "Author Ruth Moore Provides Look at Downeast Maine," *Ellsworth American*, 1972. Review of *"Lizzie" and Caroline.*

75. Spiker, LaRue, "*The Dinosaur Bite* Vivid, Vigorous," *Ellsworth American*, Sept. 2, 1976, Sect. II, p. 2.

76. Spiker, LaRue, "*Time's Web* Is Collection of Verses by Ruth Moore," *Ellsworth American*, 1973.

77. Starrett, Peter, "Novelist Likes Maine Coast—To Live Near and Write About," *Maine Sunday Telegram*, May 19, 1957, p. 6D. Illustrated.

78. Stevens, Austin, "Notes on Books and Authors," *The New York Times Book Review*, Nov. 29, 1942. *The Weir* listed as a forthcoming book for Jan. 1943.

79. Sullivan, Richard, review of *Spoonhandle, The New York Times*, June 16, 1946, p. 8.

80. Tewskbury, H. J. R., "Lure of the Automobile Depopulates Little Island off the Maine Coast," *Portland Sunday Telegram*, Dec. 23, 1928. Sub-

titled: "Gott's Island, separated from Mount Desert by Two and One-Half Miles of Water, Uninhabited for First Time in 139 Years—People Oftentimes married Among Their Own Relations but Stock Has Maintained Its Integrity and not Degenerated as Isolated Communities Sometimes Do as in the Case of Malaga Island—Houses Sell for a Mere Song." Illustrated.

81. Westbrook, Perry D., "Writers of the Maine Coast," *Down East,* Oct. 1956, pp. 31–37. Illustrated. Moore included with Elisabeth Ogilvie, Dorothy Simpson, Celia Thaxter, and others.

82. Whalen, Margaret A., "Ruth Moore," *North Country Libraries,* January/ February 1968.

C. UNSIGNED ARTICLES AND REVIEWS

1. "Ceremony Will Celebrate Author's Life," *Bar Harbor Times,* May 24, 1990.

2. "Damon Speaks for Ruth Moore," *Bar Harbor Times,* Aug. 1, 1991. Southwest Harbor Library with Dennis Damon.

3. "'Deep Waters' to Open Southwest Harbor Theatre," *Ellsworth American,* May 20, 1976, Sect. 2, p. 2.

4. "Discussion to Focus on Ruth Moore," *Ellsworth American,* Sept. 17, 1987, Sect. II, p. 6. Dennis Damon.

5. *The Fire Balloon* review, *New Yorker,* Nov. 13, 1948, vol. 24, p. 145.

6. "Former Maine Student Is Author of *Candlemas,*" *Bangor Daily News.* No date. Sanford Phippen collection, Special Collections, Fogler Library, U. of Maine.

7. John C. Willey obituary, *Bangor Daily News,* May 9, 1990.

8. "John C. Willey Dies; Book Editor Was 75," *The New York Times,* May 3, 1990.

9. "A Lively Historical Novel Which Is Concerned With People," *Bangor Daily Commercial,* March 11, 1951, p. D3. Review of *A Fair Wind Home.*

10. "Maine Novelist Is Close to Nature," *Bangor Daily News.* Review of *Candlemas Bay.*

11. "Movie Company to Start Filming *Spoonhandle* in Maine This Fall," *Bangor Daily News,* Aug. 14, 1947, p. 1.

12. "Novels Centered on Maine Background," *Bangor Daily News,* May 28, 1976, p. 7.

13. "Services Set for Author Ruth Moore," *Bangor Daily News,* Dec. 5, 1989, p. 18.

14. *Spoonhandle* review, *The New Yorker,* June 15, 1946, p. 94.

15. "Storyteller to Read Ruth Moore Pieces," *Bangor Daily News,* Feb. 24, 1992. Dennis Damon at College of the Atlantic.

16. *The Weir* review, *The New Yorker,* Feb. 27, 1943, p. 66.

17. "Well-Known Women Novelists Build Own Home of CCC Camp Lumber," *Bangor Daily News,* Dec. 10, 1947, p. 11. Illustrated.

D. REFERENCE WORKS

1. *Bibliography of the State of Maine,* G. K. Hall Pub. Co., Boston, 1962. May be found at the Bangor Public Library.

2. *Book Review Digest,* H. W. Wilson Co., New York, Vol. 39, 1943. Reviews of *The Weir,* p. 581.

3. *Book Review Digest,* H. W. Wilson Co., New York, Vol. 42, 1946. Reviews of *Spoonhandle,* pp. 585–586.

4. *Book Review Digest,* H. W. Wilson Co., New York, Vol. 44, 1948. Reviews of *The Fire Balloon,* p. 596.

5. *Book Review Digest,* H. W. Wilson Co., New York, Vol. 47, 1951. Reviews of *Candlemas Bay,* pp. 627–628.

6. *Book Review Digest,* H. W. Wilson Co., New York, Vol. 48, 1952. Reviews of *Jeb Ellis of Candlemas Bay,* p. 640.

7. *Book Review Digest,* H. W. Wilson Co., New York, Vol. 49, 1953. Reviews of *A Fair Wind Home,* p. 662.

8. *Book Review Digest,* H. W. Wilson Co., New York, Vol. 52, 1956. Reviews of *Speak to the Winds,* p. 657.

9. *Book Review Digest,* H. W. Wilson Co., New York, Vol. 55, 1959. *Reviews of Cold as a Dog and the Wind Northeast,* p. 725.

10. *Book Review Digest,* H. W. Wilson Co., New York, Vol. 56, 1960. Reviews of *The Walk Down Main Street,* p. 950.

11. *Book Review Digest,* H. W. Wilson Co., New York, Vol. 58, 1962. Reviews of *Second Growth,* p. 837.

12. *Book Review Digest,* H. W. Wilson Co., New York, Vol. 61, 1965. Reviews of *The Sea Flower,* p. 897.

13. *Book Review Digest,* H. W. Wilson Co., New York, Vol. 69, 1973. Reviews of *Time's Web,* pp. 911–912.

14. Burke, W. J. and Will D. Howe, "Ruth Moore," *American Authors and Books, 1640 to the Present Day,* 3rd Revised Edition, Crown Publishers, New York, 1973, p. 440.

15. *Who's Who in New England,* A. N. Marquis Co., Chicago, 40th Anniversary Edition, Vol. 4, 1949, p. 410.

E. AUDIOTAPE AND VIDEOTAPE/RADIO INTERVIEWS, ETC.

1. Bok, Gordon, *"Cold as a Dog and the Wind Northeast,* Spoken Ballads of Ruth Moore" told by Gordon Bok, Timberhead, Inc., 1986, P.O. Box 840, Camden, Maine 04843. Also distributed by Folk-Legacy. Audiotape.

2. Damon, Dennis, Interview with Sanford Phippen, July 26, 1990. Audiotape.

3. Dillon, Mary, Interview with Sanford Phippen, January 1991. Audiotape.

4. Gillman, Jackson, "Downeast Ballads by Ruth Moore and Others," Maine Squeeze Productions, 1987, HCR 62, Box 36A, Mt. Desert, Maine 04660. Audiotape.

5. Graves, Betsy, Interview with Ruth Moore, 1988. Audiotape.

6. Holmes, Edward Ted, Interview with Sanford Phippen, Oct. 1, 1991. Audiotape.
7. McLean, Harris, Interview with Sanford Phippen, 1992. Audiotape.
8. Phillips, Eunice, Interview with Sanford Phippen, 1992. Audiotape.
9. Rawley, Aileen, Interview with Ruth Moore, WDEA-Radio, Ellsworth, Maine, 1967. Audiotape.
10. Trask, Brian, Ruth Moore's Memorial Service, May 30, 1990. Videotape with Dennis Damon, Jackson Gillman, Donald Mortland, Sanford Phippen, and Moore family members.
11. Trask, Esther, Emily Trask-Eaton, and Sven Davisson, Interview with Sanford Phippen about Ruth Moore, October 1991. Audiotape.

F. UNPUBLISHED WORKS

1. Ames, Edward B., "Ruth Moore's Art," May 16, 1949. A paper written for Prof. Hilda Fife's Maine Writers course, U. of Maine. Fife Collection, Special Collections, Fogler Library, U. of Maine, Orono, Maine.
2. Arbor, Ann, Letters of Beloit, Wisconsin students to Ruth Moore, 1987. Arbor was their teacher and they read *The Weir* in her class. Copies in Sanford Phippen Collection, Special Collections, Fogler Library, U. of Maine, Orono, Maine.
3. Bailey, Ruth, "Maine Coast of Ruth Moore's Novels," July 3, 1967. A paper from Hilda Fife Collection, Special Collections, Fogler Library, U. of Maine, Orono, Maine.
4. Boles, Donna, "Ruth Moore," May 2, 1963. A paper in the Hilda Fife Collection, Special Collections, Fogler Library, U. of Maine, Orono, Maine.
5. Cousins, Connie, "Interview with Ruth Moore," April 29, 1965. A paper in the Hilda Fife Collection, Special Collections, Fogler Library, U. of Maine, Orono, Maine.

6. Ford, Paul G., "The Mayo Clinic," May 16, 1949. A paper in the Hilda Fife Collection on Eleanor Mayo and Ruth Moore, Special Collections, Fogler Library, U. of Maine, Orono, Maine.

7. Freeman, Doris R., "Ruth Moore's Life as Reflected in Her Books," August 8, 1960. A paper in the Hilda Fife Collection, Special Collections, Fogler Library, U. of Maine, Orono, Maine.

8. Gott, Susanna, Diary. *Gott's Island History 1852–1910*. The private papers of Mr. and Mrs. Harris McLean, Sullivan, Maine.

9. Higgins, Elaine, "Paper on Novelist, Ruth Moore," no date. A paper in the Hilda Fife Collection, Special Collections, Fogler Library, U. of Maine, Orono, Maine.

10. Higgins, Ruby, "Ruth Moore," 1960. A paper in the Hilda Fife Collection, Special Collections, Fogler Library, U. of Maine, Orono, Maine.

11. Holmes, Edward M., "Summer Island Sunday." A short story with fictionalized characters based on Ruth Moore, Eleanor Mayo, Ted and Jane Holmes on Gott's Island. Sanford Phippen Collection, Special Collections, Fogler Library, U. of Maine, Orono, Maine.

12. Joyce, Myra, Diary. *Gott's Island history 1874*. The private papers of Mr. and Mrs. Harris McLean, Sullivan, Maine.

13. Moore, Ruth, "The Bottle-Green Bottle." Story.*

14. Moore, Ruth, "Creepy." Story.*

15. Moore, Ruth, "The Enemy at Dawn." Story.*

16. Moore, Ruth, "The Gargoyle." Story. Sanford Phippen Collection, Special Collections, Fogler Library, U. of Maine, Orono, Maine.

17. Moore, Ruth, "Hungry Fingers." Story.*

18. Moore, Ruth, "Hupporunde." Story.*

19. Moore, Ruth, "The Moon and the Stars." Story.*

20. Moore, Ruth, "Paper Money." Story.*

21. Moore, Ruth, "The People Around Them." Story.*

22. Moore, Ruth, "When Foley Craddock Tore Off My Grandfather's Thumb." Story.*

About the Editor

Born in White Plains, New York on June 19, 1942, Sanford Edwin Phippen grew up in Hancock, Maine, across Frenchman's Bay from Mount Desert Island. He attended three grammar schools in Hancock; graduated from Sumner Memorial High School in East Sullivan in 1960; and received his B.A. in English from the University of Maine in 1964. He also holds an M.A. in English Education granted by Syracuse University in 1971.

Phippen is the author of *The Police Know Everything* (1982), *People Trying to Be Good* (1988), and *Cheap Gossip* (1989). He was the principal author and editor of *A History of the Town of Hancock*, 1928–1978 (1978), the editor of *The Best Maine Stories* (1986), co-producer with Virgil Bisset of the MPBN-FM series *The Maine That's Missing* (1981), and producer of the video *A Century of Summers: The Impact of a Summer Colony on a Small Maine Coastal Town, 1886–1986* (1987). Phippen's work has also appeared in the anthologies *Inside Vacationland* (1985), *Maine Speaks* (1989), and *A Lobster in Every Pot* (1990). For ten years, 1976–85, he was the Book Review Editor for *Maine Life* magazine; and before that, he wrote book reviews, theater reviews, and a humor column called "The Letter from Liverpool" (1973–75) for the now-defunct *Tuesday Weekly* newspaper of Ellsworth, Maine. Phippen is a contributing editor of *Puckerbrush Review* and his work has appeared in *The New York Times, Maine Times, Portland Monthly Magazine, Down East, Ellsworth American, Bangor Daily News,* and *Maine Alumnus Magazine.*

The founder and first president of The Historical Society of the Town of Hancock (1979), Phippen served as librarian of The Hancock Point Library for eleven summers, 1978–88. For six years, 1984–90, he served as a member of the Maine Humanities Council, retiring as Vice-Chair; and since 1990, he has been a member of The Literature Panel of the Maine Arts Commission.

Phippen has taught high school English for 28 years, starting at Bangor High School as a student teacher in 1964 and continuing at New Hartford, New York; Corcoran High School in Syracuse, New York; and currently at Orono High School in Orono, Maine. For several years in both adult education and summer school programs at Orono High School and the University of Maine, he has taught a course in Maine literature. For one year, 1987–88, he taught writing and literature courses at the University of Maine.

Currently, Phippen is completing work on a novel, *Kitchen Boy,* a play version of *The Police Know Everything,* and a script for an animated feature film for television called *The Moose Who Couldn't Fly.*